STUDIES IN WORLD HISTORY

THE TRIUMPH OF THE MIDDLE CLASSES

Charles Morazé

THE TRIUMPH OF THE MIDDLE CLASSES

*

A Study of European Values in the
Nineteenth Century

WEIDENFELD AND NICOLSON
5 Winsley Street London W1

Printed and Bound in England by
Hazell Watson & Viney Ltd
Aylesbury, Bucks

Contents

FOREWORD   xiii

BOOK ONE: YOUNG EUROPE – OLD WORLDS, 1780

1 EUROPE RISES IN THE WEST   3
  LONDON-BERLIN: A CONTRAST
    Modernism in England
    Tradition in Germany
    Elsewhere in Central Europe
  PARIS BETWEEN TWO WORLDS
  DECLINE OF THE SOUTH
    Revival in Spain
    Italian Autumn

2 PROGRESS CROSSES THE ATLANTIC   36
  MEDITERRANEAN RUINS
    The Ottoman Camp
    Arab Ruins
    Constantinople
  ATLANTIC ACHIEVEMENTS
    Servile Africa
    The Awakening of Spanish America
    Free Anglo-Saxon America

3 THE CALL OF ASIA   56
  THE DISCOVERY OF INDIA
  CHINA REMAINS ALOOF
  THE STRUGGLE FOR CENTRAL ASIA

BOOK TWO: THE BOURGEOIS REVOLUTIONS, 1780–1840

4 THE WEST AND ITS TOOLS   77
  MAN
  SCIENCE
  THE LAW

5 THE MIDDLE CLASSES TAKE OVER   100
   INDUSTRY IN ENGLAND
   GOVERNMENT IN FRANCE
   FEUDALISM IN GERMANY

6 THE MAN OF 1830   136
   DEVELOPING SOCIETIES
   THE AESTHETICS OF PROGRESS
   THE CALL OF THE PEOPLES

7 THE EUROPEAN WORLDS   160
   THE WEST IMITATES EUROPE
   England First
   The United States Governed by the South
   America for the Americans
   Africa Not for the Africans
   EUROPEAN PENETRATION OF ASIA
   Capitalism in India
   The End of the Celestial Mandate in China
   The Steppes of Central Asia
   THE CROSSING OF THE MEDITERRANEAN
   Nationalism versus Islam
   The Birth of French Africa

BOOK THREE: CAPITALIST AND INDUSTRIAL
   EUROPE, 1840–80

8 THE VICTORY OF INDUSTRY   191
   THE RAILWAYS – CATALYST OF THE INDUSTRIAL REVOLUTION
   VICTORY IN 1848
   ITS EFFECTS ON CAPITALISM

9 INDUSTRIAL NATIONALISM   216
   ENGLISH STEEL – MASTER OF THE SEAS
   PRUSSIAN STEEL – MASTER OF EUROPE
   FRANCE BETWEEN TWO EMPIRES

10 THE TOWN-DWELLER   245
   THE SERVANT SCIENCES
   THE INDUSTRIAL SOCIETIES
   THE DECLINE OF AESTHETICS

BOOK FOUR: THE CONQUEST OF THE WORLD, 1840–95

11 THE MARITIME SUCCESSES OF WESTERN CAPITALISM   273
A TRIUMPH: THE UNITED STATES
Authority Passes to the North
Large-scale Capitalism, Imperialism
A PROMISE: THE SOUTHERN HEMISPHERE
The Development of Australia
South Africa Becomes Industrialized
Ephemeral Industry in Peru
The Adolescence of Three Nations
Positivist Brazil
A REVELATION: JAPAN

12 THE CONTINENTS RESIST   311
INDIA EXPLOITED, BUT NOT CONVERTED
INLAND CHINA REJECTS CAPITALISM
The End of the Celestial Mandate
Inland China Remains Conservative
Outer China Lets in the West
RUSSIA DEFENDS ITS TRADITION
Ancient Russia in Search of Itself
The Russian People Conquer Asia

13 CHANGES IN EUROPE AND AFRICA   343
THE BURGEONING OF INDUSTRY FROM 1880 TO 1895
Outward Appearances: Financial Crises
Events in France: Industrialization
Events in Germany: Phenomenal Development of Industry
Events in England: Trade Predominates
RURAL LOYALTIES
The North and North-East: Modernization of Agriculture
The East and South-East: Prisoners of Their History
Italy: Capitalism Builds Unity
Spain: Capitalism Encourages Disorder
INDUSTRIAL EUROPE SPREADS INTO AFRICA
The Defeat of Islam
Europe's Future in Africa
The Partition of Africa

CONCLUSION

DANGER AHEAD   377
ONE CAPITALISM OUSTS ANOTHER
A SETBACK FOR THE MIDDLE CLASS
A SETBACK FOR EUROPE
A SETBACK FOR NEWTON
CONCLUSION

BIBLIOGRAPHY   395

INDEX   401

Illustrations

(between pages 208 and 209)

1 Vauxhall, one of the London pleasure-gardens
2 A song-merchant at the Gonesse Fair, near Pontoise
3 The Sultan's palaces on the banks of the Bosphorus, near Constantinople
4 An early view of New York harbour
5 Monsieur Prudhomme, a caricature by Henri Monnier
6 & 7 London life in the nineteenth century, as depicted by Eugène Lami
8 Loading cotton and tobacco in one of the Southern states of the USA
9 Mississippi river-boats being loaded with cotton at a New Orleans quay
10 The main square in Havana
11 A meal in a rich Brazilian household
12 & 13 Westerners in the Far East
14 Russian and Chinese merchants meet in a house at Kiakhta
15 A toll-gate on an English road, caricatured by Eugène Lami
16 A humorous vision of the future in 1838
17 The first steam-engines
18 A scene at one of the rolling-mills where railway engines were made before 1850
19 The opening of the bridge over the Lagoon at Venice
20 One of the first underground railways in London
21 Unloading cargo at Limehouse Dock on the Thames
22 London's slums as depicted by Gustave Doré
23 & 24 Two famous steam-ships: the *Great Eastern* and the *Normandie*
25 F Street, Denver, Colorado, in the 1880s
26 The first French railway in China, 1886
27 The slave-trade in Africa
28 Paris cafés in full swing on a summer night

ACKNOWLEDGEMENTS

The publishers are grateful to the following for providing illustrations for this volume: Bibliothèque Nationale, Paris, figures 1, 2, 3, 4, 5, 6, 7, 8, 9, 10, 11, 12, 13, 14, 15, 16, 17, 18, 20, 21, 22 and 28; Cie Gie Translantique, figure 24; Musée de la Marine, figure 23; A. Paoletti, figure 19; M. Perham and J. Simmons, *African Discovery*, Faber and Faber Ltd, figure 27

Maps

1 Industrial England c. 1780   10

2 Industrial France c. 1780   11

3 Maritime Explorations, 1760–80   34

4 Europeans in America in 1780   46

5 India in 1795   57

6 Political Divisions in Germany c. 1820   134

7 Customs Unions of 1823   135

8 Races and Languages of Eastern Europe   157

9 Cotton in the USA   165

10 America in 1825   169

11 Stages of the English Occupation and Movement of the Boer Population in South Africa, 1814–48   171

12 English Possessions in India, 1795–1815   174

13 Russia's Advance towards the West   179

14 The Conquest of the Caucasus, 1800–50   182

15 Stages in the Conquest of Algeria   185

16 Industrial England c. 1880   238

17 Industrial France c. 1880   239

18 London, Paris, and Berlin in 1790 and in 1890   260

19 Stages in the American Civil War   278

20 European Occupation and Indian Reserves in the United States   281

21 Cotton in the United States   283

22 Australia   294

23 South Africa   295

24 The New Republics of the Region of La Plata at the Time of the Paraguayan War (1865–70)   300

25 British India in the Nineteenth Century   313

26 Railways in India   314

27 Difficulties in China   318

28 Chinese Emigration in the Nineteenth Century   328

29 The Economy of Europe c. 1880   351

30 German-Speaking Population of Central and Eastern Europe
      c. 1880   361

Foreword

The year 1900 was a wonderful one, when men were proud to be middle-class, and to be Europeans. The fate of the whole world was decided around green baize-covered tables in London, Paris or Berlin. Rubber trees from the Amazons were shipped to Malaya, the vast coal seams of the Upper Hwang-Ho were being exploited at the expense of the wretched labourers, and in the north of the Upper Vaal a mining city sprang up in a few short weeks. Mobilized by steam, the planet's riches were being shifted 'from one side of the world to the other', to quote *Le Bateau Ivre*, on orders flashed by telegraph in two or three minutes. Decisions reached by boards of directors in London, Paris or Berlin affected the lives of millions of human beings who did not suspect that their right to happiness depended on quotations scribbled on blackboards in three noisy exchanges built like temples, in which raged the battles of unbridled financial ambition. Not a single detail escaped the notice of Europe's financial capitals: they fixed the price of a tram ticket in Rio de Janeiro, and the working hours of a coolie in Hong Kong. So much power had never before been concentrated in so few hands within so small an area of the globe. It was the age of triumph of the European middle classes. This book sets out to explain how this power was built up.

In 1780 the ancient civilizations of the world, whether Chinese or Indian, of the Crescent or of the Cross, existed side by side on an almost equal footing. Yet almost all were showing signs of increasing age, and especially in the rigid, undeviating routine which characterized rural life and labour. The Far East could, it was true, boast cities far bigger than London or Paris, but it had no parallel to the urban development of Western Europe – a unique phenomenon springing from the surge and ferment of new ideas around the shores of the North Sea. Curiosity, a desire for novelty, boldness, a zest for gain – these were the qualities which stimulated the progress of science and the development of trade, the great achievements of the nineteenth century. We shall attempt to recapture something of the curiosity experienced by travellers in this age of progress, in order to see the world of 1780 through the young and confident eyes of London or Paris, mutual rivals, yet each on the threshold of a great and epoch-making future. These vivid descriptions, accounts and reminiscences of Europeans fascinated by the exotic and the cosmopolitan emerge very vividly from the dusty volumes. We hope to be forgiven for devoting a hundred pages to these descriptions of a young Europe confronted with ancient civilizations (Book One, pp. 1–73).

The stage was set, the play about to begin. Proud of their science and their law, and buoyed up by their newly acquired wealth, the middle

classes emerged from the old social framework and became the champions
of action in the service of method: banks and blast furnaces, harbours and
highways, changed the geography of Western Europe, a Western Europe
which now extended as far as Berlin. With considerable difficulty, and at
the cost of several revolutions, they were to achieve their political ambitions – the destruction of the old, conservative monarchies, the proclamation of freedom of enterprise and control over as much of public administration as needed to be preserved. Never had the times appeared so rich in
hope, nor human destiny so malleable. Artists and poets, thinkers and
statesmen were anxious or elated: Romanticism discovered history and
the power of evolution. From Europe the movement spread to America,
not only to North America where that Republic so dear to the radical
thinkers was being created, but to South America too, where new nations
were coming into being on the European pattern. Even the East was stirring. Sixty years of passion and tumult, of injustice and innovation from
1780 to 1840, saw these middle-class 'revolutions' (Book Two, pp. 75–187).

From the 1840s onward the battles of the European middle class were
waged with renewed vigour; the victors had a new weapon at their disposal – steam – which made ships ten times more powerful, and pulled the
coaches of the new railways. The innovations of 1800 were soon out of
date: scarcely were the first blast furnaces perfected before they became
old-fashioned and were superseded by more powerful ones. The banks
increased their services tenfold. Yet for a time the middle classes were uncertain and afraid: in 1848 the people of Paris made their bid to dominate
progress, but without success. The hour of socialism had not yet struck, and
it was an arrogant capitalism which established Napoleon III and Bismarck in power. Both these men were eager to equal and surpass England,
and competed with each other to achieve this the sooner, projecting the
rivalry of big business onto a national scale. Thus London, Paris and Berlin
became the great controllers of world progress, because it was they who
had been the builders of 'capitalist and industrial Europe' (Book Three,
pp. 189–270).

Yet even before this European process was completed, the middle
classes of Europe had harnessed their commercial, financial and industrial
skills to conquer the world. They thrust their ruthless way across every
continent, bringing wars in their train, inciting revolts, but everywhere
triumphant. We shall review this 'world conquest' (Book Four, pp. 271–374)
in which, without even bothering to exploit the whole of their own continent (see p. 343) the middle classes of Europe forged ahead, transforming Japan, stirring up the southern hemisphere, and shaking Asia from its
torpor. Ships, roads, telegraphs and railways opened up the way for a
thousand schemes of rural and urban development. Everywhere, the past
remnants of age-old civilizations crumbled away under the picks of labour
squads snatched from their old rural villages, and everywhere buildings
and factories appeared, brought from or inspired by Europe. These were
the victories and triumphs of industry.

Yet victory was by no means complete. The vast expanse of China, wretchedly poor but still very much alive, refused to be brought under the yoke. And though the huge, patient mass of India assimilated technical progress, its surface was merely grazed by the still fragile structures of capitalism. The African, inured to slavery, might well have been an easy prey, yet Africa, that giant land of rock and water, of blazing sun and towering vegetation, cost Europe an exhausting effort. In America, the success was too great, for within fifty years it had become the leading industrial power in the world.

A wonderful year indeed was 1900: to the European middle classes, proud of their struggles and successes, proud at having mastered the world with so little loss and with only a modicum of heroic sacrifice, the future seemed secure. Yet 1900 was the eve of those apocalyptic wars in which neighbouring European powers destroyed each other, the eve of a proletarian revolution as wide as a continent, the eve of a spiritual revolution less obvious but even more significant for the future since, going far beyond anything that European individualism could have foreseen, it removed the very foundations of what had been the science of the middle-class era. At the very height of its triumph, cracks were starting in its fabric, and they eventually led to its decay (see Conclusion, pp. 375–94).

This is the epic of a middle class, an epic of science, good fortune, and world-wide influence, but also of ignorance, selfishness and chauvinism. The details of this century are already fading, although it was claimed that in it alone was achieved as much as in the whole of recorded time put together. The present book is simply an attempt to understand it, and it is meant for those who wish to do the same. The writer does not sit in judgement on the dead; his sympathies, on the contrary, are warm and human. The study of the past is not sad but salutary. The middle classes of nineteenth-century Europe conquered the world not because they were middle class or European, but because they were more capable than their predecessors, or than leaders in other parts of the world, of exploiting the technical weapons put into men's hands by the progress of science. For a century and a half, science and progress claimed the European middle classes. Science and progress choose those who serve them best.

Book One

YOUNG EUROPE-
OLD WORLDS

1780

1

Europe Rises in the West

WE are not beginning with the usual description of Europe on the eve of the French Revolution for the simple reason that it obviously never occurred to the Londoners, Viennese, Parisians or Romans of the day that they *were* 'on the eve of the French Revolution'. Their main aim was to be happy. It may be objected that every age wants happiness, but this is not true. There are times when it is fashionable to die for the sake of honour or mystic love, when 'grand passions' are all the rage, but not even in the Germany of the *Sturm und Drang*, nor in the sentimental dramas of Diderot, nor even in Rousseau's appeals for a new education, did passion reach such a pitch of intensity that it excluded gaiety, a delight in the miniature or the dainty trinket, or the love of music and intellectual amusements. Between two intensely serious ages, that of the serious Romantics and the serious middle classes, the climate of the 1780s may be summed up in the word *esprit*, by which was meant not the Spirit of the Trinity, nor the questing spirit of knowledge, the sacred guardian of progress, but 'spirit' as Voltaire defined it in his *Dictionnaire Philosophique* – 'ingenious reason'. It meant, too, the subtle pleasures of society people who implied more than they said and preferred to leave as much as they could to the imagination.

In 1785, then, society's chief diversion lay not in the fact that it was divided into three Orders, but in discovering in the first temperate *salons*, and in the delightful new coffee-houses, some ingenious novelty, some fresh source of trifling pleasure. Yet we ourselves must not be carried away, as they were, by this passion for baubles and trinkets which at the time made Matthew Boulton's fortune, and which a few years later led to the downfall of Cousin Pons. It is unlikely that we shall be, at least if we have the genuine feel of the period; for the fashionable toy of 1785 had none of the sheer prettiness, the drawing-room appeal, of its successors or of its predecessors. It represented tremendous and quite recent achievements. There was the mechanical clock, a triumph of the new technique of clock-making, or the geometrical object which ingeniously took to pieces and bore witness to the astounding new discoveries made by mathematicians; there was Chinese jade, now at long last beginning to be distinguished from jasper. These objects revealed a gentle revolution in domestic habits, and one which introduced into the daily life of Europe both scientific skill and an eagerly cosmopolitan outlook. The European discovered the Indian and the Inca, the Huran and the Chinaman, a whole vast planet that the man-about-town could now draw on for a host of minor pleasures, stuffing his pipe with tobacco, and making his own cocoa (unless, copying Africa and Asia rather than America, he preferred tea or coffee).

It was an age which perfected the art of living, which gave to Greuze's portraits a smile utterly different from that found in Da Vinci's, and a charm not untouched by sensuality. It was a delightful age when, after two centuries of strife and stormy seas, the European citizen was beginning to feel that the whole wide world was working exclusively for his pleasure. Voltaire called it 'the iron age', a strange epithet to us who are acquainted with the real iron age of blast furnaces and Bessemer converters. But we must go further in our attempt to think ourselves back into the atmosphere of the period which forms the start of our study.

The men of 1780 were certainly not living in hourly expectation of the Revolution. They neither wanted it, nor were afraid of it; in fact no one gave a thought to it, in spite of contemporary historians who profess to discover signs to the contrary even in La Bruyère's *Caractères*. What really interested those men of 1780 was the progress of science. Very few could really understand it – but the building of the Academy was almost as dear to Berliners as the King's Palace – and Parisians were already beginning to realize that the centre of their world was no longer at Versailles, but in the workshops, botanical gardens, and libraries which every day revealed something new to arouse their curiosity. Londoners out for a Sunday stroll made for the newly-built docks in the port, went to see the first steam mill, admired the first iron barge; others flocked to the lecture-halls of the Royal Society. They combined their love of science with a curiosity about technical processes which budding inventors made even more fashionable by lively expositions of the complicated procedures for measuring the earth, or observing the stars; or of the ingenuity which made hot-air balloons rise into the sky of their own accord. Aristocrats thumbed the Encyclopaedia in search of recipes for cosmetics or rare delicacies. Plates illustrating mechanics or human anatomy were studied with interest. Yet curiosity was not merely bookish and academic; it ranged far and wide. Travel had never been so popular nor inspired such a lively literature, in the tradition of Laurence Sterne.

In 1786 Goethe left Carlsbad secretly, because he wished to travel alone. He set off, like so many of his contemporaries, in search of Italy, Rome and its ruins. It is generally stated that not until Valmy did Goethe declare that 'a new era was dawning'. It was in fact on his arrival in Rome that he wrote: 'I shall live in peace and quiet here for the rest of my days. A new life is opening out before me.' The truth was that in the ruins of an empire he had just become aware of a new human dimension. When Europe discovered the ancient world of Herculaneum and Pompeii it discovered also the vast perspectives of history itself. Winckelmann, in his work on the classification of Roman remains, had fired the imagination of scholars with his theory about the various periods of ancient art; fashion too, first in England and then in France, stealthily consigned to the attic, piece by

piece, any furniture and fittings that were baroque or rococo, and replaced them by the 'antique'. The antique brought into house interiors its
colonnades and pilasters, its decorations in grisaille with their delicate
lines, and its Pompeian style; antique ruins invaded parks and gardens.
Within a few short years the 'antiquity' of Horace and Virgil took on a
new meaning. Their books were no longer regarded as immortal decrees of
fate, as well-tried guides to the poetic art, or as a compendium of prophecies. They acquired a date and were given their place in this new
classification of time and space. They assumed a historical picturesque-
ness, the finer shades of which were more readily appreciated because men
had discovered the geographical fascination of America, China and India.
There was a new art of living, a new art of feeling and thinking, an eager,
impressionable curiosity which swept over the whole of Europe from the
fogs of London and Paris to the lights of Rome. Thus was cosmopolitanism
born.

Yet this was also the age of patriotism, a new kind of patriotism.
'Patriotism' and 'nationalism' were not new concepts in 1785, but although
a sense of honour was still comparatively strong, it was linked more with
the idea of self-respect *à la Voltaire* than with respect for race or royalty.
Voltaire showed himself aware of this in his comment on the line from
Corneille: *Fille de Scipion et, pour dire encore plus, romaine.* He regarded it as
a wretched piece of affectation. But how do wars and treaties and the
European balance of power fit into the picture? Naturally the entire
political set-up, all the indispensable machinery of government, continued
unchanged, although it occupied a far more modest place in public opinion then than it does in many modern history books which claim to give a
faithful picture of the age. Vergennes' cabinet may have regarded the victorious sea-warfare being waged against England on the Western Atlantic
seaboard as a revenge for the defeats suffered in the Indian Ocean, and
honoured Suffren accordingly; yet it was not this policy of theirs which
aroused enthusiasm, but the birth of a new agricultural republic on the
shores of the New World, and the public's real hero was La Fayette, who
had gone there as a *franc-tireur* on a temporary commission; and perhaps
also Beaumarchais, who was none too scrupulous in furnishing arms to the
colonists.

The enthusiasm with which men of culture welcomed the birth of the
United States completely stifled the few expressions of regret in France at
the loss of Canada and India. The partition of Poland caused little stir, and
did little to diminish the prestige of the two monarchs responsible for it.
Louis xvi, philosopher king, reformer of agriculture and industry, patron
of the arts and sciences, and his accomplice Catherine the Great, Empress
of Russia, and 'Semiramis of the North'.

How could land cultivation be improved? How could industry be made
more prosperous? How could people be made happier? These were the
chief preoccupations which we would now call patriotic or national.
Happiness is writ large, in a place of honour, in the American Constitution.

It is not, however, our intention to embark on a sterile exposition of European politics in the 1780s, but rather to recall certain vital facts which will help to place the following chapters more firmly in their context. In the course of three centuries the Atlantic had become the central trade area, a great battlefield far more important than the sleepy Mediterranean. For two hundred years skilled sailors had brought wealth across the Atlantic and the adjacent Indian and Pacific Oceans, to the shores of Europe; and fortunes, which previously had been amassed by pillage and conquest, were now made by traders using wily and cunning tactics, diplomacy, forcefulness and powers of persuasion; and these traders were less interested in gold and silver than in a wide new range of products from all over the world on which European fashion had set a high price. The age of enlightenment was essentially and primarily the age of trade, and trade so profitable that it was able to make many and varied demands on politics as well. It was trade which gave England its economic, financial and monetary institutions, its banks and insurance companies, its credit and business codes. It was trade which dictated to England its political institutions, its Board of Trade and its costly interventions in diplomacy and war. And it was trade which imposed on the European nations a social structure of its own choosing, a society in which 'all other obligations took second place to those of debtors to creditors', in which the landowner must curb his political privileges, and was only forgiven for being wealthy provided he tried to bring down the price of farm commodities, and opened his fields to potential mine-owners and his parks to town-builders. The country labourer was forgiven for being poor (and poor at the expense of his parish) provided he would work for next to nothing in the shops, or better still in the new factories owned by prosperous businessmen. This was a society, in short, where the new hero was the man who risked his money to make still more, and who, if he failed, became a victim of the harsh commercial laws, a bankrupt without hope and with no future but a debtor's prison.

In all this activity, industry was merely the handmaid of business. It was still far from being as profitable as trade, and very far from gaining complete control over economic life. Furthermore industry had not as yet made more than limited contacts with a science still in its infancy and too young, in fact, to be of use to it. Relying on the initiative of bold *entrepreneurs*, it had to do the best it could with techniques which had been taken over from the old trade guilds with hardly any adaptation or improvement. There was no such thing as an industrial revolution in 1780; it had not yet evolved from the revolution in social customs.

This, then, was the great age of commerce, and particularly of that most important of all its branches, maritime trade. In this sphere England's superiority was incontestable: English trade outstripped Amsterdam, overwhelmed and shaken as it was by yearly financial crises; and it outstripped Nantes, Bordeaux or Lyons, although they were as prosperous as Liverpool, Bristol or Birmingham, and rather more elegant, since their prosperity had a longer urban tradition behind it. But this very tradition was liable to hamper the new maritime trade to an extent that only later became apparent. The success of London may be measured in addition by the prosperity of Frankfurt and Hamburg, which in some respects were its outposts.

The winds of fortune blowing in from the Atlantic penetrated, though not at once, to the inland heart of Europe. Danzig, first and foremost, maintained its old prosperity; Berlin was gradually improving its position. Princes and princelings of Eastern Europe, too, were attempting to set up maritime companies for trade with the Indies. There were maritime companies in Copenhagen, which was understandable, in Berlin, which was surprising, and even in Dresden, Vienna and Munich – and the Russians, too, were endeavouring to gain a foothold on the Baltic, while the old inland fairs were beginning to organize their widespread inland trade on 'maritime' lines. But these inland 'maritime companies' had a hard struggle. Eventually the princely exchequers grew tired of heaping subsidy upon subsidy. A maritime destiny is not for the asking! It is tempting to assert that from east to west across Europe there was a wide range of political and social institutions, from society on the English model to ancient feudalism, and that each different type adapted itself to an economic structure which took into account the increasing difficulties of trading companies from London to Nijni-Novgorod. This might be correct if it were not for the monarchies, whose inflexible traditions upset this neat arrangement. The monarchs, whether great or small, may have acknowledged and envied the great success of maritime trade, and may have been favourably disposed to listen to the suggestions made to them by their middle-class subjects, who wanted to lay their hands on some of the wealth pouring in from the sea and hoped to carry out on their own estates some of the improvements made by the great landowners. But these same monarchs were usually very determined to live in a royal style themselves, and not in the new tradition set up by the English kings. They wanted the heavy pomp and splendour of traditions inherited from Louis xiv.

Every German sovereign had his Versailles, and there were more architects building castles and more landscape gardeners designing parks in eighteenth-century Germany than had ever before been known in Europe. And all these rulers were looking for a Colbert to direct their trading ventures, unwillingly taking a hand themselves when the minister they hoped for failed to emerge from the ranks of their counsellors. The less beribboned the dress the greater the freedom of speech and of action; but there were endless royal fêtes in the style of the court of France; and this imitation of both France and England, more or less influenced by justifications drawn from the philosophical dictionaries, made up what was known as enlightened despotism.

Thus the economic progress which in Western Europe laid the foundations of political liberalism and created a vigorous public opinion, served in the German states to increase the lavish ostentation of the princes and often their absolutism as well. East of the Rhine there were, it is true, vary-ing degrees of despotism. Frederick II, naturally had every intention of be-ing his own chief minister (in the French manner), in sole control of the governmental machine. On the other hand, in Saxony, one of the oldest 'nations' in Germany, the Elector had followed English precedent in granting a moderately free hand to his Lutheran subjects in the discussion of and decisions on public affairs, since he feared that they would take offence at his alacrity in being converted to the Catholic Royal House of Poland. Joseph II, blindly trusting in the reason extolled by the *Encyclo-pédie*, made changes, carried out reforms, codified laws and produced such an excess of order that he brought a whirlwind about his own head.

It is not, however, our purpose to analyse the political mechanism of Europe in the 1780s. It would tell us practically nothing that we need to know for an understanding of how the Europe of the late eighteenth cen-tury became the Europe of 1900. In 1900 there were still, of course, many of the same family traditions, the same frontiers, the same parks, castles and administrative habits which had existed in the previous century, but in the nineteenth century, the princes, good or bad, saw the future of their countries taken out of their hands; and in that respect too, the French Revolution, spectacular though it was, was only one manifestation of that great whirlwind of change which was beginning to blow across Europe. It was a storm which raged, not simply from 1789 to 1815, but from 1780 to 1900.

But in 1780 it was as yet no more than a stiff breeze which had its source not in the secret diplomacy of cabinets, in military discipline, in religious fanaticism or what remained of them, but in the very search for modest pleasures, the zest for new things and the curiosity about science and the world, its geography and history. It was fanned by trade, and by the novelties turned out by craftsmen who were making China fashionable everywhere in European society. This fresh wind blowing through society seemed at first to carry no threat to the old political organism whose gnarled trunks, apparently so sturdy, were rooted deep in feudal traditions. Yet when the breeze became a hurricane they were blown down, and though restored here and there in the nineteenth century, fell once and for all in the early twentieth.

What features of the 1780s are essential to a knowledge of Europe? They are to be found, undoubtedly, not in political organisms, but in the soil of Europe, in its peoples, its countryside, its towns, its rural landscapes, its ports and factories; in the myriad activities which, pursued with toil and effort, were to change the very nature of its labours. These were more im-portant even than the Eastern question, or the Polish question, or any financial questions. We propose now to set out on a journey, a sentimental journey in the manner of Sterne, and to travel with deliberate non-chalance the roads along which the postillions of Goethe, Euler, Mauper-tuis, Diderot, Haydn and Mozart trotted in 1780. We shall not pay par-ticular attention to the big things, but confine ourselves to the small and the insignificant, and try to form an impression of everyday life which though so unchanging in appearance was of endless variety beneath the surface. It was an upheaval in this everyday life which was soon to shake the history of the nineteenth century; the explosion started in Europe but was to change the whole world.

LONDON-BERLIN: A CONTRAST

It is impossible to study here every detail of the life of Europe, which was divided into numerous countries all jealous of their individuality, at a time when patriotism extended very little farther than the parish pump. Nevertheless so important are the differences between the countries directly exposed to Atlantic influences and those still on the periphery that we may be permitted to dwell on them at the outset.

Modernism in England

Every merchant in Frankfurt or Amsterdam, every philosopher in quest of happiness and world prosperity, every sailor waiting for the wind in the tall-masted sailing-ships which scoured the globe, would have urged us to start our world tour with London. Either you liked it or you did not, this upstart city with its thriving business and swirling fog, but it set a magnificent example of the prosperity achieved by a small people, one of the least numerous in Europe, yet the most influential of all because of the irresistible power of its trade and its banking institutions. Its public buildings could not compete with the architectural masterpieces that were the pride of more aristocratic cities; indeed the interest of London lay not in buildings, but in the city itself – the city as a whole, which set a new fashion in urban comfort. We shall not spend too long in visiting the many new churches which had sprung from the fertile brain of Sir Christopher Wren after the Great Fire of the previous century: London's St Paul's was, after all, little more than an imitation of St Peter's in Rome. Let us instead look first at the streets, at traffic hurtling down the Strand at breakneck speed, or along the endless reaches of Holborn. New paving stones kept the roadway clean and level, and since it was fashionable to walk from one place to another in town, the pavements were wide, with railing along the outer edge to protect pedestrians from the throng of carriages. From wooden posts hung lanterns for use in the evenings, and the old watchmen who called the hours all through the night were scarcely needed now, at least in the city centre, since the city was so orderly, and clocks and watches were already in general use. Though there were coffee-houses all over Europe, none could compete with those of London. Only six hundred yards from Westminster were the Ranelagh Gardens with their famous Rotunda, more than sixty yards in diameter. In the middle, in a fireplace surrounded by columns, an enormous brazier supplied heat and light. Strains of

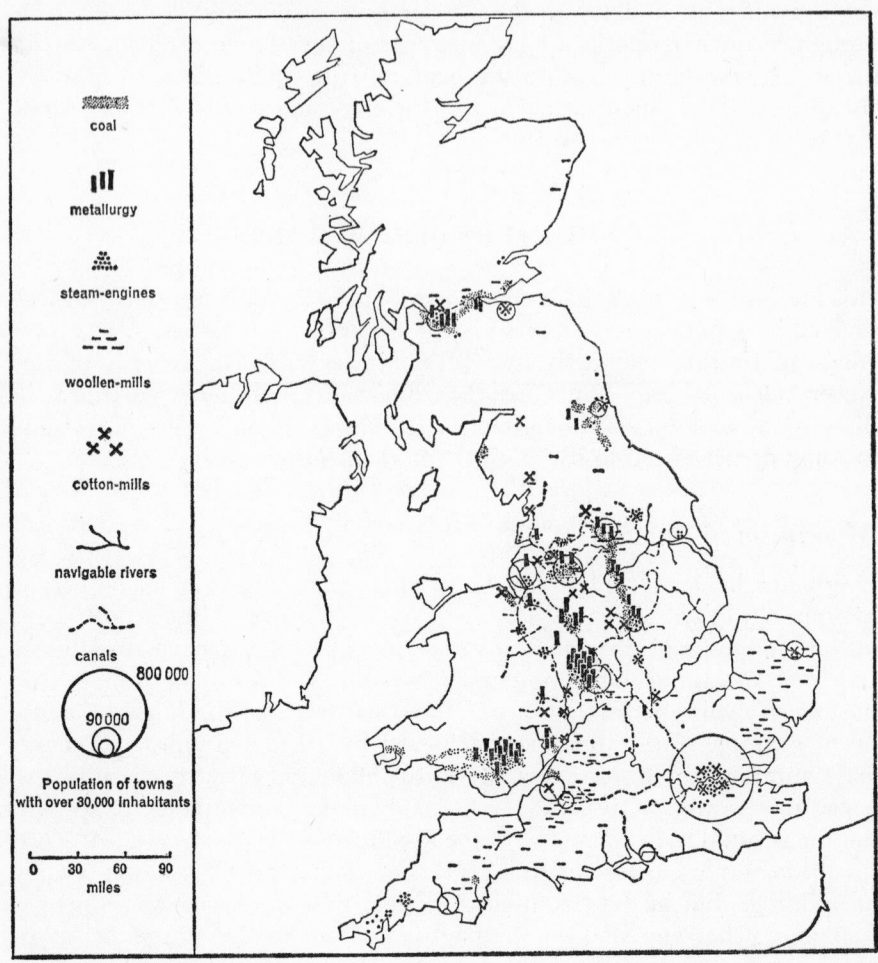

1 Industrial England c. 1780

music floated down from a raised dais, and for a crown you could buy, with rye bread and butter, those brand-new beverages coffee, tea or chocolate. For those who preferred it the rival establishment at Vauxhall could boast a rotunda in the same style, only a little smaller, but surrounded by even more spacious gardens which at night were lit by over a thousand oil lamps. A band played in the open air, visitors flocked there in their thousands, and numerous pavilions in Chinese style combined a homely welcome with the thrills of the exotic.

England also set a fashion in good living, and in home life, in what Englishmen called 'comfort' and everyone else was to call '*confort*'. English private houses had lofty ceilings, spacious staircases, and their brick walls were panelled in light-painted wood, and decorated with graceful garlands. New houses were going up all over London; the builders did not

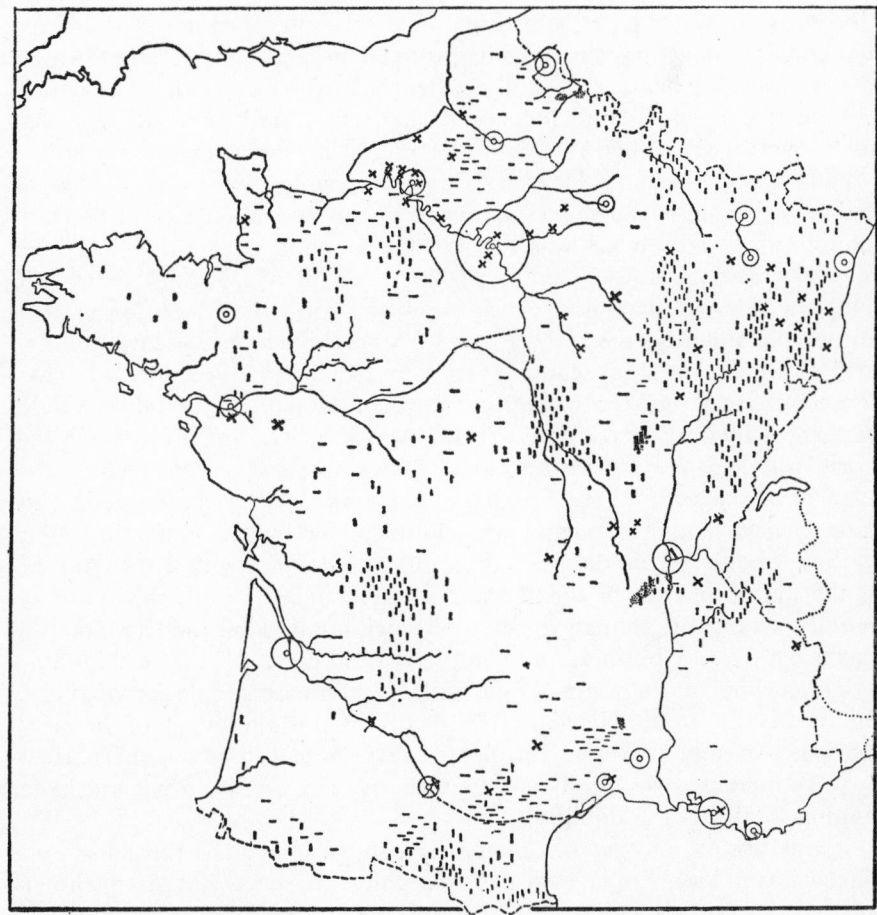

2 Industrial France c. 1780

always own the land on which they built; they leased it for sixty years and built lightly, to avoid having to hand over a still valuable house to the landowner. There were, therefore, many new houses side by side with dilapidated ones. Moreover they were uniform in style; behind those façades, miniature reproductions of Hampton Court, there were tiny houses crowded together, but also great buildings, especially in the centre of the city. The nobility had moved out of the city, deserting their town houses which were turned into business premises. Lord Montagu, for instance, installed the British Museum in his mansion. In the parks of the aristocracy middle-class houses were often built around small squares, an arrangement which combined privacy with a love of nature dear to inhabitants still new to city life. London was no longer the sprawling wooden township of Stuart times; it was already a solidly built city ready and waiting for the overcharged elaborations of the Victorian style. But English comfort implied more than a pleasant home life; it meant also clear

Hertfordshire water piped and distributed through Sir Hugh Middleton's new canal; better still it meant water pumped under steam pressure through lead pipes; and heating in well-constructed fireplaces with coal, which was more convenient and less costly than wood and had only one dis- advantage: it intensified the fog and even – it is said – affected the sun.

Hard work was the order of the day. The penny-post system for letters and parcels catered for correspondence in this enormous city of 800,000 inhabitants. At its heart was the Pool of London near which rose the colossal Customs House, almost as big as the Bank. Around them was built the City, replacing the old administration from Westminster. In- numerable small barges plied to and fro on the Thames below London Bridge, among the ships whose masts were like a swaying forest, branches of a commercial network whose roots tapped the world. Everything could be bought there. Everything was sold, even security. Nowhere else in the world was it so easy to insure oneself, for so modest a sum, against the hazards of the sea and the fluctuations of trade. To keep pace with this entirely new activity, colleges were founded for further education. The leading scholars of the day were brought into contact with a wide public in the amphitheatres of the Royal Society. But above all, this whirl of activity inexorably shaped society. The rich families left the City when it was taken over by business and commerce, and created a new fashionable neighbourhood at St James. Meanwhile the common people crowded into the East End: around Newgate with its prison, and the stench of the meat markets. Already a wretched proletariat was herded together there, their poverty increased by middle-class prosperity and by the great and con- tinuing wealth of the nobility.

It was not easy to get out of the city, so great was the throng of car- riages. Even Frenchmen were left speechless at the way the coachmen hurtled along roads which were often indifferent, narrow, and continually in need of repair. Nowhere else in Europe was there such a busy round of traffic as that which connected London with its countryside and with other towns and cities. Once this bustle had been left behind, there was the green English countryside, with its meadows and valleys, its cottages tucked away amongst trees, its small estates hidden behind hedges. These estates were not over-large but were prosperous because they were never smaller than a hundred acres, and were well stocked with cattle which were the admiration of every landowner in Europe; the cattle wintered indoors, were put out to grass in summer, and provided London with the finest meat in the world. Stockbreeding had not, however, entirely sup- planted corn. In good years England had surplus corn to sell to Portugal and Spain and sometimes even to France. Outside London it was still a predominantly rural country. There were still large pockets of land in England given over to the old systems of mixed cultivation which had sup- ported the freeholders, small tenant-farmers who had been the backbone of Cromwellian England. But almost everywhere new crops, new farming methods, and new social groups were beginning to efface them.

England was still proud of its landed gentry, who had stopped taking up arms against the court after their abortive attempt to seize power in the seventeenth century, and had destroyed the old régime by economic innovations instead. Indeed, the success of the agricultural reformer, Townshend, contributed to that of his brother-in-law, Walpole, who was for long master of London. In return the London merchant helped the agriculturist. Parliament continually passed bills authorizing the splitting up of common lands, a process which completed the ruin of the poor whilst making the fortune of the average or large landowners. Townshend, then, was one of a number who, on retiring from public life, set the fashion for studying agriculture, and made stockbreeding as important a business as the composition of a ministry. Nowhere else in Europe, Young assures us, were there such well-tended fields and such a comfortable country life. Seventy per cent of the population was still rural – a high proportion by twentieth-century standards, but small in the eighteenth century by comparison with the rest of Europe. It was large enough, however, to produce abundant crops of rye, oats and barley and the widest range of vegetables, while continuing to breed fine long-haired sheep, a tradition inherited from the Middle Ages. Yet it was hardly the golden age of country life. In the midst of this prosperity, English travellers had a good deal to say about the extreme poverty of the country people; not only were there vagrants, driven from the countryside by the disappearance of common lands and enclosures who were starting to drift towards city suburbs, but there was poverty on poor lands untouched by the reforms. In these particularly poor areas, philanthropists even did their best to keep alive some of the wise traditions of former days, by reintroducing pig-farming and poultry-keeping, small rural sidelines which had gone out of fashion. Poor countrymen had such a struggle to make ends meet that it was no wonder they were attracted when merchants offered to lease them a hand-loom, and held out the possibility of piece-work. Many middle-class 'merchants', of country stock and new to trade, made their fortunes in this way. One of the first was Sir Robert Peel's ancestor, who started a small cotton mill on his farm and employed his own family as well as the poor from neighbouring cottages, thus paving the way for the next generation's exodus to the nearby town. Such was the rise of one of the foremost families in England.

London was not the only town that made a great urban blot on the green landscape of southern England. Near the Pennines, black, sprawling patches revealed the spread of towns and mills. Though the ancient port of Bristol was still the second largest city in the country, and though development of colonial trade enabled it to maintain its position during the first half of the century, its supremacy had recently begun to be threatened by new towns which had sprung up from nowhere. They might not rival Bristol in size, but their progress was meteoric; Liverpool, Manchester, Birmingham and Sheffield soon outgrew the older centres of Leeds and Bradford. The old privileges of the trade guilds had disappeared, and those of the trading companies were broken or rather worn down by economic practice and new commercial concepts which the Law Courts, backed by public opinion, gradually came to confirm. The East India Company, for instance, was incapable of exercising its monopoly alone, and had to agree to a sub-contract in exchange for an indemnity. This indemnity, however, gradually decreased, opening the way for numerous rival companies and shipowners eager to engage in so profitable a trade. The Elizabethan guild rules, though they had never been very strictly observed, were invoked more and more rarely and then only for use against crying abuses, such as the disasters caused by the blundering ambition of would-be businessmen who took advantage of the powerlessness of the workers to put their new schemes through more quickly. But the injustice had to be exceptionally harsh, and had sometimes to end in riot, before the corporative régime was again invoked. The new political religion held that profit was the source, as well as the just reward, of creative activity.

So water-wheels soon appeared along the rivers, working the forge-bellows and grindstones of cutlery works. Ironmongers no longer manufactured their wares. Ancient villages were rudely jolted awake. Spinning-jennies, or spinning-frames, invaded the countryside in the wake of the looms, before being concentrated in certain city suburbs, in vast mills run by water-power; and steam-power was soon to follow. So factories hummed busily in places where poor country folk had settled with their meagre belongings when driven out of their small-holdings. Sometimes the small landowner became the small mill-owner. But more often than not he was pulled down to the poverty-stricken proletarian mass on which the manufacturer drew for whatever labour he needed. For this labour he paid practically nothing, and it enabled him to sell his goods at enormous profit in the city markets, and even more in country markets, where hawkers' packs were everywhere in evidence on fair-days.

All this economic activity creates the impression of a kind of vast industrial republic. Yet dominating it all was some 'prince' or, as the saying ran later, some 'king of industry'. There was Boulton of Birmingham, for instance, living in his brand-new mansion, surrounded by a veritable court of artists, poets and inventors (it was with the support of this wealthy patron that James Watt perfected his steam-engine). Boulton was the aristocratic-ironmonger who was to be associated with Wedgwood in an alliance so powerful that it obtained from Pitt's Government, along with the revision of excise duties, freer access to international exchange. Boulton went to Europe in search of artistic inspiration for his products, his knick-knacks. He made cheap reproductions of the marble statues being discovered in Italy, whilst Wedgwood drew on the arts of antiquity for designs for his pottery, ceramics and porcelain. Thanks to them, every middle-class sideboard had its china made from the local clay of the Potteries, and every middle-class kitchen boasted utensils made from the new iron. For Wilkinson, another king of industry, erected furnaces on the banks of the Severn. This iron king had been the first to put smelting and iron puddling on an industrial basis. He had ventured to span the Severn with the first iron bridge. He presented the citizens of London with an extravagant toy in the shape of a boat, made entirely of iron, floating on the Thames.

The rôle of these kings of industry should not, however, be exaggerated; though they caught the imagination of their contemporaries, they were insignificant in comparison with the powerful figures which were to arise in industry a century later. Moreover, they were very few and far between. They reflected a society in process of evolution but which, taken by and large, still kept fairly close to its classical structure. We have seen that the common people, when driven to it by the energy born of despair, could invoke the old guild rules and rely on them to force from the new masters certain improvements in wages. But the masters themselves often used these rules to check dangerous competition. The Government, and even Parliament, hesitated to do away completely with the old laws and principles. In any case they continued to accept the obligation of king, county and parish to ensure that the poor had bread and work. They were still reluctant to compel beggars to work in the workhouses, and the English state, although it soon became the model of the indifferent liberal state, was at that point still a welfare state. The Government opened workshops, particularly in London, tried to ensure that apprentices had a good training, and improved the status of journeymen, for whom they endeavoured, though unsuccessfully, to ensure a decent livelihood. The example of the early masters of industry was more potent than state initiative. Such vast fortunes so speedily amassed were an incentive to ambition. There was naturally the fear of bankruptcy, which so often resulted from rashness, but to stay idle in that rapidly changing society was to run the risk of swelling the ranks of the paupers. So every river in England became the scene of industrial activity much admired by travellers. The gap widened between the prosperous countryside and its burdensome poor, and around the new country houses there surged a tide of change which threatened to engulf the last remnants of the old, merry England.

Tradition in Germany

We move, now, from one end of Europe to the other: to the roads stretching endlessly over the monotonous plains of the Weser and the Spree. Imagine a traveller riding into Berlin in one of those light travelling-coaches, 'berlines', so swift and well-sprung that they were soon to become popular with the middle classes all over Europe. He would have to cross the barriers surrounding the city. A sightseer would be more likely to be attracted by some famous buildings (the Prince's palace, the King's palace, the building of the Academy) than by the city as a whole. Around these places, Berlin was an overgrown village with a population less than one-eighth of that of London. True, it could boast many factories, each consisting of a central workshop with a large number of home workers, often run by masters with French names. They turned out porcelain and woollen goods, particularly the famous red and blue cloth, and of course silks, all imitated from the French. They also made cotton using English processes, and – a great novelty – made a first attempt at running a sugar refinery.

But Berlin was not a workers' city, it was first and foremost a city of soldiers. The Prussian soldier was different from other soldiers: in Berlin he lived at home with his family, and so made up almost a third of the city's population. In Potsdam, nearby, there was a school which provided the rudiments of education for five thousand soldiers' children. If there were more than the army required, they were given a few crowns and sent to live with peasants who brought them up and gave them work until they were old enough for military service and were needed by the Prussian army. In England it was the merchant's way of life that threw light on the real social forces at work in the country, whereas in Germany it was the soldier who held the key to progress. In Berlin the soldier was employed in the factories in peacetime, and when he was not on manoeuvres. He took what employment he could find and was welcomed by numerous industrial establishments financed by the Royal Treasury as well as by private firms. Outside Berlin, in the country, he worked on the land, leaving it from April to May and going back for the harvest in July. We should bear in mind the type of eighteenth-century warfare in which Frederick II distinguished himself. There were no frontier battles, but heavy raids into Russia or similar expeditions thrusting deep into the heart of the country. The army might be, in fact had to be, everywhere. The sword lay beside the plough. As with the ordinary soldier, so it was with the officer. The country squire, the small country landowner of good old stock, so proud of his Teutonic past, was the best captain in the royal army. The king called him up for his wars, but also saw that he was given good seed to sow, credits for draining his marshes, and sound advice from the Berlin Academy which not only produced brilliant mathematicians, but acted as a kind of vast agricultural college, concentrating on concrete techniques of value to the economy rather than on abstract speculation. Thus soldiers and captains worked shoulder to shoulder on the farm as well as in the army. Such was the origin of Prussian solidarity. Agriculture fed the people, and filled the royal granaries. It supplied rural and urban markets, but also filled the stores of the commissariat. Industry, on which the king kept a watchful eye, provided clothing for the middle classes, but also for the army; and it was designed for manufacturing weapons as well as tools. Frederick II built up his country on the lines of a vast entrenched camp.

There were some exceptions to this general view of Prussia. There was, for instance, Breslau which it had recently acquired; the flax and hemp grown on its surrounding terraces produced magnificent linen, perhaps the finest in Europe, and a great loss to Maria Theresa; and fine woollen cloth came from the neighbouring mountains, and from the ports. But the chemical industry was a product of this double activity; with state encouragement, it made a start with the new vitriol works, bleaching mills and explosives factories.

The age-old search for yellow amber still went on along the seashore, but every month saw the opening of new glass, china and textile factories in Koenigsberg or Memel. The king encouraged it all, to enrich his country and his treasury, and sustain his policy – whether pacific or military.

The Prussian ports deserve a detailed description. Memel, the old Hanseatic town at which only seventy ships put in at the middle of the century, was loading more than seven hundred round about 1785. Stettin, the fortified town, was the storehouse for all the countries along the Oder, and handled large imports of foodstuffs and exports of timber. Amidst these growing ports, Koenigsberg was struggling to hold its own all the more creditably since the technical facilities of its old harbour were proving more and more inadequate. To keep going at all it had to send a large number of ships to its outport Pillau. The ruler of Prussia realized how useful these ports were to him; he was keen to see shipowners and merchants group together and form royal companies, and he always afforded them his protection. At Danzig (a great commercial city which was already becoming a problem to Europe's diplomatists) Frederick II had just handed over all sea-borne trade exclusively to the ancient citizens of the town, leaving the newly-arrived Prussians the quasi-privilege of trading freely on land, from east to west, and throughout Pomerania, which until recently had been part of Poland.

The rising state of Prussia gradually awoke to life and order, taking its place in Germany as a whole. Germany, while retaining its traditional political character, was nevertheless, in its turn, becoming increasingly active. A detailed description would reveal its infinite variety: in Munich industry was reminiscent of Paris; there was a great factory making Gobelin tapestries, and textile mills turning out cloth inspired by French fashion. The industry of Nuremberg continued to show that its economic roots were deep in the Renaissance; its brass, copper, silver ware and woodwork were exported all over Europe. Then there was Mainz, its cellars stocked with Rhenish wines, and Dresden, famed for its furniture, its fine shops filled with saxe-blue cloth. Each of these cities was actually the centre of a small state, whose prince, after erecting all the buildings needed, lived on the income from its customs duties, and even, when hard up, on hiring out to more affluent princes soldiers who were soon famous throughout Europe for their discipline and their cheapness. Each city was therefore the seat of a small court, often outmoded and pretentious in its way of life, but with a certain provincial charm, with its own poets, painters and philosophers, and of course its inevitable *Hofmusiker*, who was conductor, composer and orchestral manager all in one. From one end of Germany to the other, the *Bruderschaft* movement encouraged young people to indulge their passion for long rambles on which they sang together and marched in step, especially on Sundays, returning in the evening to the local concert hall where they listened to orchestral music or joined in community singing. There was a general atmosphere of *gemütlichkeit*, liveliness and good fellowship.

It should not, however, be thought that these small German capitals were hide-bound in their routines. The staid citizen, his wig tied with a butterfly bow, his long-tailed coat flapping round his thighs, who wanted nothing more novel than a clay pipe and the beerhouse, might perhaps give that impression; but German youth was already being disturbed by the turmoil of *Sturm und Drang*. The day was over when, at Jena, the great Saxon University which had been the home of the Lutheran tradition, the students commissioned J.S.Bach to write a cantata, celebrating in mythological style the praises of one of their revered professors. A small, intellectual revolutionary movement was evidence of a youth impatient and eager for emancipation. Goethe, with the complicity of the Duke, shocked the Court of Weimar with his farces; and above all Schiller, having stirred up the University of Stuttgart, was soon reduced to tramping the roads of Germany pursued by the myrmidons of the Duke of Württemberg from whose army he had deserted. He lived hunted and wretched, existing on potatoes which were rotting in his drawer, but writing *Die Räuber*, that haunting play which proclaimed that the law could never create great men, that routine and discipline only led to degradation, that liberty alone could foster genius. This eccentric poet gained a following among young people all over the land. At Mannheim he was fêted like a conqueror and even the well-bred Goethe was eventually captivated by the poverty-stricken rebel. They were moreover brought together by their mutual enthusiasm for the recent discoveries of science, since one of their first friendly contacts took place as they came out of a lecture in Jena on the progress of biology.

The origins of this revolt of German youth, a revolt which a generation later was to inspire Fichte, Grillparzer and Père Jahn, lay, certainly not in economic ambitions, but in a violent need to break up the old-fashioned framework of their narrow urban civilization, that very framework which was also hampering economic development. In any case those were years during which the entire youth of Germany travelled widely – the *Wanderjahre*. They moved from country to country, and got to know each other; without settling down in any one place, they travelled throughout Germany. Sometimes criticism of municipal life led them to the delighted discovery of nature, and, like Goethe, they identified themselves with Werther. Or else they turned plebeian with Schiller and, less eager to enjoy nature, wished to begin by destroying those 'nests of pestilence' the courts of princes: from the inevitable and bitter struggle between intrigue and love was to emerge a prosperous Germany which would have made Sparta look like a nunnery.

These young people certainly despised the middle classes for being too submissive to the prince. But the Germany of their dreams was actually taking shape before their eyes in the form of timid experiments which brought fresh vigour to old institutions: the Leipzig fairs took on a new lease of life and exhibited Bohemian glass, Silesian linen, Augsburg silverware, Hungarian leather, Dutch swords, and fashionable French novelties. There were also the Frankfurt fairs at which merchants from Italy, Holland, France and Switzerland argued over big deals near the obscure ghetto where Nathan de Rothschild was keeping a wary eye on his fluctuating fortune as he dealt in old clothes and sold carefully selected antiques cheaply to neighbouring princelings.

Most important of all these commercial cities was Hamburg, now a large city of more than 100,000 inhabitants (not counting the Jewish population). It was built in the Dutch style, and a notable feature of the enlargement carried out in 1785 was the completion of the *Herrengraben*, a new canal which cut through the ramparts and enabled more ships to reach the centre of the city. Hamburg was famous for its vigorous maritime trade which was both envied and protected by the Baltic and North Sea merchants, and neither the reviving shipping of Denmark, nor that of Sweden, which had leapt into sudden prosperity, was as yet in a position to compete with it. Moreover, this city was not only growing more beautiful, it was also acquiring entirely new industries. It already prided itself on the quality of its sugar, which was even more famous than its beer, and on the variety of its textiles. Its flourishing trade, its banks, its numerous laboratories and workshops grouped around the old sixteenth-century municipal bank, won for the city and its finances such a high reputation that its coinage, the Mark, stamped with the city arms, was valid throughout the length and breadth of Europe.

Elsewhere in Central Europe

It is impossible to pursue this economic pilgrimage, in detail, through the whole of Central Europe. We can only refer in passing to Prague, one of the most modern cities so far as its economic reputation is concerned and one of the oldest in the charm of its architecture, to the steel works of the Tyrol, to the iron foundries of Innsbruck, and particularly to Vienna – the threshold of the East, with its suburbs inhabited by Turks and Armenians who came to sell their country produce and buy ironware (scythes and sickles) and cloth. Vienna was the capital of one of the oldest monarchies and the place where the best gold braid in Europe was made.

Yet this long list of cities should not mislead us. Apart from these small capitals, Central Europe consisted of countryside of the most primitive kind. Serfdom was almost universal and had its roots deep in the soil. Just beyond the Rhine was to be found the age-old division of the land into plots cultivated on a three-course rotation, bordered by communal lands and forest – the old agricultural system which had supported the European peasantry in the Middle Ages. Whether or not the system was Germanic in origin, it was certainly Germanic in the eighteenth century. This agricultural picture naturally varied in character in every area of Central Europe, from the manorial system in the West (*Grund-herrschaft*) to feudal landownership in the East (*Gutherrenschaft*). In Brisgau and Austrian Swabia serfdom had disappeared as early as the sixteenth century. In the West,

generally speaking, feudal rights had been somewhat relaxed and were
sometimes replaced by gifts in money and kind granted to the peasants by
the lord of the manor for the tasks they did for their master; and slowly the
village community was breaking up. In fact, if not in law, the lot of the
Rhineland peasants was probably not very different from that of peasants
on the Meuse.

In the East, on the other hand, in spite of the rigorous efforts of Joseph
II, the restrictions under which the serf laboured were still very oppressive.
Peasants were even to be found working on their own lands by night because their days had been taken up with work for the nobleman's benefit.
The use of the term 'peasants' lands' does not even imply that there was a
régime of individual ownership, since the peasant lands belonged to the
village, which managed them in common. And beyond the Elbe the
farther we penetrate into Poland and the vast stretches of Russia, the more
firmly we find this communal peasant system established, assuming an
almost geographical inevitability. The nobleman was not so much a landowner as an owner of men. If he wished to mobilize soldiers, he ordered
his villagers to provide them. If he needed workmen for a factory he intended to open on his own estate, he selected the smartest of his subjects
and transported them to the site of the building. If he needed servants he
took young people from the village to be trained and educated for his
household. The village community had no option but to ensure the survival of its members through the bitter winter as best it could. Work on the
land, the management of the village interests as a whole, were conducted
according to routines of very ancient origin, going back to neolithic times.

Under this curious system the wealth of a country was reckoned not in
the produce of the land, but in manpower. When Catherine II opened a
money-lending establishment in St Petersburg in order to make available
to the nobles of her country credit facilities which would enable them to
adapt themselves to the new trends in economic life, it was human souls
which were pledged as security, the number of souls owned by each nobleman being determined by a census held every five years. It was a Russian
system, but also a Transylvanian one, and with few modifications it extended as far as the banks of the Elbe. Throughout these regions governed
by a rigid system of land tenure, there were naturally variations in economic structure between one area and another. In Eastern Germany there
were peasant holdings: individual farms, the remnants of West German
medieval colonization in Slav territory. Most important of all, and particularly from the beginning of the century, great streams of trade began to
flow along the old routes, and corn was collected in the villages for the
nobleman's bailiffs to sell in Danzig, so that he could buy with the proceeds those luxury goods hitherto unheard of by the lords of Poland or St
Petersburg. In this way the latest fashions from the great Western capitals
penetrated to the most backward society in Europe. German princes,
Russian and Polish nobility came to inherit the splendour of Versailles.
But this circulation of goods was not always easy: the roads were in bad

repair, and sometimes petered out in the fields. The roads of Eastern Europe could not be compared with French roads, nor its countryside with the English countryside.

In order to keep their merchants, so useful if the supply of luxury goods was to be maintained, the nobility and princes granted them extraordinary privileges, frequently extended to Jews, the most active of them all. This was the case not only in the maritime republics of Germany: in Russia Catherine issued a decree placing them above the middle classes but below the nobility, and excepting them entirely from all the restrictions to which the common people were subject. In Sweden, the merchant was respected. In Poland he quietly pursued his own interests amidst the quarrels of the great. The merchant may have still been incapable, even in Sweden, of exerting any permanent influence on political life, but he was gradually gaining possession of the centres of communication to which the ruling class was beginning to attach increasing importance. He started a great movement which gradually tried to dominate industrial production, not yet, of course, in great factories, but in the home industries carried on by peasants in their cottages.

Thus, under the direct rule of Frederick and of Catherine, or the indirect authority of Joseph II, there was a noticeable enlargement of the trade arteries which spread their network through the old feudal country areas. Here indeed, unlike England, there was little direct connection between the landowner devoted to the improvement of agriculture and the merchant in the city. The growth of commerce was protected chiefly by the prince, overlord of the landed gentry. In London trade was created by liberty, in Berlin and Paris by despotism. In Poland the wealthy aristocrat and his innumerable train of poor dependants paid no heed to this basic difference and wore themselves out in paying lip-service to the word liberty only to fall more easily under the autocracy of Russia or Prussia; whilst in the lands of the House of Austria, from the Low Countries to Hungary, the people mutinied against Joseph II's reforms, because they were too radical or too ruthless.

For the closing years of the eighteenth century already showed the paradoxical features of an evolution which dominated Europe right up to our own day; in the East, progress and despotism; in the West, progress and parliamentarianism. Nor were the results interchangeable. For in the West the merchant gained control of power, whereas in the East the nobility remained in power and merely sanctioned his activities. It was to be the same with industry, for though it was more robust than commerce in its first vigorous growth, it soon fell into the same rigid pattern.

PARIS BETWEEN TWO WORLDS

There are two Europes, one of the sea, the other of the continent. Between the two lies France. Where did it stand at this juncture? Was it caught up in the whirl of economic innovations which were beginning to give England its Victorian characteristics or was it still a backward country, bogged down in feudalism, into which new ideas could be injected only by the authority of the monarch? The France of Louis xvi saw many travellers: the majority, first of all, naturally, were French, but there were also Germans, English, Italians, and many of them have left detailed accounts of their travels. Yet it is difficult to gain any clear impression from them. A splenetic Italian paints too dark a picture whilst the gentle Franklin is more indulgent. A German praises everything he sees in the highest terms, with one exception – the exceedingly slipshod way in which the soldiers march. But what of Young, the inquisitive, accurate, and ruthless Young? He is by turns enthusiastic and indignant. He saw foul cesspools and splendid cities, delightful stretches of countryside and others so poverty-stricken that they were a standing reproach to the despotic régime which had caused them. Unfortunately these opinions frequently give contradictory versions of the same phenomenon. A manufacturing city in Flanders, for example, might be considered either a busy hive of industry or a wretched hell; a farm in Caux might be called a mud heap or a quaint cottage which only needed whitewashing to be better than English cottages. How is it possible to form an accurate picture when faced with such an accumulation of conflicting opinions?

It would be simple to state that France was a land of contrasts. But there were contrasts in England between the Downs and the new industrial countryside, and in Germany between the Pomeranian peasant and the Hamburg citizen. Yet if the word contrast could be applied to any one country in particular it was undoubtedly the France of 1780. It was a combination of the civilization which created the commercial supremacy of England and the feudalism which typified the endless plains of Eastern Europe. France was the country of the past and of the future. The royal apartments at Versailles, once the jewelled shrine of kingly omnipotence, illustrate the extent to which France lived in the past. Petitioners certainly still flocked there, and in the Hall of Mirrors beggars rubbed shoulders with bourgeois dressed in serge and noblemen glittering with decorations, especially at one o'clock on Sundays, the hour of the Royal Mass. The most unwashed of scoundrels could even gain access to the king's chamber, in the crowd which swept past the Swiss Guard in the ante-chamber to the Great Hall (the Oeil-de-Boeuf). The king himself used to retire to his attic, where he enjoyed working with his hands as a locksmith, and (like any middle-class father) he loved to relax with his family in the queen's private apartments. Louis xvi, the plump adolescent, behaved like a schoolboy in the midst of a ceremonial to which the valets adhered more rigidly than their masters. He was a figure-head issuing orders, a mere symbol of authority. Around him the courtiers most crippled with debt were often the most extravagant: rebuilding *châteaux*, erecting follies in a few weeks to be used for a fête lasting a single evening. In the most famous park in the world, the queen played the farmer's wife. The royal family had lost its majesty. They even turned a pilgrimage to the tomb of poor Jean-Jacques Rousseau into a fête and went in fancy dress. In a Louis xiv setting, they lived in the manner approved by Diderot.

Paris itself showed the same contrasts. In the northern and eastern quarters, the streets unpaved and unlit, there were sewers piled with offal and rubbish thrown from the houses, whose overhanging fronts made the narrow streets gloomy. The dark shops were pervaded by the sour smell of poverty. Already, around the Hôtel-Dieu and Notre Dame there was growing up a strange and poverty-stricken quarter into which honest people hesitated to venture. But at the opposite extreme were the glittering splendours of the city of cities – the Place Louis xv and its colonnades, the gardens of the Palais-Royal, its arcades, its kiosk, its gay and lively throng, the Boulevard des Capucines with its broad belt of trees amongst which rose the pagodas of the Chinese baths. There was the Temple and its famous fête; and a copy of London's Vauxhall competing with the Café de Foy and the Café Italien; all were furnished in silks, velvets, mirrors, and gave the Parisians the illusion that they were living like kings. Yet, after all, such crude contrasts have been a feature of every city, whether ancient or modern.

More detailed facts are available. An ordinary person living on bread and cheese nevertheless ate off china plates, used a knife and fork, and had a four-poster bed. It is difficult to find out how his budget was balanced. Though much is heard of incredibly meagre meals, they were almost always washed down with wine. Even outside the cities, country folk normally in rags would put on finery for High Mass on Sundays. There is Rousseau's story of the peasant who looked so poor but, on being assured that his visitor was not a tax-collector, offered him the comparative riches of his larder. In any case, the wealth of the peasant seemed to have no connection with that of the soil. Young found what he called mud huts in Normandy, and stone houses too fine to be called cottages in Quercy. This astonishment may simply be that of a man accustomed to brick buildings and confronted with the splendours of stone architecture. But, in the same vein, it was Gilbert who claimed that poverty in France followed 'industry and the wealth of the soil'. In a rich countryside, a poor peasantry; in a poor countryside, a well-to-do peasantry. The population tended to accumulate in places where the hope of a livelihood was greater. And the rich country areas were also those containing industrial towns; hand-looms were installed in the peasant farms which the merchant from the town kept going with orders carried out at cheap rates.

Yet poor though the country districts were, they were gradually shedding all traces of serfdom. The law limited the right of mortmain, a right which made the landowner complete master of the peasant's person and reduced him to the status of a serf. In the eighteenth century, French people were beginning to think this went too far. Beyond the Rhine, and certainly beyond the Elbe, it was a fact as well as a right; in England it was no longer either fact or law; in France, if the law still existed, it was not applied. Although Louis xvi had suppressed the law of mortmain in his domains as long ago as 1774, he had made it clear that he could not abolish it from the lands of his subjects without encroaching on the right of ownership. The royal Treasury, in any case, could not possibly pay the landowners the 'just' indemnity which would enable this last vestige of slavery to be banished for ever. The law courts and the high judicial courts made a practice of limiting the consequences of this right. In many estates it disappeared of its own accord, and in others famous law-suits showed how difficult it was for the lord of the manor to produce the requisite proofs from his archives when challenged. About 1781, a land-owner in Franche-Comté lost a law-suit he felt certain of winning: a vital bundle of papers proving his rights, many of them going back two hundred years, were of no use to him at all. A few formal objections disposed of them; the law was feudal, but practice was liberal.

But to return to our travellers: the Russian Karamsin found country districts poorer than those of the Neva, the Austrian Hartig affirms that the Champenois were living on cooked clover, yet the severely critical Young rated Bordeaux higher than Liverpool. North of the wide Garonne the merchants' town houses, the crescent curving around the king's statue, the lovely theatre, made a harmonious group unique in the world. And Nantes was as impressive as Bordeaux. Both hummed with activity. The many ships and the importance of their cargoes were evidence of the strength of French maritime trade. Yet nothing could be more wretched than the poverty of the Landes or the Vendée.

By-passing Clermont, which Arthur Young dismissed summarily as 'carved out of a dunghill', we move on to Lyons, one of the most famous cities on the Continent. Its 200,000 inhabitants lived packed into a small area around the finest town-hall in Europe, a seventeenth-century build-ing repaired in 1702 by Mansart after the fire of 1674. At any rate the peo-ple of Lyons thought their town-hall superior to that of Amsterdam. The eighteenth century saw the peak of its prosperity; never before had so many looms clattered at the foot of the Croix-Rousse, never such a busy hum of trade, from the Place Bellecour (then the Place Louis-le-Grand) to the Terreaux. For the previous twenty-five years goods leaving Lyons had been exempt from local customs duties, which had brought about a phenomenal increase in trade. Its most famous products were silks, and cloth of gold, and braids, which almost rivalled those of Vienna, and in recent years new products from the dye-works, soap factories and drug-factories which made the Vitriolerie quarter one of the world's finest centres of the chemical industry. The town expanded by imposing an in-creasingly heavy burden of taxation; the engineer Perrache embanked the Rhone and imprisoned it between great stone quays. In the new quarters with their streets intersecting at right angles Lyons was beginning to as-sume the aspect of a capital city; it was proud of its academies, its palaces and even its governor Villeroi, whose wildly extravagant way of life was the envy of many an imperial prince.

Such then was France, with its powerful and prosperous cities set in a countryside in which opposition to change seemed to increase in proportion to the richness of the land. Such a dogmatic assertion calls for further elaboration. Young, indeed, is a reliable guide, and he declares that the improvement in agricultural techniques was far from being as thorough in France as across the Channel. The reason for this lay in the different system of land ownership. In England the small estate had vanished. In France, on the other hand, it was so deeply rooted that the trend towards larger farms encouraged by the new technical improvements had only limited effects. We are told that many farms which were too small were broken up, particularly when their farmhouses fell into ruins because they were too costly to repair, and were leased in small plots to neighbouring farmers. But this did not mean that they ploughed more land or increased their livestock, and if their yields improved slightly in quality, production as a whole sometimes decreased. There was, of course, Rochefoucauld-Liancourt, who made a name for himself by modernizing great estates on English lines, but his example was not followed by the majority. The small farmer stuck to his old ways. For one thing, he could not read. There was therefore little likelihood that he would ever be affected by the pleas and the advice of agronomists, who were great publishers of treatises; this sort of treatise was read much more widely in the towns than in the country. There were, it is true, a large number of agricultural societies in which well-meaning people expressed pious hopes and were particularly anxious that each village should have its resident adviser capable of instructing the peasant population – a praiseworthy intention but of no practical significance. In such conditions, the work of progressive administrators often ran counter to the aims proposed. For instance, to improve stock-breeding the use of studs was extended throughout France, and these were given special protection, notably by forbidding breeding in the countryside. These studs were the admiration of travellers. Nevertheless they did harm to French livestock, which decreased so sharply in twenty years that in 1785 there was talk of suppressing them: there were not enough horses for the cavalry and Spain could no longer buy mules. It seemed far better, on the whole, to have less highly-bred animals and more of them. In consequence, because the government could not carry its precepts right into the heart of the country, its effects were crippling in spite of its good intentions. It is true that the royal *château* at Rambouillet was renowned throughout Europe for its achievements – particularly in breeding merinos; but its example was followed abroad more than in France. Botanical gardens were all the rage, royal gardens by which the government set such store that it even opened one in Louisiana in order to introduce American plants into France (cotton was tried out in the south and in Corsica); but if these royal gardens were a tremendous help to the new study of natural history, they were of little use to agriculture. The King might guide the plough, the Queen turn dairymaid; but the villein's yearly routine continued unchanged.

Similarly, French cities owed their beauty to an architectural tradition which was far more monarchical than bourgeois. The hastily built London houses may have looked less attractive, but they were the result of a surge of individual wealth and of trade, while the superb avenues in Paris and the provinces were the work of the government. The Bordeaux bourgeois, the future Girondist, was indeed rich, but the splendid layout of his city was not of his planning though he helped to pay for it. The same applied to industrial life. Wagons from Lorraine, workers from the Auvergne massifs converged at Le Creusot, and blast-furnaces were built under the active supervision of English iron-founders, particularly Wilkinson. France was making its first successful attempt at smelting with coke, but the chief shareholder was the King. Similarly, the chief shareholder in the nearby glass-works was Queen Marie-Antoinette; and again in the new mines at Anzin. Were there *any* great ventures not financed by royal capital? The Duke of Orleans worked wonders, and was a great builder of shops, houses and apartments around his royal palace. He was patron and shareholder in Central Canals, and created several industries, but it was all made possible by his royal fortune. This did not mean that the bourgeoisie were unhappy or poor – craftsmen's shops had probably never done such a thriving trade, or been so quick to carry out orders for more and more utensils for even the poorest kitchens – but it was hardly possible to find a single powerful, middle-class company creating big capital. Associations of capital did exist, those of the Partisans. The success of the Paris brothers and the fortune of Lavoisier are famous: but again, this accumulation of wealth and this organization of capital were made through royal financial channels in the service of the Treasury and derived from taxation.

Public opinion, formed by popular books extolling liberty, had no use for the Court and courtiers, yet it was just as definitely in favour of the progress brought about by the royal administration and even by the aristocracy. What conclusion can the historian draw from such a paradox? If we examine the texts of the period we find that all echo a common satisfaction in having had the good fortune to be born under an enlightened king whose youthful reign gave promise of both progress and liberty.

This hope was to persist as long as the illusion lasted that the king could be at one and the same time dictatorial enough to impose reforms and compliant enough to live like a bourgeois. The artisan, the merchant, the shipowner, who had made a fortune but had not been able to gain control of credit, looked to the king to give them what they had not been able to take for themselves. This meant in effect that they were expecting the Bourbon locksmith to create in ten years economic institutions which it had taken England two hundred years to perfect. They were expecting him to be as enlightened as Frederick II, but in a country where the middle classes, already exceedingly active, had no longer any intention of bowing down to despotism.

DECLINE OF THE SOUTH

If the Atlantic trade played such an important part in the comparative transformation of London and Berlin, it did so at the expense of the Mediterranean, which until recently had been Europe's main gateway to the world. Formerly the highways of civilization, the peninsulas were now no more than its museums.

Revival in Spain

Let us turn to Spain. It was a land corroded by the floods of gold and silver which had been sweeping across it ever since the New World was first plundered and drained dry by the victorious adventurers following the routes opened up by Christopher Columbus. The land was deserted by its sturdy peasants who had been conscripted long years ago and torn from the soil to man ships, and had left their vital work in Europe to follow the mirage in America. It was a land neglected by a people indoctrinated by hordes of monks and priests who relied on the authority of the all-powerful Inquisition to discourage every worldly enterprise of any magnitude. A land, in short, ravaged by the 'American sickness'. There are writers and philosophers in plenty who hold Spain up to a virtuous Europe as the most appalling example of what despotism can produce when it is founded on slavery and encouraged by fanaticism. They describe the ragged soldier with no thought in his head but desertion, the arrogant beggar soliciting alms with pride and receiving them with condescension, the haughty, impoverished nobleman looking to adventure for a living he will not earn by daily toil.

But Spain has its defenders as well. They show the other side of the picture, the virtuous and enlightened Charles III, setting an ideal example of economic restoration to the courts of Europe: the Inquisition curbed, the ambition of the Church restrained, economic affairs put on a sound basis, restrictions in trade removed, the currency strengthened by the creation of the St Charles bank – and even a model army, the only one in the world which cared for its veterans, and guaranteed them an adequate retirement pension. In any case, in matters of finance and commerce, the Spaniard had a sound reputation for honest dealing, and was so scrupulous in honouring his commitments that 'the whole of Europe entrusted him with its assets, and had no cause to complain'.

It was an attractive country, defying description. Everywhere, in its wealth as well as in its poverty, Spain's outlook made itself felt. And what of the countryside? There was Valencia, an outer province and one of the richest – the Orient of Spain. It produced silks, rice, oils, wine, currants, dates and palm trees. It was like a survival of the gardens of the great Arabian civilization, existing side by side with a Nordic agriculture: hemp and flax brought trade to city shops and country homes. In the central provinces of Estremadura, in Navarre, and even in Castile, there were oases of cultivation threatened by the invasion of the sheep. Indeed the Spanish sheep crossed with the Maghreb ram had a European reputation, and was highly prized in England since it produced the finest wool in the world. Yet it cost Spain dear. The enormous flocks of greedy animals, tearing up the roots as well as the stems as they grazed, ravaged the countryside as they moved ceaselessly over the land. The association of wool producers, the famous Mesta, made a fortune from these products in the Segovia market, but resisted all reforms, since it could show that tens of millions were brought in by breeding. At last, to fight this harmful monopoly, the Friends of the City had been formed, a young association or rather group of associations encouraged by the king whose aim was to revive small farming and populate waste lands lying between the large towns, too far apart from each other, in which hordes of the poor and needy were congregating. But as yet all these efforts had met with little success. It had not escaped notice that not far from Madrid good, fertile land had been broken up for the exploitation of nitre-beds, though it was appreciated that these provided the saltpetre vital to Madrid's powder-magazines, the largest in the world, relics of an age in which trade was conducted by the musket.

In this country of barely ten million inhabitants, Charles III worked miracles in raising the general income, doubling it in a few years, and making more efficient use of taxation, thanks to the land register that he instituted; yet the impression persisted that Spain was still the base for world conquest.

Foremost among Spanish cities was Madrid, an artificial city. It was, of course, admirably planned around its Plaza Mayor, a vast square surrounded by identical five-storey houses with identical balconies, and which set a pattern for every city in the Spanish New World. It was there that the famous bullfights were held. Madrid was a beautiful city, but its streets were dirty and its ways and habits seemed expressly designed to amaze the English; houses were let without window-panes, and every tenant had to bring his own when he moved in; the first floor of each house belonged to the king, and enquiries about renting them were addressed to his officials. Yet this artificial capital was also a great commercial capital. The *Deputación de los Cincos Gremios Mayores* of Madrid, which included all merchants trading in textiles, jewellery, spices and drugs, not only directed the city's economic activity but had a large stake in the trade of Cadiz, owned the largest factories in Valencia and managed others all over Spain, and its ships, for trade with the New World, continued to be the safest means of transit available to European merchants. This great commercial organization even encouraged a luxury glass-making craft long famous and which at that time made mirrors reputed to be the finest in the world.

Yet another surprise was the curious city of Cadiz, built on an island; it was a lovely town with paved streets and tall houses, its artificial character as a commercial centre emphasized by the high cost of living; its castle protected by precipitous rocks and a system of forts, was a reminder of the privileges enjoyed by the Spanish Crown in overseas trade. It was a town packed with foreigners – French, English, Dutch, and Italians – who knew that over and above their legitimate profits they could make good money from smuggling; even the court guards themselves were accomplices when silver ingots and bundles of merchandise were illicitly passed through the posterns at night, to be shipped off on the high seas as quickly as possible. And smuggling was a necessity in Cadiz, if the goods from Europe were to be paid for. In Cadiz, reputed to have the best harbour in Europe, and the most envied, the flotillas bound for America anchored – approximately eighty ships which sailed each year bearing the iron-ware, wines, cloths and oils contributed by every manufacturer in Europe. They came back laden with precious metals, raw wool, copper, tin, and cocoa.

Another port carrying on a brisk trade with the New World was the old Roman port on the Corunna peninsula. It exported to Havana, Buenos Aires and the Philippines the same merchandise as Cadiz, and received gold and silver in exchange, as well as sugar, tobacco, and raw hides. Bilbao, the pretty capital of Biscay, had taken on a new lease of life, and was beginning to feel the advantages of the expansion of sea-trade, and of the freedom granted by Charles III to his subjects to trade with the Empire. Its longstanding trade in Spanish wool and in fish (dried cod from Newfoundland and Norway) was now supplemented by trade with America.

Barcelona was an attractive city built in a semi-circle at the foot of the hills, on the coastal plain which had been the objective of so many recent battles: a new fort had just been built for it on the Monjuich, but the main sea defence of its splendid harbour consisted of a long sea-wall. The exports of Barcelona were oils, alcohols, and the most famous of all Catalonia's industrial products – fabrics. Every year more than twelve million silk handkerchiefs were turned out by its factories to meet the demands of shops all over Europe. Silk and cotton stockings and wool velvets were equally in demand. The city had an air of prosperity, with its wide, paved streets radiating out from the Plaza San Michele, dominated by the vast cathedral. Barcelona was also a busy ship-building centre and its huge yards were said to be the finest in Europe. They served as a reminder to Spain that, in addition to its Atlantic trade, there was still wealth to be exploited in the Mediterranean basin.

We cannot leave Spain without seeing what insight Goya, the most perceptive of its painters, can give us into its enigmas. In 1785, when he was almost forty, he settled in Madrid after travels and adventures in Italy. He was adopted by Mengs, an official with an official style, and became court painter to the Bourbons. He filled this role with such candid realism that it must always arouse wonder. Charles III's honesty is no less admirable; Goya's portrait of him makes no attempt at flattery, though it has captured his witty, cynical expression, rather reminiscent of Voltaire. And what of Goya himself? His is the swarthy face just visible behind the handsome Count of Floridablanca – the skeleton of truth behind the tinsel trappings of the court. Goya was commissioned to paint sketches for tapestries, and dismayed the tapestry-weavers by the minuteness of detail he put into the vintagers and harvesters, the games of pelota and blind-man's buff, and all the sturdy, muscular, animal peasant life which contrasted so strongly with the foppish affectation of the lace-bedecked landowner. He portrayed the decadence and cynicism of the royal family in his studies of the Cardinal Infanta's suite – and the smug ugliness in the face of Maria Luisa, soon to be queen. He was equally ruthless in his treatment of the wild-eyed stupidity of the litanists in St Ignatius. Of three hundred years of past greatness, Spain in its decadence had retained but one noble quality – courage in facing up to the truth. The political façades had crumbled away; what remained was the fierce, tenacious solidity of human nature reduced to its essentials.

Some mention must be made of Portugal, which political thinkers in the West were studying with considerable interest. This little country was said to be rich, for it imported what was left of the gold of Africa and Brazil. It was also said to be deeply in debt, losing the greater part of its colonial gold to England to pay for a crippling import trade. It was said to be enlightened because of the general admiration felt for the famous Pombal, who cut down the number of religious foundations and encouraged secular education. Nevertheless Catholicism was the only religion tolerated, and clerics still represented more than fifteen per cent of the population. Pombal encouraged agriculture, yet three-quarters of the corn consumed in Portugal had to be imported. He did his best to discourage the exclusive production of a single wine, highly prized in England, yet wine remained the country's chief export. At all events, it seems that he infused new life into various industries, particularly textiles, which had collapsed under the competition from England to which his predecessor Methuen had exposed them. All economic progress was utterly dependent on English shipping, and the English were the real masters of Portuguese colonial trade; Portuguese banks were working even harder for London than for Lisbon, which was only just beginning to recover from the terrible earthquake of 1755.

Italian Autumn

In Italy the evenings were more serene and men could relax and enjoy the enduring charm of its dead past. Let us accompany the cultured men of the day who journeyed there to search for treasures in the old palaces of the mother of the arts.

Many travellers went to explore Venice in this age when educated people were beginning to reflect on the history of nations. It was a source of wonder that so magnificent a city could have originated with a few wretched groups of men who had sought refuge in the islands of the lagoon during the Gothic invasions. Venice was the queen of the seas which were its very foundation. From whichever side one approached, it seemed to be surrounded by a forest of masts, large vessels between which slipped a swarm of small boats. The city itself was built on piles, which were driven deep into the waters of the canal to strengthen the low-lying foundations. Four hundred bridges connected the islands with each other and added a final touch to the artifice of a city which, as its people proudly asserted, would remain the mistress of the gods just as Rome had made herself mistress of men. Its natural defences were moreover so strong that Venice had no need of fortresses and gates to guard its treasures. But land was so scarce that the inhabitants were in constant danger of falling off the narrow quays into the five feet of water of the smaller canals. As for the Grand Canal, the widest and deepest, it cut the city in two and was spanned only by the famous Rialto Bridge. This meant that people had to use 'barques and galleys' all the time. There were no carriages in Venice, but enormous crowds of pedestrians jostling each other in the narrow squares, too cramped for the city's 200,000 odd inhabitants and their gay and lively social round, the envy of Europe, which lasted from the Carnivals (which began at Christmas) to the Wedding of the Doge and the Sea on Ascension Day.

Very few realistic paintings of these Venetian carnivals exist and the tiny figures of Canaletto and Guardi no more than hint at their bustle and movement; but the spirit of Venice still survives in a painter whose warm humanity scaled the heights of genius: Tiepolo, the last representative of the Mediterranean movement that still has a profound influence in Europe. But Tiepolo died leaving no successor and with him Venetian painting came to an end.

The Palace of St Mark – with its chapel, the famous church – was the political centre of the Republic. The Doge was still the incarnation of its power, but he did not exercise it. Montesquieu singled out Venice as the model of an aristocratic republic; in fact magistrates were chosen by lot or by election from among the two thousand noble families in a procedure in some ways reminiscent of the Ecclesia of Athens or the Roman Conclave. This hierarchy of consuls settled all affairs, but by good sense rather than by force. When there was any uncertainty the majority fell back upon a compromise – to the despair of leaders and ambassadors. The power of Venice had greatly decreased since the days when it was mistress of the Eastern Mediterranean. In 1780 its only troops were Dalmatian. It still guarded the Adriatic ports, but Tunis held out against the small permanent fleet it maintained to keep down piracy. Its trade still reflected something of past glories, encouraged by the exports of lace, cloth of gold and silk, mirrors and glass; and it still maintained a form of monopoly over Levantine drugs and Russian leather. Venice, the converging point for Alpine valleys and the southern outlet for textiles from Holland and Germany, remained prosperous at a time when the once great cities of Mediterranean Europe were falling into decadence and apathy.

Venice had most cause to fear the power and influence of Rome. It banished all ecclesiastics from its councils and forbade its dignitaries to accept any Roman benefice except that of cardinal, since this only carried authority in Rome.

Yet Rome too was awakening to new life and was the meeting-place for thinkers and artists from all corners of the world. It was there that Goethe and Mozart and David and Goya and the celebrated sculptor Canova first made each other's acquaintance. The road from Venice to Rome leads us in any case to a city about which educated men throughout Europe were talking – Bologna. They cited as a model of modernization (and of physiocracy) the *chirografo di nostro signore papa Pio VI, nel quale si ordine et stabilise il regolamento de la publica economia de Bologna*. In this theocracy the Papal letter was law, replacing the old complicated system of taxation embodied in a tangle of rigid decrees issued by the Bolognese Senate and confirmed by the Popes. The letter provided a new system favouring neither the urban middle class nor the impoverished nobility, to which were added the families of each fresh Pope; it was a law which, though it did not set the peasant free, and gave very little more to eat to those who existed mainly on chestnuts, did at least clarify the many heavy taxes and duties, delivered the state from a crushing debt, and above all freed the circulation of corn and imposed taxes on the swarms of clerics inhabiting the city, and on the convents perched on every surrounding hill.

Let us continue our journey. According to contemporaries, poverty was rife in the Roman countryside, the land was deserted, and beggars lined the roads and crowded around the doors of inns; yet food was not expensive. There was much idleness and despondency in the factories, yet there was an enormous number of well-endowed almshouses.

Where did the wealth come from that subsidized all this idleness and poverty? Over and above the revenue from his states, the Pope received a substantial additional income from the Christian world. Spain alone contributed one-fifth of the expenses of the Roman budget, but this budget, which showed an excess on its ordinary expenditure (the army was quite small), had a constant deficit if extraordinary expenditure was included. Extraordinary expenditure included the embellishment of churches (the new sacristy of St Peter's had to be rebuilt three times because of the architects' negligence), subsidies to Malta and the battle against the infidel, and above all purchases of corn from outside, in accordance with the ancient tradition of the *annona*, to give cheap food to all those who lived by going in processions. The deficit was made up by *cédula*, a curious papal currency. These notes were issued in theory against the security of gold reserves deposited in the Castel Sant' Angelo, but they were so inordinately in excess of the reserves that this paper money would have been quite worthless if the Romans had possessed any of the critical acumen which in those parts seemed to be the exclusive attribute of the foreigner. In Rome nothing was ever finally settled. An excess of Pontifical goodwill, for instance, compelled the judges to give detailed reasons for their judgements, and allowed the unsuccessful plaintiff to refer the case indefinitely from one court to another: no lawsuit was ever concluded. Everything was casual

and easy-going, and in this patriarchal, indulgent atmosphere, inexhaustible patience was required in face of the endless delays. Aided and
abetted by the climate, the people lived on next to nothing, and the nobleman lived like a king on a mere pittance. The Church provided food, the
Church organized festivals both sacred and profane; there were theatres
run by clerics in every part of Italy. The trusting nature of its citizens and
the generosity of foreigners brought some equilibrium to this strangely un-
balanced situation. From conclave to conclave the *status quo* was maintained
and prolonged, in the hope that the draining of the Pontine marshes,
which had started a long time before but still dragged on, would eventually revive a neglected agriculture. And trade was slack, thanks to customs
dues which were crippling but easier to evade, if need be, than anywhere
else in Europe. Nothing was manufactured in Rome, everything was
bought in the port at Civita-Vecchia, the outlet of the states of the Church,
and paid for out of the resources of Christendom. The population of Rome
was declining so slowly that there were still 125,000 inhabitants building
their houses with stones dug out of the ground during excavations made in
the hope of finding valuable antiques which would fetch a good price.
Mediocre architects made a living out of repairing the countless small
palaces. Coachmen and hotel-keepers grew rich on pilgrims and visitors.
Rome lived solely on its past and on its present position as the Head of
Christendom.

In fact the largest city in Italy was not Rome but Naples, a sprawling
monster of nearly 500,000 inhabitants and one of the biggest cities in the
world. The soil, on its basis of lava, was so fertile that anything would
grow, pomegranates, oranges and figs, and costly produce could be sold –
flax, oil, wines and saffron. Salt and sulphur were available nearby, from
which were made vitriol and soap. The harbour was enormous, consisting
of the whole bay protected by a small breakwater. Yet trade was slack and
the magnificent bay sheltered an almost non-existent royal fleet. The
Bourbon king lived like a bourgeois in his enormous palace: his luxury,
like that of the beggars and the swarms of monks, was the beauty of the
earth. Taxation was arbitrary, and fluctuated according to privileges and
benefices, the multiplicity of privileged lands, and the idle ingenuity of
collectors who fleeced the poor peasant right and left.

We cannot leave the south without a glance at Sicily, so rich in arable
land, with its marble quarries, its precious stones, and the coral from its
coasts. Sicily even harboured scoundrels who had the right of asylum in
the convents which enjoyed so many commercial privileges that they
virtually controlled business in Messina and Palermo. Palermo, famous for
its silk gloves, regarded itself as the capital, with its 90,000 inhabitants,
many of them impoverished noblemen, with its gardens, palaces and fountains; whilst Messina was only just recovering from the terrible earthquake
of 1783, in which it was reduced to a mass of rubble and then swept by a
dreadful fire.

The Venetian Republic, the Papal States, the Kingdom of the Two-

Sicilies, these were the backbone of the old Italy. But this group was rounded off to the north by widely differing states. One of them, Bourbon Tuscany, was just entering upon a phase of activity and almost of wealth. Here a scattered agriculture produced unusual crops – saffron, flax, broad beans, kidney beans – and competed with industry, which made fabrics and table linen, porcelain and china. It was encouraged by a shrewd and enlightened despot who was to bring fame to Leghorn, the famous free port whose ever-increasing population watched without astonishment as Greeks, Americans and Turks freely practised their own religions, whilst even the Jews had their own synagogue. All this intermingling of races was not just the living sign of a widespread Mediterranean trade flourishing at the expense of Venice and Genoa. Farther north were the rich Milanese. Milan may have been rather dull and only moderately busy around its cathedral and its famous library, but its soil was among the most fertile in Italy, well irrigated and rich in corn and rice. The Hapsburgs could have worked wonders with it if they had had any other ideas beyond crushing it with taxes. These were taxes, moreover, from which the officials raked off so much *en passant* that a bare twentieth ever reached the Court of Vienna.

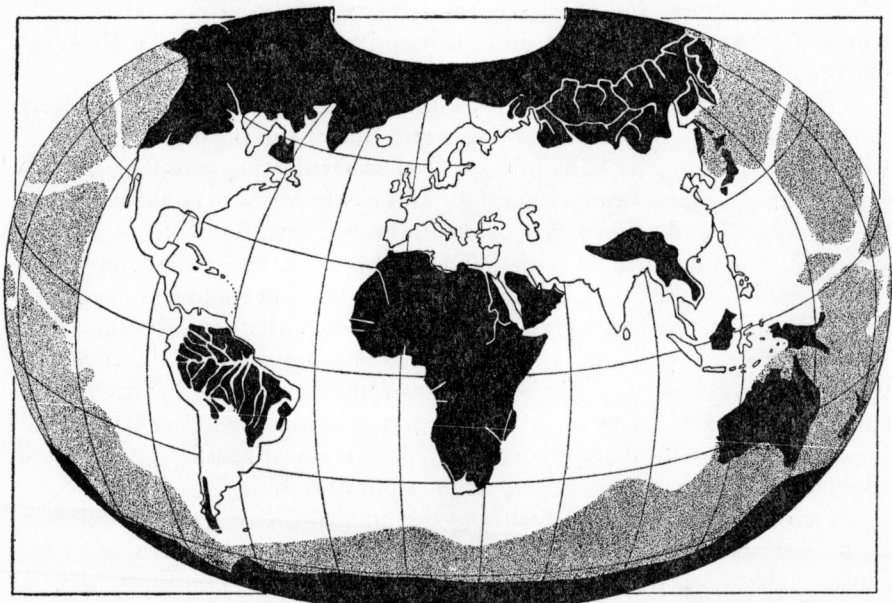

3 Maritime Explorations, 1760–80

Grey: areas explored from 1760–80
Black: areas unexplored in 1780

Piedmont still formed part of Italy, a rough mountain kingdom whose ruler was excessively ambitious and burdened his land with taxes which were borne with equanimity since they affected nobles as well as the common people. A scanty, laborious agriculture supported Turin, a clean, bright town, an arsenal, and a military as well as a commercial centre, where one could buy the silk cultivated in northern Italy. Then there was honest, poor, industrious Nice, a tiny fortress-town, enclosed within a narrow space, and with only vast ruins on the outskirts to bear witness to its ancient dignity. The countryside was only sparsely populated in a region where everything was considered in terms of strategy; and the ruler of the rock of Monaco, that tiny citadel, now depended for his living on France after having formerly been dependent on Spain.

This was Italy, then, a wonderful much-envied land whose store of ancient treasures was being heedlessly exhausted. It had no unity as a country; the military tradition of order and hard work survived only in Piedmont, a harsh state on the mountain perimeter which acted as a fragile barrier between northern Europe and the easy-going life of the south.

2

Progress Crosses the Atlantic

IN 1780 it was almost three hundred years since the West had discovered that the earth was round and had ventured to cross the oceans; the Mediterranean, the China Sea, the Indonesian seas, like the Atlantic, were, so to speak, opened by these voyages round the world. The daring of sailors destroyed the prosperous overland trade which formerly linked China with Europe through Constantinople and Central Asia. Even in the eighteenth century, two spectacular results were apparent: the Arab worlds, which had controlled the land routes, were collapsing in ruins, and the Mediterranean itself seemed to have relapsed into slumber. In contrast the Atlantic and Pacific were rewarding the bold foresight of those who had plotted the movements of the stars and built ports in every bay of the new worlds.

In this chaper we shall deal in turn with the decline of the Mediterranean and the progress of the Atlantic, leaving the Pacific for a later chapter.

What exactly was understood by Europe? Where did it end? In the Urals in the east, and on the Bosphorus in the south-east? Eighteenth-century geographers were cautious men and generally gave Asia as the eastern boundary of Europe. So Catherine II may have been a European princess, but it is by no means certain that the Sultan of Turkey deserved a similar honour. He was generally regarded as an Asiatic despot. On the other hand, could the Greeks be excluded from Europe? Some were in Athens, a little city at that time part of the Ottoman Empire and numbering no more than 15,000 inhabitants, and some were in Constantinople where they formed the most important commercial core of the city. A host of glorious memories made it imperative for enlightened Western minds to claim them as their own. On the other hand, the Serbians, the Rascians who spoke only Slavonian, were they too to be classed as Europeans?

MEDITERRANEAN RUINS

The territories which the maps grouped together under the name of the Ottoman Empire included parts of both Europe and Asia. The old régime very sensibly ignored the requirements of our modern geographical definitions.

The Ottoman Camp

The Ottoman Empire was little more than a vast army encamped on the lands seized by the successors of the Osmans. Christians, whether they were Greeks or more occasionally Latins, belonged to Europe, whereas Muslims, even if they were Serbians, belonged to Asia.

The Turks, like the Arabs, hardly ever persecuted the Christians as such; they 'protected' them for a financial consideration. In the first place, they made them pay a heavy poll-tax, and officials armed with gauges measured their children's skulls to see whether they had grown big enough to be liable for it. Merchants and craftsmen in addition paid excise duties, dues which (on the advice of Villeneuve, the French Ambassador) had just been reinforced by heavy customs duties. The majority of the subjects of the Ottoman Empire had to contribute the equivalent of one-tenth of their produce, but the whole skill of the tax-collector went into the assessment of this tenth; the fisherman returning to harbour with one hundred fish often had to hand over the ten biggest fish, the equivalent of half his profit. As for the well-dressed merchants and the religious dignitaries, it went ill with them if their voluntary contributions were not adequate. For the Ottoman had unexpected ways and means of making them pay up. He would immediately confer on them some honorary post, which made them direct subjects of the Sultan, who could then exercise his discretionary powers of life and death.

The Ottoman pretended to have nothing whatever to do with the affairs of these protected subjects. He put judges and executioners at their disposal, and at heart preferred the Christians to manage their own affairs; except for levying a special tax on any village where a crime had been committed, he would take no further interest in the criminal. If, however, the victim's family appealed for a Turkish trial, the executioner in attendance tied the culprit's wrists together, and led him to the place of execution through the motley crowd in the market place and the streets, without the spectacle arousing any particular attention. On the way, the plaintiffs were free to continue their negotiations and discuss with the condemned man the price of his ransom. If agreement was reached, the accused was at once handed back to the Christians. If poor or obstinate, the guilty man walked on to his death, chatting with his executioner if he felt like it.

It is almost impossible to enumerate here the extremely wide range of occupations engaged in by the indigenous inhabitants of the Empire; it would involve a geographical study of the whole of Balkan Europe and Asia Minor. But one feature was outstanding – the utter and universal poverty of the peasant. In Syria, when times were good, he lived on dura bread, onions and lentils; and when times were bad, on acorns. There was no question of seed selection or stock-rearing. Little donkeys drew a plough, more often than not the old-fashioned swing-plough made from a tree branch cut below the fork; the corn was scarcely ripe before it was cut and stored away in caves: every possible device was used to outwit the bands of

Arab robbers who came up from the desert. Owing to its precarious food supply, Palestine itself had barely more than 100,000 inhabitants. Syria proper had perhaps two million.

A few great cities, amongst them Damascus, were more favoured. Bread cost less there than in the surrounding countryside, chiefly owing to the requisitions of the pashas who were anxious to maintain peace in the unruly bazaars. When there was famine, old remedies were applied: it was forbidden to take corn out, provisions were collected in the city and every wagon that tried to escape was handed over to the Arab robbers by order of the pasha. In this way activities absorbing large numbers of people were maintained in the urban centres. Money was minted, damask cloth was woven, silks figured, glass blown, and the brightly coloured ceramic tiles which decorated every mosque in the Empire were made. There were charming little palaces, their clustered domes built around exquisite gardens, modelled on the pious foundations erected for the use of pilgrims journeying to the Holy Places, since Damascus was still one of the most famous halts on the road to Jerusalem and Mecca.

Yet though several cities continued to flourish, the population of the lowlands was decreasing. Syrians, Greeks and Armenians were endeavouring to escape from the casual despotism of the Turks. They set out towards Persia, and even towards Africa and Europe. Large numbers made for Russia, often taking with them the Jews who were their partners in trade.

All along the Mediterranean coast, the Franks had enjoyed long-standing privileges, of which the French in particular reaped benefits in the form of low customs duties and the special protection of the Turkish administration. In return for these, they exhorted the Christians to patience. They brought sugar from the West Indies, coffee and cochineal from Cadiz, and cloth from Languedoc, and they shipped bales of cotton and cloth, copper and silks. This was the famous Levantine trade. These Levantine ports were in a sad state of decay: they were small roadsteads with scarcely any shelter, their ancient defences repaired with stones dragged from nearby ruins; the sea-walls were strengthened and supported by the shafts of pillars taken from ancient temples or Latin churches. The harbours were often choked up with mud and sand. Acre and Tripoli were in this state of dilapidation. Nevertheless mule-trains still came down to them from Aleppo or Ramleh (at that time a French trading post). Throughout European Turkey the English merchants were active, especially at Salonica, where tooled leather, skins, and the famous carpets were on sale. Yet just as much, if not more, of this trade from European Turkey went overland to Austria, extending the Asiatic trading quarter on the outskirts of Vienna, already described.

The Turkish military machine was kept going by these remaining traces of agricultural, industrial and commercial splendour. The Ottoman Empire was little more than the indefinite prolongation of a state of siege declared by a conqueror who had never advanced beyond a military administration for the simple reason that he was not interested in adapting himself to the complexities of civil administration. Besides his privy purse, the Sultan was especially anxious to keep the coffers of the public Treasury as full as possible, since the bulk of this money was earmarked for the upkeep of an enormous military machine. But what was left of the power that Machiavelli praised so highly? Did it still number the half-a-million men referred to in the European chancelleries? It did still include a great variety of formations; the most famous corps of all still being the Janissaries, the sons of Christians, to whom were added contingents from every country in Asia. The army on campaign was a mobile state: there were crowds of Jews and merchants, representatives of every trade guild in the Empire, and the whole ministry, under the orders of the Grand Vizier (when not of the Sultan in person), accompanied, naturally, by the entire Chancellery. It was a vast, cumbersome assemblage of heavy wagons and draught animals, and in the wars against Vienna it was reputed to have numbered as many as 8,000 wagons and 5,000 camels. This moving horde had to be fed – and well fed. It was accompanied by as many as 10,000 oxen, the same number of buffalo, 100,000 hogsheads of fruit and provisions, and always by the Treasury itself, a weighty strong-box covered with vivid carpets.

Yet this vast army was not really organized; it had achieved the golden age of chaos. Between the moment when the Grand Vizier reviewed it and the moment it began to march, deserters reduced its fighting strength by one-third; the finest artillery guns in the world (the copper and tin came not only from Asia but also from Holland and England) were heavy and of varying calibre, and inadequately provided with ammunition. Moreover, shock troops were too eager for battle to wait for the artillery to prepare the way, and the latter, according to Tott, was of very little use except to sound the sunset cannon when the army was encamped for the night, which apparently cost no less per salvo than 54,000 pounds of powder, and to no purpose other than making an infernal din. This armed horde could not move about regardless of the time of year. It had to have grass for its horses and cattle. In short, even if it had still been disciplined as in Machiavelli's day, it would have been utterly unsuited to the requirements of swift, light, modern strategy. The Turkish army and its organization were the exact opposite of those of Frederick II and the enlightened despots, and this accounted for its many defeats.

In theory the fleet at least was strong, made up as it was by all the contingents contributed by Africa and Asia, but the Bosphorus itself was hardly suited to the manoeuvres of great sailing ships, and in the far Mediterranean, the Russians, taught by the English, wiped out the Ottoman fleet at Chesme. In effect, the naval strength of the Porte was reduced to a few small ships of seventy guns.

The Sultan, moreover, was not merely a military leader and a feudal overlord; he was also a religious leader, accepting advice only from the Grand Mufti who enjoyed the inestimable privilege of kissing his master's shoulder, and not only, like his other subjects, the hem of his robe. Moreover, the submission of the Mufti was maintained by tradition; even up to 1787 there was kept in the harem the symbolical mortar on which this same Mufti could be ground to powder if ever he was guilty of treason. The authority of the Ulémas, a college interpreting the law, had been worn away in dissension and vain ambitions. Therefore the Sultan was theoretically the secular and religious head of the hundred local lords who, from the Caucasus to the Atlantic, professed the religion of Mahomet. Yet the faith, like the army, had lost confidence in itself.

The military weakness and the religious shortcomings of the Ottoman Empire enabled Russia to dispute its suzerainty over the Crimea and Georgia where considerable political and religious confusion continued to prevail right up to the end of the century.

Arab Ruins

The state of independence existing in Africa was undoubtedly as serious. Egypt was the habitual refuge of every dethroned Bey living on plunder in the mountains. The Sultan's envoys dared not venture far from their palace. The Pasha paid even less homage to the Sultan than he received from his own subjects. In practice he relied on the Arabs to keep order. The Arab officer guarding Cairo was greatly feared, whether he ruthlessly enforced the law and put to death everyone remotely suspected of theft, or whether he accepted bribes and protected the powerful brigands. And under this corrupt and indecisive rule the fellah eked out a bare existence, living on barley broth, and producing just enough corn to feed the caravans passing through on their annual journey to Mecca. In this Egypt the European trader endeavoured to get a footing. Merchants from Marseilles intrigued on the spot to get a passage through to India. Sometimes the idea of Sesostris' canal was brought up again.

For although Alexandria had fallen into decadence, in spite of its harbour, Cairo, the great creation of the Arabs, was still a dream city in western eyes. Saladin's palace still stood on the hill – a group of palaces, with gardens approached by the gigantic staircase which even camels could climb. Marble and columns were everywhere, and in the centre rose the beautiful mosque. This 'heavenly city' was served by an aqueduct of more than five hundred arches – or rather had been, for it was falling into decay along with the three-storey well where oxen harnessed in circles hauled the water up from landing to landing. Lastly, there was the wonder of the city, its central lake; for eight months of the year water carnivals were held on it with gondolas and fireworks, and for the remaining four months it was turned into a garden gay with shrubs and flowers. Cairo was still one of the cross-roads of the world. The Latin Christian and the Copt rubbed shoulders with the Arab and the Jew. Asia and Africa sold their own people, along with their best incense, their aloes, their aigrettes, lacquer and ivories. Something like 100,000 inhabitants milled around the great bazaars in this famous city, a survival from the past.

Farther from Constantinople, and even prouder of its autonomy, was Barbary. Tripoli had become a desert where hardly a single passing caravan was to be seen, and where the Arabs, abandoning the remnants of the cloth and saffron trade to the Jews, lived on piracy in small city-fortresses built near the coastal water-cisterns. At Tunis linen cloth reported to be the best in Africa was woven by the lake, and there were still faintly perceptible traces of Arab civilization between the low houses covered with balconies and the gardens which surrounded the city; but inside the old ramparts, no longer kept in repair, the population was content to live on piracy. No thought was given to the hygiene of the city, swamps were allowed to foul the air and rainwater tanks were badly infected. In spite of so many risks, French merchants had gained a footing in the city, which tolerated their presence because they bought the produce of its plunder. These French merchants were beginning to ensure some measure of coastal trade, and soon Tunis became a kind of international receiver of stolen goods: even the English and the Dutch infiltrated into it. The Moorish Bey had overthrown the Turkish Bey. Even more than Tunis, Algiers was the capital *par excellence* of plunder, and the largest urban centre in Africa next to Cairo. Indeed, the luxury of some of its houses and their gardens was evidence of the success of the world's biggest venture in piracy, and attracted French and English merchants; Jews from Leghorn opened several banks there. The English even opened Gibraltar to the pirates. The French from Marseilles installed at La Calle a precarious bastion where coral fishing was carried on. As the citizens of Algiers were rich and could pay, people were beginning to trade hardware, sugar and coffee to them. But this wealth was not lasting. The price of cargoes was going down.

Finally, in the West, the 'King' of Morocco had just left his old fortress of Marrakesh to take up residence in Meknes. This was still the country of the nomad Adouans ruled by marabouts and caïds, the country of caravans which journeyed twelve hundred and fifty miles, five hundred of them across the desert, to bring what remained of Guinea's gold. This Sudanese gold seems to have aroused little interest in Europe. In 1750 a company was formed in Copenhagen to trade with Marrakesh. But the Portuguese had lost interest and abandoned Mazagan in 1767, for even though it was well provided with harbours, by 1780 preference was being given to Mogador. And anyway the same thing was happening in Morocco as in the whole of Barbary; the foolish local chiefs, flattered by the competing European traders, were too easily persuaded to grant trading privileges, and since piracy was given a free hand the large number of buyers soon put up the selling prices.

Constantinople

Constantinople was perhaps an even more important centre than London or Paris; its population was in the region of a million, consisting for the most part of Greeks and Armenians, but also of subjects drawn from every corner of the Empire and, of course, of Turks. It was a strange city on the beautiful site of the new Rome. The old city was built around the incomparable church of St Sophia, whose bold and extravagant style had been frequently imitated and improved upon by the Turks. They were proud of their large, airy mosques, even bigger than the church of Justinian, although they kept to the same architectural pattern of one great dome resting on four pillars. The harbour, the famous Golden Horn, still attracted ships from every point of the compass and merchants from all over the world. In the upper town, behind the mosque of Eyoub, the covered bazaar was a centre for merchandise from three continents. Nearby was the slave market: an enclosure for the men, a covered bazaar for the women; Jews bought lovely Georgian girls in order to teach them elegance and to sell them again at a high price. High on the other side of the harbour was the noble suburb of Pera, with its embassy gardens and palaces; lower down, in the suburb of Galata, a dense cosmopolitan crowd of sailors and adventurers milled around shops licensed to sell wine, which even attracted a few Turks. Dominating Galata was a tall fire tower, which unfortunately did not prevent the terrible fire of 1782 from devastating twothirds of this wooden suburb with its dirty, winding streets so riddled with vermin that even the fire did not exterminate them. More dangerous even than fire were epidemics, like the plague which killed off thousands of victims every year, and which was responsible for more deaths than the earthquakes. Yet Constantinople remained a hub of the world. This was not because of the harem, a monument to the vulgar and cosmopolitan taste of the Sultans, where the Sultans walked in the shady gardens among countless little Byzantine or Chinese pavilions. Nor was it because of the pretentious fortifications of the Sublime Porte, but because of the ferment of trade, peoples, customs and religions, on the shores of the narrow Bosphorus, where the history of the world seemed to be rotting away.

ATLANTIC ACHIEVEMENTS

Servile Africa

Ocean trade, however, was still a comparatively new phenomenon, a novelty which more than two hundred years of slavery had made extremely profitable.

The whole Atlantic coast of Africa, with the exception of the Barbary coast and the desert seaboard, was known vaguely as Guinea. It was one of the busiest coasts in the world, chiefly because it was on the route to the Cape of Good Hope, and the Cape Verde Islands had become one of the most famous ports of call; but it was also the centre of an enormous trade, the trade in Negroes. Compared with this inexhaustible supply of saleable humanity, and the profits it brought in, all other branches of the African trade – pepper and gold dust or ivory and Benin bronzes – seemed insignificant. Many were the battles, and bitter the rivalry, to control the traffic in Negroes. The treaties throw little light on the problem of who controlled the innumerable fortified points on the coast. Hardly had the island of Fernando-Po been wrenched from the Portuguese by the Spaniards than it was abandoned. The Dutch were more prudent and only imposed a substantial duty on the Portuguese of the Gold Coast. Yet ships from Recife managed to evade it by bringing their vessels alongside spots not mentioned in the original agreement. The French were more methodical and built a harbour, but an English ship massacred the men working on it, though no state of war had been declared. The Danes obtained permission to erect huts and stalls, but never succeeded in making use of them. Moreover, about 1755, slaves were becoming scarcer and slave-masters more choosy: it was no longer a buyer's but a seller's market, and the seller preferred to lead his files of captives towards harbours frequented by international shipping, where he could obtain a better price because of the competition. Hence the extreme complexity of what may be called the commercial geography of this strange traffic, always on the move, ever changing, not only because it dealt in men, but because of the varying rate of flow of the tidal currents at the mouths of certain harbours, the silting up of river mouths and periodic outbreaks of fever which made some ports unusable.

Nevertheless the trade was still very profitable. Great Britain sent out hundreds of ships mainly from Liverpool but also from Bristol and London, laden with ironware, glassware, guns, and printed cottons from Eastern bazaars or manufactured in the new English mills. These were Africa's main imports, and every European country tried to align its trade with that of England.

This trade, however, was not only conducted by barter, and in the closing years of the eighteenth century an oriental shell was still in use. It was a curious currency and varied in value from one country to another. The price of an African was reckoned in shells. The white man, moreover, did not go direct to the villages for Negroes; the business was done by local chiefs, minor chiefs of small tribes, who were half sorcerers, half family men; or by the more powerful potentates of Juda or Benin, pale replicas of the famous Monomotapa. It is true that at first the native chieftains sold only Negroes condemned by tribal law, but as printed calico became more fashionable and more expensive, so the tribal law became proportionately stricter. In the regions most favourably situated for the trade, the quota provided by the law was soon increased by the supply from war, and even by the abduction of the ruler's own subjects. This business of slave catching was a dangerous one, and the bodyguards of the Negro kings liked to try their hand at it. But sometimes the villagers would band together to resist and go to the king himself to complain, and then it was the bodyguard who was sent into slavery, as the king did not want to be the loser all round.

Yet the coastal native adapted himself to the situation, preferring to sell rather than be sold. Gradually the melancholy columns came from farther and farther inland. The captive's neck was imprisoned in a wooden fork, the handle of which rested on the shoulder of the man in front. This chain of slaves could neither sit down nor lie down except all together and on the orders of the man holding the first fork. It was an interminable journey. In order to keep Goree supplied the French undertook journeys which might last for months. The traders complained that slaves had doubled in price in the African markets, but they had to be sold at four times the price in American markets. Luckily the price remained low in the south of Zaïr – the Congo – which was a great advantage to the Portuguese of Brazil, who had retained their possessions on the coast of Angola while they gradually abandoned the ports in the north. Sometimes a bold spirit tried to substitute some new trade for this traffic, which was beginning to be disliked even in Europe, but it was not easy to penetrate into those central African kingdoms of which such miraculous tales were told. It was said in particular that gold was washed down in the mountain streams and was even to be found in the mud in which the natives paddled; but as yet no-one had managed to get a footing there and organize the collection of the gold efficiently enough to offset the enormous cost of transporting it. The heart of Africa was, in fact, unknown. Of that vast continent, only its capes, estuaries and coastline were known.

At the extreme tips of the continent were a few good natural harbours, and there was a flourishing settlement at the Cape of Good Hope. This was a port of call on the long voyage to the Indies, and it had been admirably laid out by the Dutch; their company had successfully discouraged rival English agents who were weary of doing battle and preferred St Helena. At the Cape, ships willingly paid a high price for fresh supplies of water, vegetables and fruit, the more so as the Dutch had succeeded in creating extensive gardens and the fruit was renowned for its quality throughout the Ocean. Carefully selected seeds and plants from an experimental garden were sold to the settlers, who cleared all the surrounding land. These settlers came from every city in Europe, and only one condition was imposed – they had to be Protestant. French settlers who came after the revocation of the Edict of Nantes did well there and consequently attracted numerous Germans. The whole of this microcosm of Europe stretched for a radius of a hundred and fifty miles and there were about 15,000 settlers in all. They were dissatisfied because the company, having distributed land free, actually had the audacity to subject them to an ownership tax, although it was already making a large profit from trade in the port. Nevertheless, the company had the forethought to build an admirable hospital, which was all the more appreciated since the agents of the great maritime companies were often paid according to the number of sailors they succeeded in bringing back to Europe alive.

Work on the land had never attracted the native Hottentot. At first, diseases brought from Europe had decimated the local tribes. Those who survived went inland hastily, retreating as the white man advanced. It was said that one Hottentot had gone to settle in the Indies where he had made a modest fortune, and then, shedding his clothes and his Western luxury simultaneously, had returned to the indolent nakedness of his fathers. The assimilation of black nations was not easy, and the story of the Hottentot was one good reason for not troubling too much about it. In 1785 the chief concern of the people of the Cape was not to assimilate the native, but to know whether or not the European settler would have the right to trade direct with ships which anchored in the ports or whether this was to remain a company monopoly.

There is no need to pursue in detail our voyage along the eastern coast of Africa. Everywhere there was a general desire to imitate the prosperity of the Cape. In the Ile Bourbon, or Réunion, were to be found horticulture and agriculture, which through the efforts of 'one of the King's botanists' were nearly as good as the Dutch plantations. There were several thousands of French people on the island who had fled there from Madagascar where the natives from the interior would make sudden descents on the coast and murder over-adventurous Frenchmen who were too anxious to get rich. These massacres of white men were sometimes led by a handful of Arabs who had lived in proximity to the natives for hundreds of years and resented European competition. Farther north, the east coast of Africa was considered even more uninviting and unprofitable: it was dominated by the Banian, the sea-faring Indian of the Persian Gulf, and the Sultan of Zanzibar.

If proselytizing Muslims penetrated as far as Madagascar, Prester John could be claimed as a glorious victory for Christianity, except that it was the Egyptian Copts who converted the Abyssinians. They stubbornly refused to listen to the Roman missionaries who attempted to prove that Christ was not only God, but also man; the Negus, who would don a crown of thorns before putting on his royal crown, punished this 'heresy' by death. A few Dutchmen, perhaps the only ones to do so, managed to settle in Abyssinia, because they were less interested in dogma than in a modest trade in ivory and spices, which did little to enliven the dreary capital of Gondar, a mud town abandoned by its population in the dry season for the comfort of tents and the freedom of the steppes.

Accustomed as we are to the amazing advance of progress on the American continent, we have to make an effort of imagination to realize what America was like in 1785, and how it appeared to an inhabitant of Europe. People were not even entirely sure where its natural frontiers were, the continent was so vast. The expedition of a group of scholars who undertook to measure the earth by triangulations taken from Peru was a most hazardous venture. Equally heroic was a Jesuit father who vanished without trace in California where he had taken his telescope to get a better view of the stars. There was much argument about the exact configuration of the north-west coast of the continent: many well-informed people were

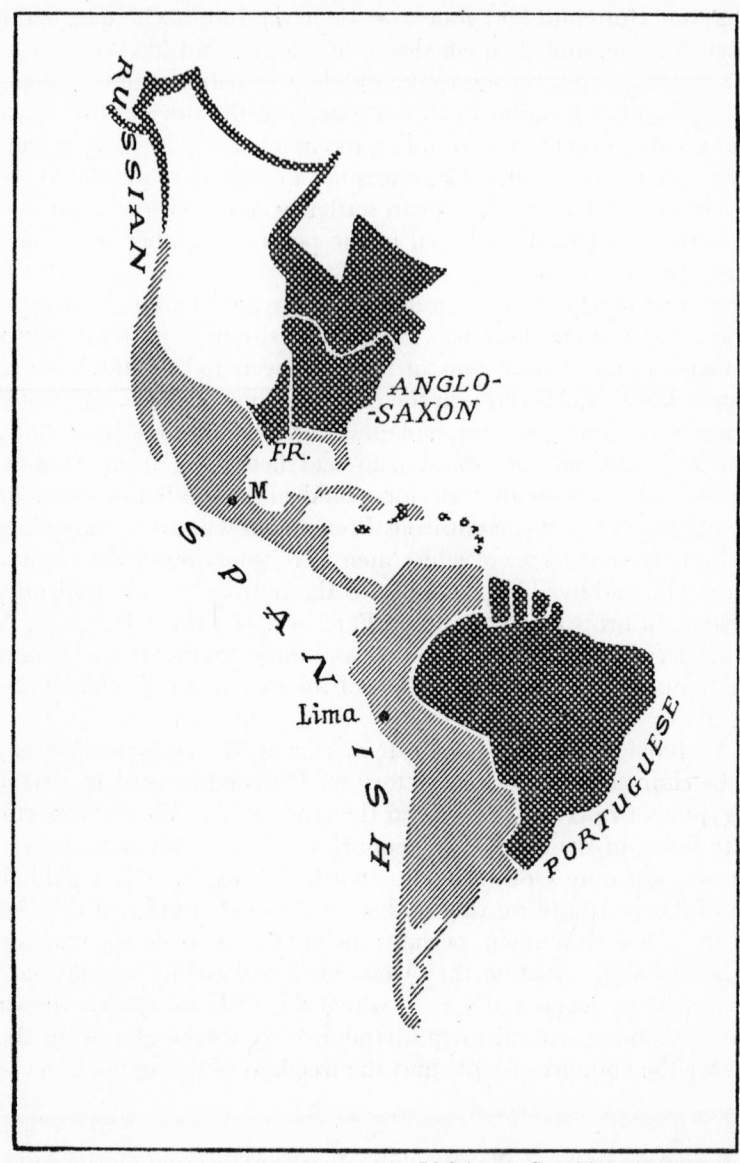

4 Europeans in America in 1780

Light grey: Spanish possessions
Dark grey: other foreign possessions

expecting an influx of Chinese into America and believed that North America was attached to the Asian continent. Almost nothing was known of the interior of this vast continent, either to the north or the south. People may have read between the lines of the more or less fanciful stories told by travellers who collected trappers' tales and believed that great Indian civilizations, prosperous but unknown, peopled the north-east of the continent. As for the great southern mountain range, there was considerable doubt as to the whereabouts of the kingdoms of Toupinambas, so fashionable in Europe. The high Cordilleras of the Andes were better known than the great range of the Rockies though certain of its peaks had been given picturesque names by French-Canadian trappers.

A further surprise for the twentieth-century reader is that economically the West Indies by themselves were as important as all the rest of the continent put together. Moreover it was only the immense popularity of the independent English colonies which prevented the whole continent from being regarded as Spanish. Brazil and England, in fact, occupied only a few scattered border strips here and there, while Spain controlled the Panama isthmus, and consequently the safest route to the Pacific coast, and might be said to have gripped the New World by the waist. Carolina could well have been French; it was English only because the Spanish had so many other possessions that they despised these sandy wastes. Throughout the New World places which are now the greatest human townships on the face of the earth were then only small settlements; taken all together, they would not have equalled the population of a single one of the great cities of Asia. In short, though the Europeans had gained a foothold on the continent and conquered the Indian cities, they had scarcely begun the economic conquest of the continent.

The Awakening of Spanish America

What remained of the fabulous Spanish Empire? It can best be assessed from its physical centre – Panama. The passage round the Magellan Straits was much feared by sailors, and merchant ships greatly preferred the route across central America. The town of Panama, rebuilt after the lootings of the late seventeenth century, was the capital of the Kingdom of Terra Firma – a pretentious name which concealed a disappointing reality: a country without culture, with only mediocre fisheries and a few pearls. Yet great wealth flowed across this poverty-stricken land, as cargoes from Europe were unloaded at the Panama docks and transported either by mule or in large barques to Porto Bello on the Pacific. Outside the trading season it was a small town with an unhealthy climate. The garrison was made up of one hundred soldiers who came to take up their stations there at the opening of the commercial campaigns. For several days merchants from Spain mingled with those from America. There was amazing bustle and activity. Under the supervision of the commander of the convoy the price of merchandise was hammered out. The Americans brought their precious metals, and Europe its manufactured goods which the Creoles were eager to buy. The market had been famous for the scrupulously fair dealing which characterized it, but by the time we are speaking of this great Panamanian trade was on the decline. We know that the Treaty of Utrecht gave the English the right to bring slaves and goods to this market in the so-called 'permit ship' (which was followed by numerous others which kept it constantly supplied). What with English competition, the unhealthy site, and especially improved techniques of navigating around the continent, the Panama trade was declining and did not recover until the famous canal was opened in 1914. Meanwhile there was a long period of trade depression in central America, although it fluctuated over the continent as a whole.

Up to the mid-eighteenth century the voyage from Callao to the Pacific coast of Chile had taken six months, following the indentations of a dangerous and broken coastline. The first captain to venture into the open sea instead of keeping to the coast did the round trip in a month and was nearly condemned for witchcraft. Nevertheless his daring marked the opening of a new era : the Panama isthmus lost its trading monopoly. The round voyage benefited Chile and its inland capital Santiago, and even more Valparaiso, which of all the harbours formerly in use was the only one to expand, because it was the nearest. In 1783 peace reigned in Chile, and white people from all over the coast were coming to settle there. There was a plentiful supply of cheap timber for building, and the peace-loving Indian (when he was not drunk on European alcohol) sold his cattle and even his children for a good price. Adequate farming was developing on the plateaux, and the mines were still stirring men's imaginations as well as contributing to trade. Sea communications drained off the coastal trade as far as Panama, whilst other trade routes brought goods through the snows and over the precipices of the Corderillas of the Andes, and from as far away as Buenos Aires. It was this latter route which was followed by the mules loaded with tallow, leather, maté tea and sometimes a few slaves who reached their new masters in much fresher condition than those taking the northern routes. In the opposite direction from Chile to La Plata caravans wound their way loaded with ponchos, wool for making cloth, whisky, and even a little gold. The country farthest away from Spain, Chile, was also the first to profit by the trade concessions which Madrid granted to all Spaniards in 1778, and Valparaiso expanded as a result.

Whilst Chile was growing in importance at the edge of the known world, new life was stirring in 'Paraguay', a vast region with vaguely defined frontiers between Brazil and the endless plains of the south. It was known chiefly for its central region and what was left there of the Jesuit missions now run by monks of various other orders. We know how successful the Jesuits were in assembling 100,000 peaceful and trustworthy Indians in villages, regulating everything by and for the Society. The Spanish merchants of Santa Fé and Cordoba, and the Portuguese merchants of Sacramento could hardly be expected to tolerate an empire which defied the principles of economic freedom and private interests in search for lands, cheap labour, and easy business. Once the missions had been destroyed, the economy of La Plata was dominated entirely by stock-breeding. The mountain stretch of the route to Santiago was hazardous, but it could not have been easier in the plains. Everywhere there was magnificent grassland, and in some places there were even cultivated fields. Thanks to its sturdy mules, the already prosperous stock-breeding industry was sure of a good

market, especially in Buenos Aires. The city's wide streets were lined with
low houses and small gardens, riotous with flowers, which stretched as far
as Santa Fé. Nearer the city centre whitewashed brick houses were already replacing those made of earth. Its 30,000 inhabitants could boast
several brand new public buildings, yet Buenos Aires had still not extended
as far as the river, and was ten leagues away from its port, La Enceñada, an
unreliable harbour bordered with huts. No one, in fact, had yet discovered
the secret of building an adequate port on the treacherous banks of the
muddy estuary of La Plata, often swollen by storms and continually
blocked by shallows. The attempts made at Montevideo to construct a
similar, rival, port were by no means completely successful. The barques
going down river managed quite well, but sea-going ships almost invari-
ably ran aground. La Plata faced inland, rather than to the sea.

Lima was the centre of Spanish rule. Peru had once been the treasure-
house of America, but was now in decline; even Lima had been destroyed
by the 1746 earthquake, like all the coastal settlements. At Callao, a tidal
wave had completed the destruction of the town. But a magnificent competition in rivalry achieved the rebuilding not only of the port but of the
capital as well, which emerged even finer than before. True, the old Incas
were sceptical when they saw the Spaniards digging deep foundations for
their stone houses. 'They are digging their graves', they said. Nevertheless,
the whole of European Peru was being built to last, the display of luxury
was a sign of its confidence. The corridor leading to the Viceroy's hall
was paved with silver. They flaunted their wealth, although the result was
disturbing: the mines were being exhausted. The cities in the high mountains were still there: Cuzco, the old Inca city, was the greatest. Its ancient
buildings had overawed the European invaders at first, though they later
affected to despise them. Its new baroque churches softened the heavy
background of the natural landscape. It still had 25,000 inhabitants.
Potosi had almost as many, La Paz fewer. Small towns atrophied in the
high mountains where the air was rarified, life hard and short; where
workers' riots were violent and managers alternated between extremes of
benevolence and cruelty. In these high lands, where a living was hard to
come by, the day had passed when the Incas could pick up at will huge
nuggets of gold from which they made vases and jewellery, when on up-
rooting a tree a hunk of silver could be found at ground level, when a few
shovelfuls of earth uncovered veins of metal which could be chipped out
with a chisel. As late as 1730, a nugget weighing forty-five pounds was
discovered near La Plata. Fifty years later there was no longer any hope
of such discoveries. The trenches gaped open, useless: pits were deepened
in vain and extended by wooded galleries, and only with difficulty kept
free from flooding. The raw metal had to be treated with mercury (of
which Peru fortunately had several rich deposits), and yields and profits
were so seriously on the wane that many preferred to invest their capital
in agriculture and in the few industries vital to the inhabitants of these
cities. In any case by that time gold and silver were no longer the country's

sole source of wealth. Llamas and pacos came down from the mountains loaded with chunks of minerals less rare but now more marketable: copper, tin, sulphur and even platinum. It was the closing period of colonialism in Peru; the creoles of Chile and La Plata were beginning to turn away, relying on their own efforts to bring them wealth. They were no longer so willing to submit to the out-dated authority wielded from the effete Spanish palaces in Lima.

In the north, in New Granada, the King of Spain had gained nothing by relaxing his restrictions, and scarcely managed to maintain the dwindling trade between Quito and the mountain towns scattered throughout this wild, rough countryside. And the Caracas Company in Venezuela only managed to survive, when ships of the Spanish fleets were no longer compelled to put in at ports along the coasts, by conceiving the idea of lending capital to agriculturists and having the interest paid in agricultural produce. Within two or three years the port of Puerto Cabello revived and La Guaira became prosperous. Caracas also found itself in an excellent position in the middle of an area producing cocoa, as well as indigo, which fetched a high price in every market in the world; but the Caracas Company was short-lived. About 1780 an economic crisis made American merchants cautious. The old organizations disintegrated, and people relied on individual initiative to take the place of the failing business concerns which could no longer be directed all the way from San Sebastian.

Mexico had a similar history. Most of the country was separated from its Atlantic port by wild mountains. On the Pacific side it sloped down more broadly and gradually stretched towards Acapulco. Its territories northwards spread over half the north American continent, where its frontiers petered out beyond Santa Fé, the tiny capital of New Mexico. If this vast area alone brought Spain as much income as all the rest of its American continental possessions put together, it was chiefly because of the silver and gold from its mines, which were being worked again. In the south of the Oaxaca country the Indian, under the whip of Spanish merchants, grew cochineal, which was in great demand for textile industries all over the world; in Los Angeles and its surrounding villages small local industry produced ribbons and textiles of every kind and improved the quality of its output by copying materials from Europe. These communities, tiny islands of new activity, were not to be compared with the great cities of the past, with the bold towers of Puebla's vast cathedral, and particularly with Mexico City. Surrounded by floating islands, overgrown with grass and trees, on its mountain lakes, Mexico City was the pearl of America. In the days of Montezuma it boasted more than 200,000 inhabitants; but even now, with its 60,000 souls, it was still in 1780 the first city in the whole of America. Its majestic square in the Madrid style was bordered by sumptuous palaces, and by a huge cathedral built on the ruins of an old Indian temple. All around were the crowded quarters of the poor, where the police were constantly on the watch; there was frequent danger of riots, especially when the Indians had drunk too freely of their beloved *pulca*, an alcohol made from the same agave-aloe which supplied him with textiles and foods. Everywhere canals were built to drain a soil liable to flooding in the rainy season. Sumptuous carriages decorated with gold patterns bowled along the streets. As in every Spanish American city, the population was mixed. Europeans were in a minority, making up barely a sixth of the population of Mexico. The rest consisted of African Negroes, half-castes of every colour, and especially Indians, who retained traces of the unusual qualities that led to the construction of the strange pre-Colombian buildings around Mexico and Yucatan, and which are beginning to attract interest and attention again after a long period of neglect.

The formation of a united Brazil was to be one of the wonders of the nineteenth century. Towards 1785, in fact, that vast country gave no signs of being a unified empire, but seemed to consist of a multiplicity of mutually suspicious and rival cities, inadequately linked with one other, and each attempting to exploit for itself the immense resources of the interior.

The Brazilians occasionally allowed their small and remote capital to mediate in local conflicts, provided it did not annex power at the expense of local interests. Moreover, the whole of the south was still uncertain of its true nationality, and had not decided whether Spanish or Portuguese was to be its mother tongue. The fine natural harbour of Bahia de Todos os Santos had no adequate deepwater connection with the interior, which was cut off by high mountains, and there was no way of unifying this huge country in which the north, proud of its longstanding wealth and prosperous sugar refineries, was acting independently. Bahia had to give pride of place to Rio de Janeiro, a more convenient outlet for the centre of the country. In these central regions were precious metals; the gold-seekers who had been trying to make a way through the hostile forests for two hundred years, at last discovered the precious veins of metal. Sumptuous baroque churches plated with gold were erected near the mines. Towns sprang up in the desert where the workers alternated between extravagant festivals and feverish labour; the subsoil was already getting worked out at the time of which we are speaking and was soon exhausted. To the task of retaining a monopoly in this wealth, the riches of Minas-Geraes, Portugal devoted all its remaining energies. Its policy towards Minas was one of unremitting severity, though it was lax enough elsewhere; it led to the martyrdom of the hero Tiradentes in 1789 as he was addressing a meeting at Ouropreto on the liberal examples of North America and France. Pieces of his body were exhibited in all the surrounding towns. The mule-tracks which led by laborious stages from the interior to the coast would soon carry less gold; but by then landed proprietors of the interior were reaching an agreement. Their efforts at land clearance were being helped by the development of the mining towns, and the merchants of the coast. These two middle-class groups, both proud of their authentic Brazilian roots, were to unite in a mistrust of foreigners that soon developed into hatred, and they persuaded their customers to feel the same.

Free Anglo-Saxon America

The Spaniards made their settlements around former Indian sites in the south and centre, but the English-speaking peoples who created the small cities in the north had proceeded quite differently. Consequently these small North American cities had neither the wealth nor the population of their Spanish rivals. New York, which still occupied only the southern part of its Manhattan peninsula, had scarcely more than 25,000 inhabitants. It had a fine Anglican church and its French, Dutch, and German chapels, but had previously been regarded merely as a fortress. Nevertheless, its people were beginning to build stone houses, with fine English fronts, and a new town hall, which was intended to be the most remarkable in America, was nearing completion. It had one of the finest natural harbours in the world, and trade with England had flourished, especially during the War of Independence: it was therefore with reluctance that New York took part in the discussions in Philadelphia which defined the new federal Republic. For Philadelphia, with its 35,000 inhabitants, was assuming the rôle of a capital and even superseding Boston, the first city of them all, the birthplace of freedom, and the first place to make a stand against England.

The admirers of the young federal Republic had nothing but praise for Philadelphia, a small gay city where living was cheap, with delightful small houses along the banks of the Delaware and its tributary, which was spanned by a fine bridge; its market-place, raised on pillars and bordered with brick arches, was particularly famous. The whole city was organized around this centre, dominated by the town hall which had its windows framed in marble, an unusual luxury in this new agricultural Republic. Philadelphia was famous also for its numerous freshwater fountains, and its tree-shaded walks stretching away into innumerable orchards. In 1785 the small inns of this potential capital were full; it was not that the delegates of the thirteen states were very assiduous in attending the Congress, but the city was crowded with petitioners. Amongst them were large numbers of demobilized officers, a threat to the new state. They had in fact formed an association of 'Cincinnati', protesting that those who had laid the foundations of their country's freedom were entitled to greater consideration, and that it might perhaps be their duty to take the destinies of the young country into their own hands. They sent their Cincinnati badge to all their friends on the continent, and particularly to the French. Every liberal-minded person in Europe followed the debate which was to give power either to the new civilians or to yesterday's heroes. The soldiers were anxious, and so were the merchants, whose safes had been crammed with paper money which had been issued for the war but was beginning to depreciate.

The newly born Republic was an object of concern to every honest soul in Europe. People dreamed of emigrating. Jefferson proposed that entry should be forbidden, and Franklin, in Paris, explained at length the difficulties and risks involved in land clearance: America was far from being the land of ready-made happiness. Philosophers and theoreticians in Europe, and especially in Paris, paid no heed: they overwhelmed the Congress with good advice. Have a fleet, said some; give up commerce and trade, said others, and concentrate instead on the virtues of agriculture. Be a democracy, said Mably. You will progress only under the leadership of an aristocracy, replied Morvilliers. It was no use! The 3,500,000 new Americans paid not the slightest attention to this flood of solicitous literature. They cultivated their land, attacked the forest, attempted to irrigate their sandy soil, worked in small workshops beside rivers and harbours, traded in the small markets which were set up at road junctions, with only one idea in their minds, to buy as little as possible; hence the falling-off of trade which would – the English hoped – lead the young Republic to regret secession. But the spirit of independence was strong: there was eager competition for the news-sheets published in Philadelphia, New York or Boston, which played up to their readers by protesting against the excessive taxes to which the war had given rise.

America, then, at that date was not industrial. The tar factories which were stripping the forests in the Carolinas could hardly be called industries; nor could the state-controlled tobacco drying plants in Maryland or Virginia, or the boat and barque building yards in Boston. During the war country families had been obliged to spin and weave, though the cloth they made was only coarse in quality. The great majority of American farmers, eager above all to devote themselves to their lands, were waiting till goods could be imported from Europe again. On the other hand, there was great variety of agricultural produce. Jefferson had interminable lists of them drawn up, the largest, naturally, being for Virginia. In the south, the warm, moist summers set a premium on possession of slaves. Was the high-minded Republic going to tolerate them? Public opinion was beginning to take notice of the not wholly disinterested protests from England. Though the state of Virginia had, for its own part, decided to forbid trading in slaves, it did not forbid the use of them. Charleston continued to be a busy port for the slave trade. Close by the southern states were islands which had remained European, and had an enormous Negro population, so that they needed to export men and import foodstuffs; consequently an easy profit in the slave trade could be made by the southern farmers. Public opinion in the north was wavering, and the feeling against slavery filtered through from London to Boston. This was a city almost like London in miniature, built like an amphitheatre around the Bay of Massachusetts, studded with fertile islands and fruitful orchards. The city with ten churches of all denominations in the style of Wren, its English-looking houses and streets, espoused the ideology of the capital against which it had revolted.

As for the west, it was a controversial topic. Briefly, these virgin lands were to be set apart for the creation of new states. It would have been condoning too great an inequality between the old colonies to allow that some of them should be hemmed in by their neighbours, whilst others, open to the west, would develop unhindered. By undertaking to create these new states the Confederation had suddenly increased in power and significance and was confirmed in it by the new state of Kentucky, formed about the wonderfully rich grasslands of the western slopes of the Alleghanies. The vast west was still no more than the perilous domain of trappers whose tracks followed the Great Lakes and the rivers. These trappers were almost all French, as the English preferred to remain near the coastal areas, even in Canada, where they settled.

About 1780, Acadia became Nova Scotia: in face of the advancing English, the French had followed the land routes towards New France, and were soon replaced by English Royalists who were themselves refugees from the United States. A few thousand families, scattered here and there, they were not particularly anxious to embark on the great adventure into the interior. As for the French on the St Lawrence, they were, so to speak, shut in on their tiny citadel of Quebec, and evolved on the surrounding plains a peasant population like that of France. They were more reconciled to separation from the mother country when they learned, through its priests, that a wave of moral laxity and irreligion was sweeping over Paris. The French court had, as we know, taken very little interest in the problem of America because, for continental Europe at least, the real centre of interest so far as America was concerned was the wonderful chain of islands which formed the West Indies, the pearls of the Atlantic. To give them their true place in the economy of the late eighteenth century would mean devoting more pages to them than to the United States itself. It was towards the West Indies that most of the slave convoys made their way. There was good money to be made from growing coffee, cocoa and tobacco in the sheltered valleys, as long as they were not too swampy, and in laying out enormous plantations of sugar cane. Mule convoys converged on the small harbours, selling the produce of the land in return for riches brought by ship; amongst these the precious metals from Mexico were most highly prized. The islanders' greatest problem was not to yield to the seductions of a climate which Europeans found delightful, but on the contrary to get rich quick by making slaves do the work. The buccaneers had learnt from experience. When they were unable to get a plot of land, they kept shops in the small towns in order to sell as dearly as possible to the planters the goods for which there was such competition when the ships tied up at the quays. The one subject of all their Sunday arguments and weekday dreams was how to get back quickly to Europe with a substantial fortune. This was especially true perhaps in the French West Indies: the Dutch were more loyal to Curaçao, and the Spanish to San Domingo. It was they who had introduced cattle-breeding, much appreciated by the French consumers who held the other part of the great island. But in the

French possessions the day of the adventurers was over. These former members of the minor aristocracy had achieved marvels at the beginning of the century by pacifying the pirates whose interests they defended against the voracious India Company.

This powerful and hated company showed, moreover, how ill it rewarded the services of its settlers. There still lingered the memory of Law's bankruptcy; he paid the settlers out in valueless paper notes, so that when the poor wretches landed on the French coast they learned that they were utterly ruined. The company certainly put up a good defence: the West Indies offered an excellent opportunity for trade, and European businessmen from every capital in Europe were no less eager to increase their profits than the Creoles were to get rich quick. But although the great ocean trade remained in the hands of Europeans, their ships did not linger unduly along the island coasts, which retained the monopoly in coastal and inland trade. This island trade sent its boats plying from island to island, and tried to expand as far as the American continent; it gradually created a network of interests increasingly capable of holding their own against the demands of the distant capital. The old governors' palaces often changed masters and sometimes flags as well. The settlers paid no heed, learning from experience that it was easier to make money in an open town, where troops of all nations were always welcome provided they paid up, than in fortified towns which were destroyed and ravaged by each fresh war. They held aloof from Europe's quarrels: they protected themselves against European competition, and exploited the Negro. In San Domingo there were already more than 300,000 slaves; the death-rate was exceedingly high, but a constant supply from Africa was guaranteed. Once Europeans had been converted to anti-slavery there was of course a decrease in the traffic; this caused the settlers some anxiety, so that they tended to keep their slaves, rather than free them as before, even though they knew that this fresh severity could lead to sudden revolts in their territories.

Thus from north to south the vast American continent was everywhere breaking its links with Europe. The break was made in the north. It was being prepared in the south and centre. The Atlantic, which had been the vital means of Europe's hold over America, was in process of becoming the instrument of American independence.

3
The Call of Asia

ALL through the Middle Ages contacts had existed between China and Europe, although they were indirect: it had taken months, even years, to accomplish the journey overland and had involved innumerable ship crossings, which almost always included the Indian Ocean. Now, during the eighteenth century, European ships established direct contacts. These direct contacts brought a revelation to everyone in the Western ports and cities in the eighteenth century, as they had done to a small group of adventurers in the sixteenth century. The products of Oriental craftsmanship, Oriental agriculture, and the manners and customs of these enchanting civilizations revolutionized European taste. In addition, the powerful European merchants penetrated deeply into several Eastern countries, and in order to exploit Western fashions they strove to transform the economic structures of the East: successfully in India, with greater difficulty in China. As for Central Asia, it was beginning to be a depressed area both economically and culturally. Its unsettled state attracted neighbouring peoples and gave them the excuse and the opportunity to intervene. The beneficiary this time was not a sea power. It was a land power, familiar with the slow rhythm of life of continental peoples: it was, in fact, Russia.

THE DISCOVERY OF INDIA

Every wealthy mansion in Paris (and of course in London, as well as its counterparts in Germany), had at least one 'Indian' drawing-room, in which, inset in the Western panelling, botanical, zoological or human scenes imitated from India were portrayed. India was just as popular as China in cultured circles, with perhaps this slight difference, that its philosophy was not quite so admired; nevertheless it probably exerted an even stronger influence on public taste. If India was less often admired in Paris than China, this may have been due to a lingering bitterness at the loss of an empire which Suffren's efforts had failed to defend against English ambitions. A more likely reason was that Indian civilization was alien to the Frenchman. It was a world at once more secret and more subtle; the improved communications had brought it closer physically, but it was as far away as ever mentally, for its passive organization remained incomprehensible to Western minds.

Eighteenth-century European thinkers found India quite inscrutable. On the one hand they were dazzled by the splendour of such potentates as Aurengzeb, the Louis xiv of India, last representative of a dynasty of kings which had enhanced the old Hindu arts with the refinements of Persia. People still remembered his throne 'encrusted with diamonds, decorated with vine-branches made of pure gold, their leaves enamelled in natural colours, the grapes being of emerald, ruby and garnet'. The famous throne had, in fact, disappeared, carried off in 1738 during a Persian raid. Yet Agra remained a vast capital city, with some million inhabitants, which a man on horseback could scarcely ride round in a single day; it boasted eight hundred bridges, a hundred caravanserai, innumerable mosques, and twenty magnificent baronial castles, so arranged that they appeared to be paying homage to the King of Castles, that of the Moghul, whose harem alone contained twelve hundred women. Merchants from all over the world seemed to meet in Agra, for not only was the finest indigo to be obtained there, but also all the produce of Central Asia and India. The nearby town of Delhi, in which the Moghul had also lived for a long time, was easily outclassed by Agra. Delhi itself was quieter than Agra, but the Prince's palace was even more dazzling, especially on high festivals when elephants bore the imperial processions in state.

Yet at the time we are considering little was left of the power of the Moghuls. The one reigning in Delhi had no longer any authority. A rival and perhaps legitimate claimant lived on a pension paid him by the East India Company, which also ensured him a refuge in Bengal and gave him military protection against the attacks of his enemy, for the finest province in India had become almost the private property of merchants.

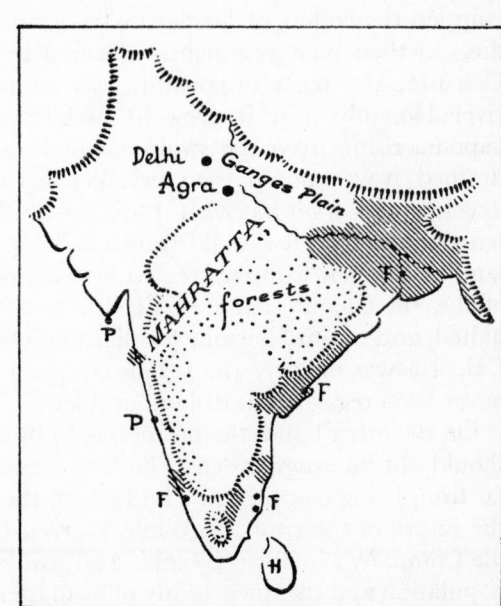

5 India in 1795

Grey: English possessions
F: France; P: Portugal;
H: Holland

The Ganges was in the hands of foreigners; not the kind of foreigner who swept down in one fierce raid to loot and plunder a territory for a season, and then withdrew to his distant lands; nor was it the foreigners who had come over the last hundred years to settle on islands in river estuaries, or in the mouths of harbour channels, where they awaited their moment to steal some of India's wealth. This time the foreigner who had India in his power was a methodical exploiter who intended not only to reimburse himself as quickly as possible for the enormous capital expended on its conquest (a conquest at first directed less against the Indians than against his European competitors) but also to organize a permanent administration of India which should be to his own advantage.

In 1785, this corner of the world presented a series of violent contrasts. Here was the shrine of Juggernaut, the most famous temple in Asia, home of the great Brahmin. Its enormous idol was covered with diamonds and drenched with perfume, and it was surrounded by attendant idols reputed to be carved in gold. From the farthest reaches of the peninsula it continued to attract pilgrims who came on their knees to cleanse themselves in the Ganges after having paid, each according to his means – but even the poorest of them generously – for the right to enter the sacred city. The most fanatical threw themselves under the wheels of the chariot in which the idol was carried. And in the middle of this milling mass of humanity were a few passive commissioners, tall, lean, fair-haired representatives of a different race, who disliked any excesses and carefully respected the natural order of things. They assessed taxes, obliged puppet princes to sign laws and regulations, and by the offer of moderate rewards or through pressure exerted by local chiefs recruited thousands of Indians whom they intended to train as workers in the factories they were opening on the coasts. They emptied the coffers of former tax-collectors, and enrolled disaffected soldiers in their own regiments, officered by Europeans. They built cities: Calcutta, the most important, was an insignificant mud-town on the river Hooghly, but it grew at such speed that, in spite of the putrid vapours rising from the swamps which only now were beginning to be drained, it was soon a great city. Yet this artificial city was to impede the development of all its rivals, Indian as well as European. The merchants' tents gradually left the old traditional capitals, cut off from their hinterland by the new frontier created by the Company. Thus the development of the old Chandernagor, built Indian-fashion on piles, was artificially halted, and the city became fossilized in its outmoded Franco-Indian form. Calcutta was already the ruling city in a country where obedience had never been regarded as dishonourable.

On the other hand, the position held by the English Company in Bengal should not be exaggerated. The transformation of India by England was far from being completed. The English themselves were not agreed about the future of the country. While Warren Hastings was strongly pursuing the Company's interests by taking advantage of the passivity of the Indian population and the uncertainty of its masters, in the House of Commons in

London Fox thundered out his protests against the Company's scandalous exactions and its criminal negligence in allowing some millions of men to die; in 1784 the Commons ordered Hastings to be impeached and to render an account of his stewardship before the Lords. Pitt struggled to induce the Lords to agree to a reform of the Company embodied in the famous India Bill, which received a stormy passage through the Commons, culminating in the suicide of Clive, victor of Lally-Tollendal, and the overbearing leader of this new conquest.

Whilst London discussed their fate, the Indian peasants were aware of the changed situation only through the presence of new officials who appeared in their villages from time to time. The majority of Indians remained indifferent to the disastrous transactions which marked the end of the old imperial India and added considerably to the hardship of their lot, which for centuries had been steadily deteriorating. This passivity of the common people was perhaps the result of their religion, which inculcated a respect for order; by degrees this had transformed the old social structure and consolidated the caste system, and may even have paved the way for the country's downfall. Certainly, at the time of which we are writing, this passivity was the country's most noticeable characteristic.

Caste did not however exclude freedom, at least in principle. It split freedom into separate compartments, as it split the whole country. The fact was that everywhere the old Indian community still existed; we have noted the survival in Eastern Europe of this communal life, which gave rise to the intellectual myth of a common Indo-European civilization. In the village the assembly settled everything, and its duty was to ensure a livelihood for all. It may have been to protect these villages that the former conquerors had guaranteed that soldiers would not enter them, and had imposed a similar obligation on the armies to ensure that they respected the educated classes. In any case, at the end of the eighteenth century, the educated *élite*, the soldiers, and the peasants, were three worlds functioning in water-tight compartments, separated from each other by an ever widening gulf: there was no mutual social contact, no sharing of even an occasional meal, and certainly no intermarriage between these various worlds. And following their example the infinite variety of artisans formed themselves into trade groups which in turn were grouped into castes, the frontiers of which were no less rigidly fixed, although difficult to define. Originally, in the days when this structure was more general than tyrannical, the individual had the right to abandon his caste, to become an outcast, with greater freedom. But later, when the structure became fossilized, the outcast's lot was disastrous, and he was rejected on every side. Certain trades came to be considered unclean or degrading (that of scavengers, for instance), and this added a new rigidity and increased the number of untouchables, the slightest contact with whom necessitated purification.

Religion in India never developed a moral conscience capable of overcoming the appalling inequalities of the caste system. Buddhism retained its admirers among the literate, and its teaching was propagated everywhere, including southern India, where it was more strictly observed than elsewhere. It did not eradicate the primitive animism of the common people which compels an Indian to remove every living, moving thing carefully from the patch of earth on which he is about to sit, saying, to God: 'I have spared the ant, Lord, do Thou put it down to my account'. And belief in the transmigration of souls also led to a respect for the order of nature: in a new life the good will attain a higher caste, but the bad may descend to the vilest of animal forms. Thus every living creature had to be respected in the eyes of the Hindi sage.

The Muslim religion also spread from the north, brought in by each fresh wave of conquerors; but even in Kashmir and Nepal where the Koran was widely disseminated it did not succeed in effacing old customs. It was propagated throughout the peninsula by merchants and craftsmen, but only served to strengthen respect for the old beliefs. Indeed, its most notable effect was to induce in those who resisted it a heightened fanaticism in the observance of the old customs. To each wave of Islamism, the peasant replied with new fervour for Hinduism.

So from generation to generation the community villages retained their differing patterns of toil, varying from one end of the country to the other, but always true to themselves. The village produced barely enough to feed itself, after handing over to other castes and to the lords their due share of rice, fruit, curds and milk, and leather. Certain castes forbade the eating of meat, others held the cow sacred, but consented to eat the ox; others would touch neither leeks nor onions 'which grow out of impure things'. To satisfy all these different diets, the peasant watched for the arrival of the monsoons, which were first spotted from the top of the Ghats, for he was afraid of floods except in specified places were they could be controlled. It should be noted that the English victory in India brought them control of a crop which was a highly profitable economic proposition: the poppy, which already grew widely in Bengal, and produced opium of a medium quality.

As for craftsmanship, its infinite variety defies description, whether in the realm of small useful articles or in skilled luxury trades, such as jewellery. Indian goods, particularly cottons, were very popular in Europe, and this popularity proved fatal for India. European trading companies were no longer content to buy ready-made produce; they wanted to develop it to order, pledging in advance enormous capital sums in order to buy raw materials, pay wages, and train workers, of whom they intended to have only the very best. Around every European settlement grew up zones of industrial activity, attracting population, the craftsmen seeking work or peasants threatened with famine: and these forces most probably accounted for the prodigious new cities of India – European settlements founded on unhealthy islands or barren sandy wastes.

Bombay, Buon Baya (in Portuguese 'good bay'), was nothing but 'a filthy islet' when the Portuguese presented it as a wedding-present to Charles II. At the end of the eighteenth century it was a new city of nearly

200,000 inhabitants, the capital of yet another principality belonging to the East India Company, and already powerful enough to send troops into the interior to conquer new lands and cities. It gradually extended itself inland, by judicious payments of gold, by negotiation or by treachery. Relying on small contingents of several hundred armed men (later increased in number), it expanded its settlements and tried to carve out a new Bengal in the west of the country. But it soon faced the solid feudal régimes of the Mahrattas. Madras, in the east, was built on a sandy, uninspiring site, with an inadequate supply of drinking water. Gossips maintained that the Englishman who settled there did so only in order to be near his Portuguese mistress who lived in the neighbouring colony of Saint Thomé. But Madras, however difficult its site, was admirably placed to attract to itself all the trade of the rival settlements on the Coromandel Coast, and had the added protection of the powerful British fleet.

This Coromandel Coast had lost the former glories of its maritime empire which had stretched as far as the Sunda Islands and across Indo-China. But it could not escape the consequences of its geographical conditions: it had two monsoons in regular succession, great ocean currents and a whole chain of suitable harbours. The Dutch, Portuguese, French and English had disputed over the bases of this ancient maritime coast, in a costly struggle which gave birth to great feats of arms, miracles of political juggling and an infinity of stories. The mastery of India could only be won from the sea; this was obvious enough, and Suffren had continually repeated it, but Clive was the first to prove it. He used the stretches of the River Ganges to effect what Dupleix with his land policy had not been able to achieve permanently in the Deccan. The interior of the Indian peninsula, together with the north-west, still formed in 1785 an island of land resistance against the maritime inroads of the East India Company, whereas the wide northern delta allowed it to push far inland.

This was India. Its weakness in the eighteenth century was that it never expected attack from the sea. There had been a few stubborn 'pirates' on the coasts of Rajputana, who had long been a source of uneasiness to the Moghuls and had attacked the sea-routes and disorganized the European and particularly the English fleets. But the Mahrattas were almost as concerned as the English to destroy this 'nest of disorder'. And although India possessed good ship-builders it was content to let them work for the Company. As for sailors, the skill of the famous Malabars is legendary. The most enlightened of the Moghuls from Central Asia had never had any great liking for seafaring activity: there was no sailor caste and no curiosity about modern improvements in navigation, any more than there was a caste for the new developments in metallurgy and armaments. The haughty Aurangzeb himself was quite content to leave to the despised foreigners the task of scouring the seas. The Moghuls must have smiled to see those down-at-heel emperors whom the Portuguese set up on the Malabar coast in order to make sure of getting their services cheap, at the cost only of a little flattery.

So it was that the old caste-divided India, though still defending itself in the centre of its vast peninsula, saw its coasts encircled by the English who had already sailed up the Ganges and were now threatening the capital itself.

It was the sea that conquered India, the sea and the ships from Europe. On each side of the Indian peninsula there had formerly existed two great sea empires. These soon fell, but were not fully supplanted by the advances of Western trade. In the west, the Moslem and Banian ships had apparently remained in control of trade along the East African coast as far as Madagascar. They were also masters of what little trade was still carried on in the Arabian Sea, and remained so until the Mediterranean trade broke through Suez and destroyed the last vestiges of this old and decaying maritime civilization. Little remained of the famous Ormuz, a huge treasure-house which still stirred dreams of adventure in any imaginative Western mind. It had been the most flourishing of the ocean ports where the loveliest of Asian slaves and the produce of the world's most cultured civilizations were to be found. But from Albuquerque to Shah Abbas war on land and sea had ravaged the dream island, and with a decadent Persia turning away from the sea, the centre of activity shifted to Basra. Basra was part of the mainland ruled by the Arabs, a rich fertile country which yielded acres of the finest corn. Shepherds from the interior came there to offer butter, leather, and above all camels in exchange for the coffee and tobacco they loved, and also for opium. All these precious commodities, which were also produced in the rich fertile lands of Arabia, aroused the envy of the desert tribes and provoked them to savage raids on the caravans bound for Damascus or Mecca. The routes from Aden and Mokha were in most respects safer, and European interests were already infiltrating along them.

But Europeans had found an easier conquest in Eastern waters, where navigators were continually making fresh discoveries; the Spaniards, for example, were busy exploring the Philippines with the help of the strange long-haired black natives who until then had been chiefly engaged in continual inter-tribal warfare in Manila. The Spaniards had succeeded in settling on the coast and had introduced European cattle, which were doing well there; and there were also ample local resources to be exploited: trees which bore abundant fruit, gold-nuggets in the rivers, and the skill of Hindus, Chinese and innumerable half-castes.

Batavia was the Queen of the Eastern Seas; its deep harbour thrusting far inland made it the finest port of the East: hence the fantastic growth of that swarming city, built on mud. Every country in the world had, at some time of the year, ships in Batavia. It was the great port of call between the New World and the Far East. This commercial wealth was based on extraordinarily rich agricultural resources. The soil was fertile when irrigated (and so much water had been taken from the river for irrigation that in 1780 its estuary was nothing but a sandbank). It produced rice, coffee, spices, and food in sufficient quantities not only for crews of ships anchored in the bay, but also for several islands in the Pacific, and sometimes supplied places as far afield as Mexico. The island of Java sold much and bought little: most goods, English hardware, for instance, had to make a long journey to get there. As a result, Batavia had acquired vast wealth in gold, which was administered by the Resident General of the Amsterdam Company.

The Dutch, who had driven out their European rivals, had no great difficulty in dominating the small local kings, or in subduing the betel-chewing, opium-smoking, feudal society which kept in its service armies of slaves, easily obtainable in the Celebes or the Moluccas; and Holland saw to it that the market was always well stocked. Close watch was kept on the labour gangs bent double over the ground, but who only a few years previously had shown the degree of violence to which they could carry their revolt. Free trade was practised by Chinese or Indians who got rich on the side and where possible sent their profits to their families at home. The Company kept as tight a watch on this illicit traffic as it did on the gangs of slaves. The Dutch might confer coveted honours on the local chieftains, and respect the Muslim religion (mixed up as it was with survivals of the old paganism), but they made it clear that all the gold must go to Amsterdam. So these islands – where so much of the work was done by slaves, these busy yet depressing cities in which innumerable small ships were built for the Pacific trade, where every type of dress, every way of life known to Asia has intermingled – constituted one of the most envied commercial sites in the world. By sheer hard work gold was extracted from the Batavian mud, just as not long before, and for the same reasons, it had been dredged from the mud of the Lower Rhineland.

CHINA REMAINS ALOOF

The end of the eighteenth century marked one of the most splendid periods in the history of China – but it probably appeared even finer in the missionaries' tales that were read in Europe. These remarkable Jesuits had been expelled from France by Louis xv in 1763, under the joint pressure of fanatics and Jansenists, and in 1773 the whole order was condemned by the Pope under the combined pressure of the 'enlightened' monarchs. Nevertheless, Father Verbiest had enjoyed immense authority in China in the previous century, and so did his successor Father Gerbillon. In 1715 the latter had even succeeded in persuading the proud Emperor of China to write to Rome, defending the Jesuits' tolerant attitude to ancestor worship, which the Emperor represented to the Pope as being a simple, pious tradition. But the Son of Heaven had pleaded in vain, and his failure must have rankled. Christianity was thus forbidden in China – but the Jesuits themselves remained in favour. People remembered that they had reformed the calendar, repaired the old wooden cannons, cast new ones, and rebuilt the ruined citadels. One of the last of the Peking Jesuits, Father Ventavon, wrote in 1764 that the Emperor and noblemen of China agreed that the Roman religion was good, 'but if they opposed that which was preached, it was from fear lest, under the pretext of religion, we should conceal some ulterior motive. They had heard of the conquests made by Europeans in India.'

The exceptional position of these few Jesuits, most of whom were at the Imperial Court of Peking, should not blind us to an extraordinary fact: the immense Chinese Empire which the Manchus had restored in Tibet, Kashgaria, Chungaria, Mongolia and Southern China, making it as great as it had been during the most glorious Han period, this Empire which was the largest in the world, bigger than the whole of Europe and yet united under one single prince, was closed completely and effectively to Europeans. The few occasional caravans which the Russians, after endless journeying across the steppes, managed to get through to Peking could hardly be reckoned as contacts ; nor could the insignificant coastal trade for which the English, Portuguese and Dutch competed along the great estuaries under the amused and scornful eyes of minor officials and Chinese merchants. The Chinese extracted every possible advantage from the rivalry and hesitations of the Europeans: when it was a foreigner who was being robbed, there was surely some excuse for violating the teachings of Confucius on the subject of honesty in business.

European philosophers read the books of the condemned Jesuits with profound pleasure, and from this reading there suddenly grew a realization of the vastness of the Chinese civilization. In the light of this momentous discovery, China ceased to be an obscure and distant example of despotism. After Quesnay, the greatest and wisest government in the world was universally praised throughout the cultured society of Europe, and particularly in Paris. Its supporters claimed that it was based on the evidence of natural rights and enlightened reason. Let us attempt to sum up what was written, and what is known today, about one of the most admirable periods of Chinese history.

'It was an attractive sight, the fertile countryside where land was never fallow, where even the mountains were cultivated on their highest slopes, built up by a hundred terraces; such mountains elsewhere would have produced nothing but brambles and bushes but here they made a delightfully fertile scene and bore three harvests a year.' Obviously China was not all one endless garden, but in the writings of the period everything came in for admiration, the forests of pine and oaks, of palms and cedars, and the many trees unknown in Europe, the *ram mu* with its everlasting wood, the rosewood with its lovely black grain, and the ironwood, so hard that ships' anchors were said to be made of it. There was an infinite variety of fruits, and herbs with a thousand virtues; and bamboo was used for every purpose. The Chinese peasant was poor, certainly, but at least he appeared to be free. The Emperor's close concern with agriculture was particularly praised. It was recalled that one of the emperors was himself a ploughman, and there was enthusiasm for the celebration of the spring festivals which in every village was presided over by the Mandarin, or by the oldest and most respected sage.

Although the Chinese peasant was obliged to hand over almost half his harvest to the state, and although he lived frugally on a little rice, oil and tea, it was quite true that the Manchu emperors in power since 1644 had done what they could by dividing hereditary estates, and trying to combine the smallholdings of three hectares; it was these smallholdings which turned three-quarters of the Chinese peasantry into small landowners, given over to agriculture and the cultivation of their land, which they fertilized skilfully with the manure that was essential if the ground was not to be exhausted by three harvests a year. The Manchu dynasty, to make its power secure, supported the slaves against their masters. Slavery had probably never been so harsh as under the rule of the Mings; slaves and servants were beaten to death without the administration making any attempt to intervene. From that time onwards, however, the brutal master risked deportation or flogging, and after several generations the farmer was regarded as the owner of at least a part of the land he had been cultivating. This was a feature of which the Western philosophers approved.

Of all the products of Chinese industry, none was more famous in Europe than the porcelain – so famous in fact that Dutch factories tried to imitate the best Chinese pieces in order to heighten the value of their own wares. In China, vast industrial centres were made up of a conglomeration of small factories organized in guilds. In Kiangsi there was King-teh, where it was estimated that more than 500 kilns and a million workmen were grouped together, and where the finest paste in the whole Empire was made; at least, the European merchants thought it was superior to that of Peking. As for the Canton porcelains, well known in Europe under the name of *Indian porcelain*, they were apparently made simply because the Chinese believed that European merchants had very poor taste and they were far inferior in quality to those of the interior. At all events this seems to have been one of the really great periods of Chinese ceramics; there was monochrome, *sang de bœuf* or sapphire blue, as in the eighteenth century, to which had been added what was known as the *famille rose*, and the *mille fleurs* pattern on a rose-pink background, the finest flowering of a thousand-year-old art.

As for silk, even Europeans recognized that it was very unevenly spun and that fabrics were not always in the best of taste. Yet certain of these silks were admired and eagerly sought after, chiefly because of their unparalleled whiteness. These smooth silks attracted foreigners much more than the brocades, which were already being made more efficiently in Europe: the Chinese never seem to have taken the trouble to spin gold and silver thread properly, and they decorated their material with gilded paper. On the other hand, the green and red dyes they produced were so good that contemporary Europeans could congratulate themselves if they could improve on them.

In China, of course, nothing was known of the mechanization which was being introduced in Europe. Nevertheless a few Chinese, so skilled at every kind of manual work, tried their hand at applying some of these new techniques ; they succeeded in manufacturing watches and guns – but these were isolated attempts which did not give rise to any real industry. Chinese civilization remained in a pre-mechanized stage. The population was so numerous that flour mills were very often turned by human labour ; water-wheels and windmills were known, but were in general too widely scattered and too expensive to deal adequately with the nation's requirements.

This predominance of manual work did not prevent China from maintaining vast cities. They were usually square in shape, surrounded by high walls with towers at each corner supported by flying-buttresses. These large towers, often hexagonal, were also to be found in the centre of the cities, close to the temples and the gateways rather like our triumphal arches, and they were a distinctive feature of old pictures of China. The population swarmed around low-ceilinged shops piled high with silks and porcelain and all kinds of glazed pottery. These represented high-class trade, since the small trader did not need a shop: the barber strolled about, with a chair on his back, in search of a customer. In the same way, most craftsmen worked only to order in the actual homes of those who had placed the commission. The bath merchant carried hot water to the house. The strolling players had no theatre: they simply used the big market places, transporting their troupe from town to town. And there were certainly plenty of towns. Father Lecomte wrote: 'I have seen seven or eight cities all bigger than Paris, not to mention several others which I have not visited. There are more than eighty cities of the first rank, comparable to Lyons or Bordeaux. There are more than one hundred like Orleans and more than six hundred like La Rochelle or Dijon.' In all, there were more than four thousand walled cities. All were linked by roads or canals, though these sounded more impressive than they actually were to Europeans who thought in terms of their own royal highways or stone-banked canals. The artificial rivers attracted special attention, particularly the Grand Imperial Canal from Canton to Peking. The Europeans at once imagined seven hundred and fifty miles of waterway bordered with stone embankments and avenues of trees. The different branches of this canal must in fact have varied a good deal, and probably included several overland sections across which boats had to be dragged over the clay soil. Another wonder of China was its daring bridges spanning embanked valleys or broad rivers; and the pontoon bridges, which opened to let boats through. The whole empire gave the impression of a vast fair, bustle and animation prevailing everywhere.

Peking, a capital beautified by the Mings, had been burnt down when the dynasty fell in the seventeenth century. But the city had been restored, and once again the traveller could admire the golden river and the marble gates, the palaces with gilded roofs arranged according to the order of the Cosmos, and all the glittering framework of the Imperial religion. In the last years of the century the Garden of Spring and the Garden of the Round Light were completed, to form what is known as the Summer Palace. French *salons* were decorated in Chinese style, but French missionaries in China were also appreciated for their skill as painters. One of them, Father Attiret, has caught the charm of these pleasant man-made valleys, watered by streams channelled from the mountains, with pillared façades supporting the gilded and lacquered structure, made of cedar-wood brought from twelve hundred and fifty miles away. In the middle of the great lake, on a rock, rose the small central palace, from which all these wonders were clearly visible.

Yet it was not only the material civilization of China which Europeans praised. Chinese medicine, in so far as it was known, aroused the admiration of many Western doctors. At a time when Western medicine consisted essentially of the application of ideas which the Arabs had taken as much from the Far East as from the Greeks, the skill of the Chinese at detecting minute variations of the pulse won them high esteem. In philosophy, too, Chinese civilization had produced achievements to equal the elegance of its lovely houses, and the size of its urban settlements.

In theory, every educated man was a nobleman, and in theory too, there had to be a school for every twenty-five houses. But in fact, if the privileges of birth had no sanction in law, they were recognized in reality, since it was difficult to achieve the Red Girdle unless one was born into a cultured family. But also, and the liberal-minded traveller consoled himself with this thought, the precious Yellow Girdle reserved for members of the Imperial families could sometimes be worn by beggars legitimately, for the Imperial families remained prolific, even after suffering the most disastrous vicissitudes of fate. In any case nobility was acquired, and maintained, by the study of texts. Children were taught the thousand sentences of the Santseking, adults the wisdom of Confucius and his commentaries. The man of letters could give a brilliant performance when called upon to make one of the traditional public speeches that were dedicated once a fortnight to some fresh virtue. Good servant that he was to the Empire and the Emperor, the man of letters could earn some of those greatly envied titles of nobility which were transmitted not to his descendants but to his forbears, and went so many generations back in proportion to the degree of magnanimity shown by the Emperor. For, side by side with Confucianism, ancestor worship was so deeply rooted that it could well seem more than just the filial piety of which the Pope had been so suspicious. The dead were laid in a richly decorated coffin and given the most elaborate funeral rites. An altar in every home was consecrated to the ancestors. For the rest the people relied on a higher power – the Tien – of which every person in authority was an emanation, the Emperor first and foremost.

China was undoubtedly tolerant. She may have feared the Christianity of the barbarous West, yet the most varied superstitions were allowed to spread. Buddhism introduced the human figure of Buddha, which was soon followed by innumerable idols installed in equally innumerable pagodas in which the clergy lived comfortably and well. Not only did the people regard them with awe and reverence, but scholars went there to meditate on the transmigration of souls, a doctrine which they came to accept. All these sects intermingled with each other and were constantly being revised. There was a continual ferment of religious enquiry and each man furnished the shrine of his conscience as best pleased him. All these differing creeds had one observance in common, the obligation to preserve, at all times, that extreme politeness whose subtle delicacy was mistakenly interpreted by Europeans as dissimulation. This politeness and its rituals arose from a great desire for goodness and wisdom, since the gesture and attitude were to control the conscience from without. The Chinaman with a barren wife was free to take a concubine, but it was his legitimate wife whom the resulting children had to regard as their mother, for the complicated marriage rites were intended to safeguard the future of the family.

The stories about these rites brought back from their long journeys by European merchants were often no more than caricatures of the real thing, for they could really know little about China. Their experiences were confined to a few sea-ports, notably Canton and Ning Po. Canton, they said, had a million inhabitants, and the influx of merchandise was immense. The river was covered with an amazing number of great ships. In fact, the draught of water was so shallow that European ships had to stay in the marshy roadsteads which were studded with islands and more than three miles from Canton. One of these islands was well populated, well provisioned; it was reserved for the French who were not a little proud of it, since the Portuguese, English and Dutch had to make do with more barren ones. Commercial rivalry was fierce between these islands. The most famous was that of Macao, but its activity was not increasing; ships were turning away from it, a sad ending to Portugal's ambitious schemes. And no one could have forecast the amazing future of Hong Kong, a stony islet at which ships from England were beginning to anchor in increasing numbers. European trade was attracted by silks and porcelain, but it was not wholly uninterested in gold either. The Chinese preferred silver, Europeans gold: hence the origin of a trade which would have been extremely profitable but for the hazards of the long journey. The English and the Portuguese went in for it on the largest scale. A certain Frenchman, too, made a handsome fortune by bringing silver from Mexican mines to the Pacific port of Acapulco, and after putting in at the Philippines, exchanging it for Chinese gold.

The Chinese scorned maritime trade. It is true, Chinese ships made for Japan, Manila, Batavia, Tongking or Cochin China. But it was only small-scale coastal shipping, the lingering survival of the old coastal trading and the empire of the seas which had been the refuge of the last of the Mings, and of the pirate Koxinga who for twenty years had successfully disputed possession of Formosa with the invaders from the north. Yet its importance should not be underestimated; it was to lay the foundations not only of the outer China which had already played such an important rôle in the national resistance to the conquerors of the land but also of the offshore China which later was to transform the Pacific Ocean. On the other hand, the Chinese kept a closer watch on the vast continental masses of which their country was part. Of the 800,000 men under arms (this figure included the whole number, even local militia, which were of very unequal value) the sections not guarding the interior of the country were massed along the famous wall, built of stone and brick, from which they sallied forth on expeditions intended to preserve peace and goodwill among friendly and neighbouring merchants, and to keep within the Chinese *orbis* the unsettled regions of Tartary and Tibet. In the course of these operations China encountered the Russian caravans. (These Chinese expeditions did not penetrate very far across the steppes of Central Asia along the route of the old silk trade towards the West but they helped to create a new route along which went rhubarb and tea.) In the eighteenth century they had the right to bring goods which were traded in Peking itself, under the eyes of the sovereign. But this privilege was often contested, since a strong faction at court accused them of abusing it. The Russians succeeded, nevertheless, in keeping the imperial privilege of maintaining a trading post in Peking.

But during the period of Manchu or, as it is more often called by Europeans, Tartar splendour, China despised these land barbarians as thoroughly as those who came by sea. These men with their strange white skins and fair hair (a characteristic of the demons of popular imagery) seemed alien to them. In reality, these European traders, like tiny insects, had done no more than touch the vast body of China with the minute antennae of their remote ambitions.

THE STRUGGLE FOR CENTRAL ASIA

Beyond the Tian-Shan and the Altai, beyond the Himalayas and as far as the frozen sea in the north and the Atlantic in the west, sprawled an enormous continent intersected with forests and mountains, furrowed by rivers and huge lakes, with seas stagnating in the hollows of low-lying land. Did this vast region stretching from Kamchatka to the Baltic belong to Europe or to Asia? The eighteenth-century Westerner had become accustomed to looking on Sweden, Poland and Russia as a part of his world, whilst Persia belonged to the East, to Asia. But when we come to survey this vast region as it was in 1780, we shall be dealing with it as an integral whole, and as part of the East.

We have seen how Western maritime trade reached the shores of Asia and began to penetrate to India and Indonesia. These sea-routes were relatively new: for ten centuries China's trade with Europe had been carried overland across this same, huge continent. The land trade had carved out economic channels too deep to vanish without trace, and which remained important since they were the channels along which Russian history began to infiltrate in the nineteenth century. What was the position at the time of Catherine the Great?

The routes from Asia to Europe were a succession of halts, post-stages precariously established and widely spaced, for the use of the great caravans whose journeys lasted many months. These routes seem to have followed three natural directions. The most famous and most direct, the 'silk route', after following the oases of the Tarim Valley, took the shortest cut across Central Asia and emerged at the end of the Mediterranean. This, generally speaking, was the route followed by the Turkish invasion; it enabled them to take over Constantinople, and it was still the backbone of their power. Persia and Afghanistan were enclosed within mountains, as if in natural fortresses, between China and India and between Turkey and Russia.

Russia was gradually establishing itself along two other great continental axes, which might perhaps be called the tea routes; the China tea transported over dry land was considered superior to any tea that had been shaken about in the damp holds of ships. Naturally, just as many other commodities besides silk travelled along the silk route, so the tea routes were also used for lambs' wool, tallow, rice and spices of every kind. These goods, on leaving Turkestan, went towards Astrakhan and the Caspian, or Archangel and the White Sea, or Gotland, Hansa and the Baltic. The first route followed the Siberian rivers, ideal for descending traffic. On these endless journeys small ships had to be made which were destroyed or left behind when the time came to leave the rivers and resume the overland trek. The building of these boats presented no problem because of the inexhaustible supply of timber in the surrounding forests. Boats had to be built for the second route also where it crossed the Caspian, and here the forests of Kazan were equally useful. The English, as we know, had tried to take advantage of both routes through Moscow to Central Asia in the heroic days of the first Muscovite Company. They still held an important position in this two-way traffic. There were English agents in Astrakhan, but that strange city built at the mouth of the Volga was also frequented by the Swedes and the Dutch, and of course by Mongols, Turks and Jews. Large numbers of Armenians were also active throughout this whole region. The curious city of Astrakhan lived on fishing in the Caspian between the two peak seasons of its commercial traffic: winter, when the sledges glided over the frozen Volga, and summer when the unfrozen waters were no longer a danger to shipping.

Three routes, then, led Europe towards China. It is difficult to imagine what this traffic must have been like, and what were the conditions of the areas through which it passed. There were tales of Tartars, and Mongols, of unarmed caravans being attacked by dangerous robbers, incidents which Borodin was to evoke so vividly in music.

In fact the status of the whole area, extending over several hundred miles north of the seas, was politically ambiguous, situated as it was between the old, solid Moscow and the domination of the Turks: there stretched undefined territories which for centuries had been a refuge for serfs escaping from Russia, for the politically persecuted, and the heterodox of all religions: it was these areas which made up the Ukraine in the west, and which extended as far as Persia. They were frontier lands where man had no rights other than those he was capable of defending. And the real rulers were the Cossacks. We know how the Ukrainian Cossacks had first offered their services to Poland against Russia, and had then entered Russian service against Poland. Pushkin has told us the history of the great revolt of Pugachev, who gathered together tens of thousands of rebels about 1773; they gained control of the Don, and threatened Moscow itself, where a section of the people were waiting for them, seeing in Pugachev the true Tsar Peter III. By the time Pugachev was captured at Tsaritsyn and drawn and quartered by order of Catherine, the Cossacks had laid waste a huge area to the east, before seeking refuge with the Turks beyond Kuban. Yet even in Pugachev's time, most of the frontier Cossacks had eventually accepted Russian authority and, in return for their autonomy of government, were getting used to their rôle as zealous servants of the autocracy. They provided troops for the army, and became involved in all Russia's military ventures, against the Poles as much as against Prussians and Swedes, while still retaining a predominant rôle in the military structure of the south. It was their detachments which accompanied the slow-moving caravans as they penetrated into the high Caucasian valleys towards Tiflis and Armenia, or into the trans-Caspian deserts, towards the valley of Syr Daria, and the ancient cities of Samarkand and Bokhara. The atmosphere of these caravans has also been described by Pushkin, and a few years later Tolstoy portrayed the life of the Cossacks which had hardly changed since the eighteenth century. The Cossack was half-soldier, half-peasant. For his work and service he received for cultivation thirty deciatins of the land which his slow conquests were acquiring for Russia, and whose cultivation, apart from producing a much-needed food supply, helped on the work of land clearance, opened up the forests, and thus made it easier to keep an eye on troublesome local tribes who retreated as their natural defences were destroyed.

The Russian army was Asiatic; it was a versatile army which adapted itself to all these different tasks. In the north and north-west it operated in European style, disciplining itself to fight the Swedes, fortifying St Petersburg, and opening up Russia's path to the west; but in the south-west it remained a vigorous, largely disorganized affair, holding off the Turkish raids or moving in a compact body to thrust out spearheads towards Constantinople. In the south-east a cavalry army was always on the alert, and sometimes ventured into Tartar territory to demolish a fort or break up a village of Central Asian bandits. The bandits would rebuild their village farther away, constructing their flimsy dwellings from the time-worn débris of the ancient Mogul capitals. Finally, to the east, merchants and peasants had created Russia's Siberian empire.

Samoyeds, Tunguzes and Gakuts passively accepted this domination without realizing its true extent. They kept their Muslim or pagan traditions under the guise of a conversion to the Orthodox Church, which was all the more sincere for being less enlightened. The Russian merchants, whether they settled down or journeyed over this immense country, caused little inconvenience to the original inhabitants, who were glad to sell, even cheaply, sable and fox skins, precious stones and foodstuffs of every kind. Moreover, the chancery of Tobolsk had scarcely any means of controlling life in the countryside. It had only the roughest idea of the position of each small wooden township, and was barely able to keep in touch with its faraway assistant-governor at Ienisseisk.

Russia was lucky enough to have no eastern neighbour. It had been able to seize Kamchatka without offending anyone at all. As for the south, nothing now remained of the brilliant medieval capitals but ruins. The irrigation canals, the marvellous oases of former days, had silted up, forming a level uninhabited battleground on which robber bands were continually at each other's throats. Central Asia was nothing but a breeding-ground of legends, which made it no easier to conquer. The Russians tried to intervene, in particular in Persia. In the previous century the cultured public of Europe had read Montesquieu's account of the admirable Persian civilization, but now it was torn apart by incessant civil wars between Ispahan and Teheran, extending from Mazanderan to the frontiers of Baluchistan. The Russians protected first one claimant and then another in the wars, and sided first with Turkey and then against it; nor did they escape without reverses, for the Persian theatre of operations was too far from Russian urban centres, and the small bands of troops who ventured there were generally cruelly defeated, decimated, and the remnants led off to slavery. Unsuccessful in Persia, the Russians fared very little better with the brilliant Emir of Bokhara. Yet if Russia failed to conquer Central Asia (and it was not in fact one of its major objectives at that time) it had, at all events, nothing to fear from that quarter. It trained armies there and drained away the remnants of its wealth. Russia, strengthened by its eastern and southern marches, could display its full strength in the west and south-west. Politically it came into collision with two states whose military power had become legendary: Poland and Turkey, two major powers which opposed each other in the mid-seventeenth century with something of the enthusiasm of Crusaders. But as we have seen, the Turkish government was no longer in complete control of its own subjects. It could terrorize them, but it no longer governed them. Much the same situation existed in Poland, whose elected king was powerless against his over-powerful vassals. In both countries the Russians found richer and more profitable battlefields than in Asia. In that part of the world at least conquest had some point: the countryside was well populated with industrious serfs and the towns were busy centres of trade. Consequently the

Russian troops, with their experience of frontier fighting, felt that victory was worth achieving. They took advantage of the frequent disturbances, inevitable in a country combining so many races and religions, which jeopardized the established authority and provided ample pretexts for intervention. Russians backed Orthodox against Muslim, Lutheran against Catholic, insinuating themselves everywhere, assuming authority in Warsaw and almost in Constantinople itself. In this way Russia began the astounding drive towards the west and the sea. To the amusement of England, it succeeded in sailing a fleet all the way from the Gulf of Finland to the eastern Mediterranean to destroy the remnants of the famous Turkish navy at Chesme.

There was a profound difference between the situation in Poland and in Russia towards the end of the eighteenth century. The great Catholic kingdom of yesterday was collapsing. Muscovy, taking a lesson from Byzantium, acquired a belt of territory stretching westward for two hundred miles. Nevertheless there was no difference in structure between Poland and Russia; both had the same social pattern of peasants tied to the land, chattels in the hands of their master (though conditions were perhaps a little less harsh in the west than in the east), and the same comparative absence of a middle class, which gave excellent opportunities to the Germans and Jews settling in Warsaw as well as in St Petersburg, Moscow or Nijni-Novgorod. They had the same nobility – a strange group composed of powerful lords with genuinely old hereditary titles and rich princes making money out of thousands of enslaved souls and maintaining a swarm of poverty-stricken nobles. These nobles were of doubtful descent, but ever ready to form a guard of honour when some looting expedition was afoot. The Tsars watched this nobility with jealous eyes and carefully supported the ambitions of the most humble against the over-powerful. Up to the time of Catherine II, coteries of noblemen and their quarrels proved almost as dangerous to the throne of Russia as to that of Poland. But Poland suffered the crucial disadvantage of having to defend herself on every frontier, while Russia could exert her full weight in the west.

In this winning game, Russia wore down Turkey and established itself on the Black Sea, the Sea of Azov, and in the Crimea. It assumed a right which the Turks were quite powerless to challenge: Russian ships, laden with corn, were already crossing the Bosphorus and new settlements were already foreshadowing the future prosperity of Odessa.

Russia was like a vast living organism, a composite biological structure, and the special skill of Catherine II lay in allowing herself to be carried along by that intense stream of life and riding its triumphant forward surge; she had no military knowledge but she knew how to select the right men capable of diverting those breaking waves to her advantage, of subduing Pugachev and the Turk, of allowing the stream of colonizers to roll on unhindered towards the limitless east, and of leading the battalions recruited from this flood of rough, primitive peoples against the weakening states which separated them from the solid continent.

Book Two
THE BOURGEOIS REVOLUTIONS
1780–1840

4

The West and its Tools

WITHIN fifty years, from 1785 to 1835, the face of Europe was transformed – but what of its political structure? A comparison of the political mechanisms in Europe at these two dates would throw very little light on the upheavals it underwent from 1789 to 1815. The disappearance of Poland was implicit in the agreement reached at St Petersburg in 1772. The modification of the imperial title (Austria instead of Germany) was a logical consequence of Joseph's policy, and the adoption by Bourbon France of institutions on the English model might also have been regarded as a predictable outcome of the trends of French opinion at the accession of Louis XVI. A politician of 1780 would not have been unduly bewildered at the picture presented by Europe in 1835; a moralist would have noted that on the whole ways of life in Germany and Eastern Europe were not so very different in 1835 from what they had been fifty years earlier.

But in Western Europe, particularly in France and England, there had been immense changes in society and habits, and a vast upheaval of what is known as 'human' geography. New blast furnaces were springing up all over industrial England, and the industrialization of France had begun. The appearance of the countryside had undergone a change, and that of the cities an even greater one. Was this the industrial revolution? This label, which we were unwilling to apply to the economic and social movements of the late eighteenth century, might well be appropriate here, if there were not to be more revolutionary changes taking place in Europe from 1840 to 1855, from 1885 to 1900, and above all in the twentieth century. It might be wiser to postpone the use of the phrase still further, with a caution induced by the vastness of the changes taking place today before our very eyes. Nevertheless, during the fifty years which included the French Revolution it would be true to say that a great new force took root in Europe and that the extraordinary surge of developments in the following century was no more than its natural flowering. There was more than a difference in degree between the slow rhythm of evolution which characterized the Western peoples from the fourteenth to the eighteenth century, and the suddenly quickened pace which gripped them in the nineteenth – there was a difference in kind. If the changes effected by the generations from 1780 to 1840 were less spectacular than those of the following century, it is nevertheless true to say that they contained the embryo of all future changes throughout Europe and the world. A turning-point had been reached in the world's history where a slow advance was to be superseded by a headlong rush, and it is this turning-point that we shall attempt to describe, and the causes of which we shall endeavour to ascertain.

Was there any outward change in the physical appearance of Western man from 1780 to 1835? There has certainly been a measurable change from 1850 to 1950, so that the question is justified. But the answer is quite definitely in the negative. From works on anatomy, from the teachings of medicine and the plastic arts, it is obvious that the human physique underwent no change, either in Germany or even in England; there was the same build amongst the well-to-do, the same bodily structure, and such physical deformities as were to be seen amongst countrymen and suburban alike could be attributed to the wretched lot of the poor in both periods. Looking at the poorest classes in the new industrial societies, one might even wonder whether the poor of 1840 were in fact worse physical specimens than their ancestors.

If it were possible at all to speak of progress in this period, it might be apparent not so much in the individual as in the masses. Amongst them it was quite obvious in Western Europe at least that a change of some kind had taken place in the lives of collective human groups, a change so decisive that from henceforward it was to dominate the whole history of the world. The revolution could be summed up in four words: man was living longer.

Whether or not this was a biological change, if not of individual man, at least of mankind in the mass, its effects were profoundly important: since he lived longer, man could make better use of his brains and the result was a sudden and prodigious enriching of his mental equipment. The combination of these two changes brought with it a complete structural reshaping of societies, which we shall discuss at the end of the threefold study which is to be the subject of this chapter.

MAN

Man was living longer, so much was evident from the statistics. In the early years of the nineteenth century in France the number of deaths was approximately 28 per 1,000 inhabitants; in the third decade the ratio fell to 25. To give a more detailed picture, in 1814 the death rate was very high, which was understandable in view of the war raging in France; yet the same was true in 1802, the year of the Peace of Amiens, which makes it uncertain whether or not the war was a decisive factor. The decrease in the death rate from 28 per 1,000 under the Empire to 26 per 1,000 under the Restoration was perhaps not wholly due to the fact that Europe was at peace. Under Louis-Philippe the average was still falling, in spite of a very heavy increase in the death rate at the time of the cholera epidemic (1832) and during the economic crisis of 1837, since they were balanced by years when the rate was exceedingly low (22 per 1,000 in 1835). Outside France the English, if not the Irish, enjoyed an even longer expectation of life, whereas in the whole of Eastern Europe the death rate hardly ever fell below 38 per 1,000. Thus the contrasts between Western and Eastern Europe, so much in evidence in the late eighteenth century, were reflected as soon as the mechanism of statistics enabled them to be recorded in a change in the balance of life.

This decline in the death rate was reflected also in an increase in population in the first half of the nineteenth century. It was nearly as high as 13 per 1,000 in England, though it fell to less than 2 per 1,000 in Ireland and less than 4 per 1,000 in Württemburg, and was even lower in Hungary. Moreover there was not the same geographical regularity here as in the incidence of the death rate. Some Eastern countries showed a marked increase, and not only Prussia (which was almost on a level with England in rate of development), but also Saxony and Russia who surpassed it very noticeably. The population increase in France, on the other hand, was hardly more than in Würtemburg. Thus the variation in the death rate was far from being the only factor in the growth of population. It meant that Prussia, for instance, had a fertility rate higher than that of England and much higher than that of France, which brings us face to face with one of the most delicate problems in this human evolution of Europe. One cannot be too cautious in interpreting these complex results from West to East. In England, after 1740, the death rate declined very appreciably. But there was also a slight decline in the birth rate, fairly adequately balanced by an increased longevity, so that taken as a whole the population did not stop increasing. This general trend, which was becoming evident in the second half of the eighteenth century, became very marked in the nineteenth century. The number of inhabitants in Great Britain and Ireland rose from sixteen to twenty-five million between 1800 and 1830, a striking increase in comparison with Europe as a whole, where the growth during the same period was only from one hundred and seventy-five to two hundred and five million inhabitants.

In France there was a decline both in the death rate and in the birth rate, with a slight time-lag in comparison with England. But up to 1830 the total population increased less, as the French birth rate dropped more quickly than the English, and the death rate fell more slowly. In Prussia the death rate remained really high; but it was balanced by a fairly high birth rate which increased the population by nearly fifty per cent, a rate comparable to that of England. It was almost the same in Austria. We have seen above that the incidence of low mortality towards 1820 was linked geographically with the establishment of major sea-trading concerns about 1780. We can now add that the birth rate around 1820 was high for those countries which in 1780 had what might be called a strongly defined political structure, as for instance English liberalism, or enlightened Prussian despotism ; whereas the political vacillations in France were linked with a relative sterility in 1820.

The fall in the death rate, as a physiological phenomenon, spread as the middle classes became richer; it only affected the working classes where they were caught up in the new tide of prosperity. This was partly because changes in the birth rate had psychological causes: it rose when the social group remained relatively stable, but fell where there was high social mobility.

The new longevity is sometimes attributed to improvements in medicine, such as the discovery of vaccine. The Englishman Jenner is credited with this though it had long been practised in Asia and was probably imported to London from Constantinople. In any case, Jenner's first inoculation took place only in 1796 whereas the longer life of the population had already been obvious twenty years earlier. The science of medicine was scarcely more advanced in the eighteenth century than in the time of Molière. It is true that some diseases which today are not defined with anything like the same wealth of detail (particularly the melancholias) were treated with some success, and this gave rise to endless comments on the closeness of the ties between mind and body. And eighteenth-century doctors paid great attention to the minute variations in the pulse and based an elaborate system of classification on them. The treatment of the humours always entailed bleeding, clysters, and a variety of potions. The list of curious practices has come to include the most fantastic remedies, which were still recommended in mid-century treatises, like the 'water of a thousand flowers' made from decoctions of fresh cow-dung (the poor ate this exceedingly economical *materia medica* raw to save money); it was used as an antipleuritic. Macquart gives a really staggering list of the remedies used in his day, but had already reached the sound conclusion that they should be avoided, particularly the drinking of various urines, a custom which was still very widespread.

By the eighteenth century, however, though medicine was not very advanced, problems of food and diet had begun to be studied. Plants and meats, milk and spices were boiled and dissected, and from these studies some very sensible conclusions were drawn. 'Cures' became 'diets', which was a step in the right direction. People no longer believed that alcohol was an elixir which ensured long life, or that white meat was dangerous. Similar researches were being pursued in cooking, and cooks, though quite unaware of the new trends in medicine, were influenced by their customers' new tastes ; they too were moving towards simpler recipes in which spices were much less frequently used. They aimed more at satisfying the appetite without blunting it than at tickling the palate by a sometimes dangerous search for new sensations. Our cooking, said one of them, must become chemical; in other words, its sole aim must be physiological efficiency.

Changes in cooking led to improvements in hygiene. It was not that anyone suspected the existence of microbes and their dangers, but more fastidious tastes and habits induced people to wash more frequently : they were less in awe of water, made greater use of soap and changed their linen more frequently. Over-elaborate clothes, tapestries, curtains and hangings, and heavy bed curtains, formerly thought to be effective in the battle against epidemics, were going out of fashion. The result was an improvement in living standards, of which the well-to-do were the first to feel the benefit, but which soon made itself felt over a widening area of the population, and if the new fashions spread much more rapidly in the towns than in the country, the latter nevertheless benefited from urban progress, which had already made considerable strides in the eighteenth century.

At the beginning of the nineteenth century, people were becoming interested in the spread of the precepts of medicine and hygiene: Louis XVIII founded the Academy of Medicine, and Bichat refused to read the 'black books' inherited from his predecessors. A thorough knowledge of anatomy became the rule among his associates. By a quite natural reaction the new school, founded by his pupil Broussais, ignored the nervous system and concentrated on repairing changes in tissues. He still overemphasized the importance of the digestive system as the source of disease; and consequently continued to use old prescriptions. It did not matter much! The pathological school was making progress and soon Laënnec's auscultation was to triumph over observations of the pulse. After 1820 clinical observations became more searching, and statistics enabled a finer distinction to be drawn between the various fevers and the diseases which had previously been mistaken for them. Schelling's abstract philosophy would hardly allow any differentiation between them, but they were to be fully classified in the first thirty years of the nineteenth century, starting with the pathological and functional disturbances of the organs, thanks to Laënnec's research on the lungs, Bouillaud's work on the heart and Bright's on the kidney. The way had been prepared for the decisive experiments of Claude Bernard.

Medicine then, was by no means a negligible factor. We shall study the general improvement in economic life later in more detail, and shall then discuss the food resources made available to mankind in the first decades of the century, the improved yield of cereal crops, the production of fine maize harvests, and the advances made in sugar beet and the sugar industry, as well as the introduction of plainer and cheaper clothes, and more widespread laundering: all these factors were even more decisive than in the previous century in contributing to the progress of mankind. Hence the explanation of the paradox: in the cities the working classes were penned like cattle in the slums and ravaged by a fearfully high death rate, but the greater luxury in the well-built areas more than balanced this appalling poverty. And the city, too, influenced the economy of the countryside from which it drew its food supply; it speeded up progress, and so helped to lengthen expectation of life. The growth and development of the city meant the increase of man's life-span.

On the other hand it carried with it a decline in the birth rate. The growing family, caught up in the rising tide of middle-class prosperity, was thrifty. Not to feed useless mouths – Malthus' great preoccupation – was also a general preoccupation of the new society. They counted their pence, planned their budget and calculated, and could do all this the more accurately since the family had begun to break up and to change its proportions. It had still been a vast collective group at the end of the old régime, and still opened its doors to newly married couples. They had their place at the common table. Several generations and innumerable families of cousins lived happily together under one and the same roof. In these conditions it was impossible to calculate the cost of a baby. Under this God-will-provide-for-the-family régime, lack of forethought was a positive virtue, the corollary of the virtue of Christian charity. It was even the cardinal virtue of the old Christian family. The change of habits which took place in the last decade of the eighteenth century led young married couples to set up their own homes. They wished to live in their own houses and to keep themselves. The large number of well-paid jobs opened to them by the widening of social life encouraged this process. The new family broke away from its own folk. It now consisted of the limited group – father, mother, child. A careful housekeeping budget was now not only possible, but essential: the newly married couple would have felt ashamed to ask their elders for help. The obligation of honour in this respect completely changed its meaning between 1780 and 1820. Since responsibility fell more and more on the individual, since each man felt master of his own destiny and responsible for his own children, young couples had to calculate their resources very carefully, and not be in too much of a hurry to start a family. The obvious result was a decline in the birth rate.

Thus the progress of urban civilization, which meant essentially an increased expectation of life, was also the cause of a decline in the birth rate. This progress in urban civilization was bound up with the development of a more individual way of life, characterized by a new pride in living. In spite of the falling birth rate, the population of England continued to increase because its general economic and social condition was at once more stable and more prosperous. France, although aware of this new pride in living, was developing in uncertain conditions, swept by the violent upheavals of the Revolution and the Empire; French parents were cautious, and the fall in the birth rate occurred even more rapidly than the increase in expectation of life. In Germany, urban civilization made only slow progress and people clung tenaciously to the old family traditions. Germans remained loyal to the old, dignified way of life and this had a greater effect on the population figures than increasing longevity, which was anyway not very noticeable.

Among the fascinating details of this new way of life let us stress only one essential point: from London to Dresden men were living longer. One consequence was that a bigger place could be found for education, and it was a wise father who urged his children – when there were not too many of them – to acquire the intellectual equipment needed to establish them in life as soon as possible on their own account. This father of a small family, looking to his own and his children's future, saved as much as he

could and invested his money to the best advantage ; so this rise in population had two main effects: an advance in education and increased demand
for credit. We shall deal with these two problems in turn.

SCIENCE

Now that most families were attempting to provide for themselves it was
no longer appropriate to trust to Providence for food and shelter. That sort
of faith and resignation was only appropriate for the very poor, to whom the
English philosophers were attempting to preach the necessity of birth
control. Even a modicum of wealth creates duties.

The French Encyclopaedists made bitter attacks on the traditional
teaching of the Church. The man who was creating science, measuring the
earth and the heavens, opened up new avenues of technique, and producing comfort and luxury, surely had the right to be angry with those
who opted out of the common tasks – for instance those beggar monks
detested by Voltaire. Side by side with the new responsibility assumed by
the head of the family, went a new reliance on science and technology.

European man in 1840 was no longer as he had been in 1780. In sixty
years a profound change had taken place. Even in the eighteenth century
the Westerner would not venture to affirm his superiority over India or
China. From the beginning of the nineteenth he no longer had any doubts
about it. However, he did not consider himself a race apart. Innumerable
representatives of the white Western peoples scattered over the face of the
globe, and particularly the Portuguese, proved abundantly that they could
inter-breed prolifically with the other human races. There was at that
time no racial problem in the biological meaning of the phrase. Perhaps
one cannot state that heredity played no part in the formation of the
intellectual equipment of the new Westerner; but in the present state of
our knowledge, it is as impossible to define its rôle as to prove it.

It can hardly be denied that the general way of life prevailing in Europe's
new cities was superior to the customs still followed in the East; and as a result the material wealth of Europe was growing at the expense of the rest of
the world. We shall not probe too deeply into religion or the arts, where
values are so imponderable, nor into manual skills, for the eighteenth century craze for *chinoiserie* – maxims, trinkets, landscape and customs – was
beginning to lose a little of its fascination, though it still served as a reminder of the Oriental's greater skill in this sphere. The real reason for
European superiority lay in the equipment used, and in the respective
mental processes of each type of mind. Brilliant though Chinese civilization was, fertile though its endless experiments were, resulting in many
effective new techniques, they had hardly anything to do with what today
we call 'science'. One essential element was missing – the art of proof by
logical reasoning.

Christopher Columbus, before becoming a courageous navigator, had to prove to all the commissions which had opposed his plans that he had an accurate knowledge of the works of Eratosthenes, of Greek reasoning and Alexandrian mathematics. Even so he relied on persuasion more than on logical reasoning. It was during the two following centuries that Europe rediscovered the Greek art of proof by reason. This new procedure was in its infancy even at the time of D'Alembert. But at last the certainty conferred by reasoning was felt, and tested, and although it was used indiscriminately for arithmetical problems or parlour games, it nevertheless fixed, from the time of Fermat and Pascal, the rigid standards by which all knowledge was to be judged.

At the beginning of the nineteenth century these mental processes which had been developing in isolation for two hundred years, began to be linked together, and the basis was laid for modern scientific method – a revolution confined to the countries of the West.

The new mathematical reasoning made it possible to see a common basis for all the experimental results which had previously been contradictory and scattered, but which now became systematic, co-ordinated, and organized around a few major principles. The system around which all human knowledge crystallized bore the name of the most illustrious of its promoters. Newton's thought, his reasoning and his calculations dominated almost the whole of the nineteenth century as they had dominated the eighteenth. In this respect Newton was synonymous with the West, and we shall see that the time when his theories were attacked at their foundation was also the moment at which European domination over the rest of the world began to slip – the end of the nineteenth century.

Newton, to the majority of the educated public, was the inventor of the theory of universal gravitation, which was popularized in France by Voltaire and his friend Madame du Châtelet. But Newton's more narrowly scientific work, known only to a small circle of genuine scholars, was much more influential than his popular theories. He condensed into a few formulae the immense body of calculations which astronomers had been accumulating for a century past (Kepler's contribution alone was enormous). These Newtonian formulae remained valid throughout the whole of the eighteenth century and for most of the nineteenth. The real superiority of Western man, as Lucien Febvre makes clear in his book *Pensées et croyances d'Occident*, undoubtedly lay in his attempt to create a synthesis which reduced everything to a single, simple whole, rejected the vague juxtapositions characteristic of Eastern thinking, and eliminated from the 'definitive' result everything which might possibly be based on instinctive intuition alone. So the attempt was made to integrate all the natural sciences in a small body of Newtonian principles around astronomy, the oldest and most rewarding subject of man's research.

Having paid due homage to the founder of modern science we can pass on to Descartes. His geometry had been just as valuable to Newton as the observations of Kepler or Galileo. For although the object of Newton's study had been astronomy, the instrument he had used in his systematizing, verifying and proving was mathematics: and Cartesian analysis in particular, which had resulted from the creative fusion of arithmetic, algebra and geometry. Let us, however, keep to the history of principles.

No period had ever been so rich in scholars as the one we are about to study, from 1785 to 1840. It is impossible to do justice to them all, or even to name them. But all envied, admired and used Newton. 'A system of the Cosmos can only be established once', declared Lagrange, who, in one of his characteristic moments of depression added, 'The mine is almost too deep already. . . . Sooner or later it will have to be abandoned.' This idea that the last word had been said in mathematics haunted the minds of that generation. In a few years' time, in Germany, Gauss and his brilliant associates were indeed to discover new lines of enquiry, but in the 1800s the Newtonian system had reached the peak of its authority.

In England, surprisingly enough, Oxford and Cambridge were inactive, and the famous Royal Society was focusing its attention on the sea. Under the influence of the current English mania for ocean travel, it was more interested in studying the surface of the earth than in speculating about mechanics. The awakening was to come in England around the year 1840 with Dalton and Faraday. The scientific method had already been introduced in Germany with the work of Gauss. But in 1800 it was the Institut de France which gave a lead to Western science, or more particularly the Académie des Sciences, whose papers were the most widely read. The Institut established the reputation of every brilliant young scientist in Europe; and Europe to all intents and purposes meant the world. It was in fact two Frenchmen who developed Newton's system to the highest degree of perfection, Lagrange and Laplace. The first, in many respects, was the more likeable. A gentle, serious, reserved genius, who was to die at 76, a few days before the collapse of the Empire, Lagrange was a true citizen of the cosmopolitan Europe of 1785. He had worked in Turin and Berlin before rejoining his famous old patron D'Alembert in Paris. Later, though sickened by the excesses of the Revolution, he nevertheless presided from 1791 to 1799 over the commission for the Reform of Weights and Measures, out of which emerged the decimal system. He was one of the first to note the limitations of the old algebra, by proving that equations of the fifth degree cannot be reduced to a resolvent equation of lower degree. He was to leave to his pupil Cauchy ('You see this young fellow? He will surpass us all') the distinction of overcoming this difficulty. He himself at twenty-three had conceived the theory of analytical mechanics: when he committed it to paper he did so almost hesitantly, with a modest disclaimer of his own work; but it was staggering in its implications. From Newton onwards, everyone was preoccupied with the problem of motion. Maupertuis had made it out to be a product of speed and distance. Lagrange made it the space integral of the amount of movement, and starting from that point, evolved a complete treatise of all the problems of mechanics. This was the end-product of Galileo's old intuitions, now translated into the language of certainty. Starting from Galileo's simple experiment of a ball rolling down an inclined plane, a tool of thought had been evolved over the next two centuries; a simple definition had resulted in an infinity of rigorous corollaries with far-reaching applications. Newtonian mechanics in its entirety was reduced to a perfect whole, the single centre of which rested on this definition of motion; and this mechanics was adequate to account for all the scientific discoveries made up to that date.

At about the same time, applying these principles to astronomy, Laplace, a Norman peasant, a son of the Revolution and an admirer of Napoleon (who made him Minister of the Interior), and who finally gratified his childhood ambition by becoming a Marquis under the Restoration, not only re-examined and co-ordinated the old problem of probabilities, but earned the title of the French Newton for his work in elucidating some of the most subtle and difficult points in the *Principia*. Newton had postulated the interference of God in establishing order among the planets disturbed by comets. Lagrange pursued his calculations further and God was done away with. Thus the mechanism of the heavenly bodies gave the system its final precision. 'God?' Laplace said one day to Napoleon, 'I need no such hypothesis.' And his certainty of mind might well be summed up in these terms: 'A mind which knew all the elements existing in the world today would know the future.' After Laplace, the impetus given to research within the framework of the Newtonian *Principia* was to continue, but the system had already begun to be disproved and attacked at various points.

The great importance of the series of discoveries which started with Kepler and proceeded by way of Descartes and Newton to Laplace was its attempt to embody in a few simple formulae, strictly deduced one from the other, the whole of man's knowledge of the heavens. Its finest achievement, to which Galileo, Descartes, Newton and Lagrange all contributed, lay in the formulation of mechanics, an instrument of extreme accuracy which was henceforth to be used by scholars working in the most varied fields of experimental research. It gave them a number of exact definitions on which the precision of mathematical reasoning could rely. As a result, analytical calculations could be amazingly effective in observations of the phenomena of heat, electricity and the composition of matter. Their effect was to translate all observations into terms of mass, motion and force, the three keys of this new mental equipment.

It is not therefore surprising that the heyday of the Newtonian system coincided with an amazing outburst of scientific activity which in a very short time was to change the state of experimental research, and to create modern physics and chemistry. All this may almost be said to have originated between 1785 and 1840, although we must give due credit to certain outstanding predecessors. In these years the new sciences, now expressed in a mathematical form common to all, became interdependent. It was rare for an experiment performed by one branch of science not to benefit all almost equally. The historian's chief difficulty lies in deciding with which of these experiments to begin in order to make his point clear.

For the sake of convenience, let us take the problem of fire. If the worldly philosophers of the eighteenth century were a little too prone arbitrarily to confuse lightning, combustion and light, it was because the experimenters of 1780 were working in separate compartments. The ascent of paper balloons filled with hot air was certainly spectacular, and seemed to confirm the Aristotelian theory of an 'essentially' light fluid, fire, which contemporary chemistry called phlogiston. In a few years, however, phlogiston went completely out of fashion since it put forward only a superficial explanation and one which could not be verified. And it was the idea of mass, apparently so far removed from that of fire, which made sense of combustion. It is a strange story.

There is no need to describe Lavoisier's experiments in detail; let us go straight to his conclusion: 'Combustion does not change the weight or the mass of the bodies which are its agents.' This has been summed up in the famous phrase: 'Nothing is lost, nothing is created.' Thus the permanence of mass, Newton's basic principle, made its official entry into the study of combustion and created chemistry. For a hundred years substances had been weighed in order to verify the *Principia*. They were to go on being weighed for another hundred years, but now in the interests of chemistry. It was a problem which engaged the attention of every scientist, Dalton and Berzelius, Avogadro and Gay-Lussac, as well as the solitary recluse, Ampère. Gases combine in volumes which bear a simple relation to each other: hence the idea of mass led to that of the atom, an old word, but a new concept. The list of simple substances grew longer; with the help of probability theory Mendeleyev compiled a long list towards the middle of the century, not only of those which had been successfully isolated by experiment, but also of those likely to be discovered. Calculus aided in the analysis of matter. With the help of mathematics, the science of chemistry began its triumphant and irresistible course.

Lavoisier, working on combustion in relation to mass, may have abandoned the study of fire, but this in turn was taken up by mathematicians. First, fire was treated as a fluid, a caloric, and as such raised once more questions of mechanics applicable to gases. Count Rumford, a restless traveller who came from America and ended as a baron of the Holy Roman Empire, suggested the idea of a relationship between heat and work. The taciturn Fourier, a friend of Napoleon and a member of the Egyptian expedition, and later Prefect of Grenoble, devoted his spare time to the translation into mathematical terms of well-established experiments, eventually arriving at the analytical theory of heat which was to permit the perfecting of Dalton's calculations. Another Englishman, Hamilton, studying the kinetic energy of gases, confirmed the heat-work equivalence which was to be most clearly expounded in the treatise by the German Helmholtz in 1847. And the idea of work, a mechanical idea which had originated from Galileo's experiments and Newton's principles, began to dominate the science of fire, or rather the new physics.

This new triumph of mechanics was still incomplete when another phenomenon emerged under its laws – electricity. The first essential in the preliminary stages was to make qualitative distinctions between substances which were conductors, non-conductors or insulators. In 1780 this knowledge had been acquired. By 1800 all cultured Europe was waxing enthusiastic about an amazing novelty. Static electricity, produced in the famous Leyden jars, had been known for a long time, but no-one had succeeded in producing a continuous current. Then came the day when Galvani made frogs' muscles move with brand-new electricity obtained by the contact of separate substances. Carrying this experiment further, Volta set up the first 'pile' – by piling up alternate plates made of two metals. Thus electro-statics were followed by electro-dynamics. Next the pile was observed to present a whole series of chemical phenomena. The fact that the new electric current was useful in making analyses of substances, particularly of water, served to confirm Dalton's theory, and added to the list of simple substances. The next step was obviously an attempt to determine the quantity of electricity proportionate to the mass of simple substances which it isolated. In this way chemistry furthered electricity, and so repaid its debt: electricity became measurable, and in its turn came within the scope of calculation and mechanics.

One of the problems which had preoccupied Newton, and many less brilliant thinkers after him, was that of the mutual attraction between masses of matter. In order to measure the mutual attraction of two bodies, the French engineer Coulomb had invented a small but extremely sensitive balance, consisting of an axis suspended on twisted threads. The balance had been most effective in measuring magnetism. Using this highly sensitive balance, Oerstedt in Copenhagen observed that an electric current acted on the magnetic needle. Magnetism, incredible though this might seem, came within the sphere of electricity. Ampère in France and Faraday in England took up the problem again, and the result was the magnificent series of definitions which enabled mechanical mathematics to define the relations between the two phenomena more accurately. The work of Joule and, particularly, of Gauss soon made it possible to define magnetism and electricity either in terms of heat or in terms of work. When Faraday came to review the whole problem he realized with rare insight first that electricity was not unconnected with the atomic conception of matter, and secondly that like magnetism it defined 'fields' which might easily explain with greater accuracy the notion of distant attraction, which had been suggested by Newton in the eighteenth century.

There remained the problem of light. Newton had conceived the idea of particles moving in a straight line. But Young and Fresnel showed that light behaved like a wave mechanism. These ideas were very confused, and the question was not cleared up until Maxwell discovered that the ether indispensable to the wave mechanism was linked with the fields of electricity and magnetism. Although this was not discovered in the first half of the century, the first steps towards this brilliant conclusion had been taken.

To sum up: towards 1850, with the addition of mass (and the atom) and the magnetic field, all the experimental sciences came within the province of general mechanics of which Lagrange had been the greatest exponent. The laws of mechanics had first been applied to the field of astronomy, and every year they led to new discoveries (Leverrier's detection of Neptune is one example), so that by now they dominated scientific knowledge.

Naturally the mathematician of 1840, who was expected to work in so many and such varied fields, was very different from his counterpart in 1800. If this chapter began with the name of Lagrange, it can end only with that of Gauss, his near contemporary. Gauss was probably the most formidable mathematician of any time. Grandson of a gardener, and son of a Brunswick workman, he discovered at the age of ten, on his school slate and entirely by himself, the laws of arithmetical progressions. Poor and lonely, pathetically devoted to his prince who was defeated and wounded at Jena, Gauss was a man of genuinely simple heart; but his achievements are difficult to summarize, since they cover so wide a field. He discovered the meanings of complex numbers and at the same time of Euclidian geometry. Fermat's theorems were mere child's play to him and he discovered congruence. He had made his name by solving a most forbidding calculation, that of the irritating planet Ceres, which disconcerted astronomers by the difficulty of its trajectory. Gauss was also universally known for his contribution to the study of electricity. He was, in fact, the very incarnation of the mathematician of 1854. Lagrange had been afraid in 1780 that the sciences might have reached the end of the road: Gauss gave them new life, with consequences which we shall study later.

The members of the French Institut and of the Royal Society, and the professors of the new German universities, were not all physicists or chemists. In Paris Cuvier was the permanent secretary of the Académie des Sciences. And indeed biology, like medicine, was far from being swallowed up by the all-powerful mechanics. It was not until the end of the century that the chemist Pasteur broke through the old discredited science of medicine, and Mendel was to die without seeing the triumphant conclusion of his observations and calculations. Yet we should not be misled: although general mechanics and the new mathematics did not fully invade the field of biology, it is still true that some attempts were being made to subject medicine and biology to mathematical disciplines.

Voltaire declared that 'it would be very odd if laws which governed the universe made an exception of man, that minute inhabitant of a planet'; and this dictum seemed to inspire the great discoveries of 1785. Linnaeus, in his system of nature, classified man as a primate along with all other living beings. Buffon had demurred on this point, but the idea had gained ground. Gall still surrounded his curious phrenological observations with a mass of doubtful hypotheses, but Muller discovered the specificity of the nerves, and Marshall Hall proved, on the whole conclusively, that a whole area of human physiology acted in accordance with automatic reflexes. La Mettrie and his extraordinary machine-man had little effect on medicine, which had already reached the threshold of the experimental stage.

The mechanistic influence penetrated gradually into the study, not of man as a whole, but of his component parts. Bichat had already declared that the body was merely the sum total of its component tissues. Soon Van Beer showed that the egg was not the adult being in miniature, but an original mechanism from which must be developed every kind of tissue. From then on biology was no longer limited to natural history: the study of the cell became its chief preoccupation. Certainly, the study of the substance of the egg and of the cell was not yet free from the vitalist principles which had permeated eighteenth-century biology, much as phlogiston had in the realm of physics. Nevertheless, biological experimentation was already moving towards the principle of the conservation of energy, which was fairly generally recognized in that field after 1850.

Above all, biology was in many ways already penetrated by the important new study of chemistry. From 1828 an organic substance, urea, was obtained by mechanical synthesis. The work first of Priestley in the eighteenth century, then later of Saussure, and finally in 1830 of Liebig, led to the discovery of the carbon cycle, showing how chlorophyll used solar energy to return to the ground the carbon extracted from it by living organisms. Lavoisier's discovery is an instance of a biological process present everywhere in nature which conditions, if not defines, life itself on the face of the earth.

The earth and the globe themselves became the subjects of experiment. As early as the eighteenth century an English geologist had stated that the process which had formed the earth's crust was still going on, and that the geological strata to be seen in quarries originated solely from the deposits laid down in marshes, lakes and seas. At the same time, in Lyell's *Principles of Geology* (1830), fossils were no longer treated as freaks of nature but as evidence of the world's history; and it was not long before the ice ages were identified (1840).

It was precisely this study of fossils which was to make the reputation of Civier, a thorough man who reorganized the classification of the whole animal kingdom 'arranged according to its organization'. Attempts were made to calculate the age of the earth. Lamarck was already suggesting the possibility of evolutionary development and Malthus was outlining the struggle for survival; biological science was approaching Darwin's great mechanical synthesis. Finally, statistical method was starting to be used in anthropology, following the lead of the Belgian Quetelet; the average height of French conscripts, and the head measurements of Scots, were registered on graphs drawn up according to Gauss's probability theory.

Now comes an important question. All this preoccupation with mechanics in fact concerned only very few men in Europe. Can they legitimately be credited with a power equal to that of the businessman, the soldier, the

European adventurer who was making his way all over the face of the globe? All this science which had accumulated in a few generations round the turn of the century was to be transformed in the second half of the nineteenth century into a new and formidable industrial force; but in what way were industry and the already vigorous economic activities of Europe in 1800 indebted to it?

There is no simple answer. The best we can give here is that the new industry and the rapid growth of Europe in 1785 both had the same sources as mechanical science. They developed simultaneously and each helped the other.

A few examples will show how this came about. James Cook opened up a new outlet for European activity, the world of the Pacific Ocean. He charted it accurately, and his charts were more reliable than those of Bougainville. But he was only able to do this because he possessed the balanced chronometer which one of his contemporaries had invented in 1761; because Newton's system had definitely fixed the positions of the heavenly bodies; because magnetic phenomena were more clearly understood; and because he discovered the cause of scurvy and its cure. Most significant of all was the point of origin of these great maritime discoveries; the Royal Society sponsored an expedition, not to find new lands, but to observe a conjunction of Venus and the sun: so it was an attempt to apply Newton's *Principia* which led to the discovery of a new world.

Humboldt's career is equally revealing. A German by birth, he was drawn to Paris because it was the capital of the sciences, and became the pupil of Gay-Lussac. He climbed the Andes to study decreases in temperature and magnetic variations, and by drawing up isothermic charts he revealed the conditions which gave rise to tropical storms. In this way he originated the science of cartography. Humboldt applied it to biology and showed the distribution of living beings over the earth; Darwin, still a young man, was to do the same on the *Beagle*, chartered in 1831 on behalf of the Royal Society, in order to establish a chain of chronological measurements. In 1848 Huxley carried out similar work in Australia; man discovered the world in the course of verifying his scientific hypotheses.

The physical and natural sciences were advanced in the course of astronomical research, and every collation of findings in the astronomical, physical and biological sciences made the voyages of merchant ships and warships less hazardous. The spirit of experiment which resulted in scientific achievement in the field of general mechanics also furthered industry by sending Europeans over all the oceans of the world.

Yet it was not only through the direct contact of scientific research and the techniques of navigation that science contributed to the rise of industry. It did so by inspiring all human activity with a kind of mechanical certainty which aroused a spirit of enterprise and spurred Europeans along the path of profit-making and industrial power. We shall not go as far back as Locke, the doctor and experimenter, who extolled liberty because it would encourage the establishment all over the land of a vast system of individual economic experiments. England may have left theories and mathematics to the French, but from 1785 onwards it became a major field of industrial experiment.

Many works on metaphysics systematizing ideas taken from England and France were produced in Germany in the late eighteenth century. Kant's syntheses had barely been completed before they were surpassed. The extension of the sphere of mathematical reasoning and the certainty of logical proof considerably reduced the field of intuitive imagination. From Leibnitz to Kant, the metaphysicians had been allowed a wide range of territory, but after Hegel their right to it was abruptly disputed, because science believed it could provide more conclusive proof than metaphysics of the efficacy of Western intellectual tools. On the ruins of its metaphysics, Germany was to erect the finest group of laboratories the world had yet known.

French theory, English experiments, and the sudden new developments in Germany brought about a revolution in the mental equipment of Western man. Young people in Europe were learning less Latin and Greek : new engineering schools, new or rejuvenated universities, and mechanical workshops offered an education in keeping with the modern trends. Public lectures and specialized periodicals enjoyed an unprecedented popularity. It was no longer only scholars and men of letters who were socially acceptable, but engineers, for it was they who created wealth. In order to make their task easier new rules of property and credit were drawn up and to these we must now turn our attention.

THE LAW

'*Quid leges sine moribus.*' The question of the relationship between law and customs in late eighteenth-century Europe lends itself to an infinite variety of treatment. There is certainly no lack of material. French writers of the day filled volumes with their ideas on this great problem. The English too, though more reserved, had never before discussed at such lengths law and individual rights, freedom of opinion, the suppression of slavery, and the possibility of improving the law to bring about an improved way of life. It is all too easy to be swept away by this tide of polemic and discussion; the main points must be kept clearly in mind.

The first essential to bear in mind is that 'civilization', a word newly coined at that time, was almost synonymous with ordered customs and good laws. The noun 'civilization' was new but the verb 'to civilize' had long been in use and meant to judge in the civil courts a case first brought before the criminal courts. The advantage of the civil procedure over the criminal was, in Europe and particularly in France, considerable: one prohibited torture, the other allowed it. We know the horror aroused among eighteenth-century thinkers by the question of torture, and its ghastly instruments; a decree of 1670 had limited the use of these methods but only to the extent that a man due to be executed in public was not to be killed in the secrecy of the torture chamber. English law had already abandoned this barbarous custom, and Catherine II had followed this good example, at least in her declarations. Louis XVI finally abolished torture in France. Civilization was making headway, and civilization meant first and foremost sound justice and good laws.

Voltaire, as we know, praised English law, which, though doubtless harsh, was at least applicable to all alike. Now the basis of this equality was *Habeas Corpus*. Every imprisoned person could obtain from the High Court of Justice the right to be brought at once before his judges ; they released him if the reason for his arrest seemed insufficient, and the person responsible for his arrest was punished, even if he was a minister. England, therefore, did not acknowledge the separation of powers advocated by Montesquieu. The executive was subject to the judiciary, the highest political authority in England. As for the law, it was made by Parliament, which in certain exceptional cases could even suspend *Habeas Corpus*, as it did for instance during the revolutionary wars. But when this suspension came to an end in 1801, a law of indemnity, retrospectively applied, brought to book those officials and ministers who might possibly have abused it. England's fine example was not followed by any other European government; on the continent preventive detention remained almost discretionary and, above all, the agents of the state could not, whatever happened, be summoned before the ordinary tribunals. In all that concerned their administration, they had the privilege of a special jurisdiction and of administrative tribunals. This special jurisdiction meant that some remnants of the privileges of absolute monarchy survived into the nineteenth and even the twentieth century, under cover of the separation of powers. It created, side by side with the law, administrative law.

Thus in England an ancient practice ensured equality and liberty for every citizen. Those two words were interconnected not only in the theory of power but in the popular conscience. And the power of these two ideas, closely linked with each other and with the practice of *Habeas Corpus*, can well be imagined. Whenever there was a forbidden meeting or a discussion in the press, any sanction taken against an opponent might, at the request of any citizen, lead to a public enquiry before judges. Public opinion could make itself felt not only through Parliamentary elections, but also through the citizen's permanent right of appeal to judges who could themselves be tried for flagrant injustice. Every debate on the interpretation of the law made Parliament more careful to draft its laws clearly. Nowhere else in the late eighteenth century did public opinion have this power. In England anyone who knew how to wield it had a power capable of challenging that of the Government itself. It was in this way that the opposition to Lord North's cabinet had so brilliantly made itself felt, and because of this, too, many famous politicians were enabled to begin their careers. One of the most remarkable was Wilberforce (from 1780 to 1833), who brought about the abolition of slavery in 1807;

he was a private individual but a powerful leader of the Englishman's
conscience. This broadening of public opinion did much to regularize
justice, and to secure its uniform application throughout the country.

Legal practice and jurisprudence were progressively made more explicit
and available to all. In other words, the problem of a code of laws was
hardly ever posed in England, and certainly if it had been it would have
presented very great difficulties. For the laws, even the oldest of them,
remained on the Statute Book, and accumulated in increasing numbers
even when they contradicted one another. Only very rarely did Parliament
deliberately repeal them. This was not important, since it was the judges
rather than the executive who were responsible for administering this
varied and contradictory body of laws, and the judge was guided and supported by public opinion which in this way continually created laws
though a subtle interplay of institutions. It is easy to imagine how difficult
European jurists, and particularly the French, found it to analyse this
situation. In general they admired its results and to produce a similar
régime in France, the Constituent Assembly determined to create an
elected judiciary power emanating directly from the nation.

But it required long practice to give this type of legal system any sem-
blance of uniformity in dealing with the innumerable customs, letters
patent and statutes; and new laws made by the elected legislative power
were continually being added. In default of such practice the central
power had necessarily to take the initiative in co-ordinating and systematizing the collective body of laws, so that the role played by *Habeas Corpus*
in England was taken over on the continent, though in a very different
way, by the legal code. The code was in effect an attempt to reduce the
laws to order ; it had to provide the courts with a practical instrument,
indispensable if judgements were to be uniform throughout the country;
this instrument defined obligations accurately, and unconditionally an-
nulled former decrees, at least in so far as they affected matters which had
been duly codified. In this way, however, the legislature gained the upper
hand over the judiciary then being organized.

The legislature was predominant, at least in France, from 1790 to 1800.
For the code was probably considered as a mere collection of ancient laws
rather than as a new law in itself. It was regarded at the time as a kind
of editing process, a putting in order, a popularization. From this point
of view it could be regarded as the work of the executive. A code which
would throw light on a legal dispute was obviously needed everywhere in
Europe, and often it worked out to the advantage of monarchical authority
– a point on which there is more to be said.

One need only recall the authority which Justinian, Theodosus and
Tribonian acquired from their efforts to draw up practical collections of
laws. Colbert, in his attempt to introduce a little order into state subsidies,
grants, the navy, civil statutes and, with the help of Savary, into commerce,
had created separate codes for each, though these were still referred to as
statutes in *Parlement*. In this respect Colbert was a worthy successor of

Marillac, and a predecessor of Pontchartrain. But the codes grew too numerous. In Lorraine the existence of a Leopold code did not prevent the town of Nancy from having one of its own. Codes were fashionable throughout the whole of Europe: Charles of Sicily, Frederick of Prussia, Catherine of Russia, to mention only the most famous, set to work compilers who, as they could not co-ordinate laws and customs in common use or choose between conflicting ones, left the courts bewildered. It was to bring order into the law that the revolutionary assemblies undertook in committees the mammoth task of logical clarification which was to result in the first systematic code, and to endow words with a new meaning and significance.

Voltaire had complained that in travelling one changed laws as frequently as horses. The influence of Roman law and of legal bodies had not superseded local customs. Doing the best they could, jurists commented on existing fact and dealt out exhortation and advice, as did Pothier in his treatises. Consequently, in the constituent and legislative assemblies of Europe the jurists were becoming masters of the law. The Convention decided to tackle the problem forthwith. It initiated the great undertaking entrusted to Cambacérès. When he became Consul it was Tronchet, president of the new Court of Appeal (*Cour de Cassation*), who directed the work. Their chief aim was to produce a clear result and one which would take into account traditions (even canonical traditions) and the laws of the Revolution, as well as the opinions of Bonaparte.

In spite of warnings like those expressed by Savigny, the compilers tended strongly towards the practical; they reproduced rather than innovated, co-ordinated as best they could, drew on southern law for matters relating to the dowry, and relied on Pothier's precautions for the law of contracts. Above all they were selective. Once the Civil Code was drawn up, the famous law of the year XII repealed Roman laws, regulations, decrees and local usages – everything in short which might hinder its working. The judges, suddenly delivered from the burden of innumerable ancient records, wielded the same instrument from one end of France to the other.

The basic inspiration of the new code is to be found not so much in the introductory remarks of Portalis as in the code itself, and if after so many centuries of effort it was comparatively easy to draw up, this was because property and ownership could at last, and for the first time, be accurately defined in simple terms. Quit-rents, revenues, and feudal dues had been swept away, and with them went a thousand doubtful points which had complicated the labours of eighteenth-century judges. Details are unimportant: the crux of the matter is contained in one phrase: property was unfettered and free. Property still meant real estate, for the definition of personal property remained obscure : France's industrial and financial experience was still too brief to have produced effective legislation. In spite of this gap, the improvement was remarkable. The vast procedural machinery and its paralysing delays were abolished. That 'every man should know the law' could become a concrete reality. Economic activity was at long last freed from the dead weight of the old legal procedures, although in time new and unwieldly legislation grew up around the interpretation of its clauses.

Most important of all, no sooner had the French code been promulgated than it conquered Europe. The Empire introduced it into Italy and Holland, and it was adopted in Frankfurt, Danzig, the reconstructed Poland and Illyria, Westphalia and the Swiss Cantons. After the fall of the Empire, many countries which had adopted it recast it, though such a process involved great difficulties, especially in Holland and Germany. Meanwhile, a *Revue de droit français* was published in Mannheim throughout the century, and the decrees of the French Court of Appeal were followed by half Europe. In this way the French code was introduced into Rumania, Italy, Louisiana, Argentina and Uruguay. If it was not universally adopted, it was at least imitated in principle. In Saxony an attempt was made to clarify the old Germanic law; Spain endeavoured to overcome the particularism of the *fueros*; the new American republics followed the fashion, while in Russia Nicholas eventually fulfilled Alexander's ambition by publishing his own compilation.

The success of the French commercial code of 1807 was less marked, for though the Revolution had settled the question of property, it had made little progress in solving the new problems created by commerce. The French commercial code, therefore, remained bound up with the old cautious precepts of Colbert; and the rest of Europe was understandably reluctant to adopt it. After 1870 France acknowledged the superiority of the German-inspired commercial code.

The real significance of the French attempts at codification is not easy to define. It was not really weakened by the vagueness of its enactments on personal property and commerce, since its chief value lay in its insistence on the uniformity of the national law. Person and property were no longer differently defined according to whether they were inside or outside a town's gates, or on opposite banks of the same river or of any of the other innumerable divisions which had existed for centuries on the land. If the code did not fully succeed in being really European, it did at least stimulate every nation in Europe into drawing up its own national code. It thus strengthened the national unity of a divided Europe; it also showed the advantages of a complete revision of legal traditions, and opened the way for the great reforms necessitated by the new economic structure.

Land was now free, and its produce belonged to its owner, who felt every personal incentive to improve its yield and to extend his business. Uniform contracts meant that men in different parts of the land could group together for a co-ordinated effort. Now that people were free of local restrictions they could be mobilized within the nation in the service of a better economy. The restrictions imposed by out-dated traditions on present-day activity were finally lifted. If a clause proved to be harmful, it could be abolished by the legislative power and replaced by another without overtaxing the scruples of the judge or the uncertainty of the plaintiff. Thus, by degrees, continental Europe was catching up with England; public opinion, stimulated by economic progress, demanded that authority be as flexible as in England in adapting the law to everyday needs. Political changes, the appeal to constitutions, the revolutions in nineteenth-century Europe, were all results of this need for a flexible and continually renewed code. The people of western Europe had entered an age of major industrial development and had now acquired the means to free themselves from the restricting effects of past traditions. The living had to free themselves from the dead.

This attempt at codification, a new characteristic in Europe at that time, was not confined to the law. Weights and measures varied to an extent that seems as strange to the modern mind as the variation of the old laws from town to town, and from province to province. There were as many 'leagues' and 'pounds' as there were domains and manors, in fact more: a measure needed only to be registered and published for its use to become legal. Furthermore, peasants and craftsmen often cared very little whether the measures they continued to use were registered or not. The skill of the merchant and the trader was based on a knowledge of the innumerable and deceptive differences, and the question was still being asked quite seriously in the eighteenth century what use the trader would be, and to what would his skill be reduced, if measures were unified. But it was obvious that most Englishmen found quite enough risks and worries in trade without the addition of this particular hazard. By a slow process initiated in the eighteenth century and concluded in 1767, England had reduced and co-ordinated its system, keeping two pounds (one of which was a troy pound for precious metals), one mile, one quarter. The subdivisions of these measures still remained fairly complicated, the ordinary pound consisting of sixteen ounces, the troy pound of twelve.

A similar process was slowly being carried out in continental Europe but it was far less advanced than in England, and in that sphere too French logic tried to speed things up. The Constituent Assembly was the first to set up a commission for the unification of weights and measures, with its members drawn from the leading mathematicians of the day. First they rejected sub-multiples of 12 (and 244 and 976) or 4 (and 16 and 512) in favour of division by 10 and the power of 10. Enumeration had proved the superiority of this 10 basis. Why, asked Legendre, try to push an hexagonal tenon into a pentagonal mortise? Then they looked around for a basic unit of measurement – the metre. Their first idea was to fix it by the length of a pendulum beating once per second at zero altitude in latitude 45°. This was a typical physicists' idea, and it would certainly have facilitated the many calculations of mass which, as we have seen, were so important. This, however, seemed too daring to the majority of the commission. It chose a fraction of the earth's meridian, though there is not the least connection between it, a Great Circle of the earth (a very uncertain quantity in any case) and the current system of length or weight; but it was one way of keeping close to the earth. After the decimal division and the metre, the entire system of weights and measures was founded, and usage was very greatly simplified.

Unfortunately, the old usage persisted and the law sanctioned it by assimilating the fathom to two metres, the pound to half a kilo, and so on. The metric system nevertheless replaced a number of provincial measures which could be fitted in to the new measures. However, though it became legal in France in 1801, it was not made compulsory until 1840. Its success in Europe was linked with the adoption of the code, but was more lasting and on the whole more widespread. The German Empire adopted it in 1872, Europe and South America followed suit. In 1864 it was even legalized – though little used – in England, and then in the United States: it had made its way round the world.

This adoption of a system that rejected any concrete meaning of the units of measurement in favour of simplicity of calculation represented an intellectual advance as important as the transformation of the legal code. In this case too the new system was divorced from the original connections with man (*pouce, pied, coudée*, etc.), from the requirements of agricultural work (*journal, ouvrée*) and from historical traditions. The metre and its combinations are purely mental concepts. The abstract measure was widely adopted; trade was simplified and was based throughout the world on two major systems.

After the reform of measures came the successful introduction of the decimal system into money transactions and coinage; and in France francs, décimes and centimes were soon tied to a fixed weight of silver with a definite standard. This freed commerce from all the old apparatus of money-changers, and left the merchant free to concentrate on the quality of his goods, and the banker on the quality of credit.

Credit was now the important issue. Commercial good faith could no longer be concealed behind a jingle of weights, measures and coinage. Administrative and commercial accounting had everywhere abandoned Roman figures and the use of tokens in favour of Arab numerals and written transactions, so the new units of measurement could now deal accurately and clearly with everything that could possibly be written down in precise figures. The old ways of assessing were replaced by the single question of how much trust one could place in the signatory of a contract. The problem of confidence, or what is now called credit, could at least be limited and defined even though it could not be completely abolished.

The metric system was a guarantee against numerical error, and the code against legal error; but no government department, and no system of law or of measures could define the *economic* value of an undertaking and its owner. It was in this sphere of credit that the speculations and risks of private initiative had full play.

One remark in conclusion: from now on, the rough and tumble of competition was to be between individuals and not between families. The old Christian family group, the *gens*, which in our study of population we saw breaking up, was, as we can now see more clearly, being replaced by individuals personally responsible for their debts and contracts. Civil affairs were removed from Church jurisdiction and made the sole concern of public administration, not just from a wish to secularize, nor because a desire for progress had arisen to complement and supplant the desire for God; nor was it merely because the state was more anxious to watch over its citizens who would furnish its armies and elect its organs of government; it was also because the concepts involved in the code and in the new forms of financial transactions dealt primarily with the individual, and so the individual had to be identified beyond all shadow of doubt. A man giving credit was no longer satisfied for his debtor to be designated merely by his Christian name; this now became just a forename to avoid the confusion that it had created, even when accompanied by indications of trade, or place, or by various nicknames. Each child of course had its Christian name, but each must now have its proper surname and each citizen his civil status. Already in the eighteenth century the use of the family name had spread from the nobility to a few commoners. Now it became general and compulsory for all, though the more accurate date of birth was preferred to the date of christening, and the birth certificate to the baptismal certificate. This finally put into effect the aim of theorists who had advocated credit and attributed the failure of the law to the casual, unbusinesslike methods of the *ancien régime*. No obligation, whether family, religious or social, could now supplant that of debtor to creditor. While science encouraged the development of a philosophy and a moral outlook independent of God, whose effects on family and population have already been noted, the law now recorded, and safeguarded, the individual's new position in the economic society.

Now at last we can embark upon a study of the new man at work, and observe his vicissitudes and his reverses.

5

The Middle Classes Take Over

ALTHOUGH the elements of large-scale industry were present in Western Europe at the close of the eighteenth century, the age of far-reaching industrial changes had not yet begun. In our opinion the industrial revolution took place later than is generally held, especially since the work of Paul Mantoux. These changes did not, of course, all occur at the same time in every country in the West. They came early in England, and late in Germany. In France especially they were accompanied by a spectacular political revolution, which many historians, particularly in France, place at the beginning of the new era.

We have already seen how progressive England was, the land of Newton, with its advanced legal system, and the reforms in weights and measures. Above all, it had already acquired a political and social structure which could easily be penetrated by new financial institutions. It should be borne in mind that the London Bank was established in 1695, soon after the second great political revolution of modern England. The Bank of France was founded soon after the French Revolution. The Bank of Germany was established soon after the unification of the country by Bismarck. The financial history of Europe, echoing the Dutch example of two centuries earlier, is a chronological record of the gradual penetration from West to East of the economic institutions to which the great Atlantic trade had given rise, and the effects of which we discerned in the geography of Europe round about 1780.

But the industrial changes did not take place at the same time as the developments in credit. A whole century elapsed between the institution of banking and that of England's vast industrial development. This time-lag was reduced to a few years in France. In Germany a unified banking system was set up at the same time as economic and political unity was achieved.

INDUSTRY IN ENGLAND

In England a large-scale development of credit and banking preceded the introduction of mechanization. A law of 1693 allowed groups of less than six persons to set up as bankers. By 1786 a great many had done so and the following six years were 'the golden age' of banking activity. In 1793 there was not a city in England without its bank. Such an abundance of credit stimulated trade, made corporate institutions more flexible and developed a spirit of initiative and an attitude of mind willing to take economic risks. Thus the revolution of 1688 led to economic progress as well as to the development of parliamentarianism. In short, the machine age was becoming established in England without provoking the terrible upheavals with which it was to shatter political institutions in the rest of Europe.

In maritime trade the powerful East India Company, in common with others, was still defending its monopoly against the state's attempts to reform it. It had held out against the interests of the American colonies, and against accusations of brutality brought against it in India. But this monopoly, which had remained almost intact legally, was being gradually relaxed on the economic plane; the Company delegated its powers widely, since it had not the ships, the equipment or the agents to deal adequately with the rapidly increasing trade in the Indian Ocean. The same attitude may be observed on the part of all the great companies. Private initiative was responsible for most of the maritime trade. Even quite small companies, with only a little capital at their disposal, could charter ships at their joint expense.

Trade fostered credit and was also furthered by it: with each addition of a new settlement in India, each discovery of a new and hospitable Pacific coast, each opening of a new port in the Spanish Empire, there was a strengthening of the credit system and capitalism which formed the centre of England's economic life. At its peak about 1786, it was ready to enter into competition with France by a reciprocal lowering of customs duties. This step was not without risk, since France in 1785 could boast a production quantitatively superior to that of England in almost every sphere and particularly in what is known as heavy industry. In the luxury trades the superiority of Paris was overwhelming.

At that time England held the lead, not in industry, but in agriculture. There again, it was the result of two hundred years of agricultural effort following the secularization at the time of the Reformation. Between 1780 and 1830 this effort was at its height. Young noted it with pride. Young's forty-five volumes of the *Annals of Agriculture* were the favourite reading of kings, lords and gentlemen farmers from 1784 onwards. It was also the time of the wholesale passing of Enclosure Acts which changed the entire landscape of central and western England. At much the same time techniques of specialized stock-breeding on a large scale were perfected, by men such as Bakewell, whose horned cattle were at first the object of ridicule (it was said that they were too dear to buy, too fat to eat). Lastly, tuberculosis was finally stamped out from cattle in the most fertile areas of England.

Towards the close of the eighteenth century this meant the end of numerous small farms whose tenants lived on the produce of their own fields and on the general widespread use of common land. The smallholder had either to raise the money needed to increase his holding by

purchasing common lands and the plots of his poor neighbours and enclosing them, or to renounce his independence and get out to the town,
driven from a countryside where stock-breeding required an ever-decreas-
ing labour force. The yeoman of earlier days was in an even worse position.
Possession of a house in the old countryside with its common lands had
meant, if not wealth, at least a secure livelihood. When there were no more
common lands the yeoman too had to make for the town. The English
countryside was emptying, and the era of medium or large estates began.
A property of one hundred acres was considered small, one of three
hundred average. This gives some indication of the size of the English
estate in contrast with the minute plots on the Continent, which still bore
the mark of the old feudal system. These large estates were regarded by
Arthur Young as the chief sign of his country's agricultural progress.

The segregation of rich and poor on English soil was also aggravated by
circumstances arising from wars with France and the rest of Europe. The
disappearance of the small farm, with its pigs and cows, its farmyard and
its kitchen garden, brought about a change in diet and made it necessary
to rely on foreign aid; and this coincided with a time when imports from
Europe became more difficult and costly. It was, of course, impossible to
bring butter, eggs and milk from America. Prices went up. In 1785 corn
was two shillings a pound; this was thought expensive, yet it reached four
shillings in 1805 and six shillings in 1811. The fortunate victor of the battle
of the enclosures found himself comfortably off, and never before had he
earned so much money. Good land quadrupled in price between 1780 and
1800. In such conditions the struggles for power in the villages (and eventually in the House of Commons) to obtain bills of enclosure became more
numerous.

Yet these high prices worsened the situation of the poor. It was no use
cutting down on food, going without meat, and eating nothing but por-
ridge and whey; the poor were haunted by famine. There was no longer
any question of beer, not even the home-brewed ale which masters used to
serve at the common table in the good old days of collective living, when
there were freeholders and the agricultural worker was a companion
rather than a paid employee.

Under the old régime it had been considered one of the essential duties
of a lord to feed his dependants. In the new régime of *laissez-faire* the
landowner no longer had any such obligations towards his employees. He
engaged them if he needed them, and dismissed them when he had no use
for them. Nevertheless in England old tradition was revived in face of the
rising tide of poverty. The period 1785–1840 was to see the great debates on
the Poor Laws, which vacillated between strictness and leniency and revealed the country's fear of infection by a Jacobite revolution if poverty
was too rife, and the feelings of pity aroused in the minds of philanthropists. We shall only outline the essentials: Pitt at the start favoured a broad
interpretation of the tradition; the parishes were to feed the poor without
requiring them to enter workhouses. The poor, driven from the land, some-

times wandered from parish to parish in search of work. When the French Revolution was at its height in 1785, Berkshire affirmed the right of the poor to a minimum of food, and its decision was confirmed by a law. This minimum was to be found from local taxation, and employers in town and country took immediate advantage of this to lower wages, deducting the amount contributed by the parish.

From this point Malthus's gloomy predictions began to be fulfilled. The poor man, thus encouraged, would have every incentive to relapse into indolence; if he was married he would have swarms of children; humanity would be wrecked on the shoals of poverty. The big landed proprietors who paid the taxes protested against this relief, asserting that agriculture provided it for the benefit of industry; parishes which agreed to feed their own poor now turned away those of neighbouring parishes. So from law to law, from restriction to restriction, the lot of the non-producer became increasingly hard. In order to earn a living the poor had to work in the notorious workhouses, grim places which took husbands from wives, mothers from their children, gave only a minimum of food and imposed a harsh discipline. Schemes were devised to turn people away from country workhouses and to thrust them into the industrial towns, so as to lighten the burden of taxation and bring down the birth rate. Meanwhile, various worthy souls urged the rural poor to resume the traditional tasks of gardening and small farming. Cobden, in direct contrast to Young, reckoned a country's wealth by the number of pigs he saw wandering around a cottage.

Two distinct classes were beginning to emerge from the agricultural revolution: first that of the landowners, most of whom adopted the way of life of the upper classes. They had top-boots, guns, comfortable furniture and even the new-fangled piano in their country houses. Their sons and daughters dressed like children of the nobility and sometimes even succeeded in getting into the same schools. The classes who benefited from agrarian change were drawing closer together around the land-owning country gentleman, a process clearly illustrated in sentimental English novels of the early nineteenth century: young ladies of modest birth could marry lords' sons and aristocratic daughters went so far as to marry well-dressed commoners. The local vicar conducted these ceremonies with some emotion and, if he was a young man, sometimes turned his own thoughts in that direction. These were the impressionable, romantic years of the new rural England, described by Mary Webb. Everything seemed to be blending together and fusing into one common society. The heart could concentrate on its own problems with all the more interest and emotion because social barriers were frailer. But a considerable barrier still separated landowners from farmers, even if they were well-to-do and farmed in a big way.

The real poor ended up in the overcrowded city suburbs and the filthy slums. They and their wives and children worked in cotton mills, mines, foundries, and for a mere pittance with the terrible threat of unemployment always hanging over them. There was unemployment with every crisis – whenever the supply of cotton from overseas was held up, when the market was saturated, or when the mill owner was refused the overdraft he asked for from the local bank. If he then hastened in his carriage to London and met with a second refusal justified by a rise in the discount rate at the Bank of England, his factory would close down and the resulting poverty was frightful. But there was also unemployment when the employer's business was going so well that he started getting rid of his old plant and replacing it by mechanical looms driven by water and steam. So far as the worker was concerned there was nothing to choose between unemployment due to prosperity and that due to a crisis. The poor, the common people, became as it were a reservoir on which industry drew according to its needs – human raw material.

There was plenty of it: in 1790 Manchester had 50,000 inhabitants, and in 1830 it had almost 250,000. Many other cities and towns (Glasgow, Birmingham and Liverpool) were increasing at a similar rate. The rural world was being drawn into these privileged centres: contingents of Irishmen, rough and stout-hearted, came to swell the migration. A few cities, it is true, were developing more slowly; Bristol, a former great port, was beginning to lose its relative pre-eminence, as were the old centres of the wool trade. On the other hand, London was incontestably the most powerful city in the world. It can be estimated that at the beginning of the nineteenth century only twenty-eight per cent of English families were living on agriculture. Even if country craftsmen, those who had village workshops or worked in their own homes for city manufacturers are included, the rural population figures barely reached fifty per cent. It was more than a century before France was to achieve the same proportions. The figures indicate the extent of the English industrial revolution.

Let us examine the technical aspects of this revolution: we have discussed the many remarkable inventions produced in the eighteenth century – power-driven looms and spinning jennies, coke smelting, the growing use of hydraulic power, and the first steam engine. Though these various inventions had proved their worth and had been applied here and there, to the general admiration, by the end of the eighteenth century they had not yet been brought together into great industrial concerns. Ten years later the position was very different.

The first large textile establishment equipped with steam-driven machinery was opened in Manchester in 1806. There were fifteen of the same type in 1818. In 1823 there were probably 10,000 mechanical looms in the country. In 1830 this figure had risen to 50,000, although there still remained 250,000 hand-looms in use in town and country. These were weaving cotton, a product for which mechanization was particularly suitable. Wool kept closer to tradition, and carpets were all woven by hand up to 1850. In 1830 the power-driven woollen loom was still an exception. The setting up of the mechanized silk industry apparently dated from the 1820s in Manchester, though it was not systematized until the end of the century. Fulling by hydraulic press was introduced only at the very end of the eighteenth century and reached Dundee in the 1820s. The application of chemical processes, following on the discoveries of Berthollet, was first tried out on the industrial scale in Scotland in 1814.

Similarly, there are few signs of a revolution in the metal industry before 1825. In 1789 one-quarter of the production was still dependent on charcoal. The war of course gave it a formidable impetus. Until 1820 all foundries made guns. Production stepped up from 70,000 tons in 1789 to 260,000 in 1806, and 700,000 in 1830. Puddling was not introduced before 1793 and did not penetrate to Scotland until 1830. As for steel, people were still complaining in 1830 that far too much was being imported from country mills in Germany or Sweden. The use of steam-engines was being extended at the same period. It is true that in 1786 Watt himself had built the plant of the London Mills (the Albion Mills), and soon afterwards a steam-engine was working the pumps used for London's water supply. But the greatest novelty of all dated from 1816, when *The Times* was printed by steam, and other newspapers were soon to follow suit. In 1831 Glasgow could boast 328 steam engines, of which 60 were on ships anchored in the Clyde.

In agriculture, there were no harvesters before 1850, but from the late eighteenth century threshing machines were becoming widely used and a few of the great landowners even had steam-driven ones in 1820. At about the same date a mechanical haymaking machine proved fairly successful.

In short, the beginning of the industrial revolution in England, too often attributed to the previous century, coincided with the Revolution and the Empire in France, and the first cycle of the changes it brought about was to continue until after 1840. The statistics of external trade confirm this view: foreign trade rose from 500,000 tons about the mid-eighteenth century to a million just before 1789; but it reached five millions in 1800 and continued to increase at the same rate up to the middle of the nineteenth century.

It had been trade which, in the eighteenth century, had brought greater flexibility to English institutions on the eve of the capitalist revolution. Trade profited greatly by the resulting changes and in turn stimulated more change. The old corporate medieval practices disappeared, and in particular the fairs. Sturbsidge or Stirbitch vanished, and in his place appeared the new figure of the commercial traveller with his order book and his samples. In the cities wholesale warehouses sprang up claiming that they offered the whole year round the prices that prevailed at the fairs: the result was a change in the habits of the customer (who no longer confined his purchases to certain seasons, but spread them out over the whole year), and fresh scope was provided for exchanges and bank credits had to be increased.

New banks were continually founded. In London there were sixty-nine in 1797, and about seventy-seven in 1808; the secretary of the Local Bankers' Association reported two hundred and thirty country banks in 1797 and almost five hundred in 1804. At that time there were three banks for the 4,500 inhabitants of Abingdon and six for the 7,000 of Boston in

Yorkshire. The numbers continued to grow; in 1810 there was a total of eight hundred local banks. There was competition for custom in the small towns. Banking found its way even into the most remote country districts. In the the cities banking houses controlled the fortunes or ruin of businessmen. Everyone applied for credit. During the 1810 crisis Baring told a parliamentary committee that the bank had granted credits of five to ten million pounds to humble folk, even to workpeople who had broken their contracts and gone into business on their own accounts and who 'had scarcely a hundred pounds to their names'. Moreover in spite of the war metric currency was still in circulation, India and China were ceasing to be sellers and becoming buyers, and money which had formerly moved from West to East was beginning to move in the reverse direction. The East India Company asked the Bank of England to buy as much as £100,000 worth of silver in 1803. The circulation of Bank of London notes increased continually. It rose from £11 million in 1790 to almost £18 million in 1804, and these figures give only a faint idea of the total circulation of notes issued by all the banks. Indiscriminate advances to the Government had forced Pitt to suspend convertibility in 1797 and the suppression lasted through varying fortunes until 1820. Not only Treasury Bonds, but many other kinds of notes increased the circulation of paper money still further.

It is easy to see how the cautious Mollien in France could simultaneously admire the English Government's good fortune in having so much money available without an adequate basis of precious metal, and also speculate on the weakness of the English system. One of its strong points, however, was the wisdom of the Government which, after the unfortunate experience of 1797 (and learning from the contemporary experience of France), steadfastly refused to borrow too much from the Bank. However excessive British circulation may have seemed, it was deliberate, justified by trade and by the briskness of business.

Crises were inevitable in this young economy, and the periodic recurrence in ten-yearly cycles was already making itself felt. In 1783 the first great wave of change began, and in 1804 the English were forced to sue for peace; they were uneasy about the future of the Nordic trade, since the Scandinavians and Russians seemed to be favouring France. The most serious crisis broke in 1811, caused by the blockade set up by Napoleon at the far end of the Baltic in one of the most vulnerable areas of English trade: he had control of Danzig, the source of corn and wood. In England the price of provisions rose violently, the war with the United States made maritime trade precarious, stacks of unsaleable goods piled up in the London warehouses, and merchants faced with ruin went from bank to bank begging for credit which was refused them even at the highest rates of interest. Finally the excessive boom of the preceding years and the over-sanguine hopes raised by the opening of Rio de Janeiro to English trade had given birth to so many dubious ventures that a cleaning-up operation was inevitable. It occurred quite spontaneously, but brought widespread poverty and wretchedness in its train. Napoleon's defeat in Moscow and Wellington's advance through the Iberian Peninsula restored hope and confidence in business ; but the crisis was slow to resolve itself. and was indeed intensified in 1815 when supplies were no longer needed for the army and the allies. One can understand Thackeray's disillusionment and moralizing tone in describing *Vanity Fair*, that society in which fortunes were quickly made and as quickly lost, so that middle-class families were ruined just as they seemed about to succeed on the social ladder to the aristocracy.

But although the role of *entrepreneur* was hazardous and required qualities of daring and courage, the real sufferers in these crises were the common people. Up to 1815 England lived in dread of popular revolts on the Jacobite model. Once Napoleon had been defeated, riots broke out in London and Manchester, and Wellington's armies were called out to fire on the people. These were not the first revolts bred of poverty (they had already occurred at the end of the eighteenth century): the Luddites, the machine-breakers, banded themselves together, threatened factories and burned down mills. Ruin and despondency followed these explosive outbursts, though usually they did not last long. Yet the Government feared they might become widespread, which accounted for the mistrust of workmen's associations like that of the muslin and cutlery operatives in Glasgow in 1787. In 1797 (in the name of *laissez-faire*) a law had been passed against workers' coalitions, though associations of employers were tolerated if not encouraged. The only resort left to the workers was the old corporative law, the *ancien régime* tradition of protecting the poor, which it became increasingly difficult to evoke.

Yet it is worth noting that however tragic these crises were in England they never seriously threatened the English economy. They gave an astonishing character to certain great parliamentary debates: in 1811, for example, the party favouring the re-establishment of convertibility opposed those who wished to maintain the Restriction Act of 1797. Ricardo and the orthodox economists pointed to the depreciation of the pound, which had lost forty per cent on gold, fourteen per cent on the franc, and seven per cent on the Dutch florin; and they urged the Government to submit to the discipline of the gold standard. But to do so would have meant slowing down the borrowing drive and the war effort, and might possibly have meant making peace with Napoleon. Patriotism must prevail ; each man must exert himself to the full so that England might successfully balance on the tightrope between popular revolts brought on by the crisis, the threat of overloaded credit, and the danger of relaxing the war effort. Thus while European countries were counting soldiers and cannon, the English in their island were counting pounds sterling, credits and gold reserves. The crises of 1785–1815 were revolutionary, but in different ways on opposite sides of the channel. In England they were economic, in France political; in England social, in France military.

When peace had been restored, the English crises continued to recur in a ten-yearly rhythm which began to intrigue economists, and soon became the chief object of their study. And these crises became increasingly serious as capitalism became more firmly established. The 1825 crisis was regarded as a catastrophe comparable to the great fire of London. Nevertheless, the growth in volume of American trade, particularly with the new nations of the south, the prospects of a rich trade in the eastern seas, and the considerable profits made by the new English factories had at first provoked a feverish activity in the 1820s; new mills were being opened everywhere. In order to amass the necessary capital, appeals were made to a public eager to buy shares and bonds even from the Government. This speculation soon led to inflation of their currency; the price of consumer goods rose, the drain of gold began, the Bank reserves were endangered: in short there was a sudden tightening up of a credit, a rise in the discount rate, and notes of all kinds were suspended. The bold speculator had to sell; immediately prices fell by more than thirty per cent; a vast wave of bankrupts engulfed England. This provoked an equally grave disaster in the United States, which were linked to England by the cotton trade.

Once this cruel cleaning-up operation had been completed, life was resumed again, and there was a cautious return of initiative. So as to give credit a wider range a new law freed the issue of credit entirely except within a sixty-five mile radius of London, where the privilege of the Bank was maintained. In 1836 there were 670 private banks in England. Industrial opinion remained vocal about the weakness of its representation in Parliament. There were only fifty businessmen out of six hundred MPs. The clubs embarked on a campaign, the press increased its circulation by demanding electoral reform, workmen let themselves be persuaded by the organizers that reform would mean cheaper bread and free beer. In 1825 Huskisson put through a bill making workers' associations legal and setting up a scale of customs' duties which lowered the price of imported foodstuffs and raw materials. Finally, in 1832, under threat of a popular revolt to which the memory of recent events in Paris lent an added terror, Parliament passed the electoral reform which opened its ranks to representatives of the new industrial cities. The electorate was not greatly increased, rising from 650,000 to 800,000, but this was enough to create an atmosphere favourable to a number of social reforms.

These reforms had not been fully assimilated when a fresh crisis arose, a complicated one which recurred in successive waves from 1836 to 1839. There was a scramble for gold between England, where speculation surpassed even its peak period of the 1820s, the continent, where industrial progress was just beginning, and the United States where reconstruction on a vast scale was in progress to the accompaniment of violent convulsions in the cotton market. At one moment it was in America that there was a shortage of gold, and seven hundred banks suspended payments; the next was in England, which had to obtain as much specie as possible from Hamburg. In 1833 the problem of the renewal of the monopoly of the Bank of England had arisen. Finally, in 1844, Peel's famous Bank Charter Act separated the banking and issuing departments of the Bank of England so that it should be protected from financial crises even at the risk of an excessive limitation of credit.

In 1844 such strict measures harmed no-one, so great was the degree of prosperity which had returned, but in 1846 signs of a fresh storm began to appear ; we shall return to this, since it marked the beginning of a new age. We should just note here that all these crises, though particularly dramatic in England, affected the rest of the world too and particularly the countries of continental Europe, where they resulted not in discreet forms of credit but in violent popular or military revolutions.

GOVERNMENT IN FRANCE

It is curious that when so much historical research has been done on the closing years of the old régime there should still be so few reliable analyses of the mechanisms which unleashed the Revolution. Graphs of prices show a crisis linked to the drop in the price of corn, which reached its lowest points in 1777, 1785 and 1786. Yet England had gone through similar crises, and had shown no trace of revolutionary symptoms beyond a few popular agitations from which the capitalist régime had emerged even stronger than before. It is true to say that the economic crises which swept over the West during the period of 1780–95 proved fatal to only one political régime – that of Versailles. They shook Austria, but did not overthrow it. They in no way undermined the Prussian monarchy, and actually strengthened the English system. The reasons for the destruction of the old régime must then be sought in the régime itself ; the economic crisis merely provided a climate which fostered their violence.

The monarchy of Louis xv had benefited from the expanding economy of the eighteenth century. It had been an unusually prosperous period for France as well as for England. Agricultural methods had improved and industry had expanded; new goods were produced (cheap cottons, loom-woven silks, porcelain and glass), maritime trade increased, making Nantes and Bordeaux the major sugar ports and Marseilles the chief Mediterranean port; all this brought France new growth and prosperity. But the old monarchy, prosperous enough in years of calm, had lost the power of producing remedies for times of stress. England, as we have seen, drew on credit for resources to meet the strain, but there was nothing comparable in France. Was it the fault of Louis xv or Louis xvi? The unfortunate Louis xvi at all events could no more be blamed for this deficiency than he could be given credit for the prosperity which marked the early years of his reign. It was not the king nor yet the court which proved incapable of erecting the structure of credit which was essential if economic crises were to be surmounted: it was the whole of society.

French society was still constructed on an archaic pattern, its only resource in time of crisis being (as it had shown in its reactions to seventeenth- and eighteenth-century crises) to make new rules, whereas since

Cromwell's time England had dealt with crises by creating liberty. French society, if it had been alone in Europe, might possibly have been able to survive by the rule-making procedures of a previous age. But the machinery for making these regulations was too cumbersome and in-flexible to keep pace with the fierce international competition which the expansion of commerce had brought about in maritime trade since Utrecht, and in overland trade since the trade treaty of 1786.

Louis xvi's enlightened ministers and the lords at his court who were interested in industry attempted to introduce into France the economic techniques of English society, though by so doing they rendered the old French monarchic procedures effete. Thus Louis xvi was by turns too orthodox in a progressive France or too progressive in an orthodox France. The revolutionary ferment spread without difficulty through the monarchical body, which had lost its old, protective shell and had not yet acquired a new one.

The English remedy for the 1785 crisis was credit. Why was there no equally effective credit in France? The reason was that French society, unlike that of England, was so constructed as to restrict its own credit. First it had no bank. The very word 'bank' was forbidden. When some Swiss financiers adapted an idea originally proposed by a Protestant group backed by the speculator Panchaud, and opened the *Caisse d'Escompte*, they did not dare call it a bank. Its title was confirmed when Necker took over the ministry. This bank, as if ashamed of itself, was so careful not to fall into the same errors as the Scottish financier Law that it managed its credits with excessive caution, limited its clientèle, stood out against Calonne who was expecting it to contribute too much to state finances, defended itself even against Necker, and by dint of remaining in the background managed to keep going until the introduction of the *assignats*. But France had no state bank. This *Caisse* neither could be, nor wished to be, the leaven of French modernization.

Of course there were shipowners, industrialists and merchants in some French cities and particularly in the ports who ran a credit bureau in con-nection with their business. But French middle-class businessmen were basically against credit. They had no confidence in the banknote. They wanted gold, and the premium they placed on it (as Colbert would have wished) led to a result which surpassed the wildest dreams of the mercantile fraternity. France was draining gold from the rest of the world. By 1785 she had become the gold reservoir of the world. It was in order to pay for this gold that she had rejected the financial advantages offered by paper currency.

Bank credit has become so familiar to us since the nineteenth century that its full social importance is sometimes overlooked. If a collective group is to be trusted to put notes into circulation, to use them to give support to businesses in process of reconstruction, to expanding industries, or to businessmen in temporary difficulty, it is essential that every member of that group, or at least the majority of them, should feel a sense of solidarity and should play the credit game without cheating. In France in 1789 nothing could have been further from this position. La Rochefoucauld transformed his estates at Liancourt and turned them into a modern farm, finer probably than any in England; but he did this out of his private income. The model farm at Rambouillet was created out of the king's privy purse. The Duke of Orleans may have founded textile factories, porcelain or pottery works, and opened his royal palace to merchants, but this again was done without borrowing and out of his own resources. The same applied to the industries launched by a few great aristocrats. When the Azin mines were finally opened up, when Le Creusot was smelting with coal and Indret forging steel by English methods, and when textile mills and metal works appeared all over France – in each case it was done with ready money, accumulated from landed property, and without resorting to credit. Of course the innumerable small craftsmen who continued to make articles to order in their own homes, with a partner and two or three apprentices in a shop at the back of the house, had not the remotest idea what credit was. They had no stock. The protection afforded the craftsman by the corporate system, the guarantee it gave him against competition, meant that he had no need of credit.

Although there existed in France influential merchants like those in England, they were not clearly distinguishable from tradesmen. The name financier was more often used for those people who were exclusive experts in matters of credit, who met to discuss the price of stocks and shares in the Hôtel de Soissons, the first exchange. This was not merely a question of nomenclature. The financier drew his resources from administration of the royal taxation. It was from the state and the authority he derived from his administrative office that he derived his power, and not from private credit. English credit, on the other hand, was sufficient unto itself without any kind of outside help.

In fact the French financier, so despised since the days of La Bruyère, had some excuse: not only did the government turn to him in its difficulties, but it was on him that the Treasury itself usually relied for most of its ordinary resources; moreover whenever the middle classes had a little money to invest, it was to the king and the government that they entrusted it, in preference to banks or merchants. They bought not only government stock, but also those posts which sometimes, before 1789, carried a title and conferred nobility on the holder. A vast swarm of solicitors, attorneys and recorders throve on lawsuits which proliferated under the corporate régime, and the most shrewd and go-ahead members of the bourgeoisie became lawyers. The centralizing monarchy, originally established to see that justice was done, had created for itself a bourgeois society in its own image; it was more concerned with dictating the law than with creating banking.

A society of this kind could hardly therefore expect to display financial flexibility when faced with a crisis. A few powerful industries directed by aristocrats and financiers, a few bourgeois merchants practising financial self-help, living on their own resources and never entirely without landed

property, could afford to await better days and prepare a few timid reforms in their industrial methods. But the industrious lower middle class
was strangled by the inelasticity of the currency based on gold; and the excessively zealous government refused to debase the alloy used for the gold.
In time of crisis, there was no possible way of escaping a deficit.

This social economy based on metal was controlled by archaic governmental methods – in other words by restrictions, controls and regulations.
When gold ceased to circulate, it was essential to stop goods from circulating too. Turgot had had a bitter experience of this: by an over-hasty relaxing of control over the circulation of goods he had set in motion a wave
of bankruptcies. Every crisis in the old structure inevitably called forth the
old remedies: hence the economic significance of the feudal reaction which
was evoked whenever economic activity was threatened. The threat itself
almost always came from the land, from a bad harvest.

A bad harvest meant an impoverished peasantry, dearer bread, craftsmen without orders, industry without credit or work, workers without
pay: at such times as these, the weight of rents and of taxes was a grievous
burden, so heavy that it killed taxable assets. The treasury emptied; and
as a final resort launched loans which no one took up. In the general unrest and mounting poverty, the privileged aristocrat (or cleric, or wealthy
bourgeois), whose landed property enabled him to finance himself, won
on every count. He could expand his business and his estates by exploiting
the downfall of others; he alone had reserves of wealth on which to draw,
and it was to this man of influence that the government had to turn for
help for its own treasury, before it could even begin to think of asking for
help for the nation's strangled economy.

The eighteenth century had seen the appearance and growth of a
generally enlightened public opinion; but it had had no possible opportunity of acquiring financial techniques. Although the salons and cafés,
the aristocrats of the court or of industry greatly enjoyed discussing tools and
methods of agriculture or industry, they knew nothing at all about banking. They were content with a sound currency and a pure metal coinage.
When poverty and unrest increased, it was not therefore lack of credit
which was blamed, but the king, the court, or the regulations. English
liberty was praised everywhere, not because it was seen as the basis of
credit, but as a symbol of increasing prosperity which was believed to be
due solely to its political virtues. The American experience had failed to
educate public opinion on this point. It was to political liberty in itself that
people gave their votes, and not to the financial apparatus it supported.

The argument as to whether the French economy in 1785 was rich or
poor has continued from Michelet to Jaurès, but no definite conclusion
has been reached. Economic activity apparently throve when times were
good and slumped when times were bad. France appeared flourishing or
wretched in turns, and although people managed occasionally in periods
of prosperity to put something aside for a rainy day, they were never in a
position in times of adversity to call on credit or to draw cheques on the

future. The result was a series of lean years, when savings were exhausted and the country was reduced to hopeless misery. The government, with its treasury empty, could act only as it was authorized to, whilst the worried artisan from sheer force of habit looked solely to the king to solve all his difficulties. It was on this colossal note of misunderstanding that the Estates-General met in 1789.

The government learned during the nineteenth century that only a strong issue of paper currency could save the country in these grave crises. England had learned this from experience. Louis XVI, on the contrary, gave honest Necker his head, and Necker's honesty was the only thing in which the bourgeoisie had any confidence at all. The lawyers of France gathered in the Salle des Menus Plaisirs at Versailles, with a mandate from the Third Estate to defend honesty and integrity. The government talked finance, the Third Estate replied in terms of virtue; no real exchange of views was possible. The Revolution grew out of the most fruitless arguments at the very moment when, as we have seen, England was meeting the crisis by developing its banks.

The monarchy foundered because of its inability to organize credit in France, because it summoned the Estates-General who were no wiser on the subject, and because it doubled the representation of the Third Estate without acquiring a single additional financier in the process. The greater the number of members associated with the deliberations of the Third Estate, the more lawyers they included. These eminent lawyers were entrenched in the routines of everyday procedure; they had been brought up on Montequieu's reflections and Voltaire's sarcasm (though Voltaire had strongly suspected that there must be some great economic force at work beneath the law, which he had never been able to identify); they were stirred by Rousseau's sentimental outpourings; they dreamed of a strong society built for virtue by virtue. It was all very abstract; what France needed was accountants, while what she had was lawyers: instead of counting acres of land, the length of roads, bales of wool or cotton, they discussed the rights of man and of the citizen. The treasury was empty, the assembly filled it with a constitution. It revived all the points raised in France in the impassioned discussions on American independence. The masterpiece was drawn up, and the great principles of 1789 were laid down; and indeed it *was* a masterpiece, for in the world of that day it would have been almost impossible to find an assembly more competent or better prepared for the task. Its members were well matched from the start, since they shared a common education and long years of common practice.

The assembly was crystal clear when it came to translating into legal terms two centuries of experience. The 'claims of citizens' must be based on simple and incontestable principles. It was an attitude of mind reminiscent of general mechanics; and it reflected the spirit of deduction which had created philosophical speculation in France, to the detriment of the old Christian faith. For long years the French *parlements* had been twisting the law they were charged to apply in order to foster liberty, property ownership and security. In corporate lawsuits they had done their utmost to protect the inventor and the innovator: decrees which conformed too closely to tradition were bitterly criticized by enlightened society, attacks on the liberty of conscience were condemned, and judges who applied the royal laws strictly were pilloried by opinion. Landowners arriving with carriages full of dossiers to support their ancient rights had been dismissed summarily, to the delight of all Paris, and backed by the honours list of the *Encyclopédie*. In order to condemn the Jesuits, the progressivists had made them appear ridiculous. It was this whole century of struggle and controversy that was summed up in the final song of victory celebrating the natural and inalienable rights of man; and it gave to the *Déclaration* the strength of its style and structure. Moreover, the cosmopolitan culture of 1789 had left its mark on these French texts, which drew on the lessons of English or American political experiments; there were also reflections inspired by the virtuous Chinese emperors who were depicted climbing to the top of a hill to proclaim their good intentions before the supreme being. It was this cosmopolitanism also which gave the *Déclaration* its universal appeal.

It would be difficult, therefore, to overestimate the power and the effectiveness of the enormous intellectual achievement which emerged from the commissions of the revolutionary assemblies. They shaped the development of the new era of European and world thought and gave Europe the tools which were to help it assert itself. In all that concerned ideas and intellectual concepts – law and the code, the fixing of measures, the metric system – the revolutionary assemblies did magnificent work, but they failed signally on the vital practical problem of the organization of money for purposes of credit.

For all these masterpieces of intellect had no practical significance when it came to monetary and credit techniques. Eventually, of course, after a great many speeches, they had to tackle this fundamental problem which had formerly been the province of the monarchy but had now to be dealt with by the assembly which had taken over the monarchy's responsibilities. Though desperate appeals were made to it, it fell into the most fantastic error: there were in the Constituent Assembly a few rare economists like Condorcet, a few practical men like Talleyrand, and a few (far too few) experienced bankers like the farmer-general Lavoisier, or the outstanding Dupont de Nemours. All urged the assembly to think long and hard about Law's fiasco. Law had tried to sell his colonial companies in banknotes; the assembly was contemplating selling Church lands in the same currency. How was such a mistake in monetary technique possible? First, because all the reserves which had supported the French economy through the crises of the eighteenth century had been derived from landed property; but more particularly because the vast majority of the assembly consisted of lawyers; they were convinced that the fundamental difference between Law's disaster, still fresh in memory, and the new experiment was embodied in a new legal statute which would be an adequate safeguard:

such an innovation would in itself be enough to validate, in 1790, what had been disastrous in 1718. We quoted above the anonymous preface to Law's *Money and Trade Considered*, laying down the conditions of sound currency. It went on to say that these conditions existed between persons equally subject to the law, and that credit thus meant simply trusting in the laws themselves. This may be a legal theorist's view of the economy; it would hardly be that of a banker or a technical expert. From lack of experience, France, unfortunately, was about to embark once more on the same adventure. From 1791, there were two prices in France, one in cash, the other in *assignats*. In a country accustomed to gold, there should have been twice as many psychological precautions taken to ensure that a correct relationship was maintained between the note and gold. In actual fact far fewer precautions were taken in France than in England.

Thus this magnificent assembly of lawyers, deservedly immortal for its work of codification, was about to plunge the country into a series of regularly recurring catastrophes, the effects of which were evident right up to the mid-twentieth century. Yet the real responsibility lay not so much with the assembly as with the whole of French thought and French society, which rated legal expertise higher than understanding of credit. The basic lack of this credit, which the assembly dismissed as a minor issue, was soon to split the whole of society, and bring to the scaffold most of those who, far-sighted or otherwise, had been connected with this fatal blunder.

The crisis of 1789 necessitated a widespread recourse to credit. Far from organizing this remedy, the constitutional monarchy which was evolving in France actually destroyed the financial framework of the old régime. The break-up of the court and the departure of the great noble families and financiers (apart from one of the wealthiest, the Prince of Orleans, who stayed in Paris to watch over his own concerns) destroyed the classic consumers' market at the same time as it emptied the treasury. The *Caisse d'Escompte* disappeared, engulfed by the assignats before being officially suppressed in 1793. An immense floating population of unemployed emerged from the suburbs in search of non-existent bread. There was looting in the countryside and rioting in the towns. The panic did not create a climate favourable to credit. The old economic masonry of the old régime was crumbling. The unemployed, instead of seeking bread from the factory, the exchange and the bank, shouted for it under the windows of the town hall. French society was too dependent on the land, and on landed property; the sale of national property encouraged this tendency still further; capital either went underground, or was used for speculating on the price of land. Industry came to a standstill. The Anzin mines were paralysed, and the blast furnaces at Le Creusot went out. The economy was dying – in fact it was dead.

Two important events showed its passing. First the rise of a socialist government on the ruins of legal liberalism, and second the success of mass-recruiting for the army.

In fact only a socialist-minded government could maintain an economy without credit, and the Committee of Public Safety, under the guidance of Robespierre, actually rushed full speed ahead towards the steep and slippery slope. Credit was dead, so the whole credit structure, not only the *Caisse d'Escompte* but the trading companies, the capitalist groups and the *bourse*, might as well be destroyed. Banking operations, in the estimation of all good members of the Constituent Assembly, were deals in stocks, no more and no less. Trade in merchandise was speculation or monopoly pure and simple. So death to stock-jobbers, speculators and monopolists! Thus the liberal economy, hounded from its very last strongholds, was replaced by the vast and improvised machinery of a planned economy: requisitioning, maximum prices, maximum wages, and maximum everything. Yet the decrees of Ventôse were beginning to tackle the problem of a redistribution of land in favour of the poor. Although the value of the assignat was low, the terror checked its further depreciation. It did not matter whether the note was covered by gold or not, or what its real value was. Any citizen who was dishonest about its value was obviously a bad patriot, a suspect, and a case for the dreaded terror. It was not for gain, or handsome profits, that the factories kept going, or reopened in the worst possible economic conditions in every French canton administered by Paris; it was not for profit, nor from fear of a ruthless government that saltpetre was raked from the cellars, or that Monge drew up plans for fortresses and guns; it was from politic belief in the threatened mother-country.

A patriotic dictatorship was substituted for a liberal banking system; influential merchants, theorists, or lawyers who had come up from the Gironde to Paris to establish the government of their dreams, had a rude awakening: they either perished on the scaffold, or were proscripted, or were relentlessly hunted down. This continued as long as the Committee of Public Safety was able to equip its armies by requisitioning, to the sound of the *Marseillaise*, and to ensure fairly adequate food supplies to the cities by the compulsory mobilization of all available resources.

Yet one man, Danton, saw the position clearly. Before making a dangerous deal with the speculators, he had advised the republican armies not to hesitate to seek in the liberated countries a livelihood which the Republic itself could hardly provide. The army was the great outlet for the working people, particularly in towns, where they were thrilled by the great patriotic adventure planned in factories now deserted by their customers. Mass conscription became inevitable with the destruction of the economy even before it was ordered by the famous decree. Thus the towns with a reduced population stopped feeding the troops of the sections. As the national army increased in size so the revolutionary troops diminished, and the more successful the regular army, the more precarious became the position of the Committee of Public Safety which had brought it into being. The well-known phrase 'victories swooped down on Robespierre like furies' is a most apt description of the position in which that extraordinary moving spirit of this epic now found himself. It seemed to him that the

Republic was lost and the brigands triumphant. By brigands he meant the financiers, merchants and commissaries.

However formidable the work accomplished by the Committee of Public Safety it could not succeed. It had aimed at a lasting reform of society, but it could not possibly hope to build the permanent apparatus of a vast controlled economy with no monetary basis. Monge, a fine geometrician, had had no training in economics. No-one in the country really believed in the permanence of reforms which were called 'revolutionary' precisely because they were exceptional and temporary. Men and capital went into hiding, waiting for the return of a bourgeois peace, while the very fact that France was the gold reservoir of Europe meant that capital was all the easier to conceal. It needed only a slight shift of majority in the Convention, engineered by men who resented Robespierre's enquiries into the affairs of those who were doing well out of the régime, for gold to reappear once Robespierre was overthrown. It was even being squandered openly by dandies and spendthrifts. It set up a new economic current which galvanized the old society into new life, and led the Convention, in spite of itself, towards the re-establishment of the bourgeois economy. Then the strange world of the Directory came into being, a motley crowd made up of speculators in national lands, businessmen from the old régime, who had been living hidden away in little back shops, experts in the mobilization of military production, and foreigners whose alien status offered them a certain security against the Tribunal and who could take advantage of the stable currencies of their own countries. There were marvellous business openings for the Swiss, a subject on which Benjamin Constant dwelt at length in his diary. Beside, or above this financial élite which now emerged from its hide-out, were the revolutionary leaders who had managed to avoid both the guillotine of Fouquier-Tinville and the 'dry guillotine' which followed it. They had succeeded in keeping their posts by the adroit game of co-operation, first under the Convention, and then under the assemblies, councils and ministries of the Directory. They were to attempt to take their place in the revival of business.

Between the two groups, financial and political, it was not always easy to achieve agreement. The wealthy bourgeoisie mistrusted the Jacobites. But the political group was equally suspicious of the old hands who had toadied, first to Pichegru, then to Sieyès, and finally to Bonaparte. It also mistrusted the whole political see-saw of the Directory, whose chief aim under the fiendishly clever direction of the superb intellect of Citizen Barras was to keep Thermidorians in key positions at all costs. It was a policy furtively plotted in governmental councils, at parties and at the famous balls given at the Palais du Luxembourg, all spick and span for the occasion, or in the glittering, recently opened Hôtel de Salm, around the petticoats of Madame Tallien, Madame Récamier and Josephine de Beauharnais.

But the well-to-do remained suspicious. The *assignat*, whose depreciation had been checked by the terror, fell in value until it was a worthless piece of paper. The *mandat territorial* which replaced it was no more successful. Credit was not restored. Nevertheless, the conditions in which it could be restored were gradually being established; the political situation of 1790 was more stable, and new economic measures took into account the bitter experience of the past years. The Constitution of the year III made property ownership and liberalism secure: the legal, bourgeois revolution was an accomplished fact. The Constitution abolished everything that went beyond the bourgeois revolution towards socialism and recreated a kind of court life. Relief at the ending of the terror brought artisans' shops back to life. Orders poured in for fabrics, furniture, building work, house decoration and knick-knacks, and there was less fear of unemployment; this lasted as long as the armies remained on a war footing and were mainly stationed beyond the frontiers, since they could be maintained there without placing any strain on the country's precarious economic revival. The stubborn patience of the peasants, of the *Pères Goriot*, was rewarded, and they enlarged their farms with national property. The peasantry again enjoyed a secure livelihood, and again began to invest its money. The *Caisse d'Escompte* reopened under the name of the *Caisse des Comptes courants*.

Who protected this newly emerging credit? Who was on the council of this new bank of issue, a bank which still did not venture to disclose its name? There was Le Couteux, a Rouen manufacturer, a former deputy, cautious and self-effacing. There was Claude Périer of the famous Grenoble family of cloth manufacturers, who bought the Château de Vizille and a block of shares in the Anzin mines for next to nothing. There was Perrégaux, a Swiss banker, who had adroitly survived the vicissitudes of the Revolution, along with other fellow-countrymen like Mallet, Hottinger and Delessert – the whole circle which revolved around Madame Récamier. For the benefit of a carefully selected group of known and trusted industrialists and merchants, a sound note based on sound credit was brought cautiously into circulation, but there was no intention of putting it at the service of the Directory. The great number of *mandats territoriaux*, printed by the Directory itself, were exploited for their rapid loss in value.

It was in this divided and ill-assorted society, protected from foreign invasion by a now disciplined army, that the destiny of the régime was to be decided. The Directory held its ground so long as Barras remained in power, as he kept with him the other politicians who had survived the Revolution. But once the peasants felt secure, and the craftsmen had work, they tended to push to the fore at elections men quite out of sympathy with the members of the former Convention. Barras, aging, disillusioned and overworked, planned to retire to his great estates, to round off a most successful career in a philosophic calm worthy of the eighteenth century. Mutual uneasiness in face of the unknown future, whether too royalist or too Jacobite, drew politicians and financiers together in a common desire to safeguard the system of co-optation which had proved so successful in government as well as in banking during the previous four years. This rapprochement, engineered by Sièyes, was aimed at dividing the spoils as they were – banking for bankers; good, permanent senatorships for the politicians; and power for Sièyes himself, who would use the army to protect the whole arrangement. Two factors were omitted from their reasoning. The first was the army, which had to be kept mobilized away from the cities and even, if possible, from the frontiers, while the second was Bonaparte, shocked at the realization that the ultimate end of this arrangement was the enrichment and consolidation of a privileged few, solidly united among themselves.

Bonaparte, it is true, was an ambitious general, but when all was said and done, no more dedicated, meticulous or loyal individual had ever come up against Barras. He could turn his hand to any task, small or large, private or public. Guglielmo Ferrero has rightly stressed the submissive and sometimes beseeching tone of his letters to the Directory during the Italian campaign: after all, his first victories (whose significance was not yet apparent, as they followed six years of victories) could barely serve as sufficient explanation to the republican Government for the major changes that the General, brought by the exigencies of war from Italy, sought to introduce in the Directory's plan.

Bonaparte had already done some hard thinking in prison. Hoche had been removed from the same army of Italy, and but for Thermidor might have suffered the same fate as Custine. But Bonaparte, with that singular patience he was so often to display during his married life with Josephine, bided his time, like the true soldier he was; and soon the fact that Sièyes' associates were by no means disinterested began to attract attention. Bonaparte may have hesitated to throw grenadiers into the assembly, but he had no hesitation whatever in relegating Sièyes to the presidency of the Senate in order to assume complete power himself in a matter for which, after all, he bore the full responsibility.

But the first consul could not change the pact concluded between politicians and financiers. The former were comfortably esconced in the Senate with a permanent income. The financiers had their bank, the *Banque de France*, in which they held magnificent directorships enabling them to keep the advantages of credit exclusively to themselves and to their friends; these advantages had cautiously been kept secret because the bankers refused, at first uncompromisingly, to take charge of the French economy. Parisians all, they were interested only in Paris, their Parisian friends and a few provincial notables. Above all a magnificent concession had been made to the bankers: the *Banque de France* was to take over the *Caisse des Comptes courants*. This had been dissolved, and the bank's working capital, which was vital for a large circulation of paper money, would have to be much more substantial than that of the *Caisse*. Thirty millions were needed, of which the bankers had put up only two millions. The state alone could provide the rest. In England the financiers of the bank had lent to the state, but in France the state lent to the financiers of the bank. The bank's cash balance, in fact, was ensured by realizable assets, by the securities of the Treasury's Receivers-General, by receipts from tolls and duties and by the proceeds of the state lottery: this was a return to the financial techniques of the old régime, basing credit on the cycle of taxation. Thus, the society of the Consulate had much in common with that of the old régime: dynasties reappeared, dynasties of senators, only too pleased for the Consul to adopt the hereditary principle for his office, since they were eager to establish it on their own account; and dynasties of financiers unobtrusively introducing their own hereditary succession into the governing body of the *Banque de France*. Both dynasties were content to see the Consul aspiring to the Empire, since they were delighted at the opportunity it would give them to sport the finery of counts, dukes and princes.

Mollien, however, rightly denounced the narrow-mindedness of these 'fifteen heads of business houses who brought to the bank only a concern for their own affairs, and who assessed the future of the bank only in terms of their own personal fortune'. No great skill was needed to make credit available to industrialists out of the state's money and the proceeds of taxation. It was no more than had been done by the financiers of Louis xv, in fact by all those of the old régime, from Jacques Coeur onwards. It would have been better to choose other men with a wider outlook, but perhaps they had emigrated to Italy or England. At any rate they were not to be found in that 'arid, sandy waste', which was how Bonaparte described French society in 1800. It was the very mediocrity of these *parvenus* which eventually led to the curtailment of their ill-earned privileges after the crisis of the 'united merchants' in 1805. A governor of the *Banque de France*, Deprez, had persuaded the bank to pay good notes for the promised Mexican piastres, which never got safely across the sea because of the battle of Trafalgar. The new franc was again subject to the risks of Law's system: Napoleon imposed a governor of his own choice on the bank and ordered it to open branch banks. In short it was to follow a policy which would serve imperial France more effectively and the interests of the governors less exclusively.

Although the basis of the new French financial credit was restricted, it was fairly sound. This time the technical as well as the legal conditions of the Code were fulfilled, since Mollien had taken a lesson from England and safeguarded them effectively. This newly found credit developed all the better because the army, founded in the crisis at the end of the eighteenth century, was not disbanded and in the course of its military advance through Europe introduced into the French, that is the Parisian, market something of the economy of continental countries. Napoleon was only a soldier; he brought military solutions to the problem and those military solutions were accepted by civilians whose business concerns they affected. A peaceful Empire would have been quite inconceivable in 1805.

Neither the mediocre Sièyes nor the detested Talleyrand could possibly have organized the immense changes involved in bringing back the enormous numbers of soldiers under arms into the factories, mills and countryside. We know how severely the 1785 crisis had hit France because it had developed so late compared with England, and because it had a surplus population which ended up in the army rather than in industry. In 1805 it was even further behind. Had the *Banque de France* been founded in 1720 at about the same time as the Bank of England (although this was of course inconceivable at the time), its credit would possibly have been enough to stave off the French political crisis. In 1800, it came too late to repair in a few years the results of a hundred years' time lag. The French economy needed the war, with its expedients and its blockade, in order to take advantage of a continental market even more backward than its own was compared with England. It could not have existed in a framework of European liberty, which was the real reason why no serious protest was ever made against the Napoleonic adventures. The Emperor could play about with his soldiers just as he pleased, since no-one in France would have known what to do with them if they had been returned to civilian life.

Thanks, however, to the providential blockade, French activity awoke from the lethargy of the Revolution. It experienced some periods of brilliant success and dominated the rest of the continent. It would be all too easy at this point to pour out floods of statistics. We know that Napoleon liked to keep an inventory of the civilian population as he did of his troops. He naïvely assumed that a prefect could state how many citizens were at work, and what kind of work they were doing, just as a general can account for his soldiers, his ammunition, and the uses to which they are being put. He sent out questionnaires and demanded replies within a fortnight – only just about time to put a few approximate figures on paper. It was less risky for a prefect to over-estimate his Department than for a general to over-estimate his resources.

The career of a typical industrialist will illustrate the rapid growth which followed the blockade. Charles Ballot gives the main facts about the life of Ternaux. He was the son of a Sedan wool manufacturer, a man unfortunate in business who had been set on his feet again by Guillaume Louis to such good purpose that, even in 1789, he employed more than three thousand workers, some concentrated in the town itself, but a large number dispersed throughout the surrounding districts. Though he supported the legal revolution enthusiastically at first, in 1792 Ternaux protested against the treatment meted out to the king, and left France in some haste in order to escape the fate of his colleagues of the municipality who perished on the scaffold for taking the same attitude. He contrived to liquidate his assets on fairly good terms, and was apparently able to get most of his capital out of the country in gold. At any rate, he opened a business house at Leghorn in order to sell German cloth in Italy, a not unprofitable venture. He visited Germany and England, where he observed the new mechanization. He returned to France under the Directory and tried to restart his business, although in somewhat desultory fashion. Under the Consulate he increased his fortune, especially in Sedan, and made his business one of the finest in France. From Sedan he turned his attention to Rheims, where he took two people into partnership, for he needed the high-class cloth which was made only in the city. In the Rheims area, all the work was done in the countryside. Ternaux and his partners regrouped the workers into a huge new factory in the city and provided them with English looms. Then began a period of outstanding success furthered by the blockade. He bought a secularized convent here, an abandoned warehouse there, or a whole plant which was rusting away. In Paris he and his brother opened a large joint business-house, which was the nucleus of the whole concern. In short, from Sedan to Louviers, from Verviers to Leghorn, all the wool in continental Europe came in the sphere of influence of this brilliant French businessman. In a former convent in the rue Mouffetard he proceeded at vast expense to try out machinery made by Douglas or Cockerill. With the help of several ingenious colleagues, he himself invented an apparatus for dyeing. With considerable daring he ordered fleeces by the land route from central Asia for super-luxury goods. He secured tools and workmen from Spain for bleaching merino wool, which had only just been introduced into France. He acted as adviser to the imperial administration which showered medals upon him. He recommended everywhere the machines he had proved successful. He was the first to try out great concentrations of workers, which were still considered rather risky. He had fifteen hundred workers at Ensival, and five or six thousand in Rheims (and the number was increasing); he expanded his business from Leghorn towards Genoa and Naples and from Bayonne to Lisbon. He controlled Germany, visited Russia, and opened a mill in St Petersburg. It should be noted that the shrewd Ternaux made widespread use of what was to be known as a trust eighty years later; theoretically independent businesses were created, each with its own commercial reason for existing, and in which Ternaux did not figure by name; but in reality he directed them because he controlled their capital. The establishment in Paris only had a small number of employees but inevitably became the centre of this vast network with its ramifications throughout Europe. It was in Paris that the markets, and more important still, the credits, were shared out; it was both a bank and an exchange whose existence was closely linked with that of the continent. This immense structure of industry and credit was solid enough to withstand political crisis. Ternaux continued to be the model industrialist under the Restoration, and in the closing years of his life, under Louis-Philippe, the aged Rouget de Lisle, still a prolific hymn-writer, composed for him the *Chant des Industriels*.

There were under the Empire a few other businesses similar to Ternaux's, such as those of Bauwens and Richard Lenoir, but their numbers were fewer than in England. It should be added that Ternaux, being a wool merchant, was in a privileged position. Cotton merchants had had no difficulty in dominating the continent, imposing high prices forced on them by a blockade which cut off their supplies of raw material. Then, before they had completed the courageous process of converting their plant from cotton to wool, the fall of the Empire brought a drop in prices so that the return of free cotton ruined them. Ternaux himself had had some experience of the limitations and dangers of imperial protection; his business in St Petersburg and Lisbon collapsed even before the end of the Empire. Richard Lenoir's bankruptcy was complete and total.

Nevertheless, the temporary success of very large business enterprises led to great innovations, especially in the introduction of steam-engines. The first great factory was that of Périer's, built on the hill at Chaillot near the steam-pump which had been supplying the western quarters of Paris with water since the early years of Louis xvi's reign. The mills at Chaillot made not only heavy plant, but mining equipment (which replaced the armies of horses previously used) or rolling-mills and even parts for organ-builders; but these mills almost went bankrupt during the Revolution. Orders had flowed in from the revolutionary government (especially for guns), but instead of the half million in cash they had been promised, they were merely entered in the great debt book for three per cent stock! There again it was the Empire, its protectionist policy, its blockade and its credit (the state bills were discounted by the *Banque de France*), which at Chaillot and elsewhere in France saved Périer's various enterprises. Other flourishing businesses were started in Lyons and Digoin, and it was claimed that French steam-engines were even better than those of Watt.

Strangely enough, the French metal industry did not share the trend of progress in textiles or in the use of steam. Le Creusot, the outstanding success of the old régime, made no innovations until about 1830, and France made no move to introduce coke smelting. 'Those who so glibly suggest the substitution of mineral fuel for vegetable coal', wrote a metallurgist in 1814, 'seem to have no idea that it will involve an almost total reconstruction of the blast furnaces, refineries, machinery, and workshops . . .' This was a task obviously beyond the means of French industrial credit, so that France's metal industry continued to operate on the old lines with very little cast steel and almost everything in wrought iron, forged in tiny foundries scattered all over France. The price of this iron, which was in great demand and produced in small quantities, rose in France as much as it dropped in England. The products were no better, and the ironmasters were no richer, since wood was dear and came from forests that had been over-exploited, and capital resources were too closely bound up with the land. This landed capital brought in large returns only at the cost of deforestation, and was thus self-destructive.

Dearer cotton and dearer iron were two factors which explained the dissatisfaction of ambitious industrialists. The consumer had to protest against the high prices resulting from the economy of the blockade. In Europe as a whole and even in France industry was becoming strong enough in 1812 to stand up to English competition in textiles, and obviously had more to gain than to lose from a resumption of liberal economic relations across the North Sea. Napoleon was well aware that he was helping to keep the malcontents quiet by allowing so many infringements of his blockade, but these breaths of fresh air were by no means enough to satisfy an economy which was becoming increasingly self-confident. The point at issue was the system itself: was it worth while to conscript all those thousands of men into the army when industry could perhaps make good use of them? People said that the blockade, all things considered, was doing more harm than good. They were getting tired of the war and felt confident (sometimes rather blindly) in the possibilities of an economic peace, especially since France also experienced the crisis of 1811–13; as usual, the severity of the crisis was attributed more to the political régime than to the actual structure of expanding capitalism.

Thus the very notables who had summoned General Bonaparte, thrust him into a position of power for life and then made his position hereditary, were now beginning to complain about the ogre. They plotted and barely concealed their impatience after the *débâcle* of Moscow. They were ready for a change, and for a return to the political situation as it had been, provided of course that their property, their code, and their place in the social hierarchy was guaranteed, and that the privileged few were allowed to retain their hereditary titles.

It was this that made the return of Louis xviii very much simpler. The monopoly of the Bank was to be confirmed and even extended, the governor once more becoming the tool of the directors, while the provincial branch-banks (which Paris regarded as costly and almost useless) were to be suppressed; the imperial Senate would move up en bloc to the House of Peers, and the King would then be able to settle into the usurper's chair without undue dislocation of the economy. The return of the Eagle was a bad business, the Bank refused to co-operate, credit went underground and the great ones fled. The officers on half-pay and a group of liberal-minded patriots did, it is true, attempt to create a new constitution, but they could no longer rely on the powerful conspirators of 1799. In the House of Peers, established again after Waterloo, it was the former conspirators who were the most ruthless at the time of Ney's trial.

All things considered, those who had done well out of the economy had been right not to fear peace and the return of Anglo-European collaboration. From 1815 to 1820 French industry was in better shape than that of England. Lyons, Lille (and the mining towns of Roubaix and Tourcoing, which were growing as rapidly as Manchester), Normandy, and of course all the ports, took on an air of modern prosperity. In Paris there was speculation in everything, including patterned fabrics, perfumery, luxury materials, corn and iron. A great wooden shed was hastily erected to deal with the sale of Stock Exchange securities and state funds, into which, in response to the appeal launched by the Rothschilds and Laffitte, flowed the savings which had accumulated during the blockade. The shops were lit up at night, to the delight of foreigners who were always fascinated by that exquisite French taste which made the fortune of the merchants. Though heavy industry developed only slowly, merchants were rapidly growing rich. In peasant workshops in Auvergne they collected cloths and fabrics woven by employees in their own homes from the raw materials with which the merchants had supplied them, and they operated on the same system in Flanders and Cambrésis. Skilfully exploiting the cheapness of rural labour to bring down prices in the big factories, the merchants then made these the excuse for lowering the country worker's wages still more, so that the poor man soon had to set his entire family to work long hours in order to make his old loom produce the money needed to supplement the income from his inadequate little field. In Paris, in the cities and in the trading ports, however, the middle-class businessman was thriving, and displayed his luxurious possessions in the sumptuous mansions which former aristocrats, who had now been ruined, let out in flats or sold to speculators.

With the coming of peace, the consumers' markets were greatly expanded. Officials, clerks and a whole lower middle class of artisans, shopkeepers, officials and employees bought specially treated cotton or Calais linen so that they looked as if they dressed in silk. Stendhal rightly noted in France what Carlyle noted in England: a transformation of society the like of which had not been seen for four hundred years. Among the lower classes, there were growing up innumerable families who managed to imitate the aristocratic way of life in some way or other.

Nothing is so persistent as a nation's taste. The France of 1820 still remained true to the impeccable taste which for two hundred years had characterized the Louvre and Versailles. The label 'quality' was applied to both noble blood and to good merchandise. Work done by hand in a craftsman's shop or in a family workshop, even when the articles concerned were only cheap, were regarded as very superior to shoddy English trash, turned out by some anonymous machine. The shopkeeper, who shared this attitude, encouraged the natural trend to hand-made goods. This in turn reinforced the lack of enterprise of the industrialists, who were in no hurry to change their way of doing things. The lesson of Colbert had been too thoroughly learned to be really understood. France produced luxury goods for the lower middle classes, as she had formerly produced them for the courts of Europe.

These 'luxury goods', however, had to fall in price all the time if they were to be produced in ever-increasing quantities. More and more workmen were being absorbed by the small artisans' workshops; wages were very low, and very little trouble was taken to give the workmen a thorough training. In spite of this, in the absence of a courageous policy of mechanization these cheap luxury goods were much dearer than the corresponding English article. Though some might sell in London where fashion and snobbery made them popular, they could barely hold their own, even in France, against English products. This explains why the chief aim of French economists was to protect French 'quality' against the unfair competition of English mechanization. The apprehensive demands of the old corporate spirit had been transferred to a national scale; and they were soon translated into a systematic protectionist policy.

Under the Revolution and the Empire, protectionism had been introduced under the guise of patiotism and had brought wealth to the new
middle class. After the Restoration it assumed the prestige of tradition. At
first d'Artois did indeed try to re-establish international commercial exchanges, but from 1816 to 1826 customs duties were imposed and increased. Both the aristocrat who sold timber from his forests and the owner
of a small iron-foundry were anxious to impose duties amounting to 120
per cent on iron smelted in English coal blast-furnaces. Duties on coal were
lower, since France got very little from the Loire and Anzin mines, but
they were high enough to ensure colliery profits and slow down the progress
of iron-smelting with coal. The superiority of French silk was assured:
consequently there were no restrictions, but cotton fabrics were absolutely
prohibited.

Thus under the Restoration the state was still the indispensable protector of industry, just as the king had been the protector of the guilds.
The whole administrative machine invented by the old régime and rebuilt by the Empire continued its role of promoting and controlling industrial activity. Civil engineers, mining engineers, foresters and surveyors
trained by the polytechnics and the mining schools (including that of
St Etienne) inspected, granted or refused permission for new installations,
drew up reports for the government on measures of a general nature, and
brought useful inventions to the notice of their ministers. In short they
kept an eye on activities in general and based their recommendations on
their conscientiously compiled statistics and on the battery of forms so
dear to the administrative mind. Meanwhile the courts based their judgements on the Civil Code, which as we have seen was better at dealing
with questions of landed property than of industry; and in any lawsuit
almost always pronounced in favour of the owner of the field or meadow
against the industrialist who wished to use water from the river for his
mill. Provided the French middle classes could control the state, they were
content to see it clamp down with all its authority on progress.

But now in 1828 the ruling aristocracy wanted to put noblemen in all
the high administrative posts. The great feudal landowners wanted to
take over all the responsibilities of the monarchy. The administration
even drew up a liberal scale of tariffs on the pretext of bringing down
internal prices. It was obviously a favourable moment for the landed
nobility who had been untouched by the crisis which was now sweeping
over France just as it had swept over England earlier; but a bad one for
the lower middle classes who were feeling its effects. They began to complain of tyranny. Old feuds flared up between the merchant and the aristocrat, between the shopkeeper and the court. The young journalist Thiers
rapidly made a name for himself in politics. The elections went against
the king, who was anxious that the trade licence of an industrialist or merchant should no longer count as a qualification for the electoral roll, a
proposal embodied in the Third Ordinance which was one of the causes
of the revolution of 1830.

When the progressive Thiers came to power he tried in vain to introduce into France industrial freedom on English lines, and particularly freedom of trade, the lowering of tariffs and the stimulus of economic competition. Some of his reforms were accepted; for instance, after the rapid development of cotton weaving it became possible to import cotton warp; but within a very short time strong coalitions of interests again brought together the protectionist allies of 1820, the landed proprietors, metallurgists, shopkeepers and artisans. The English crisis of 1840 was even more fatal to Thiers in the sphere of economics than of politics. Guizot reassured industry and France went back to the guardian state which meant peace and security – or did until the crisis which began in 1846. The new government thought of lowering protective tariffs, and steps were taken to bring this about in 1847, but only tentatively, since the monarchy of Louis-Philippe fell before it could be carried through.

Beneath these changes of régime, the increasing cohesion of the administration was maintained. The administration sent out questionnaires, collected important information about English methods and practice, and made every effort to disseminate them in all earnestness. It gave particular encouragement to the early attempts at coke smelting and to the use of coal in iron foundries. It organized exhibitions with the collaboration of the chambers of trade and the Society for the Promotion of National Industry. It continued, in short, to control activity throughout France, that curious country which rebelled so bitterly against political authority only to fall the more readily under the sway of administrators. Not that the latter were without merit. They had the finest mathematical training in the world, they built many new schools, they encouraged initiative by the offer of prizes and developed educational facilities in the academies in Paris and Lyons at a time when England had not a single school of engineering; they carried out experiments the results of which, in a typically French way, were studied with a view to acquiring a clearer grasp of the theory that lay behind them.

It is understandable that in such conditions the problem of credit was solved in ways entirely different from those adopted in England. The bank expanded very little. The first move the *Banque de France* made under the Restoration was to close its provincial branches, and it was with something approaching reluctance that it reopened fifteen of them after 1836, driven to do so by the rapid progress of the large iron and textile areas. Its policy, nevertheless, remained extremely rigid, in striking contrast to the freedom with which notes of all kinds were allowed to circulate in England. In France, parallel with the issuing bank, there were the influential private banks in Paris, run by a handful of aristocrats and great landowners, which are still known today as *la haute banque*. These were at one and the same time stimulating and cautious. They included a considerable number of newcomers: Jews, Swiss and English, and did very little business in the provinces. There, small capitalists, solicitors, landowners, merchants, and sometimes industrialists formed associations to provide the necessary floating capital. But there could be no question of very big deals. It was not until the thirties that industrial concerns like Le Creusot, technically well equipped since the end of Louis XVI's reign, could emerge from the grim series of bankruptcies which in France affected even excellent English technicians between 1780 and 1830. Even the mines in the north of France emerged only by a miracle from a series of financial difficulties, which explains their desire for inflexible customs duties.

Whilst in England appeal for capital by joint-stock companies had met with great success, this system was almost unknown in France. A joint-stock company could be founded only after three favourable reports by a commission specially selected by the Council of State and the Minister of the Interior. Almost always, where the best businesses were concerned, major arguments were produced to prevent the company from being set up. In moderately important businesses, resort was made to the old procedure of the *commenda* already laid down by Savary and Colbert. This was the method by which a joint-stock company had to be set up.

There had also been surprisingly little development in insurance in France; life and fire insurance had existed in England and Germany since the beginning of the eighteenth century. In France a tentative attempt had been made to introduce them on the eve of the French Revolution, but had failed. It was not until the end of the Restoration that insurance really began to take root in France, and even then only because a great number of foreign companies had established themselves in the country to exploit the French market. On the other hand, the French system of government stock was brilliantly successful. People like Balzac's '*Père Grandet*' bought stock. The Paris *bourse* speculated particularly in stock. Thus roads and canals were not built, as in England, by private initiative; in France they could be constructed only by the *Ponts-et-Chaussées*, which was financed from the state budget.

This was the paradoxical situation in France; it was continually changing its government, and was continually critical of fiscal arrangements but nevertheless put its sole trust in the administration and state credit. This was in fact a prolongation into the mid-nineteenth century of the situation we noted in 1780, a country at the meeting place of two great economic systems: that of England, dominated by public opinion, and that of Germany, where economic power preserved a despotic structure.

Nevertheless new equipment and methods were introduced into France in spite of all these procrastinations; industry emerged in a stronger position from each of the economic crises which took the form of political revolutions in France. Modern methods of iron-smelting were introduced in the forties, particularly around the Massif Central, in the east and the north. Many small family concerns had to close down in face of the competition from the new blast-furnaces and rolling-mills. Similarly vast concentrations of textile industries sprang up around new centres like Roubaix and Tourcoing. Mulhouse was an excellent example of creative effort, comparable to the most ambitious of English ventures. In 1828 Charles X called Mulhouse the capital of French industry and in 1846 Heilmann's carding-machine attracted the attention of manufacturers all over the world to Mulhouse. It was near the newly awakening Germany but was separated from it by such rigid customs barriers that a Western manufacturer declared it was easier for a camel to pass through the eye of a needle than for a needle to get into France.

That gives an indication of the extent of French protectionist policy and of the unifying role of the administration. The raw materials essential for industry in Alsace had to be brought by long hauls from Le Havre, rather than from the nearby Rhine. The difficulties which French geography put in the way of the co-ordination of industry were one reason for the severity of protectionism and French bureaucracy. The extent of these impositions could be judged by the number of wagon convoys making their way across the country; France was huge by the European standards of the time, but gained little help from its contours and its rivers.

Hence the importance of the constuction of the railways, which were to reshape the economic map of Europe. Some were started in the forties, and opened up a completely new age just as decisively as they had done in England, perhaps even more so.

FEUDALISM IN GERMANY

In 1785, as we have seen, a new Prussia emerged, centred on Berlin. It was to undergo many vicissitudes before its eventual triumph: for although the central European economy had been brilliant in the gay days of the old Nuremberg, the variety and importance of its resources at the opening of the nineteenth century had hardly affected its archaic structure. Its map, even more than that of France and England, bore the imprint of history. The whole of the Rhine valley with its attractive scenery, its village fêtes, its vineyards and its trade, was reminiscent of France. Beyond the Elbe and the Oder, the forest which fringed the cultivated zones was a reminder of the comparatively recent date of the agricultural settlements on the edge of the Slavonic clearings. In the north, polders and dikes, pumps and windmills and village houses, strung out in line according to the exigences of irrigation, showed the influence of Holland. In the centre, the vast stretch of open country, with its clustered villages and its strips of land divided up in accordance with the old tradition of three-year rotation of crops, betrayed the persistence of the forms of collective agriculture that have left their traces also in Lorraine.

There was not one but several Germanies. Not that the political states which shared out these plains and varied uplands so unevenly between them made any attempt to conform to the boundaries of this economic maze. It was rather that each state included within its borders both urban and rural traditions, as well as a variety of landscape; as if each one had enlarged its old Germanic core with conquests to east or west and with settlements on newly colonized lands. This was even more pronounced in the east than in the west, where a more western structure preserved the independence of traditions and increased the number of compact little states, duchies, free towns and ecclesiastical principalities. In Prussia the fragmentary structure of the lands inherited by the German dynasties could be seen in miniature, and the variety of domains that ensued seemed better protected in the east by the protective and paternal Empire than in the west. Germany as a whole showed little sign of the progress that Arthur Young admired. It seemed as if it was still too enmeshed in past history to be ready to enter the industrial era.

The combined population of the twelve largest cities in Germany barely equalled that of London or Paris. Almost eighty per cent of the German people were, it is true, dispersed over the countryside. Urban development was hampered by the rural structure, for just as each village formed a compact group in the centre of the lands for whose collective cultivation it was responsible, so too many cities such as Berlin were primarily composed of farms exploiting the surrounding lands. It would not give the right impression to say that German cities were large country towns. To a Frenchman a country town is a commercial rather than an agricultural entity; the produce of the land is sold there, it is true, and rural progress is given a certain stimulus; but the French country town is not the collective owner of the land. Almost everywhere in Germany the bonds uniting the small town with the surrounding countryside were very close; they formed a single community for which tradition, strengthened by the laws of the princes, fixed in detail the class and occupation of each inhabitant. The peasant could not set up a shop in the town, nor the craftsman from the town take up agriculture. Each given community had its fixed quota of bakers, butchers, harness-makers and blacksmiths. The peasant belonged to the peasant class and the artisan was immutably fixed in his artisan class. Private ownership rarely succeeded in breaking into this closely knit society of rigid traditions. The capitalist merchant made little headway except in the largest urban centres, and even there he had to worm his way in between the innumerable corporate regulations and privileges which kept each man in his place, forbade competition and prevented centralization.

Ever since the eighteenth century many princes had tried to encourage individual ownership – an easy task both in the extreme east and the extreme west, but for opposite reasons. In the east, the conquest of the Slav lands had benefited those, like the country squires of Frederick II, who not only owned the lowland serfs but also ruled the towns; and it had especially benefited the direct owners of fairly large estates which they were gradually learning to farm in the English way. In the west the smallness of the states which were stimulated by competition with the Rhineland or Hanover, and their ready access to information because each minor prince had his industrial advisers (Hanover was directly influenced by London), had contributed to the prosperity of the merchants and of the owners of medium or large farms, which were also worked by modern methods. The task was not so simple in the small courts of Saxony and the south, particularly in Bavaria, where the old system of small country estates persisted, a régime which, though less profitable, was equally tenacious. But though the agriculture of the old Germany had some westernized enclaves, industry had not yet felt the impact of the West.

The metal industry of the Westphalian countryside which became so famous at the end of the century was still being carried on in conditions similar to those under which craftsmen were working in Paris and the provinces. At Solingen knives were made by the dozen, but only to order. The metal did not come in bulk from blast-furnaces, but was smelted at home, by charcoal of course. When orders were scarce, the blacksmith in his leather jacket worked in his fields. In the east, especially in country districts, the Saxon and Silesian cloth industries had only very old-fashioned looms scattered all over the region, dependent on a few merchants in the towns (the forerunners of the great twentieth-century merchants) who drove around the flat countryside in covered carts distributing raw material and order-sheets, and collecting the goods when manufactured. Often, in those 'extremely progressive' regions, which were almost entirely free from the old constraints of class, the peasant could have a loom, and stabilize his income by working through the winter.

There was no sign that the Industrial Revolution was at hand, and no hint of changes like those taking place in England. Even the crisis of 1785–95 stifled the Colbertian attempts of Frederick II and the enlightened despots by forcing a return to the old ways.

Not that the cities were uninterested in progress. In 1798 the works of Albrecht Thaes, who purported to explain the methods of English agriculture to his fellow countrymen, met with some success. The great landowners derived some benefits from it. Soon this body of information was circulating in the universities (Thaes was professor in the University of Berlin from 1809 to 1812). Ministers were influenced by his teaching, and they not only proposed the marling of sandy soils, the advantages of potatoes or beetroot, and the careful selection of stock in breeding cattle and sheep, but also the legal reform of the law about land.

It was into this curious medieval Germany that the French revolutionary forces erupted. Once the army of the princes was disbanded, since Austria was powerless and Prussia remained hesitant, Hoche, Moreau and Napoleon swept from victory to victory. The west was able to put up a stouter resistance because of the solidity of its urban organization, as Custine learned to his cost, but once that dike had been breached, the troops spread out where they wished, even as far as the plains of Poland. Moreover in the towns the common people eagerly welcomed the popular revolutions, while in the rural principalities the frightened and apathetic princes were taken by surprise.

Once victory was achieved the French occupation in western Germany found an economy sufficiently like that of France to ensure the triumph of the new administration and the new Code. All along the Rhine French prefects or the king of Westphalia built admirable roads in networks graded like those of France. They introduced the new legal system, and freed the peasant from the lingering remnants of feudalism. They applied the Cartesian principles of the French officials to municipal administration. The prestige of French currency and credit was all that was then needed to modernize the Rhineland, since it was ripe for these changes. Farther east the situation was not the same. Whether the princes in their anxiety hastened to join the French alliance, even to the extent of furnishing contingents of troops, or whether they passively waited for the victors to impose their terms, the old social structure baffled the imperial administrators, who could not, in fact, do without the local dynasties if they were to conduct business at all. Thus Prussia could be dismembered and lose the outlying western possessions which were too far from the centre, but she could not be suppressed. Napoleon, east of the Elbe, could act only in accordance with the old feudal system: he was forced to abandon all thought of direct rule.

Nevertheless, in those areas which were not affected by French activity, French ideas still made a certain impact, backed as they were by the prestige of brilliant victories. Moreover in Bavaria, Swabia, Saxony, and especially in Prussia, the advantages of private ownership, free enterprise and codes abolishing serfdom appeared all the more attractive since the French legal system facilitated the introduction of technical improvements learnt from England. This marked the beginning of the slow, difficult and spasmodic emancipation of the German peasants. In fact, the French Code had succeeded in France, and partially succeeded in western Germany, only because its way had been prepared by much past history, and by a hundred years of progress of which it was merely the culminating point. Elsewhere, even in anglicized Hanover, any ruler who might have wished to follow in the footsteps of Joseph II would have been similarly disillusioned. Reforms were not introduced into Hanover until 1831. Elsewhere there were quarrels, discussions of principle and interminable debates; in Brandenberg, for example, Marwitz was torn between his fear of exposing the defenceless peasant to violent capitalist competition and his desire to bring new vigour to the state.

This was the climate that prepared the way for the cautious Prussian legislation of 1807 and 1808, and explained the courageous attempts and the disappointments of liberal ministers and the difficulties and evasions of the dynasties in southern Germany. It explained, too, the fragmentary and incomplete character of the reforms attempted in 1807, 1808, 1811 and 1821, but not carried out until 1860. It was the colonized lands in the east, where the authority of the Junkers was paramount (based both on ownership of private lands and on authority over the serfs of the communal villages) which made the easiest transition from the old régime to the new capitalist régime. This explains the relative modernity of Prussia compared with the small states of central Germany.

The liberation of the peasants was not achieved without hardship on their part. The traditionalist country squire made extensive use of his rights to induce the serf to work on his land, which the latter was the more ready to do since the squire continued to supply him with certain commodities which had otherwise to be bought commercially, or protected him against war and above all against famine. The squire exacted from his peasant not gold, which was extremely rare, but provisions in kind of a sort which would not upset the economic balance of the village. Reformers who were familiar with conditions in France and England realized the advantages of a redistribution of land which involved suppressing the common lands, and breaking up the collective villages. It enabled them to enlarge and enclose their own estates and carry out improvements which increased German agricultural returns by more than five per cent from 1800 to 1815 and by more than fifty per cent from 1785 to 1850.

Thus the land began to produce bigger harvests after 1820. Stretches of waste land were cleared and marshes were drained and methodically farmed. Above all two new crops, potatoes and sugar beet, made astonishing progress. Merino sheep were an outstanding success; by 1830 Saxony was breeding more than any other country, surpassing the France of Rambouillet and even Spain. There were fewer horned cattle but more good meat and good leather. The population increased. This increase, already apparent even before 1830, presented the old Germany with unexpected problems. The squire, of course, the new large-scale landowner, used paid labour, but not in sufficient numbers to provide a steady livelihood for all these extra people who were no longer protected by the old paternal feudal traditions. The surplus population had to build up its life outside the old class barriers, and was to form the nucleus of the new industrial force.

Here and there industry showed fresh signs of life, in places where it already had deep historical roots, especially in Silesia. It was a prosperous time for the merchants, who sold good wool-cloths not only throughout the whole of Germany but also in the external markets which they were gradually penetrating. This trade formed the basis for the great commercial capitalism of nineteenth-century Germany; its origins were modest but it soon grew in importance. Westphalian industry felt the repercussions of this extension of markets and surplus manpower. In 1821 the Prussian Government set up a *Gewerbe Institut*, the counterpart of France's *Conservatoire des Arts-et-Métiers*, to spread the new industrial techniques. It attempted to extend the original French road system from one end of the monarchy to the other, and succeeded in doing so in the western half. The problem of capital was a difficult one: nevertheless, after 1830 prosperity stimulated a remarkable accumulation of capital in the towns.

In 1830 Borsig, a former pupil of the *Gewerbe Institut*, opened a foundry in Berlin: by 1847 he was already employing 1,300 workers. In the Rhineland, at Ruhrort and Oberhausen at about the same date, ventures on a similar scale introduced smelting by coke using English methods, and made Westphalian steel famous for its high quality. Sometimes peasants who had previously been blacksmiths became paid workers. At Essen the foundations of Krupp's fortune were being laid. A more sensible way of mining coal was already being adopted: in 1793 each coal mine employed on an average three to five workmen, then larger concentrations developed, and the total number of miners in Germany quadrupled between 1837 and 1845. The output of these men gradually increased as more steam-engines

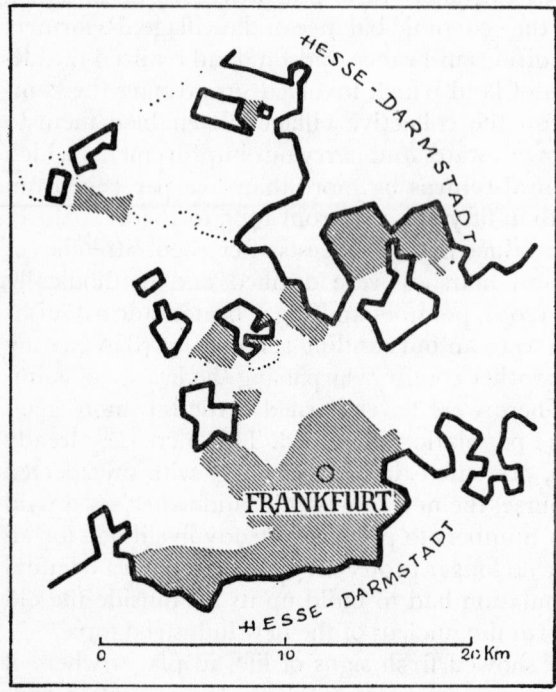

6 Political Divisions in Germany c. 1820

Grey: areas belonging to the city of Frankfurt
Bordered by thick line: areas dependent on Hesse-Darmstadt

came into use. Finally, since capital attracts capital, the success of the metal industry attracted to the Rhineland the textile industry, which had already established itself at Elberfeld and Crefeld by 1845.

We saw that Frederick II attempted, in the eighteenth century, to imitate Colbert. With this impetus, Germany continued to advance until the opening of the nineteenth century, and in the next half-century the founding of a western system of land-ownership and liberalism replaced mercantilism.

This was the background of the German revolution of 1830: a liberal constitution introduced representatives of commerce and industry into the princes' governments; above all, throughout the whole of Germany, the development of modern activity led to an increased circulation of goods, with a wider appeal to more extensive markets.

But to go back to 1815: trade was at that time hampered by the multiplicity of customs barriers. So long as the economy had remained crystallized around small towns living in an almost closed system, this multiplicity of duties strengthened the authority of the princes and justified the fragmentation of the country: each princely family, often divided into several branches, administered its state as a landowner does his estate. But Prussia, because she was really a state, had been the first to realize the need for customs reform. This could not be achieved independently in Prussia since it was split up by so many tiny independent principalities; in particular the main body of Prussia was separated from those possessions on the Rhine which had been granted it by the Congress of Vienna.

Then began Prussia's historic struggle to achieve a customs' union in northern Germany. At first the princes stood out against it. Their tiny enclaves which refused to be integrated into the Prussian customs system, and which relied on the Diet and the authority of Austria to defend their liberty, were then transformed into a veritable smugglers' paradise within the Prussian economy. The three *anhalts* in particular made a handsome fortune out of the Elbe, and it took twelve years of patient effort on Prussia's part to persuade the princes, one after the other, of the advantages of a common administration: the minor dukes only allowed themselves to be persuaded after having been granted exorbitant advantages. Nevertheless, gradually, the idea of a customs' unions gained ground. In

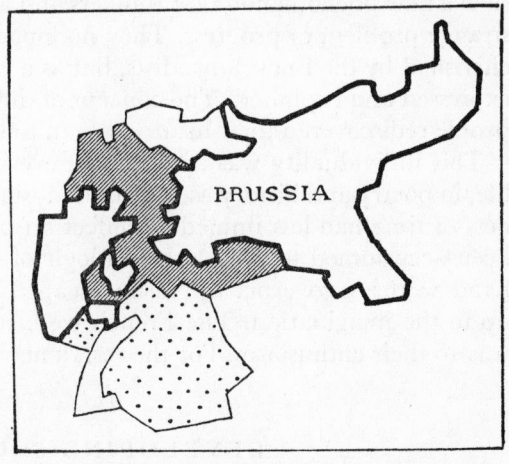

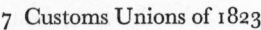
7   Customs Unions of 1823

Thick line: Prussian
Customs Union
Grey: Customs Union of
Hanover
Dotted: Customs Union of
Bavaria-Württemburg

opposition to it, however, another system of unification extending from Hamburg to Saxony cut it into two while at the same time, in southern Germany, Bavaria and Württemburg had united in a common organization orientated towards Austria.

The task on which the Prussian ministers were engaged called for the greatest patience; they tried to take advantage of every trifling difficulty experienced by the princely régimes. Whenever a crisis started in England and then touched off a political revolution or a ministerial crisis in France, it also led to structural modifications in the German economy and presented yet another opportunity to the advocates of union with Prussia. Soon the south was drawn into the Prussian system and the cohesion of the centre began to break down. From 1840, just as the development of railways was about to begin, Prussia's leading position in the customs system was no longer in dispute.

6
The Man of 1830

In 1830 Europe was shaken by a series of revolutions. They brought about no fundamental change in the political structure of the Continent, but they revealed the profound modifications which had already taken place after half a century of technical progress. The social hierarchy was no longer a stable reality fixed by an immutable decree of providence. It was a turmoil of ambitions, failures and successes, which were undermining the old *élites* in order to make way for the new ones. This rapidity of change was such a new phenomenon that thinkers and artists became fascinated by the strange problem of progress. They no longer saw it as an abstract idea so cherished by the Encyclopaedists, but as a concrete reality which could be expressed and exploited. The concept of time took on a new meaning, and people rediscovered their history, began to be aware of their individuality.

This individuality was apparent in every sphere, in family as in social life, in poetry and history as well as in music and painting. The new awareness of time had less immediate effect on peoples who for long years had been accustomed to the Cartesian logic of space; those who, on the other hand, were less governed by reason, escaped into this new dimension opened up to the imagination. The French were cautious but the Germans gave way to their enthusiasm. For the rest, a new spirit was everywhere abroad.

DEVELOPING SOCIETIES

Society in 1830 – the very words conjure up portraits by Ingres, caricatures by Daumier, noisy theatrical first nights, the flashy successes of worldly musicians and also the easily provoked revolutions in which Alexandre Dumas covered himself with glory. It was a tolerant and fanciful age, passionately searching for happiness; from 1815 to 1870, the arts profited from the long period of peace.

Yet this picture is too dated and unlike Paris as it actually was in the 1830s. There was in fact, no such thing as *a* society of 1830, any more than there had been a single *ancien régime* society from Dresden to Rome or from Prague to London in the heyday of cosmopolitanism. If one cannot point to a uniform society in the eighteenth century, it is even more difficult to do so in 1830. There was not *one* society, but a multiplicity of societies, looking for common ground but coming into conflict in the arena of experiment and experience that Europe had become in its transition from the traditional age of the past to the industrial age of the future. There were different rural societies from east to west, and the capitalist societies varied from city to city, and from nation to nation; and each of these separate societies was divided within itself into watertight compartments, mutually ignorant of each other. Cobbett's England may have seemed modern, but here and there were country districts in the north and east where small landed gentry still made their own beer and bread, and spun and wove their own cloth just as they did in feudal Germany. It is equally difficult to make an accurate assessment of rural society either in the France of François le Champi, in Germany or in Europe as a whole. About 1830, in a journey from west to east, from north to south, one would encounter in turn a fine modernized farm around its manor house subscribing to the *Annals of Agriculture*, and the most wretched peasant hovel owned by a serf in fact or law; and in the same place we may see a small well-to-do land-owner, already sporting a white cravat. All this world was moving slowly, but it was moving. The very small farm had almost disappeared from England at the very moment when it was becoming more firmly established in France, while Germany from its feudal tradition was evolving the beginnings of the medium-sized farm. Old and young alike were begin-ning to take an interest in the outside world, and the newspaper was be-ginning to reach a country public where groups met together to read it in common.

It is difficult to assess the moral basis of the society of the old régime. According to Montesquieu it was honour, a conception which lost its appeal at the end of the eighteenth century and changed its meaning in the nineteenth. It could hardly have been loyalty to God, loyalty to the king or loyalty to an eternal moral law, for these sentiments would not have been thought 'intelligent', and 'intelligent' was the fashionable adjective of the day. 'This age', wrote Carlyle, 'is neither heroic, nor philosophical, nor religious, nor moral. It is, more than any other, the mechanical age.' This tendency was evident throughout spiritual as well as material life; in other words the mechanistic conception which science was evolving had affected moral life. It was best shown in Bentham, who meticulously calculated pleasures and pains in order to prove to his own satisfaction that the balance was favourable to virtue, by which he meant wisdom applied to work. Ure went on to say that Providence has assigned to man the glorious function of immensely improving on the products of nature by skilful initiative. In this way a link was established between moral and industrial mechanics and between moral and commercial book-keeping.

In this world where industry and commerce were already being personi-fied everywhere as allegorical figures, proudly displayed on the façades of great new buildings and on the front pages of newspapers, and referred to in the edifying proclamations of private and public men, the universal criter-ion soon became the mutual trust which could be established between businessmen. This trust was based as much on business ability as on the honouring of a contract which was legally binding for the parties concerned. In England a man was said to be worth £1,000, £10,000, or £100,000. In France he was a man of first-rate or third-rate credit, a grading which determined his social career, his opportunities of accumulating capital, and his chance of getting a good discount. And side by side with the traditional organs of justice new institutions grew up; boards of directors of large business concerns, governing bodies of banks, and most important of all, the board of directors of the bank of issue. If a request for credit could surmount all these obstacles and be favourably received by the highest authority, the phrase used of a merchant that 'his word is worth its weight in gold' was literally true, since his request for credit ended in the issue of paper money which was everywhere accepted as the equivalent of gold. The new ambition was to have sound, reliable credit, and the new dream was to hold a directorship in one of the most influential companies.

A man with credit could enlist the wealth of others in addition to his own wealth. He could then be in the main stream of business: buying, selling, and increasing his capital. He borrowed to enlarge his sphere of action. He employed 100, 1,500, then 3,000 workmen. What was more difficult and even more praiseworthy, he commanded a market in which prices were aligned on those of the shrewdest dealer. It was up to him to choose carefully the nature of his business, the quality of his raw materials, his equipment and his partners. Steadily he climbed the ladder of the new aristocracy, that of industrial power. The grandfather was a peasant, the grandson was educated at a public school and ended by becoming a baron and a member of important councils ; such, with various origins and vicissitudes, was the career of the Peels, the Radcliffes, the Cobdens and all the rest of that influential and vigorous English society. This was also the *cursus honorum* of several ancestors of the great French textile families. They were successful because they followed the stream of progress: they were prepared to abandon the old traditional agriculture when necessary, they ordered hand-looms, they settled in the centre of the towns when mechanized industry, especially cotton, was concentrating there; and they aimed at a national and then an international market.

There was, however, a fundamental difference in this respect between France and England. Ever since the disastrous days of the Stuarts, who had misused their absolute power to confer upon themselves any number of financial privileges, English merchants had done their utmost to put their banks beyond the reach of royal greed. Democracy, according to Bentham, was necessary to reconcile the individual interests of the sovereign and the corporate interests of the financial aristocracy. Pitt (as we have seen) came to regret his excessive recourse to bank credit. The parliamentary régime was meticulously careful in respecting the free play of credit institutions. Gladstone refused to be a member of a commission on railways which he himself had urged should be set up, because his in-laws had powerful interests in railways.

In France the picture was quite different. The Bank, created just when the established power of the financiers balanced the rising power of Bonaparte, soon grew accustomed to a certain measure of subjection to the Emperor. In addition the successive changes in régime – republican, consular, imperial, monarchist, imperial again and finally parliamentary, first under a Bourbon and then under an Orleans prince – put the ruling aristocracy in a very unusual situation: there was always the fear that a revolution or a *coup d'état* might at any moment endanger its position. Virtue, in its eyes, consisted not in preserving as rigidly as possible the separation between political and economic power but, on the contrary, in maintaining the most rigid control of both at the same time. It would, naturally, be absurd to think that all the privileged people and all the politicians in England were as scrupulous as Gladstone, but the difference between English integrity and French shrewdness had so many consequences that it must be stressed.

It was Chateaubriand who said: 'Just as you can tell a stag's age by the branches on its antlers, so today you can tell how many places a man holds by the number of oaths he has taken.' After 1830 the stag's antlers sprouted more branches than ever. In 1835, Talleyrand remarked: 'Yesterday there were only six of us in the House of Peers . . . we were all former members of the National Assembly, and we were more than eighty years old.' On the governing body of the Bank, founders, or the descendants of founders, were in control. It was a demonstration of the superb skill and shrewdness of a small body of men who had succeeded in weathering every storm simply because they had happened to be present at every successive debate and every council which had selected the ruling powers of the various régimes. And this group brought to the parliamentary life of the 1830s the lessons of the republican, imperial, and monarchist years. No matter of moment could be put through without close agreement between political and industrial power, which the small body of men at the top were best placed to bring about. Credit was dispensed by the middle classes, but always with considerable assistance from taxation. If sometimes the state asked the Bank for too much, it was because the Bank had always asked for a great deal from the state. The best instance was to be afforded by the railways, financed by the state and run by private companies whose profits were guaranteed by the state. This arrangement was a survival of the liberal régime, as well as of habits of mind and traditions of work inherited from the old régime. It took England more than a century to free itself from its old ways and establish the credit of its currency and of its Bank on a relatively independent foundation; France, building up its parliamentary and bourgeois system in haste, had to use such materials as were left over from the monarchy and the style of the building was affected accordingly.

Each generation, of course, added new blood to the direct heirs of the old régime (now greatly aging), but it was easier in France to make a career in politics than in business. In England the parliamentary leaders had first proved their mettle in industrial life. The middle classes grew up in the shadow of power before actually crossing its threshold, and fame, esteem, and an effective hold over public opinion was sometimes achieved by men who remained outside all public office. The best example was probably the amazing Wilberforce, who could have made a brilliant career in Parliament, and who might well have been prime minister, had he not chosen to remain a private individual in order to launch his formidable and successful campaign against the slave trade and slavery. This initiated a magnificent movement of national unity, and converted innumerable English consuls who had formerly been procuring slaves into apostles of the freedom of labour; and this was at a time when there was an emigration movement of whites who were not at all anxious to enter into competition with the negro. The career of a Decazes, a Guizot or a Thiers in France, is in sharp contrast to this, since they first made their name in politics, and consolidated their fame by a term of office before they plunged so advantageously into the economic stream. Decazes achieved a dukedom before he built Decazeville. Those who, like the Périers and Laffittes, made their name in credit and industry before achieving political fame were far smaller in number. Even so, their early beginnings were closely connected with the opportunities for profit offered by the good old days of the *assignats* and national property. Whilst in England the origins of the influential families of the 1830s have to be sought much earlier than the eighteenth century, in France the new Gouin concerns, still very insecure in 1848, were an isolated instance of success achieved by a family already engaged in business in the provinces under the old régime. It is not exaggerating the contrast to say that the great French bourgeois rose to power within thirty years, and that they looked like *nouveaux riches* beside the English middle-class gentlemen whose fortunes had taken one hundred and fifty years to make. The roots of the new society were planted deep in the hothouses of imperial protection. The French economic tree did not take kindly to the open air. Just when Cobden was risking his fortune to ensure the triumph of free trade in England, French industrialists were fiercely protectionist. This was how Mimerel, a northern deputy, addressed the House: 'I like to think', he said, 'that it is not the Government's intention to disturb the nation's industry in its possession (*sic!*) of the country's custom.'

Obviously these habits were also the result of a difference in standards between English and French produce, though the latter had been superior to its rival even under Louis XVI. Then, too, as late as the middle of the nineteenth century, the consequences of customs of the old régime, whereby the bourgeoisie used law and jurisprudence to establish itself in France, were still operating; in England, however, it was almost in spite of the law that the middle classes were established. Of course the contrast with the English outlook was far more marked the farther east and the farther away from the Atlantic one went; ever since the sixteenth century the Atlantic had been bringing commercial and economic novelties to Europe. In Germany the real bankers were still the princes; they dominated with all the weight of their treasury the activities of any institutions which issued bank-notes. Apart from a few business centres, Hamburg, or Frankfurt, private credit remained hesitant and every enterprising businessman had first to take the road to the court. It was quite hopeless for the bourgeoisie to dream of breaking free from these restraints in 1848. Germany had, it was true, a growing number of small manufacturers who were to achieve great wealth. These were like the Verlegers, whom Gerhart Hauptmann describes in his moving tragedy, *Die Weber*. The Verlegers went round distributing work to country mills just as English merchants had done in the seventeenth century, and others in the eighteenth. But whereas in France and particularly in England this type of middle-class merchant tended to disappear and make way for large-scale banking and industry, in Germany he still remained the only conspicuously active element in the economy of the 1840s. What was achieved from 1785 to 1899 in France and other nations with new middle-class dynasties, only came about in 1840–6 in Germany. There is an obvious paradox here, but one which a little thought will explain. The more revolutionary the origins of the bourgeoisie, the greater the dependence of industry on the state.

These differences between the various middle classes also throw light on the differing social problems. In Germany there was not, properly speaking, a labour problem before 1848; this does not mean to say that there was no poverty among the working classes. There was still the poverty characteristic of the old régime, which looked, sometimes with justification, to the old-style feudal overlord who was in honour bound to protect and feed the poor. In France and England the problem was different in kind. The bourgeois state held aloof in principle from any intervention in social problems, the regulation of which must be left to the natural course of events. But while in England political power, perhaps because it was relatively independent of economic power, had never entirely shed its feudal obligations (laws for the protection of the poor and old guild rules, for instance), in France the political power, which was closely linked with middle-class interests, became much more radical in the application of *laissez-faire*. The point is worth examining in greater detail.

At the beginning of the nineteenth century English workers could still invoke the Elizabethan Long Law, which by organizing the guilds had given their members and apprentices a certain protection. This law had never been repealed. In France it would have been quite unthinkable, after the Constituent Assembly had passed the radical measure introduced by Le Chapelier, for the workers to appeal to regulations laid down by Henry iv though they were contemporaneous and almost identical with the Long Law of Elizabethan England. In London there existed a body which, though more limited in its application than the French national workshops of 1848, could have been regarded as socialist in character had it not been inherited from the old régime. It was the Corporation of the Poor of the City of London, whose workshops dated from the seventeenth century and had increased during the eighteenth century in the great urban centres. In 1832 there were more than sixty-seven corporations of this type, the Gilbert Incorporations. Of course, industrialists frequently attacked the disadvantages of the system and the idleness which was said to prevail, in the workhouse at Oxford for instance. Nevertheless, it did represent a living foundation, based on tradition and law, on which social legislation could build more easily, and it prevented the growth of socialist ideologies, and the temptation to experiment, in which for centuries England has indulged only with moderation and restraint. At first people's fears were aroused by the Malthusian doctrine and workhouse life was made into the dreadful caricature of charity denounced by Dickens in *Oliver Twist*. But eventually philanthropists raised their protests, not only in a private capacity, as Robert Owen was to do, but even openly in Parliament itself by people such as Lord Ashley and his friends, with the result that England was a century in advance of France in the foundation and application of labour laws.

Dickens had begun to stir up a great wave of sympathy for the victims of industry and a materialist civilization; he praised the nobleman who protected the people and his philanthropic friends in the middle classes, such as Pickwick; he violently and scornfully condemned the rest of the middle classes, for whom business was merely business, and thus helped to create a parliamentary opinion in favour of improving the lot of the worker. At this time the landed aristocrat himself, worried by the manufacturers' propaganda in favour of free trade which was threatening the price of his produce and especially of his corn, and worried by the railways which were cutting across private property and whose profits threatened road and canal shares, developed a lively enthusiasm for everything that might restrict the extortionate profits of industry, and advocated particularly a rise in the cost of labour. He supported the formation of corporations and clubs which protected the interests of specialist workmen. All this ended in the recognition of trade unions, the control of female and child employment, and the legal ten-hour working day. Greville vividly described the curious nature of these debates about workers, in which the ruling classes who held the reins of power were disturbed by the great wind of reform which was blowing from the Conservative side, disconcerting the Liberals and investing the Tory party with a youthful and reforming role. He wrote in his diary that he did not remember ever seeing anything like the scene which followed the ten-hour bill of Lord Ashley; some voters did not know how they should vote, and simply voted with their friends; the whole affair was awkward and unpleasant.

In contemporary France on the other hand, a large majority, untroubled by doubts or distress of any kind, were whole-heartedly behind the government in its ruthless suppression of the workers' riots in Paris and Lyons. Even stranger were the comments of d'Argout, Minister of Trade: 'Whatever the worker's lot may be,' he wrote, 'it is not the manufacturer's business to improve it. . . . There is no law compelling a scale of wages to be fixed for any particular industry. If there are contracts, they affect only those who have signed them, and the government is not only powerless to insist on their observance but positively cannot interfere in the matter. If the boards of arbitration let themselves be drawn into the affair, the court of appeal will quash the case.'

Thus the French bourgeoisie of 1830 was solidly united in its demands for state aid for itself in the name of the nation, but refused similar assistance to the workers in the name of liberty. The aristocrats who had not rallied round the new bourgeois order were driven out of the House of Peers, electoral pressure kept them out of the Chamber of Deputies, and the obligation to take the oath kept them from the higher administrative offices. Thus, although urbanization, industrialization and banking were much less advanced in France than in England, the people in power were exclusively middle-class. They were so firmly entrenched that there was no possibility of a new policy based on the charitable tradition of the old régime.

The English working class had never lost faith in the possibilities of the parliamentary system. However half-hearted and long delayed electoral reforms might be, it remained confident, organizing itself to struggle within the framework of established institutions for right of entry into the legislative councils. The first signs of socialism did not appear in a struggle against the state, nor in legal battles, but in practical issues of everyday life. In France, however, the entire legislative body presented a united front against working-class hopes. A solution along the lines of co-operation or philanthropy was never a practical possibility at any stage. The bourgeois state in its entirety would have to be dismembered, along with legislative and administrative machinery closely integrated with it. Socialism took refuge in revolutionary theory. Substitution of a social republic for parliamentary machinery was the most moderate of its demands. Idealists called for the total suppression of the state, which offered to the workers nothing but the bayonets of the soldiers and the prosecutions of its police.

The importance of these differing legal outlooks between France and England cannot be too strongly emphasized. In England a body of traditions inherited from a previous age was powerful enough to influence conduct and affect legislation, and thus inhibit any solution which was too radically middle-class. In France the revolutionary tradition, which caused workers and bourgeois alike to rise up against anything reminiscent of the old system, enabled this newly emerging middle class, which really controlled the state, to consolidate its position. Neither the workers nor their supporters fully understood the fundamental explanation until Marxism came forward with a new and radical solution, and one which was this time radically anti-bourgeois; that was the idea of the inevitable class struggle. It was the result of the legal rationalism in which French socialism originated, rather than the consequence of actual material conditions of middle- and working-class life. So the people's new *Marseillaise*, the *Internationale*, gained ground in France. It was yet another instance of the stubborn persistence of the theoretical turn of mind in France, which already in 1789 had preferred the abstract theories of right to the realism of credit, and now in 1830 preferred the abstraction of parliamentary government to the reality of industrial experiment.

It is important to note that working-class poverty was no less appalling in England than in France. It might even be argued that it was worse. We hear of the hardships endured at Cambrésis by workers living on starvation wages, for which an entire family had to work for ten to twelve hours a day, and of the scandalous state of degradation of the 'dangerous class', mostly made up of the unemployed who 'squatted' in the ruins of filthy dwellings in the heart of Paris, where the pickpockets and depraved murderers emerged at nightfall, and where the descriptions in Eugène Sue's novel are not at all overdrawn. But Dickens gives us ample proof that the horrors in the slums of London and Manchester were every whit as dreadful as those of Paris; this urban poverty was probably even more widespread geographically on the other side of the Channel where industry expanded more rapidly and more extensively than in the French countryside. French philanthropists were unanimously of the opinion that in the south and west the old cities devoted to trade and agriculture remained clean and tidy, sometimes even welcoming the poor, and did not develop the horrors of the industrial and particularly the textile cities of the north.

England had her Benthamite theorists at the beginning of the century, but by 1830 their popularity was on the wane, to the advantage of pragmatism. Middle-class France remained devoted to theory, the attitude of Thiers and Guizot. This bourgeois theory was opposed by a rigid and uncompromising working-class theory – socialism.

French socialism originated at one and the same time from the great hopes which mechanization had aroused in the mind of Saint-Simon and the doubts it awakened in Sismondi. Saint-Simon proposed a reorganization of society which was to take advantage of the railway to establish universal peace, and use technical progress to banish a useless aristocracy and abolish landed property, since the idle rich frittered away the income from this in empty pleasure. In any case he placed the magnates of industry or banking at the top of the hierarchy. In contrast, Sismondi, struck chiefly by the squalor of working-class slums, blamed technical progress and even suggested that research laboratories should be closed. The disciples of Saint-Simon, after the riots and revolutions of 1830, blamed the idle industrialists and bankers for all this poverty. Bazard demanded that the tax paid by labour to capital should be suppressed.

The basic idea of a profound transformation of society was clearly stated: there must be an end to the exploitation of man by man; it must be replaced by a collective or communist structure, ensuring a fair distribution of labour and property. Opinions varied on this point too; Proudhon insisted on the logical conclusion, 'property is theft'; he wanted to do away with any kind of state. Louis Blanc, on the other hand, hoped that universal suffrage and the establishment of a republic would result in socialized factories and workshops being organized by the state.

In England, Owen tried at first to put socialist experiments into practice and almost succeeded, in 1830, in grouping the workers' syndicates (authorized from 1822) into a vast trade union, and so virtually founding a labour party. And although he failed, it was nevertheless on these lines that the English working-class movement was to be organized fifty years later.

French socialism, on the contrary, provided an essential political content to the philosophy of Hegel and Feuerbach which had a formative influence on Karl Marx in Germany; and Engels helped his friend to a better understanding of socialist Saint-Simonism. Even Leroux contributed to the German theory of the irreversible tide of history which leads from capitalism to socialism by the gradual dwindling of profits. Later observation of English industrialism was to round off Marx's thinking. From a French seed, socialism grew into a European tree – the brotherhood envisaged by Gracchus Babeuf, revived on modern lines, in revolt against the injustice which enabled the idle rich to profit from other peoples' labour; socialism prepares to call on the workers of the world to unite.

THE AESTHETICS OF PROGRESS

It has been said that the man of 1830 was by temperament a Romantic; we shall try to clarify the meaning of this new feeling by suggesting that the Romantics had discovered history, and that their new perception was an awareness of time.

Gently, almost imperceptibly, this new spirit had been evolving since the middle of the eighteenth century. Greek perfection had, of course, been studied for centuries, discussed, held up as an example, and judged far superior to the moderns, but now this admiration for the antique took a new turn. Lebeau's fine description of the house of Caylus will serve as an illustration. 'The hall of his house was reminiscent of ancient Egypt. The first thing you saw was a handsome Egyptian statue five feet five inches high. The staircase was decorated with medallions and curios from China and America. In the house itself you were surrounded by Egyptian, Etruscan, Greek and Roman gods and priests and magistrates, amongst which a few Gallic figures hardly dared show themselves.' He had casts made in Malta of two Phoenician inscriptions, the deciphering of which led to much competition. He founded a prize in the *Académie des Belles Lettres* to encourage the study of the customs of ancient peoples, and to prevent artists from making mistakes through ignorance of historical costume.

This new passion for antiquity seized the whole of cultured Europe when news of the excavations at Herculaneum and Pompeii were made known, and received a further impetus when Champollion deciphered the hieroglyphics. German universities opened numerous centres for historical studies, and philology replaced the old aesthetic appreciation in classical studies. In short, cultured emphasis shifted from beauty to historical truth.

We have already had occasion to mention the love of antiquity which gave a new fascination to Rome in 1780 and filled first English and then European interiors with a whole new range of ornaments and knick-knacks. It had an astounding success in England, where the fashion began, especially in country houses. It was the age of Chippendale, which repre-sented the modern manner of the early industrial era. It seemed as though the middle classes wished to evolve their own interpretation of antiquity. Middle-class taste tended first of all to adopt 'perfect' lines imitated from Greek and Roman models. The design of antique bowls, vases and jars, the lines of folds and drapery were carefully studied and copied by many European craftsmen, particularly those working in England under the direction of the potter Wedgwood, or the iron-founder Matthew Boulton. The same influence was apparent in the delicate scroll-work which decorate Adam interiors in England; in the small and delicate pieces of furniture carved by Riesener for connoisseurs at the French court. Marie-Antoinette in particular loved Riesener's skilful work. The same influence can be seen in the modifications – made during the course of building – to several charming German palaces, especially in Potsdam, so as to insert a few straight lines into the elaborate rococo which was suddenly discovered to be too servile an imitation of French taste. It was this same taste for classical decoration and furnishing, though in a very unadorned and humanized form, which developed into the Biedermeyer style in Germany and Austria. This taste for the antique, which originated in the first half of the eighteenth century in Rome, where it was passionately debated by artists of varying talents and of all nationalities, was made fashionable in Ger-many by Winckelmann and later by Goethe himself. It was a fashion which commended itself to the new middle-class families all the more readily since the decoration and type of furniture it inspired was simpler to make and less costly to reproduce in the workshops of the master cabinet-makers and carpenters than the extravagant fancies of late baroque. The middle classes, first of England and then of France, per-suaded Europe to abandon complicated and delicate veneering and fussy motifs and use full-grained woods, particularly the new mahogany. This English taste, which combined classical form with middle-class simplicity, took a firm hold on Europe, remained in favour during the time of the Em-pire, and found its full expression in the Louis-Philippe style. The triumph of the Pompeian style in Parisian decoration was apparently complete at the time of the Directory when even women's fashions were inspired by what was believed to be Roman. Talma and Joséphine de Beauharnais built their mansions around classical marble patios. It was not only in the minor arts that the Roman style was successful; the fashion affected everything.

In 1780 David electrified artistic circles in Rome with his three Horatii, proud and resolute, their faces expressing the courage and military virtues of Rome. The painting shows three arched porticoes, three women, three swords and three heroes; the perfect symmetry of their attitudes was intended as an expression of Roman discipline. In David's art antiquity was not yet a history lesson. It was an attempt to convey an eternal virtue by means of a noble style, bold design and unequivocal colours. In his studio, David, as we know, preserved a rigid discipline. This pageant-master of the revolutionary festivals and painter of the rising imperial fame was indeed convinced of the absolute value of his art and when his days of activity and fame were over he passed on his aesthetic certainty to Ingres. We have only to compare his early portraits with the famous *Madame Morel* in the Louvre. But Ingres was a pupil with ideas of his own, as we can see by comparing the *Danse de Léonidas aux Thermopyles* with *Thétis suppliant Jupiter*. Even in later life David was still fascinated by the depiction of movement, in painting as a means of expressing courage, manliness and the doing of great deeds. The majesty of Jupiter, on the other hand, is conveyed by his immobility and by the sculptured lines of his throne, while Thetis, sinuous to the point of distortion, foreshadows in the young artist the aging painter of the voluptuous Odalisques of a later date. Antiquity was no longer a reservoir of controversial subjects for vast canvases or a source of all the virtues, as it had been at the time of the Revolution. With Ingres, classical perfection turned middle class.

Long orations in classical style had been much in vogue in the Revolutionary assemblies. The use of Greek and Roman first names, which had persisted so long in other Latin countries, only went out in France with the return of the most Christian kings: it persists to this day in the south. This taste for things classical reached its peak with the style known as the 're-turn from Egypt', which was to the lower middle classes what mansions built on Pompeian lines were to the rich and fashionable. They chose Jacob furniture in their houses and admired the triumphal arches of Percier and Fontaine. This style symbolized the destiny of the middle classes, who were unable to reorganize the economy which the Revolution had destroyed and suffered the Empire until the moment of defeat.

The taste for antiquity had created not only English knick-knacks and the Louis xvi and Empire styles but also a new outlook; it focused attention on the dimension of time which the eighteenth century had hardly noticed. The problem of time had, it is true, obsessed Pascal and religious thinkers, and led to mysticism, but it also led many great minds to irreligion. Men shrank from its mystery. After 1780, however, the notion of time became more human. It was no longer linked with metaphysics but with nostalgia and history. First the English, then the French, put ruins in their parks, where fine old trees were preferred to model plantations. The death of a young woman left them inconsolable, their grief was lifelong, and Chateaubriand's description of the funeral of *Atala* set a fashion in literature. The love of history was mingled with melancholy at the irrevocability of life, for which neither divine goodness nor unbridled orgies could afford consolation any longer; when the old poetic forms were revived in the poems of André Chénier, melancholy was their predominant theme. All intensity or delicacy of feeling was submerged in the vague, un- defined concept of evolution, a reflection of the great tide of life itself.

When Jouffroy delivered his lectures to an enraptured student audience at the *Collège de France* in 1825, his subject was 'The Problem of Human Destiny' ; and when Christianity became fashionable again, it was sup- ported not by arguments from the Word of God or from Holy Scripture, but from the history of the early days of Christianity.

Even before the triumph of economic individualism and the rights of freedom, men were trying to read their destiny in history. Poetry, the theatre and philosophy no longer shrank away from the problem of time, while the middle classes were no longer afraid of it since they realized that it was on their side. Every businessman, every family which had left the countryside to build up the new urban civilization, was acutely aware of it. The middle-class economist too, continually proclaimed it, or demon- strated it by theorem and corollary in the manner of Bentham. However harsh and unjust the industrial society might appear to be in its ruthless treatment of the poor, it was its stubborn determination to fit itself for its task which in the end relieved the wretchedness it had caused everywhere in its earlier stages. Time would bring redress provided man held fast to the idea of freedom.

Time as it was experienced by the artist or studied by the philosopher and the historian and which distinguished human beings from each other even more than space – this was the theme of romanticism. In its treatment by Stendhal, Michelet or Edgar Quinet it was a great theme, for it dealt with the history of individual man and the history of mankind.

A comparison of the same Napoleonic story seen through the eyes first of David then of Gros (Bonaparte visiting the plague-victims at Jaffa or the battlefield at Eylau) reveals the effort that was being made to seize the historical moment and to derive emotion not so much from the majesty of the whole as from the realism of detail. There was as yet no sureness of touch in the realism : corpses were piled on top of each other or, in Géri- cault's paintings, starving wretches writhed in agony on a raft. It was a realism in which carefully built up detail, as with David, and only later, with Daumier, captured a vivid, fleeting impression. Géricault was not content simply to ask his friend Delacroix to act as his model for the men on the raft, but actually went to the Hôpital Beaujon to paint the dead and the dying.

It is often said that romantic painting, like the new history, was revolu- tionary or, to use the then fashionable word, liberal. True, when we admire the vast canvases of the time on the walls of the Louvre it is not easy to distinguish the conservative from the liberal. Already in 1819 Delescluzes was protesting against this over-simplified conception of art which inter- preted paintings in the light of political ideas. But this conception did reflect the novelty of this new trend and the dangers it held for the traditionalists. It is perhaps absurd to see in the *Raft of the Medusa* nothing more than a devastating criticism of the Minister of Marine. The Minister himself was most tactful ; he commissioned a picture from Géricault as acknowledgement of his genius, but the subject was to be the *Sacré Cœur*. Géricault, disappointed, declined the offer and left for England.

Time cannot be expressed on canvas as easily as space. The French Romantics, as we know, owed much to the English painter Bonington. He showed them how to capture, in a rapid sketch, a single fleeting mood of the landscape he was painting, or a burst of sunlight on a passing cloud. The effects of light achieved by Constable and especially by Turner were truly remarkable: the fact was that painters who had been seeking to express feeling through line since Watteau's time had at last discovered colour at the very time when chemistry was enriching the artist's palette. Decamps was a chemist and Delacroix kept his pallettes as he did his sketches. It was through an interplay of colour, as Goethe had foreseen even before Chevreul, that the surface of the picture might be made to evoke time, which was now the most important element in human feeling.

Géricault was undoubtedly the first great French painter to use the new English methods. His *Horse Stopped by Slaves*, painted in Rome as early as 1816, did aim to show movement by the play of muscles, using colours typical of Michelangelo, but in *Racing at Epsom* in 1821 it is the colouring of the sky and the ground which gives an illusion of speed.

Another painter who was feeling his way simultaneously towards realism and the use of colour, trying always to make the surface of his canvas express time, was Delacroix. He had begun by trying his hand at historical subjects (*The Massacre of Scio*, 1824), before turning history into the symbol of the victorious advance of the Revolution (*Portrait of Liberty*, 1830). Now art concentrated passionately on movement; but barely had the great victory been won, when it seemed as if inspiration had suddenly run out. This happened at a time when society was becoming more orderly; Casimir Périer was selected for office rather than Laffitte, before the choice finally settled on Guizot. All this intense effort at synthesis, which had led painters to exalt time with a simultaneous use of history, colour and realistic detail, began to slacken and become diffused, as if exhausted by its own success. Finally Delaroche, Isabey and Decamps achieved little more than cold, anecdotal history, foreshadowing the worst banalities of the following generation. Dupré and Théodore Rousseau also limited themselves to the delights of colour in landscapes in the manner of de Cuyp; and even in Africa Delacroix did not discover the splendid scenes which had inspired the 'Orientales' of a previous generation, but an opportunity for accurate descriptive painting.

From the end of the eighteenth century German literature had also rebelled against the French models of the age of Louis xiv, and had substituted praise of the transitory and ephemeral for their ideal of unchanging man. This too was an attempt to bring time into art. In 1767, Lessing, meditating on Winckelmann's discoveries, was fired with enthusiasm for a group of classical sculpture (a late example) and wrote a book on the

Laocoon. The plastic arts may have found difficulty in conveying an impression of time, but poetry was the natural medium for its expression. It was at Goethe's suggestion, as an act of self-discipline, that Schiller immersed himself in historical studies. He read everything that had been written about the revolt of the Swiss cantons, and the result was *William Tell* written in one draft and performed a few months before the premature death of the man whom Wagner considered the finest representative of the 'young Germany'. It is worth considering Schiller's career more closely: before achieving *William Tell* with its masterly analysis of events and character, Schiller had been experimenting and was first carried away by political idealism (a phase in which he wrote the mediocre *History of the Netherlands* and the play *Don Carlos*); then, gaining in power and self-confidence with his studies of seventeenth-century Germany, he wrote his *History of the Thirty Years War*, which led on to the fine *Wallenstein* trilogy. In this he already reached a level of objectivity which he proudly announced to Goethe as a victory. 'Wallenstein does not interest me', he wrote. 'He does not seem to me to be noble in any of his deeds.' In his *Maid of Orleans* he altered the tragic ending and idealized the harsh reality in a last revolt of his artistic temperament; it was his last historical failure, for then came *William Tell*, which was acknowledged in Germany as his finest dramatic masterpiece.

Faced with the extraordinary intellectual career of this German poet, whose dominating interest was history, it is interesting to reflect on the progress achieved since the tentative rationalizations of Corneille. Schiller had thought deeply over the outline of philosophy which Emmanuel Kant had at first entitled *Prolegomena to all Future Metaphysics* before he confronted the human mind with his two famous *Kritiker*. In his philosophy time was a prerequisite of feeling. Schiller held that man's destiny could be fulfilled in the harmonious combination of instinct and morality, and though he never learned Greek, the Greek world, as it appeared through the admiring eyes of poets and tragedians of his day, seemed to him as dangerous as the Kantian rigidity. Thus it was that Schiller opened the door wide to German Romanticism. Goethe held out longer than any of the rest against this assertion of instinct. His Greek tragedies, though separated from Racine's by a hundred years, have all their consummate art.

Just as French Romanticism originated when the classical art of David and Ingres was in its prime, so German poetry too experienced this simultaneous tendency towards classicism and romanticism. But though Goethe was more successful with classical style than Schiller, he too shared Schiller's preoccupation with history, as witness his *Egmont* and *Torquato Tasso*. He also had a great sense of the reality of daily life and succeeded in giving it nobility in *Hermann and Dorothea*. His long life span enabled him to be a contemporary of David, Gros, Géricault and Delacroix, and he expressed in his poetry everything they had attempted to capture in their painting – the flow of history and the sense of realism; and his verse had both music and the brilliance of colour to evoke the destiny of man. This was achieved most

successfully in *Faust*. *Faust* is no incarnation of liberty. The most classical,
the most antique of the German poets mistrusted to the very end this idealization, this abstraction which was so characteristically French. But *Faust*
is a poem in praise of movement, and of man's genius for seeking happiness,
which he finds only in creative action, in the creation of material wealth.

This juxtaposition of French painting and German poetry is an extreme
over-simplification of the essential characteristics of romanticism. France
had her poets too. Vigny, the aristocrat, also defended the concept of truth
in art, though more concisely than Schiller (a plebeian) had done in the
Maid. He held that truth enables a man to achieve self-mastery when he is
in danger of being ruled by his instincts. The brief sketches in his *Servitudes
et grandeurs militaires* contain more realism even than Goethe's *Dichtung und
Wahrheit*. Nevertheless, French dramatic poetry developed late in comparison with that of Germany. When the historical plays of Victor Hugo were
raising storms of protest on the Parisian stage, Schiller, who had profoundly
shocked the theatres at Mannheim, Stuttgart and Dresden in his youth, had
been dead for twenty years. Germany was probably more responsive than
France to this new exciting awareness of time.

Above all Germany was a century in advance of France in music, an art
which is probably more concerned with time than any other. We cannot
attempt a summary of that period of musical history which included all the
greatest geniuses. We shall merely note the contrast: at a time when Mozart
had been dead for more than twenty years; when Haydn had just died
and been mourned in Germany and in England as the greatest musical
genius of all time; and when Beethoven was at the height of his fame, it was
Rossini who was drawing the fashionable crowds in Paris. In 1810 it was
Rossini who conquered the French capital and made the fortune of the
Théâtre des Italiens. It is understandable that the *Barber of Seville* should be
preferred to Mozart's *Marriage of Figaro*, although it was composed in a
fortnight, so enchanting is Rossini's airy lightness; but a great many inferior
imitators were also successful. It could only be the poor taste of the French
public that made them prefer Donizetti and Bellini and later Auber,
Hérold, Offenbach and other Cherubinis. Kreutzer, solo violin at the
Théâtre des Italiens, whose admirable technique was learnt from Viotti,
never played the sonata which Beethoven dedicated to him, and this is
the only reason the idolized composer of *Lodoïska* and *Aristippe Ipsiboé* has
been saved from oblivion.

The French looked for flourishes, lightness, charm and grace in music
and above all not too much emotion. They certainly did not want the torrent of feeling that was sweeping through German music at that time.

The difference was not one of national temperament but of psychological
and social climate. This can be illustrated by two parallel careers : Meyerbeer, born in Berlin of a rich family of Jewish bankers, made money in
Vienna out of Italian music, and later had a great success in Paris where he
found in Scribe a librettist worthy of him ; and he enriched French opera
with the *Huguenots* and the *Prophet*. This 'nobody', as Wagner called him,

stifled the early career of Berlioz. Mendelssohn, born in Hamburg of a rich Jewish banking family, was lucky enough to please Goethe and to be influenced by Johann-Sebastian Bach. He was a tremendous success in London, and later in Leipzig and Dresden. He founded the Dresden academy which became the musical centre of the new Germany, and supported and encouraged Schumann there.

While France was content with light music which copied the technique of the eighteenth-century Italians, and even ignored the lessons learned from Glück, Germany was experiencing an extraordinary musical development. The eighteenth century had defined the scale, and the orchestral instruments. With Haydn the structure of symphonies and sonatas marked a distinct departure from the old *Suites* and the new and classical architecture of composition was introduced. Mozart, a master of emotion as well as of the keyboard, surprised and disconcerted his contemporaries by the unexpected daring of his phrases and musical confessions. But he still belonged to a generation which travelled cosmopolitan Europe. He had made a tour of the capitals: Munich, Vienna, Brussels, Paris, Milan, Rome, and Naples. He could almost be said to have composed to the trotting of horses. Austria, however, was more open to European influence than Bach's Thuringia. The new feeling for German concentration, its enrichment and its diffusion by and through Europe originated from Vienna and from the palace of the Esterhazys. They were the great patrons first of Haydn and later of Beethoven.

At the turn of the eighteenth century the final improvements were being made to the pianoforte, which was gradually replacing the harpsichord. The piano with hammers did not need a double keyboard to modify its *forte* and its tones, and it inspired Beethoven to write one of his most magnificent sonatas. But with Beethoven the era of cosmopolitanism was at an end. He was no great traveller, for his life was lived on an inner plane and his geography was purely musical. Like his masters, Beethoven at first avoided the expression of personal feelings in his music. But, even though he could no longer hear it, music became his only outlet for self-expression after 1810; his physical handicap shut him in upon himself completely, so that at the end of his life the only way in which he could express himself was by scribbling on scraps of paper and above all by pouring all his deepest emotions into his compositions. Almost as soon as it had been defined, musical form was enlarged and altered by this tremendous revelation, which amazed and shocked well-bred society and even disturbed Goethe, as he confided to the young Mendelssohn. The great movement in space which had characterized the generation of 1780 was followed by this passionate exploration in time.

The new generation in German music began where Beethoven had left it. The changes in the design of instruments led to a vast improvement in the technique of instrumentalists and made possible a great delicacy of touch. After Clementini the outstanding pianists were Moscheles and Clara Wieck, who became Schumann's wife, and Paganini became the leading violinist. Music had reached the point where it could express every feeling from the outpourings, joys and sorrows of Schubert to the passions, violent emotions, leaping enthusiasm and melancholy of Robert Schumann.

This flood of music from Germany and the Rhine was received with enthusiasm by the rest of Europe, except by France. Wagner was then in his adolescence. This music was brilliant at expressing the inexpressible; it was beyond the sphere of poetry and conveyed the passage of inner time. It burst upon the theatre, giving romantic drama a power which the artificiality of opera in general and Italian opera in particular had never been able to achieve. Beethoven's *Fidelio* and *Egmont*, even more than Mozart's *Don Juan*, gave added depth to feelings which the words had done no more than state. Musical drama burst into new fields with Weber's *Freischutz*. Only music could express all that magic and witchcraft, and give dramatic life to the dialogue between man and Satan which stretches human stature from heaven to hell. The psychological destiny of human history was once more rooted in the Middle Ages which the eighteenth century had so little understood. Their seething unrest found even stronger expression in romantic music than in the drawings or the poetry of Victor Hugo, and provoked an even more violent emotional reaction than did the pseudo Ossian revivals.

This age of emotion which ignored the boundaries of reason and argument found its finest expression in music, thanks to the daring new combinations of sound. Eventually even France proved receptive to the new art with Delacroix in the 1840s. The circle of admirers surrounding the young Chopin, who was supported, tyrannized, cared for and overwhelmed by the impetuous George Sand, was still small, but it was very enthusiastic. The Pole's rival, Liszt, was a virtuoso as well as a composer, and his liaison with Madame d'Agoult shocked polite society. One of the most amazing representatives of all this passionate young generation was Berlioz. The composer of *Benvenuto Cellini* never became wealthy, for his work was too unlike the popular Italian operas filling the theatres, but he was an important symbol of what was to come. His life, like that of the Brontës, was spent in the imaginative creation of tremendous passions, although in reality he indulged in little more than moderately sentimental adventure. His *Symphonie fantastique* was an attempt to portray the history of his love and he used music to convey his deepest feelings. In his search for self-expression he included in his music the drums of an execution, the *Dies irae* of the Gregorian liturgy, and a witches' sabbath. The man was, indeed, a symbol of the great gulf between a society which was a hundred years behind the times in matters of taste and a young generation which suddenly and brutally erupted with its *Sturm und Drang*.

It may be true that France was a hundred years ahead of Germany scientifically and probably politically, but its sensitivity at that time seemed blunted. French painting had never been so brilliant, but it was sixty years since Lessing had shown that painting could not be made to express time. Time was poetry and music; it invaded German metaphysics, and broke out in the sufferings of the young Goethe and of Schiller fifty years earlier than in Victor Hugo's *Légende des Siècles*. It poured out in German music sixty years before it brought unhappiness to Berlioz and, even then, was surrounded by a society still unwilling to listen to him.

The French power of rational thought had been fruitful, especially in the technical field, but it was closely linked with a love of order. After 1840 it was through a wave of disorder that the face of Europe was transformed; it was swept along by great storms, and a wild speeding up of time. The result was the age of romanticism and, later, a new realism which destroyed the old economic structures. The most striking concrete expression of this was the railway.

THE CALL OF THE PEOPLES

In the nineteenth century Europe was undergoing major political changes, in which the railways played a considerable rôle. They were not always the organ of progress, however. The countries which were already almost united in 1830 were consolidated by the coming of the railway in 1870, but those still unprepared saw new bands of steel, forged by the old empires, tightening around them. In other words Germany and Italy on the one hand, and the Austrian Empire on the other, emerged from the railway revolution in a stronger position. The principle of nationalism won the day across the Alps and the Rhine, but was unsuccessful among the Slav peoples. In order to understand this fact properly we must think ourselves back to the eve of 1830. It was as if every possible nation was hastening to proclaim its right to exist before the railways were built, so that it might be acknowledged as a nation by the transport system which defined the political boundaries of Europe for over a century.

The reasons for this strange situation must be sought in the increasing speed of means of communication which preceded the building of railways and made them popular. The comparative ease of travel, the improvement in postal services and the optical telegraph (as well as the marches of campaigning armies) passed ideas from one end of Europe to the other. These ideas aroused the interest of the uneducated and unsophisticated mass of the people. As we know, catchwords and slogans can generate currents of enthusiasm: for instance, Victor Hugo's magnificent metaphors acquire their full meaning in the context of this Europe of 1830. He called the theatre a point of focus for the poet and a resounding echo. Hence specific phrases or lines of dialogue drew an eagerly responsive public whenever they were spoken on the stage.

Let us consider only three words: firstly the word *race*. Hitherto its meaning had always been very aristocratic or possibly even feudal. It was used by the nobleman to describe his ancestral descent. Used by a royal line, the word took on a special majesty; the Bourbons for example were 'the third race'. But the revolutions had placed these titles of nobility within the reach of other social groups. True, the newly-rich bourgeois of 1830 would probably have been mocked had he spoken of his 'race'. But used collectively, to refer to a whole people, the word race now conferred a kind of ennobling dignity. Already Sièyes, in his defence of the Third Estate, had laid the foundations of his popularity by attacking Boulainvilliers, who had claimed that the French nobility were descended from Germanic conquerors and held their privileges by right of conquest. If that were so, said Sièyes, the Gallic people must drive them out and exact a military revenge. The dubious proceedings of the terror might thus be justified by being called a military operation. Augustin Thierry later adopted this strange theory, and based his *Histoire* on the principle of racial conflict.

Doubtless the young intellectuals living, learning and loving in nineteenth-century Paris were sometimes suspicious of this concept, charged as it was with a suspect mysticism. Michelet and Quinet forcibly condemned the very idea of race. Yet neither of them was insensitive to the new dignity of the *people*; they were proud to be identified with barbarians, and the new status the word conferred, for it was after all the people who should be the rulers and not the kings. The time was now ripe. Chateaubriand hesitated to claim that race carried all the essential values; he cited Christianity and Jerusalem. To this Bible Michelet was to answer with the *Bible de l'humanité*: the people achieved their highest dignity not in the Church, but in universal brotherhood on earth. This revival of the concept of inheritance and traditions necessitated wide reading. Philosophy came first with the admirable lectures of Jouffroy at the *Collège de France*; then history, which resulted in the discovery of claims to nobility not of sovereigns as in the past, but of previously little-known collective groups now quite suddenly invested with importance. In this search the French people naturally earned the gratitude of humanity; for they graciously acknowledged the claims of many peoples besides themselves. Edgar Quinet pursued German studies and as the son-in-law of a Rumanian poet also studied the 'eight million men who are knocking imploringly at the threshold of our Western societies'. A chair of Slavonic language and literature was founded at the *Collège de France* and offered to the famous Pole Mickiewicz, who was a poet, conspirator, philologist and crusader of the emigration, as well as being inevitably an inseparable comrade-in-arms of Quinet and Michelet.

If 'the people' in the singular retained its prestige in the twentieth century (for reasons connected as much with the industrial socialism which followed on the railways as with the feelings of 1830), the peoples, in the plural, were still regarded with a certain suspicion at that date. This was probably because of the sense in which the word had been used by the monarchy (royal or imperial), when 'our peoples' suggested the art of dividing to rule. Avoiding the use of 'peoples' in the plural, nationalists preferred to say 'nations'. The 'nation' had acquired the glory of the Revolution, and the word had marched round Europe covered with victorious standards. The two words 'country' and 'nation' enabled every man to cherish his belief in the essential goodwill of others. At the moment when the outburst of German patriotism was causing uneasiness in France, Quinet himself was trying to rescue the basic idea from excesses.

The man who best expressed the idea of nationhood was probably Mazzini, the remarkable moving spirit of 'Young Italy', a secret society which began the struggle for the unity, liberty and independence of its country. Nations could be defined in terms of geography, history or language, but Mazzini discovered a hidden force of faith in one's country. This was the heyday of 'nationalism', when the word was first introduced and meant an alliance of peaceful peoples. Not that Mazzini refrained from action. He was the heart and soul of every plot, and the force behind every riot. He not only constituted the rallying point for Italians eager to free themselves from Austria, but also united the Swiss of the regeneration and courageous Poles in his Young Europe movement.

In every country in Europe the new words and the impressive demonstrations which accompanied them met with extraordinary success. The princes were incredibly indulgent to these movements. University professors famous for their devotion to their country were honoured. Historical studies and the old traditions of folk culture were held in high esteem. At the same time the cult of the national language took on a new meaning.

In Germany, German had been the major language for the last fifty years, thanks to Lessing, Goethe and Schiller. But it seemed as if the long eclipse of German by the French of monarchic society was now provoking a widespread reaction, based on the new and omnipotent philology led by Fichte, with his *Discourse to the German Nation*. A political ideal was beginning to form in Germany, though it was only conceived in general terms at that date. Fichte was not the only successor of Kant to play an important part in its development: soon Hegel was preaching the idealization of the state. The historical and particularly the philological schools made rapid strides: they lauded Alexander for regrouping cities into an Empire, they began to discover a kind of grand march of history from India to Europe, in which the nineteenth-century Germans were to be the torch-bearers. Congresses were held at which the doctrine and dogma of Germanism were discovered; they were tentative and isolated at first but soon grew in number until a great organization was formed covering all the universities and giving strength to the new nationalism.

There was perhaps less eagerness in Italy than in Germany to make claims on history. During his ambassadorship Chateaubriand had, in 1829, diagnosed the real significance of the Italian *mal du siècle* as a need of national brotherhood. Austrian rule was more unbearable in the peninsula than in the small German states, for in Italy the Austrian really was a foreigner and a barbarian. The people of Italy, energetic but without staying power, expected great results from acts of bravery which too often ended in abrupt defeat.

In Poland hopes of a new spiritual country lingered on even in 1830. The King of Prussia had allowed Polish to be used alongside German in administrative documents. Through the indulgent goodwill of Alexander and the liberalism of Grand Duke Constantin Czartoryski, the University of Vilna attracted a brilliant group of Germans and Poles, while in Warsaw Linde was drawing up a great Polish dictionary. All this activity was alas brought to an end by the catastrophe of 1830. Whilst the 'pilgrims' relapsed into mysticism, the Polish fatherland was stifled by Russianization. The Prussian part of Poland was spared for several years. All the remaining intellectuals and conspirators took refuge in Germany to become a source of great uneasiness to Nicholas, and soon to the King of Prussia himself, until William IV finally expelled the suspects. But of all the masters of Poland, Metternich was the harshest; when Galicia was rebellious, he allowed the peasants to be incited against the nobles in a terrible medieval rising, and a price of ten florins was paid for every nobleman's head. Then many Poles gave up all hope of salvation for Poland, except through the salvation of all Slavs, and resigned themselves to the idea of a Russia which would protect the Slavs against the Germans.

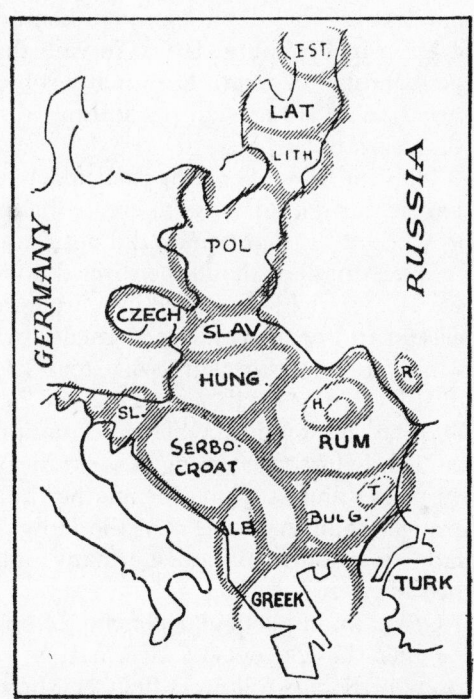

8 Races and Languages
of Eastern Europe

This Slav feeling is very marked in Kollar's work. Czechoslovakia, in fact, lies at a remarkable crossroads; the Czechs are neighbours of the Poles, but also understand the aspirations of the Austrian Slavs, an ocean of related peoples with Hungary like an isolated island in the middle. And although Prague was surrounded by German influences it was protected by its mountain shield. It was affected by the great philological and literary

movement which swept through the German universities; the works of
Herder were eagerly welcomed, translated and expanded. Szafarzik published his *Slavonic Ethnography* in 1842. It was estimated that the European
Slavs, numbering approximately eighty millions, were divided into fewer
groupings than the Germans, although they were more numerous than the
latter. The old peaceful virtues and the civilizing influence of the Slavs,
which had already been praised by Herder, were remembered. The old
traditions had to be honoured once more and the Slav languages allowed
to enrich each other in order to strengthen racial unity. The list of great
men who contributed to this task is too long to quote, but their names are
to be found on the pedestals of statues in almost every east European
capital. Serbian and Bulgarian histories were written, grammars were compiled and old legends revived, while a whole spate of poetry resulted from
this revival of the ancient unity of the Slav peoples. But Latin was still
often the only common language between one people and another, and
the Hungarians, who oppressed the Slavs dependent on Pest all the more
ruthlessly as their own national pride became stronger ('a Slav is not a
man'), put Croat deputies into difficulties when they forbade them the use
of Latin in Pressburg. It was in vain that enlightened Hungarians feared
the explosion of wrath of so many subject peoples; Kossuth, the very incarnation of Hungarian patriotism, was the most intractable defender of
Magyarization.

Thus the Slavs were not particularly united in spite of Kollar's affirma-
tion; it was no light task to create for them a common language, and the
presence of the Rumanians did not simplify it.

These divisions made the shrewd policy of the Austrian Empire all too
easy. Prussia had succeeded in uniting the Prussian country squire and his
peasant in one patriotic movement. In Austria, the Magyar or German
commander was in charge of Croat soldiers and could count on the old
loyalties of the local men. Thus, in face of the irresistible movement of
German nationalism, Slavonic nationalism could not succeed soon
enough, before the coming of the railways reinforced the framework of the
Austrian administration for another hundred years. Its structure became
stronger than in the days of the Holy Roman Empire, although Vienna
had to lose control of both Germany and Italy at the same time, because of
the railway.

Germany in particular benefited from the system of ideas which bound
together the concepts of race, nation, country and language. The philosophy of Kant's followers first set Marx thinking, but it exerted an even
more active influence through Engels, thanks to the innumerable chairs of
philosophy which were springing up like mushrooms in Germany. These
new teachings revealed affinities between the agrarian civilizations of eastern Europe, the German agrarian civilizations and all the communal
civilizations of India about which little was known in detail but whose
originality was being studied with the greatest interest. These teachings
also revealed similarities between the roots of German vocabulary and

those of Asian dialects; Aryanism was on the move throughout the vast Indo-European world. It ignored anything which did not fit into its system. With the conception of race, it idealized this vast community of peoples; and with the concept of nationhood it exalted the two finest incarnations of its age-old traditions – the German fatherland and the German language. The German scholar was soon proud of having been the first to express the inexpressible quality of historical stories, and made a religion out of the movement for German unity which was fostered by the railways. He was soon ready to sacrifice the French type of liberty and fraternity, and freedom and brotherhood on the English model, to his new god, Germanism. Grillparzer had become the champion of this new Germanism by exalting the victory of Hermann the Teuton over Augustus the Latin in the woods of Teutoburg.

7

The European Worlds

MEANWHILE the map of the world was being radically altered. In 1770 America belonged to Europe, and the legal traditions of what was known as the Colonial Pact kept the New World in a state of subjection. Fifty years later, Europe had almost entirely lost its hold on the New World. Yet America was shaping and moulding itself in the image of Europe. It was in order to be Europeans in the fullest sense of the word, and to enjoy all the privileges of that distinguished title, that America defended the rights of its citizens and established its rights as a nation. European trade reaped a handsome reward. What the old monarchies lost, the new middle-class business circles gained. A new conception of power came into being, less legal and military but more economic and financial. It enabled the sea-faring peoples, and particularly the English, to continue their successful advance into Asia. This proceeded easily in India, but with greater diffi-culty in China where the continental mass provided a stronger resistance to seaborne ventures. Russia continued its conquest of central Asia; and France was extending its influence to the southern shore of the Mediter-ranean and Africa.

THE WEST IMITATES EUROPE

Napoleon had attempted to subdue sea-power by land-power. It was cer-tainly easier to keep a fairly accurate reckoning of the strength of armies on the march than to estimate the power of millions of tons of shipping sailing the seas of the world, and the Emperor as a result had underestimated English sea-power just as he underestimated the power of English credit. It was very difficult for him to gauge its size, since even in the seas of Europe he could not see the real currents of the English economy. He had no feel-ing for a sea-based economy. Napoleon's political and administrative ideas came to him from his entourage of newly-rich, already described. These continental Swiss, brought to power by the Revolution, had not known the old seafaring military or mercantile aristocracy. The Revolutionary block-ade followed by the continental blockade of the Empire had ruined the maritime tradition, which was a very much more serious loss than the purely material one of the fleet. Even at that time, in spite of Cugnot, Jouffroy d'Abbans or even Fulton, steam-powered ships were no more than useless toys, and the sailing-ship still reigned supreme. Ships could be built with comparative ease, so the construction of a great fleet took only a few months, and there were plenty of sailors along the French coasts; but the trained officers for these ships were lacking; thus no sound appreciation of naval affairs reached the Tuileries, especially after the critical affair of Deprez and the United Merchants.

England First

Meanwhile, the English and American fleets were acquiring mastery of the seas. The English navy had been rapidly enlarged until the whole of coastal England was familiar with the heavy wooden ships. They ceaselessly patrolled the North Sea, and kept a day and night watch, strengthened after the setting up of the camp at Boulogne, and continued until Napoleon had fallen. All naval shipyards were building at great speed, so that in 1815, 20,000 ships sailed over the routes of this new sea-empire. Naturally vast quantities of wood were required for the building programme, since for each warship four thousand fine oaks had to be felled. For a considerable time English forests had been devastated by the requirements of the fleet. It was slow and costly to bring wood from America. Therefore England began to consider the enormous forests of northern Europe near at hand; the key to England's freedom was to be found where supplies of wood could be obtained, from Norway, Sweden, and the vast forests of Finland. England had to keep the passage through the Danish straits open at all costs, for in addition to wood it obtained corn and meat by the same route.

Napoleon's destiny, however, led him towards the Mediterranean, and his rashness ended in the disaster of Aboukir Bay, although at that very time any hostile move by the Nordic neutrals was enough to cause England alarm. When there was a possibility that these neutrals might gain Russian support, England was so terrified of seeing the roots of its naval power cut off that it was constrained to make peace, at the Treaty of Amiens in 1802. In the story of Bonaparte's love affairs we may have possibly the microcosm of the Empire's fate. We know that before the young and brilliant officer made love to Josephine in order to please Barras, he had turned away from Désirée Clary after a brief and idyllic affair. Désirée later became Queen of Sweden as wife of Bernadotte, who re-entered Paris as victor in 1815. Napoleon had taken no interest in these Nordic states. Even in Holland he had failed to benefit from the lessons that the clever and adaptable Louis had learned from his subjects. He never attempted to conquer Denmark. It is true that when the Grand Army camped in Poland in 1811 and found itself in direct control of the eastern Baltic, England's position was made even more critical. But this was not a deliberate move in a systematic policy of intervention designed to harm Britain's northern trade, and Napoleon never exploited the advantage it gave him. He was pursuing a continental policy which came to grief in the wastes of Russia and perished in the flames of Moscow just in time to save England.

So England remained certain of receiving regular supplies of wood and could continue to build its fleet unhindered. The only source of competition that might cause anxiety was in its former American colonies. There, too, shipbuilding yards were buzzing with activity and there was no shortage of wood, of course. Within a few years the fleet of this newly-born nation amounted to more than half the English tonnage, and took its place as the second in the world. In 1792 the Americans landed in Japan, where they successfully disputed the trading rights of the Dutch in 1797. This was a success without a future, but it forged a first link, and turned the United States from the coasts of England, whose superiority was still manifest in the 1812 wars against Washington.

Nevertheless, from 1780 to 1850 Suffren's country was still devoting immense thought, calculation and ingenuity to the improvement of sailing-ships, in seeking to lighten the wooden hulls, and to make the greatest possible use of the frame. When the British navy made its last sailing-ships in about 1830, it copied French models. However, it is true that the United States also benefited considerably from French improvements; with a daring use of capital provided by brand-new shipbuilders, they produced the clippers which were the most extraordinary sailing ships in the history of the sea. These ships had long, narrow lines, carrying an immense area of sail (more than forty times that of the hull) and sailed so fast that between 1825 and 1850 they had reduced the North Atlantic crossing from 25 days to less than 10, with 3,000 tons of cargo. This was swifter and much cheaper transport than was provided by the first steamships.

Every expansion of the maritime economy favoured the commercial activity of London. The blockade certainly harmed England's markets in Central Europe, but it also forced England to exploit its sea-power more fully and the more distant markets which England had already begun to exploit after the Treaty of Utrecht were still bringing in profit. From this point of view the Emperor's intervention in the Iberian peninsula forced the two American monarchies to play the English game. When the court of Lisbon was threatened by Junot it had turned with some hesitation to its 'natural protectors' the English. While Braganza was crossing from Portugal to Brazil, the English admiral had ample time to indoctrinate his protégé and to wrest a firm trade treaty from him. When the stocks of English manufacturers threatened the economy of the capital, as much as possible was dumped on the quays of Rio de Janeiro; the taste for English luxury goods soon spread in the old colonial city thanks to the relative cheapness of these surplus products. Not only the Portuguese courtier, but the native Brazilian had small palaces built, furnishing and decorating them in the same style as he adopted for his carriages, his finery and his fêtes; in this way this new court consoled itself for its exile. In exchange the English ships brought to London precious metals, Brazil-wood (a dye product still widely used) and several raw materials in the way of metals. English banks arranged credits for the Brazilians and supported the founding of a state bank in Rio de Janeiro.

Although English pressure on Brazil was heavy and sometimes tactless, it was more effective than the exhibitions of impatience staged by British admirals in the Spanish ports and especially in Buenos Aires, where Beresford and Whitelock failed to stir up public opinion in spite of the weakness of the Spanish Viceroy. The outcome benefited only Deliniers, who boasted of his victories to Napoleon (1807–8). Nevertheless Napoleon's invasion of Spain, the cheapness of English foodstuffs which the great agricultural countries eagerly demanded, and the example of French and American ideas, led to a wide revolutionary movement which started in 1810; its effect was to detach Spanish America from its European court and draw it more and more into English economic channels.

But before dealing with this English economic victory in Spanish America, let us pause to describe the changes taking place in the United States. The example of their prosperity, following on their independence, had important repercussions on the whole of the continent.

The United States Governed by the South

The thirteen colonies were far from being the largest state in either population or size immediately after achieving their independence, but their subsequent transformation was the quickest history has ever known. In less than seventy years the Americans had, as it were, exploded all over the continent; the area they occupied rose from one to eight million square miles while the population grew to about fifty millions.

By the peace treaty, England had given up to the victors not only their own lands but all English territories from the Alleghanies to the Mississippi. Thus when the constitution of the new federal republic came to be drawn up the colonists had to decide in whose hands the authority over so many new lands should lie. The states opening on to the west and in particular Virginia wished to extend their own authority in that direction. On the other hand, the states shut in on the Atlantic seaboard, who were restricted by old frontiers which cut them off from the west, feared the excessive expansion of their rivals and intended the unoccupied lands to be used for the creation of new states. They proposed that for the time being they should be governed by the Federal Government. Winning their point in this matter, the small but often highly developed states ensured the authority of a central government which the bigger states, particularly the less developed ones of the south, did not accept without reservation. The political destiny of the United States could be seen in their constitutions; the means at their disposal looked less promising at first sight. They had achieved incredible results in the great open country, but the means they had used were imported directly from Europe at that date. For the first fifty years there was nothing unusual about the American economy. The north-eastern states still remained more maritime than industrial, while their harbours were first fishing-ports and then shipyards, building those beautifully designed ships which were to become the models of the world's last sailing fleet. If industry was progressing, it was still at the craftsman stage, since so much English equipment had to be imported. In the south, more and more cotton was being grown; it soon replaced Indian cotton in the European market because it was produced cheaply on virgin lands and it was processed better than the cotton of the Old World, and because Whitney had already invented the picking machine. Finally, the triumphant westward advance of the settlers passed the Alleghanies and moved on towards the rich lands of the Mississippi. This unceasing conquest of new territories gave American families an almost boundless faith in the resources of their lands. The birth rate was high and the death rate relatively low in a population which closely followed all the medical and hygienic precepts of the most up-to-date Europeans. The native population increased and trebled in fifty years.

This process was of course helped by immigration, though this remained moderate; over this same period it accounted in all for less than half-a-million Europeans and Negroes. There were many Anglo-Saxons who felt quite at home in this new England which had adopted the customs of the old country; and the Irish already realized that cultivation of the land was more rewarding in this expanding economy than in their own island. Large numbers of Germans made their way from the plains of the Rhineland to Hamburg, and then sailed via England to the shores of America, particularly to Pennsylvania and Maryland. They were welcomed there by fellow countrymen who still remembered their own language, but they soon learned to speak nothing but English so that they could merge as soon as possible into a new country which they adopted so wholeheartedly that they often even changed their surnames.

The Negroes were still being dragged there in droves in almost as great numbers as before independence. Several states had, it is true, adopted a free constitution, forbidding slavery. Pennsylvania in particular had proclaimed the right of free birth: the children of slaves were to be freed. The slave trade had been condemned by the Congress of Vienna and the English, who had been the greatest dealers in black ivory during the previous century, were now the most fanatical in spreading the ideas of Wilberforce and keeping a watch on the seas. But it could not be denied that cotton was a lucrative crop, thanks almost entirely to the Negroes. The slave trade enabled shipowners, even those from the north, to make handsome profits. Nearby Cuba was a prolific slave-market and one in which there was very little risk. In short, the Negro population continued to grow, all the more since they had large families. In 1808 the Federal Government condemned the slave trade in principle, but it was another twelve years before the measures which were slowly enforced began to restrict it. After 1820 the trade continued, but under cover and at increasing cost; it became, in fact, so expensive that it was finally abandoned – although not until 1830.

The increasing production of cotton, tied to this forced importation of Negro labour, was probably the outstanding feature of American life at this date; however swift the westward advance of northern agriculturists,

it was more than equalled by the expansionist policy of the southern
farmers. The advance towards the Mississippi in the south was also a
much easier proposition. At first it came up against the frontiers of France
and Spain, but both readily relinquished their claims, one in 1803 and the
other in 1819. New Orleans entered the Union, but what was most important was that all the lands from the Mississippi to the Pacific ceased to be
legally French and were opened to the triumphant advance of American
farmers. Southern expansion extended to Florida and the north of the
Gulf of Mexico as well.

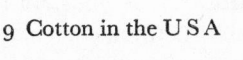

9 Cotton in the U S A

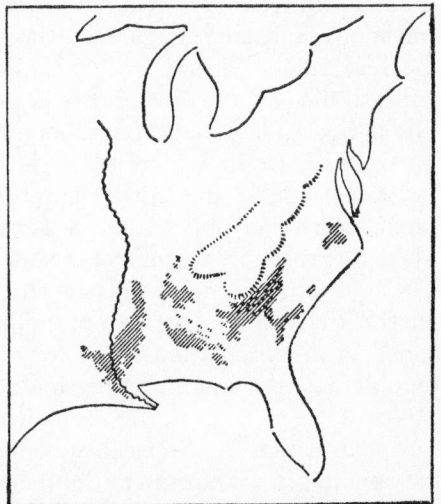

Black dots: in 1790
Grey: in 1840

    This first phase of American history was an age of good relationships.
Quarrels between the supporters of Hamilton or Jefferson died down, and
a measure of balance was achieved between those who wished the centre
of gravity of the Union to be kept on the Atlantic seaboard and consequently advocated political, administrative and monetary centralization,
and those who wished all efforts to be concentrated on the new lands of the
west and south. As the number of inhabitants in the interior grew, however, their claims acquired greater weight and led to changes in the
American structure radical enough to provoke the upheavals which followed in the time of Jackson.

    This southern hero, victorious general of the Florida war, had offered
himself as candidate in the Presidential election at the head of a new party
called the Democrats, whose policy was to defend the interests of western
farmers against the industrial and traditionally commercial east. Once
elected, he reorganized the administration from top to bottom, suppressed the central control of the bank, circulated easy credit, and issued a
great variety of banknotes, sometimes barely covered by local banks whose
policy was often exceedingly reckless. This transformation in the structure
of credit was the American equivalent of Europe's 1830 revolutions and
was caused, moreover, by the same economic crisis.

The Mississippi became the great economic artery, navigated by the first steamboats which brought to New Orleans a volume of traffic greater than that of New York. A few years later, the shores of the lakes proved to be ideal sites for industry and towns, especially as all this constructive effort gave a marked impetus to mining activities to the north of the Alleghanies in Pennsylvania, which turned out to be rich in raw materials such as iron and coal, and soon became a great producer of steel.

In the meantime, the old rivalry of north and south continued. The north's economic successes had perhaps a more solid foundation, but those of the south were very real, and in any case more spectacular: with their enormous lands and magnificent horses, the aristocrats of the south were the real rulers of the newly acquired territories. They dominated the political life of the United States in practice, following a militant policy at this period. Their determination to conquer added almost two million square miles to the Union, through the annexation of vast Mexican terri- tories. In fact, in the thirties large numbers of planters had crossed the Mexican frontier and settled in Texas with their slaves and their cotton. Mexico was barely in control of such a vast and remote land any longer. The agitation kept up by the new settlers (which gave some Frenchmen the illusion that they might be able to stage a come-back in America) soon ended in the foundation of the free State of Texas in 1835; and the new republic lost no time in requesting admission to the Union in 1840. The causes of the ensuing war are somewhat obscure and complicated, but the ease with which the Mexican was defeated immeasurably heightened the self-confidence of the gallant Southerners. American troops even marched as far as Mexico and imposed their own peace terms. This war was the expression in the United States of the European crisis of 1848, and was brought on by the same economic depression.

The duality of America assumed a more serious aspect after that date. The quarrels between the industrial Northerners and the cotton-planters of the South with their immense territories had been kept in check for some time while both sides were so prosperous. But strife recurred on a grand scale when the vast state of Texas was colonized by slavery. In 1820, with the entry of Missouri as a state supporting slavery, the South had undertaken to confine the penetration of slavery to latitude 36° 60'. But in 1850, the Southerners were talking like masters, and regarded themselves as the em- bodiment of triumphant patriotism, and the new chivalry. From the ranks of their aristocracy came the best orators, the most convinced and the most convincing politicians. The new Democrats, in the name of the Patriotic Union, persuaded a majority of Northern electors to adopt the conciliatory attitude which was vital if the Union was to be preserved. In 1850, the Northern states consented to pursue runaway slaves on their lands in order to return them to their Southern owners.

Despite the Southern progress, the North was often said to hold the upper hand. Between these two old antagonists of North and South, the West, which had also continued to grow, was to play the part of umpire.

In the 1840s in fact, the advance towards the West was all the more rapid since the lands on the right bank of the Mississippi were the richest in the Union. This was the black earth zone, whose fertility soon became legendary. Bridges were thrown across the wide river, and ships provided excellent transport for agricultural machinery and heavy sacks of corn and maize. The industrial Middle West had a strong vested interest in this cultivation of virgin lands, since it manufactured the ploughs, harrows and a whole range of implements for the new country. These products were continually being improved, and the revolutionary new harvesting machines caused a sensation when they were displayed at exhibitions in Europe. As the Americans penetrated beyond the banks of the Mississippi, they began to realize the immense resources of the Rocky Mountain area. The feeling gained ground that a country that was so rich and so free must be a new earthly paradise, and great religious movements swept the country: Methodism became a little more tolerant, opening its ranks to Episcopalianism and Anglicanism, and everywhere there was a strange respect for any form of religion; the most curious new doctrines were widely accepted and credence was given to the most disconcerting manifestations of religious eccentricity. There was the curious story of the Mormons who discovered a new bible written on leaves of gold, and announcing an American Messianism: all who followed the word of Smith belonged to the chosen people. The peculiarity of this doctrine and of its polygamous way of life stirred up such harsh persecution of the Mormons that they fled to the rich alluvial lands on the shores of the Salt Lake, protected by wide stretches of desert and rock in what was later called Utah. In the Salt Lake they discovered a new Dead Sea, into which flowed the little Jordans of a new Promised Land.

Such, then, was the vast and complex experiment in which the rival doctrines of the chivalrous, victorious aristocracy of the South, the hardworking and industrial middle classes of the North, and the conquering peasantry of the virgin lands of the West, carried away from time to time by great whirlwinds of Messianic mysticism, were being pitted against each other on a chess board the size of a continent. In the second half of the century, before they became united around the railroads, the United States went through an appalling civil war. But well before the middle of the century, the miracle of their territorial, economic and demographic expansion attracted the attention of the other Americas which now aspired to independence in their turn.

America for the Americans

We have described the relative importance of the cities of the Spanish Empire; and they were also the crucible in which a very unequal society was being forged. Their population consisted of small traders, creoles, and sailors, grouped around ports whose equipment was provided by the government and whose activity depended upon trade, stimulated by the liberal measures proclaimed by Charles III. Their new-found prosperity was based on trade between the agricultural hinterland and industrial Europe. From 1810 onwards, it was clear that industrial Europe meant first and foremost England. All this mass of ordinary people living in the port cities were in no sense an *élite*, but it was they who kept the shops and streets busy and provided the contingents of volunteers who were called on to deal with each new political crisis. The new nationalism was beginning to develop out of these recurring political upheavals.

Above this urban population the aristocracy fell into three major groups. First there were poor creoles of humble birth who had made a large fortune out of trade or the exploitation of lands surrounding the towns. They were beginning to emerge as leaders and figureheads for the new patriotism which had nationalism as one of its chief ideals. Side by side with them were many aristocrats who had only recently arrived in the colony, but who were firmly settled there and began to rear families; they continued to exert a great influence by their personal conduct although their official duties imposed by Madrid were coming to an end and they were increasingly tending towards local patriotism.

Finally there were the officials, every one a Spaniard and essentially a monarchist at heart, who were there only to fill the lucrative posts dispensed by the capital. They looked down on the creoles, and even on those of their predecessors who had finally opted for the New World. The more local patriotism developed the further they were driven into isolation, and they soon became suspect. This minority had at its disposal troops and income from the Treasury which consisted chiefly of customs receipts, and was bitterly resented by the merchants. In a short time the officials found that the creole and half-caste peoples, most of the middle classes and some of the aristocrats were solidly turned against them.

As English merchandise and the prosperity which accompanied it increased in the ports, the conflict between nationalists and Spaniards became more intense, and before long it was spreading to the interior. Planters and stockbreeders could obviously not be expected to have any very clear ideas about politics, but they were loyal to a few leaders, most of whom were great landowners won over to the defence of local interests. Soon the clergy itself was drawn into the conflict. The half-castes saw the struggle as a chance to bring out into the open all the bitterness and uneasiness they felt at the presence of the Spaniard. All these factors combined to create an atmosphere of seething unrest which resulted in the collapse of the old Viceregal administration. For a time the re-establishment of the legitimate monarchy in Spain calmed tempers, but the old Christian interests loyal to the monarchy carried the day only because of their hopes that Madrid might reform the viceroys and open the doors of the government to local interests on the spot. However, Madrid, which was wholly taken up with plans for restoration in Europe, had little interest in these overseas territories except for the income they brought in by taxation. Consequently in 1818 and 1820 uprisings broke out everywhere.

From Mexico to Chile all was unrest and upheaval, although the out-

breaks were not sufficiently large or uniform to engulf the whole of Spanish
America at once. It was a case of each city defending its own patriotism,
and involving only its own hinterland in its activities. There were innumerable independent rebel centres which leaders like San Martino or the 'polytechnician' Bolivar could not succeed in linking together. Iturbide's Mexico formed an isolated group at one end of the Empire, and the Rio de la

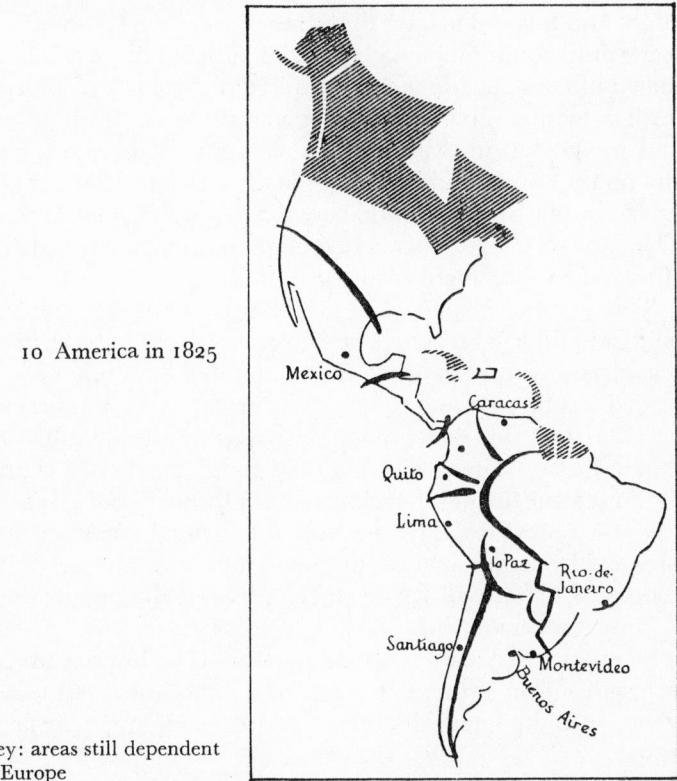

10 America in 1825

Grey: areas still dependent
on Europe

Plata republic of Buenos Aires at the other end. In between there was no
uniformity in the string of capitals from Santiago to Guatemala, although
everything was happening in them simultaneously. This excessive fragmentation, which did not prevent Spain from being defeated, militated
against the setting up of a creole empire. San Martino, discouraged, left
his America to end his days in the calm retreat of Boulogne-sur-Mer.
Similarly Bolivar and Iturbide failed in their later attempts at empire-
building. The economics and the politics of Spanish America remained
enclosed within small states, each constructed around its own city.

Inside these states none of the political or social problems had been
solved by the defeat of Spain. The rural population who lacked any economic or political education continued to be the devoted soldiers of inland
leaders and of the great landed proprietors. These two groups, anxious to
remain masters of their own fate, had to defend a very lax federal law

against the centralizing tendencies of the small capitals which were the seat of the government in each new republic. The landowner-captains were always ready to fight, and could in a few days improvise a formidable cavalry which was raised on their own estates where there was an abundant supply of horses, servants and retainers. They wanted to dictate their own law to the city. The city, for its part, relied on its population of merchants who were now in control of the ports, the market and customs revenue; and it could always find from among the conflicting groups a leader who could count on enough popular support to raise infantry. This leader then built fortifications, and exploited the lack of unity of the country leaders; with a mixture of daring and diplomacy, using money from trade and weapons from Europe, he then tried to impose the authority of the city on the countryside. Thus, even after the break-up of Spanish America, each republic had its quarrel between city unionists and country federalists. The quarrel was to persist throughout the nineteenth century, and its effects are still evident in the twentieth.

This was not a quarrel of ideas; any catch-phrase borrowed from the political and legal disputes of Europe was only used to disguise the respective claims of town and country interests. The more important the part played by the port and the city, the greater was the success of the unionist party. It was this which enabled Rosas to establish his famous dictatorship in Buenos Aires which endured for a quarter of a century; he built up the Argentine during that time but finally encountered the resistance of the city of Montevideo. The interminable struggle between Buenos Aires and Montevideo ended in a partition of lands and interests on both sides of the Rio de la Plata, and led to the creation of the new country of Uruguay.

Only one region succeeded in avoiding the general pattern of urban and rural enmity because it was too remote in the interior and still too loyal to its organization of tiny villages carved out of the forest. This was Paraguay where an Indian majority preserved its autonomy in the face of two Spanish states.

These three examples will be enough. It is not necessary to enlarge on the theory of the system of European settlement in Peru, whose capital was cut off from the vast lands it controlled and which had now to be content with the old Indian territory enclosed within its ancient frontiers. It would also be too complicated to attempt to explain in a few lines the strange destiny of Mexico and of various states in Central America, where the poor white, the Indian and the half-caste formed an alliance against the aristocracy loyal to Spain.

Let us next consider the origins of Brazil. The country had given asylum to the Portuguese royal family, and when John VI of Braganza returned to Europe, he made a secret agreement with his son Pedro advising him to proclaim independence on his own initiative if the yoke of Lisbon seemed too heavy for the Brazilians; for they had also felt the stirrings of nationalism and were claiming that only men born in the country had the right to make its laws. At all events, the wise policy of the Braganzas succeeded in preserving the unity of this vast land where revolts in north and south did not result in final separation since each side always accepted in the end the flexible and easy-going rule, undemanding and always open to reform, which was exercised from the palaces of Rio de Janeiro. Pedro I was proclaimed constitutional Emperor in 1822. He abdicated in favour of his son Pedro II after the crisis of 1830, and a ten-year regency followed.

Africa Not for the Africans

South Africa had been in a state of flux since 1780, and especially since the beginning of the nineteenth century when the Dutch governors, with their rigid and restrictive administration, handed over the Cape to English rule. The white settlers, who were Dutch and French at the time of the Netherlands Company, loaded their *trekken* and set out for the northern plains in defiance of the official ban on such adventures, under the tolerant eyes of their new masters. In this movement, the migrants came up first against

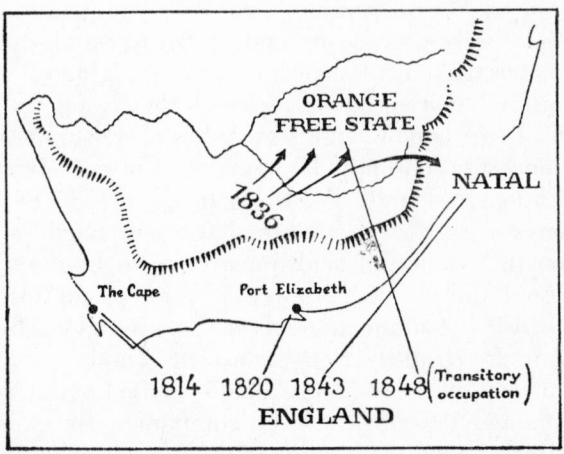

11 Stages of the English Occupation and Movement of the Boer Population in South Africa, 1814–48

the Hottentots and then against the Kaffirs. The Negroes, who were themselves conquerors coming southward in search of independence, at first retreated before this invasion from the sea. Some allowed themselves to be won over and once more found themselves slaves; indeed slavery was abolished only in 1834, when there were more than 30,000.

While the old population was spreading out over the northern plains, new arrivals were landing on the coasts; the English were now settling at Port Elizabeth before succumbing in their turn to the call of the interior. Two races, two languages and two legal systems, both from Europe, were struggling for influence. Sometimes the Englishman imposed his ways and sometimes he respected his Dutch neighbour, who nevertheless acted as the African had done before him. The Dutch fled from the new conqueror, set out across the plains, passed the Orange river, reached the Vaal river, and crossed it in 1837, disputing the land with the Africans the more stubbornly the farther they moved away from the ports where they had landed, the more so since the English anti-slavery movement was affecting their traditional colonial economy. The Kaffirs, threatened in their retreats, turned to large-scale reprisals, burning lands and destroying the white man's herds in a merciless battle which dominated the mid-nineteenth century. But when the English army intervened on the side of the settlers, the Kaffirs embarked on a gigantic programme of suicide; in a paroxysm of mystic frenzy, they destroyed their own herds and their own farms, and by this act of collective folly laid the country wide open to the invaders.

With the Kaffirs subdued, the Dutch could press on to the territory of the Zulus, when there were fresh battles, and fresh victories won at a cruel cost.

EUROPEAN PENETRATION OF ASIA

The new Latin-American states were an opportunity for England. In each there were cities to be built, ports to be improved and agriculture to be modernized. English technique, English material and English capital found profitable investments, although these were not always completely secure, for each economic crisis brought disaster to the most adventurous business concerns. Through large-scale buying of brazil-wood at a time when artificial dyeing was already being introduced, the Rothschild Bank suffered several losses; and the Barings invested too heavily in Argentina. But on the whole the fields opened up to England's merchant shipping and trade still seemed limitless. Obviously in this rapidly increasing trade, British businessmen realized the prodigious benefits they stood to gain from free trade from 1840 onwards. If there were no customs duties to pay, the new overseas nations would choose London as the site of their financial, commercial and industrial companies. Every improvement in technique strengthened the position of the London market.

The English had also to reckon with competition from the United States, which was already showing signs of a lively ambition, especially since the Americans still feared an invasion by England. The Monroe doctrine had an economic significance: it was designed to dispute with London the task of providing America with the equipment necessary for its development. But the United States had its hands full already with its own lands in the west, and economically Buenos Aires, Rio de Janeiro or Callao proved to be closer to London than to New York. Moreover, England had the great good fortune to possess enormous advantages not only in the Atlantic Ocean but increasingly in the Pacific and Indian Oceans. In 1825 Tasmanian fishermen settled at Portland. In 1836 a settler went to live at the place on the Australian coast which later grew into Melbourne. In 1830 a company was formed to exploit the south coast which distributed lands to many colonization societies. In 1835 Adelaide was founded and named after the wife of William IV. The rapid growth of India was the most important of all.

Capitalism in India

In India, in the nineteenth century, English capitalism was trying to encompass one of the oldest of Eastern civilizations. Nowhere else was there such a direct and ruthless clash between two worlds, two ways of feeling and of reasoning, and two ways of life, between an invader equipped with every available industrial tool and peoples nourished by traditions laid down like alluvial deposits by tides of invasion through the centuries from every part of Eurasia. It is difficult to describe this vast encounter between Europe and Asia in a few words and we must leave out a great many aspects of it, although to an Indian philosopher the truth could only be arrived at through a study of every single aspect.

It is tempting to confine our attention to military history. In that realm Western superiority was so overwhelming that our traditional historical studies concentrate on it with a thoroughness which at least has the merit of being obvious. Wellesley's battle against the Mahrattas, and the bitter struggles to seize the remains of the Mogul Empire after the capture of Seringapatam, the occupation of the Punjab, the control of the routes to Afghanistan and Persia, the conquest of the Gurkhas, and the subduing of the Rajputs in 1789–1823, are well known. However, the details of this story would reveal ways of fighting very different from those of European armies at the same period; much of it was a continuation of the eighteenth century conflicts and in many respects it was also a battle against the remnants of the French experiment. But although the Directory confirmed the winding up of the French East India Company in 1796, many French officers stayed on to become advisers to Hindu princes, with an authority heightened by the brilliant victories of Napoleon. The English learned a great deal from the struggle. They had to face resistance which, although unskilled, was liable to break out at any time, and had also to deal with a disconcerting subtlety in negotiation. The cruellest Indians showed themselves to be the most loyal once they had been defeated, while the smooth-tongued were the most dangerous in peace-time, since every term of a treaty had to be endlessly re-discussed, re-negotiated and enforced. The last blow struck by Indian resistance was the famous revolt of the Sepoys, whose notorious massacres provoked a bloody reprisal.

The English learned to take advantage not only of the religious rivalry between Muslims and Hindus, but also of the infinite number of conflicting interests which divided princes and empires; and to exploit the myriad local rivalries which could sway potentates from one policy to another. All these eventually ensured the dominance of the merchants who, though few in number, were in close touch with each other through the new techniques of communication, particularly the optical telegraph; they were

also bound together by a community of spirit and feeling born of their belief in the superiority of European civilization.

England continued with the conquest of India and installed fortified
posts in the frontier regions. At the same time it changed the structure of
its Indian policy. The commercial privileges of the Company came to an
end in 1813, although it was to continue to administer the country until
1865. Above all, English civilization modified the structure of this huge
country's institutions.

When it first occupied Bengal, the Company's great task had been to fix
and collect the land dues in spite of a punctilious but intermittent supervision by parliament in London. It took a lesson from the experiences of
the Moghuls, and retained the services of the *zamindars*, a kind of farmers-
general who were responsible for the land tax on a contractual basis.
Gradually, however, their functions were divested of all the traditional
subtleties which had made them so flexible; the *zamindars* then became
landowners in the European style, possessing gigantic estates of which they
were merely the tax-collectors. The peasants, who had previously been
subjects of the Treasury, became tenants with a precarious tenure. This
system had every kind of advantage for the Company. It spared it the
trouble of going into Indian affairs in detail, and gave security to its allies

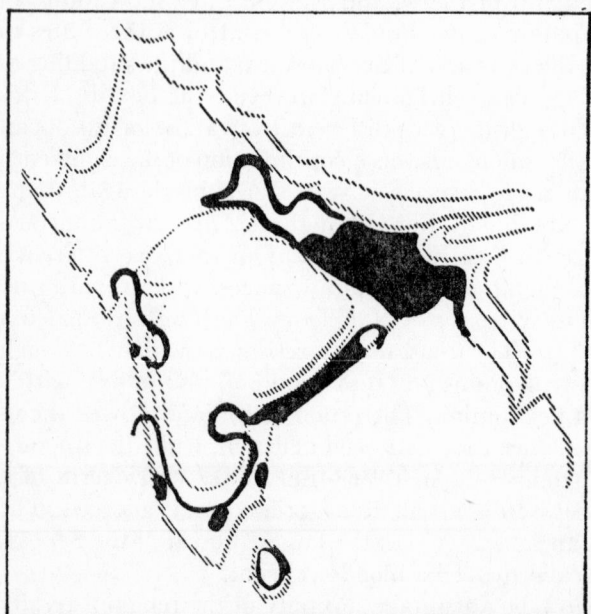

12 English Possessions
in India, 1795–1815

Black: English
possessions in 1795 and
their extensions by
1815

(an unheard-of legal gift) since they had become its accomplices in the exploitation of the country. Thus the system of large estates was able to
spread southward as far as the presidency of Madras.

However, there were quick reactions against this brutal irruption of
property rights into a civilization which knew nothing of all the
rigours of land-ownership in Europe. The most far-sighted Indians

persuaded the English administration that if the right of property was to be adapted to an Indian economy, its beneficiaries would have to be more carefully selected from the complex hierarchy of rural society. The farmer and the *rayat* were obviously more suitable to assume this rôle of land-owner than the faraway and indifferent tax-collector of former times. The *Rayat-wari* system was therefore developed after 1830 and was particularly strong in the centre and south of the peninsula; or was re-established in Madras and penetrated as far as Bombay. The occupant of the field became its owner. On the other hand, of course, it was on him that the full burden of heavily assessed taxation fell, although it was revised every thirty years. This dual system of ownership, by *zamindars* and *rayats*, created two classes on European lines in a proud society in which previously the honorary rank of the castes had been only incidentally based on wealth. There had been great landowners, particularly in the north, and average landowners more frequently in the south. However, both gradually became aware of the enormous advantages of the European system of property rights. This *laissez-faire* economy absolved the landowners from all obligation to care for their tenants, once the rent assessment had been discussed and then fixed for a long time to come. Even the *rayat* soon became a person of property since he farmed out his land to one or more peasants without rights. It was these peasants who had ultimately to bear the full weight of the new money-based social pyramid.

A further innovation was that the landowner, whether great or small, paid the land tax in money, and consequently exacted his rents in cash. This marked the end of the era of transactions in kind, when the whole collective life of a community had centred around the distributions of food, organized in the centre of the village. Reforms which were so profoundly revolutionary did not penetrate easily into all the country districts of India.

The old communal rules persisted in the south, where the village groups supervised the distribution of the monsoon rainwater collectively; this was then stored in innumerable artificial cisterns and rationed out on the lands during the dry season. The same continuity of tradition persisted in certain northern regions, particularly in Kashmir, where a marvellous network of canals distributed the waters from the Himalayas. Proud traditions were also preserved elsewhere in the regions not subject to European rule. In these incompletely assimilated areas, governmental power was hardly represented except by commissioners or residents stationed near the local ruler, whether he was a powerful prince or a village chief. These commissioners had full power in theory, but were in fact reduced to incessant negotiations and endless palavers. Gradually a *modus vivendi* was reached in these areas, sanctioned by the central government; it tended to establish uniform practices and thus to set up an Indian law, but it did not succeed in eliminating the many varied local traditions.

Naturally the English tried to establish civil and criminal codes of law on the Western pattern, and to create some unity in the legal system. They had to be satisfied with laying down clear rules which took no account of the caste system although they did allow Europeans to have a special legal system of their own. They had to give up all idea of geographical uniformity; there were laws rather than one universal law, and although the principle of ownership was recognized in some districts, it was far from being generally accepted. However, it was widespread enough to have brought in its train an extensive circulation of money, which in turn created new relationships between men. Many landowners, and even more tenant-farmers, had to borrow from a money-lender, whose importance in rural society thus increased considerably. In many cases the peasant's subjection was closer and harsher under the régime of mortgage and money-lending than under the old communal village system, even when the latter was at the mercy of great and powerful feudal lords. It is difficult to say whether this new Western system of ownership can prove lasting. Today as formerly, numerous cases are quoted where whole villages disappeared as a result of political disturbances, vanishing into the forests and hiding there for long periods, awaiting a suitable moment to return. They would reappear twenty or thirty years later, rebuild their villages on the old site and according to the old rules, and resume their communal life of work and mutual assistance.

However precarious these new social structures which Europeans were initiating in India may have seemed, they did nevertheless show concrete results about the middle of the century. Of course, much fairly fertile land remained fallow. The English occupation, which was almost comically small in number, did not include any settlers anxious to clear great stretches of land since manual work was considered beneath the dignity of the European. The half-castes were no more anxious to undertake it; as for the Indian, the very idea of leaving his ancestral land was repugnant to him. Consequently there was very little radical clearance of land. In general the old crops continued to be grown by the old methods, which were often quite efficient and brought in several harvests a year on the rich lands of the Delta.

The various kinds of rice were carefully cultivated, since they formed the basis of the local diet. The villages tried to sell a surplus, especially since under the new system they needed to have money. As rice sold well, the poor in India lived on millet, sorghum and all kinds of minor cereals. In addition to cereals, the pulses – there were as many different kinds of peas as there were districts – and the oil-crops which mainly consisted of flaxes or sesames for which there were innumerable uses in a village community, sometimes sold fairly well in the market. Lastly the traditional cotton attempted to compete successfully with its new rival from the United States, at least for internal consumption.

The End of the Celestial Mandate in China

China remained a vast besieged fortress. In the previous century Kien-Lung had ensured the autonomy of the Middle Empire; of the previous

Christian population he retained only a few isolated Jesuits (for example the president of the Court of Mathematics) and a few Western technicians, mainly artillerymen. He felt powerful enough to exact tribute from foreigners, and admitted the Portuguese, who had been in Macao for two hundred years, only as Chinese subjects. But the seventeenth son of Kien-Lung, his successor, Kia-King, was not left in peace; for the first twenty years of the century, he had continually to dismiss foreign embassies from Russia, America, England and Japan which came to request commercial privileges. The English were particularly persistent. In 1808, for instance, after Admiral Drury had been expelled from Macao he hit upon the idea of going up to Canton, where he was met with a stiff cannonade and turned back; this added one more rebuff to the many administered to those who had been trying to get through to Peking and the Summer Palace for twenty years. For a time the Westerners hesitated. The Dutch abandoned the attempt in the face of Kia-King's obduracy, while the Spaniards were content to slip in under cover of Portuguese privileges; the Russians sent embassies and gifts brought by caravans in even greater numbers than before, but without much success, while the King of Sweden relinquished his privileges to the Göteborg Company. France kept up the illusion of protecting the Catholic missionaries who were forbidden by the Empire but were tolerated by the local potentates fairly generously.

There was another reason for the restlessness of Kia-King's reign. Conspiracy seemed to be rife in every district of China and the time to proclaim the end of the dynasty's rule appeared ripe. Secret societies flourished; that of the Water Lily, for instance, even managed to get a footing inside the Peking Palace. This unrest became even more widespread under Kia-King's successors and the period of the great troubles began. Arrests and executions did not prevent the spread of the secret societies in Canton or Honan. The court was overwhelmed with alarmist reports; it was thought that the Society of the Dryads of Heaven and Earth had been exterminated, but its cells proliferated all over the country and its members incited what was later known as the Taiping rebellion. Religious quarrels, too, grew more bitter, in particular the conflicts between Muslims and Chinese. In Kashgaria a descendant of the prophet tried to remodel the state to his own advantage and evoked the law in the name of the Sultan of Constantinople. Everywhere the Muslim population was becoming stirred by the great news of progress from India and the West, and resented Chinese obstinacy.

In this disturbed atmosphere the persistence of the English paid dividends. Even after the previous stinging rebuffs, Lord Napier attempted to get through to the Emperor in 1833 but died of exhaustion. In 1839, the Guild of Canton Merchants, acting on orders from Peking, pitched 21,000 cases of opium from India into the sea. Rarely had a spectacular gesture such sound moral justification, although China itself had long been growing the poppy. But it was a direct blow at the Indian economy and a threat to the rapid development of that vast empire which the English were having some difficulty in controlling. This time England despatched fifty ships and five thousand men, instituted the blockade of Canton and sailed up the Pearl River. The court at Peking grew worried and there was a hasty treaty. Canton, Amoy, Foochow, Ningpo and Shanghai were opened up to British trade and consuls were established there. The Chinese had to pay a high price for the opium which had been destroyed, as well as the entire cost of the war. Above all, the English obtained possession of the small island of Hong Kong, facing the Sino-Portuguese settlement of Macao. The small squadron quickly established a station, a port and a resident there. The port became thronged with English and American ships. The town of Victoria was begun in a hastily-chosen creek that proved to be often devastated by typhoons. Macao declined in importance and the ungrateful Spaniards left it for Amoy, soon taking with them the Portuguese themselves. Canton lost some of its trade to the new English harbour, which was soon fitted out with European equipment. True to the liberalism which had already brought such rich returns to the capital, the English Government declared Victoria a free port. Following in England's footsteps the whole of Europe now tried to get a footing in the Chu-kiang estuary. In 1845 France obtained privileges and had her right to protect missionaries confirmed. Then the United States made a treaty, followed by Belgium, Norway and Sweden.

So the vast land of China was beginning to lose its coasts to the seafaring activity of the West, led by England, with the United States following in its wake. Of all the old powers, Russia alone resisted the lure of the sea.

The Steppes of Central Asia

If Catherine II had created the illusion of being an enlightened despot thanks to the philosophers, it was with Alexander I that Western institutions began to creep in. The French Revolution held no terrors for him in its early stages, but on the contrary showed him how powerful ideas of reform could be. Passionately devoted to new ideas, he tried to spread education, opened grammar schools – where Pushkin was educated for instance – encouraged an almost free press, and no longer used banishment as a way of dealing with his political opponents. He delighted in the company of Speransky, a man of humble birth and a son of a Greek Orthodox priest, whom he made his private adviser. This mathematics teacher dreamed of setting Russia on the road to liberty. He secretly admired the new developments in France and drew up plans for a reform of the legislature and administration for the Tsar (the only republican in his Empire). At the Ministry of Justice and later as privy counsellor and secretary to the Imperial Council, he tried to apply these reforms, but their effect was shattered by the French invasion, which revived the old Russian patriotism and caused the reformer to be exiled to Perm.

After his victory, the aging Alexander was disillusioned. He professed liberalism in Paris and recalled Speransky to St Petersburg, but lacked the courage of his convictions. He veered from one doctrine to another as the mood took him, promised the Poles liberties he failed to grant, and detested Metternich but nevertheless aligned his policy on that of Austria. His fine proud nationalism turned gradually to mysticism. When the Tsar

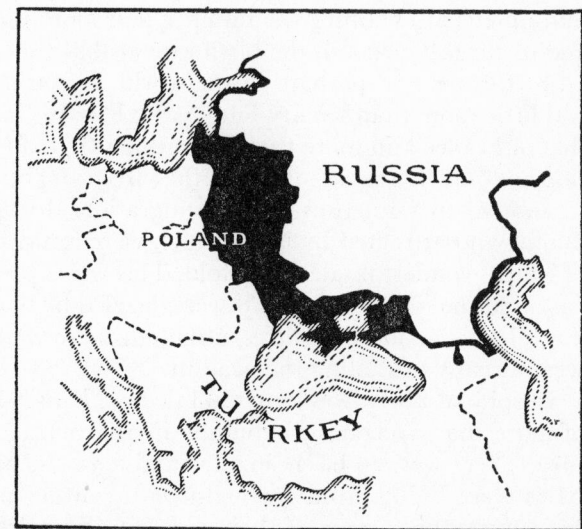

13 Russia's Advance towards the West

Black: Russia's advance from 1770–1800

hesitated, all Russia hesitated too, and this indecision continued under the reign of Nicholas I. Nicholas brutally suppressed the liberal decembrist movement which had hoped to take advantage of his accession to impose its reforms but he defended Greek liberty against Turkey and the Holy Alliance. In 1830, political uncertainty drove the Tsar into a suspicious autocracy. Education was closely supervised and the press spied upon and stifled; Poland was annexed after its unsuccessful revolt. The prevailing feeling in Russia was one of danger. It was obvious that maritime Europe, after breaching the Mediterranean and India, was now threatening central Asia by penetrating and settling there. Russia's counter-attack led her to the Crimean war.

This political vacillation on the part of Russia sprang from the dual nature of this vast land, which bordered Asia on the marshes of Kazan and shared a common frontier with Europe in the west. At each swing of the pendulum, however, Russia was drawing closer to the West. Nicholas I had entrusted to Speransky the drafting of a code, which was in itself a typically French approach, although the forty-eight volumes of this gigantic general collection of laws could be little more than a codification of the old ukases, treatises and manifestoes. They were followed by a more systematic résumé in fifteen volumes, intended to guide judges, but not to tie them down. Alexander II made a treaty with the allies of the Crimea and abandoned Persia to English influence, a move dictated by the fact that Russia's internal problems had demanded his full attention.

Russia was on the move. It was a huge country which defied all statistics and disconcerted the observer by the apparent uniformity of its peasant countryside, although this impresssion concealed subtle differences. Great changes took place in its population from time to time. At the end of the eighteenth century it had something like thirty million inhabitants. By the mid-nineteenth century the number had more than doubled. In Moscow and its neighbourhood, the birth rate at that time was probably the highest in Europe and perhaps in the world. It is true that expectation of life was little more than twenty-four years; Russia's infant mortality was twice that of France and more than three times that of Norway. Yet the population not only increased, owing to the birth rate, but shifted from one region to another in numerous internal migrations driven hither and thither by famine and attracted by lands which were reputed to be more fertile, and of which wonderful tales were told. This was especially true of lands in the east, and the starving peasants were dazzled by these rumours of imaginary paradises. The urban centres, although there were not many of them yet, were already attracting the peasant.

In spite of Boris Godunov's old decree, Russia had only very few towns of more than 100,000 inhabitants in the middle of the nineteenth century. There were to be six in 1870 and ten or so at the end of the century. Mills were built. From the eighteenth century onwards, the nobles had been regrouping some of their serfs into factories, which were vast compounds often in the country where the families lived together, each in its *isba*, and worked with rudimentary looms. Mills like those in England were introduced only very slowly, chiefly for cotton. Concentration in the mines took place more quickly. From 1816 something like a thousand tons of gold had been extracted from the gold-bearing sands of the Urals. In the Altai, in Transbaikalia, they were working silver-bearing lead, coal, and soon, beyond the Caucasus, naphtha, which was already very valuable.

It was perhaps a little too early to claim this as an industrial awakening in the first half of the nineteenth century. The migrations originating in the country districts in Russia were similar to those in western Europe. But although some led to the towns in the same way, others led more often to other regions, to the vast empty lands bordering the old Russia and to the vast stretches of Asia. Here the old traditional activities had been affected by England's seagoing trade and were dying out, so that the old economic centres in the heart of the country were decaying and consequently being left wide open to Russian expansion.

The Russian world was a strange one for the Westerner to understand. Its economy, compared with that of France or England, seemed static and backward and yet was continually growing. Like the American world it was surrounded to east and south by an enormous area over which it was free to expand. There was nothing unusual in whole villages and bands of peasants leaving their homes because of an epidemic or an economic crisis, or simply in pursuit of a mirage, at the call of a preacher announcing the promised land. It was more through this voluntary movement than through transportations, although these, as we know, played an important part, that Siberia was peopled by Russians. In addition the frontier nations on her borders continually protected, controlled and assimilated these advancing elements of Russian civilization. The continual extension of Russian territory, whether by migration or by political infiltration and conquest which was considerable even in the eighteenth century, reached astounding proportions.

This dynamism was perhaps precisely the result of the apparent confusion characteristic of everything Russian. Property had no clearly defined boundaries nor the law, religion or the country itself, except in the west where it met the German Empire. Imperceptibly one passed from Russia proper to 'marches', where the peasant was still a soldier as well and was obliged to answer the call of military leaders. But the soldier who had come from the interior also wanted land so that he could become a peasant. Those who had been unfortunate in the land they had received arranged matters between themselves and set up a *mir*. Officers and high-ranking leaders received a fairly large portion on which they settled as lords or middle-class landowners. In every case the Russian Empire acquired new lands. Life in these marches was always turbulent, although it was not so wild as it had been: in the west Poland had been conquered, the Ukraine had lost the last remnants of its military organization, and its Cossacks no longer fought except at folk festivals. Turkey, too, had lost its aggressive power and no longer disputed possession of the Black Sea, and there was no longer any danger from Persia. There were no more bitter struggles for the narrow passes leading into the closed river basins of central Asia which had made it for a time the fortress of Eurasia. Persia remained inactive between her two new rivals; the Russians were threatening it from the west while there was the English menace from the south. English shipping enabled Afghanistan to continue to keep order in this part of the world, just as the Bactrians had done in former times.

There was one main reason for the decline in the land power of the great Hakemite Empire of the noble Bactrians, which was still strong enough to defeat an English force. This was the inevitable decline of the great trade currents which had run from Asia to the Mediterranean and from India to Scandinavia, for it had been under their influence that these river basins of the Balkash, the Aral, and the Caspian had become the trade centres of the old continent. Every city was decaying and almost in ruins. Thus the old civilization was collapsing and the old empires were crumbling from the Black Sea to the great mountains of Tianshan. The vast mass of Russia was expanding continuously, not only towards the primitive Siberia offered to Boris Godunov, but equally towards the lands of the Muslim Empire.

It is true that the Russian drive southward was in quite a different category. The Scythian, Byzantine and Muslim civilizations had left much more decisive traces of their passage, and the population retained certain habits of work and of trading, while sometimes even a military discipline and some remnants of political organization remained, although its extent naturally varied from one region to another. From the end of the eighteenth century Russian penetration spread out through the Caucasus; at the beginning of the nineteenth century the mountain barrier was crossed and Tiflis was reached. The Russian stream then flowed easily down the depression towards the Black Sea and the Caspian and spread southward unchecked until it met resistance from Turkey which defended the Euphrates, or from Persia. The Russians then turned towards the northern chain and cleared the valleys of all remaining pockets of resistance. It was an easy conquest, owing partly, perhaps, to the fact that the Muslim overlord was disliked by the native population, and the Christian welcomed the orthodox soldier as a liberator, since they both practised a rite inherited from Byzantium.

At the time of the conquest, the Turks had decimated the handsome Georgian races which had been the pride of the slave-dealers in Constantinople. Afterwards they had massacred as many Russians as possible, whether venturesome soldiers or incautious settlers, and had reduced the

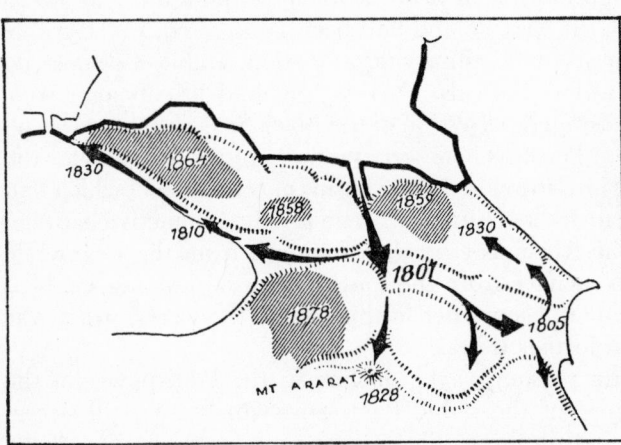

14 The Conquest of the Caucasus 1800–50

rest to slavery. Slaves and sons of slaves were therefore awaiting the arrival of the liberators. Once they had conquered Erivan and Mount Ararat, the Russians controlled the holy places of Armenian Christianity, which they treated with a respect which was all the more effective politically because it was genuine. The news of the restoration of the famous monastery spread throughout Turkey as far as Constantinople, where the Armenians controlled trade. The Tsar was considered as protector and saviour by all the Greek Orthodox Christians and he had no choice but to assume the title. The Armenian merchant preferred to remain where his business was, but the poor man and the peasant often left Turkish Armenia to breathe the free air of the new Russian Armenia. It is difficult to judge the extent of these movements of peoples, since they were offset by a gradual return of Muslims from Transcaucasia towards lands which had remained politically Turkish, but the military frontier soon became also the ethnic and religious frontier.

Russian civilization was nevertheless advancing in the wake of its small armies. To consolidate his authority, the Tsar confirmed the great lords in their possessions, and even granted them lands when they had none of their own, but on the slightest suspicion they were confiscated and redistributed to soldiers and officers. Russian peasants in their turn crossed the mountains and obtained plots of land which they quickly organized into *mirs*. Finally the boatmen of the Black Sea and Caspian brought to the gates of Baku and Batum the promise of increased trade.

THE CROSSING OF THE MEDITERRANEAN

The eastern opulence which had characterized the Mediterranean during the Middle Ages had been brought by the rich traffic from China, through Persia to Egypt. It had launched wave after wave of prosperity throughout North Africa. The real reason for the decadence of the southern Mediterranean lay in the decline of central Asia. The advance of Russia and the inactivity of Turkey led to the independence of Egypt, and left the states north of the Atlas Mountains to their own devices. They had to make the best use they could of such maritime traditions as were left to them by resorting to piracy on the high seas.

At the same time Atlantic traffic was entering the Mediterranean through the English Straits of Gibraltar. In this case, however, it was not English maritime trade which replaced the old economic system of the continent; this time it was French settlers who crossed from one shore of the sea to the other, from Europe to Africa.

Nationalism versus Islam

In 1779 Persia had selected Teheran as its new capital. It was a strategic move to enable more effective mobilization so that Georgia might be saved from the Russian threat. However, the move proved useless, since Persia, which had remained a feudal empire, could not put up any resistance to the Russian campaigns of 1804–13 and 1826–8. The diplomacy of Abbas Kajar attempted to play off the English against the Russians in vain. The English had allowed themselves to be beaten in Afghanistan by troops whom the Persians had often dominated in the past. The Persians could hardly hope for aid from France. The imperial victories had indeed made a deep impression throughout Asia, but there were no French troops available on that immense continent. The only Frenchmen there were archaeologists and scholars, although they were made very welcome. Consequently Persia had to accept the Russian advance. But a nationalist *élite* which was coming into being intended to place responsibility for the defeat on the outmoded traditional education, and the old Islamic religion, which was paralysed by sterile disputations. A new Persia was developing, and the old Persian rock began to emerge through the sedimentary deposits laid down by Islam.

The same process was apparent at about the same time in Turkey after the loss of the Crimea, when the Khan had embarked too late on essential reforms and the Sultan Mahmud II dissolved his janissaries. An admirer of Napoleon, he tried to remodel his army on modern lines. This plan was thwarted by the joint action of France and England at Navarino in 1827 – a repetition of Chesme. Fortunately the French wrecked Western plans by supporting Mehemet Ali in Egypt. Turkey succeeded in using diplomacy where Persia had failed; its leaders succeeded in holding out and even tried to follow up military reforms by administrative reforms which gave the Turks some redress against the old, rigid practices of Islam. Sultan Mejid's readiness to reform led to a reconciliation with Mehemet Ali, who was quite content to be a life-ruler of Egypt.

Istanbul was now developing into the capital of Turkey rather than the centre of Islam as it had been previously. Like Persia in the east, Egypt in the west was striving to become a nation, but the fellaheen were far from being a people in the modern sense of the term. After having massacred the Mamelukes systematically, Mehemet Ali, a Turkish official of Albanian stock, appealed to all men of ambition in the Mediterranean world including Lebanese, Greeks, Jews, Albanians and even French, to set up an Egyptian aristocracy. He needed a language which could be mutually understood by so many different peoples; the choice was a kind if composite Arabic which the fellah was slow to learn.

He sent 120 students to Paris, while he encouraged trade, developed cotton-growing, built villages and developed the towns. From 1800 to 1845 Egypt's population trebled. A new nation was breaking through the rigid structure of the old Islam.

At about the same time, the Moroccan empire was deprived of its most important source of wealth and prestige. The Moroccans had taken a great part in the continental activity of the African slave trade. It was they who had recruited supplies for the great Turkish and Indian markets, which had profited the Sultan of Zanzibar in particular; and they reaped further advantages later by directing this traffic from central Africa towards the west and the growing market on the Atlantic coast. The suppression of the Negro trade, at first in theory by the Congress of Vienna and later in fact, robbed them of this source of gain, while at the same time allowing the Westerners who had set foot on African soil to appear as liberators; this obviously acted to the detriment of the race and religion of the lords of Islam. The growing power of Western naval resources was also restricting the income from Atlantic piracy, especially that of the notorious Salé pirates; thus Morocco gradually lost one of the sources of revenue which came up from the Niger towards the Mediterranean.

Through its geographical position between eastern Islam, cut off from its Arab and Turkish bases, and a western Islam cut off from black Africa, Algeria became a wide corridor wide open to the claims of the north.

The Birth of French Africa

France certainly cannot claim a place on the high seas comparable with that of England; but she made good use of the Mediterranean. In 1789 Marseilles had 100,000 inhabitants; by 1816, after the ups and downs of the Revolution, the figure was the same. Thirty years later the population had doubled, while numerous minor industries were beginning to grow up around the port. Shipping in Marseilles increased in the first half of the century from 400,000 to 2,000,000 tons. The old and inadequate harbour had to be doubled in size by the addition of two large new docks in 1844. Marseilles became the largest commercial port after London and Liverpool; there was competition from the Italian ports and from Austrian Trieste, but they never seriously challenged Marseilles. This was partly because it was a vital stage on the quick post route from London to Calcutta. The overland route was preferable since the horse was still quicker than the sailing-ship; the journey was made first across France and then across the Asian isthmus, so that the only part for which sea travel was necessary was from Marseilles to Cairo.

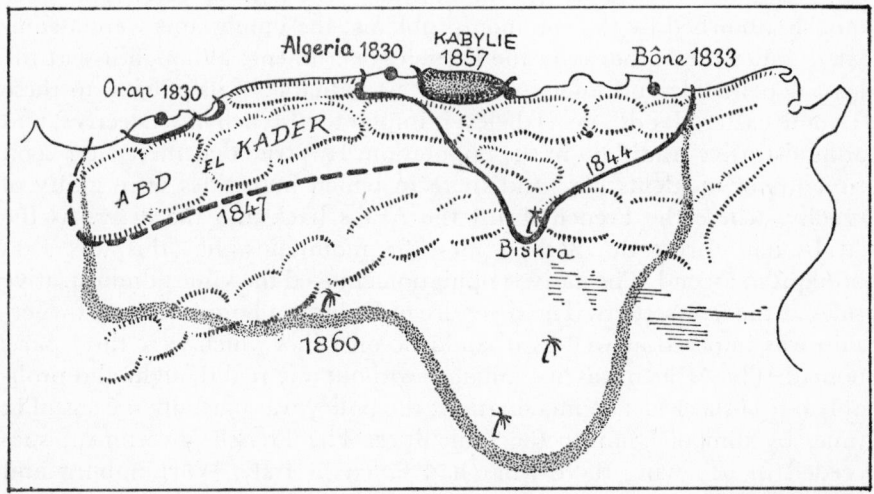

15 Stages in the Conquest of Algeria

Thick line: 1844
Dotted line: 1847
Grey line: 1860

However, the supremacy of Marseilles was assured because it became a French bridge-head to Algiers. The capture of Algiers in 1830 might well have seemed an achievement of naval power, and England viewed it with misgiving. After a few years it became clear that the Barbary Coast was now nothing but a position in which the remaining wretched chiefs, corrupted by plunder, lived out their lives. They died out because the seas were more efficiently patrolled *à l'anglaise*. Beyond this coast the continent still had to be conquered, however, and there was only one army available for the task. It exacted a high price for its services. It was the French army, forged in the Emperor's wars, and tired of resting on its laurels for fifteen years; it was still tenacious enough to transform this French expansion southward into a national epic. What neither Charles x nor Louis-Philippe had foreseen soon became a reality. Algiers could not be conquered by sailors, but had to be defeated by land. Thirty years of warfare costing six thousand million francs with hundreds of thousands of men lost in battles that were always hard and often frightful, put Algiers between the Seine and the Rhine and between Paris and Brussels, as Lamartine remarked in 1846. France, thrust out of north-east Europe by the treaties of Vienna, was advancing southward on a wide front.

First came soldiers and soon after them the settlers. Frenchmen were hesitant about crossing the sea. In 1831 the authorities had to enlist 4,500 Parisians 'whom the misfortunes of the time made permanently available to the hands of agitators', to constitute a first contingent of volunteers. The Spanish, Italians, Maltese and other peoples from the old Mediterranean regions were readier to volunteer. The protection of Bugeaud's military police afforded them in Algeria a way of life which differed little from that to which they were accustomed in their own countries. The racial and other tensions to which this immigration might have given rise were quickly absorbed by the common problems; the immigrants were assimilated under the authority of the French government; although it sent the least dependable and sometimes the least valuable of its officials to these 'remote eastern lands', nevertheless it implanted French laws, decrees, and administrative traditions in the population. It is true that there were soon rumours of incidents here and there in which both sides were guilty of cruelty, where the French thrust the Arabs back into the desert as the Arabs had thrust the Berbers into the mountains, but this was soon brought to an end. The native population enjoyed the same administrative rules as the new settlers. The structure of European bourgeois land ownership was imposed as well as it could be on tribes which were three parts nomad. The African was 'assimilated' without any real thought and probably out of sheer lack of imagination; the policy was partially successful in time, by dint of ignoring the difficulties. The French government succeeded in achieving there what had failed in Italy, Württemburg and Holland. Reassured by the presence of this government, which was strong just because it was completely unaware of the difficulties, French immigrants grew accustomed to the idea of crossing to Algiers, and African France was born.

North Africa returned to what was really its natural geographical role at this time; it became once more a part of the West, after having been an extension of the East for so long. The English, who took fifty years to realize what was happening, and the Turks, who did not care, made no move. Algiers became the first city of North Africa after Cairo and Algeria was the first region of European Africa after the Cape. Thus there were to be two Mediterraneans: the French Mediterranean in the west, Turkey's in the east; England sanctioned this situation as long as she could enjoy free access to both currents of trade which led to the Red Sea and the Persian Gulf via Gibraltar and Malta.

At that date Saint-Simon was considering the possibility of a reconciliation of peoples, and the title he gave to his reflections was 'The Mediterranean System'. In doing so he may have over-emphasized the connections between the destiny of the Mediterranean and that of the world in general and he may have considered the planet on too small a scale, but he believed, perhaps rightly, that mankind was witnessing a tentative revival of what the *pax romana* had been eighteen centuries earlier.

Book Three
CAPITALIST AND
INDUSTRIAL EUROPE
1840–80

8

The Victory of Industry

A VARIETY of fates, covering in all a period of some two hundred years, have been allotted to the industrial revolution by different historians. At all events, it was the revolution of 1848 which marked the triumph of industry. Technique and industry are not synonymous. The establishment of great industrial concerns presupposes a general effort on the part of the people, with migrations of workers, the construction of towns, the digging of canals, and the surfacing of roads. In short: a whole new organization of labour affecting millions of men is necessary and this profound transformation lasted all though the nineteenth century. If that is what is meant by the industrial revolution, it is premature to apply the term to the inventions of the eighteenth century. But there was a crucial period in the nineteenth century, 1845–55. Railway building had been started all over Europe, but the work had to be interrupted everywhere since the effort was too great for the means available. It was this interruption, the unemployment it led to and the helplessness of societies whose ambitions outran their means which provoked the revolutions of 1848. These were the decisive battles in which capitalist industry was at stake. It was at this point that railways became the most powerful weapons of the new economy, and thus ensured the triumph of the new capitalist structure.

THE RAILWAYS – CATALYST OF THE

INDUSTRIAL REVOLUTION

The improvements in industry and agriculture during the 1830s had profound repercussions on the circulation of goods. This was the golden age of canals and stage-coaches. England already had a network of roads which covered most of the country, although their quality was not very good. They were famous for the density of their traffic and for the jolting they gave to the traveller. The new surfacing invented by Macadam did not improve them to any marked degree; the dressing of tar did not become general until the second half of the century, and meanwhile the weight of traffic, especially of coal and iron, pitted the surface with ruts and holes. These English roads were, moreover, private property, and the tolls had to cover not only capital expenditure but continual upkeep which was cheap only because of the cheapness of labour. The swing-gates along these toll roads were at that time one of the most familiar features of the English countryside. In France the road system continued to be maintained by the state which had reorganized the *Corps des Ponts et Chaussées* for this purpose in Louis xv's reign. This road system, extended by the great road-builder Napoleon, continued to grow after the Bourbons had been restored to power; the flow of traffic was centred around Paris, so that the cities and frontiers could be served by direct roads; there were passes for crossing into Italy, Spain or Switzerland. But the quality of the roads was still very mediocre. The metalling was very shallow, and after a few weeks of bad weather the road could often not be found, since it disappeared into the fields.

On the rest of the continent the years were marked by a parallel development: in Austria roads were built radiating around Vienna while in Italy the French and Austrian roads were carried on over the Alps towards Brindisi. The Prussian Government, in particular, had expended vast efforts and great expense to link Berlin with the Westphalian network. In the new western provinces, it came across the sections of road laid down by the French Government. Because it was most anxious to complete this sector, Prussia postponed the construction of a road system in its eastern provinces, which explains the still archaic nature of those roads or rather tracks, which are almost impassable in wet weather, especially in swampy areas. All the German states energetically competed with each other in trying to ensure better communications, especially with the great international artery, the aorta of German trade, the Rhine.

On all roads traffic was beginning to be controlled by powerful coaching companies; this was a novelty in contrast to the general pattern of individual transport in the previous century. Two famous companies were operating in France: in one, the banker Laffitte had interests (Caillard, Laffitte and Co.), and the other was that of the *Messageries Générales*, the very wealthy successors of the former *Messageries Royales* created by Turgot. There was a new fashion for travel which kept the post-stages busy; it was illustrated in engraving, and celebrated in the popular theatre, poetry and music. The new stage-coach caused quite a sensation, with its touching departures, its eagerly awaited arrivals, and its bustling journeys. It sometimes met with tragedy when the route lay through forests barely opened up, where bands of highwaymen still lay in wait. It employed a large number of stable-hands and managers and drained the surrounding countryside of manpower and horses; horse-breeding had never before been so lucrative. Obviously the means used for travelling in 1830 were not very different from those of preceding centuries. Nevertheless the quality of the roads, the excellence of the organization and the relative comfort of well-sprung, light-wheeled carriages enabled postillions to drive coaches at high speed; the psychological love of speed has its first origins in this development in road traffic.

The canals were being developed as rapidly as the roads. Every river in Europe in 1830 carried those famous tow-barges which seem so strange to us. Although less popular than the new stage-coaches, they were greatly favoured by the new tourist, because they were more comfortable, travel was more picturesque and safer, and finally because of the accommodation on board, which sensitive souls preferred to overcrowded stage-coaches. On the great rivers there were numerous ports and inns, some of which were well kept. The slowness of the trip was enlivened by entertainments on the boat and on the river-banks. The Loire was famous for its tourist attractions, but the Rhône was rather frightening, providing the traveller with many a thrilling tale, especially when it was swollen with flood water, so that the boats had to shoot between the piers of the bridges.

In order to connect these rivers with each other, canals had been dug everywhere, and were even more comfortable to sail on than the rivers. Michel Chevalier had cause to complain, in 1838, that France's rivers were not worthy of her canals.

France possessed a fine system of waterways and the Canal des Deux-Mers with its large dock at Béziers was no longer the finest. France's Central Canals, which had been begun under the *ancien régime*, were improved during the Restoration, when work in the north was resumed and the length of waterways was doubled. Under Louis-Philippe, whose family had always had extensive interests in the building and leasing of canals, effort was concentrated in the north and east, and again the network was doubled: the Marne was connected with the Rhine, the Rhine with the Rhône and the Aisne with the Marne. All of this was made possible by the tolls levied on the boats which used them, bringing good profits to contractors and farmers.

In England, private enterprise had achieved an improvement in transport comparable to that effected by the *Ponts et Chaussées* in France. This early part of the nineteenth century was a time of great expansion and progress, and was known as 'the age of canals'. Nevertheless, the most ambitious projects, particularly the Caledonian Canal opened in 1831, had not fulfilled the hopes of their constructors, and in spite of heavy governmental subsidies could never pay the interest on the heavy debts incurred, thus discouraging shareholders. On the contrary, numerous small canals and all river transport brought in handsome profits, especially where they enabled the coastal trading ships to penetrate inland.

In Germany the great preoccupation at this time was to make the Rhine, which was already used by large ships, more suitable for navigation below Ludwigshaven. The Elbe and the Oder naturally carried a great deal of traffic. There was some talk of canals, though very little work was done on them. The great transport problem facing Germany was an administrative and political one; how to reduce the multiplicity of controls and customs at each frontier, since each state, however tiny, regarded itself as the exclusive owner of its waterways.

In 1830 a technical revolution took place on the rivers. Barges were still often towed by horses, but already the slow boats hugging the banks were being outdistanced by the new steamboats, which could travel in midstream. Some of the old bridges over the Loire had had to be reshaped and sometimes replaced by light iron foot-bridges to give room for the funnels of these new boats. Steam made boats less subject to the uncertainties of wind, currents and sandbanks. In Germany the crossing of the Baltic Straits was made by steamboats which penetrated into the very heart of the continent without any transfer of cargo. In France and England steam shipping was developing, so that the same ships could be used for sea and inland transport. The great English ironmaster Aaron Manby, who later transferred to Charenton and then to Le Creusot, had built his own iron steamship in 1822. It was greatly admired by the Parisians, and he professed to prefer it to all other means of transport for the journey from London to France. In 1832 a small iron steamship, the *Alburkah*, performed a great feat by sailing up the Niger.

This sudden expansion of trade on roads and canals gave a great impetus to economic growth within each country and throughout the whole of Europe, while the invention of the optical telegraph encouraged it still further. The great wooden arms invented by Chappe during the Revolution and first used exclusively by the state had soon begun working for trade. They topped every tower and height in Europe. In bad weather they stopped, showing that there was bad visibility at some point on the route. The Berliners, strolling through the city, could tell when bad weather was on the way by the breakdown of the Western telegraph.

Thus in 1806 there were indications that the countries of Europe were drawing closer together, and that a greater solidarity was developing between provinces and between nations. Following the telegraph came cargoes of goods, and then credit began to spread from town to town and from capital to capital. The *Banque de France*, which had resisted the opening of provincial branches for so long, had to establish many under Louis-Philippe and had to compete with the provincial banks of issue by setting up branches in the chief cities of France. In England the spread of local banks was too strong to be checked by the development of these London banks. In Scotland in about 1830 there was a sudden increase of issuing banks, which even went so far as to put one-pound notes in circulation. Peel was incensed but neither governmental pressure nor crises were able to make the Scots see reason. Yet the note and credit of the Bank of England, and particularly of the London Bank, were going from strength to strength. In any case, the influence of the City extended as far as the highlands, where it played the rôle of supreme regulator. The fluctuations of market prices could be followed in detail from one end of the continent to the other, so that people risked their capital farther and farther over the frontiers. They used the already existing banking networks, consisting of the Rothschild, Baring and Hope banks, from London to Paris, Amsterdam, Frankfurt, Berlin, Vienna and Naples, widening their scope and consolidating them. It was in this way that European solidarity was created; it enabled the *Banque de France* to lend part of its gold reserves to support the Bank of England in a crisis on several occasions, in 1825, 1839 and 1847. In the same way, the Bank of England opened its discount system widely to French paper money. English capital was invested throughout the whole of Europe, encouraging local money to come out of its hiding places and swell the credit put at the disposal of the great industrial concerns; a new era was opening up to European industry. It was then that the railway really came into its own.

Once more the French were theoretical and systematic, for they planned before they acted. They had a railway system before any railways. There was the well-known Saint-Simonist movement, which was a curious intellectual group where logic merged into mysticism. Its promoters dreamed of a vast Mediterranean railway system as the forerunner of a world system, which would ensure the brotherhood of nations and universal peace for all eternity; the more generous their estimates of the advantages and benefits to be reaped by business concerns from swifter and safer transport, the more persuasive their arguments became. It is true that this splendid theory was adopted only by a small *élite*, chiefly in Paris, but it was a most influential *élite* consisting of Jewish and Protestant bankers, although also including a few solid directors of the *Banque de France*. It was an *élite* of engineers and also of polytechnicians who were to ensure a fine future for the pupils of their school for generations to come; senior ministry officials were also involved. Enfantin was not just a quaint mystic who wore his waistcoats buttoned down the back, for as a polytechnician he had the entrée into banks, ministers' bureaux and the yards of contractors engaged on public works, and was on familiar terms with old school friends of the *École Polytechnique*. This small enlightened *élite*, confident, ambitious and eager, exerted the greatest possible pressure on the French Government, and tried to convince the outside world. It almost succeeded in a series of missions in Italy, Spain and Egypt, where it was already busy with a project for a canal between the two seas.

But Saint-Simonism should not lead us to overlook the importance of Leipzig, another centre of thought where Frederick List was trying to get new ideas adopted in Germany. List's liberalism and unionism had brought misfortune on him, but had also led him to evolve a national system of political economy. When he was freed from prison and exiled, he travelled in America and France; he returned convinced of the necessity of a customs union and a railway system. He preached his message from Augsburg to Magdeburg, lectured to businessmen, and made his name as a journalist. He was soon influential enough to have a say in the formation of governments and in particular that of Prussia. Of course, List's activity came several years after that of the Saint-Simonists, but it had more speedy results, for the German railways were built before the French.

The English had no famous schools of engineers, and lacked theorists. But they went one better and set a practical example. Since the eighteenth century English coalmines had been making use of railways, and the cost of maintaining roads and transport was saved by installing small trucks on rails running from the mine to the river or the coast. In France, Anzin copied this method, and so did a number of small metallurgical and mining centres all over the continent but especially in Belgium. Thus the English posed the problem of the railways on a wider scale, for it was now a case of providing them not simply for an industrial firm but for a whole industrial area.

The decisive step forward in the progress of railways was the replacement of the horse by the locomotive. George Stephenson, a clock-maker, believed he had discovered the secret of perpetual motion at twenty-five. Then one of those English farmers whose social status was peculiar to England, as we have seen, taught him enough mathematics and physics to enable him to become director of a coalmine, whose owner helped him to perfect a steam engine which drew the coal-trucks. Having taken out a patent, Stephenson founded a locomotive works near Newcastle. In 1829 he won the competition organized by the Manchester-Liverpool Railway Company with the *Rocket*. In 1834 the Newcastle-Carlisle Company still kept up its stables, but in the following year it bought an engine from the firm of Stephenson and Company. Parliament approved. In 1835 the victory of the locomotive was assured for in March of that year the three coaches *Expedition, Social* and *Prospect* were drawn by the Stephenson *Rapid* from Blaydon to Hexham.

The railways had won the day and the countryside was transformed almost overnight. English metallurgists were working at full pressure and new blast furnaces, gigantic for that time and producing a hundred tons a week, sprang up everywhere, but especially in the Midlands, and in Scotland where there was formidable industrial development round Glasgow. By 1830 England was turning out two thousand tons of iron per working day, and rolling it by steam-power, for steam-engines were gradually replacing water mills. This iron made the safest rails in the world. New companies were busy snapping up capital and credit to make trucks and engines. Others hastened to obtain parliamentary sanction for the creation of new lines, in a frantic rivalry which led to fierce arguments about sites for stations in the towns and in country areas about the routes for lines. Astonished countrymen first saw surveyors, followed by gangs of navvies, invading their fields and meadows, digging and building, bridging rivers, and constructing lines along the sides of hills and mountains. A terrific fever seized the country, and technicians succeeded in stepping up production to such a degree that it exceeded local consumption and left a good surplus for export to the continent in a few short years. The great railway fever lasted forty years, and changed Europe and the world.

Naturally, in the early stages things did not always go smoothly and there were many difficulties. It sometimes took a long time to obtain credit. In order to attract it, innumerable construction companies put forward magnificent plans which were reasonably economical on the surface. Barely had the company been formed than technical progress and more accurate calculations forced an increase in the weight of rails and the solidity of rolling stock, while at the same time the law imposed more numerous precautions affecting brakes and signalling; the cost of labour was continually increasing and the salaries of technicians rose rather than went down, so that a company's actual outlay was always more than had been foreseen in the original estimates. Public opinion was disturbed, and canal and toll-road owners organized great campaigns against the railways, inveighing against their dangers and the ruin they would bring to rash investors. They lobbied Parliament with their objections to this unnatural craze, which would ruin the solid, safe transport of former times and drag the whole country down with it to disaster.

Moreover, the navvies scattered all over the countryside sometimes broke down fences, and robbed farms and cottages. It was said that no good could come out of this wild, beer-swilling mob. In 1839, a parliamentary committee was told that the railways were a calamity, but the railways replied to these protests by increasing their capital, strengthening their safety measures, and declaring their faith in ultimate success.

The gradual opening of railways along the classic routes of coaches and canals was a tremendous boost for the new mode of transport. Above all, the few great noblemen who dominated conservative opinion began to use the railway for their own journeys. This desertion of the canal and the road by the kings of public opinion was a notable event. It must be admitted that great efforts were made to make the stations comfortable. They were equipped with handsome waiting-rooms with a buffet in the middle where the staff were instructed to refuse tips. It was thought that the railway would drain away travellers, but would leave goods for the roads and canals. Up to the middle of the century a famous glass manufacturer had transported his fragile wares by water, but from about 1835 goods were piling up in the stations, and more trucks had to be built hurriedly. The great metal and mining concerns had their own rolling-stock which they used on the railway companies' lines by mutual agreement. Meanwhile the dividends paid by the inland waterway companies and the toll-roads decreased sharply. On the Birmingham Canal they fell by eighty per cent between 1825 and 1838. There was also a change in the method of calculating railway costs and fares. The railway charges had been previously based on the old traffic on the canals and roads, but after a few years the new traffic was found to be much higher than had been foreseen for the railways were now attracting a new type of customer.

Many people who had not been in the habit of travelling were now fired with a longing to see what a train journey was like, and very soon acquired the habit. Crowds of third-class passengers who had never travelled before invaded the stations and trains. Merchandise also seemed to be attracted by stations. There was naturally a corresponding decline in road traffic, although this only affected the main highways. On the minor roads serving the area around the stations there was such an increase that the organization of road transport and the administration of road maintenance and construction had to be overhauled completely. But the canals themselves survived in these widespread changes. In high society, and even among humbler folk, the railway craze was so strong that it left its mark on the country's whole way of life. It affected language too, and it was fashionable to talk of matters being 'in train', or of 'steaming ahead'. The phrases were used first of business but then even of one's love affairs, for the Victorian age truly came into being around an iron cradle.

England's transformation was soon followed by that of Europe, although the English economic methods could not be exported very easily. The power of British capital, allied to the easy circulation of money and credit, meant that the new economy could develop without intervention from the state. Parliament, torn by conflicting arguments, usually approved the creation of new companies without discussion. General laws, debated at great length, obliged companies to take more technical and financial precautions, compelled them to keep their prices down, and insisted on reductions for soldiers and officers, or Sunday trips for city workers. In fact these laws aroused the opposition of the railways, who were encouraged by Cobden and his associates to proclaim their rights of ownership as vehemently as their opponents proclaimed the rights of the nation in matters which went beyond individual ownership. For some months Parliament gave a committee something approaching plenary powers over the railways. This Committee of Five (known as the 'five kings') achieved very little, for it was swept along by the current; the most stubborn aristocrats ended by being appointed to the governing bodies of the railways, and the Government reduced intervention to the minimum among so much intense competition.

This English pattern could not be reproduced on the continent. It was the new state of Belgium which set the decisive example here. Almost as soon as it came into existence, the Belgians made it a point of honour to prove the vitality of their new state by constructing a network of railways which was the best co-ordinated in the world. They planned a junction at Mechlin, connecting Antwerp with France and Ostend with Germany. After brief discussions in 1834 Parliament voted by acclamation that these national enterprises should be undertaken by the state. Within two years Brussels was connected with Antwerp and within ten years the plan was completed and the system flourishing. Soon other lines were added although they were privately owned. The Belgians had almost caught up with England by methods which were a model for their neighbours.

The history of French railways began with the small mining railway connecting Saint-Etienne with Andrézieux, which was first drawn by horses and oxen and then by engines ; it was to this little railway that Vigny referred so slightingly in his *Maison du Berger*. This entire industrial civilization seemed unaesthetic, dangerous and inhuman to a public brought up to the slow trot of stage-coaches. Thiers' sceptical sallies are well-known. But the Pereires and Rothschilds persisted in their battle, supported by a troop of Saint-Simonists and by many people who came back from a journey to England praising the advantages of this new form of travel. Small companies sprang up on all sides while Government and Parliament willingly granted permits which appeared to affect only suburbs and industrial areas.

However, in the offices and councils of the financiers a general plan was being worked out. The small line from Paris to Saint-Germain was built by Pereire in 1835, not as an amusement for Parisians but as the fore-runner of a great section running along the Seine to Le Havre. English investors had barely regained their outlay from their own country's railway development when they began to take an interest in French lines, particularly the one between Amiens and Boulogne; it was this that obliged the Rothschilds to acquire the Paris-Lille line with all haste. In 1842, just when the Belgian network had proved its worth, agreement was reached on a great general plan. From Paris lines were to go to the Channel and Belgium, to Nancy and Strasbourg and to Lyons and the Mediterranean, and there were to be two lines to the Pyrenees, one through Toulouse and the other through Bordeaux.

It was all the more important that the Saint-Simonists had won the battle of principle and law, since in the private ventures that had been started the small companies were doing very badly, using poor quality material and spending their efforts in a search for illusory profits which the suburban lines could not bring in. The view that the state should take over the railways, following the Belgian example in every way, was widely held. The protagonists of free ownership fought back and tried to keep profits and initiative in their own hands. The result was an uneasy compromise with the state meeting the very heavy cost of the substructure, as it had done for the roads; the *Ponts et Chaussées* laid the bed of the track and were responsible for excavations and embankments, bridges and tunnels. This substructure was to be given with substantial credits to the companies who were to lay the rails and purchase the necessary rolling-stock. For a number of the most profitable lines, notably that between Paris and Lille which was backed by the Rothschilds, a purchaser was easily found. The deal provoked the first quarrels between the Rothschilds and the Pereires. For other lines, the state built the substructure before knowing whether companies would be found to buy them from it so that progress was very slow and very unequal, according to the part of the country concerned.

But eventually, about the middle of the century, the system was beginning to work; Paris was connected to Belgium, the Channel and the Loire, and tracks were already being laid towards Troyes and Dijon. Certain venturesome spirits embarked on the manufacture of rolling-stock. On his return from a study trip to England, Gouïn, the banker's son, opened a construction centre at the Batignolles, getting men from the *Compagnie du Nord* and various bankers together on his board of directors. Using English methods, he built locomotives and coaches in works that occupied the present site of the *Gare Saint-Lazare*. The metal industry was gradually developing Le Creusot which had been practically inactive since the days of the Constituent Assembly; it restarted its furnaces after 1834, and rapidly developed under the initiative of the Schneiders its new owners. This metal industry made full use of English technique, and sometimes of English technicians.

At Creil a powerful industry developed, backed by the *Compagnie du Nord*, although rails and plant still had to be imported from England. There was very little rivalry with the canals and roads, for agreements had been reached with the large coaching companies. In fact in the heroic days of the Parisian railway the bodies of the stage-coach were taken off their wheels and, with their passengers still inside, were lifted by crane and put with their axles on the rails! The rivalry with canals and rivers did not become apparent until the triumph of the railway was a foregone conclusion.

While French railways were developing, plans were also going ahead in Germany. The exhortations and predictions of List were producing results. In Leipzig in 1833, he had published his pamphlet advocating a Saxon railway which would be the first section of a German railway, for in his opinion the centre of the whole German railway system must be Berlin. The company building the first sector from Leipzig to Dresden in 1839 received help from the Saxon Government. It was not quite completed when a second line was laid down in the suburbs of Nuremberg and the King of Bavaria prided himself on having inaugurated the first railway in Germany.

People wondered whether the kings of southern Germany, the teachings of List, the enthusiasm of Rhenish manufacturers and even the progress of the *Zollverein* were to overcome the hesitations of Prussia. There was no lack of medical men to declare that the speed of the trains would make passengers ill and even mad, or that a journey through a tunnel would give rise to immorality. Nevertheless, the iron fetters were about to close on Werther's poor, beloved Germany. Although the Prussian authorities were worried at not having completed the Western road network, and although the roads in the Pomeranian east had not even been started, they were persuaded by the wildly enthusiastic Crown Prince Frederick William iv and sanctioned the Leipzig-Magdeburg line and the development of plans for a wide network linking the Rhine, Berlin and Magdeburg. In 1842 work was proceeding all over the country; the Prussian Government adopted a vast plan for the whole of Germany and, above all, agreed to ensure a minimum rate of interest for the companies constructing these various lines.

Numerous central German states constructed their own internal lines on their own account. Bavaria abandoned private enterprise in order to progress more quickly. Towards the middle of the nineteenth century, Munich was linked with Berlin and Stettin with Hamburg, and railroads penetrated to the heart of Prussia from the Rhine. At the same time in Vienna, the state, realizing the political importance of a rail network which would draw together the unequal members of the old monarchy, had already linked Prague and Cracow with Vienna in a line which ran on southward to the Dalmatian coast through the difficult Alpine terrain. By 1848 the railways in Germany and Austria covered twice the mileage of the French railways. In order to make it one of the most formidable in Europe, the German network now needed only the line from Mainz to Bonn along the historic

Rhineland gap, and the link with Berlin around the Black Mountains.

These German railways were cheap, and rapidly fitted out, and it was soon clear that they were the most efficient and would bring excellent returns. In central Germany land and labour were cheap, and the terrain not difficult enough to need great engineering skill. Here, as in America, the railway often preceded the road and the canal. The demand for raw materials, rails, sleepers and rolling-stock increased rapidly, and was no longer met by imports from England. Prices rose and the potential profits spurred on the Westphalians, Silesians, and contractors from every industrial area in Germany. The Siemens firm in Berlin was one of the first to exploit the situation. Schemes were undertaken which would meet the demands. The age of prosperity seemed as if it would never end. When the customs barriers were opened in 1834 a vast number of wagons was waiting near the old frontiers for the day when transport would be cheaper; as soon as the breach was opened the railways moved in.

Towns were changed and expanded and the old rural industries were now being concentrated in the capitals. People were so eager to invest money in railways that they started undertakings (as at Frankfurt) which were even more rash than the most imprudent of English schemes. Blast furnaces were started and steel works expanded their rolling-mills; a kind of industrial nationalism was aroused, and people believed that German steel was the finest in the world. The urban proletariat, which was building up at the expense of the countryside, volunteered for these new industries, and for the food and sugar industries which were soon added to the list. In a few years this industrial upheaval radically altered the meaning of the *Zollverein*.

The first aim of the *Zollverein* had been to decrease the customs duties levied on goods and to allow Germany to profit by the cheapness of new products, particularly from England. The aim now, which List had foreseen and advocated, was to raise the duties, not at the internal frontiers, but at the external boundaries of the German zone, so as to protect the newly-emerging local industries. Cheap sugar was brought down the Rhine from Holland, and the commercial towns had been pleased to get it; but ten years later they were objecting to the *Zollverein's* policy of low prices. The Prussian Government took note of their protests and raised the tariffs, and the towns applauded the measure; thus the new sugar industries were protected. It was now raw materials and not manufactured goods which were being unloaded from the clumsy barges along the Rhine, while trucks loaded with refined sugar were travelling in the opposite direction from before, going from south to north and even trying to get into Holland.

This sudden change in the economic significance of the *Zollverein* and the comparative flexibility shown by the Prussian Government increased the effectiveness of measures still further. Inside the new economic frontiers industrial growth was phenomenal and capital everywhere was wildly stimulated. The *Gewerbe Institut* developed its researches in industrial chemistry. What had been the land of craftsmen and peasants was now becoming that of a substantial chemical industry. The cultivation of sugar-beet and potatoes opened up a vast market for the new manures and for the products of distillation. In ten years Germany changed from medieval agriculture to modern industrialism.

Here we must leave the railways for the time being. In the rest of Europe, by the middle of the nineteenth century Italy still had only a very few lines. American railways will be discussed elsewhere. A further general point must be made: the development of communications by water and by road was linked with that of the optical telegraph as we have seen, and the development of the railways brought another innovation, the electric telegraph.

Gauss had linked his observatory at Göttingen with his physics laboratory by an electric wire. He offered his invention to the railways in Saxony but they could see no particular use for it. The idea was taken up in England however, and was soon a great success. From station to station the electric wire announced the trains, and ensured the smooth and continuous flow of traffic. The prodedure was then adopted in Germany as well as in Belgium and France, and all the European railways took up this convenient method of signalling. England was the first to extend the use of this railway telegraph to the general public, and thanks to the alphabet invented by the American Morse, the system was already very popular with the public in 1846. In 1848 the Siemens firm experimented with a submarine cable at the bottom of Kiel harbour, and in London there was soon talk of a telegraph which would link Europe with the continent and New York.

VICTORY IN 1848

We have noted that economic crises recurred every ten years, affecting England in particular. One of the crises in this cycle occurred in 1846. England dealt with it in its usual fashion, reforming the economic structure in the midst of a wave of bankruptcies, while the continent was swept by the famous revolutions of 1848.

It is first important to note that prices had been decreasing continually, slowly but steadily, from 1815 to 1848, with only brief upward trends. Agricultural and industrial wages had followed the same graph closely and life was hard for the poor. Poverty sometimes exploded into revolts, especially in England and France, although they were easily suppressed by the state, which was responsible for the maintenance of order. It was seen as normal to respect freedom in all disputes about wages, as long as they remained on the economic plane and were thus favourable to the industrialist. It was regarded as equally normal for the government to bring maximum pressure to bear to prevent these impoverished men from making too violent an appeal to public opinion.

But the continuous drop in prices was no less upsetting to businessmen. They paid a little less for their labour and raw materials, but the economic

advantage thus gained was largely offset by the difficulty they had in selling their goods; nobody would buy except at very low prices. The more
widely they resorted to credit and drew cheques on the future, the more
embarrassed their finances became so that they were soon on the verge of
bankruptcy. They had to make continual appeals for funds to the shareholders and in the enormous surge of activity the smallest monetary resources played their part in bolstering up credit. This was to be seen in the
ruthless manner in which the bank rate was raised on the eve of a crisis.
In England, where the structure of banking organizations was particularly
hazardous, these spectacular rises ruined several local banks and their
clients with them. However, this brutal eliminating process did ensure the
vigour, the *savoir-faire* and the market-sense of those enterprises which survived; after every crisis they proceeded to grow rich on the spoils of the
vanquished. The *Banque de France* had come to the help of the London
Bank and French gold helped England to find security for its credit, which
the English based less on gold than on industrial activity. In a time of
crisis the English capitalist structure called on France's more orthodox
system to nurse it through the growing pains caused by these fundamental
changes.

A further interesting point which must be stressed was the efficiency of
the circulatory system in England. From an industrial or rural area
ruined by the crisis, both middle and working classes could move away to
a more prosperous district fairly easily. Thus although it entailed hardship
the economic balance of the country was effectively established. It is
therefore easy to see why the crises did not seriously shatter the public's
confidence in economic freedom. Public opinion supported the ruthless
measures taken against agitators who threatened economic liberty. Thus
there was little outcry against the terrible verdict passed in London on the
agricultural workers who had marched on the capital demanding a
minimum wage; two were hanged while 420 were deported to Australia.
But ships leaving English ports for overseas at this date did not carry convicts. A growing number of immigrants were fleeing from the poverty at
home, especially from Ireland, but also from Scotland, Wales and the
more backward areas of England. Emigration increased from 2,000 a year
in 1830 to 30,000 in 1850. These emigrants went to settle in Canada, New
Zealand, and Australia. Thus, by force of circumstances, and thanks to
improved communications, England achieved greater internal stability
after each upheaval and populated her Empire at the same time.

It would be inaccurate to claim that the English Government paid no
heed to the nation's economic interests, for indeed they were the subject of
endless debate in Parliament and the heated passions aroused by the Corn
Laws were a matter of common knowledge. At a time when the whole
English tariff system was moving towards considerable reductions in
duties and the abolition of restrictions, imported corn was subject to excessively high rates of duty. This meant dearer bread in the towns, but it
also meant that the landed interests of the aristocracy were firmly

protected. It was not so much the workers as the industrialists who protested, for they were eager to grasp at anything which would justify a drop in wages and would thus extend their security margin and their capital. Eventually in 1846, after long hesitation, Sir Robert Peel accepted a gradual reduction in the duties on corn with a view to their eventual abandonment. This victory for urban interests was made possible only by the growing weight given to the towns in the electoral reform bill of 1832.

In any case, England had an economy which was flexible enough and credit which was firm enough to bear the gradual slight decline, which characterized these years of industrial development, without too much harm. On the continent the same decline acted on an economy that was still more rural than industrial, and thus delayed the start of industrialization; for people hesitated to invest their money in view of the risks being run by credit. If the *Banque de France* was so ready to lend money to England at a time of crisis, it was because it granted credits with extreme caution and watched its reserves jealously. The industrialists followed rather than initiated progress, clinging to the protection of the state rather than dissuading it from intervention in economic life. Apart from certain industrial areas of Prussia, the same attitude was prevalent over the whole of the Continent.

Let us now examine the effects of the crisis to west and east of the Channel. The collapse of credit in 1846 appeared at first sight to resemble preceding crises. Ten years of successful speculation had thrown doubtful securities onto the market and they had to be eliminated. But the great difference now was that credit was largely tied up in the railways and metal industries. Thus bankruptcies were particularly numerous and spectacular. The help given by the *Banque de France* did not prevent the Bank of England from acceding to Cobden's request that its cautious policy be abandoned and separating the departments of credit and issue. It thus repudiated Peel's Act of 1844, because a large number of notes was needed in circulation. The extension of paper currency and credit accompanied the huge rise in the bank rate which was to go up to twelve per cent for the general public. Moreover, the effects of the passing of the Corn Laws were only superficial. In fact, while the price of wine was falling, that of corn was very high, even outside England; in England itself the bad harvest of 1846 was followed by the good one of 1847, but throughout the rest of the world there was a succession of bad harvests, especially in America. In Danzig, which was the Chicago of that period, prices reached fearful heights. At the same time the potato harvest was disastrous, for in 1845 the plants were damaged by a disease which spread from Ireland to Holland, from northern to southern France, and affected Germany and Italy. The peasants were ruined and famine ravaged both town and country. The combination of low industrial prices and high agricultural prices could not possibly have been worse.

In England the unrest grew. The Working Men's Association drew up its People's Charter and demanded annual elections based on universal suffrage. Orators travelled the country while meetings and strikes increased. O'Connor proclaimed the need for an armed rising. It was in this atmosphere that Marx and Engels conceived the idea of the class struggle. But gradually the movement petered out ending in 1852 in the absurdity of a monster petition which proved to have far too many fictitious names. The safety devices of the English economy came into action and good business recovered at the expense of indifferent business, giving a renewed impetus to concentration. Great numbers of people left their homes by rail or by sea, and many emigrants left for the colonies or the United States. Good harvests all over the world ensured the country's food supplies from 1852 onwards, for foodstuffs were now being imported on a large scale. Soon newly discovered gold in America was available to give security for notes courageously increased by credit. The bank rate came down to a reasonable figure, and the Act of 1844 was re-established. Once more the crisis had strengthened British capitalism and the conservatives returned to power. *Tout va très bien, Madame l'Angleterre.*

On the continent, the picture was very different. In 1847 agrarian unrest created by bad harvests spread throughout country districts everywhere, from Holland to Sicily and from Berry to Poland. In Italy peasants met in the villages, camped out all night in public squares and cheered emissaries who came from the cities to address them on such subjects as freedom, republic and union. Sometimes they demonstrated under the very windows of the princes' palaces, demanding constitutions in the belief that these were synonymous with prosperity. All over Europe police posts were attacked, and a succession of riots stirred up the regions affected by the food crisis. These revolts assumed a national character in Galicia and Cracow. In Germany there was acclaim for the Union and for the liberalism of Frederick William in granting a *Landtag*. Metternich was afraid of being overwhelmed, but during the winter of 1847-8 the princes thought of going back on their concessions.

In France the workmen had demanded bread and in Lille had plundered the bakeries, for instance. They had been severely censured, had pleaded guilty and shown themselves repentant. Calm returned when the summer harvests reached the markets. But although bread could be bought again, credit still remained just as rare and just as expensive.

The lower middle classes persisted in their demands for reform, which may perhaps have been inspired to some extent by political ambition, but which were also rooted in anxiety. Financial worries were common to small businessmen with falling incomes, to small capitalists whose company dividends were poor or non-existent, to shareholders whose plight was similar and to whom the railway companies continued to appeal for fresh capital even though they had paid no dividends, and lastly to small shopkeepers who were finding customers few and far between and the wholesale merchant ever more exacting. This fear turned to anger at the sight of the new power wielded by the privileged few of the Bank, of industry, and of the railways, for the state drew largely on receipts from taxation to build the substructure of railways and support big business. The lower middle classes wished to have a share in these great concerns protected by the Exchequer. First they wished to have their own representatives, men like themselves, in Parliament. They persisted in this campaign, supported at innumerable dinners where the privileged few of the régime were condemned in speeches and song. They demanded reform, sometimes by the light of Chinese lanterns, so that the lower middle classes added fuel to the flames of popular discontent.

The two anxieties merged into one, and at the first opportunity they exploded. It needed only an incident under the windows of Minister Guizot, whose stubborn and Anglophile ideas convinced him that his Government would be strengthened by riding out the storm unmoved. But France was still only half aware of the laws governing the new liberal economy which tended to reduce the rôle of the State. The National Guard cold-shouldered the king of the opportunists.

French chartism was at first less exacting in its demands than that of England, but it soon began to move towards socialism. First it demanded universal suffrage and then drew up varied and wide-embracing plans for a reformation of society although there was little agreement between the members of *La Réforme* and those of the *National* on that subject. The bourgeoisie paused for reflection. The suburban workers, whose opinion carried great weight with the man in the street, went boldly ahead. They listened to those who came to address them, and delivered inflammatory speeches in squares and clubs. They were no longer demanding only universal suffrage under the windows of the *Hôtel de Ville*, for they wanted bread, guarantees of work, a social republic and the red flag. The bourgeoisie realized with astonishment that they had opened the door to a social revolution.

The provisional government in Paris was torn between those who respected property and the Code, and those who wished to set up the socialist state, open national workshops, initiate a large-scale enquiry into the condition of the working class and discuss the workers' lot in a commission meeting in the Luxemburg. The monetary crisis was getting worse. The *Banque de France* had to be forced to issue a large quantity of notes, and even in small denominations. Proudhon would have liked credit to be free; it was obvious that it must at least be easy to obtain. An attempt was made to open discount banks in every administrative area. There was also an attempt to set up branch banks to benefit the great trade corporations. Notes and money were in wide circulation again, and although this tended to raise prices debts were settled and the bourgeois were now anxious for a different reason. They were no longer alarmed by bankruptcy, but rather by economic communism, and at elections and in clubs and newspapers they began to call for order at all costs. At first their hero was General Cavaignac, who savagely suppressed the Parisian workers as they protested against the closure of the national workshops, but the days of June 1848 witnessed ghastly reprisals. Then the providential man of order appeared in the shape of Prince Louis-Napoléon Bonaparte, nephew of the great Emperor. The peasants, impelled by fear of communism, rushed to support the winning side, and Louis-Napoléon was elected President of the Republic.

There was socialist agitation, a great deal of disorder and too much bloodshed, but the real result lay chiefly in the new credit and in the new and large circulation of banknotes. The banks set up by the Republic, which was anxious to have a social policy, were to be separate from the state. They were only to survive if they could live off their own capital. The task of supporting the national, communal, and departmental budgets was taken from them, especially when the moderate majority insisted on a reduction in public expenditure. Thus the institutions with socialist tendencies avoided state control and passed into the hands of liberal capitalism.

In Europe the news of the February Revolution in France stirred up political unrest. Metternich fled from Vienna while republics were proclaimed in Budapest and in Rome. In Turin Charles Albert was only able to canalize the agitation by declaring war against Austria. In Berlin, King Frederick William IV summoned a *Landtag* and declared himself ready to assume the leadership of German unity. However, parliamentarians of all the states were making for Frankfurt, where a German parliament was eager to bring about national unity. As we know, this enthusiasm was short-lived. The Russian army, coming to the support of its 'faithful and loyal' ally the Austrian army, was soon victorious over the Hungarian rebels, and this enabled the Austrians to defeat the Italians. The Prussian army dispersed the remnants of the Frankfurt parliament. There again, order was restored. The new and lasting outcome of all this unrest was that the order which had been restored was not the old order. First, a new step had been taken towards the abolition of serfdom: in Austria for instance the young Kudlish, the only peasant deputy in Europe, took advantage of the short-lived parliament elected by universal suffrage to put through the abolition of serfdom as well as a whole series of agrarian measures which soon had their effect in the most highly-developed regions of Austria. The peasant had to buy back his rights, for ownership was respected, but his eventual status was that of unquestioned owner of the land. In 1848 Austria took the step taken by France in 1789, with middle-class approval. When the Emperor was restored to full possession of his political rights, he revoked every political concession except this one profound social reform. In Munich, Stuttgart and Berlin far-reaching agrarian measures were adopted in the same way. No doubt serfdom had been abolished there in theory but many steps had still to be taken before abolition became a reality. The German peasantry did not emerge from the events of 1848 with the same status as its counterpart in England or France, but very important concessions in line with the French laws of property and ownership had been made and not even the most reactionary régimes dared to withdraw them subsequently.

Thus the revolts of 1848 were an explosion of liberal nationalism which failed, although their effect was to shake the feudal structure so thoroughly that it gave place to a capitalist and bourgeois law, supporting individual ownership, based on a code like that of France. The year 1848 saw the last ineffectual flicker of Romanticism and the first great victory for capitalism.

Eastern Europe then became middle class and shed its tenacious traditions, its feudalism, castes, trade guilds and time-honoured ways of life. It entered the age of codified law, which was kept well up to date by great elected assemblies, and guaranteed the owner his land and the industrialist his credit. In Frankfurt, Rome or Paris there had been little mention of railways, but it was they which had broken up the rigid framework of credit based on personal estate; and by their demands a new monetary and financial world was created, enabling the railways to expand into new areas. The agricultural crisis activated a revolution in the urban industrial economy. Order was re-established in Europe as in England, for gold from the New World no longer enriched either an antiquated feudalism or a radical socialism, but rather strengthened the financial economy imposed by the railways, which gave its shape to capitalism.

ITS EFFECTS ON CAPITALISM

The 1848 revolution saw the definitive failure of socialism. French theorists who had severely criticized middle-class indifference to poverty as being barely concealed under an affectation of charitable virtue, could not seize power in spite of the vehement eloquence of Proudhon, who dominated the debates in the republican assemblies; they could not even prevent the disastrous failure of the national workshops which were a caricature of the dreams of the first socialist age. Outside France, English chartism collapsed in ridicule, for the worker across the Channel was definitely no revolutionary. In Germany, Marx and his friends had tried to take advantage of the revolutionary movement to win support for their own brand of socialism. After having launched their celebrated manifesto in Paris, they had gone back to Cologne to replace the too liberal *Kölnische Zeitung*, on which Marx had been a collaborator some years earlier, by the *Neue Kölnische Zeitung*. But Marx was expelled in 1849. The crisis of 1846–8 deprived English landlords of the precious Corn Laws and the feudal lords of eastern Germany of the gangs of serf labour and Austria of serfdom itself. Middle-class capitalism was the great victor. From 1850 onwards it was to flourish with extraordinary vigour with the new supplies of American and Australian gold.

It was in February 1848 that Captain Sutter discovered several grains of gold dust at the foot of a waterfall in the Californian mountains. In a few weeks thousands of men rushed in from all over the Union. San

1 Vauxhall, one of the London pleasure-gardens

Chantons sans céſſe,
Vive la Foire de Gonéſſe.

2 A song-merchant at the Gonesse Fair, near Pontoise. Parisians would travel there in order to 'buy the secrets of happiness'

3 The Sultan's palaces, which were built on the banks of the Bosphorus near Constantinople. The boats are full of courtiers returning from Scutari, where there was a famous mosque

4 An early view of New York harbour. On the left is a ship-yard; in the background, the tip of Manhattan island

5 Monsieur Prudhomme: one of the caricatures through which Henri Monnier took revenge on the middle classes for not recognizing his talent

6 and 7 London life in the nineteenth century, as depicted by Eugène Lami.
Above, evening prayers in a London household; *below*, early afternoon traffic

8 Loading cotton and tobacco onto a sailing-ship in one of the Southern states of the USA

9 Mississippi river-boats being loaded with cotton by Negro slaves at a New Orleans quay

10 The main square in Havana, surrounded by the church and the governor's palace. This classical town plan was used throughout Latin America

11 The amicable relationship between master and slave in Brazil is shown in this print depicting a meal in a rich household

12 and 13 *Opposite above and centre*: Westerners in the Far East. (*above*) An early view of Hong Kong; (*centre*) Portuguese colonization at Macao

14 *Opposite below*: Russian and Chinese merchants meet in a house at Kiakhta, an important stopping-place on the tea-route

15 *Above*: A toll-gate on an English road, as caricatured by Eugène Lami

16 A humorous vision of the future in 1838: air-ships were a serious proposition at the time

17 The first steam-engines: ships built like sailing-boats and wagons like stage-coaches

18 A scene at one of the rolling-mills where railway engines were made before 1850

19 The opening of the bridge over the Lagoon at Venice

20 and 21 *Above*, One of the first underground railways in London; *below*, unloading cargo at Limehouse Dock on the Thames

22 London's slums, as depicted by the famous nineteenth-century engraver Gustave Doré

23 and 24 Two famous steam-ships. *Above*: the *Great Eastern* (which was used for cable-laying) in about 1860. *Below*: the *Normandie* in about 1886

25 *Above*: F Street, Denver, Colorado: a thriving new town in the America of the 1880s

26 *Below*: The first French railway in China: the opening of the line from Tientsin to Chingyang on 20 November 1886

27 In Africa. The slave-trade: Arab merchants leading slaves towards the coast

28 In Europe. Paris cafés in full swing on a summer night

Francisco, which had just been a village in March 1848 when the treaty whereby Mexico handed over California to the United States was signed there, rapidly became a town buzzing with activity, and with huts being built at top speed. Immigrants flocked in from Europe and China, attracted by the prospect of the sudden and fabulous fortunes which a few lucky placers had made. After 1850, systematic exploitation of the mines led to the installation of more efficient plant. Gold flowed over the American continent and soon over Europe.

At about the same time gold was discovered in the alluvial deposits in the colony of Victoria in Australia, then in the quartz itself. Although less spectacular, the effects were similar to those of the American finds. In the ten years following 1850, the world production of gold was ten times greater than in the ten preceding years. As is well known, the French had always preferred metal currency, and welcomed the gold with a special enthusiasm; the state struck an impressive quantity of coins, striking five hundred million in 1845, for the world's gold found its way more readily to France where it fetched the highest price. The circulation of gold increased in other European countries also, and the banks of issue, in particular, filled their vaults. In this gold rush the English were more cautious after their long acquaintance with problems of values, and the upheaval in the gold market brought hardly any changes in the prices of the metal there. It is true England also minted new coins, but took advantage of it chiefly to establish her banking system more firmly. The influx of gold, which was exclusively Australian, had at first little effect on the prices of goods, but it developed credit with a paper currency. The minting of this money increased England's metallic circulation by almost fifty per cent, but the use of the banknote and especially of the cheque increased by a far higher proportion. The use of the cheque became so widespread in England that shopkeepers and farmers adopted it as the only possible way of doing business although it was almost unknown on the continent. Cheques were often used for amounts of less than two pounds. Even if he had an income of only fifty pounds a year, the Englishman immediately opened a bank account. In 1885, payments in metal currency represented only one per cent of the London Bank payments and six per cent of those in Manchester.

The Act of 1826 granted complete freedom of issue, except in an area of twenty-six miles around London, where the privilege of the Bank was absolute. There was a good deal of argument about the exact meaning of this privilege; for example the question arose as to whether provincial banks could open an office in London, the main centre of business, without losing their rights of issue. When it was ruled that they could not, many banks nevertheless settled in London and forfeited their privilege of printing. Only the Scottish banks put up a firmer resistance to this extension of the privileges of the Bank of England. On the other hand, the right of issue was losing much of its significance, since the remarkable development of payment by cheque meant that there was less resort to the note.

Settlements between the great deposit banks were made neither in metal nor in notes, but were transacted in the accounts of a clearing house, which dealt with transactions amounting to several hundreds of thousands of pounds every year.

The London and Westminster Bank, one of the most important of the English private deposit banks, soon became a model for every bank in Europe, for it had a reserve capital of less than three million pounds, and held approximately twenty-two million in deposits. Such influential private banks, established as joint stock companies, had to resort to the Bank of England only rarely, so the latter did not need to be unduly anxious about its insignificant gold reserves which were barely one-third of those held by the *Banque de France*. The privilege of issuing paper money, a relic of the royal right of minting money, was therefore by-passed to all intents and purposes by the gradual improvement of English banking procedure. At the same time the Bank of England enjoyed a monopoly of issue which it was in process of acquiring without the intervention of the state, since the development of banking led all the provincial banks to settle in London, near the clearing house. It was a masterpiece of liberalism to co-ordinate the free activity of the English economy in the capital without any pressure from the political power. In this way financial centralization was achieved purely by private initiative once the need for it had become apparent.

French banking evolved on very different lines. In order to meet the credit crisis, the provisional government had recommended the establishment of departmental banks and of trade credit societies when it was reforming the *Banque de France*. Most of these establishments, whose capital was to be provided partly by the state and the departments, were stillborn, while others lingered on for a month or two before wasting away. On the other hand, the *Comptoir d'Escompte de la Seine* became a private concern, and flourished under the name of the *Comptoir National d'Escompte de Paris*. The *Banque du Département du Nord*, which became the *Crédit du Nord*, was equally fortunate, as were several trade banks, particularly that of the *Entrepreneurs de Travaux Publics*. The unusual feature about the composition of the *Comptoir National d'Escompte* was that the Council of State had allowed it to set up as a joint stock company. Within a few years the *Crédit Mobilier*, the *Crédit Industriel et Commercial*, the *Société Générale*, the *Société des Dépôts et Comptes Courants*, and other companies were established to benefit from this new way of accumulating capital.

Not all these new banks were as prudent as their English counterparts by any means and this point is worth dwelling on. After 1848 the *Banque de France* had the monopoly of issuing notes for the whole of France, because the local issuing banks created by Napoleon I and Louis-Philippe had been absorbed by the *Banque de France*, whose notes were the only ones in circulation. It was the state which had made this decision and had settled the problem of monetary unity by authoritarian measures. A few bankers, under the Second Empire, protested against the right of monopoly exercised by the *Banque de France*, which had been imposed on the whole of the country by the state. Very little use was made of payment by cheque, and compensation was meagre. The wide circulation of metal currency was a sign of a restricted paper currency, but this meant that credit was scarce and was based entirely on the *Banque de France*. The latter, taking no risks, consequently piled up in its coffers considerable reserves of precious metals, proud of the fact that it could now maintain a steady discount rate more easily than England. It also gained great satisfaction from being the gold-controller of Europe. Whenever a sudden drastic rise in the English bank rate sent businessmen, and even the Bank of England itself, as we have seen, hastening to Paris in search of precious metals, it was to the *Banque de France* that they turned. Although it was attacked by those who accused it of stifling credit, on the other hand it was defended by those who found its caution reassuring. It was a difference of opinion which further enlivened the quarrel between the Pereires and the Rothschilds.

As we know, Jewish bankers played a vital part in the building of the railways. Pereire, a railway enthusiast, and Rothschild, the largest holder of free capital in France, had at first been prepared to undertake the great task in complete agreement. Rothschild, content with holding the *Nord* and the English connections, was one of the directors whose word carried most weight in the *Banque de France*, while the Pereire brothers, their heads still full of Saint-Simonist projects, were interested in vast plans covering Austria, Spain and the Mediterranean. They financed the great development of the economy of the south although even so they were obliged to open a credit institution, the well-known *Crédit Mobilier*. But because they could not use it for the issue of paper notes, and had tied up the funds entrusted to them too quickly, the Pereires embarked on a struggle to deprive the Bank of its privilege of issue. They believed that the mere right of minting money would enable them to possess the wide credit necessary for the bold financial policy on which they were launching out. It so happened that when Savoy was annexed to France, the *Banque de Chambéry* brought its banknotes and its privileges within French frontiers. The Pereires and their friends seized the shares of this bank and tried to turn its notes into rivals of those of the central bank. The *Banque de France* then asserted its rights, Chambéry lost its rights of issue, and soon afterwards the *Crédit Mobilier* went into liquidation.

This incident occasioned a great quarrel between theorists for or against privilege; it was above all a demonstration of the solidity of the rights the Bank had acquired, while no-one doubted the right of the state to confirm its privileges any longer. This situation was all the more paradoxical since the state was in the hands of Napoleon III who was a firm supporter of the Pereires and the *Crédit Mobilier*. The underlying cause of this paradox lay in French scepticism about cheques, for the development of bank money lagged more than half a century behind England. It was to be chiefly the work of Henri Germain, founder of the *Crédit Lyonnais*. His patron of 1863 was mainly anxious to attract large deposits by guaranteeing them against theft and fire so that he insisted on the effective help the

Bank could give industrialists and merchants by insuring their cash service itself. By making wise use of these deposits and by a cautious policy, the *Crédit Lyonnais* was able to open branches in Paris and Marseilles, so that it was soon as powerful as the *Crédit Industriel et Commercial* and then outstripped it. It even surpassed the *Comptoir d'Escompte*, and soon the *Crédit Lyonnais* became the leading French deposit bank. From 1860 it was the major bank to introduce cheques.

But there is little reason for suprise in the difficulties encountered by the cheque between 1860 and 1870. The *Banque de France* was regarded as the most reliable of all issuing authorites, and French specie reserves as the most powerful stock of gold in the world; between notes and gold as the two methods of payment, there was very little room for the cheque. It is difficult to believe that France's reserves could not have kept the deposit banks generously supplied, perhaps as much as, and even more than, the English reserves. But it kept a good part of its cash-balance in gold, which held up the full development of French credit institutions until the closing years of the nineteenth century.

In England there was security and in France hesitation, but in Germany there was an irresistible wave of enthusiasm which led to the rapid growth of credit institutions from 1840. There were a great many note-issuing banks in the Germany of the confederation, because each prince had his own currency. Hamburg had one of the soundest banks of issue, whose *marc banco* was esteemed throughout Europe and served as a standard for the whole of Germany. Nuremberg still had its old seventeenth-century bank and its florin, while a large number of private establishments were also manufacturing notes with a restricted circulation. In this scheme of things the Bank of Prussia held a pre-eminent position which was strengthened by the place Prussia had assumed in the *Zollverein*, but it still could not contest the superiority of Hamburg. In short, the legal position of the German banks was similar to that of the English, in that there was plurality of issue. Bank money, and banknotes, increased in competition with each other, and the future of the four great and famous banks which were to dominate the destiny of capitalist Germany after 1880 had already begun to take shape. The *Dresdner Bank* was connected with the progress of the iron industry in the Rhineland, and particularly of Essen and Krupps. The *Deutsche Bank* operated in the countries of central Europe. The *Darmstädter Bank* and the *Disconto Gesellschaft* carved out a place for themselves; indeed bills on the latter increased from six to forty million marks between 1855 and 1862.

In spite of the confusion of currencies which brought the southern florin into conflict with the northern thaler, whose rivalry was sharpened by that of Prussia and Austria, and despite the difficulties encountered by the Union thaler which Prussia tried to circulate through the economic channels of the *Zollverein*, and the difficulties experienced by the Congress of 1861 in defining a mark, the German public, which hitherto had been so cautious, had the greatest confidence in the banks and unhesitatingly supported credit. One example will serve to illustrate this. An old soldier, Friedrich-Wilhelm Raiffaisen, was Burgomaster of a Rhineland village; he was anxious to help the peasants, and launched a corporate movement of agricultural banks, after the famine of 1847. Schulze-Delitzsch, a Prussian judge, took the lead in a parallel move to help the artisans in the towns. From 1860 there was a widespread development of mutual credit societies, with unlimited liability, which granted loans to their members. They met with tremendous success and their offices sprang up all over the country. By the time the Empire was an accomplished fact, every large village and naturally every town had its bank. The *Raiffaisen* and *Delitzsch* banks helped each other. In one generation the practice of credit had penetrated every layer of society, for the bank attracted savings and could grant extensive credits. Almost a quarter of the German peasants were affiliated to a credit society. The situation, though not exactly similar, was comparable to that in England, and radically different from that in France.

France appeared to be a conservative and routine-loving country in its loyalty to gold, but this continued dependence on gold could be regarded as misplaced loyalty to an outdated rural structure. In 1852 Napoleon III tried to mobilize rural savings by founding the *Crédit Foncier*. It was the state which took the initiative here again, although misguidedly, since the *Crédit Foncier* was used to finance the transformation of the towns and to speculate in urban land in the main, while playing a very minor part in rural improvement. This example fully confirms the impression that France was hanging back between two rapidly developing countries in the general development of capitalist institutions between 1850 and 1880.

The development of new financial structures was rapid throughout Europe. Belgium had a substructure of credit on the Anglo-German model, and from 1848 there was unity of issue as in France. This derived from the merging of the Bank of Belgium and the *Société Genérale*. Italy had so large a number of note-issuing establishments in 1848 that there were more banks than there were states, since the number was increased by several private banks, but nevertheless there was no easy development of credit there. If there was a move in favour of unity, the Sardinian Government brought pressure to bear on the banks of Turin and Genoa and even restricted, although it did not suppress, the privilege of the southern banks after victory had been won. If there was a desire to encourage agricultural savings the government of the new Italy proclaimed freedom of issue, but failed to create any of the necessary institutions. In Spain the situation was similar to that in Italy. The southern limits of the great capitalist thrust passed just south of Vienna, included the plain of the Po and Barcelona, but extended no farther, while the northern limit of this European capitalism was Stockholm.

Naturally enough this picture of monetary Europe is almost the same as that of financial Europe. Long-term credit found its ideal vehicle in the joint stock company which was already widespread in England and it soon began to appear on the continent. In Belgium there were about one hundred in 1850, and almost three hundred in 1860. Contemporary France was still loyal to the limited joint stock company; although each company could be established only by a special law in each individual case. In this way banks and railway companies came into being, but finally a general law was promulgated in 1867. Eighty societies were established in 1868 and two hundred and twenty-three followed in 1870. Prussia continued to authorize them in the French way, although the Hansa towns had been legalizing their joint stock companies on the English system ever since 1843. Apparently over Germany as a whole limited liability companies were by no means rare, and in the excessive division of power characteristic of confederate Germany even the system of authorization itself had not prevented a fairly substantial rise in the number of joint-stock companies. When a long and detailed decree was issued on the subject in 1884 under the Empire, several thousand societies already in existence hastened to conform to it. Everywhere the banks made sure that newly-issued shares were taken up.

In England practice preceded legislation but in France the law came first and imposed the economic structure. In Germany the economic system came into being of its own accord, preceding the law.

We have said that on the continent the 1848 crisis was the result of the inadequacy of capitalist equipment, and the weakness of banking institutions. From 1850 onward this inadequacy was overcome, and consequently the railway programme could be resumed on a grand and imposing scale after a few months of stagnation. From 1850 to 1870 the length of track in Great Britain went up from 6,000 to 15,000 miles, that in France from 2,000 to 12,000, while German track rose from 4,000 to 12,000 and Italy's railways increased from 500 to 4,000 miles. By 1870 Europe's railway system was almost completed.

Capitalism and railways developed together. Nevertheless, relations between the state and the railway concerns were not entirely compatible with the varied credit structures we have observed. Once again in the case of the railways the political geography of Europe in 1870 played an important part. It ranged from English liberalism to eastern state control and the French structure seemed like a hinge between the two. For whereas in England the companies were free and controlled by the interplay of competition, in France the system was very curious; the companies were free, but sought help from the state, which granted it only by imposing its own control. The imperial regulations made many private companies link up into large networks which prevented them from competing with each other in practice. In fact, the tendency of French companies to resort to the state always seems to have been strengthened by economic necessity and by the difficulty of obtaining substantial credits. In Germany it was different, for the Prussian Government was interested in the railways for military reasons and constructed strategic lines. It was also concerned for political reasons and thus acquired the Hanover, Hesse–Cassel and Hesse–Nassau lines. The southern states were in search of a free port on the inter-

national Rhine, but Prussia seized the Rhineland traffic, thus vitiating the
king of Bavaria's efforts to defend his own railway system. The private
companies, which appear to have done good business until about 1880 at
least, since their mileage then was three times larger than that of the
Prussian state, were soon bought back by the German Government.

The telegraph remained quite independent of geographical differences,
because it was in state hands all over Europe after 1870 only America remaining loyal to the principle of private industry. In England, telegraph
systems were in the hands of the railway companies until 1870, but this was
an arrangement which proved most inconvenient in practice, so the English
Government bought the lines and entirely reorganized the system. In
Germany from 1849, the year in which Berlin was linked up with Frankfurt, there was great activity. Soon all the cities in Germany were connected by a system of electronic wires which belonged to the state until
they came under a federal ministry in 1871. In France Napoleon III was
passionately interested in the development of the telegraph system. From
1851 to 1854, he had all the Paris prefectures interconnected; for political
reasons he made this service available to the public in 1851, so as not to
increase the budget and antagonize French middle-class public opinion.

Here then was capitalist Europe equipped with powerful means of communication in the railways and the telegraph. This iron framework was a
great support for the newly developing industries, particularly the iron
and electrical industries. It also brought about a new imbalance between
town and country: banks, railways, and telegraphs opened up a new era in
the history of the development of the Western countries. However, at this
point we have to cease to consider Europe as a whole. A glance at the map
of the telegraph system reveals how it reinforced the importance of the
capitals and of national frontiers, for although capitalism triumphed from
one end of Europe to the other, it sometimes acted as a spur to national
rivalries.

9

Industrial Nationalism

ONCE victorious, the industrial revolution transformed the political structure of Europe. First it strengthened the power of England, which had been shaped by commercial liberalism and big business for more than a century and a half. Every new achievement in industrial and financial techniques was initially an English victory in the nineteenth century. It was therefore with fervour that the subjects of Queen Victoria supported economic liberalism and its technical apparatus. Germany had only narrow outlets to the sea, but possessed such rich mines that in a few years she became a first-rate power. The railways united Germany and enabled it to consolidate its position and spread out over the continent before turning its attention to the sea. It annexed a piece of France. France was a maritime power, although less well equipped for this rôle than England and was also a continental power, but was less well endowed than Germany. Thus it was uncertainty about its future which made France hesitate between the maritime world and the continent of Europe, concentrating on each in turn, only to win and then to lose what it had wanted in both spheres. The French had their railway but had lost Lorraine and Alsace; they had lost the coveted Mexico as well, but were now firmly entrenched in Asia and Africa.

ENGLISH STEEL – MASTER OF THE SEAS

In England the 1846–8 crisis was simply one of those ten-yearly crises which had already occurred in 1825 and in 1836–7, and which returned in 1857, 1867 and 1874. The financial outlook remained the same. The joint-stock banks, pressed by their customers in difficulties, turned to the London Bank, which increased its discount rate to protect its relatively small reserves. Although it was normally at two and a half per cent, it could rise as high as ten per cent. When credit reached this exorbitant figure, a number of over-adventurous businesses had to give up the struggle and go into liquidation. Production and trade adjusted themselves, the demand for credit became less urgent and the bank rate fell to its normal level. Life went on as before.

There were two almost immediate signs of recovery: plant and equipment improved greatly and the geographical distribution of industry changed, at least until 1880. Between 1830 and 1850 for instance, blast furnaces were already forty-eight feet high; these iron monsters leapt up even higher in the following generation and reached eighty feet or so. In 1880 they were to be one hundred and ten feet high, and were then able to turn out the enormous quantity of three hundred tons a day. Up to 1850, the great geographical innovation was the development of iron-smelting in west Scotland, where the comparatively limited supply of ore was soon exhausted. In the following years the industry opened up, first in Wales and then at Middlesbrough in Yorkshire, so that in a very short time the modern products of these ironworks were providing tools and implements for Lincolnshire.

During the same period old blast furnaces were closed down and dismantled, because their capacity was too limited; and to compete in price mass production was necessary, since it alone enabled valuable by-products to be recovered and ore and fuel to be used more sensibly. In spite of improvements in coking (in France and particularly in Belgium, which discovered how to recover the gases long before England), Durham alone must have wasted 45,000 tons of sulphur a year up to 1880. But English industry could afford this technical wastage because of the excellence of its commercial organization.

England was the first to make use of one technical advance, however: the substitution of steel for iron, the outstanding event of this period. From 1850 to 1860, the production of iron rose from three to four million tons; it fell to half this figure in 1880, because steel from England was just starting to conquer the world. For many years previously, Durham and Staffordshire had been making steel by the puddling process, and one big railway company, the North-Eastern Railway, had gone over to the new metal, which was more durable although more expensive. The English admired and envied the machines for mechanical puddling which were already in use in Cincinnati in the United States. In 1856 Bessemer made the startling announcement that he had discovered the possibility of converting iron into steel without the use of fuel, and by a speedy process. This was the famous 'converter'. At first this unexpected step forward left ironfounders sceptical and uncertain, but at the 1862 exhibition Bessemer was able to show tools and weapons made from his steel. The customer was convinced, and gradually iron was replaced by steel. Once again the example was set by the North-Eastern Railway, which substituted Bessemer's cheap steel for expensive puddled steel. This move was soon followed by all the companies. Rails were cast in steel, and were so strong that they largely compensated for the extra cost incurred. First railway engines were made of steel, ship's engines and their new propellers came next, until finally the ships themselves were steel built. In 1870 225,000 tons from a total output of 240,000 tons of steel were made by the Bessemer process. In 1883 more than 500,000 tons of Bessemer steel were turned out; this was its peak production period, for there was already competition from a new source – Martin steel.

T.M.C.—8*

Bessemer's process certainly had several drawbacks, the chief of which was that it required ores of specially high quality. These had to be imported from Sweden and Germany, so that some English mine workings had to be abandoned. The solution of the problem was discovered by two cousins, a Welsh chemist, named Gilchrist, and an official of the Thames Police court, called Thomas. Both of them were passionately interested in metallurgy, and realized that if the converter was lined with basic materials the phosphorous ores could be used as well. Throughout Europe the new patent was rapidly adopted.

The period 1850–80 was the heyday of English steel. Steel was made into flat plates and in 1854 the *Clytemnestra*, a steel ship, triumphantly weathered a cyclone off Calcutta. In 1868 Lloyds began to question the safety of iron ships, and by 1885 iron had disappeared from the British navy. This success speeded up the disappearance of wooden ships and sailing-ships, since steel could be adapted to all the new improved techniques and was ideal for parts subjected to great strain. The main shafts of ships driven by propellers, and the crankshafts of steam engines (particularly the new double-expansion steam engines which needed longer axles) are examples.

The rapid growth in the use of steel emphasized the importance of standardization as an invaluable commercial necessity. The idea was first tried out by Whitworth in his own mill and was soon adopted by the Admiralty, shipowners and of course the artillery services. Engine parts, screws and bolts, ship's propellers and tools in general had to be reduced to a few main types, so that spare parts could be stored in readiness in arsenals and ports of call. Any mechanical damage could now be repaired quickly, whereas it was slow and costly to forge a replacement for a broken part.

In about 1880 the supremacy of English steel was such that the English had understandably neglected certain aspects of their industrial development, as we have already seen in connection with the use of coke. English coalmines were soon surpassed by those of the Borinage in swifter and more efficient cutting and better lifts, safer pit props and more efficient ventilation. Soon even the French mines were accusing their English rivals of holding human safety cheap in order to bring down running costs and so conquer markets, although the reproach was not entirely justified, since the geological siting of the English pits made them much easier to work and less dangerous, and thus less expensive.

We shall not dwell on the growth of the textile industry except to say that the number of spinning-frames rose in thirty years from 200 to 245,000 while the output of each machine had almost doubled. The output from the looms more than doubled, although their numbers had increased by barely fifteen per cent. All this showed a vitality that was still unique in the world. But nothing was comparable to England's triumph in the manufacture of steel. Undoubtedly it was steel that held the key role, just as cotton had done almost a century earlier. In conclusion, we shall mention the success of machine-made cement, for it was a discovery which held great things for the future. At the end of the eighteenth century a Kentish labourer, following the fashion, had given the name of Roman cement to the 'plaster' he got from the clayey chalk of Kent, which 'took' far more quickly than the traditional hydraulic limestone. In 1824, Joseph Aspdin of Yorkshire achieved exactly the right mixture of sandstone and clay in a cement that he named Portland, and after 1870 cement was made on an industrial scale.

With steel for ships and engines, coal for steam and cement for harbours, England had all the essentials needed to keep and strengthen its economic domination of the seas. In 1845 many wooden sailing-ships were still being built in England after French models, particularly the famous *Sans Pareil*. Out of a total of 3,400,000 tons, the English fleet contained only 170,000 tons of iron shipping, but it had performed miracles from 1855 to 1860, cutting down the time for a voyage to Australia from eighty-three to seventy-eight days. But it was still too long a voyage, since the American clippers were already faster. But within half a century, steel accounted for ninety per cent of England's tonnage, which had trebled in the meantime; this vast substitution had obviously had its problems. Cunard had been one of the first to go over to iron and steam, but it was unwise at that early stage to move too quickly. This could be seen in the notorious *Great Eastern*, which was 692 ft. long and sixteen times as big as the biggest other ship afloat; it was so huge, requiring as it did a coal reserve of 12,000 tons, that it was never able to find enough freight and passengers to cover the cost of the North Atlantic crossing. It was turned into a collier and then a trawler, but always ran at a loss; the ship ended its career as a cable-layer, but the only person to make money out of it was its last purchaser, who had it broken up. This lesson in caution was not forgotten and the subsequent progress of the steamship was irresistible just because it had been carefully planned. The steel steamship was the invincible weapon of British commercial imperialism.

The English certainly used it with courage and boldness, and with a breadth of outlook rarely found on the continent. In England, it was accepted without question that it was unwise to attempt to protect the nation's industries, according to John Stuart Mill. He went on to say that in normal business dealings foreign goods were hardly ever imported except when it was in the national interest. He believed that it was absurd to base a general political system on the obviously unlikely possibility that war might be waged against every nation in the world at once and on the assumption that a country could be blockaded like a city if weak in sea power. In short, Stuart Mill admits that the state may intervene to protect a new and weak industry, but only as a purely temporary measure, and only in so far as this industry gives proof that it is vital to the nation.

These were not only Mill's opinions, but those of the great majority of English people, who were convinced of the benefits of free trade at least as far as England was concerned. We have already spoken of the importance of Peel's repeal of the Corn Laws in the late 1840s. The consequences were not long delayed, for from 1850 onwards a quarter of the population of

England was living on foreign bread; this was an adventurous policy for that time, although it made the fortune of the Rouen mills. The imports of cattle doubled between 1850 and 1853, while butter was brought from Ireland and Brittany and even from Portugal, Holland and Denmark. If the Admiralty still felt a lingering uneasiness at the thought that half the wood used in England came from Scandinavia and tried to protect local forests in consequence, its anxiety was short-lived. England naturally imported wool from its colonies, but also well-made Saxon cloth from Germany. England imported all its cotton and imports of ores exceeded exports; this trend became more and more pronounced as time went on. Exports of coal rose steadily on the other hand. Iron exports rose from 200,000 tons in 1839 to 600,000 tons in 1849 and reached 1,300,000 tons in 1853.

The likeliest source of rivalry to England lay in America. The United States were past-masters in the preparation of wool; their Singer sewing-machines were unrivalled even in England, their agricultural tools were widely used in the English countryside, and the competition of Scottish products was still very largely ineffective. England ceased to compete in certain areas; wooden articles, for example, could never be made as cheaply or as attractively as those from Germany and English children loved the German toys. The English could never hope to make clocks better than the French, or watches comparable to the marvellous products from Switzerland, while it was impossible to compete with certain French luxury fabrics such as silks or fine woollens from Roubaix or Saint-Quentin, or leather and skin boots and gloves, although Manchester tried to compete with French silks in the English market through the efforts of Huskisson, Jacquard's rival. The Lister loom, too, tried to produce woollen goods to equal those of the famous Heilmann of Mulhouse. An attempt was made to process English glass for light-house lamps, for the manufacture of which France had enjoyed a monopoly until that time.

Businessmen in London were sometimes impatient at the exclusiveness with which France shut herself behind customs barriers and resisted the entry of English goods, iron and coal in particular, although other markets offered British trade ample compensation for this restriction.

Since English products sold well, England had little need to expend her energy in making objects it was more convenient to buy from its neighbours, especially as all transport benefited the merchant navy, and any deal helped its market. In the absence of customs' duties, transit via Liverpool or London did not add to the cost of goods significantly, so that in consequence these great English commercial centres became the nuclei of world trade. As the years went by the English improved their sales technique, for whether it was a question of presenting samples, guaranteeing the quality of a consignment or fixing a fair price, their word was law, and they made the most of their skill. But since it was also to the advantage of the continental merchants to make use of this same skill, profitable transactions continued to increase. Cobden was right, for England became the commercial centre of the world.

The English were great handlers of money as well as dealers in goods, since they were the best informed and the most skilled in taking advantage of financial opportunities. There was always someone in a good position to suggest to Argentina, Brazil or Peru, and obviously even more easily to Canada or India, a plan for building a railway, a harbour, or a lighthouse, or for opening up a market. From 1850 to 1880 England invested one thousand million pounds in the world, or more than one-tenth of all the capital invested in Great Britain itself. This capital brought in orders for English industry, including more than £160,000,000 worth for railway material alone during the same period. Of course, not all these investments were sound. More than £3,000,000 were lost in rather risky ventures in Confederate territory during the American Civil War, although weapons made of the new British steel were effective on both sides. But when the fluctuations of markets beyond its control caused Britain anxiety, it could always fall back on its imperial markets; for instance, investments in India between 1870 and 1880 rose from forty to two hundred million pounds sterling.

All this capital brought in good returns, and the English could afford to see their import figures surpass those of their exports without undue alarm, because the revenue from capital, added to profits from freight, insurance and brokerage, more than made up the trade deficit. England had been the great trading nation of the eighteenth century and became the great industrial nation of the nineteenth century because industry was used to further trade, which explains how it brought such rich rewards. The wealth of England's economy came from a combination of genius for trade and flair for business, even more than from the steel on which industrial power was based.

This was important in shaping English politics; England never experienced the shattering upheavals of the 1848 revolution. It was not that it escaped the agricultural crises which brought famine to Europe and impelled the peasantry and the growing urban proletariat out of their traditional submission. Ireland in particular was badly affected. The financial crises of the time also affected England and indeed were more dangerous there than in any other country. The ravages of unemployment which inevitably accompanied the closing of mills were more widespread in England than elsewhere, and resulted in the structural reorganizations which were such an important feature of England's economic life every ten years, as we have seen. However the mass of human beings whom the agricultural and financial crises drove into the public squares was quickly absorbed by English trade, English railways and English ships, so that before they had the chance to foment serious political troubles they had embarked for parts of the world where labour was needed. It was this fact which, in retrospect, gives its real meaning to the success of the antislavery campaign in a nation which had profited so much from the slave trade in the previous century. In 1849, emigrants from the British Isles to the United States numbered 300,000, of whom two-thirds or more were Irish. Australia, too, absorbed a good number, particularly for work in the gold mines. This emigration was essential if the social balance of the home country was not to be destroyed. Thus each period of crisis was also a period of mass exodus and more than two and a half million emigrants must have left between 1832 and 1880. They were all the more willing to go since they often found at their destination centres of English activity prepared by English capital and equipped with English material.

The crises which led to political unrest or even revolution in continental Europe worked to the advantage of an England equipped with powerful steel ships, and actually increased its world commitments in the prevailing atmosphere of free trade. Moreover this vast emigration was not left to look after itself since the philanthropic associations, which on the continent were concerned with finding bread and work for the down-and-out, devoted their energies in England to finding them a place on a ship which was leaving. The administrators of the Poor Law slowly awoke to the implications of this new solution, but many emigration societies were set up as well, including a Female Middle-Class Emigration Society in 1861. All this activity was co-ordinated by the Colonial Land and Emigration Commissioners, who alone sent more than one hundred and twenty ships to Australia and never ceased to work for the improvement of conditions aboard, for conditions in the early stages were tragic and deplorable.

Thanks to this effective safety-valve, the social and political evolution of England continued without too much upheaval. From over a million, the number of poor kept by the parishes in workhouses fell by half in 1880. This lightened the poor-rate, which had been very heavy at first, and soon the excessive strictness of the rules was relaxed and the poor were allowed to work outside the workhouses. The growth of savings banks, soon to be followed by the establishment of the Post Office Savings Bank, the co-operative societies and the mutual aid societies proved useful to the *élite* of a proletariat not too weighed down by poverty. The dangerous class had been reabsorbed by emigration.

The middle classes in power were less uneasy at the prospect of 'educated' workmen organizing their own clubs and unions. Those who gave the lead were the luxury-trade unions like publishing and they were followed by the Mechanics Union, which soon became the most wealthy union, and by the Union of Building Workers. A fairly high membership fee enabled them to provide reading-rooms and schools, to undertake large-scale investigations and to publish journals. Thus the workers played their part in educating public opinion, which was very important in England, as we have seen, and which enabled a middle-class public to acquire at least some knowledge about the problems of the people. In 1871 these unions, which had long been recognized in fact, were recognized in law, and were allowed to consult together and to organize strikes. The power of the unions then became dependent on the size of their membership rather than on their resources, so that subscriptions were lowered to allow the inclusion of non-specialist members; the Miners' Federation in the 1880s increased its membership from 36,000 to 200,000, for example.

Tolerance was the outstanding political quality of the English middle-class business community. Self-confident and proud of the benefits it had reaped from the triumph of free trade, it welcomed the continued political successes of the Liberal Party, which had come into power at the time of the repeal of the Corn Laws, and had remained in office without too much difficulty until 1867. The type of man admired by this liberal middle class is typified by two leading politicians of the day. Palmerston, or Dear Old Palm, as he was called, is the first. His background was beyond reproach, for he was educated at Harrow, Edinburgh and Cambridge; he had entered Parliament as a Tory in 1808, and had held office in the Ministry of War. As a young man he had viewed the continent with a somewhat supercilious nationalism, but was soon won over by the commercial and industrial middle class. While the Tories had been greatly disturbed by the revolutions in France, Palmerston saw in them the sign of England's supremacy. Soon his enthusiasm for the new England took him over to the Whigs, and as Foreign Secretary he found it easy enough to deal with Guizot and Thiers. He supported free trade from 1846, and had so clear a conception of continental politics and of England's opportunities that Peel recognized in him a potential statesman. This Whig, who had become one because he realized the rôle played by economic affairs in the destiny of peoples, supported and admired Louis-Napoleon Bonaparte: preferring that Saint-Simonist to the man he called 'that scatterbrained windbag de Tocqueville'. Such bold views brought him into conflict with public opinion, which was less ready to shed its traditional opinions in the matter of liberal policy and slower to understand the bonds which bound liberalism to industrial progress. Palmerston had to withdraw from power for a time, but on his return in 1852 he threw himself into the military alliance with Napoleon against Russia. He himself regretted this rashness, for although it ended in the common victory of the Crimea it had involved the country in a war which was not only unprofitable but possibly even harmful. He blamed Napoleon III for the Crimean war even more than for his uncoordinated policy in Italy and said to him in 1861, 'Between you and me all is over'. Nevertheless, he successfully negotiated the trade treaty opening up France to English goods. As he grew older, Palmerston continued to take an interest in armaments, especially in the navy, but by that time the star of Gladstone was already rising.

Gladstone, too, had received a very upper-class education at Eton and Oxford, and had also started as a Tory exercising his administrative talents at the Board of Trade, in conjunction with Robert Peel. In 1842 he had the courage to introduce a tax on income, while in the great debate centred around the Corn Laws Gladstone had first hesitated and then announced his conversion to liberalism. During the Crimean War, he rallied to the defence of Palmerston, whose successor he eventually became. As Chancellor of the Exchequer and leader of the Whigs from 1865, he remained the leading exponent of English liberalism, opposed to every war and to every constraint, even when exercised by England in Ireland. From a burning

religious conviction he derived a political doctrine which advocated un-
wavering support for the peaceful conquest of markets. So solid were
England's economic bonds with the world that it could easily afford to
renounce its army as an aid to maintaining its international position for all
that was needed was to preach liberalism. Gladstone maintained that it
was necessary to grant Canada and Australia freedom to govern themselves, while rejecting all military intervention in South Africa, and on the
continent in 1870–1. He ended his career in a supreme struggle to win for
Ireland the Home Rule which English opinion refused and stood firmly
by his convictions, even though it meant a breach in the Liberal Party.

The history of the great English Liberal Party hinges on these two
careers. In Palmerston's day it still believed in the need for armed intervention and played a risky diplomatic game on the international chess
board, but under Gladstone it was concerned only with England's moral
position, neglected diplomatic and military procedure, and relied entirely
on England's immense material success. It was an approach which left a
wide field for manoeuvre open to the Conservatives, which Disraeli did his
best to exploit. He was a negotiator of consummate skill, and sought to
carry on the great imperial tradition, which was revived by the Imperial
Federation League in 1884 at a time when international competition was
beginning to threaten English supremacy and was jeopardizing the future
of liberalism. It was this new Conservative spirit which refused Home Rule
to Ireland, strengthened British naval power, intervened in South Africa
and in the world at large, when the golden age of Bessemer steel and the
financial and human pre-eminence of England had passed its peak.

The country's internal affairs, too, reflected its economic development.
New men went into Parliament on the wave of the industrial success
achieved by the new middle classes. The electorate was enlarged by fresh
classes of the population, who were given schooling in the growing towns,
and the result was the reforms of 1867 which appreciably enlarged the
electoral body. Thus England symbolized the power given to the Westerner
by his commercial, industrial and banking tools.

PRUSSIAN STEEL — MASTER OF EUROPE

Of all the countries of Europe, the 1848 Revolution was most successful in
Germany. Traditional historians usually maintain the opposite, because
attempts at the political unification of Germany failed in 1848. It is true
that in a country where feudal traditions were still so strong these first
seeds of liberalism fell on stony ground: a brief uprising that was quickly
checked left its supporters full of bitterness, disheartened those who had
planned it and led the philosophers to doubt idealism. However, the shock
of 1848 did eradicate the remnants of feudalism and prepared the ground
in Germany for the new harvests of capitalism.

In Prussia laws had been passed in 1816 and 1821 to liberate the peasants wherever the provincial states wished to take advantage of the measure. The events of 1848 in Prussia are easy to interpret: archaic legislation led to popular uprisings and Manteuffel granted the farm-labourers (*spannfähig*) the right to claim their freedom. There were no longer any of the intermediate powers to bridge the gap between state and people as Montesquieu had advised; and the monarchic state profited from the economic progress of the people. The remnants of serfdom were soon eradicated from Württemberg and Bavaria too. In 1847 German agriculture was in fact still enslaved, whereas by 1870 it was free practic-ally everywhere. This emancipation worked to the advantage of the well-to-do peasants. In a few years, the laws applying to land tenure in Germany became similar to those in England and France, but the social structure of German agriculture was closer to the English model, which, as we have already remarked, was more suited to the rapid adoption of modern methods. It is true that there were still differences between Bavaria, where half the lands were divided into tiny holdings of something like twenty-five acres, and Mecklenburg where sixty per cent of the lands consisted of estates larger than 250 acres; but even in Bavaria *métayage* was disappearing fairly rapidly, and the average peasant farm was soon larger than fifty acres.

Up to 1850 there had been some division of common lands, but though the local lord took his share individual peasant farms hardly ever benefited by it; the village's portion remained, in fact, undivided. It was only very gradually, as the country's industrialization progressed, that the German peasantry went over entirely to individual ownership. The result of this evolution was that communal holdings were not divided into lots, but leased out *en bloc*, which greatly facilitated attempts at redistribution. Germany differed most from France (and even from England) in the way in which the peasants left the countryside; the exodus of the poor peasants happened at a time when the railways were already in existence. The new proletariat, instead of collecting in great numbers near the nearest towns, could choose areas where industry was already flourishing or go directly to one of the great ports from which they embarked for America – generally for the United States. From 33,000 in 1844, German emigration rose to 250,000 a year in 1854; the trend was strong enough to attract the most underprivileged workers from the east, those of the 1810 *Gesinde Ordnung*. This decree gave to the employer (but not the worker) the right to break a contract and thus gave him the means of imposing pitiless discipline. The German emigrant was soon replaced by the Polish immigrant in these power levels of rural life.

German production improved as that of England had done a hundred years earlier, and at first this progress helped to strengthen the exporting position of Danzig, still a great European supply port in the middle of the century. Twenty years later the situation was reversed, and Germany be-came an importer. This reversal of commercial trends took place in a single generation there, whereas in England it had taken almost a century.

It proved how quickly German agriculture had adapted itself to the new resources of rail-borne trade, which meant that any country need produce only what it could grow cheaply and at a substantial profit. Yields of corn at the end of the century were to reach twenty-five hundredweight to the acre in Mecklenburg, far surpassing those of France. Potato crops grew in size too and production went up to forty million tons a year, six times that of England. Such decisive progress was not achieved without good technicians. The first problem tackled by the German school of chemistry was that of the land. In the 1850s specialist schools began to appear in the small towns, and at Hildesheim for instance there were twenty-two peasant schools in 1870. Obviously the food industries also benefited from these new methods; sugar production rose from two hundred thousand tons to a million between 1860 and 1885.

From 1850 to 1880 the proportion of Prussia's rural population fell from seventy-two to sixty-four per cent, and the change in Saxony was even more rapid. The cause lay largely in the increase in coal production over the same period; it went up by eighty per cent in England, but almost quadrupled in Germany, and the number of mines more than doubled. From 1860 to 1875 Germany's iron production quadrupled (in France it doubled). Steel production in 1880 was higher than in France, and half that of England, which it surpassed in 1900. This progress was due also to the high concentration of the new German concerns. Foreigners were amazed to find that each German coalmine employed on an average eight hundred workers. Through the influence of the joint-stock companies, the number of big concerns in the Ruhr was reduced from three hundred in 1858 to fewer than two hundred in 1870. Naturally, work processes were continually being improved, and more modern methods adopted. In 1840, ninety per cent of Prussian iron was being smelted by wood; by 1860, eighty-eight per cent was produced by the use of coke: that was the real significance of the 1848 revolution in Germany.

Germany had, of course, bought a good deal of plant and equipment abroad, though only what was absolutely essential: in the 1840s its production was almost equal to the needs of consumption; in 1857 it could supply no more than sixty-six per cent of them; ten years later Germany began exporting. Berlin's coal consumption from 1840 to 1870 went up from 30,000 to 800,000 tons. Here again, progress was the result of co-operation between research and industry. In 1858 a mines committee of the Ruhr brought together fifty companies and embarked on a programme of extensive research. This committee organized production and opened a rail factory at Dusseldorf in 1850, a zinc works in Upper Silesia in 1860, and a tin works at Cologne. In this way Germany continually had new groups of producers systematically studying markets and techniques. Borsig was still one of the leaders of Berlin in 1860, and later came the *Hörder Verein*. These industrial 'general-staffs' formed a nucleus for the great cartels, as for instance the famous Westphalian cartel of 1876 which was soon called on to control half of Germany's production.

This modernization was not brought about without suffering and poverty. In 1850 there were more than 200,000 peasants in Prussia who were spinning and weaving flax. During the 1848 crisis they had suffered terrible hardships, dying by thousands; and the organization of the flax industry was achieved only at the cost of these painful social changes. About 1850 there were still 250,000 hand-spinning frames in Germany. There were no more than 30,000 in 1882, and these remaining weavers were to prove far harder to get rid of. But the brutality and poverty of those years were the price that had to be paid for the progress of the new textile industry: in 1846 Germany exported nearly all its raw wool, but twenty-five years later German mills were using all the raw wool of the country and more was being imported. This coincided with developments in American stockbreeding which were already making cheap wool available. In Germany, cotton did not – as in England and France – act as a spur to the textile industry: there was very little of it in Germany in 1850. The fact was that Germany was forging ahead at tremendous speed. She did not suffer too much in the process: Elberfeld, Stuttgart and Breslau began to import cotton. In 1866 almost 70,000 tons of raw cotton were already being imported, and ten years later, owing to the incorporation of Alsatian industry, the quantity had almost doubled. Elberfeld and Crefeld, encouraged by this success, were even competing with London in the world silk market.

Finally, when we come to consider German trade, it is important to remember that the late development of German industry in comparison with England and France led to a much more rapid rate of progress. Germany profited from the example of Western Europe in particular. As Germany depended on manufactured goods or on machines for rapid modernization, it imported them in better conditions from countries whose great desire was to sell, and so to lower their prices. When Germany bought rails for its railways before making its own, when it selected the best foreign workmen before its own were trained, or when it used the best available machine-tools before manufacturing them for itself, it did so cheaply. These useful transactions were made easier because the commercial and customs systems were fairly flexible. After the 1848 crisis, German industry was first protectionist, in order to defend its production against foreign invasion; then, when Germany wished to speed up its modernization programme, which was already well under way, and to begin exporting, it went over to free trade. In 1880 List's prophecies came true: Germany had become an industrial country. Like all industrial countries at that time, it then reverted to protection. Here, as in England, there were three phases, and here too they closely followed the chronology of politics. Let us see how they did so.

In France the freedom of individual initiative had been proclaimed by the Revolution of 1789; in Germany the old corporative way of life collapsed in 1848, together with the last traditions of serfdom. It is impossible to go into all the details of the economic liberation which was achieved in very different circumstances from one state of the confederation to another; but everywhere it was hastened on by the anxiety of each not to be outdone by its neighbour. Thus all the old, small seigniorial capitals with their care-free way of life which had lasted until the middle of the nineteenth century, were turned into economic centres in the modern style in the space of one generation in this general stampede.

Between 1854 and 1859 factory chimneys appeared all over the country. Since the liberal movement gained strength in Germany there had been a marked increase in credit, which enabled the new industry to benefit from the habits of mutual aid and trust inherited from the corporate methods of former days. This movement of credit was as strong in the country as in the towns, and depended on the fairly large class of average landowners, so that it only developed where employment increased. Commercial com-panies were organized around the new railways from Liège to Bremen and Hamburg and along the first great trunk lines serving Cologne, Crefeld and Dortmund, which were the centres of gravity of the new Westphalian iron industry. In the east the Berlin-Magdeburg-Leipzig triangle covered the areas of traditional Saxon craftsmanship. The south was less well provided for, except perhaps in the region around Baden along the Rhine. Prussia was already moving towards free trade, whilst Bavaria and Württemberg were protectionist. Inside the *Zollverein* there was incessant quarrelling between the two groups. In the north, the metal industry became independent between 1854 and 1864. Imports of iron went down from 125,000 to 100,000 tons, while the output of iron rose from 400,000 to 900,000 tons. The time of high protective tariffs was over. The produce had to be marketed and foodstuffs had to be bought cheaply to feed the new working class. In short, tariffs had to be lowered. In the south, however, industrialization was slower, and to adopt low tariffs would have meant disrupting Germanic economic solidarity in favour of Prussia. Prussia furthermore refused to modify the heavy transit dues on German wines exported by Bavaria and Württemberg. The Austrian Government realized that the new industrial development of Prussia threatened to tip the balance to the north, especi-ally if Germany bought foodstuffs from other countries instead of from Bavaria. Austria itself was forced to adopt protectionist policy, since it was at the start of its own economic expansion. After the 1848 crisis Austria was able to impose its customs policy on Hungary (which naturally favoured free trade since it exported a great deal of corn); and since Austria also aimed at controlling the German market, it posed as the protector of the southern states.

There were disputes within the *Zollverein* as well as within Germany as a whole, but as public opinion gradually began to take shape, fostered by the new press and by the progress of credit and trade, the change of outlook began to tell in favour of the north. The Association of Economists was founded at this period and a union of German industrialists was on the way. All these new bodies favoured a progressive policy which advocated the lowering of tariffs and the development of trade. Prussia was already in a similar position to England's as an importer of raw materials and food-stuffs, and an exporter of manufactured goods. The commercial and financial structure of Prussia was sound, particularly since the reorganization of the currency (which was increased and readapted to the new circulation of money). A new commercial code was carefully worked out, and measures were taken to help the workers (*Gewerbe Freiheit*), although nothing would help them more than cheap bread.

The Austrians in their turn, under the leadership of Brucke, were attempting to profit from the new railway junction with Trieste. This had now been completed after many setbacks, and it was hoped to use it to revive the Mediterranean trade and to serve all central Europe; but it proved impossible to divert to Trieste the route from India for which Marseilles, Genoa and even Brindisi were competing. Support was given to the trading companies (the Lloyd-Triestino), a loan society on real estate was set up (the *Hypotheken Bank*) and, most important of all, the famous *Oesterreichische Kredit Anstalt* was founded with the assistance of the Rothschilds. Eventually Austrian currency was reformed. Encouraged by this advance, Brucke tried to intervene in Germany's customs disputes in order to gain some advantage for himself, but without success.

In fact although progress in Austria was rapid between 1850 and 1860, it was less than in most countries. Bremen, Hamburg and the Baltic ports profited from the growth of Atlantic trade. Hamburg opened trading centres in east and west Africa. The Hansa traded with Zanzibar, and Bremen's connections with the United States were strong enough to bring the *Nord Deutscher Lloyd* into being. The *Berliner Handels-Gesellschaft* was founded in Berlin and the *Disconto Gesellschaft* was adapted to large-scale international trade. Trade on this scale led almost inevitably to free trade. Even Switzerland lowered its tariffs and after the Crimean War Russia began to send corn across Germany, to the great advantage of Nordic trade. Above all, France had just signed the famous treaty of 1860 with England and a similar one with Belgium, and had also made overtures to Berlin.

The threat of a commercial treaty between Berlin and Paris was very disturbing to Austria. At that time Austria had just lost the war with Italy. Napoleon III, indeed, had not managed to secure the total victory for which he had hoped, but he had disrupted the Austrian economy, and was apparently aware that by inviting Prussia to sign a commercial treaty involving a lowering of tariffs he could further its expansion at the expense of its Austrian rival. The damage to Austria was all the greater since it put the countries of southern Germany in a great difficulty. The old *Zollverein* admitted all the German states on an equal footing, and the *Zollverein* council could proceed only by a unanimous vote; a single veto blocked every resolution, as the dispute of the 1850s had abundantly shown. All Prussia's proposals had been systematically blocked by Bavaria and the council hardly met again after 1850. In 1858 Bismark denounced what he regarded as sabotage and advised the ministers to withdraw from the *Zollverein*. In signing a trade treaty with France, Prussia knew it was running the risk of breaking up the union if Bavaria should reject the new customs policy. It was a reasonable risk to take, since Austria could not offer the southern states any economic openings as good as the natural outlets to the north.

The Austro-Prussian economic battle began in 1862. Brucke had died in disgrace. Hamburg had sold itself to the highest bidder and was now an ally of Prussia. Bavaria tried in vain to keep opposition to the Prussian plan alive by seeking to arouse greater German enthusiasm for a Germanic union including Austria. A plan for a Franco-Prussian treaty put an end to this once and for all. Economic requirements are the most compelling of all. The *Zollverein*, including Bavaria, had to give in. Bismarck granted Austria most-favoured-nation treatment: this was not a great concession in the circumstances since Austria was economically cut off from Germany.

Prussia's victory was all the more significant since in the course of the negotiations on the treaty with Paris, the *liberum veto* was not used. The legal rights of Bavaria and Württemberg became meaningless once Prussia could threaten to dissolve the *Zollverein*, on which both were economically dependent. Prussia controlled the outlets to the sea which were essential to the economy of southern Germany. In a few months the old constitution of the *Zollverein* was replaced by a new one in which each country was represented by a number of votes proportionate to its population, and a customs parliament was to make decisions according to majority vote. This move in 1867 made Prussia the master of Germany.

As Clapham aptly remarked, Bismarck achieved German unity not so much by blood and iron as by coal and iron. Prussia's vast industry won the greatest victory of the nineteenth century in the field of economics. When Prussian troops defeated the Austrians at Sadowa, and when later the customs parliament was created, the foundations of the new Prussian Empire were laid several years before the ceremony at Versailles. The fierce economic competition in the 1860s placed Prussia in an invulnerable position.

After Sadowa, Bismarck only demanded economic concessions from the defeated Austrians who were forced out of the English and French markets to make way for the German economy. This was in spite of opposition from the trading states of the north, which were still anxious about this southward deflection of trade currents. This demand of Bismarck's had serious consequences for Austria; since the Austrian customs régime could no longer be imposed on Hungary. The latter, an agricultural country, accepted the autonomy decree of 1867 which destroyed the economic unity of the old monarchy.

Let us return to Bismarck in 1868. The economic and military victory over Austria turned a difficult internal situation to his advantage. He had only been called to power in 1862 because William I despaired of getting a parliament dominated by merchants and industrialists (particularly by Schulze-Delitzsch) to approve the credits needed for the reorganization of the Prussian army proposed by Roon. Bismarck's success was therefore a double one, since by opening up unlimited prospects to German finance he rallied the industrial opposition. All the currents of public opinion that had been against the *Zollverein's liberum veto* were now, at the instigation of the economists and influential merchants, transformed into a patriotic campaign which even infected Bavaria. It brought about unanimity in Germany which Bismarck was able to exploit against Napoleon III by enticing this ill-starred man into the diplomatic and military traps which he and Moltke had prepared for him.

In any case, Bismarck could hardly have been caught unawares in his struggle against the liberals, for he had been watching the progress of the German working-class movement and its growing opposition to the middle-class programme since 1862. When the unfortunate Lassalle, who had fought for the unity of the working class, was killed in 1864, he was less regretted by Marx (who accused him of collaborating with the middle classes and of putting his trust in such middle-class institutions as universal suffrage), than by Bismarck, who later adopted some of his theses. Bismarck had probably intended to harness this working-class power against the middle classes if the latter had continued to impede the military measures desired by the king of Prussia. After the victory of 1870–1, however, Bismarck no longer needed to woo the German worker's party, since he had the support of the merchants and industrialists. On the contrary, now that the workers were becoming united under Bebel's leadership into a social democratic party they had become increasingly dangerous and Bismarck was soon to think of fighting them.

In 1871, Bismarck saw not only the last states enter the *Zollverein*, but the customs parliament, previously only an economic organization, become the Parliament of the Empire and a political entity. The king of Bavaria was now personally in favour of the Empire and was carrying public opinion in south Germany along with him. He himself suggested that the imperial crown be offered to William.

Then a new phase opened. The unassuming Delbruck, that model official who had presided over the destinies of the Customs Union and remained true to the policy of liberalism, was compelled to leave his post in 1877, defeated by the new crises and by the new needs of the economic empire. Bismarck, now Imperial Chancellor, was putting through emergency laws against socialism and inaugurated the protectionist *Realpolitik* which opened a new phase of German history. Once unity was achieved and strengthened by modernization of the economy, Germany's main requirement was to orientate industrial production towards those world markets which were still free – those of central Europe. The great German banks then concentrated on an intensive exploration of central European markets, and were already turning their attention to Turkey (it was perhaps significant here that Roon was a geographer and Moltke had been military adviser to the Sultan). The steady progress of the German economy opened up to it the European routes across the Mediterranean; Austria had failed to create an outlet to the Mediterranean via Trieste, but now German credit was attempting to obtain one through Constantinople.

Now that Prussia had conquered Germany it intended to dominate all central Europe, and eventually to be the head of a great continental empire.

FRANCE BETWEEN TWO EMPIRES

In 1848 France had been the focal point of the revolution; in February of that year France had again stirred up the waves of unrest which appeared to have died down in southern and eastern Europe. But by 1849 order was restored in France. Whilst revolutions or wars continued to shake southern and eastern Europe, France, through the mouth of Lamartine, was already counselling calmness and restraint and preaching reconciliation. Then the new Republic adopted a constitution with a monarchical executive power, and elected neither the poet Lamartine nor the Republican General Cavaignac, but a prince with the magical name of Louis-Napoleon. The revolution was an urban phenomenon caused by the weakness of French credit institutions which suddenly collapsed under the weight of the railways. The restoration of order appeared to be a rural achievement, since universal suffrage gave the peasants a greater voice in the nation's affairs. This is worth considering in more detail.

In 1848 French peasants were still not very different from what they had been in 1800. There had of course been some technical advances as we noted throughout the first half of the century, but there had been little structural change and no appreciable transformation of rural society. In 1862 France still had 2,400,000 farms of less than twenty-five acres, and in practice even the large holdings were no bigger than a hundred acres; only just over 150,000 farms were larger than a hundred acres. Compared to the English or German country estate in the middle of the century the French estate remained small. Consequently the number of small land-owning farmers was still enormous, more than two million. There were almost as many gentleman farmers as agricultural workers, and the latter, too, often possessed small plots of their own. We shall not reconsider at this point the legal importance of the civil code, but merely emphasize that the agricultural scene of 1850 in France was not basically different from that of the eighteenth century.

The result was that however marked the urban development of France might be, it did not play as decisive a role as urban development in England or Germany. There were twenty-seven cities with more than 20,000 inhabitants in 1800; there would be at the close of the century forty of more than 40,000 inhabitants. France's rural population was still seventy-eight per cent of the total population in 1866; this proportion was higher than in Prussia, or in Germany which was in other respects still so close to feudalism. Whilst France's cities, with their enlightened and progressive *élite*, had brought out their civil code for the world to copy fifty years earlier, launched Proudhonian socialism ten years earlier, and had recently welcomed the manifesto of Karl Marx, the French countryside was still the most conservative in the world. The roots of a land-owning peasantry went very deep, for as Marc Bloch has so clearly shown, they were already vigorous under Louis XII. It is not easy to estimate how much agricultural equipment was being used on French farms. The number of ploughs seems tremendous, simply because it included even the wooden swing-ploughs which twentieth-century geographers found still in use only a few years ago. On the other hand there were very few hay-making and mowing machines, and mechanical threshing machines were possessed by only a very few great landowners. The rural world, even that of the well-to-do, was by no means over-enthusiastic about the American or Scottish techniques so popular in England and even in Germany.

Indeed, this dominance of the countryside enabled France to produce all the corn that was needed in good years and to be self-sufficient in food supplies; this had been Colbert's aim and was the chief goal both for the monarchy of the old régime and for Napoleon I. The price of bread was still taxed as before. Agricultural societies existed in great numbers, and many of them appear to have been half a century old, but their effectiveness had increased hardly at all. The Restoration had encouraged agricultural shows and Napoleon III was to take an even greater interest in them. Fortunately, Flaubert used one of them as a setting for a famous episode in *Madame Bovary*: the rustic pictures he gives of rich, progressive Normandy would not have displeased Young, but Young had been dead for nearly fifty years.

On the big farms, farmers continued to try out improvements in sheep-breeding. French merinos tried to compete with the sheep of Spain, and even more with those of Saxony and England. But there were no startling changes in French cattle: their numbers rose only from twelve million to thirteen million, whilst those of sheep actually went down from thirty-two million to thirty million. For agriculture was advancing very slowly indeed. Throughout this period the vine was a basic element of the rural economy; except in years when the crops were affected by mildew, France produced ample wine, the consumption of which had risen by fifty per cent between 1840 and 1870. The area sown with wheat increased by thirty-three per cent between 1850 and 1870. The production of sugar was developing slowly, and in 1870 it was not a quarter of that of Germany. The cultivation of beet, however, made the fortune of several modern-minded landowners, one of whom was Morny. The area sown to corn and beet was apparently increased, mainly at the expense of fallow ground. This was excellent, but the increase in production was not accompanied by an improvement in quality: French yields were barely half those of Belgium and Holland, and were fifty per cent lower than those of England and Germany.

In these circumstances, it is surprising to find that the reign of Napoleon III has acquired such a high reputation in the field of economics. In actual fact, all the effervescence of this period hardly affected more than one-third of the total population. The Prince declared on the ninth of October

1852: 'We have vast uncultivated lands waiting to be cleared.' An ab-
surdly small credit had indeed just been granted for the development and
improvement of Sologne, and several rural areas hoped to receive a similar
life-restoring gift. In reality the Sologne credits went to a small railway.
The most memorable part of this famous speech, in which occurred the
phrase 'the Empire and peace are one', was the sentence: 'There are roads
to be opened up, harbours to be dug, canals to be finished, our railway
network to be completed.'

The credit crisis which had overthrown Louis-Philippe arose from the
massive demands for capital put forward by the railways. There were half-
finished excavations for tunnels and embankments, and ballast was waiting for the rails; lines already laid down were waiting for their rolling
stock; stations were half-built in Paris and other cities. All these projects
had to be completed.

This was the period when efforts were being made throughout Europe
to attract all possible trade and business to the ports and towns along the
great transport routes, so as to gain a few months' lead over competitors
and create habits which would hold good for the future. Austria, as we
have seen, was improving Trieste. The Lloyd-Triestino line already possessed financial resources and a fleet of ships which were superior to those
of all French or Italian competitors. It now needed to establish a flow of
trade from Amsterdam or Antwerp to Trieste that would be powerful
enough to divert the English traffic to India which had previously gone via
France. In order to retain its geographical advantages France needed to
secure the Paris–Marseilles link as quickly as possible. Neither north nor
south of Lyons was there as yet the least idea how the companies were to be
organized. There were urgent problems in west France too: Bremen and
Hamburg were starting a regular service with America modelled on the
English services, and Le Havre and Rouen were not yet in any position to
compete.

The capitalism of Louis-Philippe had failed. A socialist programme had
been sketched out by the provisional government, but had met with no
success. Acting at top speed, the republican Government had at once given
work to the many thousands of unemployed who had been left stranded
beside the half-finished tracks on which work had been interrupted through
the financial embarrassment of the railway companies. Thousands of
building workers were still wandering idly about Paris. State control, and
socialism were suggested by a very small group of economists. There were
bitter arguments on political theory in the clubs of the young Republic,
but they were all overruled by one grim, inescapable reality: the Government could not procure the necessary resources, for if the French investor
had previously been reluctant to lend his money to the railway companies,
he was not now going to hand it over to the Treasury of the social republic.

We have seen how in 1848 suggestions had been put forward for a
tentative reform of credit, which became the basis of the new French
capitalism. The shortage of money which had lasted since 1846 ended in

1850 and as a result the position of private enterprise, and especially of the railway companies, improved. As a rebuttal of socialism, Thiers had hastily thrown together *Propriété*, a curious and childish book, a collection of platitudes, in which he defended landed property without giving any detailed answer to Proudhon's claims on the subject of credit. But capitalism was making such fair weather that everything, even Thiers' lightweight performance, combined to speed it on its way. The Constituent Assembly had already decided to respect the companies' privileges. Then the task of the executive gradually became clear: Louis-Napoleon Bonaparte, who had been elected by countrymen, or in other words by landed property, used the authority bestowed on him by this rural majority to extend credit based on personal estate (*crédit mobilier*). Once they had been given power the companies, in order to get the capital they lacked, launched preference shares of small amounts which could be taken up by a wide public, even in country districts. The state guaranteed these shares, in other words it exerted all the power of its institutions to push their sale. In addition the state decreased its budgetary charges as much as possible so that taxation could be lowered and all available financial resources could be concentrated on private enterprises. Thanks to this situation, which had been imposed on him by events, Louis-Napoleon appeared as the saviour of both town and country. The workers resigned themselves to the situation, and the capitalists accepted the Prince's authority.

We have spoken of Palmerston's sympathy for Napoleon III; it was now to have practical results. England's railways were much more advanced than those of France, and had already reached the stage when all the essential lines had been built and were fully operative, so that any further projects would be of only minor importance. As a result, English investors were looking around for new schemes for their capital – and where could better opportunities be found than in France? After all, the British Empire's great natural routes led from the Channel (through the Parisian basin and the Rhone Valley) to the Mediterranean and on to India. Soon ships crossing the Channel were bringing France material, rails, and above all capital, more even than the considerable amounts imported under Louis-Philippe. The capital was carefully followed up and watched by English businessmen sitting on French boards of directors. It was clear that the companies were entitled to better contracts with the state than those of the 1842 law, and the Government had agreed to grant them. But in negotiating these additional concessions, the Government took the opportunity to ask the companies owning the best lines to take on in addition branch lines which were more difficult to place. Thus France's great network of railways came into being. This solution of the problem of the railway-building crisis of 1847–8 was natural and inevitable, but credit for it was given to the head of the executive who in consequence was able to proclaim himself Emperor without appreciable opposition.

Actually, in so far as any clear economic opinions can be attributed to Napoleon III, they would have led rather to a kind of state socialism. But the author of *Extinction du Paupérisme* was making the middle classes uneasy. Napoleon III gained power only because he had renounced the application of his own principles. True the officials of the *Ponts et Chaussées*, who were polytechnicians and consequently Colbertians and inherited a tradition going back to the old régime, were only half satisfied with a solution which gave to engineers of private companies a responsibility and an authority which they felt belonged only to themselves. Their engineers took good care of the roads, but the roads now took second place to the railways. The canals, at all events, would have to be publicly administered, since they represented the only means of transport capable, it was said, of moderating the high fares exacted by the new railway companies. But a great canal scheme was hardly feasible. Already in 1852 the Midi Canal had had to be handed over to the *Compagnie des Chemins de Fer du Midi*. Plans were drawn up, but to be carried out they would have needed much more money than Napoleon III could raise, since he had done all he could to stimulate investment in private initiative. Moreover, the legislative body was most watchful, and within a few years it placed the disillusioned Emperor in an untenable position.

At first the wave of optimism was general; the railway programme absorbed all the vagrant unemployed and continued to attract workers away from country districts. Towns grew at the same time as shares rose on the exchange. Shares were taken up so readily that it was necessary to apply for double the amount desired in order to get any at all. The new banks made handsome profits from the sale of all this paper and increased the number of their customers. Satisfaction was widespread in England. Austria was defeated in the race to the Mediterranean. Prussia was just as successful in its efforts to push German trade in the direction of the North Sea, but this prospect still caused no uneasiness in France. Paris was in holiday mood. The Emperor took his full share in these rejoicings; this was the brilliant life he had dreamed of. Millions, millions, *châteaux*, a civil list, wrote Victor Hugo, who added: 'I have been down into the cellars at Lille. I have seen those black tombs.' It could not be denied that not all branches of industry derived equal benefit from the new developments and the contrast they afford deserves examination.

Surrounded by the luxury of his court and the riches of the *parvenus*, Napoleon soon forgot his intention of stamping out poverty, which was still acute, particularly in the textile areas. Spinning and weaving had flourished during the Restoration and the July Monarchy but their economic prosperity was achieved mainly at the expense of the workers (what a magnificent field of observation for Marx!). A good deal of the work was still being done in the countryside, and since many French weavers often owned a small field (unlike their English counterparts), they could afford to accept the continual drop in prices imposed by the merchant who brought their raw material and orders. But the fall in wages was more disastrous for the wretched city workers, crowded into cellars or, in Lyons, in hovels built into the hillside.

The requirements of French fashion, ever-changing, which sought to give each buyer the impression that he was acquiring 'a unique article' which would earn him a reputation for originality anywhere in the world, prevented the large-scale use of modern looms. Fine, detailed work of this kind was ideally suited to the sweating system. The isolated worker suffered severely from the luxury character and the renowned high 'quality' of French textile productions.

The home cutlers were a little more fortunate than the weavers, particularly in Auvergne, but also in Poitou and Champagne; they kept alive an outmoded commercial and industrial structure which nevertheless succeeded in exporting to European markets because of the originality of its craftsmanship.

In heavy industry, on the other hand, everything had to be sacrificed to mass production. At the end of Louis-Philippe's reign, coal seams were discovered to the south of Lille. Working began when the companies took advantage of the new credit, after 1850. Then pits opened at Lescarpelles, Courrières, Lens, Loos, Béthune and Saint-Omer. In twenty years production rose from five to thirteen million tons. The production of the north and the Pas-de-Calais alone almost equalled the total output of the old mines dug out of the periphery of the Massif Central. Mining in France had to contend with difficulties unknown in England, and consequently French prices were thirty per cent higher, but there was a good French market for coal and so production was easily absorbed. From 1851 iron output reached the 1846 figure of 600,000 tons, and then it was trebled in twenty years. The steel output was soaring, but could by no means compare with that of England, though Napoleon iii had done his best to attract Bessemer to France and to appoint him adviser to numerous ironmasters. At Le Creusot and Hayange converters appeared after 1863. There was a geographical displacement just as there had been in England, particularly towards Denain and Anzin. Large concentrations of industry were taking shape in the centre and east. Under the direction of Schneider there were 10,000 workmen at Le Creusot, which thus ranked as one of the major industrial centres of the world. At Rive-de-Gier under the direction of Pétin-Gaudet there were 6,000 workers, and 5,000 under Wendel at Hayange. The price of rails dropped by half, but the French still preferred iron rails to steel and became as a result the second largest producers of iron in the world after England. Old centres like Commentry, Fourchamboult and many others remained busy, and by 1850 seemed assured of the same future as the industrial areas of England. In comparison with the swiftness of change in Germany, French industry made only moderate progress, and Paris remained stubbornly attached to individual craftsmanship right up to 1878.

Napoleon iii was an observer of this industrial scene rather than its instigator. Yet it was only natural that he should believe in his great destiny, for this dreamer came to power at the very moment when gold reestablished a credit system and he appeared as the country's saviour.

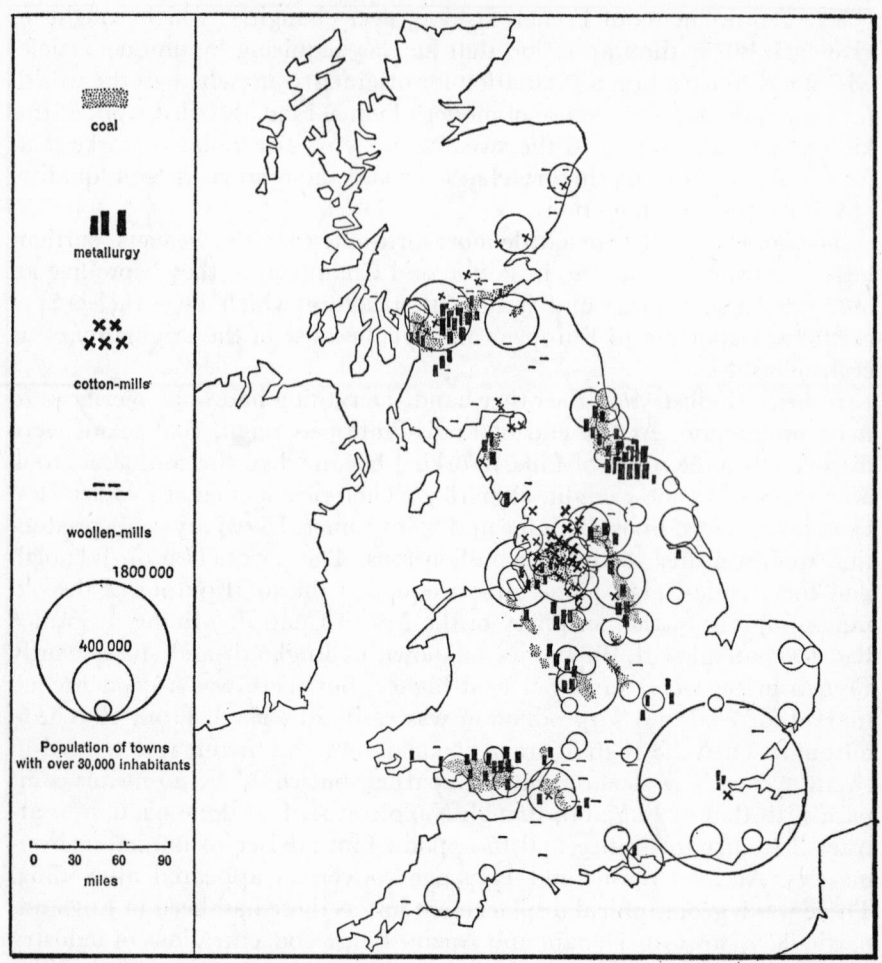

16 Industrial England c. 1880

Nevertheless his inactivity irked him. He thought himself called on to realize the most grandiose projects of the Saint-Simon school, particularly the Mediterranean system. A new edition of de Tocqueville was a sign of the revived popularity of the United States in France. It was the fashion to compare England and America. The Anglo-French industrial bloc was envisaged as playing a similar rôle in Europe to that of the Atlantic sea-board on the American continent, in which case central Europe would assume the rôle of the great central American plains. The Chicago of Europe was to be Constantinople. The westward expansion of the United States must have its counterpart in Europe in a great economic conquest reaching out towards Asia. Shipping companies were started on the Mediterranean. At first the French lines were far inferior to the Lloyd-Triestino, but soon the *Messageries Maritimes* won for France, with English consent

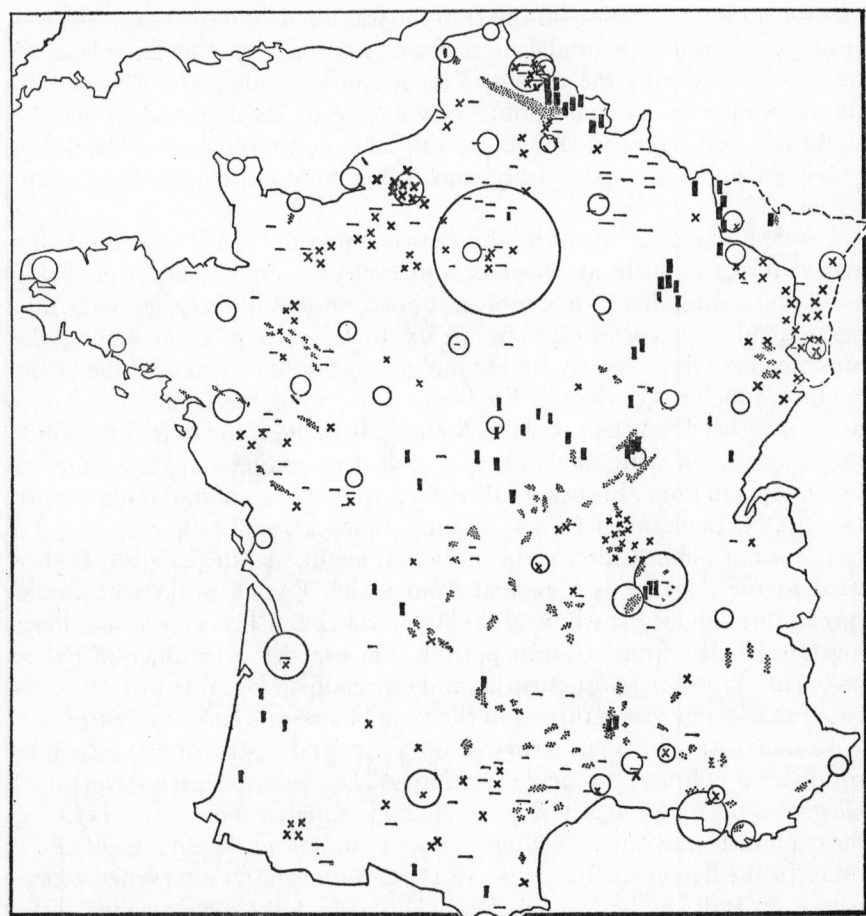

17 Industrial France c. 1880

and capital, a supremacy all the more easily achieved since Algeria was a
French outpost in 'the East'. Palmerston, seeing in Napoleon III something
of the qualities which attracted him in the great English industrialists, gave
his support to the Black Sea adventure. The French battalions in Rumania
and the Expeditionary Force in Crimea were the pioneers who were to take
large-scale trade and industrialization eastward in their wake. The French
negotiated the building of railways in Greece and the digging of the Suez
Canal in Egypt. Syria could provide Europe with an even better supply of
horses than Kentucky!

The dearly-bought victory of Sebastopol gave England cause for thought.
Trade was less attractive if it was going to involve war. The dangers were
out of all proportion to the profit, and England was already so deeply involved in India that she had no intention of taking on unlimited military
commitments on the continent of Europe. The Treaty of Paris was a vic-

tory for trade: navigation on the Danube was freed, and the Black Sea was closed to all warships; and England was well pleased. But Napoleon III was carried away by the weight of his military prestige, and although in the beginning he had no doubt been sincere in his desire for peace, he could not stop halfway. He went on to take an interest in the Danubian provinces, in Serbia, and in Italy, and at that point England no longer supported him.

England had no doubt of its ability to conquer the world by trade, using armed forces as little as possible, and such a conquest, far from being costly, brought in handsome profits. France, on the contrary, fell back into her old military vocation: it was easy to levy troops from among the humbler French peasantry barely integrated into the economic life of the country, much easier than in England where young men tended to follow in their fathers' footsteps. So the French abandoned the maritime policy they had shared with England, and turned to continental expansion, as Germany had done. France tried, in fact, to make the best of both worlds. It imitated England in China; French diplomats and admirals settled *à l'anglaise* in Cochin-China and Cambodia; again, like the English, France tried to use Algeria as a Bengal from which French settlement would spread throughout the whole of the Arab world. But France was also looking towards her frontiers, and putting into practice a continental policy favouring Prussia against Austria, and especially favourable to Italy, provided this favour was returned in the form of a regrouping of territories.

In short, Napoleon III, weary of the court and castle round, turned to continental politics for a new diversion. At last he saw a career worthy of his genius opening out before him. He had rendered too many services to the capitalists (not always willingly) not to profit from their neutrality for a time. In the five years from 1859 to 1864, Napoleon III intervened everywhere. In Italy, he helped on a unification which the development of the railways was organizing from within. Having succeeded in this, he tackled Germany and Mexico (he had even thought of Scandinavia). But the industrial power of the United States was much stronger in America than that of France. The Mexican *débâcle* was followed by the tragic death of Maximilian. Similarly, the economic power of Prussia was stronger in Germany than that of France.

The disaster of Sedan was foreshadowed by the blunders of Napoleon III's internal policy: from the moment when he broke with the English alliance and departed from the policy of a capitalist peace which he had promised at Bordeaux, the Emperor found that in France itself he was mistrusted by the majority of businessmen. He held the peasant mass of electors and the majority of the urban lower-middle class by the prestige of his victories. Thiers, who had again become the mouthpiece of public opinion, realized this very well and did his utmost to widen the rifts separating the Emperor from the upper-middle classes whose diplomatic difficulties were now beginning.

In the early years of his reign Napoleon III had renounced his own social policy, and had been forced to allow the free development of bourgeois capitalism. Nevertheless, using the prestige his victories gave him, he had tried to make French capitalism benefit from technical progress. This aim he sought to achieve by forcing the industrial feudalisms, created in the first half of the century, out of the hothouses in which they had been enclosed by the protectionist laws. In 1860 he signed the famous commercial treaty with England which put French industries on the defensive and compelled them to make reforms. The result was a storm of angry protest against this abuse of this executive, which was taking advantage of its right to ratify treaties, in order to interfere in internal economic policy.

However, certain industrial changes were made, especially in the textile industry, although these were mainly the result of an acute crisis which hit Europe from 1863 to 1866, known as the cotton famine. The American Civil War ruined the Southern plantations which supplied the bulk of the raw material for Europe's cotton industries. In spite of England's attempts to support the South, European spinning-mills closed down, and an appalling poverty settled over Lancashire and northern and eastern France. Manufacturers adapted themselves to the situation as best they could. A change over from cotton to wool involved modification of plant; buying cotton outside America meant forging commercial links with India and Egypt and many merchants did attempt this, especially the enterprising Mulhouse industrialists who made the Le Havre *bourse* so prosperous. From this crisis the French textile industry emerged transformed. Although there were still 200,000 hand-looms in use for cotton-spinning in France in 1867, there were already 80,000 driven by power, 47,000 of which were in Alsace. As a result of a magnificent effort which had been particularly intense during the past two generations, and of which Heilmann had been one of the most distinguished initiators, Alsace became one of the world's great cotton centres. Normandy also was acquiring new spinning-frames, and in Flanders many small firms were being squeezed out of business and replaced by stronger ones. In consequence, a parallel change was taking place in the woollen industry. In 1860, imports of raw wool amounted to very little more than home production; twenty years later they were to be four times in excess of it. There again, Napoleon III was a witness of the phenomenon rather than its director.

The only point of his programme which he was able to carry through nearly as he wished in the 1860s was the transformation of the towns. The Emperor was unable to direct the economy himself, since the legislative body (the mouthpiece of the industrial middle classes) wished to maintain it on a private footing, especially by reducing the budget to extremely moderate figures; but he secretly helped certain of his own friends, bringing the whole weight of the state to the aid of his protégés. Amongst them must be specially mentioned the Pereires, whose banking activities we have already noted. Any *entrepreneur* who took part in the great plan for transforming the cities, particularly Marseilles and Paris, could count on the secret support of the executive, especially its Parisian representative,

Haussmann. Advances were readily agreed to by the *Crédit Foncier*, they were given the backing of municipal finances and enjoyed a certain amount of governmental complicity in the delicate matter of accounting. All the financing of this urban reconstruction was done behind the scenes. The Emperor, who practised international politics in alcoves and in the discreet privacy of watering-places, carried on economic reforms in estate offices, publishing offices of business jourals *à la Mirès*, and behind the fences of demolition yards.

The real advance achieved by the French economy in iron, textiles, commerce, banking, and even agriculture made new building projects fashionable. Louis-Philippe had already had the idea of finishing the Louvre of the Bourbons. Bonaparte took the scheme in hand. Meanwhile all the new rich were building themselves mansions and *châteaux* in the provinces, hesitating between the style of the *grand siècle* or that of feudalism, the Gothic which Viollet-Le-Duc's endless reproductions had made so fashionable.

The whole of France was hard at work building itself houses ; there was speculation in the price of town sites, and by dint of borrowing impressive fortunes were built up. To speculate was to head straight for a title and those who succeeded were soon installed in lordly homes. The lower-middle class was lost in admiration of these amazing achievements. It could no longer recognize its broken-up streets, its demolished suburbs. A wind of pride was blowing, inflating the vanity of the townspeople, filling them with self-importance at being caught up in all this bold and feverish activity. After buying railway stock on the recommendation of Mirès and the securities offered by the *Crédit Mobilier*, the petty bourgeois dipped into his purse again for the debentures of the *Crédit Foncier* when Mirès suggested that he, too, might like to invest in real estate. Far more cautious, however, were the great financiers and all those who had learned wisdom from the accumulated experience of several generations, and the conservative and orthodox Rothschilds figured as defenders of tradition.

At first Napoleon III was delighted at seeing the country thus transformed in accordance with Saint-Simonist ethics and aesthetics.

All the kings of the earth paraded around him at the solemn opening of the exhibition of 1866. He may really have believed that he had only to follow the dictates of his ambition, and that the future would condone all his rash financial ventures, whose irregularities he tried to conceal. At all events, after 1866, the fear of bills being called in began to haunt his nights. Haussmann's fantastic accounts made credit uneasy. The Pereires, abandoned by the Bank, led to the downfall of the *Crédit Mobilier*. The railways, indeed, were doing well out of lines which were profitable to run, but the system of secondary lines was not yet completed. The leaders of industry, shaken by the cotton crisis and preoccupied by the enormous calls being made on them by the modernization of their businesses, grew anxious at the foolish waste of money on wars and imperial cities.

The political and financial world, remembering the closing years of

Louis-Philippe, believed that the resources of credit could be reinvigorated only at the cost of political reform. It was in these conditions that the legislative power was granted a control over the budget all the tighter for being accompanied by a reform in the rules governing public accounting. By that time, however, the accounts had already become hopelessly entangled and suspect. Napoleon III had to abandon his recently adopted protégés. Although he was able to get Mirès out of prison, he could not prevent Jacob Pereire from selling his priceless collection of pictures and his brother Isaac from being twice disqualified for electoral corruption, or Haussmann, his favourite administrator, from being sacrificed to the liberals.

In the last months of the régime it seemed likely that the liberals were at last to assume control, and rescue the country from the crisis to which imperial adventures had led it. The legislative body attempted to canalize all the credit still available for those industrial concerns which were badly in need of it. Economies were ordered in every department of public expenditure including, of course, that of war. Unfortunately, however, the revolutionary changes brought about in Europe by the railway gave rise on every hand to rivalries which strained the 1815 frontiers to breaking point. The consequences of the imperial ventures in Mexico, beyond the Alps, and especially across the Rhine, began to appear at the very moment when the Emperor had exhausted his credit in unspectacular adventures in landed estate. There was no longer, Thiers said, a single mistake left for him to make.

Napoleon III had completely lost control over the machinery of politics, and was powerless to check the economic forces welding Hamburg to Munich, Venice to Rome. Ministers who had believed that their finest achievement would be the dismissal of Haussmann suddenly found themselves confronted by an insolent and cunning Bismarck. They declared war, in spite of the hesitations expressed by Napoleon who was bolstering up his courage with Eugénie's compliments.

It was a terrible year. The German railways did excellent work in concentrating troops; after all, they had the Rhine as their axis. The strategic moves were written on the railway map: France dispersed her troops, which were captured at Metz and Sedan before they had struck a single blow. The Tuileries and the lovely, new Paris were burning under Bismarck's eyes.

Socially the France of 1871 was in the same situation as in 1848. In May the Commune resumed, and lost, the struggle of June 1848. The middle-class business world again tried out a line of action which previously had always succeeded: as in 1815, 1830, and 1850 it allowed itself to be edged out of power, and underwent the revolution and the following reaction, only to emerge with a firmer grip on the reins of economic life. That was the real meaning of France's famous unheavals. Once the storm had died down, the same Thiers, the Montalivets, the Dufaures, Fraissinet the Marseilles shipowner and Freycinet the Ariègle engineer, all came to the fore again, until such time as the thriving industry of eastern France brought Jules Ferry to a position of authority. Their object was still a parliamentary régime, supported by sound business ventures. So the Republic resumed the building of railways, the best of which would be sold to private companies and the rest run at the expense of the taxpayer. It put forward a gigantic plan for canals and ports. French gold which had been in hiding now flowed in from all sides. Within a few months Bismarck was amazed to find that the Republic had freed France from German troops. It animated urban activity where streets, squares, houses, theatres (above all the Paris Opera) were completed according to the prescribed plans. Credit recovered and French firms were soon building railways in Greece, Spain, Algeria and Tunis, and making plans for Indo-China. Again, as before, the army, reduced to inaction in Europe, set sail for conquests overseas.

The break between Napoleon and the bourgeoisie occurred, as we have seen, towards 1865. By 1880 this same bourgeoisie had rallied to the Republic. More tenacious than the successive political régimes through which it had passed, modern French industrial capitalism, born in the *salons* of the Directoire and matured under Louis-Philippe, now entered upon its most successful phase.

10
The Town-Dweller

EVEN in the loneliness of exile, Victor Hugo never lost his faith in progress; it was his religion and he wanted to make it that of his people too. Baudelaire was more sensitive to the gloomy life of the streets in the new industrial towns, where a mass of human beings crowded together still secretly longing for the country life they had once known. The towns were tyrannical in their demands. They kept scientists and able men hard at work, forcing upon them tasks far removed from the cultured dilettantism which had been so delightful and valuable a feature of the old philosophical studies; these tasks were dictated by the needs of French industry and had to be carried out within a fairly rigid research organization, subdivided into specialized branches. The tasks drove millions of navvies and labourers to work. As for beauty, the townspeople were indifferent to it; insensitive to Daumier's criticisms, they revelled in reproductions of Meissonier, in the affected landscape painters, and in Millet's peasants praying in the fields. The important thing was to build quickly; style did not matter – Gothic, Greek, Louis XIV or Louis XV. Everything was grist to the architects' mill, nothing was too good for this greedy, uncouth bourgeoisie. Against this decadent taste, there were few rare reactions from a group of artists who detested the Philistine, bourgeois order. There was Courbet, painting crude, earthy men of the soil, and Wagner, celebrating the legendary heroes of olden days, the pure-hearted hero uncorrupted by gold.

THE SERVANT SCIENCES

In our discussion of the first half of the nineteenth century we ranked science before law as one of the motive forces of European life. In the second half, railways and banks were put in the foremost place, and science was relegated to a subordinate position. We must now examine the reason for this.

Science had lost its amazing coherence. Gone were the days when one single mathematical concept could give rise to a thousand experimental applications. Mathematics was divided into specialized branches separated if not by actual contradictions, at least by lively quarrels between the supporters of irreconcilable methods. As for the applied sciences, physics and chemistry, they were now almost independent, and depended as much on industry as on intellectual circles for the fitting out and successful working of their laboratories.

Confronted with this vast and strange phenomenon, the philosophers were unable to synthesize. Up to the time of Kant, philosophy had kept closely in step with scientific discovery and had even sometimes succeeded in disentangling the fruitful elements in it from the sterile. The Kantian philosophy, including its cosmogony, was a fairly good description of the Newtonian spirit. Once Kant had gone, it endeavoured to continue along the line of its own deductions. It tried, especially with Hegel, to deduce from these premises all the movements and the whole future of the world. But the *a priori* nature of this philosophy of identity, which blindly followed its own path, forced it to part company with the natural sciences. As each fresh discovery was made in these, leading to a correction of earlier ideas, it finally became obvious that the mental equipment of 1800 was no more than a shell which had to be broken out of. Hegel and the pure idealists continued to reason about this henceforth empty shell until Hamelin so sadly and humbly confessed their failure. The renewal was not to take place until the twentieth century when a new Newton was to mark an epoch calling for a new Kant.

In 1862 Helmholtz could write: 'The crucial proof [of the Hegelian identity principle] would have been in the natural sciences . . . at that moment [the Hegelian philosophy] failed utterly and completely. Of all the scientists not a single one could be found to follow these ideas. The philosophers accuse the scientists of being narrow-minded. The scientists retaliate by telling the philosophers they are crazy!' This admirable, mutual contempt reveals something besides mere pique; from now on it was no longer possible for one single man to embrace within his own mind all knowledge, to grasp the common nature of all methods.

The middle of the century was marked by one outstanding phenomenon, the division of scientific work. The encyclopaedic outlook was dying out. Each scientist entrenched himself in a domain which was exclusively his own, and so numerous were the discoveries being made that from one speciality to another, from one type of laboratory to another, no one had either the time or the inclination any longer to venture rashly into fields other than his own. Mathematics itself was split up in order to meet the requirements of such varied sciences. The old, sacrosanct unity of science was replaced by the doctrine of compulsory specialization. These specializations, however, and the techniques of laboratories which were beginning to fit themselves out with new equipment, did not in the least mean that each scientist was isolated within his own restricted sphere. On the contrary, the publication of scientific journals, the quicker postal service resulting from steam, the telegraph and soon the telephone, and travel, were to enable scientists specializing in the same subject to keep in close touch with each other and to cross all frontiers. There was a scientific internationalism which forced specializations to develop on what amounted to a world scale yet at the same time bound them ever more firmly to themselves.

The division, through discipline, was also reinforced by work in the universities. The mid-nineteenth century was the great age of university organization, or reorganization, of systematizations such as that suggested by Auguste Comte. The practical result was the formation of research groups in which students and assistants gathered around a professor for some special piece of work, applying a group of methods centring on one particular subject. This change in the universities took place extremely rapidly in Germany. In England, Oxford and Cambridge renounced their medieval universalism, of which Newton had been the finest flower, to open large numbers of specialized laboratories such as those directed by Maxwell, Cavendish or Forster. France, which had led the world between 1800 and 1830 because of the strong centralization of her Institute, found it more difficult to abandon this universalism, and resisted specialization. The wretched conditions in which Pasteur and Branly had to work, the hard lot of so many contemporary scientists, emphasized the slowness with which France was adapting itself to the new conditions.

Before embarking on a concise study of the scientific disciplines, we must explain some simplifications imposed by the need for brevity. We have abruptly cut the century in half and stressed the turning-point between 1840 and 1850. It is hardly necessary to point out that the break was not so clear-cut. If the record phase of the nineteenth century began much later than 1850, it started, as far as mathematics were concerned, at the very moment when Lagrange's rational mechanics was at the height of its popularity, for mathematicians were already assessing its results and preparing the next step. We must now return to Gauss, with whom we ended the last chapter.

If Lagrange and Laplace were men of their time, Gauss was well in advance of his. In his calculation of the trajectory of Ceres, he still showed his adherence to the Newtonian school, and it was by this calculation that the brilliant German established his reputation, entered the ranks of the great calculators, and ensured his own livelihood and his academic future. Similarly his work with Weber on electric physics was in the context of his time. But behind this imposing façade, which in itself would have been enough to make a man famous, another Gauss was concealed, a silent, secret worker, who accumulated the most extraordinary discoveries in his *Notizen Journal*. They were in a style so elliptical that some still remain an enigma today. This journal, written between 1796 and 1816, made quite a sensation when it was published in 1898. It is not therefore surprising that even *Disquisitiones arithmeticae* published in 1801 (and still published in Latin) opened up pathways so new that contemporaries failed to recognize their significance, and their extraordinarily rich potentialities became apparent only when they were taken up again by the generations of Dirichlet and Eisenstein. He was working on the monogenous analytical functions of complex variable from 1811, but his conclusions remained secret until

Weierstrass rediscovered them forty years later. In spite of his undoubted genius, Karl Friedrich Gauss lived with difficulty on his meagre income, sometimes bitterly disappointed at having only three pupils – 'one of them was mediocre and the other two ignorant'. He was less known than the learned Pascal, since he had no understanding sister to help him on the road to fame. He used to say jokingly that he had been able to count before he could read. At seven he had fathomed, quite unaided, the mystery of arithmetical progressions and could do instantly in his head the interminable sums with which his country schoolmaster burdened his young pupils. It was in this country school that he discovered the binomial theorems.*

Gauss's work on differential geometry was more spectacular still. The problem arose out of cartography – how to represent a curved surface on a plane. About 1820, as we have seen, a great deal of work was being done on representations of the globe. Studying in a new way how to determine the position of a point on a surface, Gauss analysed multiplicities in two dimensions: he then generalized his method, and ended with multiplicities to the nth dimension. This method of work enabled him to solve the problem of the map by distinguishing the conform representation which preserves angles from that which preserves distances; but it also showed the possibilities of mathematics in cataloguing any type of space whatever, even of more than three dimensions. The analytical functions of complex variables played an important part in this. And it was the conditions of calculus which, for those who were eventually to use it, gave the definition of space which most conformed to the phenomenon studied, much more than the conditions of sensitivity which played so great a role in the Kantian critique. A new age was opening in the history of man's mental equipment.

And now we move to the remote borders of Europe, to an obscure Russian university, which Alexander 11 had tried to stimulate by giving it new foreign professors, especially German or Viennese. At the whim of the imperial government Lobachevsky was in turn museum director, professor, rector, or merely a private individual, a suspect, whose movements were watched by the police, but through all these vicissitudes his unfailing passion for research resulted in a striking achievement: the definition of a surface (pseudosphere) which would enable several parallels to a straight line to be drawn through a single point. In 1855, at the age of 65, on his university's diamond jubilee, Lobachevsky presented his *Pangéométrie*, which he had just finished dictating, as he had become blind. It went right back to Euclid in order to escape from his postulates and start off again

* Every student of higher mathematics is indebted to Gauss for a clear geometrical explanation of the meaning of complex numbers, and of the i (the square root of -1) so mysterious to the uninitiated. The *Disquisitiones arithmeticae* already foreshadowed the important new definition of congruence, which had led the study of uneven numbers out of the impasse in which it had remained since Fermat. Gauss returned to this subject in 1825 and threw new light on the problem of the congruences of quadratic binomials. He wrote a paper on cubic congruences which was found after his death. This work opened the way fifty years later for Dedekind, to whom modern students of higher mathematics owe the idea of the 'Dedekind cut', so useful in the new presentation of differential calculus and imaginary numbers.

along paths which the old geometry had neglected in an attempt at recti-
linear simplification. Its mathematics became exceedingly complicated*
but the main thing was that the tools needed to deal with the scientific
problems of 1850 were now ready to hand. This new mathematics did far
more than revolutionize philosophy, which for the next fifty years
abandoned all attempts to understand it: it provided practical methods
which simplified and activated the thinking of the experimenters in the
physical and chemical sciences.

While this revolutionary new theoretical work was being carried out in
eastern Europe, France still had Hermitte to carry on the great tradition of
1800. It seemed at times as if the Polytechnic and the University were in-
tent on preserving the tradition of Laplace by clinging to the system and
putting every possible obstacle in the way of Hermitte's 'pernicious
originality'. Fortunately the aged Cauchy and the whole German school
supported the young 'dreamer' in his application of elliptical functions to
equations of the fifth degree; and the way was opened for his pupil, Henri
Poincaré.

The theoretical work of the east Europeans brought a new diversity into
mathematics and it is easy to understand why philosphers looked back
wistfully to the age of enlightenment, when it seemed as if the whole life of
the mind could be illuminated from one single source. Their attitude is accounted for by the diversity and the enormous complexity of the mathematical concepts which emerged from Gauss's revolutionary theories. To
take just one example, there were interminable (and often friendly) arguments between the two protagonists of the rival German schools, Kronecker
and Weierstrass: for the former, everything was number, for the latter,
analysis. The field of thought covered by mathematics had become so vast
that its extreme frontiers were in violent contradiction with each other.
But it was so productive of ideas that, no matter what the demands of the

---

* It is important at this juncture to stress the importance of Riemann. He was born in 1826. As
a young man he had mastered the nine hundred pages of Legendre's *Théorie des Mondes* in six
days. At thirty-three he defined the terms of an arithmetical problem with which Fermat had
been giving mathematicians sleepless nights for the past hundred and fifty years. At twenty-four
he discovered that it was possible to establish a mathematics which would do away with all distinctions between the gravitation of electricity, magnetism and thermostatics – thereby fulfilling
the dream of the early nineteenth century, but more important still, enriching geometry so immeasurably that a thousand new avenues were opened up. Gauss had suspected the importance
of the analysis of position, the forerunner of our modern topology. From Gauss's uniformity of
complex functions, Reimann, using the work of Abel, deduced the reasoning for a critique of
multiform functions, the complexity of which he reduced by presenting a new interpretation of
the plane and of space. We shall merely state here that in inventing a new geometry of surfaces
Reimann made as much use of the obverse as of the reverse of the plane, and eventually evolved
a general theory of the functions of the complex variable. The aged Gauss encouraged the young
Riemann at Göttingen. At that period it seemed as if the whole story of mathematics was concentrated in Germany in the persons of Dirichlet, Kammer, Kronecker and Weierstrass, all of whom
took a great interest in the young mathematician. In 1860, in a memoir on a problem of heat con-
duction, Riemann, drawing inspiration from his geometry, perfected the reasoning from which,
in the twentieth century, the theory of relativity was to emerge.

natural sciences might be, they could almost always be profitably met; mathematical diversity encouraged the dispersion of scientific work.

We saw that at the close of the great creative period from 1800 to 1845, the problem which proved most resistant to the magnificent synthesis of the time was that of thermo-dynamics. The first person to tackle the problem was Sadi Carnot, the son of the 'organizer of victory'. Sadi Carnot made a theoretical study of the working of the steam-engine. It had been thought that just as the old mills were turned by the action of falling water, so the steam-engine worked under the effect of the fall of heat. Actually, Carnot had gone into the subject far more thoroughly, as the discovery of his papers was to show. The same careful observation is apparent also in the work of Lord Kelvin: not all heat is transformed into work. Joule had calculated the relations between the electricity expended and the heat produced in a conductor. Now, in theory, if the gravity machine is reversible, the heat produced by work is incapable, even in theory, and without friction, of reproducing the work which has engendered it. This is all the more important since in machines a vast amount of energy is irrevocably dissipated in heat, for theoretical as well as practical reasons. Furthermore, the new theory led to the liquification of gases: all that was necessary was to make them work. Faraday liquified chlorine, and by the end of the century hydrogen had also been mastered. Most important of all, however, were the first industrial consequences of thermo-dynamics: the improvement of steam-engines and proof of the superiority of internal combustion engines.

In 1860, using Lebon's gas, the Belgian Lenoir produced his combustion engine. It was costly to run, using 3,000 litres of gas per horse power; a Nottingham engineer improved it by preliminary compression, then a German from Cologne claimed to have solved the problem – consumption fell to 300 litres in 1870, and eventually to 100 litres in 1890. The engine was ready and waiting only for petroleum.

Meanwhile advances in chemistry had been no less revolutionary. If Berthelot occupies a special place in the history of chemistry it is mainly because of the lucidity of his expositions, the convincing simplicity of his experiments. He was proud to be known as the creator of organic synthesis, of which he was the chief popular exponent. At times in his work he failed to give due recognition to some of his predecessors, to Berzelius, for instance. It is true that this brilliant Swede never abandoned his scepticism on the subject of organic synthesis in spite of convincing discoveries. However, Liebig in Germany had succeeded in achieving the synthesis of formic acid and urea; lactic acid was to follow. The Alsatian went one better, with the synthesis of ethyl alcohol, thereby opening up innumerable avenues to industry.

The most important outcome of the new organic synthesis was artificial dyes. There were, of course, many mineral dyes already in existence. Pliny had described the Roman processes for making ceruse (white lead). Nevertheless, most high-grade dyes were obtained from vegetable products, indigo, campeachy wood (log-wood), brazil wood, and until 1880 competition from traditional dye-stuffs limited the industrial application of chemistry to the dye industry. Eventually, however, the new methods were adopted in all the great industrial dyeworks, as much for the novel brilliance of the colours they produced as for their cheapness. A number of German researchers were successful in this field. One of them, in 1826, distilled indigo and isolated aniline. Then a series of related substances of the same family were discovered, in isolation, in Germany towards 1850, when Hofmann perceived the basic unity of these substances and started large-scale industry. The explosives industry, too, dated from the 1850s. Up to that time, gunpowder was merely the mechanical mixing of a substance causing burning with a combustile substance. But the discovery was then made that organic compounds could be combined with nitric acid. The explosive power of gun-cotton, of picrate of potassium and of nitro-glycerine made a terrifying impression on contemporaries, heightened by the results of the first practical tests, the effects of which in every case greatly exceeded expectations: scrap-iron and rocks seemed to have been volatilized.

There was so much rapid development during this period, that a number of important new products went unnoticed at first. The development of the rubber industry is an example. In the eighteenth century rubber was merely an object of curiosity. About 1825, in Glasgow, Mackintosh invented the raincoat, but if this peculiar garment was exposed to a too-hot sun it softened and ceased to be waterproof, and if it was exposed to cold, it cracked; all that Mackintosh got out of it was the honour of having given his name to a garment. About 1850, the American Goodyear discovered vulcanization; he had just gone bankrupt in an agricultural implement business when by a lucky chance he happened to heat a mixture of rubber and sulphur. 'Vulcanized' rubber resisted solvents, cold and heat. Goodyear's fortune was made: his firm soon grew to a huge concern, which dominated the American market by the close of the century. The new raw material was used not only for office erasers; it was drawn out into sheets, cut up into elastic, moulded into half-spheres out of which Lejeune in Paris made his celebrated balloons. It was hardened into ebonite, a valuable insulator for the new telegraph and telephone apparatus, and the development of pneumatics soon followed. This rubber was at first collected in the Brazilian Amazon; it was so profitable that a permanent shipping company was started on this dangerous river. Then trees were bled in Java, and there was a widespread search for these precious forests in Gaboon, as well as in China.

But it was electricity which effected the biggest change in industry. Ampère, one of the last great admirers and pupils of the *Encyclopédie*, carried on from the experiments of Oerstedt, and in 1820 demonstrated the relationship between electricity and magnetism, and propounded the law of induced currents. But he did not realize the full significance of his discoveries.

The implications were far-reaching. The foremost scientists, about 1850, doubted the possibility of inducing a current by mechanical means. In order to obtain high tensions, they continued to pile up voltaic elements on the model of the giant pile which had been in use for the past fifty years at the Polytechnic. This was not appreciably improved upon by the discovery of thermo-electricity. These piles supplied the current for experiments which soon moved out of the laboratory into the field of industry, one of the most important being electrolysis. Then the electric arc gave light and heat at temperatures never reached before, which enabled Berthelot to achieve his spectacular syntheses. Measuring instruments of ever-increasing sensitivity and resistance were devised. In 1880 an international congress determined the units of electricity which were to apply all over the world. Meantime, electricity had begun to have its effect on industry.

In 1831, Henry in the United States and Faraday in England carried out the decisive experiment which Faraday was the first to publish in a famous report to the Royal Society in London. 'Twenty-six feet of copper wire, one-twentieth of an inch in diameter, were wound round a cylinder' reported the *Annals of Physics and Chemistry* thirty years later. Into this apparatus was thrust a magnet: 'There was an immediate deviation of the needle.' It was the first electro-magnetic generator. In the following year, Hachette, the son of an Ardennes bookseller whom Monge had put in charge of the physics collections at the *École Polytechnique*, and who had just become a member of the *Institut*, read a paper by the son of a laboratory instrument maker: it dealt with a spark machine, which was probably the very first alternator. It was still of very low power. All over Europe men were at work inventing apparatus. In 1869 Gramme invented the machine which, according to the *Institut*, was capable of everything the pile had previously achieved. Gramme was a strange man. He appeared in Paris at the age of twenty-five in 1856, after attending free classes in Liège, and found a job as moulder in a lamp-glass factory. He taught himself by reading small treatises and dictionaries, and turned the kitchen of his small flat into a laboratory. Later he worked under Ruhmkorff with intense dedication. Finally he succeeded in building his continuous current dynamo which at first was greeted with scepticism. He perfected it and founded the *Société des Machines Électromagnétiques*. In 1880, at long last, he received his first reward – 20,000 francs. Meanwhile he worked with Fontaine and studied the problem of the flow of an electric current. In 1890, the Society was turning out something like one thousand dynamos a year, the largest of which could keep 3,600 lamps alight on a consumption of 350 horse-power.

All these new industries which emerged from the laboratories were to change society. Before discussing this important aspect, it is worthwhile considering the mental and moral effects of these discoveries, particularly of the new strides which were being made in biological research.

Buffon had already put forward the tentative idea of linkage of creatures, but the pettiness of the criticisms that followed, particularly those of

Diderot, whose chief aim was to annoy the Sorbonne, detracted greatly from the significance of his ideas. More important theories were proposed by Erasmus Darwin, a strange poet, a doctor by profession, who obtained some success with his *Botanic Garden*. The English are proverbially fond of their trees, their island flowers, the wild life of their countryside (Erasmus Darwin also produced a zoonomy), and English rural society, unlike that of France, was as we have seen largely middle-class. It had leisure, and yet retained close connections with the towns. All the English took a close interest in agricultural experiments, cross-breeding, and seed selection; the successes of breeders and planters were discussed, appreciated, imitated, and the country was like one vast biological laboratory. Erasmus Darwin, then, was a doctor, so was his son Charles, and his grandson Charles was to have followed in their footsteps, but at Cambridge it became clear that he preferred hunting, dogs, gaming, and insect-collecting to medical studies. His career was typically English. He met in a club a member of the *Beagle* expedition who suggested that Darwin should go with him. His father was doubtful; his uncle Wedgwood, of Etruria, decided that he should go. Charles Darwin had paid no particular attention to the ideas of Lamarck, or Geoffroy Saint-Hilaire, or Chambers. He observed, noted, collected, and brought back from his cruise a huge mass of documents, which he endeavoured to put into some sort of order. He read hardly any theoretical works beyond the one which all England had been discussing for the past forty years, Malthus's *Essay on Population*. He read it in 1838 for entertainment, he said, and suddenly discovered the idea that favourable variations tend to be preserved, and unfavourable ones to be destroyed. This gave him a theory on which to work. Darwin said nothing about the causes which, in one and the same species, differentiated the innate qualities of individuals. But he explained with the utmost clarity how, of these innate qualities, those which have a survival value give to the individuals possessing them an advantage which enables them to live longer and to secure a mate which will propagate a durable race. Darwin formed his theory in 1844, but he worked at it for another twenty years, so that a year before publishing his own work, he learned that Alfred Russell Wallace had just arrived at the same theory, also from a study of Malthus. Darwin engaged in no recriminations, finished his book, published it, and won immediate fame.

In the bitter controversy which followed, he received valuable help from T. H. Huxley, who was known as Darwin's bulldog. A vast campaign of criticism and a violent quarrel of principle was unleashed. The Anglican clergy and all the Christian churches fulminated against the theory which made man 'a descendant of the apes', and relegated him to a position as the first of the primates. The Bishop of Oxford defied Huxley at the British Association, and sneeringly asked him whether it was through his grandfather or his grandmother that he was related to the monkey. It was Huxley who put into words the reason for Darwin's success (the first edition of the book had been sold out immediately). The *Origin of Species*, he said, supplied the working hypothesis they had been looking for. But he realized also the limits of this hypothesis: all good agriculturists, for whom Darwin soon wrote *The Variation of Plants and Animals under Domestication* (1868), know that the offspring of different, though related species, is sterile. The chief difficulty of the theory was therefore apparent at the outset, but did not hinder the popularity of the work. It was fairly popular in France, thanks to the materialists (as the socialists were called), who thus at one fell swoop, as they thought, got rid of the Revelation and final causes. In Germany, Haeckel declared that the new revelation was even more certain than universal gravity and that it should be taught instead of the catechism in all primary schools. And England buried Darwin (who died soon after the publication of his book) in Westminster Abbey near Isaac Newton.

The way to a solution of the difficulties inherent in Darwin's theory was opened up in 1865, though it was more than thirty years before this was realized. Mendel, abbot of a monastery in Brno, embarked on a series of experiments on the cross-fertilization of peas. He found that certain hereditary characteristics were indivisible and unchangeable units, and that particular hybrids, though similar in appearance, possessed in their germinal cells a pair of characteristics proper to each of the species which had participated in the cross. In this way he originated an atomist conception of biology, though its full significance was not recognized and exploited immediately. Before this could happen, Bateson and Devries had to study mutations.

In 1872 Darwin published *The Expression of the Emotions in Man and Animals*. He attempted to show that man can really be considered as ending the biological evolutionary series. This new publication of Darwin's gave great stimulus to the development of anthropology. Already Quetelet had been at work measuring conscripts. The shape of skulls was studied, racial demarcation fixed. Each race was defined by a group of interrelated characteristics. The geography of the European races was studied, their geological antecedents were traced. In 1856 human remains were discovered at Neanderthal; in 1886 more were found at Spy. A cousin of Darwin, Francis Galton, studied the transmission of the mental qualities of the individual, and stressed the importance of heredity. He drew graphs based on the work of Gauss similar to those which Quetelet had used. The final conclusion of all this research was, however, that the influence of environment had been overestimated. Education can and must foster only the best strains – an idea which became the ethics of eugenics, soon to become so popular in Germany.

Whilst English biologists were publicizing these extraordinary new theories, France seemed to be proving the evolutionists wrong. We shall deal at a more appropriate time with the work of Pasteur; he, too, was the butt of persecution. On the other hand, Berthelot, the friend of Renan, was a fairly typical example of the modern French approach. He embodied the militant secularism of the late nineteenth century which was in revolt against all the old religious ethics. In 1870, from one end of Europe to the other, to have a scientific mind, to be practical, meant to support the doctrine of evolution.

Thus, at a time when man was covering Europe with a network of railways which were to give him the greatest industrial power the world had yet known, Darwin showed him the immense historical perspective of his destiny. A new pride can be seen in the works of some Western intellectuals. The gradual development of this philosophy can best be illustrated by comparing John Stuart Mill and Spencer.

At thirteen Stuart Mill had read most of the Greek and Latin authors and a wide range of other books. Born in 1806, he was consequently steeped in eighteenth-century thought, and inevitably became a disciple of Hume, imbued with the learning of a previous generation. As a result he resisted the main research work of the nineteenth century, the exploration of the problems of evolution. But he did believe that the value of mental activity lay, not in the formal discipline it imposed, but in its capacity to enrich by experience and to co-ordinate a world of associations which created characteristics. It was this belief which enabled him to avoid Bentham's uncompromising hedonism, and to arrive eventually at a philosophy of general happiness, the greatest happiness of the greatest number. He followed this doctrine so far that he had no fear of communism, and condemned individual ownership of landed property since the land belonged to all alike. From this religion of humanity, he believed that we were justified in postulating the idea of God.

Stuart Mill had been employed by the East India Company, the suppression of which in 1856 left him without employment. Spencer, who worked for the London–Birmingham railway company, was a victim of the 1848 crisis. Born fifteen years after Stuart Mill, he was brought up in complete freedom by his father, a teacher who let him read every biological work on which he could lay his hands. At first Spencer was attracted by the doctrines of calculated ethics, but like Stuart Mill believed in a kind of communism of the land. Later he met the full force of German Romanticism through the works of Carlyle and Coleridge, and he discovered behind the evolution of societies a kind of permanent imperative, a mysterious force which might well be life itself. Society was no longer a mechanism, but an organism.

Everything was evolution, but the actual direction this evolution was taking still remained to be discovered. On physical theories, he concluded that evolution is an integration of matter passing from indefinite homogeneity to definite heterogeneity. We shall mention later how much of this he owed to Clausius. The most important point was that Darwin's conclusions had been adopted: the mind adapts itself to external conditions; natural selection ensures the success of the best adaptations – which explains the intellectual studies made by psychology, and the effective combination by association of elements supplied by experience. Finally, though there is some evidence that he agreed with his German models in their theory of race, Spencer believed that evolution in general tended towards individualization. Society, militarist and monarchical in its early stages, tends to become industrial and liberal. He based his theory very largely on evidence provided by the entirely new and original study of savages. Thus he ended by rejecting the ideal he had at first adopted – agrarian communism. Biological evolution leads man to a perpetual improvement of his lot, the supreme triumph of which is political liberalism. Moral progress, imposed by force of circumstances, ends in individualism.

This was a cycle of mental evolution which ended in a curious way. First the mathematical liberalism of Bentham was rudely shaken by the crisis caused by the development of railways: people began to envisage a socialism *à la Saint-Simon*, even *à la Proudhon*, and for a short time middle-class society felt uncertain of its moral foundations. Then the drive for progress and modernization began again, in spite of Schopenhauer's scepticism, and biological science was taken to give a new basis for the middle-class liberalism in which England so implicitly believed.

THE INDUSTRIAL SOCIETIES

Both the natural sciences and the exact sciences seemed now to be furthering the ambitions of industrial enterprise. It was the knell of the old ethics, the triumph of uninhibited individualism.

We know how Flaubert's hero laconically summed up his sentimental education during the revolutionary days of 1848 – 'Je me réforme'. This kind of reform was apparently highly successful during the twenty years which saw the reappearance in France of manners as dissolute, though not as elegant, as those associated with the *roués* of Louis xv's reign. In Haussmann's new Paris, there were certain streets where gentlemen of fashion installed their mistresses in sumptuous apartments. Morny was outstanding in that strange society where literary *salons* were opened in the houses of the *petites amies* of princes of wit or wealth: the poets paid discreet (or even open) court to them. Moreover, many of these Egerias, having got themselves accepted, succeeded not only in living a decent life, but sometimes even affected a certain austerity; and at all events they remained faithful to their man. Those of the bourgeois who were less fashionable, or less wealthy, made love to the Cardinal demoiselles.

Men had no aim but pleasure; Napoleon iii held a series of imperial fêtes in which the new wealth showed off its ostentatious luxury, in which Offenbach made fun in music of the old heroes and the ancient gods, where the waltz reigned supreme and crinolines were even more costly than the hoops so fashionable under the monarchy. But if the Emperor set an example of infidelity in the Tuileries, Eugénie was the very incarnation of the dignified outraged mother, for while the demi-monde was busy enjoying itself, virtuous boredom was the fashion in well-conducted families. The dreary evening parties at Compiègne showed what were the chief preoccupations of this virtue: to ensure the future of one's children, to arrange advantageous marriages and uphold religion and self-control. One town council went so far as to reward the latter by offering a prize to a citizen conspicuous for the moderate size of his family. The *Académie* set personal goodness amongst the virtues. Immorality and virtue had, at all events, one effect in common – a lowering of the birth rate. Fortunately, longevity was still on the increase owing to a number of factors. There was a better distribution of food supplies thanks to the railway, and a slight improvement in the lot of the workers; industries followed in the wake of the modernization programme which accompanied the completion of the railway system; standards of hygiene improved in the cities whose slums had been swept away by Haussmann's demolishers. This improvement in living conditions almost made up for the infant mortality rate; if the number of marriages increased slightly, families with few children kept the total population of France almost stable: from approximately thirty-six million in 1850, it rose to thirty-eight million in 1870, but the annexation of Savoy accounted for almost one million of this increase. It fell again to thirty-six million after the Treaty of Frankfurt, and from then on, after the usual post-war bulge, there was a marked drop in the fertility rate, and in the total number of births: in 1888, the number of deaths was exactly equal to that of births. From 1880 the total figure of the male population was stationary.

This was true of Europe in general after 1880, but not in the preceding thirty years. It is true that in England the 1848 crisis caused an abrupt drop in the number of births, but a rise in the birth rate had immediately accompanied prosperity. In the 1870s the gross reproduction rate was higher than that of the 1840s and expectation of life was increasing as satisfactorily as in France; but the death rate, unlike that of France, fell from 234 to 191 per thousand between 1840 and 1880. From 1860 to 1880, therefore, England's population increased at almost the same rhythm as in the previous forty years. Thus from approximately twenty million in 1840 it reached almost forty million in 1880. England's population doubled during the period when that of France remained nearly static.

The growth rate in Germany was similar, perhaps even more marked. There again the drop in the birth rate during the years of crisis was soon made good. The gross reproduction rate in 1880 almost equalled that of 1820. Although the increase in longevity had not quite kept pace with that of the West, the net reproduction rate nevertheless rose from one hundred per thousand in 1840 to more than one hundred and fifty per thousand in 1880. From 1880, in Germany, as in England, the gross reproduction rate suffered a setback, though it was more than compensated by the fall in the death rate. But already the numerical superiority of the populations of Germany and England was assured. If France possessed more inhabitants than England and Germany put together in the eighteenth century, in

1880 the population of England alone equalled and surpassed that of France. By 1860, the population of Germany had equalled it; it surpassed it by fifty per cent in 1880. Demographically France had fallen far behind by the time of the railway revolution, a critical stage in the human evolution of Europe.

The consequences of these statistics must be obvious. It is true that the relative numbers of the populations of the three countries were not very different even up to 1860. But there is no doubt that the psychology of a people in rapid expansion is not like that of a stable people. Whilst England was flooding the world with emigrants, and Germany was responsible for a great movement of peoples, particularly towards America, France could barely populate the regions which its political and military power was still strong enough to hold. Neither Indo-China nor Mexico ever looked like being lands in which Frenchmen would settle. Emigration was limited to North Africa and was numerically smaller than that from Spain and Italy. Jean-Baptiste Say asserted, as it had been fashionable to do in eighteenth-century France, that the departure of families (and of capital) weakened nations. Between two dynamic powers, France drew false wisdom from the past.

Over and above these differences, there was one element common to the population throughout Europe. A new civilization was developing between 1850 and 1880 which led to an increase in numbers and also to increased expectation of life. The essential instrument of these new developments was the town. The growth of towns was concurrent with that of the railways, since it was the existence of urban centres, already firmly established, which attracted the railway and only the stations in big towns paid handsome dividends. Traffic paid its way between industrial cities, whereas country lines were costly to run. But if the towns helped the development on the first railways, the latter in turn brought enormous benefits to the towns. They mobilized labour and facilitated the transport of the many gangs of workmen from the country needed by the government contractors laying the lines. In 1848 the *Nord* alone employed 40,000 workmen. There must have been hundreds of thousands of workers whom the railway attracted from their fields and pitched into the towns. As a result the towns grew at an appalling rate. The crowds of workers lived where they could, in towns where the demolition of the old quarters, the creation of squares and streets had upset old ways of life. The lodging crisis passed through critical phases, and speculation in lands and houses was rife, in spite of the risks. New houses were so dear that they stood for months without tenants, and building societies went bankrupt because they could not meet their bills over such a long period. Then the new quarters filled up, but not as before with rich and poor intermingled from one storey to another in the same areas. Only the rich could afford to live in the city centres ; the poor were pushed out to the periphery. The rag-pickers no longer swarmed in squalor around Notre Dame but took refuge in the area of the fortifications. Dingy suburbs encircled the rejuvenated towns.

It was of course the railways which brought food supplies to these masses of human beings who descended on the old towns. Almost from the moment of their inception they were making special arrangements for transporting provisions to the towns. In Paris the building of the central markets began in 1851. Companies lent capital to agriculture; contractors engaged in public works diverted the gangs of men no longer needed by the railways on to irrigation projects. In 1859 the old Moulin-de-Pertuis canal was re-opened and lengthened, and became the Cadenet canal, irrigating something like five thousand acres in Vaucluse. Two years earlier the Carpentras canal had been begun, planned to irrigate more than fifteen thousand acres. The railway was soon carrying an entirely new kind of freight intended to feed the towns it had populated. Modern methods of stock-breeding and cultivation, the development of slaughter-houses, the perfecting of mills, a whole body of changes benefiting the railway and increasing its profits, supported the increasing population of the new towns. Changes in the countryside also had similar effects on population. Better harvests were being produced with less labour, and the result was a surplus population which took the train to town. Whenever the population of a town increased new industries were attracted into the suburbs. The progress of the great textile mill made competition so fierce for the old country hand-loom weavers that they were gradually disappearing, worn out by the work of a day of more than twelve hours which scarcely brought them the price of a kilogramme of bread. In 1840 one third of the inhabitants of the Auge area were engaged in weaving; two generations later there was barely a loom to be found in the district. It was almost the same in Flanders and the Lyonnais: the town drew in the rural craftsmen, after the harshness of the struggle for survival had forced them to reduce their expenses to the barest minimum. In the old days in the countryside people looked to providence to feed their children; in the town everything had to be bought. If the bourgeois, eager to rise in the social scale, reduced the size of his family, the worker soon followed suit. And soon this new economic fashion spread even into country districts, first amongst the well-to-do, then wherever the railways took modern ideas – a little more hygiene and far fewer children. Since the population continued to increase because people were living longer, there was no resistance to this new outlook.

The reign of the towns meant the reign of capitals: the population of London doubled in thirty years; from approximately two million it rose to almost four million in 1880. The area of the city grew rapidly, absorbing great new suburbs, while at its centre the old city was almost completely uninhabited, so that all its unfurnished buildings could be set aside for trade: in 1880 it had only about 50,000 instead of the 200,000 there had been in 1840. It was because it was given over to offices that it could fill up during working hours with a crowd of more than 700,000. Night and morning an enormous migration set in between the periphery and the centre – a phenomenon which amazed the foreign visitor. But the vast cost of this daily migration made it logical to extend the Sunday day of rest to include

Saturday, and later resulted in the institution known in France as 'la semaine anglaise'.

The surface area of Paris developed less, since its centre remained over-populated, and it was rather in the new quarters, the most expensive of which was the Elysée, that the new offices appeared. But the population

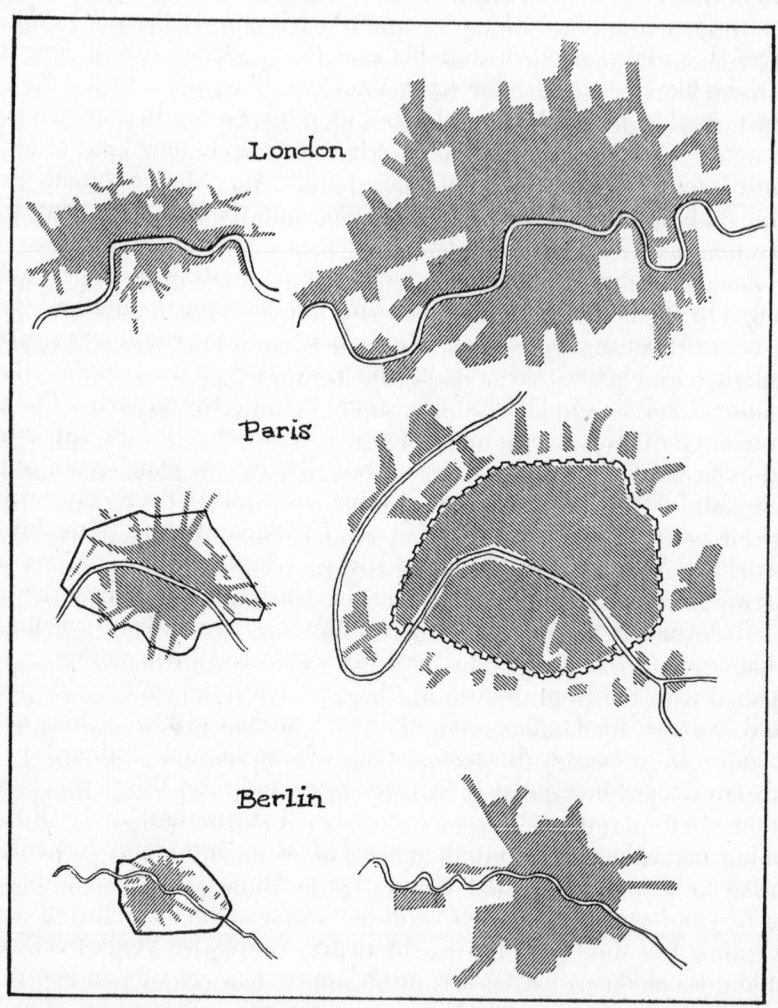

18 London, Paris, and Berlin in 1790 and in 1890

piled up in the capital at almost the same rate as in London; from something like one million in 1840 it went up to more than two million in 1880. Within the same period, Vienna grew from 400,000 to 700,000 inhabitants.

But the most spectacular growth increase took place in Berlin. At the opening of the century it had barely 150,000 inhabitants, but by 1896 it had more than 1,300,000. Berlin, which only a short time before had not been one of Germany's biggest cities, became one of the largest in the world. It took over from Danzig the role of corn exchange, from Breslau the role of textile capital, and from Essen that of iron capital (around the Borsig works there now stretched a huge black suburb). The University of Berlin was the first in Germany. The native population of Berlin included less than thirty per cent of Germans because there were so many descendants of French and Slav immigrants, so it was not by the power of race, as the Germans claimed, but by the power of industry (in which they were dominant) that Berlin became the key-city to Germany's future. In London, which had developed from trade, and in Berlin which had developed from industry, the destinies of the middle classes were comparable. But in Paris, a city still bound up in its long history – they were different.

Into this radically urbanized society the industrial results of scientific research were introduced. They created new middle-class dynasties. We have described how electricity had emerged from the domain of pure research. The Siemens family demonstrated how it invaded industry. There were ten of them, brothers, from the same farm in Hanover and born between 1816 and 1836. By the end of the century they were the masters of the most extensive and successful group of factories in Germany, the new industrial Germany. At eighteen, Ernst had enlisted in the artillery. He became passionately interested in electricity, took out patents in galvanoplasty, and, once he was appointed director of the Berlin Arsenal, he invented the electric mechanism of underwater mines. At the same period he directed the installation of Prussia's electric telegraph. He resigned from the army in 1850 and founded a company for making telegraphic apparatus. He installed equipment in Berlin, northern Germany and Russia. He helped to install telegraphs in South America and South Africa. He competed with the English even in London itself. His firm became that of *Gebrüder Siemens*, for he had summoned his nine brothers to assist him. He was courageous enough to take on dangerous operations (like the Transcaucasian telegraph) and he also kept up to date with new electrical inventions. In England he learnt how to make submarine cables and was soon teaching his teachers. He adopted Gramme's machine and perfected it. In 1880 he astounded casual visitors to the quinquennial exhibition in Paris by running a small electric railway, and it was he who installed Berlin's trams. The nine brothers spread all over the world. Two went to England and stayed there; Karl was to become a baron and in 1883, as we have seen, he invented a new process for making steel. Friedrich was the inventor of a famous gasogene furnace which, through its ingenious system of heat recovery, appreciably lowered cost prices in metallurgy. Hans founded glassworks in Dresden and Bohemia. Gas, distillation, iron and steel industries as well as electricity, telephone and telegraph, all came from the *Gebrüder Siemens*.

Electricity was not alone in creating an influential middle class, for another branch of research invaded industry – chemistry. The whole world, in 1880, acknowledged that the Germans had a genius for chemistry, and one of those who best justified this opinion was Justus Liebig. About 1820 this talented pupil of the Gymnasium at Darmstadt, the son of a druggist, was working for an apothecary. He spent most of his time reading his way through the municipal library which had just been opened, concentrating especially on periodicals dealing with the new science. He was drawn to Paris, since all the great and learned theories were being formulated there, and worked there with Gay-Lussac and his collaborators, notably Dumas. Now a brilliant scientist, he returned to Germany and founded a small university in Giessen which he was to make famous, and where he established the world's finest laboratory. It soon acquired an international reputation. He found credits easy to obtain in the 1840s when industrialization was just starting in Germany, and eventually he was made a baron. His subsequent career was typical of every official of that time – he became a member of the German Academy, and a corresponding member of those of France and England. His great speciality was the analysis of plants and living organisms, the analysis of what is known as organic chemistry. It consisted in measuring carbon and hydrogen by oxidizing them, and he discovered constants in them which he expressed in radicals (C_2H_5). He never lost sight of the practical application of his work. Studying fats, he discovered the basic products of meat extract, and when studying changes in alcohols did not neglect to analyse the bouquets of the most famous wines. In continual contact with industrial firms, he was also one of the first to take a systematic interest in agricultural problems. He was responsible for important discoveries in the nitrogen cycle, and in the course of his work in this field he paid as much attention to the detailed procedure of Chinese agriculture as to the recklessly wasteful methods of Western farming. As a jam manufacturer, he made an enormous fortune.

The evolution of the industrial society presents curious paradoxes: whereas in Germany, the home of authoritarian régimes, scientists often adopted business careers, in France, thanks to the close connections between French power and the middle classes, French scientists often ended up in the seats of power.

The work of the Frenchman Jean-Baptiste Dumas was parallel to that of Liebig. He made a special study of alcohols and ethers and contributed to the discovery of the amides. Like Liebig, Dumas founded an institution, the École Centrale des Arts et Manufactures; but unlike his German colleague, he did not make a fortune in industry. He began, like Liebig, by being an apprentice-pharmacist from 1848 to 1870, but he became a Deputy, Minister of Agriculture and Commerce, then Senator. As President of the Paris Municipal Council he initiated major improvements in hygiene and in the supply of drinking water, and demonstrated the impurity of water from the Seine. The pursuit of science in France during these years led to power just as surely as American or German industry led to wealth. 'What a miracle of chemistry', wrote an Empire caricaturist. 'Retorts distil politicians!' Like Dumas, Berthelot ended up as a Minister, after being a Deputy, then a life Senator. The career of the Alsatian Kuhlmann serves admirably to illustrate the two roads to success; via industry in Germany and government in France. He was both an industrialist in Germany (he founded the complex industries in Loos which was to become so well known) and a politician in France (General Adviser and Governor of the Lille Mint). The two different attitudes certainly existed in the powder industry. The greatest precautions were necessary in the industrial preparation of these products, since they were so dangerous to handle. Between 1865 and 1870 terrible accidents had horrified public opinion. In San Francisco, Hamburg and Stockholm nitro-glycerine wrought such havoc that there was talk of banning it by international agreement. It was then that Nobel discovered that mixed with ethyl alcohol and especially with silica, nitro-glycerine was no longer explosive on percussion, but had to be detonated. This 'dynamite' exploded when ignited. In 1878, eighty victims died through the carelessness of a cavalry lieutenant who had brought a packet of dynamite too near an inadequately extinguished brazier. Work went on ceaselessly to obviate these dangers, and above all to explore the possible applications of this new power. The vital question was, who should control it, businessmen or the state? In France the state took over and opened the gunpowder factory at Donges, whilst it authorized a very few private factories under its own control, and entrusted the direction of them to Berthelot. Elsewhere it was private capital which assumed control. Nobel was at the head of a consortium covering Germany, Austro-Hungary, Italy, Spain and the United States.

In conclusion it is worth mentioning the amazingly successful industrial career of a German chemist, Hofmann. He had been Liebig's pupil in Giessen and London, then in Berlin, where he earned a good enough reputation for himself as a scientist to found the *Deutsche Chemische Gesellschaft* in 1868. He then became 'official scientist' and a corresponding member of the great academies. In 1845 in Giessen, he had already analysed the ethyls and alcohols and discovered aniline in pit-coal. The whole new dye industry drew its roots from coal, which made it economical. It could be independent of costly vegetable imports since aniline, though difficult to purify, produced first a good black, then, properly treated, could give a red and a yellow. Another of Liebig's pupils working on indigo at Giessen enriched the range of synthetic colours and also worked in the *Deutsche Chemische Gesellschaft*. Aniline proved dangerous to handle because it was so toxic, yet in 1870 its industrial production increased greatly, and by 1890 had reached more than one thousand tons a year.

We shall not pursue further the history of all the chemical industries, ammoniac, soda, and later petroleum and celluloid. All had their part to play in the rebuilding of society; everywhere they contributed to the development of the towns; everywhere they contributed also to a reform of fashion.

THE DECLINE OF AESTHETICS

Industrial fashions had triumphed under Napoleon III. Parisian iron-founders could barely keep pace with orders for reproduction of old weapons, not, of course, in wrought iron, but in cast iron, since they were only meant to decorate halls and vestibules. After improving on the Louis Quinze style, the Faubourg Saint-Antoine then did the same for that of Nuremberg. The taste of the imperial court had not always been exquisite, but the taste of the new public opened the way to all manner of reproductions. Haussmann's new buildings gave a fairly good idea of this second-hand style in their interior decoration, which tended to luxuriate in innumerable fussy and elaborate imitations in every conceivable royal style; it was quite the thing to have a Henri II dining-room, a Gothic hall, a Louis XIV drawing-room, a Louis XV boudoir, and Louis XVI chairs. All these apartments were indiscriminately decorated with plaster or staff work. Even the cabinet makers tried to copy all these flourishes and their admirable craftsmanship did not compensate for the general lack of taste.

In all their reproductions, craftsmen were not content merely to excel; they wished to improve. Compare the imperial eagles of the First and Second Empire: the first made no claim to zoological accuracy, and was rather heraldic in inspiration, the second was a carefully observed copy of the eagle in the Jardin des Plantes. A scientific pretentiousness was substituted for an aesthetic sense: we have only to read the five volumes of the *Dictionnaire raisonné du mobilier français* or the ten volumes of the *Dictionnaire raisonné de l'architecture française* (1854–72), written by the famous Viollet-Le-Duc. This librarian's son was one of the first officials in the new Department of Historic Monuments; he first repaired then restored the Sainte-Chapelle and Notre Dame, Saint-Sernin de Toulouse, the Château de Pierrefonds, and the ramparts at Carcassonne and Avignon. His art aimed at scientific accuracy, inspired by learning and erudition. His popularity was as immense and as lucrative as that of Meissonier, the son of a chemist, and a prolific painter of the type of picture for which fashionable society paid fantastic sums, and which claimed to surpass in accuracy of historical detail the old Dutch masters themselves whom he was copying. When he wished to paint 1814, he made innumerable sketches of ploughland under snow to reproduce its exact appearance. His grenadiers were correct down to the last gaiter button, and he kept them on his easel until his imagination had encompassed every detail. It was the technique Flaubert used later to amass a wealth of detail for *Salammbô*.

Erudition in art! This was not exactly the kind of truth to which Vigny has aspired. Barely one generation had gone by and art was claiming to be 'scientific'. Was the old conflict between the artist and the bourgeois, between the poet beloved of Murger (who died in 1861) and the Philistine, at last dying down? In actual fact, although the so-called regard for truth which inspired artistic production satisfied the taste of the wealthy middle class in the case of a Meissonier or a Viollet-Le-Duc, and incidentally made their fortune, it was far from pleasing everyone. First of all Viollet-Le-Duc could not overcome the opposition of the young pupils in the *École des Beaux Arts*, who would not let him teach. Above all there was a certain form of truth which continued to arouse the violent dislike of the new society for, as Paul Mantz wrote, it 'touched the extreme frontiers of realist art'.

But before discussing this new aesthetic which originated in France, we should stress an important European aspect of the aesthetic revolution. The official taste of French imperial society left much to be desired, but it was no more dubious than the taste which prevailed in Germany or England. Munich was intended to be a new Athens and its creators were busy improving on 'Greek art'. In Berlin, too, Greek architecture on the grand scale was going up in stucco and brick. The Old Museum and the National Gallery, in a pompous Corinthian style, were no better than the Grand Theatre. Churches were constructed by the gross in every conceivable style in a vain attempt to capture for this city, which had sprung up so rapidly, the old historical traditions of the older capitals. At least one thing could be said for Germany's stations – they were enormous. Popular painters also went in for the large historical canvas: in painting the *Death of Wallenstein*, one artist reproduced the condottiere's ring so perfectly that the public mistook it for a real diamond. Menzel wasted a good deal of time in this sort of work. As for the English, they built in two styles, the Greek and the Gothic; their railway-stations looked like classical temples or cathedrals. In England, as in Germany, the statue in iron or cast-iron with an incredible wealth of dancing figures enjoyed a vogue which achieved its peak in the Albert Memorial. Germany was to be more sensitive than England to the lessons of French realist art, and in both countries alike the real reaction against this distressing modernism took an entirely different direction from that in France. We have seen that France's population figures in the 1860s revealed a trend which was not to be evident in the west and east until the 1880s. In 1860, just when the French were introducing realism in art, Germany and England were expressing their originality only by a return to Christian inspiration. At that time their demographic conditions were still those of a previous age.

This Christian aesthetic was expressed in England by the Pre-Raphaelite Brotherhood, founded in 1848. They drew a whole range of imagery from medieval legends and the books of the Bible which was essentially poetic in inspiration, although they endeavoured to depict it with extreme accuracy. Though they claimed to have revived the art of Botticelli, they achieved only Rossetti. The corresponding movement in Germany was that of the Nazarenes, founded well before its English counterpart, but more enduring. It drew its inspiration from Christian Rome, and its members carried sincerity to the point of conversion to Catholicism. They admired Perugino, but also went in for vast compositions like those of Michelangelo.

In short the plastic arts in the two great industrial countries hardly ever surpassed the level of the most mediocre Parisian artists. Occasionally, especially when faced with the sarcasm of the new generation from 1860 onwards, they did introduce several new and original features.

We can now return to discussing the French realist movement which was far more than just a novelty. It began before Courbet, and its earliest expression was in *genres* which owed much to England; the caricatures of Daumier and the drawings of Constantin Guys. Baudelaire, as we know, was a great admirer of Guys. This Dutchman by birth had learnt from the English how to sketch in with deft strokes the characteristic attitudes of people and scenes from everyday life. Baudelaire again was one of the first to appreciate the quality of Daumier. Daumier's work was so much greater than that of Descamps that it is doubtful if he owed anything to Rowlandson, who had amused the English public at the expense of Napoleon I. From the indifferent material supplied him by real life and his third-rate journalists, Daumier built up a world, the restless, bewildered world of the railway age. He drew countrymen crammed together in a railway coach, lawyers defending the speculator, the people crushed by counter-revolutions, a whole collection of simpletons hastening to offer their money to rogues, scoundrels running the whole gamut of corruption, and lastly, lording it over all these humble folk, the newly rich bourgeois, pot-bellied, pompous and moralizing.

Two artists and a poet – Baudelaire, who is sometimes accused of having too limited a range, although it was he who captured to perfection the astounding originality of those bewildered human beings, of the cities which were growing around them like prisons and shedding their wan gaslight over all.

It was not easy to express this new way of life sincerely. Flaubert, who described provincial manners which aped those of Paris, and Baudelaire who allowed his friends to publish his poems, were both pilloried for outraging good manners. Daumier had plenty of time in prison to reflect on the unprepossessing features of Louis-Philippe, and Courbet was almost as unfortunate.

In the city Courbet saw little beyond his *Parisiennes*, who lived beside the Seine and looked as if they had stepped out of the *Fleurs du Mal*. But his country scenes were very different. On the fringe of the romantic movement a new landscape school had sprung up which shunned contact with towns. Corot, the son of a shopkeeper at the Pont-Royal, was swept off his feet by a love of nature as intense as that of Goethe. He had brought back from his travels in Italy, along with the inevitable historical pictures, paintings of classical ruins and landscapes. Then, snapping the last links which bound him to the Italian style and to history, he went to live at Ville-d'Avray and gave himself up to the beauty of a sea of indeterminate treetops, to the charm of everything that was vibrant with life 'from the plants and the flowers of the Île-de-France to the quivering of birches and willows'. At first mocked and scorned, and caring not at all, since he received an allowance from his father, he finally became most successful, but not before he had reintroduced into his misty landscapes the silhouettes of nymphs, fauns and dryads. There was nothing in Corot's landscapes to shock art lovers.

The paintings of the Barbizon school were somewhat cruder in style. In the last months of the reign of Louis-Philippe this school turned the forest of Fontainebleau into its open-air studio, painted trees à la Théodore Rousseau and ponds à la Daubigny. But there again, the artists who settled on the fringe of cities caused no one uneasiness. Their most typical representative was after all Millet, a painter in clogs it is true, but a painter of clean and decent human beings, whose peasants only harvested in broad daylight and prayed without despair. Millet's peasants easily made the artist's fortune, because they disconcerted no one.

It was a very different nature with which Courbet brutally confronted this public living in a whirl of business and not daring to look poverty in the face. Here were no Parisiennes strolling in the country, but human beings whose lives had been bound up with the land, but who were now being uprooted by the cities. Official criticism voiced the indignation of the bourgeois: the faces of the Ornans peasants accompanying the famous Enterrement were not sad or moved, they were grotesque and unbearable. There was all the difference in the world between Courbet's baigneuses and Corot's nymphs. The former so completely disregarded all conventional and academic standards of beauty that at the Salon, Eugénie de Montijo pretended not to see them. Proudhon accused those who scorned his favourite painter of hypocrisy: he called it hypocrisy to reject those slightly reeling curés in the Retour de la Conférence; and hypocrisy to refuse to see the world as it really is – a world in which the harsh law of work deforms bodies and shatters dreams. Proudhon, whom Courbet painted with his family, put into words what the new socialist art was to be; Courbet was regarded as a dangerous revolutionary. After the Commune he was obliged to flee to Switzerland: he was held responsible for the demolition of the Colonne Vendôme and was expected to pay for its reinstallation.

With Courbet, painting had embarked on a new mission; it was no longer concerned with historical and anecdotal erudition, but with helping men to see, and to see themselves as they were.

In 1867 Courbet, with that rebellious spirit and boisterous assertiveness which were always his characteristics, had a wooden shed put up on the Cours de l'Alma in order to show his principal canvases which the official salons had rejected. It was not long before a second shed appeared beside it, to house the paintings of Manet.

In France, then, painting was revolutionary in trying to teach men and to remind them of what they are. In Germany there was no painting. The complex problems and conflicts aroused by the nation's rapid growth could only be adequately expressed in a torrent of music. Wagner was born in Leipzig in the year of the Battle of the Nations, which left him an orphan. He came of a musical family and he was a pupil at the famous St

Thomas's school in Leipzig. Bach, Goethe, Beethoven and Weber dominated the traditions of this small corner of Europe. When he was twenty, Wagner, who had already composed several important works, found a job in a theatre and quickly made a name as a conductor in the cities of eastern Europe which had some pretensions to musical ambition. In the course of his travels he got to know Western and particularly Italian music, and came to Paris hoping to succeed there. He travelled by sea from Riga: a stormy voyage which inspired him to write the *Ghost Ship*, the libretto of which, but not the music which Wagner had just composed at Meudon, was accepted by the Opera. French taste remained loyal to the Italians. In order to make a living Wagner had to turn journalist, music critic, copyist, and it was with no regrets that he made his way back to his small German towns. He crossed the Rhine in the year in which Victor Hugo published his *Rhin*, which he intended as a pledge of Franco-German reconciliation. When the musician came to the river which he was crossing for the first time, he saw in it the bitterness of his Paris failures and, overcome with emotion, swore loyalty to his German fatherland. The small German theatres were delighted to accept his *Ghost Ship*. Schumann realized that the new German music had at last found its fulfilment, liberated from all foreign influences. Wagner became director of the Dresden Opera to which Weber had brought such distinction; it was the era of *Tannhaüser* and *Lohengrin*.

Then Wagner discovered the true significance of his musical drama: music was not an end in itself, it was only a means of evoking the deep significance of man and his destiny. Arias and recitatives were dropped, since their significance was one of form alone: musical architecture was built up of motifs conveying an idea or a sentiment, a fate or a character. This music perfected the theory Glück had advanced against Puccini. It also exploited to the full the revolutionary freedom which Beethoven had introduced into his later symphonies, and rediscovered and enriched the lessons of John Sebastian Bach with new orchestrations. Wagner was a revolutionary in every way. In Paris he protested against the materialism of bourgeois society which cared only for entertainment and nothing for art. In Dresden in 1848, he threw himself passionately into the liberal national movement, going as far as Proudhon in his demand that money should be divested of its power to work evil. It was to be the regeneration of humanity by love. But all this fine enthusiasm suffered a serious setback when the reaction set in against the liberals and Wagner had to take refuge in Switzerland, where he did some serious thinking and discovered Schopenhauer.

Schopenhauer was a strange thinker, and very typical of the Germany of the 1840s. He knew Kant, and unlike the great philosopher's disciples applied himself in particular to the critique of practical reason and discovered that idealist logic was an illusion, because it shut man up within himself and because the world is will. Biology, so popular in Germany, supplied him with numerous examples of this pressure exerted by nature on living beings in order to force them into the paths it wishes them to take.

Without enormous self-control, man can be nothing more than the puppet of the will, which bears him along in the direction of the general current. The popularity of *Die Welt als Wille und Vorstellung* did not become apparent until long after the first edition of the work, but it had then been considerable, since it gave the vanquished of 1849 an explanation of their defeat – the defeat of an over-abstract philosophy which had failed to recognize the imperatives of the inner life.

Wagner's time in Switzerland was spent pondering on life and composing. He wrote a whole series of theoretical works in which necessity and its counterpart, love, were depicted, as in Schiller, as the foundations of destiny. It was essential to destroy selfishness, and to burst asunder the hard shell of hypocritical habits which shut the heart off from the great creative surge of human history. Schopenhauer believed that music was the only art capable of expressing the will, all other forms being merely presentation. Wagner was eager to prove him right. He started on his *Tetralogy*, the *Nibelungen Ring*, the history of the pure-hearted hero who destroys the power of gold. He said in music what German painters had been trying in vain to express in their great legendary and historical canvases, the story of Siegfried, soon a symbol of the chosen being, the chosen race which was to rid the world of the rule of those who lived for gold. (Wagner had already written *Du judaïsme dans la musique* in 1850.) The vast *Tetralogy* led from the *Rheingold* to the *Götterdämmerung*, and its completion was delayed only by the love idyll *Tristan und Isolde*.

Wagner hoped that Tristan would be successful in Paris, since it was based on a French legend. It was his second attempt to please Parisian audiences, but it too ended in failure in 1860. Parisians did not take kindly to music which educated, preferring that which entertained. Wagner then drifted from place to place in Germany; the frontiers were reopened to the exile of 1848. Then from the depths of distress he was suddenly transported to the height of good fortune. When Ludwig II of Bavaria succeeded to the throne in 1854, he responded to Wagner's appeal of the previous year: 'The Prince who supports me in my work will ensure for his name undying fame.' Then Wagner's music poured in a vast flood over the whole of Germany, arousing a great wave of enthusiasm which so dazzled Wagner that he was moved to write a doubtful parody of the fall of Paris. But it also enabled him to realize his dream of Bayreuth, though not without difficulty.

This again reflects a contrast between France and Germany. In the work of Courbet, France grasped the whole human significance of a moment of time with great lucidity. In the work of Wagner Germany exalted feeling and traced its evolution from the biological origins of man through to the deliverance of the *Graal* in Paradise at the end of the road. The French remained true to painting, the possibilities of which they had been exploring for one hundred and fifty years – and the Germans to music with which they had enriched Europe during the same period. The reason was that the French, swept up in spite of themselves into the industrial whirlwind, had never really become reconciled to it, and retained a wistful longing for their rural past. Germans, on the other hand, felt that they had been given a new chance when the exploitation of coal restored their country to the political supremacy it had lost four centuries ago. They could now draw a new certainty from Darwin's theories, and the 'historical appeal' to race was revived which German philosophers had been propounding at the beginning of the century.

Apart from the few creative geniuses of the age, the ordinary life of the people seemed to be overlaid with a cheap veneer of artificial and official aesthetics. This may well have been because man was still resisting the adaptation of himself as a human being to the great new industrial style of the cities. Hugo, exiled from Paris, far from the great cities, could continue to be the bard of progress. But Baudelaire, who was actually living in the garden of the new Paris, could only pluck from it the Flowers of Evil.

As a result, some poets and painters at the close of the century attempted to leave Europe, since they believed it was sullied by industry. But time was pressing, for the rest of the world was following hard on Europe's heels.

Book Four

THE CONQUEST OF
THE WORLD

1840–95

11

The Maritime Successes of
Western Capitalism

WHILST the continent of Europe was changing as a result of the greatest
technical innovation mankind had ever known, sea traffic also was being
transformed so as to carry the news to every coast in the world, and with it
the produce of the industrial miracles of Europe. The instrument of this
expansion was first and foremost the ship. In 1885 it was more or less in the
middle of the transition which was to lead in less than a century from the
sailing-ship, directly descended from the *Santa Maria* of Christopher
Columbus, to the steel liner driven by turbines. In 1885, every harbour in
the world was still a swaying forest of masts and shrouds, but there was
already one steamship to approximately half these sailing-ships.

Naturally Great Britain played a decisive role in this transformation. In
1850 steamships accounted for barely six per cent of its total tonnage, but
it was still the only percentage of any consequence in the world. In 1870,
when England's rivals were tentatively going over to steam, the proportion
of steamships in England rose to nearly twenty per cent, and had reached
seventy-five per cent by 1900 – a proportion almost equalled by all the
western powers from Italy to Holland, Germany and the United States.
Only France still remained loyal to sail with half her shipping, partly because there was not enough export freight and the holds had to be filled
with sand; and also because the forests still provided wood which was
relatively cheap.

The engineer Fulton, encouraged perhaps by Napoleon, but certainly
discouraged by the *Institut de France*, returned to the United States with his
proposed steamboat. Its first trials on the Seine had not in fact been too
conclusive. England made the first voyage under steam to India in 1825.
It was a long voyage, of course, but relatively simple, since the entire route
lay along coasts where the ship could put in to refuel, in easy stages. This
was an important advantage, for if these ships of traditional tonnage carried
enough coal for the whole voyage they had no space left for cargo. The
progress of the steamship was therefore bound up with an increase in tonnage, and that in turn with the progress of ship-building. In that sphere
England achieved miracles. The substitution of iron for wood in the construction of hulls was enormously to her advantage, since her metal industry
was powerful and her forest reserves exhausted. But an iron hull attracted
marine deposits – colonies of barnacles which broke up its line and reduced

speed. At first the builders merely edged wooden keels with iron. Then came the triumph of Bessemer steel, which kept the hulls completely clear.

In 1838, however, two cargo ships hastily fitted with steam-engines had crossed the Atlantic, and soon influential companies were founded. They were prepared to risk the financing of these costly ships, in view of the substantial returns which would accrue from regular swift transport, free from dependence on fickle winds. At that time the ships were called mail packets. There was the Peninsular and Oriental to Spain, the Mediterranean and India; the Cunard to the United States; the Royal Mail in England; the Collins Line to the United States, the *Messageries Maritimes* in France, and the *Compagnie Générale Transatlantique*; and before long the Hamburg-America Line in Germany, as well as the *Nord Deutscher Lloyd*. These companies could be certain of success, thanks to the vast strides in technical progress which transformed naval architecture between 1830 and 1860. Research was being carried out on the shape and resistance of hulls, engine power was increased and its weight per horse-power decreased by more than half; the condenser was adopted, the double-expansion engine was invented, and swifter engines did away with gearing; the propeller was substituted for paddles, subsidiary engines were fitted to move the vast rudder and, most important of all, accurate sea charts were compiled which did away with the slow, dangerous empirical method of taking soundings near coasts in order to find the deep-water channel.

By 1880 the triumph of the new lines was assured with the Cunarder *Gallia* and the *Compagnie Générale Transatlantique*'s *Normandie*. This had a capacity of 10,000 tons, and was equipped to take more than a thousand passengers; it was driven by steam, but in a good wind by sail as well. In this battle the rival companies met with varying success. The United States were powerful in 1860, but abandoned competition at sea during the tragic years of the Civil War. Though they resumed it in 1880 with a new fleet from which sailing ships had almost completely vanished, they could no longer catch up with England's lead. England faced stiff competition from 1850 to 1870, but was then unchallenged until the close of the century; this explains the English debates on shipping about 1860, and the unconditional return to liberalism towards 1880. Above all, England had one tremendous advantage: since it had at its disposal ports of call along every single route and excellent engine-coal (the early steamships were afraid of spontaneous combustion), it kept all the world's great ports supplied with its steam coal. It was the great purveyor of coal to the new ships, whose ports of call were dictated by the need to refuel. It sold coal all the more easily since English ships could offer it cheap and take it as freight on the outward voyage. They returned to port with a variety of the raw materials which England imported from all over the world, through markets increasingly controlled from London. English coal exports rose from three million tons a year in 1850 to nearly twenty-five million in 1884. One last detail explains England's predominance: the sailing ships carried their own repair outfits, but this was not the case with steamships. Damage

could not easily be repaired except in ports specially equipped for the purpose. Moreover, these ports had to be fitted out in a special way and stocked
with spare parts. The modern ship, like the railway, set the problem of
standardization on a world scale, a requirement which naturally put the
most advanced countries even farther ahead. Since England provided the
coal and repair-yards it could impose its norms on ship-building all over
the world.

This rapid rise of the steamship changed the rhythm of the world. The
voyage from New York round Cape Horn towards the Golden Gate of
San Francisco was shortened sufficiently to compete with the overland
routes until the intercontinental railways were completed. The southern
hemisphere, India and China, were brought nearer to the ports of Europe.
Competition in the speed of transport reached such a pitch that a saving
of a few days could be vital. The triumph of naval techniques opened
up a commercial future for an old, and oft-deferred project, the Suez
Canal.

The connection of the Mediterranean with India interested England all
the more since its original settlement in Bengal was now spreading over the
whole peninsula. By using the Afghan camel, English enterprise solved the
Suez problem, and an army of camel-drivers ensured transport from the
Mediterranean to the Red Sea. The French had long been planning a
canal: Leibniz had already submitted a project to Louis xiv. Bonaparte
rediscovered traces of the ruins of the canal attributed by Pliny to Rameses,
and commisioned Lepère to see if it could be reconstructed. Unfortunately,
Lepère subscribed to the theory that the two seas were not on the same level
in spite of the observations of Laplace and Fourier. It was not until Enfantin
invented an instrument capable of obtaining more accurate triangulations
that this so-called difference in level was finally disproved in about 1846.
A French vice-consul in Egypt, Ferdinand de Lesseps, presented with unexpected leisure by the 1848 revolution, sketched out the great financial
plan which from 1854 appealed both to Mohammed Sahib and to Napoleon iii. Even then it took five more years to collect the capital, since
English financial circles were unco-operative; then ten years work. It was
a mammoth task which required a special type of dredger and machinery
which, in spite of the cheapness of labour, had to be of twenty thousand
horse-power. At long last, the Empress Eugénie opened the canal in 1869
to the strains of the music of Verdi, who had composed Aïda in the Egyptian style for the occasion.

In 1867 Charles Dilke prophesied that France would soon realize that it
had spent millions for the benefit of England, and he doubted whether this
vast capital investment would pay. He was right on the first point, wrong
on the second. Ten years later shares had risen by twenty per cent and dividends were higher than those in average English business. But in addition
Disraeli had had the Khedive's share bought by the British Government.
England's profits from Suez in 1879 were enormous: nearly two million
tons of English freight were using the new canal, ten times more than the

French. Subsequent progress continued to affirm this superiority of England, as Suez turned out to be a measuring-rod of sea-power.

Now that merchandise could be transported so rapidly by sea, orders, commissions and returns had to be speeded up still more. This led to another invention. In 1870 the telegraph cable connecting India with England was inaugurated; a message addressed to President Grant could soon be sent from Delhi to Washington using the two cables from India to England, then from England to the United States of America. The age of cables had been initiated in the 1860s from Norway to Africa and from Nova Scotia to the Gulf of Mexico. This second link was made possible by a more efficient use of rubber, and in spite of many failures. Until about 1862, three-quarters of the cables already laid at vast expense were of very little use. Then the money invested began to show returns in 1870, by which time the world network was more advanced. In 1872 Vladivostok was linked with China and Japan, and with England and Norway on the western side. In 1874 the Brazilian Company founded by Mauá, with English help, linked Rio with Recife and Lisbon via the Cape Verde Islands. The great financial centres of Europe at the heart of this gigantic spider's web grew accustomed to commanding and following the economic activity of the entire world in detail and day by day. They soon penetrated into the heart of the continents, taking advantage of the progress made by railways and telegraphs, which were always guided by European and English capitalists and technicians.

We have seen how the coming to power of liberal capitalism had coincided with the onset of periodic crises, which shook the economy of the new industrial countries: England, the United States, France, then Germany. The vast extension of sea-borne trade brought this régime of cyclic crises into every country in the world, and the swifter a country was developing, the more violent were the crises it experienced. The great new economic powers began to share the chronology of Europe's crises.

A TRIUMPH: THE UNITED STATES

In the middle of the century, when railways and steel ships were starting up in Europe and were available to transport emigrants escaping from its countryside, the United States was also making ready to receive them. There were brand new trains waiting to welcome the immigrants and to carry them into the interior, and the railway companies often engaged the newcomers, especially the Irish, as workmen in their own yards, on tracks, embankments and building-work in the new towns created by the railway companies.

The first American railway linked New York and Philadelphia and proved to be so profitable that several companies competed for possession of it. Rivalry between companies was sometimes absorbed by amalgamation. New routes were sought: a line went out from Baltimore towards

Ohio and the Mississippi valleys, comprising twenty thousand miles of track. Rivalries were sometimes taken up by the states, each subsidizing its own line: then competition went beyond all limits and the new lines were sometimes laid parallel to the old ones, especially in the east, where economic and urban development already provided plenty of passengers. Towards the south the railway continued to be less in evidence and less dependable. At the same time steamships were appearing on the great lakes and rivers, and in the north-east the development of canals was as rapid as that of the railways.

Above all the west was being populated, even along the Pacific seaboard where gold had just been discovered near the old Spanish settlements of San Francisco. Towards 1848, ironically enough, the adventurous crowds set out for Eldorado. To go from east to west was hardly feasible, nor was it wise. It was still necessary to cross wide areas occupied by hostile Indians. These pioneers first travelled southwards, either by sailing along the coast or by an overland journey, to the point where the continent narrowed and where there were fewer wide-open spaces to cross. They then took ship again on the Pacific coast, sailing northward towards the area of the placers. The journey was a tremendous adventure and through it the Americans learned to know the deserts which entered into their natural psychology and became part of their folklore – particularly Arizona, which had just been seized from Mexico. The richness of the seams transformed the settlement pattern of the Pacific coast. Perhaps the placer did not always bring wealth, but exploitation of the gold-seeker certainly did. The traders' stores and stalls attracted merchants and industrialists. Around the mining centres, the rich soil of the Californian valleys was soon used for agriculture, and population spread along them as far down as the Bay of Angels, Los Angeles. The rumour of all this new activity spread across the Pacific, and San Francisco began to expand and turn into a strange Chinese city where the sons of heaven achieved miracles in the commercial exploitation of the white man, a scornful but easy customer. If he was too poor to become a shopkeeper, the Chinese coolie accepted work under contract in the mines and the new concerns which were springing up on all sides – largely thanks to this source of cheap labour. Railways were built running parallel to the Pacific coast.

The Californian gold-rush had already halted and the economy evened out in a steady populating of the country, when gold was discovered in Colorado. Taken in hand more promptly by large-scale American capitalism, it was more quickly controlled. By the time Colorado had created in its turn a settlement around its gold-bearing valleys big enough to claim the title of state, the great battle of South and North had begun on the shores of the Atlantic.

It was a battle for or against slavery, but its significance went much deeper. Abraham Lincoln, the son of a Quaker, supported the cause of the poor peasants against the rich financiers of the eastern seaboard. He had worked on his father's farm and built his own house. On one of his trips

down the Mississippi he had been incensed by the arrogance of the Southern planter and the poverty of the Negro. He embarked on various trade
ventures, most of which were unsuccessful. He worked desperately hard to
pay his debts. In this way he learnt how to speak to the section of the
American people which lived by hard work and suffered so intensely from
the repercussions of the general economic crises brought on them by the
capitalism of the coast. His electoral victories were as much those of the
western pioneers against the middle-class easterner as of the anti-slavery
supporters. This made him an even more formidable opponent for the
Democratic Party which was controlled by Southerners and the rich men
of the east and had dominated the elections for twenty years. Abraham
Lincoln had married into an old Virginia family. Now the least break in
the solidarity of South and North meant that the new world from the
west could irrupt into the cosy deliberations of the federal capital of the
Atlantic coast. Lincoln had already inveighed against the injustice of the
Mexican war, and had exposed the frontier incidents which served as pretexts for the Southern cavalry. He denounced the machinations of the
South against the independence of Cuba. His election to the presidency,
though far from resting on a large electoral majority, nevertheless signified
the end of the old democratic compromise: the alliance between the rich
of North and South in the name of the Union.

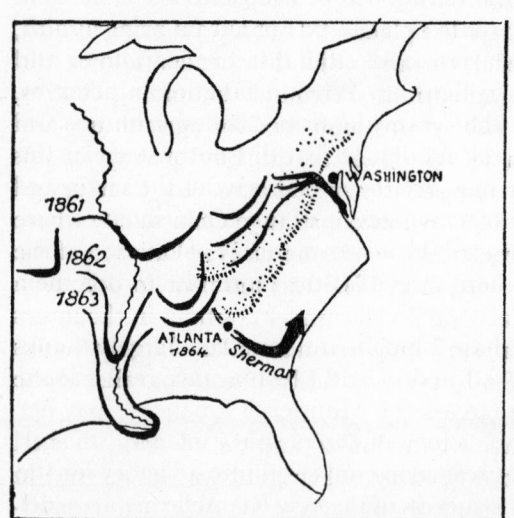

19 Stages in the American
Civil War

War broke out: when Southern and Northern troops came directly face
to face on the banks of the Potomac, either the victory was indecisive or
the ground remained in Southern hands. On several occasions the
Southerners directly threatened Washington. The last Northern victory,
the famous Battle of Gettysburg, was no more than a successful stand by
federal troops solidly entrenched along the hill-tops against the assaults of
the Confederates. The defeat of the South was due to the fact that its

positions could be turned by the west; Grant marched along the Mississippi, leading troops recruited from western volunteers and conscripts equipped by Northern industry, transported by Northern railways, outclassing the South's river flotillas. The troops attacked the fortified towns along the river, and broke through at last on to the territory of the Confederate states: the capture of Wicksburg opened a wide breach to the eager North. The Southern cavalry and their loyal Negro troops fought heroically to defend the South's one railway junction, the city of Atlanta, but it fell, and the entire transport equipment of the Confederates was in the hands of the Union.

Authority Passes to the North

Lincoln's victory meant not only the abolition of slavery, but the end of an aristocracy and almost of a civilization. This most tragic and bloody of civil wars had the same significance as the 1848 revolts in Europe – the disappearance of a world in which the social hierarchy was based on the possession of lands and men, the disappearance of the world of the horse and the sailing-ship, of sophisticated luxury and vague law, of great orators and illusory pretence. The defeat of the South had really been implicit in the 1840s when traffic in the port of New Orleans caught up with that of New York, when the decadence of Charleston had become obvious, when the track of the Southern railway carried into the mining area of Birmingham the proletarian and capitalist civilization of the North. But the South went down fighting. When a fanatic, an actor by profession, assassinated Lincoln the tyrant, he firmly believed he was defending a democracy on the Greek model. Defeat did not just mean the emancipation of the slaves. The new Southern poor saw in the victory of the North the merciless invasion of a civilization of machines, shopkeepers, technicians, methodist preachers – all the advance rabble of the expanding urban way of life which made them grieve all the more bitterly for their old rural civilization.

During the presidency of Abraham Lincoln, insidious rumours were current in Washington. His wife loved luxury and extravagance; she adored her husband, but did not hesitate to ask the Minister of Finance to pay her thoughtlessly incurred bills. The victory of the people's infantry, though commanded by Quaker generals, was soon converted into a victory for the businessmen who cashed in on the success of the new Republicans. In order to win over the western farmers, the new Federal Government had made large distributions of land during the war (the Homestead Act followed in 1870). Each head of a family had the right to a plot of one hundred and sixty acres if he farmed it. This meant good business also for the dealers in agricultural material: the mobilization of young countrymen made it essential to mechanize agriculture.

The period of reconstruction saw the heyday of big business, especially during the two terms of office of the war hero General Grant. He was powerless to check the whirlwind of speculation which swept like a tornado across the length and breadth of the United States during the first years of peace. Up to that time it had always been the policy of the American Treasury to liquidate its internal debt at the earliest possible moment. During the war, however, there had been a considerable issue of Treasury Bonds (*Greenbacks*), but their withdrawal from circulation would have provoked a drop in prices, and caused serious embarrassment to all the new land-holders in the centre and west who had incurred debts in order to increase and stock their lands, as well as to farmers who would have to sell their produce more cheaply while still paying the same price to the land-owner. Already Jackson, we have seen, had dismantled the cautious banking system favoured by the easterners. Grant gave a new lease of life to this policy of easy credit and generous guarantees by the state. Agriculture undoubtedly benefited as a result: the Timber Act of 1873 helped settlers engaged in afforestation, and four years later the Desert Land Act was to help those practising irrigation. However, the chief beneficiaries of this governmental generosity were undoubtedly the large-scale speculators.

There had been an enthusiastic programme of railway building during the war when their strategic advantages were obvious. The development slowed down when the thickly populated, economically equipped areas of east and west were more or less covered. The centre remained empty; it was still unpopulated, and no immediate profit was expected from it. Technically, however, the problem of linking the thickly populated east and the rapidly expanding west had to be solved. This was carried out in 1869; through the high passes of the Rockies, which had to be crossed through the high Californian valleys at heights of nearly 10,000 feet, over daring wooden bridges thrown across rivers and vast lakes, the junction of east and west was achieved at Promontory Point. It was celebrated by a huge fête, where most of the people were Chinese, since it was Chinese labourers who had built the substructure.

As for capital, though some was American, it was chiefly English. But shares were dropping on the London Stock Exchange, and dividends became insignificant. True, the ease with which the great American companies manipulated their assets and liabilities played some part in this, but the crisis of 1873 was also partly responsible since it was a poor year for agriculture and railway freight receipts fell accordingly. Railway law needed revising and, above all, an end had to be put to the disastrous competition which allowed two or three companies to operate the same route. Before any attempt was made to remedy this competition the government granted enormous advantages to the companies, including possession of a twenty-mile strip of land alongside the tracks they were laying down. Thus the railway companies were no longer just transport companies but actually huge land-owning companies, which attracted more English capital to the United States, and mobilized all the financial possibilities of America.

Unfortunately the 1880s were again critical years. More than three thousand companies went bankrupt, and some of them in circumstances of the utmost publicity. One of these was the company of Jay Cook, who had more irons in the fire than any other speculator during those years of reconstruction, who had built the Pacific Coast railway and founded the North Pacific Railway Company. There began to be a regrouping of interests. A pool was set up between several of the central companies, Chicago-Burlington-Omaha; each set aside for the pool half of its profits,

20 European Occupation and Indian Reserves in the United States

Grey: Europeans
Black: Indians

divided again according to the number of shares. These agreements were arrived at partly for technical reasons; it was essential to co-ordinate time-tables over this immense continent, divided into five time-zones; the gauge had to be standardized, a problem to which the first eager pioneers had given no thought whatever; their hasty and often precarious tracks, with their over-sharp curves, their too steep gradients, their flimsy, temporary bridges needed reconstructing. Steps had to be taken to cut down the excessive number of accidents, to organize signalling, to adopt better brakes, as for instance the Westinghouse in 1873, to make automatic coupling safer, to replace iron by steel wherever possible, and to make passenger coaches more comfortable. It was the age of epic ventures: Vanderbilt, head of the Grand Central of New York, declared war on the Pennsylvania Company, though himself threatened by ambitious opponents in the region of the Great Lakes. The procedure of the struggle was always the same: first lines were built parallel to those of the rival one sought to ruin, then a fares war began. The travelling public benefited by each battle, but suffered as a result of each victory, and the English shareholder always footed the bill, both of the battle and the victory. Vanderbilt's successful rival on the Great Lakes was for a time the first great king of the American economy – there was reason to fear that he might gain control of more than sixty thousand miles of railroad. In the centre and west, another kingdom was taking shape: that of Jay Gould. So much rivalry was, however, ruinous. In order to bring it to an end, the bank took away all the profit from the struggle. In 1885 the banker John Pierpont Morgan formed a syndicate powerful enough to persuade the serious competitors to make peace and to eliminate the adventurers who had come on the scene too late. The result was an equitable sharing out between the Pennsylvanian and the New York companies, and a repurchase of the Baltimore and Ohio; a unification movement went on from east to west, the development of the south was completed, and the American railway network became the admiration of the world because of its density, its technical qualities and the efficiency of its personnel and equipment.

The development of railways gave birth to new financial structures – pools, syndicates, trusts and holdings – and also brought changes in landed property. At first the central areas benefited from an enormous increase in value once the railways were opened and this added to the importance of the gift given to the railways by the Government. Above all the agricultural movement benefited from the vast transport facilities offered to men and foodstuffs. This period, during which the great transcontinental lines were being built, also meant the end of the frontier.

The frontier was the vast area where the settler reached the limit of 'civilized' lands, in other words lands protected against the Indian and under some measure of legal jurisdiction, and which were being opened up and developed in the normal way. This frontier was guarded by the Federal Army, but it was continually advancing, pushing before it Indian tribes and their herds of buffalo, enclosing them into their last reserves. The railroad now cut up into sections the belt of unexplored territory which framed the Rockies, an area of high grassy plateaux where agriculture was often difficult. But stock-breeding, not only of buffaloes, but of cows from the east and from Europe, flourished around the ranches, great farmhouses built of wood, solid as fortresses, and well able to defend themselves against the new immigrants. There was no need to worry about the cattle, except to protect them against theft: the cowboys kept guard over the prairie where the cattle grew and multiplied as on the pampas of the Argentine. The meat trade made considerable headway, especially as the cowboys' equipment was cheap and rudimentary – some good strands of barbed wire, a lasso, stout ropes and of course the indispensable Colt. In 1880, Buffalo Bill, the last of the frontier heroes, was twenty years old. Agricultural resources were beginning to be exploited. In Wyoming, Cheyenne already had more than ten thousand inhabitants, and the grave of La Ramée, a French trapper who died in the seventeenth century, had become Laramie, a small industrial centre, with five thousand inhabitants grouped around its station. From north to south of the high plateaux, colonization prospered and spread till it engulfed the islands of population which the search for and the exploitation of gold had brought there. Denver was no longer merely the site of a famous mint; it was a great capital of one hundred thousand inhabitants, the intellectual centre of this new country, with a slaughter-house nearly as famous as the one in Chicago. The technique of slaughter and preservation of meat was soon better than the methods used in the countries of the plain, and at La Plata. The canning and refrigerating industries were already making it possible to expand into European and world markets. A transformation was taking place in the Americans' diet, up to then based on cereals, which had given them the 'pasty face' at which the English poked fun; now they were eating more milk and meat and less bread and maize.

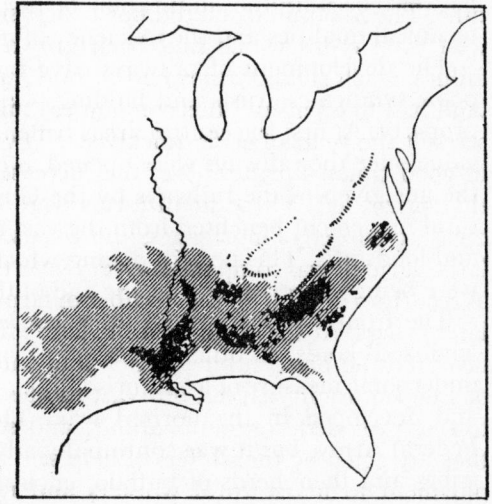

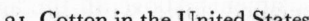
21 Cotton in the United States

Black: 1840
Grey: 1890

To the west of the prairies the small farm came off worst in comparison with the large estates, but in the middle west it was still firmly established, though in very varying forms. Between Omaha, the third abattoir in the country, and a city which won the admiration of Europe for the speed of its development, and Burlington, the terminus of the famous railroad, stretched Iowa, which took its name from the Indian 'blockheads'. Its territory with its perfectly geodesic frontiers was cut up into districts each of thirty-six square miles, then divided again into square miles each of which was split into four lots of one hundred and sixty acres in conformity with the Homestead Act. It was the best example of agricultural colonization in the 1880s; the streets of the little towns and even the field-paths were fixed in accordance with parallels and meridians. Sometimes traces were found of the first inhabitants, those who had cleared the forests, in the shape of caves hollowed out of the chalk hillsides or primitive houses built of clods.

The farther east one went, the more the agricultural scene became like that of Europe, particularly in the region of the Great Lakes where the Irish and the Scandinavians found soils and climates which were familiar to them. They built farmhouses which were exact replicas of the lovely country houses in their own country. On the east coast, even in the highly developed Massachusetts, a thorough enough search could reveal traces of a European land régime introduced two hundred years earlier by the Dutch. Towards the east also, crops were more varied. In New England there was an intensive polyculture. On the eastern grasslands there were no longer great herds wandering about over the arid grass, but small groups of animals confined to the stable in winter and providing milk, butter and cheese made on small farms and sold in village markets. In the south the cultivation of cotton, after a slight setback, continued to develop.

But everywhere in 1880 the small farm was on the decline. The farmer, even when presented with free land on virgin soil, could not make a fortune. The unfamiliar soil did not take easily to European crops, and in the west even crops which had been grown successfully in the east were a failure. Each small farmer had to find out on his own what resources the land had to offer, and this condemned him to a low standard of living. As a result the years of crisis quickly swallowed up the resources accumulated in good times. Furthermore, the increase in the number of farms meant that prices fell. These small farms were weighed down with an ever increasing burden of mortgages, and were sometimes sold to speculators or to large agricultural companies. Every year thousands of them were deposited as securities or sold. So the number of farmers began to exceed that of small landowners. At the same time the laws affecting afforestation or irrigation favoured the big combines. Rich and influential landed companies, often of English origin, carved out vast estates for themselves where they built towns, provided communications, and sold lots to small farmers whom they attracted by their offers of help and advice. Above all, they gave employment to many rural workers and ran agricultural concerns on industrial lines.

Thus, in California, there was one farmer irrigating as much as 1,200 square miles. A model farm in Minnesota covered 75,000 acres and owned 200 threshing machines, filling 75 wagons a day with corn at harvest time.

In a country where a small farm was approximately 125 acres, and a large one might be the size of one of Europe's smaller states, mechanization made tremendous strides. In 1880 the new threshing-machines drawn by large teams of forty horses were very popular. On the other hand, agriculture continued to be extensive rather than intensive. There was practically no use of manure, little study of the land, little research into genetics, yet the virgin soil gave good yields – almost too good, for soon there was difficulty in selling the harvest. Maize rotted in the fields, or was burnt, or used as fuel (1889). Nevertheless new products were added to the great harvests of corn, maize, cotton, and sugar-cane, especially in California, where the orchards had shown how profitable fruit-growing could be. Between the years 1880 and 1890 trees were planted in thousands, in millions, then in thousands of millions. This new development opened up a type of work that favoured concentration and only required seasonal labour at harvest time. Vegetables were little grown except on the outskirts of eastern towns. In 1887 the Hatch Act was passed providing for some of the money derived from the sale of state land to be used for the setting up of a fund for research into problems of land and soils. The best way of helping the farmer was to teach him about this new soil, instead of letting him find out for himself often at the cost of his own ruin.

Naturally the small farmer had long protested against the heavy burden of taxation, the dearness of credit, and the arbitrary and apparently haphazard way in which the railway companies fixed their rates, which were proportionately higher the less competition there was, hopelessly ruining the settler who had pushed far into the virgin lands. Of the farmers' associations, the oldest and biggest was that of the Grangers, which had grown to such an extent within seven years that, by 1874 when the crisis first became apparent, it already had something like one and a half million members. It tried to secure cheaper credit, less brutal evictions, lower transport rates. It intervened in political life against the trusts, the over-powerful financiers and the vast English concerns known as the Bonanza farms.

The farmers who had been given an unsatisfactory deal made common cause with the growing proletariat in the towns. In fact after 1874 immigrants no longer rushed to obtain free land immediately on disembarking, preferring to crowd together on the outskirts of ports. Wave after wave of them piled up in New York, and no longer moved off into the interior. If some did leave, it was because they were attracted by the growth of an industrial or commercial town. In the one year 1882, the United States took in from overseas almost eight hundred thousand immigrants, fewer English and Irish than before but more Scandinavians and particularly Germans, who went to swell the towns in the east or the middle west. The big capitalist companies were pleased to see them and made the most of the newcomers, since they accepted any terms and so sent down the price of labour in the factories. The large factory owners even went as far afield as Europe, especially to the Austro-Hungarian Empire and southern Italy, to recruit Slavs, Hungarians, Slovaks and Italians. These people were poor enough to accept any contract and only realized the severity of the terms they had agreed to after they had settled in America.

The Chinese recruited in China were so numerous that Congress had to put a complete stop to the immigration of orientals, and even to forbid the return of the many who had gone back home from the lands and cities of the west to pay a temporary visit to their relatives in China. In spite of this ban, a clandestine trade continued for some years in landing these sober and industrious Chinese on the Pacific coasts, making the old Chinese city of San Francisco bigger than ever and providing the fruit-growers with cheap and docile labour.

In any case, half the inhabitants of New York in 1880 had been born elsewhere, and three-quarters had at least one immigrant parent. The city had nearly two million inhabitants but, vast though it was, it was getting ready for a fresh expansion. It drained the surrounding districts, particularly New Jersey. This was a fairly widespread phenomenon in the United States and its significance was even greater than in Europe, where at about the same time honest folk were beginning to lament the flight from the countryside. Mushroom towns like Denver and Omaha sprang up within a few days. About 1890 this term 'mushroom town' was a fashionable way of describing cities like Kensington in Pennsylvania, which built five mills in two months and covered five square miles of a clearing which was soon being served by twenty-five trains a day. Speculation in urban land in the 1880s was one of the best possible investments. A town plan was traced out on the ground, the site of the public buildings was fixed, and the lots set aside for private houses were sold at a high figure. Sometimes speculation was unsuccessful; the wooden huts rotted on the spot. At other times, towns sprang up in a few months and profits were fabulous. Sometimes, after an existence of a few years, the town would disappear, sucked in by more fortunate neighbours, or moved *en bloc* from one state to another, from one resource to another. In 1885 Pithole City had houses, hotels, a station, a theatre, and public buildings; by 1890 nothing and no-one remained except ten or so obstinate creatures who had deliberately invited ruin by staying behind.

The queen of the cities which changed the map of America in the general surge and upheaval was Chicago. In the seventeenth century Joliet had made a cautious study of the ramifications of these marshy lake flats. In 1830 about a hundred people built huts on the site. Suddenly a town sprang up: land was drained, a port built on the lake, a railway constructed, and steam navigation turned Chicago into the great economic centre, the communication nucleus of the whole Federation. It was the meeting place of the committees co-ordinating the whole body of railway traffic and the transport rates between states. There was even some thought of making it the capital of the United States. St Louis, the great centre of the Mississippi, was outclassed. Then came catastrophe; the whole city, hastily built of wood, was burnt to the ground in 1871 and for six square miles nothing remained of it but a mass of charred debris. The vast column of smoke drifted south-east across the whole of America and almost half-way across the Atlantic. But the new city developed even more rapidly. In 1880 only one-quarter of the inhabitants were American born; Czechs, Slavs, Irish, above all Germans, vied with each other to recon- struct the city behind its frontage of parks stretching for twenty-five miles along the lake. Though the ground had to be drained, stakes fixed and deeper and deeper foundation piles driven, and though the houses were constantly threatened with ruin, the buildings being erected were more and more audacious. A vast hotel catering for thousands of travellers included among its public rooms a theatre to accommodate eight thousand spectators. In 1890 buildings of ten, fifteen and twenty storeys began to go up. The height of the New York blocks was equalled, then exceeded. Chicago was well fed. Its slaughter-houses were the best in the world, surrounded by vast paddocks where several thousand cattle grazed, providing half a mil- lion tons of fresh meat and almost a thousand million tins of meat. The trains were already being driven by electricity and carried millions of pas- sengers a year.

Detroit was as yet only a small township near Chicago, but a new and rapidly prospering city came into being around the Pullman coach-works. The entire population of the mushroom towns could be fed without diffi- culty, because of the cheapness of agricultural produce, and new inhabi- tants were easy to recruit thanks to the great waves of immigration and migrations within the country. The people all depended on industry, which was vigorous enough to ensure handsome profits.

The gold fever had died down. The centre of gravity of the gold mines had moved from California to the interior (the eastern fringe of the Rockies from Arizona to Montana) where, moreover, it was silver rather than gold which brought wealth to the great concessionary capitalist companies which had gradually eliminated the lone prospector. Iron ore was being exploited on the shores of Lake Superior, and coal in Pennsylvania. Re- search was carried out, and iron and coal were mined to the south and east of the Mississippi. Better still, just before the Civil War reserves of mineral oil had been found in Pennsylvania.

Oil was not entirely a novelty since Genoa had been lighted by oil as early as 1802. The small Italian deposits were probably used as a result of lessons learnt from India and central Asia in the seventeenth century, but this was, however, a rare local phenomenon and had no economic signifi- cance. Up to about 1880, oil was merely a pharmaceutical product used particularly in the treatment of ulcers. In 1859 a retired American officer was digging a well in Oil Creek, Titusville, when oil suddenly spurted out: up to that time the Indians had collected it only by dipping rags into pools, but now it flowed out in such abundance that they did not know what to do with it, and it even fouled the rivers. Whilst Berthelot, Mendeleyev and other scientists were constructing strange theories about the origins of the new liquid, Rockefeller built a first refinery at Cleveland. There the various products were sorted out, benzines, lighting oils, greasing oils, tars, each of which sold well as the invention of suitable apparatus enabled it to be more widely used. From 1851 lighting by hydrocarbide attracted the admiration

of visitors to the great international exhibitions, although their admiratio
was tempered with awe because of the risk of explosion. Oil ignites a
thirty degrees. It was therefore essential both to improve lamps, whic
were merely modified versions of the old carcels, and to regulate the refinin
of lamp oil so as to produce a more stable product. But in any case th
smell of the first lamps meant that they could be used only in kitchens an
domestic offices. In 1890 the oil-lamp first appeared in the drawing-room
Between 1880 and 1890 Europe increased its imports of schist oil tenfold; i
Germany and in Russia, where vegetable oils were costly, oil was soo
being used to light the large city streets. Paris did not commit itself unt
1880.

The small producer could not long compete in this swiftly expandin
market. Though it had been considered a simple pharmaceutical produc
at first, oil was soon found to be good for lighting, though it still had to b
purified. It was a useful fuel, but its sale had to be organized and a vast re
fining plant had to be built. For twenty-five miles around Titusville, well
were dug and crowned with pointed covers and wooden derricks. Over th
country as a whole the yield of the wells decreased, but production in
creased, because the field of discovery was extended as far as Californi
Production could barely keep pace with demand, particularly as oil cook
ing stoves had been invented and large English shipping companies wer
thinking of burning oil in their ship's boilers, and were even busy exploitin
Indian or Indonesian oils. Refining soon became a flourishing industry
and was much improved by the distillation of its costly by-products. Eve
before 1800 cracking had been introduced. The movement of oil from th
oil fields of Pennsylvania and Cleveland or Pittsburgh became so great tha
the first pipe line had to be constructed. New York, Baltimore and Buffalc
with their very powerful pumping-stations, became the world's great re
finery centres. On the edge of the Alleghany Mountains, carefully guarde
stocks were stored in great tanks, lit exclusively by electricity ever since th
terrible disaster of 1880 when a river of fire threatened to burn Titusvill

Michael Pupin may have deplored the fact that Americans had no tast
for pure science, but they had a genius for its practical application. I
1876, the Philadelphia Exhibition displayed the telephone; its vibratin
element was still primitive, but was improved in the following years unt
eventually it became the microphone. This transition from Graham Bell'
telephone, strictly acoustic, to the electric telephone gave the world a nev
network of telecommunications. It was the achievement of a man who
more than any other, was typical of the age – Thomas Alva Edison. I
1880, Edison was thirty-three. He was the son of a Dutch gardener, origi
nally a second-hand dealer who had emigrated to Michigan. At the age o
twelve he was earning a living, and was one of the many youngsters whon
the railway companies exploited as cheap labour, especially in America
He edited a newspaper in his goods truck for the use of travellers. He hac
a genius for doing the unexpected. As a telegraph employee he forgot to b
there to transmit or receive messages, but invented a device which made hi

presence unnecessary. He caused a stoppage on the line, but invented the duplex telegraph (two telegrams being transmitted simultaneously along the same wire), and soon a quadruplex system. The Western Union Telephone Company made his fortune. In 1877, he invented the microtelephone which led to the telephone and the telegraph and ultimately to the telephonograph, and which was was fantastically successful in the United States. Edison was a strange man, a jack of all trades, and a great reader, who had a genius for picking out of learned European reviews the tiny detail overlooked by other technicians, and from which he at once succeeded in deriving a wealth of riches. In turn millionaire and near-bankrupt, he invested everything he possessed in research work at his huge laboratory at Menlo Park, and drew lucky every time he played the dangerous game of double or quits.

One of the most outstanding inventions of the Menlo Park genius was undoubtedly the incandescent lamp. It deserves a few lines to itself. In 1878 Edison was bored. He visited the laboratories of a great American arc-lamp manufacturer, and realised the inconveniences of this lighting system which consumed enormous electrical energy and gave a dazzling light, but an extremely localized one. The problem of electric lighting could only be solved if the light could be subdivided. Then only could it compete with gas. Back in his laboratory Edison put aside all his photographic apparatus and applied his mind to gas lighting. He studied costs and concluded that electrical lighting could be profitable, on one condition: the solving of this problem of subdivision, which the world's scientists believed to be insoluble. Up to that time the electric lamp had been studied in isolation, whereas it should be regarded as one part of a much larger problem. The carbon had to be reduced to a very fine filament and brought to incandescence not in free air but in an evacuated glass ball. At first the filament consisted of a trace of carbon on paper; it lasted only a few minutes. Edison considered replacing the carbon by iridium or platinum, but they were too fragile. He passed from carbon to everything he could lay hands on in the way of raw material. He sent an assistant to China and Japan to bring back bamboo, which he drew out into the finest of filaments, and then found a Japanese farmer who made a fortune out of supplying it to him, since other researches undertaken by Edison in Florida, Cuba and the South American forests were unsuccessful. The cost price of the lamp was almost two dollars. Edison founded the Edison Electric Illumination Company with branches in Chicago and New York, whilst waiting for his patent to be bought in Europe by Emile Rathenau. The reason for this prodigious commercial success was that Edison offered his two dollar lamp to his customers for one-fifth of its price – forty cents – reckoning that the flood of orders would soon justify mass production and the construction of powerful Gramme dynamos. His gamble proved justified and enabled him to win a substantial victory after years of hard credit, suspicion and near bankruptcy by equipping with electricity all the great cities of America, then of the world.

Electricity, like oil, showed that in future industry would have to be conducted on a large scale.

Large-scale Capitalism, Imperialism

The law of Pennsylvania, then the Sherman law, in 1880, prevented Rockefeller from controlling affairs outside the state. The oil-men decided to hand over shares to trustees, reliable people who, without any legal façade which could give the law a hold, were actually in complete control of production and distribution all over the United States. Millions of miles of pipelines enabled the distribution to be independent of the railways. Thus alongside the railway pools the great oil trusts were founded.

In metallurgy, too, holdings were created. The cotton textile industry still retained a character reminiscent of its distant origins (almost a century old), wheat moved from the north-east, where its produce was sold and traded, towards the south where it was produced, but the metal industry developed by a process of concentration analogous to that of the railways and which the Sherman Anti-Trust Act hardly affected at all. The Bank, which had acted as referee between the railway rivals, played the same rôle with Pierpont Morgan and soon with Carnegie. In this industry the enormous and costly plant had to be renewed every five years because of technical improvement and mass production resulted in such low prices that small businesses which could not raise the capital needed to keep up with frequent changes of plant had either to give in or to get out. In fact from 1864 the Bessemer processes were familiar in the United States and all the Pennsylvanian valleys were equipped with converters. Cheap steel contributed substantially to the progress of the railroad. Barely fifty years later the furnaces invented by Siemens and Martin were rivalling the converters and turning out steel of even higher quality. Then came improvements in blast-furnaces and cokeries, requiring new types of coal and recovery plant. Chemical industries combined with the coal industries and enabled prices to be lowered throughout the entire metal industry. In short, there was a whole chain of technical revolutions which pushed along the canals towards the lakes, and towards the new coal-beds (Birmingham was developed in Alabama). This all-conquering and powerful capitalist industry was well on the way to becoming the first and finest in the world; in 1890 it was producing more cast-iron than England. At the same time the total power of American steam-engines produced was greater that that of France and Germany together.

Finally, America's vast resources of cheap timber proved most advantageous to the paper and cellulose industries. Reserves of sulphur were discovered in Louisiana and Texas, which freed the United States from dependence on imports. The Michigan copper mines and later the Montana mines were the finest in the world. Between 1880 and 1890 the United States moved rapidly into the lead of capitalist industrial civilization.

The Civil War had interrupted the development of the United States navy at the precise moment when steam was replacing sail. On the Atlantic this vacuum gave England the advantage; on the Pacific no rival had a base sufficiently near to prevent the Americans from making astonishing progress: their penetration of the Pacific had been going steadily forward from the middle of the century, a continuation of their westward drive which had taken them from one ocean to another. They had got used to regarding the great ocean as theirs, as much theirs as the great desert. In 1867 they had bought the vast region of Alaska from Russia. The Russian shipowners, who had done so much to explore the Bering Strait and had established their posts as far as the Russian river to the north of San Francisco, were obliged to retreat. Similarly the United States installed itself in the Hawaian Islands while claiming, this time, to respect the rights of the independent state of Kanake. This was a strange state, in which the natives had learned from all the sailors of Europe both to despise their gods and to fabricate a kind of constitution on Western lines. Now it was full of sailors from San Francisco who ousted all the others, protected ports and soon the whole state. Before long all the whites on the islands regarded themselves as Americans. The place was also an excellent stepping-stone to the Philippines.

After 1885 the land conquest of the American continent was completed. The great capitalists were dreaming of profits at sea. It was thought rather risky to venture outside the protection of the star-spangled banner and of the laws passed by Congress, but they were being pushed into the venture by the very success of their industrial expansion. From 1880 to 1890 coal-production rose from sixty million tons to more than two hundred and fifty millions. The iron of Lake Superior was inexhaustible: iron output quadrupled. The first task, in any case, was to rebuild a fleet.

Unfortunately, however, America's very success led to a crisis of over-production: prices dropped in three great waves from 1873 to 1897. It was a period which American historians acknowledge as being difficult to describe: there were agitations and violent disturbances, contradictory measures were passed by the authorities and the reactions of public opinion were unpredictable. Inevitably the ebb and flow of crises profoundly affected a nation where economic factors were so decisive. When prices were rising, farmers bought equipment, small farms pushed out westward, the mills paid good wages. When prices fell, the agricultural population flowed back to the east, increasing industrial unemployment, accusing speculators of robbing the little man. Huge combines were, in fact, buying up cheap the lands of ruined farmers, and enormous trusts were regrouping mills which had not a sufficiently sound financial basis. There were bailiffs running to call in mortgages but also strikes touching off more strikes and involving vast numbers of people: 750,000 railway workers supported the claims of the Pullman employees.

Naturally, here and there, appeals were made to the Government. When it decided to mint silver money, it brought new hope to the owners of those mines which had an excessive production, breathed a little oxygen into rarified credit, and sent up prices, but it also compromised the currency. Similarly, if the Government fixed high customs tariffs it consolidated the market for American produce but also sent up the cost of living. The Republicans, who had been in power since the Civil War, were rent by endless quarrels. These divisions were turned to good advantage by the Democrat Cleveland who was twice elected to the White House, swept in for a second term by a tidal wave: an increase of 400,000 votes and an absolute majority in Congress. But Cleveland's two terms of office disappointed even his own supporters, for his solutions were self-contradictory, and his rigorous honesty was no more successful than the expediency of his opponents.

Nevertheless from all this confusion there emerged several important innovations. One was the creation of the Civil Service. Ever since the days of Jackson, more than ten thousand high administrative posts had been regarded as the perquisites of the party in power, and a change of government had involved even crossing-sweepers in a nation-wide upheaval for the benefit of supporters of the new majority. This system was now done away with, and the new-style officials were recruited by competition. The universities, too, were organized. The colleges were grouped into faculties. Wealthy patrons competed with each other to provide handsome endowments. Following their example the big business concerns abandoned their rule-of-thumb methods and set up research departments, created a permanent body of technicians, and embarked on a more systematic study of markets. Estimates were made of productivity and returns, on lines suggested by Taylor, the economist and statistician. The United States began to realize that it had reached its natural, geographical limits, and must now organize itself in depth. Immigration was restricted and customs barriers were erected.

But the United States had also to face the same intrinsic problems as Europe; the chief one was to find external outlets. The most venturesome spirits talked of colonies. Cleveland opposed this suggestion as forcefully as he could. He refused to annex the Hawaiian Islands as the American Minister in Honolulu, who had made all necessary preparations, urged him to do.

In 1897 there was a rise in prices, at first tentative, then more marked. Then the Republicans came back to power, supported by a reorganized capitalism. The National City Bank had important interests in the Pacific and also in Cuba, where it financed a major part of the sugar crop. Most of the newspapers had fallen into the hands of one important trust: the Associated Press. Public opinion was being schooled to a condition new in American history: imperialism at the expense of European possessions. A new era was opening for the United States and for the world.

A PROMISE: THE SOUTHERN HEMISPHERE

Within the space of a few years not only did the activity of Latin America make such strides that it was in a position to compete with Europe, but the new lands in the southern hemisphere began to acquire economic importance.

The Development of Australia

Up to the middle of the century, Australia had been regarded merely as a place of deportation, to the indignation of the few settlers already there. These settlers were thrusting back a strange indigenous population which had retained little of its matriarchal traditions beyond customs so hard on women that the tribes were already decreasing in numbers even before the fatal invasion of the white man. In thirty years, however, the population of Australia rose from 300,000 to almost 3,000,000 inhabitants. This advance was helped on by an influx of Chinese strong enough to disquiet the English majority. The increase was largely due to the rush for gold, which was discovered there in 1851. It was this gold which led to the development of the ports which had regular services to England, and of the railways already spreading over the south-east and tentatively pushing out across the desert towards Palmerston. The telegraph had also recently been introduced and it was proposed to continue it across the sea to Ceylon and Vancouver. But the English contingent was not yet in a position to threaten the power of the squatters who had appropriated immense lands in spite of the laws; they owned thousands of acres each, on which only the rabbit, unwisely introduced, vied with them for the grass on which they grazed their vast flocks of sheep. These flocks were reckoned in hundreds of thousands, and their wool, sold to Europe, kept these lords of the land in princely luxury. Nevertheless, the towns had to be fed too, and around them the landscape was being marked out into fields of a European type. The ground was then divided into enclosed farms of average size, on the English pattern.

In 1885 there were three distinct zones and three types of society: on the coast, a landscape like that of England; farther inland, feudal land-ownership; and, tapering off towards the desert, an area peopled only by explorers and adventurers, bent on discovering a country still fraught with danger. There was one all-important city, Sydney, near Botany Bay, where the convicts had landed in former days. In fifty years Sydney had become one of the world's great cities, with almost four hundred thousand inhabitants. It was the queen of the south, a city of gardens and parks, a centre of learning, and above all a great capitalist city; it acted as the gateway through which English goods could reach a whole continent.

South Africa Becomes Industrialized

In South Africa, liberal England did nothing to hinder the expansion of the Boer state. She handed Orange over to them in 1854, then, after various vicissitudes connected with those of Gladstone's party, the Transvaal in 1874. Meanwhile the English in South Africa were grouped along a line of advance which pushed deep into the northern lands; they drew their supplies from the southern ports and particularly from the Cape.

The efforts made to reproduce the atmosphere of England did not prevent the Cape from developing a composite style of it own. Whites, blacks, Malays and Muslims from the Sunda Islands made up a population of fifty thousand inhabitants in which the half-caste was predominant, at least numerically. The lovely gardens of former days were now occupied by villas where the Europeans were installed as masters, directing the work of their employees and tenants, running business in the towns, and directing agriculture over large tracts of the surrounding countryside. They grew corn, and tried out viticulture, which made a promising start. Nevertheless, some foodstuffs had to be imported, especially since the ports, and particularly Port Elizabeth, had to provision passing liners. These ports were linked by railway and handled the bulk of the shipping. The South Africans relied on stock-breeding to pay for the imports, once the Dutch had acclimatized the cattle so profitably. In 1880, the bulk of the profit came from a most curious source – ostrich breeding. In twenty years the number of ostriches had risen from eighty thousand to almost one hundred and fifty thousand. The whim of Europe's best-dressed women had made its feathers as valuable as gold. In order to keep a monopoly of this magnificent trade, bringing in millions, the authorities strictly forbade the export of the eggs which all the breeders in the northern hemisphere coveted.

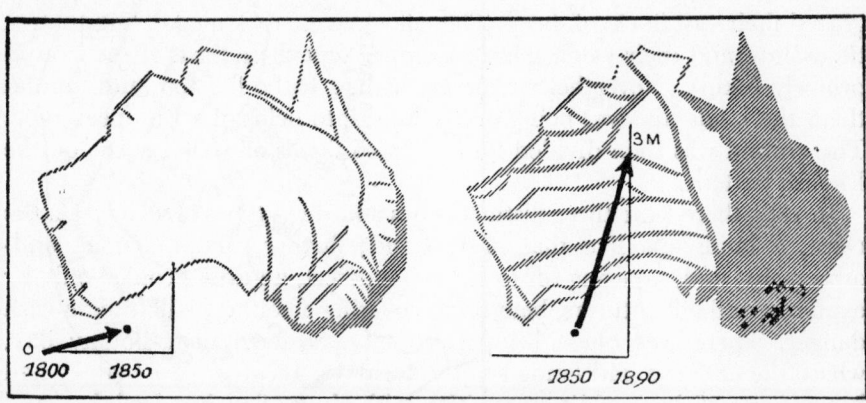

22 Australia: pattern of settlement and pioneer routes

The ostrich egg was then watched just as carefully as the tulip bulb had been two hundred years earlier. The vogue, unfortunately, proved just as ephemeral. In 1885 a caprice of fashion changed Europe's habits, and the Cape abandoned its ostriches and turned to more stable resources – the mines. Already the coal-seams had attracted Cornish miners, then copper was discovered, then when deep holes were being dug, diamonds came to light, not far from Kimberley. In 1887 alone seven tons were extracted. Police, guards, capital and covetousness abandoned the ostrich farms for the sites which yielded these precious stones, and the diamond-cutters of Amsterdam made them into the loveliest jewels in the world. Thus in spite of the rudimentary equipment of the first mines, and the cheapness of Negro labour, Kimberley experienced all the bustle of an up-and-coming industrial city, and speculation was rampant, just as in America.

Farther north, in the Boer republics, there still prevailed the grand old tradition of stock-breeding, carried on by the isolated Calvinist patriarchs who lived cut off with their families in the middle of several thousands of acres, which they left only once or twice a year to take communion in a chapel isolated in the great expanse of the veldt. These huge estates were split up by inheritance, under the control of the Government of Pretoria. Pretoria, a large town full of huge country houses, watched like a father over the social evolution of the surrounding plains. Families were prolific and medium-sized farms rapidly increased at the expense of the ancestral lands, a process not so very different from that which changed the face of the pampas and created new nationalisms there.

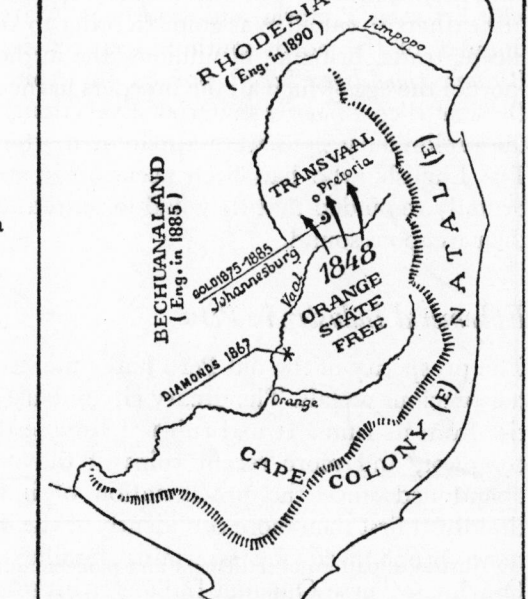

23 South Africa

South Africa;
movement of the
population from
1848–90. See map 11,
p. 171

Deposits of gold had also been found there, but of too poor a yield to warrant exploitation in 1880. Then came a sharp rise in the price of gold; with the invention of new mining plant and the discovery of dynamite, the number of prospectors increased, and bankers began to take an interest. By 1884 speculators were taking an interest in the little railway from

Pretoria to Lourenço Marques; Germany supplied the material and the English capitalists at the Cape, Natal and Kimberley had shares in it too.

The great diamond king was Cecil Rhodes, who grouped all the mines into the De Beers Mining Company. He became the head of the Chartered Company, of which the Prince of Wales was one of the chief shareholders. Then he was Minister at the Cape in 1890, undertaking the colonization of Rhodesia. The railway pushed on and the old Boer stock-breeding was threatened on every hand by the new urban development. This was stimulated by gold in spite of the heavy taxes imposed by the Boer administration. Johannesburg rose from three thousand to one hundred thousand inhabitants in ten years (1896). The increase was bound up with the influx of innumerable Britons who claimed civic rights from the elderly Krüger, which the local government was afraid to grant. Already India was beginning to pour in a labour force which rivalled that of the Negro. A whirlwind of conflicting interests raged around the old patriarchal farms: the Dynamite Ring, the dynamite trust, hesitated between giving substantial support to the Boers and rallying to English interests. The German firm of Krupps undertook to provide, with the help of Le Creusot and the approval of William II, the vast material needed for building a railway between Pretoria and Lourenço Marques capable of stealing the thunder of the north–south railway envisaged by Cecil Rhodes. The *Berliner Handelsgesellschaft* poured in capital and technicians, and the *Deutsche Wagon Fabrike* material. Everything was building up to the war; the preliminary signs were apparent in 1895, and it broke out in 1898. The English, who had been accustomed to win without fighting, were brutally reminded that they had forgotten to keep their army young and their weapons sound.

Ephemeral Industry in Peru

The prosperity of the old Peru had come from her mining resources and her precious metals. The dreary city of Cuzco seemed as if it would never rise from its ruins. It had ruins of Inca settlements abandoned since the conquest, and more recent ruins of the palaces of Spanish noblemen, abandoned since the proclamation of independence and taken over, timidly at first then more confidently as the decadence of the town became more pronounced, by swarming families of half-castes and even by Quichuas. These Quichua Indians, with stern, forbidding faces, did little to enliven the small city of barely thirty thousand inhabitants. They only showed signs of animation and fell to prayer during the processions in honour of *Nuestro Señor de los Temblores*, behind whom they may perhaps have thought to see the tutelary power of their own gods. For as upper Peru was progressively deserted by its conquerors the old religion and the old customs revived, and supplications to the moon and the sun and the expectation of some fresh natural catastrophe brought a measure of relief to the melancholy lot of the great Indians.

On the other hand, Lima was becoming a brisk and flourishing city, animated by its port of Callao six miles away, with which it was connected by a tree-shaded road and a busy little railway. Callao was sufficiently prosperous and well-armed to have held out against a last Spanish attempt to retake it in 1866. Callao was the major gateway to Chile, the sister-nation on the edge of the Andes, and to Europe; and it was also an attractive holiday resort, gay with swallows. In Lima the two-storey houses built around a patio in Moorish style lined the approach to the old cathedral with its silver pillars. But Pizarro's cathedral was no longer without a rival: a Chinese pagoda was there as a reminder that the Pacific was no longer the limit of the white man's world, but a zone of communication with the Chinese world. The Chinese had been landing in great numbers for several years; they survived the coastal climate better than the Creoles, who succumbed helplessly to fever and childish diseases. Whenever there were Chinese and Negroes to do the work, the white man managed to get rich, in spite of the indolence of the dispirited Indian. Thus gradually a community of more than three million souls grew up in search of a national ethnical identity. The basis of its agriculture was still the tasty Indian maize, now improved in quality, and the various kinds of potato; but to these were being added wheat and barley, banana trees and sugar, and attempts were being made to grow coffee and cocoa, and even cotton (though the latter was only a passing phase). There were fewer agricultural innovations on the vast territories of the old landowners than on medium-sized farms where the state tried to install new settlers, and where England, as usual, tried to establish agricultural companies. The English also tried to scrape the last ounce of precious metal out of the mines, but very little gold, silver or mercury remained. Industry was almost non-existent.

In this context it is surprising that the magnificent railways were built. They were of no great length, but had immense difficulties to overcome, especially the rocky shelves more than twelve thousand feet high, which blocked the approaches to Lake Titicaca and the rich and coveted metal deposits on the high Bolivian plateaux. No financial help was available from Bolivia, for the suspicious Indians were anxious to defend their national heritage. The capital came from the guano trade. These deposits of seabird lime on the islands were first exploited in 1840. They were estimated at some tens of millions of tons, and the Quichuas had already used them in farming. European agriculture offered a good price for guano, more than twenty times its exploitation price in the 1860s, and ships by the hundred awaited their loads. In vast quarries, the armies of Negroes and Chinese hacked down the yellowish-grey manure, the new Peruvian gold. By 1880 Peru had exhausted all its reserves, and had built its railroads and a telegraph; but had still twenty years to wait before any industries were started. It was an insecure society, and no parliamentary régime could last in it. Order was preserved only by a military dictatorship.

The Adolescence of Three Nations

Chile, the sister-nation, continued to side with Peru against Spain every time that country made an unwise move. But Peru itself was Chile's major enemy on account of a stretch of coast which Chile won in battle in 1851 and 1881. This conflict must have had very deep roots, for even before the European conquest the rebellious Araucanians had waged war with the Quichuas. It was from this struggle that they had learned to stand up to the white invader. These proud Indians were not defeated until the twentieth century, and then they were only quelled with alcohol or absorbed by cross-breeding. In the eighteenth century the Araucanians had seized Spanish wives. In the nineteenth century the Creole Chilians married Araucanian wives. In 1880 the pure Araucanian was in process of disappearing. Yet this interbreeding did not prevent the white population from retaining its predominance: it doubled its numbers between 1780 and 1810 to reach the figure of seven hundred thousand. By 1880 it was already more than three million strong. An aristocratic republic emerged, governed by the big farmers and industrialists without too much difficulty after the revolutions of the thirties.

On the arable lands, which were fairly rich though not very extensive agriculture developed on the American pattern. It was already largely mechanized, and its prices could compete with those of North America. At all events Chile fed the Pacific Coast on European standards, even producing the best wine in the New World. The success of this agriculture encouraged immigration, and Chile was one of the few countries to which Frenchmen were willing to go. The average-sized farms in the vicinity of the towns developed around the latifundia of former days. The industrialization of Chile, encouraged by European capital, grew rapidly from 1840 onwards. Since the country remained unexploited till comparatively late, it still possessed gold, silver and copper: and the foundries were prosperous at a time when the telegraph and ships used copper wire and sheet copper. The Peruvian guano was almost worked out but Chilean nitrate appeared inexhaustible. It was the industrialization of Chile which led Germany to supplant England and France in Chile's activity and external trade. It accounts for the fact that Chile could even create great financial companies in which the local governor fought against European influence. Above all, it explained the success of the Chilean capitals. There was Santiago with its luxurious shops sheltered by portals, Valparaiso where the *Sud-Americana* Company acquired a large share of the Pacific trade in the face of international competition; and Punta Arenas, the most southernly city in the world, a centre of sheep-rearing on the fringe of the sub-Polar latitudes. So although Chile was on the southernmost tip of the world, it formed a small but prosperous nation on European lines.

In 1880, the whole of Argentina was hardly more populated than Chile. As we have seen, the landscape of the eastern Cordilleras and the Upper Parana showed certain affinities with that of Europe and was suitable for winegrowing and corn, but the plains of La Plata were, by their very immensity, far more unusual. The northern plains were soon colonized for their sugar-cane, and the central plains developed a modest agriculture on European lines, especially on the outskirts of the towns and in particular Santa Fé; but the greater part created an economy and a society of an entirely original type. The problem here was not to wrest the land from the Indian (Pampians and Patagonians had retreated before the white man without too much of a struggle) but to organize it. Millions of horned cattle had bred from seven or eight animals landed by a Spaniard and a Portuguese about the middle of the seventeenth century. The abundant grass made this herd the biggest in the world; by 1860 the counting of heads would have been an utter impossibility, for no-one knew the boundaries of properties, or to whom the cattle belonged; no-one even thought in terms of land-ownership. A methodical German traveller, Brackebusch, was amazed that an Argentinian could have acquired almost a million acres for a trifling sum. But in this ocean of grass, what really mattered were the homesteads, the places where herds could rest, the *querencias*, near a spring, a drinking pool, if possible near a grove of trees. For the rest, the guardians of the flock, the bow-legged gauchos, lived with their herds. When they were hungry, they slaughtered an animal, carved out what they required for a meal, sometimes retrieved the hide if they were not too far from the drying rooms, and burnt the remains of the body if they could spare the time. Horses, bulls, and cows were caught by lasso, and stopped by having their pasterns broken. There was little or no sharing of land between the sons of landowners, and very little sharing of transit zones and heads of cattle. Their fratricidal quarrels sometimes turned into revolutions, and Buenos Aires was shaken by revolutions caused by disputes between great landowners. These quarrels were the more violent the nearer they were to the cities. Around Montevideo, Santa Fé and Buenos Aires ownership and property – the words and the reality – assumed increasing importance, a more definite meaning, in proportion as the urban civilization inspired by Europe developed. The problem of boundaries became more bitter, battles more violent. The alliances of great landowners became armies of horsemen disputing the great river valleys and fighting for control of the capital cities, and the towns tended to be organized like fortresses. It was for this reason that the Argentine, or rather Buenos Aires, could be held successfully by the Rosas dictatorship. For Rosas the vital point was to keep under the authority of the city all the plains of La Plata. Against Rosas there stood out the gauchos of the northern La Plata, of Montevideo, which the vast estuary effectively separated from its Argentinian rival. From this conflict a new nation emerged – Uruguay, supported by Brazil, the southern part of which also consisted of a large tract of pampas, where the Rio Grande do Sul felt itself as gravely threatened as Uruguay by the centralization policy of Rosas.

This quarrel of the gauchos gave rise to the most extraordinary adventure in South America in the nineteenth century: the tragedy of the ambition of Paraguay. Here and there the Indians had succeeded in defending a section of the land, but on the Upper Paraguay where the Jesuit missions had flourished more than a million Indians had founded a proud nation, quick to take offence, swift to violence, handing down the office of dictator-president from father to son in the Lopez family. In 1857 Solano Lopez proudly reckoned his subjects at more than a million and a half. In 1870 he launched them into the most pitiless of wars against a coalition of Brazil, Argentina and Uruguay. The struggle lasted five years. Its violence may be estimated from the census of 1877 which revealed that Paraguay now had no more than three hundred thousand inhabitants, chiefly women. It is true that the difference in numbers had perhaps psychological as well as material causes: it revealed the indifference of many families in the interior towards the 'census of defeat'. Yet it was not impossible that the victims numbered something like a million. Around its capital, the little Spanish-American city of Asuncion, Paraguay withdrew

24 The New Republics of the Region of La Plata at the Time of the Paraguayan War (1865–70)

into solitude, the women inheriting the bitterness of their dead kinsmen. Yet this war served to make the frontiers clear and definite, and also crystallized the mentalities of three nations, the three republics of Argentina, Uruguay and Brazil.

Argentina and Uruguay evolved on parallel lines. Gradually the limits of property were fixed just as the nation had fixed its frontiers. The vast estate was still subdivided into huge *estancias*, but there were already some smaller agricultural units. The great ports open to emigration offered the newcomers a civilization similar to that of Europe. In 1876, Argentina, on the American pattern, divided the state lands into lots of 250 acres, distributed free to farmers on condition that they farmed them efficiently. This small farm changed the character of the towns, since it attracted shops, small trade, and craftsmen. Articles made on the spot by the European emigrants were substituted for manufactured goods imported from Europe. Cloth was still being imported, but fewer ready-made garments were brought into the country and weaving had already been started.

Suddenly and swiftly Buenos Aires began to expand. The houses, which up to then had been single-storey, rose higher. Hard stone was brought and mansions in Victorian style were built along the old streets. These were only twenty-two yards wide in conformity with a decision of the Indies Council, and they now stretched out into long boulevards. This over-rapid growth led to widespread epidemics, cholera and yellow fever, which claimed tens of thousands of victims. A sewage system had to be constructed, artesian wells sunk, and the distribution of water organized. Gas lighting was installed in the city. All this development entailed an enormous movement of money. In new marble palaces, the banks vied with each other in vulgar ostentatious luxury to attract the confidence and flatter the vanity of the rich. On the verge of bankruptcy, they telegraphed London, and London replied by sending credit. With it came English styles, furniture, and plant for handling goods or building railways. Within a few years the Spanish township became an Anglo-Saxon capital, the residence of the gaucho leader a great capitalist city. But though the style was English, the basis of the population, the proletariat of the city, was more and more Italian. About 1890, out of the four hundred thousand inhabitants of Buenos Aires, there were three times more Italians than Argentinians. It was the same in Montevideo.

The countries of the La Plata had to pay interest on all this new wealth and all this capital of European origin. Nothing could be easier; the casual, unorganized stock-breeding of 1860 was replaced by organized stock-breeding, in which Uraguay led the way.

The cattle were now branded by irons, watched over by the owner who chose the animals in good condition for the abattoirs, the *saladeros*. These factories were built on the American model: slaughtering and cutting-up were done on the conveyer belt system as in Chicago. The carcasses were carefully cut up, the skins were properly treated, and the meat was salted or dried, then loaded into the new ships for which steam ensured a swift and regular service. Argentina and Uraguay fed Brazil and Europe. England was one of the best customers for this cheap meat, and became quite accustomed to this tough diet until the invention of ships fitted with refrigerating plant provided a more palatable fare.

Positivist Brazil

Brazil was the largest country in the Americas after the United States, and almost equal to it in area ; nevertheless it was one of the most backward in the world towards 1880 in that its social structure was based on slavery. This was the chief concern of the small *élite* of intellectuals which brought something of Europe's social and intellectual outlook to the tiny capitals from the Rio Grande do Sul to Ceara. These cities gave an outlet to the sea for the vast, almost unpopulated states which stretched away into the interior towards the impenetrable forests. The intellectuals called for the abolition of slavery, particularly those attached to the law faculties of Recife and São Paulo where the law taught was strongly impregnated with French liberalism. In São Paulo they went so far as to found a Republican Revolutionary Party, which was prepared to break away from the rest of Brazil. They aroused some sympathy in the urban middle classes and even in certain rural areas where the farms were small, but the rulers of Brazil clung to a slave régime and expected the Emperor to maintain it.

Pedro II, though he was liberal in temperament, was also well aware how profitable slavery was to the Brazilian economy: it was slave labour which, in the eighteenth century, had worked the gold and diamond mines of Minas Geraes, and which had given Brazilian agriculture its present prosperity when the mines were exhausted. The staple crops were sugar and cotton in the north, and above all, from the beginning of the century, coffee in the centre, in the beautiful valley of Rio Paraya which linked Rio de Janeiro to São Paulo. Here the old court families had carved out large estates for themselves, where coffee grew of its own accord and supplied half the world's needs, in spite of rudimentary equipment. It was transported on mule-back to the markets and ports. These coffee barons constituted on the whole a fairly amiable aristocracy, professing a certain superficial liberalism and a somewhat *risqué* modernism provided it did not involve any threat to the ancient foundations of their wealth. However in the 1880s Brazil, like the rest of South America, was swept by a great wave of rejuvenation.

Just after the war with Paraguay, the southern frontiers were more clearly laid down and the huge prairies of the Rio Grande do Sul were organized around Porto Alegre, and those of Uruguay around Montevideo. There too, republican and anti-slavery ideas rook root all the more easily since gaucho stock-breeding did not use slave labour. Farther north, European emigration populated small cities with Germans who introduced the customs and architecture of traditional Germany and supported the reformers. In the centre, commerce was beginning to transform the urban centres of São Paulo, Rio de Janeiro and certain privileged towns of old Minas. Average-sized farms came into being which could no longer afford to buy slaves (the trade was practically abolished from 1850) but which made a strong appeal to the immigrant and the settler, particularly the Italian. At the port of Santos tens of thousands of these immigrants landed to grow the new coffee. Since currency was limited, the settlers were often paid with gifts of land or small farms, which were not large enough to provide them with a livelihood, so that they remained dependent on the landowner, but were sufficient to keep their alligeance so that they were anti-slavery. All these immigrants, these *agregados*, increased the number of electors supporting reform. The prosperity of the central regions provoked an appeal from the poorer sugar-growing areas of the north, the bastion of loyalty to the Portuguese dynasty, which were fast losing their population to the more modern areas. Lastly, the very prosperity of coffee and its trade led to accumulated capital and closer ties with the countries of Europe, especially England ; and all the capitalist organizations on the European model began to erect buildings in Rio and São Paulo in their usual palatial style.

The English had been watching developments in Brazil for some time. In 1807, they had asked John VI to put an end to slavery, and he had promised to comply. More effective than preaching was the display of new power with which financial capitalism dazzled the coffee barons – the power for instance, of Mauà, who built the railway from São Paulo to Santos for the transport of coffee. He was the moving spirit behind the great enterprises which carried the railway over the maritime sierras towards the vast plateaux of the interior; he founded banks, of which one in particular played a great part in the development of Buenos Aires and Montevideo; and he installed the transoceanic telegraph cable. It is true that after he was abandoned by Pedro II, he fell into bankruptcy in his old age, but the impetus towards a new capitalism had been given. The settlers, the small and medium landowners, the urban middle classes, strengthened by the success of the great maritime liberal capitalism on the European model, soon developed such self-assurance that the coffee barons were swept away. The Emperor gave way, and was glad to do so. In 1874 the law of free birth was passed (the children of slaves were to be born free) ; in 1888 the Empire abolished slavery and foundered along with it, to be replaced by a republic of Paulist inspiration in 1889.

Economic changes had paved the way for this dual, peaceful revolution of society and of the state by 1880; and the intellectuals were already preparing the way for the legal framework. The Brazilian middle class *élite* was only too well aware of England's century-old economic ambition and its pressure on Portugal, and at the same time they strongly admired French culture, which had already had a great influence in the eighteenth century in Lisbon itself; consequently they preferred capitalism on French lines to English capitalism, although the latter had built their harbours, their railways, and their telegraph. The young Brazilians of 1880 were positivist, and preferred to entrust the leadership of the country to scientists, technicians and theorists rather than to bankers. The part of Auguste Comte's teaching which particularly appealed to them was his polytechnician's belief in well-co-ordinated legal systems, in scientifically planned projects. Paraguay's young, victorious army studied Auguste Comte in its military academies just as many middle-class citizens in Rio read him in their libraries. The fanatics fostered in Rio itself a positivist cult which was far more successful than its counterpart in Paris. The most ardent of the Brazilian positivists accused the Parisians of hypocrisy. The new flag of the Brazilian Republic bore Auguste Comte's motto: Order and Progress.

This admiration for positivist technique led Brazil towards industrialization. From the eighteenth century mineral resources had facilitated the process, then coffee, cotton and sugar gave rise to the subsidiary industries of bark-stripping and drying, and the manufacture of alcohol. Now a search was being made for coal; the immense deposits of iron were being mined, and work had begun on currency reforms. The hopes of the new generation of Brazilians were not to be realized all at once, naturally. Buenos Aires reached the industrial stage more quickly than Rio, at the beginning of the twentieth century, simply because the mountainous forests of Brazil offered greater resistance than the Argentinian pampas. The economic policies of Brazil were ruthless but, together with the battle against the trees, achieved a good deal of land clearance. Brazil represented one of the most characteristic areas where European capitalism supported pioneer developments in the Americas. Ironically, the methods increased in efficiency just as the pioneer zones themselves were disappearing, swept out of existence by the success of capitalism in the United States. This efficiency enabled great numbers of people to be displaced to the interior of Brazil, and towns were created there which immigrants from Europe soon came to fill, so that the foundations were laid for an urban proletariat. As a result the rise in population was enormous. From three million inhabitants in 1880 it rose to fifteen millions in 1890, so that Brazil became in this respect the leading nation in South America.

A REVELATION – JAPAN

Towards the close of the century an entirely new topic was beginning to enliven conversation in political circles and to provide subjects for caricature in the illustrated papers – the great power of the little 'Jap'. The Americans had been following the evolution of the Pacific peoples fairly closely, whereas Europeans were less well-informed and therefore astounded by this revelation. A revolution was in fact taking place in east Asia and its results were noticeable throughout the following fifty years. The change in Japan was all the more surprising because of its isolation. In earlier chapters it was possible to devote long pages to the Asiatic problem without a single mention of Japan. The Japanese remained enclosed within their islands, and exerted hardly any direct influence on the rest of the world; and if their art, their historical remains, their language and their admirable paper were known and appreciated beyond the frontiers, this was due, paradoxical though it may seem, to Chinese merchants. Maritime China was in fact much more internationalized than insular Japan. Classical Japan had been built around entrenched camps at Yedo, the seat of military power which had defended Japan in the Middle Ages against the Tartar invasions and had withstood the great Kublai Khan. The feudalism arising from this military power had become so deeply rooted that the Shogun, the leader of the Daimoys, had become more powerful than the legitimate sovereign, who was reduced to the rôle of pontiff in his ancient palace of Kyoto. These Shoguns had at first welcomed the navigators from the West, and this people which had formerly proved so widely receptive of Buddhist teaching from China seemed prepared to offer the early Christian missionaries excellent prospects of evangelization. Yet barely had the conqueror's weapons been discerned behind the preacher than a violent reaction wiped out both Christianity and Christians in a sudden, sharp upheaval. In the eighteenth century Japan was closed to newcomers from the sea, as it was to those from the continent. The whole *raison d'être* of the Shogunate lay in the strong moral obligation felt by the Japanese to defend themselves against the foreigner.

Japan was less attractive to Western capitalism than China, and at first seemed to resist its infiltrations more firmly. The ports and deltas of China, which were after all very near the Japanese coast, were becoming Europeanized, and the whole of the Pacific was being commercialized by Western influence, as much through the activities of emigrant Chinese as by white men from Europe or America. But the Japanese proudly maintained their independence. Towards the middle of the century, however, pressure was becoming so strong that in a few years their resistance broke down. At first the Russians had tried to obtain in Yedo what they had obtained in Peking: they failed. Then the Americans appeared in force and in 1852 Commodore Perry made his entry at the head of a squadron. The Shogun authorized foreigners to trade in Japanese ports, but his capitulation did not mean that Japan as a whole had capitulated. At first foreign ships, especially steamships, were objects of curiosity and interest. Small local potentates had bought a number of these vessels and so acquired overwhelming prestige, but they left them to rust uncared for in the estuaries. Then the people themselves began to revolt; after all they had been taught to mistrust the foreigner for a thousand years. The Western fleets replied to the rioting by a cannonade. Then popular fury turned against the Shogun, understandably enough, for the régime had lost its *raison d'être* once it had become powerless to protect the country against the foreigner. One after the other the Daimyos acknowledged defeat. One set the example by knocking down his castle and ploughing up the land on which it had stood. Popular hopes now centred in the ancient Kyoto dynasty; it issued orders to the Shogun which he was powerless to carry out. Then the Mikado left his old palace, and installed himself as ruler in Yedo, out of which he created Tokyo as his capital in 1869. Tokyo, the capital of the east, was already 400 years old, and had been built around the palace of the Tokugawa Shoguns. All the Daimyos had built their own dwellings around it and had soon filled them with servants and dependants. In the eighteenth century it was a vast city, perhaps the biggest in the world. Strangely enough, although Japan had placed excessive restrictions on external trade it had always had an extremely active internal economy. Tokyo was, in fact, less like a city than a gigantic conglomeration of villages with innumerable temples, connected by lovely avenues along which sped thirty thousand rickshaws. It was not, however, organized like our Western cities: its population had almost vanished on the fall of the Shogun, then it reappeared when the new government was organized. Tokyo was a *parvenu* in comparison with Kyoto, the capital, which was a religious centre and the very shrine of the celestial dynasty. It was built on the lines of a beautiful garden and divided into two regions: that of the imperial palace and that of the day palace, the seat of the Shogun's representatives. Kyoto was a city of refinement, elegance, tradition and perfect craftsmanship, but after 1869 it became a museum city, with a thousand temples. Tokyo expanded with new activity and was largely run by businessmen, the overwhelming majority of whom went over lock, stock and barrel from the Shogunate to the Mikado.

One of these businessmen became famous. The name of Mitsui conjures up one of the most formidable economic forces of the nineteenth century. It had been borne by a Kyoto merchant in the twelfth century, and in the sixteenth century it was still the name of a merchant, but one living in Yedo in the service of the Shogun. In the seventeenth century Hashirobi Mitsui was perhaps one of the most original pioneers of modern business: he went in for publicity on the grand scale. On rainy days (it rains a great deal in Japan) he gave away to his fellow-citizens magnificent free umbrellas bearing his name in large letters. Mitsui was the government's banker, the biggest capitalist in Japan. In fact Japan had been a capitalist country since the eighteenth century. Its Shogunate structure cut it off from the rest of the capitalist world, but inside its forbidding walls the most obvious of Western economic methods were practised. At the beginning of the nineteenth century large numbers of Japanese business apprentices travelled to the West to study the techniques of banking and commerce, property and law. Several members of the Mitsui family travelled in the United States.

The events of 1869 were not therefore a miraculous transformation, but rather the inevitable resolving of a paradox; for hundreds of years Japan had existed as a capitalist country in isolation, though all its neighbours had been won over to capitalism. There was no tidal wave when the trade dikes eventually collapsed: Japan took its natural place in the modern world, for which centuries of development had prepared it.

The Mitsuis gave their full collaboration to the Mikado of the Meiji era. The first essential was to give the country a flexible monetary structure. The Mitsui Bank was to serve as a model for the national banks which quickly increased in number, and for the Bank of Japan which co-ordinated their efforts. Paper money was no novelty. However, its circulation increased considerably. An increasing number of officials had to be created and paid, to import plant and offer capital to go-ahead businessmen. The state itself turned *entrepreneur* on a large scale. It prospected for deposits of coal and iron, and exploited them directly; it undertook cotton manufacture and bore the cost itself if any of these enterprises failed. If, however, they succeeded, private capitalists benefited, since in that case the Minister of Industry and Commerce, an associate of the Mitsui, proclaimed that in the name of liberalism these factories which had proved their worth were to be resold to private owners. Mitsui, Western fashion, knew how to play public interest and non-intervention against each other. Just as the government of Louis-Philippe defrayed the costs of the railway companies in order to sell them at a higher price, so the Japanese state created industry in order to sell it back to private enterprise.

If the Mitsuis were obviously the chief beneficiaries of this operation, they were not the only ones. Another famous success story was that of the Mitsubishis, but it was more sudden and spectacular: the founder of this family was only an unknown peasant in 1853. He was the trusted agent of the Daimyo of Nagasaki, and in 1868 became the owner of all his commercial concerns. He owned warehouses and ships, and increased their number. It was he who supplied the Japanese troops with transport for an attempt on Formosa in 1874. His power grew so quickly that it soon offended Mitsui. The latter, head of the 'liberal' party, blandly argued in favour of giving a justifiable twist to liberalism in the name of the general welfare of the nation (1870); the government was to have its own merchant fleet. But this government fleet bungled its affairs. Mitsubishi, who had succeeded in winning over to his side the best naval personnel, was able to buy back the state equipment at cheap rates. In 1882 Mitsui made a fresh effort. In 1885 Mitsubishi won another and similar success: this *parvenu* had become the master of Japan's sea-going trade. He had learned how to defend his interests in the new ministerial offices, he also had his own party which he called 'progressive' and his own political orators. He soon extended his activity into innumerable new branches, banks, business concerns, iron mines and so on.

Thus in Japan as in Europe political and economic activities were closely linked. And after the changes of 1869 the political framework was apparently the same as in Europe: the Supreme Committee corresponded to our Cabinet, and was, like it, anxious to have a supporting majority in the legislative Council, which corresponded to our Parliament. But under the superficial labels deep-seated differences did exist, precisely because Japanese capitalism was not a creation of 1869. It was Hashirobi who drew up the Charter of Ancestors which laid down the age-old traditions which were to remain valid to the present day. Two principles of this code deserve special note: first, 'the fortune of the dynasty depends on the harmony between the various families of which it consists. They should remain united in one group, remembering that an isolated branch is quickly broken. Next, each family must choose a head who will lead it intelligently, ready to seek advice but taking the decision on himself.' Thus family organization helped capitalist concentration. Mitsui had merely repeated the essential points of ancient tradition, so capitalism inevitably acquired such a directly feudal flavour throughout the whole of Japan. The influences that affected capitalism affected the state too. The Emperor was not only referee between the parties, but continued to be the incarnation of god, and therefore high above any constitutional suggestion. This attribute of his gave a very special significance to the privilege of direct access still enjoyed by naval and military commanders. It meant that the armed forces, as in the days of

Shogun feudalism, retained an important place in the nation and represented it more fully than the representative assemblies. Capitalism had
long known how to play on this military omnipotence; it should be remembered that Mitsui had been the banker of the Shogun, the military
leader. The new business families formulated their policy as much in the
war councils as in the councils of the parties. It was as easy to secure
national unanimity for programmes of capitalist expansion as it had been
to secure it during the past thousand years for rejection of the foreigner.

Therein lay the real meaning of the events of 1869 in Japan, which
adopted Western-style capitalism and promptly conquered it instead of
resisting it as before. The obvious course for Japan was to take full advantage of its place at the centre of the enormous bustle of activity which had
erupted from the white man's world and which was in full swing all around.
Japan joined in this activity, increased its vigour, and directed it to Japan's
own advantage. Japanese capitalism only needed to copy Western methods
to reach quick success, which explained why Japanese patriotism, forged
by a thousand years of the Shogunate, was so quickly shaken. The Japanese
peasantry soon became landowners on the French pattern, but here it was
not, as in the West, new land legislation which drove the rural population
to the towns, since agrarian 'reform' was a logical continuance of the past.
Instead of paying the state a rent, they paid it a tax: the structure of land
tenure was not upset.

In Japan, the increase in the urban population was not due to agrarian
changes, but to the new conception of national honour which had been
Malthusian but now tended to favour larger families. This rise in population filled the ports, the barracks, and the suburbs. After 1870 the population increased by more than three hundred thousand a year, and in 1890
Japan had the highest proportion of children and young people in the
world.

All this surplus needed feeding. This was achieved first by more intensive
agriculture, or rather horticulture, since the Japanese peasant worked only
with spade and pick on tiny plots. One single crop, rice, could give a yield
sufficient to feed the forty million Japanese. It was carefully sown by hand,
grain by grain. Fish was more often used as manure than as food, since in
that way it was more profitable. So Roman law, the return of which had
encouraged stock-breeding in England, brought no modification of agricultural techniques in Japan. Fresh activity in the ports, combined with
the introduction of new techniques, may possibly have led to improvements
in fishing, and to a more efficient exploitation of the fabulous riches of the
sea. But the huge old nets, almost a mile in length, drawn by a hundred
men, already brought in thousands of salmon. On the whole, there was
little change in the country's food supply, and industrialization never experienced the relatively slow phases which resulted in the West from the
requirements of agriculture.

It is probable that in these conditions the reform of the Japanese economy
was accompanied by a greater incidence of poverty. The disappearance of

the Shogunate caused the people much hardship and suffering. Patriotism led to an increase in population, but it also had to teach endurance and patience to the starving. Theoretically the new political statute ensured for the workers crowded into the new factories the right to complain, to organize themselves and to resort to strikes, but in fact the terrible law of 1890 severely punished those who resorted to 'defamation' in order to ensure the success of a concerted action. The police force, in which most of the previous feudal guards of honour had taken refuge, could easily use this law as a pretext for putting any leader in a position where he could do no harm. At the turn of the century the strike of four hundred railwaymen was considered unique. With workers' unions paralysed, the bosses could play the father to their employees, and readily granted them advances on scandalously low pittances, so putting them at their mercy, sometimes for generations. Given these starvation wages, and the traditionally meagre diet, Japanese goods could astound the international market with their cheapness. Already the Japanese merchant was insinuating himself into every European capital; polite, gentle and modest, he excited more curiosity than fear, and won on every count. From 1870 on, Japan was integrated into large-scale Western capitalism, and was subject to the rhythm of its crises even as early as 1873. The same expansion and development took place in Japan that accompanied the railway age everywhere. Railways and post offices were built, large-scale trade was initiated, and an enormous inflation of notes and credit followed. The 1873 crisis in Europe meant a crisis in Japan too: the monetary system was readjusted and industry reorganized. Japan was then in a position to take ample advantage of the few years of prosperity around 1880.

The volume of business rose in three years from two to forty-eight million yen; then came the European crisis of 1883, as a result of which the building of Japan's railways was suspended for many years and the currency was in danger in spite of the continued daring of bank credit. Then, when the Japanese were thrown back on themselves, they supplied their own needs and rearmed, with the result that the iron and textile industries were booming. When prosperity returned, there was an extraordinary increase in the number and activities of business companies, unused capital was pooled and a feverish activity began on the railways, whose network was still further extended. It was the beginning of Japan's greatness, followed by the victory over China and the occupation of Korea.

Thus this famous series of crises which marked the years 1875–95, and brought about profound changes in Europe, as we shall see, produced a new phenomenon in Asia, the power of Japan. Korea more or less vanished before it. Japanese capitalism, together with Japanese diplomacy and armed forces, seized hold of the country in one fell swoop and directed its exploitation everywhere at once within a few weeks. This was, of course, the work of the Mitsui trust which founded a company in 1890 for the development of civilization in the Far East. But Mitsubishi was not idle, either. In 1893 he provided not only the ships needed for the transport of troops and horses but also auxiliary cruisers; he was in control of Korean shipping and also of its rice trade: both penetrated into China, set up factories in Manchuria, and established a skilful commercial apparatus intended to oust Russian competition from all their trading posts.

It is impossible here to go into the full details of this activity, decisive though it was in the evolution of the Eastern world, yet its significance must be stressed. Tokyo competed successfully with Peking, the city of the Manchu dynasty. The situation had taken a strange turn since the days when the Kublai threatened the coasts of Japan, compelling the Japanese to shut themselves up in their island. The effectiveness of Western methods was proved to the whole of the East. In Japan every village of six hundred inhabitants was legally required to open a school. Colleges were founded, universities had thousands of students, generous endowments were given to encourage education throughout the whole country. To the School of Medicine in Nagasaki, which was already half a century old, engineering schools were added, then a whole series of faculties, of universities which often recruited their first staffs from Europe or the United States. Foreign engineers and professors were, however, used only to educate the Japanese as quickly as possible, since their whole aim was concentrated on learning enough from the foreigner to be able to take his place. This activity and its success drove the Chinese to a strict searching of conscience, with what effect we shall observe later.

12
The Continents Resist

THE great world conquests of Western Europe had been achieved by sea. It remained to be seen how far they could penetrate inland. England and France would have to impose their own legal and intellectual structures on these new countries if they wished to ensure the success of capitalist industry, and industry itself would have to adapt to worlds whose heritage and entire outlook were so unusual and different; and if industry did become established in any new country, it remained to be seen if it in turn would lead to the adoption of Western institutions, Western ways of feeling and thought. In fact the outcome was different in each of the three major countries: technical success and spiritual failure in India; in China, success on the coasts and along the great navigable rivers, but failure in the interior; and finally, a unique result in Russia. Russia had been orientated westward since the sixteenth century, and Peter the Great had built his capital on the sea, but in the nineteenth century Russian interests turned to the vast expanse of Asia. In Western Europe the railways had secured the future of an industry that was geared towards export, but in Russia the railways served to consolidate an enormous continental bloc. In spite of external resemblances, no Russian achievement had quite the same meaning as any similar achievement in the West. In short, from the late nineteenth century, it became clear that there were limits to the assimilation of Eurasia by Europe. Because central Asia was less affected by Europe's revolutions it was the more affected by the slow Russian migrations, which consolidated a vast Empire.

INDIA EXPLOITED, BUT NOT CONVERTED

The Indian Mutiny is generally regarded as a turning-point in Indian history. Up to that time the peninsula had been run in the name of the Moghul Emperor by the East India Company. After the Mutiny, when the Company was abolished in 1858, a chain of events began which terminated in the celebration in Delhi in 1877 when Queen Victoria was proclaimed Empress of India. This may have represented a western triumph in the technical sphere, but was certainly not where customs, way of life, and religion were concerned.

It is impossible to deal adequately here with an event as important as the Indian Mutiny, and a brief outline must suffice. Lord Dalhousie was the most ardently modernist of governors. He worked to increase the Company's possessions substantially, extended them beyond the continental frontiers, and pressed for the modernization of the whole country. Progress was his religion, and he hoped that a vast technical expansion would bring back prosperity to India and reconcile its divergent races. He rushed changes through too quickly (hampered perhaps by the Crimean and Chinese wars), and precipitated the catastrophe, exactly as the over-hasty modernization of Europe in 1846 had brought on the revolutions. Almost as soon as it was annexed by the Company, Lucknow was the scene of a terrible revolt (1847) which soon spread to the neighbouring city of Cawnpore. The corpses of Europeans were piled up by the notorious Nana Sahib, who was never captured by the police, and there were sieges and counter-sieges. Eventually the Sepoy revolt was crushed by the electric telegraph and the mobilization of troops transported along the first railways and roads, and by the new swift steamers. Lucknow became one of the most Europeanized cities in India. The town was started in the eighteenth century, then fortified by the Frenchman Claude Martin in the early nineteenth century, until the old Rajput shrine became a formidable English arsenal as well as the English garden city of modern India. Dalhousie saw himself as the most progressive of governors, but he was, in fact, the cause of a terrible war. Nevertheless, modernism had gained a footing.

In the economic sphere new crops were more readily introduced in lands subjected to the new régime of ownership. The output of corn grew in proportion to the English and European demand, and even exceeded it in the 1880s, when the quantities exported increased fiftyfold. Vegetables from Europe, too, were being grown in market gardens on the outskirts of the great new cities. The demand from England in particular increased the production of coffee and tea. Coffee had been introduced before the English conquest by Muslims who imported it from Arabia. Tea was hardly known at the beginning of the nineteenth century except as a wild plant. The Company sent for workmen and young plants from China. In the middle of the century joint stock companies boldly launched out into tea-growing and the tea trade, and speculated so heavily that they went bankrupt. In the 1880s work was resumed and pursued more methodically; in ten years, exports to England increased fivefold. In London, tea from Bengal and Ceylon threatened the popularity of China tea. Then there was the strange story of opium: its sale was so profitable that the Company and the Government organized its cultivation under supervision, and the best land was set aside for it in Behar, Bengal, the Punjab and the Central Provinces. Elsewhere it was forbidden. The Government also organized its sale in China and Indo-China and the profits were so considerable that in 1880 they represented more than one-tenth of the revenue.

Although Indian rural life was transformed, the old spells of famine persisted. The violence of these cataclysms had not diminished during the past century: in 1868 in the Punjab there were more than a million dead. Over a million more died two years later in the plains of the Ganges, a region which contained the poorest peasants, though it also had the biggest estates and the richest lands in India. In 1877 all the previous appalling records of disaster were broken, and several million people died; whole districts were depopulated and corpses strewed the towns and villages of Hyderabad, yet at the same time Bombay, Madras, and Calcutta were loading on to English ships their usual cargoes of rice and corn destined for export. Profit took precedence over all other considerations. With a monetary system replacing the old régime of collective mutual help, it was probably the poverty of the Indian peasants rather than insufficient production which was at the root of these great catastrophes. It is true that the government authorized distributions of corn and provisions, but the quantities were hopelessly inadequate. India had, in fact, reached the critical point at which the European régime was beginning to drain off the most substantial of her exportable resources, but had not yet built up technical equipment sufficiently to meet local requirements.

In the south the old dikes had been rebuilt, in the north canals had been redug and strengthened, and the admirable river network of the Ganges had been developed. But European scientists still knew too little about Indian land conditions and peasant psychology to be able to effect any

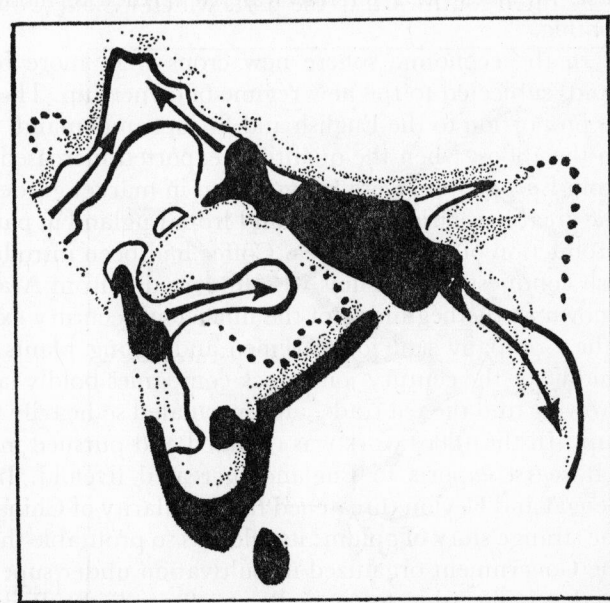

25 British India in the Nineteenth Century

Black: 1815
Arrowed: 1855
Dotted: after 1890

appreciable improvement in the old traditional methods of farming. Great efforts were made in about 1880 to combat excessive money-lending, a habitual sore in countries with an old structure invaded by Western capitalism; but apparently they had little success. The effect of capitalism was all the worse because, though the draining away of local resources by the railways ensured a better redistribution of products, in certain areas its chief effect was to deprive the country of the products it needed in order to send them to the great export ports.

The Company's first great achievement at the beginning of the century was the construction of the highway from Calcutta to the Peshawar passes. That great trunk road with its network of subsidiary roads penetrating the countryside, covered in all some one thousand, two hundred and fifty miles. On the roads the cart replaced the ox with pack-saddles, and a good police patrol carried on the old tradition of guaranteeing the inviolability of the leader of the caravan. In 1834 the Company authorized merchants to penetrate into the interior of the country. At about the same time the optical telegraph system was completed. With the 1850s the new steamers appeared on the rivers, laden with merchandise. In 1853 Lord Dalhousie, who had been a pioneer of railways in England, succeeded in putting through one part of a great programme of construction when he opened the first line from Bombay to Thana. Within twenty years the backbone of the railway system linking Bombay, Calcutta and Madras had been completed. The contracting companies were all the bolder since in India, contrary to English custom, the Government guaranteed their profits: this was partly because the railway played an important strategic role in the country. Soon, it ran alongside the road from Calcutta to Peshawar and penetrated southward to the ports which looked towards Ceylon.

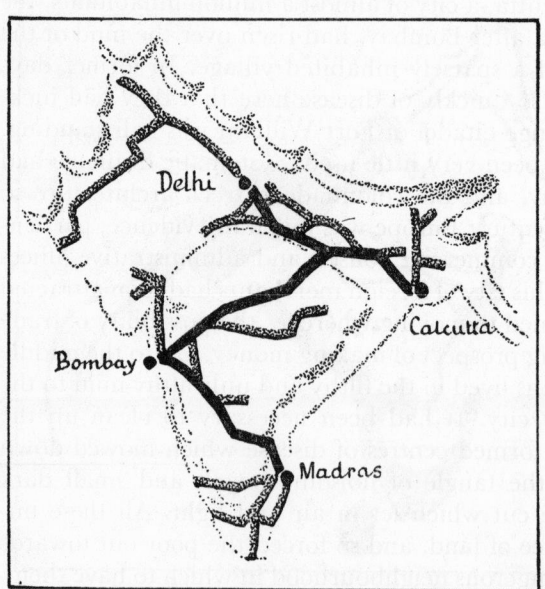

26 Railways in India

Black: 1870
Grey: 1880

All this railway building attracted capital from London. The example was infectious: local princes undertook the construction of local railways at their own expense (often with an amazing disregard for such problems of co-ordination as the gauge of the lines). Gradually the wealth amassed by the princes joined forces with European capitalism. The electric telegraph was at first reserved for the state, but it became a public service after 1854, and from 1855 the postal service included almost three thousand post offices.

The areas to benefit most from these changes which were transforming the old India were chiefly the coast and the powerful chain of cities erected by the English a century earlier. For if the interior of India changed little, the seaboard was transformed. Agra and Delhi, which had been the capitals of the old Moghuls because of their strategic importance, had again it was true become important junctions, thanks to the railways. But though travellers still visited them to admire the remains of mosques and palaces and to search for treasures in the shops of the stone and marble carvers, most of the magnificent palaces were being used as barracks for English soldiers. Agra lost two-thirds of its population. Delhi, the capital of all the empires of India, and scene of Queen Victoria's Durbar, was in turn eclipsed by a modern administrative Delhi which carried on the imperial tradition; yet this small modern city of one hundred and fifty thousand inhabitants seemed almost insignificant in comparison with the splendid ruins of old Delhi. These magnificent remnants of vanished continental empires which had lasted nineteen hundred years, covered an area of some sixty square miles, though they were now overgrown with scrub and brushwood.

In striking contrast, Calcutta, a city of almost a million inhabitants, the second city in southern Asia after Bombay, had risen over the mud of the Ganges delta on the site of a sparsely inhabited village. In former days European sailors had died so quickly of disease here that they had nicknamed it Golgotha. The huge citadel of Fort William was still standing, though after Plassey it had been very little used. Systematic drainage had made the site more healthy, and the colonnaded Greek architecture so fashionable in nineteenth-century Europe was much in evidence, particularly in the massive banks, commercial houses, and administrative offices erected by the capitalists. This city of foreign merchants had soon attracted crowds of Indians, accustomed to moving wherever the possibility of trade or work held out the alluring prospect of making money. Up to the middle of the century, all the Indians lived in the filthy and unhealthy mud to the north and east of the new city. It had been necessary to clean up the native quarters, since they formed centres of disease which mowed down the conquerors. Through the tangle of noisome hovels and small dark streets, great avenues were cut which let in air and light. All these improvements sent up the price of land, and so forced the poor out towards more distant outskirts, a dangerous neighbourhood in which to have them.

Calcutta was a success, and Bombay was an even greater one. The uninhabited island had undergone an even more spectacular transformation. At high tide the sea flooded the low-lying areas, so that the Europeans had to overcome it to build the city. Towards 1840 the caravans from Suez unloaded their English cargoes for India into Red Sea ships, and Bombay was the economic centre of the west coast of the peninsula. In 1860 the American Civil War deprived Europe of cotton. India's entire cotton harvest was collected in Bombay and sent through Suez or round the Cape to London, Le Havre and Hamburg. In 1869 the Suez Canal ensured for Bombay the place of the first city in southern Asia. Asia was changing from year to year almost visibly. In the prosperous 1860s the English in Bombay declared that they would make the city bigger and more flourishing even than London. The restoration of peace in America led to some bankruptcies and disillusionments, but nevertheless the city continued to grow. There again it was necessary to battle against epidemics, transform swamps into boulevards, eradicate cholera and the plague, and find a pure water supply. There the prevailing style was not so much Greek as Italian in the Lombardy Gothic, and around this European enclave of *nouveaux riches* the huge suburbs spread out into the nearby forest.

Calcutta and Bombay became industrial centres. We have already seen how in the eighteenth century the urban depôts attracted country cotton weavers. A century later factories were being built in the suburbs, and the weavers left their old looms to swell the urban proletariat. The concentration of Indian cotton manufacturing in the 1860s marked the end of the old rural weaving and mobilized raw material to the advantage of the coastal merchants, whose trading activities were even beginning to alarm Europe. The cotton industry attracted others, silk, jute, and also lace, and before long the need to keep all these factories supplied with machines led to the creation of a metallurgical industry.

Yet the development of European industries and the introduction of European plant and equipment did not necessarily imply any radical change in the Indian way of life. The English offered increasing rewards for the killing of snakes or wolves, but the people continued to worship them. A ruler still passed solemnly through a hollow cow of specially melted gold in order to become a Brahmin, which meant that any organized system of cattle-breeding was, as yet, out of the question. A few Christian missionaries acquired some little authority, but only in so far as they respected the caste system; the clergyman being carried from place to place in a litter did not dare to greet his brother evangelist on foot if he was an outcast. The poor people were ready enough to be converted to Christianity, but since they made it unclean by their contact they limited its influence.

After 1870, widows no longer threw themselves on the funeral pyres of their dead husbands, but the priests of Kali continued their human holocausts and did not lack suppliers. Siva, the favourite god of the trinity, underwent several surprising metamorphoses, and even acquired a blonde moustache; people worshipped the statues of the most ruthless English generals, and even the Prince of Wales. After all, for the English themselves, the traditional religion was a good instrument of government: it was understandable that the administration preferred it to Mohammedanism, especially to the intractable Wahabites who went regularly to Mecca to renew their faith and declared India to be the land of the Holy

War. This sect aimed to reinstate the former rulers of India and tried to win Persia over to its cause; this alarmed the English sufficiently for them to increase the number of guards on the great routes to Islam. The English had the telegraph on their side, and were backed up by realistic Muslims, but they gave up the attempt to convert the mass of the people to the capitalist and liberal way of life.

The last resort of the moneylender or usurer was to present himself at his debtor's house, dagger in hand, and threaten to kill himself on the spot and to bring down an everlasting curse on the family; this course of action succeeded where the regular courts had failed. Before 1858 the Company had made little attempt to develop education on a scale comparable to the tremendous needs of the population, and was less enterprising than the local potentates. In 1877 the entire activity of the great city of Bombay was brought to a standstill by a curious strike: the English municipal police had insulted a number of coolies. Passivity was India's reaction to the invasion of technical progress. This passivity was surely not so much a sign of weakness as the ultimate and decisive strength of India.

INLAND CHINA REJECTS CAPITALISM

The story of China at the close of the century was indeed a strange one. The Westerners were under the impression that they had conquered the dynasty: in actual fact they had strengthened it in its reactionary and conservative power, and had restored the old Manchus, who were being threatened by a wave of revolts and reforms which was affecting the whole country.

The End of the Celestial Mandate

The opening of the southern ports had not completely satisfied the commercial ambitions of the West. The cunning of the Chinese merchants of Canton was legendary, and the Europeans had the impression that China was selling them only what she wanted to sell. They therefore aimed to approach nearer to Peking, and open the ports of northern China. In 1856 the execution of a French missionary and the confiscation of a British ship provided an excuse for a fresh campaign: the time was admirably chosen, since China was being overwhelmed by the greatest disasters yet suffered by the Manchu dynasty.

The Taipings had been growing in strength since 1830. Starting from Kwangsi, the band was continually increased by conspirators who had been trained by secret committees for two generations. It seized Hankow, Kiukiang and Nanking in succession between 1852 and 1854, and constituted a serious threat to the north. They reached Tientsin and the Peking government became alarmed, since all the prosperous regions were affected.

Then catastrophe came. The Yellow River, the Hwang-Ho, left its bed, and people told how in 1780 the Emperor Kien-Lung had got together an army of workmen to dig a canal sixty-two miles long, capable of diverting the flood-waters of the 'Incorrigible River' towards a lake. The upkeep of these secondary canals and of the dikes which protected the surrounding countryside called for continuous effort, especially as the dikes were at a lower level than the river-bed. The civil wars disheartened the peasants and depopulated the regions where work was most urgent. In 1851 a breach almost a mile long opened up along the middle course of the river. For two years it gradually grew wider, and the river spread over the northern plains, until it found an adequate outlet some five hundred and sixty miles to the north. This left on the one hand the vast marshes of the old flood area, in places fifteen miles wide, and on the other deserts of sand between the walls of the old dikes. These useless ramparts no longer protected anything but an eternally drought-stricken tract of land. Villages were destroyed and cities abandoned, the countryside was choked with mud, flooded or dried up, and millions perished. Many complaints were directed towards Peking but with no result. If the Emperor was so powerless, people argued, did it not mean that he had lost the favour of Heaven? Was not this a sign from Heaven that the dynasty's rule was at an end? In 1870 there occurred a fresh breach, fortunately a less serious one, on the

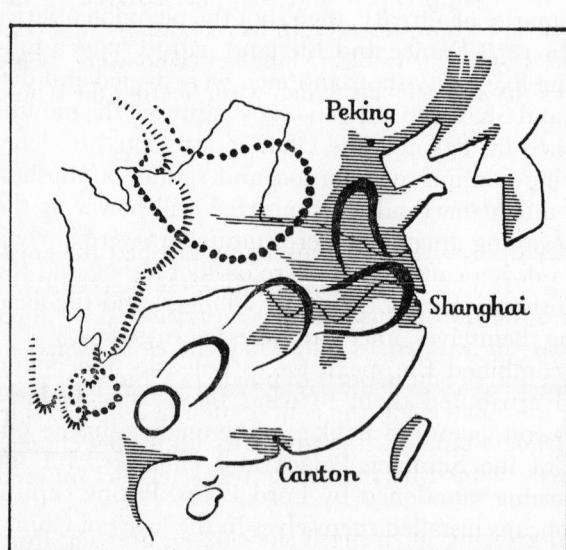

27 Difficulties in China

Dotted line: Muslim revolts
Thick lines: Taiping revolts
Grey: the Great Plain areas

south bank. A period of insecurity followed; the great canal had been cut into sections by the immense cataclysm, and liaison between north and south could no longer be effected except by the sea, which was controlled by foreigners. It seemed the end of the old China.

These great upheavals, which turned the discontent of the masses against the Emperor himself, were no new feature of Chinese history. They usually heralded the downfall of the dynasty. The legality of such a procedure was sanctioned by tradition: it was the method by which the Mings had ousted the Mongols. The situation was aggravated this time by the Muslim movement. This had reached China along the southern routes from India and along the northern routes from central Asia, and was provoking the usual unrest wherever it went. In 1855 a quarrel developed between Chinese and Muslims who were joint exploiters of a silver-bearing lead mine. The Chinese officials lost their heads, appealed to Peking and the Muslims were massacred. A wave of fanaticism (the real cause of the Anglo-French incidents of 1856) led to fears of a St Bartholomew of Muslims and Christians. An aged Muslim priest, Mateh-Sing, organized the resistance. He had travelled with the merchant caravans, visited the Arab worlds, made the pilgrimage to Mecca and Constantinople, and had witnessed the superiority of the seafaring nations. Soon, under his orders, thousands of men embarked on a campaign. They, too, marched northward and swelled the number of their troops from stage to stage of the march to Peking. Meanwhile disturbances were continuing in Kashgaria.

It was therefore in favourable conditions that the French and British attempted once more to force the Chinese stronghold. In spite of the Indian revolt which weakened the English expeditionary corps, the combined forces seized Canton and settled there (1858–61). The Chinese hedged. They accepted the preliminaries of a treaty, then shot the plenipotentiaries who came to negotiate. In 1858 France and England had to stage a full-scale war: in all, something like thirty thousand men were armed and dispatched towards Canton and Shanghai. In 1860 they captured the mouths of the Pei-Ho, and marched on Peking. The Chinese attempted to delay this advance by alternating cunning negotiation and sudden ambushes. Their action was not so much the result of concerted will-power as the effect of the confusion prevailing at court, where counsellors were at each other's throats, and half a dozen conspiracies were on foot at one and the same time: the central authority hardly existed any longer, and the local chiefs did not agree among themselves, uncertain whether to give way or to fight to the death. The combined European forces failed to understand these inconsistencies and attributed them to what they called Chinese duplicity. After the hard-won victory of Palikao, they made a furious onslaught on the gardens of the Summer Palace and embarked on the notorious looting and burning sanctioned by Lord Elgin. Peking capitulated. This time the Europeans installed themselves in the heart of China: they insisted on having their ambassadors at the court, and exacted handsome compensation for all the damage suffered by their protégés. Above all, their greatest victory was to ensure that Tientsin was opened up to international trade. It may have seemed that China would at last take its place on the list of great powers enrolled in the economic system of Europe; but this was by no means the case. Once again China's infinite complexity got the better of its conquerors. These were proud at having secured a treaty which brought the Manchu ruler from his sacred altar and gave their ambassadors the right to come before him without the kow-towing due to a descendant of the gods and master of the world, so they had now but one idea: to support the dynasty against its internal enemies. In 1861, then, the French and British turned their arms against the Taiping, who retreated, making a stand here and there, then disbanded, but not before large sections of their troops had descended into Indo-China, creating endless difficulties for the French troops. By 1864 the Taiping menace was averted. There remained that of the Muslims. In 1860 Mateh-Sing agreed to sign a treaty with Peking, but the holy man exacted merely trifling conditions, then failed to persuade his followers to continued obedience. The unrest continued until 1873. At Tali an independent sultan reigned for several years, attempting to recreate a southern Muslim empire; and until 1877 Kashgaria too was organized into an independent Muslim state under Yakub, who was proclaimed Emir by Constantinople and Commander of the Faithful by Bukhara.

If the Muslim resistance was broken, it was thanks to the help Peking received this time from Russia. Yakub, before defending his Kashgaria against China, had defended it in the name of China against the Russian claims. In 1871 it was the Russian technical missions which suggested to Peking the raid against Yakub; it was not therefore surprising that he was defeated. For a time in 1881 the Russians thought they could settle in the western part of the Kulja territory, but even Kulja returned to China. In short, after twenty years of crisis the Manchu dynasty won a comparatively unexpected victory with the help of the Europeans, who did not fully understand its significance for several years to come.

Inland China Remains Conservative

Towards 1868, a Chinese embassy, led by Westerners and presided over by a former American minister-plenipotentiary, travelled everywhere abroad to prove that this time China was well and truly converted to international collaboration, that 'crosses gleamed on the hilltops', that there were profitable openings for trade, and that progressive ideas were gaining favour there. It was all an illusion. The reality was very different. In 1870 some thirty Frenchmen (including the Consul) and French protégés were massacred at Tientsin. In 1873 there was an extensive massacre of Muslims of the Szechwan in south China in the kingdom of Tali, whose 'celestial king' had committed suicide a few years previously by swallowing gold. It wiped out his former followers. Eighty per cent of the population of Mongtze were assassinated. Tali was reduced to six thousand inhabitants. It was said that the number of victims ran into millions; certainly any subsequent Muslim coup in China was impossible. Though China allowed a few Englishmen to visit Tibet, which she wrote off as useless, she opposed English penetration of Burma, towards Yunnan. In Peking, the real authority fell into the hands of the Dowager Empress Tzu-hi who clung stubbornly to power. The Europeans had to wait for help from Japan before they could really penetrate the Middle Empire.

Nevertheless the Western world did reap something more than mere rebuffs from all these expeditions, embassies, and investments of capital: though the Chinese continent remained closed to them, they had a fairly firm hold on the ports and the seaboard. It was also in the Chinese imperial tradition that rebellious intruders should be in permanent possession of the outlets to the sea, to which the continental victors had driven them back. It was the logical consequence of the growth of coastal China, whose surplus population of industrious workers and skilled traders poured out across the Pacific. They were absorbed into the meshes of Western capitalism and in turn strengthened capitalism along the very borders of the inviolable Asiatic continent.

In 1880 then, there were two Chinas: one vast, impenetrable, remaining proudly loyal to the traditions of the Middle Empire; the other, intangible, mobile, efficient and growing in wealth, spilled out from Tientsin and Shanghai towards Saigon, Batavia and Singapore and even to Callao, Lima and San Francisco, which developed into the largest Chinese city outside China. Each needs understanding in its own right.

There was no difference between Chinese agriculture in 1880 and in the previous century, except that the Europeans knew it better and evaluated it more accurately. Consequently they praised it a little less fulsomely and it was noticed that the Chinese left considerable stretches of good land lying fallow. Moreover, much of the land was sacred, that of the pagodas, the cemeteries (which could apparently only be brought under the plough with each change of dynasty), and some territory belonging to the Emperor. In short, it appears to have been only in Shantung that more than half the land was cultivated. Another surprise was the scarcity of trees. Outside eastern China, with its forests and spinneys, there was hardly anything but bamboos growing around the sacred places and around a few privileged dwellings. The Chinese peasant had no fire in winter; he dressed in furs if he could, or put on several garments. For cooking, a tiny fire of twigs or roots served to cook food cut into very small pieces.

But the genuine merits of this agriculture were also studied scientifically. The harvest was rich in lands where the loess was deposited in layers several yards thick, where the streams cut steep cliffs, and where embanked tracks wound along the marshy hollows through the capricious waters. There, the soil was continually being renewed. The German chemist Liebig praised Chinese thrift and wisdom. Nothing which could benefit the land was neglected: refuse, human manure, crushed and powdered bones, ashes, everything, in short, was put back into it which could be recovered from organic waste. With his ancient rudimentary tools the Chinese peasant continually lightened his soil by breaking up the clods, levelling out the irregularities in the ground, finishing off this careful work with feet and hands, getting rid of every single weed, calculating irrigation to a nicety, analysing by long practice the least variations in soil so as to sow at the most suitable time of year the seed which experience had shown to be most likely to do well. It was gardening, rather than agriculture, a technique of perfection which continued to be held in high esteem; the Emperor himself opened the working season by planting a field near his palace. There was little livestock. Land was too scarce to be left for pasture. The larger-scale stock-breeding which the northern conquerors had wanted to reintroduce had always been quickly rejected. The ox and horse were pack and draught animals, old friends whom it would have been unthinkable to eat. It was permissible, on the other hand, to eat the pig and that very special delicacy, the duck, which the children guarded in enormous flocks beside pools or calm rivers. The farmyard was well stocked, and methods of artificial incubation had long been practised, as well as the correct feeding needed to produce good laying hens. Thus the Chinese succeeded in getting a living from their land.

Nothing, as we know, is more difficult to study than the system of Chinese land-ownership. Its history includes phases of collective village ownership, and of great feudal estates. In about 1880, at all events, there was no such thing as a single system of ownership. Observers noted that there were undivided lands, where families shared the work and the harvest. There were also small farms crowded close together, each of only a few hectares, which managed to keep a large peasant family alive. Ownership, moreover, implied responsibility in a country where famine was always just around the corner. The village headman could be beaten for having permitted lands to lie fallow, and after three years he had the right to take them away from their owner and to hand them over to someone more industrious. Then, too, since the tax on land was very light, there were great estates, so big that a part could sometimes be set aside for stock-breeding.

The peasant had to get all his food and indeed all his livelihood from his land, and in the same way the craftsman was responsible for every process involved in making the objects of his trade. Vases, materials, furniture, tools, wicker baskets, were fashioned by him right through from the raw material to the perfect finished article demanded by rigorous Chinese standards. Moreover, many peasants were also craftsmen: they grew, spun and wove their cotton themselves. Thus manufacturing secrets were handed down from father to son, from one family to another; the quality of enamel, of dye, of fabrics, could vary, yet be perpetuated from generation to generation in a well-guarded secret. A family without children (and in Chinese eyes that was a calamity, a punishment sent by Heaven which broke the continuity of ancestor worship) also meant the end of a manufacturing secret, an irreparable loss to art or industry. There were some larger enterprises to obtain salt by drying sea-water, and to extract coal from the seams. Bamboo was still the chief raw material for tools. These old traditional methods did give a limited opening to Western techniques; miners from Europe and a few machines were actually landed, and local groups were formed to work them, but only on the edges of the country, in Manchuria, near the sea coasts in Formosa or Pe-chih-li.

Everywhere the workmen tried to protect themselves. They had their own associations, which were more like groups of comrades than unions, drawing their strength from discipline. Strikes were always hunger-strikes and the workmen held out until they died if necessary in order to make an obstinate employer yield. Moreover, the claims advanced were always for such a small rise in wages that harmony, except in an agricultural crisis, was not broken for long.

Transport in the interior of the country remained the same as it had been for centuries. Heavy junks were towed along the rivers, and were dragged from one river to another, often by sliding along short stretches of clay. Most transport was still carried on the backs of men or animals, not along roads in the ordinary sense, but along tracks which crossed rice-fields and pools on flat stepping-stones. The towns were very varied in appearance; many were both town and fortress, surrounded by walls as thick as they were high, pierced with gates which were shut at night. Outside were great encampments like a fair in which all the commercial activity was carried on. There was always the juxtaposition of the Tartar and Chinese city. During troubled times, the outer town vanished, and the inner town shut itself up in its redoubt. Once peace was re-established, the bustle returned. The insides of the houses, at least of the well-to-do houses with their courtyards gay with flowers, were as clean as the squares and streets were dirty and stinking, at least in the late nineteenth century. Peking had greatly declined. Acres of unoccupied land and cemeteries stretched away even inside the ramparts. Some temples were better cared for than others, buildings were falling into ruins, and some of the palaces were deserted. The city may have lost a fair proportion of its population, and Bertschneider was probably right in putting its inhabitants at no more than half a million.

Inland China, in 1880, was full of gigantic ruins, but life was slowly returning to them. On the Upper Hwang-Ho in the heart of the rich loess country and amongst the coalmines already reckoned the richest in the world, the great city of Hangchow, the starting-point of the Muslim rebellion, had completely disappeared, razed to the ground in the repression which followed. In the district around Sining, merchants still went about armed, and business deals often ended in a pitched battle. A few large cities had been comparatively well preserved by their walls, as for instance Lanchow (which was re-built in European style and had kept its cannon-foundries and cloth factories). The Fuen-Ho basin, which derived so much wealth from its thick salt deposits, had been devastated by the Taipings. In the region of the Upper Hwang-Ho the population, which numbered approximately eighty million in 1840, had fallen by half in 1860, then picked up again about 1880.

On the Yangtze basin the devastation was equally great. The twelve thousand salt-pits at Tsuliu-Cheng were resuming work. They still used bamboo for their drilling, and after patient efforts over many years they had reached depths of several hundred yards. The workers forcibly opposed the introduction of European methods which many wealthy mandarins wished to adopt; they claimed the credit for extinguishing the devilish fires which had lit up the nights of the civil war. At Chungking an English consul had reorganized the great trade of this urban centre in 1878, and its prosperity was now reviving. The people were no longer reduced to baking rolls out of the greasy local earth. At Hankow, or rather in the group of three 'tributary' towns which had had nearly eight million inhabitants in the eighteenth century, the population began to come back and rose within twenty years from one to two or three million. Business was exceedingly brisk, but no longer based on the fabulous wealth of the subsoil as in former days (though the coal trade was starting again and doing well, owing to steam navigation which was developing on the Yangtze). The bulk of the trade was in tea, which accounted for the prosperity of the rich European quarter where English and Russians lived side by side. Downstream the famous ceramic centre of Kingte had not regained its past glory and seemed to have lost its trade secrets. But Nanking paid a heavier price than any other for its transitory fame as capital of the heavenly king of the Taipings (1853–63): the city was razed to the ground, its inhabitants were massacred or dispersed. Nevertheless it came back to life and retained its character as an intellectual capital.

As for the interior of China, it presented a picture of human desolation on land which was the most fertile in the world and which had been the longest inhabited by human beings. The Westerners took advantage of the disorganization to line their own pockets along the navigable rivers.

Nearer the coasts, the spectacle changed. In the ports business grew from year to year and was becoming increasingly international in character. China was importing the notorious opium. The Imperial Government had resigned itself to the fact; it had gone further and entrusted to an English official the organization of customs and duties, in order to extract as much revenue as possible from the accursed herb. China – and this was something new – was also importing part of her foodstuffs. This was, indeed, an innovation, since the Middle Empire had prided itself on being independent of foreign countries for its food supply. As for China's exports, silk was still, as in former days, a great source of wealth, and so increasingly was tea, which had become the habitual drink of the Anglo-Saxon world, whilst the poverty-stricken Chinese had to make do with elder leaves. It is interesting that the silk and tea trades had also kept to their two old continental routes: not this time, however, towards the Mediterranean, but towards Moscow across Russian Asia. All this expanding trade was not the exclusive monopoly of Europeans. The Chinese themselves took an active part in it, and with growing success, so skilful were they at manipulating money. Sometimes, too, they showed themselves to be intrepid sailors. China was familiar with paper money long before it became current in Europe and she even perfected Western improvements. Eventually the

Chinese gained a monopoly of commercial coastal shipping, ousting the Europeans and restricting them solely to large-scale international trade.

There were few railways. Technicians and financiers from England and America drew up imposing plans, but the Chinese Government rejected them all. Short lines ran along the quays in the ports, and in a few mining districts. One line had experienced a real popular success in the suburbs of Shanghai, but the Chinese Government bought it and dismantled it in order to transport the material to Formosa. Similarly, very few steamers plied the rivers; porters and boatmen monopolized the river traffic. Everywhere China tried to prevent the commercial influence of the barbarians from penetrating inland with its hated equipment. Thus the contrast increased between inland China which clung to old traditions and maritime China which had been seduced by Western trade. The great city of coastal China was Shanghai, which was fast becoming the largest mart in Asia. The Peninsula Company, the *Messageries Maritimes*, and a growing number of companies of all nations had their offices there and their place on the quay. Western banks and trading firms tended to make it their administrative centre for business in all the free ports. From Shanghai they tried to control the river trade, concentrating more on that of the Yangtze towards Hankow than on the famous but obsolete Imperial Canal leading to Peking. Shanghai, an old city, already recorded in the fourteenth century amongst towns of the third class, was very decadent in 1870 when it numbered barely 50,000 inhabitants. In 1885, an abrupt expansion raised their number to more than 350,000, and the foreign quarters comprised more than 3,000 English and French (5,000 when troops were stationed there).

This prosperity of the new Shanghai contrasted with the ruins of its neighbouring rival Hangchow, the ancient city of Quinsay, celebrated by Marco Polo as the city with 1,600,000 houses and 12,000 bridges. In the seventeenth century it had an estimated circumference of one hundred miles, and there were still two million inhabitants in 1850. It had no more than half that number in 1880; the war against the Taipings had reduced it to a most appalling scene of desolation, but it was still charming nevertheless, with its picturesque ruined pagodas and its overgrown gardens. Shanghai and Hangchow were opposites: two Chinas in confrontation.

This swift progress of maritime China revealed also the amazing adaptability of the Chinese, under the aegis of Tsai-Chin, the God of Trade. Their sobriety, their moderate tastes, enabled them to make rapid progress in competitive Western ways. They observed the Europeans carefully, but at the same time, partly from national pride but also out of an innate critical ability, preserved their own way of life and dress. They realized the superiority of certain foreign techniques, and tried to assimilate them. They had always been brilliant scholars, and were equally quick to assimilate new ideas from the barbarian foreign devils when they were travelling in Europe. Schools and newspapers were started. The Shanghai *Journal* had eight thousand subscribers in 1877. Maritime China was rapidly becoming modernized and the Japanese were working towards it even more than the Europeans. At first no one took these little Japs seriously, they looked so quaint in European dress. Loti in 1890 informed his French readers that 'the Japanese look like little old men, shrivelled and bloodless'. They were 'aware of their mummification'. Loti poked good-natured fun at this 'tiny, obsequious race, tainted with congenital affectation and an ineradicable apishness'. Writing at the same time, this same Loti praised the great and powerful Chinese, so majestic in his noble silken robe. Unfortunately he proved a false prophet. In 1895 the affected monkey crushed the incarnation of noble majesty. England, which had assured China of its goodwill, advised it to come to terms with the victor with all speed. The United States and Russia, more far-sighted, were becoming alarmed at the progress of Japan, which they were anxious to contain. After its victory Japan retained only Formosa and control over Korea. Russia had taken the measure of China's weakness, and now built a railway across Manchuria towards Port Arthur. Europe followed suit; it was the break-up of China. But although Europe was busy carving off pieces of the China seaboard, the aged Dowager Empress Tzu-Hi kept the centre of the Empire intact for another fifteen years. The story is a fascinating one.

In 1885 a book entitled *A History of the Japanese Revival* appeared in Canton. Its author, an educated young Chinese who had studied for a long time in Japan, insisted, and quite rightly, on the role played by Japanese patriotism in the changes which had been inspired by the West and which were intended soon to supplant it. The book met with violent opposition from the conservatives, who ridiculed this pretentious author and his ambition to be a modern Confucius. Nevertheless his appeal awoke some echo. The young Sun Yat Sen explained that the Young China Party was created in order to associate the throne with the much-needed reform movement 'in the hope that the aristocrats of Peking might come to understand the principle of constitutional government' and to beseech them 'in all humility to move towards a form of liberal government'. In 1898 the young Emperor was persuaded by his entourage to read the modern Confucius. He accepted the principle of reforms; the subject of the traditional mandarin examination in 1895 had been 'Confucius has said: *They were three*'. The problem was to transform the mandarin circles into schools where European and Chinese learning would be imparted at the same time. It was necessary to create cadres and to refashion the law, and something in the nature of a code was drawn up. If there was as yet no question of a ministry on European lines, or of a responsible cabinet, at least there was envisaged the creation of government departments one of which would deal specially with agriculture, the printing of technical journals, and the purchase of machinery. Furthermore, there was to be an attempt to reform the army on European lines.

This Chinese army was an interesting body. It consisted of a few corps organized on European lines; some bands hastily levied by the provincial war lords for a definite action; and the two most famous and important elements, the Eighteen Corps of the Green Flag and the Eight Banners. The Eighteen Corps were composed of Chinese but dispersed over the eighteen provinces and employed chiefly in the preservation of law and order and on certain public works; the Eight Banners was an army of Manchus and Mongols. It was they who ensured the security of the dynasty and who, in other words, were in complete control of the Tartar cities. These fortresses set in the middle of the great Chinese cities were a perpetual reminder of their defeat and subjection. These corps were the great beneficiaries of the Manchu régime. They were loyal to the old dynasty and the old principles, especially since soldiers and captains had received substantial grants of land on which, once they had settled, they brought up prolific families. Although they were of little use in a modern war like that with which Japan was threatening China, they formed a strong conservative element against which the reform party was broken. There were approximately three hundred thousand men in the Eight Banners, and the most dangerous were the sixty thousand who occupied Peking and guarded the palace; those occupying nearby Tientsin were also dangerous. The young, reforming Emperor forfeited all hope of success by threatening the privileges of these old seasoned troops, particularly as the old Dowager Empress Tzu-Hi was quite ready to oppose her grandson and assume the old, venerated, traditional authority. The small reform group was well aware of the threat: it appealed to the modern contingents commanded by Yuan Che-Kai, a young and brilliant general, the only one who had shown a clear grasp of Korean affairs, a friend of the reformers who in every possible way supported and accelerated his success and his career. Yuan Che-Kai arrived in Peking and the crisis was precipitated. The young Emperor put himself in his hands. The general weighed up the difficulties that reform would entail. He temporized, and warned Tzu-Hi. In a violent rage the Dowager Empress boxed the ears of the young Emperor and had him shut up on an island in the imperial park. Counsellors were executed or exiled, and Yuan Che-Kai was master of the situation. The privileges of the old China were restored for the benefit of Tzu-Hi. The age of reform had lasted only a few months and came to an end in September 1898.

Outer China Lets in the West

The failure of the reform movement in China which ended by closing the country to direct Western influence, at least during the few years preceding the proclamation of the Republic, should not lead us to underestimate the increasing importance being exercised by 'overseas China'. Three to five million emigrants kept up the traditions of Chinese trade throughout the whole of maritime Asia in innumerable ports on the Pacific archipelagoes. These shopkeepers, merchants, and bankers were the indispensable middlemen between the native populations and the great European business firms. They were rarely liked; the superiority of their culture shut them up within themselves behind a barrier of politeness which often re-buffed the casual, easy-going European, who nevertheless could not do without these valuable collaborators. At heart the Chinese always re-mained loyal to their Empire; it was this loyalty which made them abandon their indigenous wives and daughters, though they regarded it a point of honour to keep their sons and bring them up in the Chinese way,

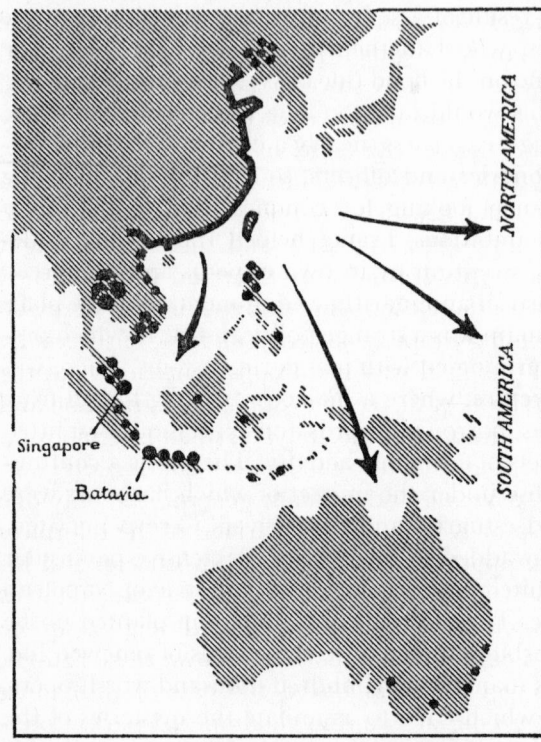

28 Chinese Emigration in the Nineteenth Century

and if possible in China itself. Their greatest ambition was to acquire as soon as possible the sumptuous coffin which would bear their bodies back to the land of their ancestors. These Chinese controlled the middle branches of the trade of the archipelagoes, and in the Indo-Chinese peninsula they possessed entire cities, like Cholon, forming colonies totalling more than a million men.

Obviously the waves of emigrants in the last decades of the nineteenth century could not preserve this aristocratic character. On the contrary, the movement was almost a repetition of the slave trade, bringing a million workers to the lands occupied by the whites: one hundred thousand to the United States of America, nearly one hundred thousand to Australia or Peru. As on the old Atlantic slave ships there was a frightful toll of human life, partly because of the exceedingly primitive conditions on board, and partly because of fearful revolts which sometimes ended in the total dis-appearance of ships, passengers and cargo. But at this high price, and thanks to several agreements between the Chinese and the reception countries, new Chinese colonies were founded in most of the new worlds in the Pacific.

In Indo-China, direct Chinese influence even exceeded that of the immigrants. The proximity of the great Empire and the long tradition of subjection had preserved habits of work, of reasoning, and of feeling which even threatened the Annamites' own way of life. The human population of Indo-China was in fact the result of a series of waves; the Chinese wave pushed back the Annamites, who had themselves ousted the Moi. The latest wave was French, borne on the flood tide of Western capitalism. The causes and significance of this would take too long to describe here. One important factor was Gialong's eagerness, nearly a century ago, to be surrounded with French missionaries and officers, so that for the following hundred years any Frenchmen looking for conquest had found this a favourable ground for their ambitions. France helped Indo-China to detach itself from China, then, swept on by its own impetus and reinforced by the power of its new industrial and maritime equipment, took the place of its former master. This Annam was a strange political state in which prefectoral institutions were intermingled with mandarin customs. There was a strange civilization in the cities, where a dialect was being forged from three or four major languages, borrowing words and expressions best fitted to describe the changing facets of economic activity. There was a continuous influx of new merchandise under the impact of which harbours were widened and deepened, and estuaries and great rivers were penetrated. Yet another new quarter was added to these already extensive peninsular cities. It introduced the architectural decorations of the style of Napoleon III into the monsoon climate. The old roots of Catholicism planted in the seventeenth century, then forbidden, began to show signs of renewed life, attracting communities of as many as one hundred thousand worshippers. Strange sects were founded which tried to assimilate the mysteries of the West into the traditions and customs of the East. And here again the influence of moral and economic forces proved stronger than the direct action of the immigrants from France: there were less than a thousand officials, whether officers or businessmen, in Cochin-China in 1881; but Victor Hugo was revered by everyone.

The Europeans were paying a good deal of attention to south-east Asia; the French especially profited from it. At almost the same time that the Anglo-French war was developing in China (1858), a French fleet bombarded Tourane in order to avenge the execution of Christians in Annam. But a landing attempt failed and the admiral decided to divert his attempt to Cochin-China. He took Saigon, and entrenched his position so thoroughly that the Emperor of Annam was compelled to confirm him in possession of it. In 1862 a naval officer succeeded in making a protectorate treaty with the King of Cambodia. The main preoccupation of the naval officers, not disavowed by Paris, though not exactly encouraged, was to find a way through into China. They had soon to recognize that the River

Mekong was no use to them in their project. The activity of the French Far-Eastern fleet then turned northward to Tongking. In 1873 Francis Garnier succeeded in seizing Hanoi, but could not hold on to it for long. Ten years later, more strongly supported by a French ministry (which was soon, however, disavowed by Parliament), the French fleet succeeded in occupying the whole of Tongking and forced recognition of its protectorate over Annam itself. China, which was claiming a right of suzerainty over these countries, acknowledged the *fait accompli* in 1884. Siam recognized the French settlement in the Indo-Chinese peninsula: the interplay of Anglo-French rivalries enabled Siam to remain an independent state and safeguard its freedom.

In 1885, England, uneasy at the progress France was making, established a footing in Burma, not without a tough war which dragged on until 1898. The English also retained the Malay peninsula, a former Dutch possession on which Singapore had been created in 1819. In 1824 they bought back Malacca from Holland and developed and systematically legalized their authority there by a series of protectorate treaties from 1874 to 1889.

The outcome for Malacca was rather different. This insignificant remnant of a once flourishing maritime kingdom had been taken over by the English in 1824 from the Dutch, who had themselves taken it over from the Portuguese. England's chief preoccupation was apparently to compete effectively with the splendid port of Batavia, which she had been forced to return to Holland when the Dutch legitimate monarchy was restored. The principal weapon of the English was economic freedom which, as we noted earlier, acted as a powerful attraction. The more Batavia surrounded itself by barriers, the more Singapore congratulated itself on its liberalism. Dutch ships had a monopoly of the one: the other had the privilege of sheltering all the rest of the world's shipping. The harbour of Singapore had to be continually widened and deepened. Along its shores a mushroom city was growing in the mud of the foreshore, bustling with a hundred thousand inhabitants drawn from every race in the Eastern world, and governed by a handful of Englishmen. They were responsible for directing raw materials, especially the new rubber, to English markets; the local trade and its profits they left to the Chinese, who, as elsewhere, assumed control.

These same Chinese numbered more than two hundred thousand in Java, where again their trade 'flowered like the lotus' and was even more influential than that of the Malays. As for the Dutch, they had little interest in shops. The Netherlands Government was more preoccupied with discouraging any European venture not strictly necessary for the exploitation of the island. Their own particular form of exploitation was a curious system initiated in 1832 by the Governor Van den Bosch. Since the English style land tax was far from covering the expenses of the colony, he replaced it by the 'system' partly inspired by old local customs which became famous. One-fifth of the natives' land was brought into cultivation by the government or by concessionaries, and farmed in modern plantations, coffee, sugar, spices (and soon rubber), the largest of the profits going to the Dutch exchequer. At first it was amazingly successful, and aroused the admiration of numerous economists, then it declined when the regulations had to be relaxed and slavery was abolished in 1861. The growth of transport and the development of the railways after 1870 possibly account for the increase in population which trebled during the century. It reduced the peasants' holdings to minute plots, often collectively farmed; rice was the only crop they could grow which would support so many people. This did, in fact, explain the rapid rise of Batavia. The harbour had silted up; the city, several miles away from the coast, had had to select a new port in deep water, and the residential areas had abandoned the marshes and moved up to the inland plateaux. Two Chinese cities were included in the settlement. It was curious to see the luxuriant vegetation of the wealthy quarter trained into formal gardens in the Dutch manner, restoring to the name Batavia something of the authenticity it had lost when the canals in the first city, dug like those of Amsterdam, had silted up. The Dutch were well aware of the necessity for keeping their prestige intact. They had been accepted by these kindly Javanese who had successively welcomed so many different peoples of such varying customs and religions; the Javanese still had a great respect for the numerous Arabs and the Muslim faith; the Dutch could probably have got both their language and their religion easily accepted, but they chose to forbid both to the natives, at least until 1870. By so doing they left the door wide open to Chinese civilization.

RUSSIA DEFENDS ITS TRADITION

Russia was entering an era of far-reaching reforms which might have made its enormous empire into one of the great middle-class capitalist nations.

Ancient Russia in Search of Itself

The originality of the Russian intelligentsia should not be underestimated. They were recruited partly from the aristocracy, and even from the ranks of the clergy, but chiefly from a middle class still indeterminate but everywhere respected, even at court. These intellectuals had a shrewd knowledge of European methods, and knew and loved their own country too well to rush into blind imitation of them. The great reforms of the 1860s were by no means a hurried copy of Western laws, as is evident from the temperament of those mainly responsible for them. Milyutin was State Secretary in Poland, which had rebelled again and been defeated again; he was the brother of a Minister of War who held his post for twenty years and was one of the conquerors of the Caucasus. Milyutin was convinced of Russia's greatness, and had no intention of aligning Russia with the West; and if he hated the nobility, it was not for the same reason as the French liberals, but because he wanted to liberate Russia's ancient traditions from their state of aristocratic hypertrophy. Samarine, after ten days' imprisonment, had been paying the penalty in Siberia for a biting satire on social life in Riga, in which he showed no love for the German aristocracy, a Western aristocracy settled on Russian soil. He was an ardent supporter of reform, but chiefly from his desire to revive the Russian rural peasant community. In Russia, the abolition of serfdom was part of a historical process and was nothing to do with the principles of 1789. It was the rejection of a feudal institution, Western in character, more or less artificially grafted on to the country in the fifteenth century in imitation of Europe.

At any rate that was the theory of the mystical reformers who ardently championed the Russian spirit. In practice the reforms of Alexander II, which liberated the serfs on the great imperial estates and then those of the nobility, posed problems which the legal expert of the reform movement, Prince Cherkasky, could not solve without resorting to Western legal and financial procedure. The peasant's real independence could only be secured by giving him complete ownership of a plot of land. The fundamental problem was therefore one of ownership, as much for the newly freed serf as for the former dispossessed seigneur, who demanded compensation.

Of course, wherever possible (as in the Ukraine) it was the peasant community, rather than the individual peasant, which was given the benefit of the reforms, but this did not simplify the financial problems. A credit organization had to be set up which would enable the new landowner to pay yearly instalments on the total amount which the seigneurs wanted to receive in a lump sum. When it came to starting this credit technique, it was once again Western institutions which offered the most appropriate experience on which to draw.

A similar situation arose with the reform of the Zemstvos. In principle there was no question of liberalism on the Western pattern, but of bringing the Russian land once again under its old traditions of government and local administration. All the same, the creation of departments and officials, and the clarification of judicial powers, involved recourse to reforms on the Western model. All this surge of new ideas demanded an educational programme, an expansion of the teaching service, and encouragement of the press. Inevitably this meant opening the door to Western ideas, which flooded in whilst the old local culture and the Russian tradition proved more difficult to diffuse, since they were vague and unformulated.

The new Russians were therefore in a paradoxical situation: they disliked Western capitalism yet were compelled to watch it irrupting over their frontiers in increasing measure as they tried to rid the country of Western feudalism and get back to the old Russian institutions and their own modes of thought. The reformers were eager to shake off the Europe of yesterday and get back to a more distant past, but it brought them up against the Europe of today.

It was not therefore surprising that the 1880s were years of confusion.

Probably never before had the entire cultured *élite* engaged in such profound heart-searching, nor had the diseases of collective psychology ever broken out in stranger forms. The most spectacular was that of nihilism, of which one of the first victims was the reforming Tsar himself in 1881. Paradoxically his successor, in order to ward of nihilism, tightened the framework of autocracy and gave back to the nobility some measure of privilege. He entered into the famous agreements with capitalist France which resulted in reconciliation with the hated England; and Russia's financial future was put at the mercy of speculators on the Paris *Bourse*. But it was a paradox only in appearance, since it was profoundly characteristic of the economy of the Russian people to stand at the crossroads between the maritime civilizations and those of vast Eurasia.

The future of Russia still lay in the balance at this time. The people were zealous and hard-working in the 1880s. The prospects of agriculture were certainly far better than those of industry. Russia was still one vast village, but a village whose system of land-ownership was exceedingly difficult to define. There were small landowners on the French pattern in the West, Poland or the Baltic countries, and apparently a few also in the south of the Dnieper and Don region. The majority were settlers of foreign extraction: notably the Cossacks, and those in the Urals, who became farmers but remained organized in hierarchies. In those regions, therefore, there were estates with a social class structure similar to that found in the West.

However, on the majority of lands, the Russian usage prevailed. It was not the individual who was the owner, but the village. The law of emancipation authorized the formation of individual farms but some Ukrainians rejected individualism to group themselves into *Mirs*. Even Germans from the Volga pooled their lands. Land was not united under the collective authority of the village in order to improve agricultural techniques: for as a rule the work was still done, if not by individuals, at least by families. The predominant motive was the desire for a brotherly sharing of liabilities. Taxation, conscription, and financial arrears were borne not by each family, but by the whole village, and it was now the village which fixed each man's share in proportion to his potentialities. The village fed the children, widows and old people, and asked only small tasks from them in return. When the demand for education began to spread, the village sometimes set up a fund in order to start its own school, or more often to send selected children to the school in a small neighbouring city. At periodic intervals the village redivided its lands into plots, so that each portion constituted a balanced farm which bore some relation to the capabilities of the person who was to run it. In case of uncertainty the plots were allocated by lot.

These redistributions of land were made on a basis of 'souls', that is to say of able-bodied men capable of giving the land all the attention it required. The method by which the reallocation was carried out varied greatly. In most cases the sharing out took place every year, but it might also be only every two years. There were fairly rare instances where the custom of sharing had been abolished, but even in these cases solidarity persisted and the harvests had to suffice for all. The *Mir* takes pity on everyone, said the proverb. There were various methods of sharing which deliberately created inequalities in favour of the most deserving, or of the families who had most men, equipment or cattle; two horses equalled one soul. Receipts and expenditure did not always balance at the end of the year. The village sent labourers and craftsmen to the town, especially in winter; all who could earn a little money by some sort of work brought it back to the community, and if there was still a deficit it was the village which was in debt and the mortgages were collective.

Of course land belonging to the nobility was governed by laws which which were much closer to Western practice. Men of the middle class and merchants also bought land in quantities large enough to displace the peasant and bring ruin on villages the population of which then moved off to the growing town. As in Europe a century earlier, the advance of progress created the agricultural then the urban proletariat. 'Where I settle, the mujik no longer sings', was the saying traditionally imputed to the moneylender, who acquired possession of whole villages and appeared on the scene whenever hunger and disease were rife. The moneylender paid the taxes and the debt, but was then the owner of souls, or, taking advantage of the new law, the owner of lands which the peasants were forced to leave.

The traditional social structure varied in this way from one part of Russia to the other, and the people's existence and their way of life also varied a great deal according to local resources. In the north they existed chiefly on fishing, hunting, and trade in power, game and furs; and they were more dependent than elsewhere on corn. On the shores of the Caspian the fishermen who were also organized in communities caught more fish, it was said, than all the fishermen between Europe and Newfoundland. In the sparsely populated areas, villages selected their fields from the vast stretches of land which belonged to them, since they could not farm them all. There were said to be enormous *Volosks*, consisting of groups of hundreds of villages. Sometimes the lands had to be wrested from the forests, which were devastated so rapidly at this time that the price of wood dropped to a tenth of what it was in Europe. As a rule, empty lands were sought, the population increased more quickly there than elsewhere, and then the *Volosks* split up into *Mirs*. Sometimes also villages rented tracts of land by the year on the fertile lands of the south belonging to great landowners or to the crown. On these new lands agriculture was somewhat haphazard. After three crops of corn and two of flax in five years, the land was left fallow. Many rich private individuals also rented land belonging to the crown or to great landowners, in order to practice a similar itinerant agriculture.

In general, Russian agriculture remained extensive: there was little use of manure and not much attempt at seed selection; the techniques employed depended solely on the chances of the great migrations. The fairs tended to encourage the production of cereals which were much favoured for export; the poor cereals were good enough for the mujik, and wheat was usually sold. Thus the export movement continually increased. Formerly it had brought handsome profits to the large landowner, enabling him to live in Parisian luxury and follow court fashions. Now commerce had an influence on the whole of rural life, from the moment when the smallest village had to muster enough money to pay the state the arrears of a heavy land debt together with the taxes. Commerce was relatively easy when the farms were those of the rich black lands of the south. The sacks of grain piled up at Odessa, putting Russia at the head of all the world's leading grain exporters during the first half of the nineteenth century. In 1880 Russia was still second on the list. In default of corn, flax was sold. The demands of Western industry had become all the heavier since Russian prices were extremely low, and Russia became the leading supplier in the world. On the other hand although the immense pasture lands of Russia were ideally suited to stock-breeding this had barely been begun. This may have been due to carelessness, or to the influence of religious fasting. Whatever the reason, the cattle were of poor quality and nothing was done to turn them into a paying proposition; but the country was rich in horses, the mujik's faithful friends.

Rural trade brought the introduction of new crops. The innumerable orthodox Jews faithful to their race and religion in south-west Russia had not made a great success of cultivating the lands on which Catherine had wanted to settle them as farmers; but they had succeeded admirably in stimulating trade in the frontier region of the Ukraine. In the region of Kiev initiative and capital were soon available to develop a vast beet-growing industry, and this in turn was followed by a sugar industry. The potato, too, did very well in Russia. Beet and potato were used instead of barley in the manufacture of alcohols from which the state derived very substantial revenues.

Prosperous villages ran small industries on their own: craftsmen provided the basic requirements of the collective, including, of course, icons. In these crafts some villages were fortunate enough to find an additional source of income, as there was considerable demand in western Europe for the many wooden articles, for the famous Russian leather and for lace. This small village or 'cottage' industry was, however, steadily declining, threatened by competition from the new urban concentration. The new mills could deal with millions of hides at a time; distilleries and refineries were grouped together, and a few major flour mills were replacing the number of small ones distributed throughout the country. Eventually some of the major industries became as concentrated as their counterparts in Europe; this was especially true of textiles, fats, and even at this early stage metallurgical and chemical products.

The first locomotive was apparently assembled in 1825 by technicians from the New World. At first there was merely an assembly shop, then a state depot, and by 1880 Russia was making one-fifth of its own locomotives. The Government also increased facilities to foreign contractors and there were already more than two hundred works, each employing more than three hundred men. An intensive search was being made for coal; the Polish mines were being exploited, and also the Donets mines which had been discovered early in the century and fitted out with rudimentary equipment during the Crimean War. In about 1880 the Gruchovka mines began to turn out enough coal for the Black Sea and Don shipping. In this basin alone, production was stepped up in fifty years from a few thousand tons to more than a million. Seams of coal were near at hand, and the Crimean War revealed how superior the strategic value of this mining area was to that of the distant Urals. So an industrial Russia was gradually being built up and the network of railways was providing its framework.

Noblemen were eager to increase their incomes, villages were being driven to commercialization, yet Russia's roads were primitive in the extreme. They were earth tracks not kept in repair, so that in spring and summer they were nothing more than quagmires or dust-bowls. Serious transport was conducted on sledges during the winter when there was always a firm, solid track for five or six months and ice bridges across the rivers. Groups of countrymen were past-masters at exploiting natural communications and at the opening of the railway era achieved greater speeds than the first steam trains.

The huge rivers naturally made splendid trade routes. The old shipping had used heavy wooden boats sometimes built for a single trip and demolished at the end of it. Then, with the arrival of the steamship, these wonderful natural arteries came into their own and carried vast quantities of grain in the middle of the century. The system of interjoining canals dreamed of by Peter the Great had never been realized, but in spite of a late start the railways were built in record time and completed the river network by about 1870.

At first trains drawn by horses linked the Don and the Volga. Then Nicholas II, it is said, marked out the line from St Petersburg to Moscow with a ruler. However that may be, the railway completely by-passed a number of important towns, and the roads were so bad that it took more time to get from a town to its station than to cover the whole distance by rail. In 1880 however, almost twenty thousand miles of track were opened. Their special gauge separated them from those of Europe. Above all they emphasized the natural centre of Russia, Moscow.

Moscow was in process of becoming the first city in the Empire. Its population was almost equal to that of the capital chosen by Peter the Great. It retained in its plan something of its curious eighteenth-century appearance. However, the seigniorial parks had been divided into lots on which had been built small houses clustered around parish churches, and which were intersected by wide avenues of trees. All these suburbs were themselves grouped around the city, the fortress and the Kremlin. Economically, the new centre was constituted by the railway stations of the five big Russian lines, the combined traffic of which was twice that of St Petersburg. Thus in the suburbs of Moscow the aristocratic mansions and the monasteries were being shouldered out by the new factories; the spinning mills, weaving mills, dye works and distilleries employed more than fifty thousand workmen.

Nevertheless in 1880 St Petersburg was still undeniably the capital, although it had less industry than Moscow and it would have had even less but for the luxury trades – tapestries, mirrors, porcelains – all the accessories of court life. The presence of the Government attracted the wealth of the country as well as the great banks. In an economy still largely dependent on Europe and the sea, English, Jewish and German finance contributed to this convergence of wealth and income.

Moscow was the city of popular and religious publications, and St Petersburg was the centre of scientific and literary works and of luxury publications. The two cities were a contrast: one with its classical palaces and French gardens, and the other with its elaborately Eastern churches and monasteries standing in remnants of forests. The two economies were a contrast; one agrarian, though this did not prevent the peasant from experiencing disastrous famines and the ever-present evil of usury; the other was commercial and piled up cargoes of foodstuffs on the quays of the Baltic and the Black Sea for England to buy cheaply. It was almost as if there were two Russias.

We shall stress later the efforts, first of De Witt, then of Stolypin, to make the capitalist system prevail, but here at the outset we should do well to recall the essays written by the young Lenin. They constitute an admirable study of capitalism in Russia, and emphasize its ill-adapted, artificial and dangerous nature. It is important also to stress another important fact: the Western powers dominated the maritime worlds because their economic liberalism was so attractive and their financial resources so powerful, but the Russian influence grew strong in continental Asia for quite other reasons and by very different techniques.

The Russian People Conquer Asia

The Russians who were acquainted with Siberia realized that it was not empty. Ethnographers in 1880 had already described several successive layers of civilization to be found there. The peasant admired its curious cattle and particularly the pig known as the *chude*, which was also the name of a very ancient people who had probably come down from the Altay. The empire of these Chudes extended as far as the Dnieper, and it was almost certainly they who came into contact with the Mongol conquerors from whom the Siberian peoples inherited their high cheek bones and slit eyes. Centuries of common life, in which there was increasing intermarriage, and the endless movements of tribes from one end of the country to the other, resulted also in the creation of a composite religious life. This predisposition to amalgamate worked out to the advantage of the Russians who were always in a majority; there were several millions of them in comparison with barely one million natives. The Russian was good-natured and sentimental. Even if he were a merchant, he adopted the orphan and welcomed the Yakut or the Tungus. In the vast spaces of Asia races probably co-existed more than anywhere else in the world, yet there was no racial problem, barely even a national one. There were only human beings who suffered together, toiled together, and certainly tried to get rich, but without forgetting the consolations of the heart and the blessings of solidarity. In the crucible of a nature so vast and overpowering, man became more human.

The backbone of this Asiatic world was the Altay, the Gold Mountain, a solid mountain range which separated Russia from Mongolia and China. Even greater efforts were being made than in the previous century to extract its wealth of gold and silver, which in the past had contributed to the greatness of the Chudes. The mines belonged to the Tsar and if yields had been fairly good up to about 1870, it was due to the forced labour of political prisoners or to the cheapness of serf labour. Then interest in gold began to wane, partly because fantastically rich seams of coal were discovered in the Kuznetsk basin. The attraction exerted by these distant countries was far from diminishing. Barnaul had been growing for the past century and already had twenty thousand inhabitants. It was almost like a capital on which the slow-moving convoys converged. Tradition, allied of course with self-interest, ensured the caravan leader the respect of the peoples. Traffic was not much improved by the convoys of steamers sailing up the Ob, where the imperial foundries were situated. It was around such small centres as these that the Russian peasant showed a desire to settle, though they were forbidden imperial lands. At first the police generally ignored them or pretended to do so; then the peasants began to grow crops, to harvest them, to build villages. When attempts were made to drive them away before an over-lengthy occupation gave them indisputable rights, they wept and pleaded and wrote to the Tsar, asking to be allowed at least the delay necessary for a reply to be received – a reply which never came. By thus letting the situation drift from delay to delay, Russian obstinacy conquered Siberia and the peasant was firmly settled on the land.

This slow infiltration of the peasants began to oust the old hunters, although they carried on their activity as before. Yakuts and Tunguses continued to pay their taxes in furs. These furs were world-famous and came from more than fifty different animals, amongst them marten, sable and black fox. Hunting provided food too, but less than fishing in the lakes or inland rivers, which were as big as our Western seas.

The deportees provided an *élite*; those who survived the lengthy convoy built the rudiments of villages around small army or police forts, and created small towns where each man did his utmost to acclimatize himself to exile, to live in mutual love and friendship an existence whose torturing fatigue ended only with death: they discussed and read, and small cultural centres sprang up in the heart of Siberia. The deportees were fairly well received by the population. They were regarded less as criminals than as unfortunates. The arrival of a new contingent brought a little novelty: the newcomers were bombarded with questions and asked for news of events in the faraway country in the west. Life's true values were prized. Dynamism could certainly not be expected from these peoples, but the new land easily guaranteed a minimum of subsistence. Escapees were taken in, hidden, assimilated, and the police soon got tired of looking for them.

All the time peasants were continually arriving to swell the population. They came in bands, bringing their *Mir* with them. Their agricultural methods were undoubtedly haphazard; they did not use manure, or select seeds, but the best possible use was made of local resources. A period of fallow refreshed the land, new plots of which could easily be found when the old ones were exhausted. The lands were carelessly farmed, and weeds competed with corn. Whole herds sometimes reverted to the wild state. Nevertheless something had to be sold to pay the tax, to buy rudimentary tools, and to acquire the necessary luxury of a bowl from Europe or leather boots. A primitive local industry attempted to make articles cheaply if they were expensive in the shops because they had to be bought from the caravans. Thus a few hamlets began to look like villages, and then like miniature towns. The centre of these was often the tavern in which the miner, the peasant, and the merchant came to drown their sorrows in potato whisky which the Government readily allowed to flow since it brought in a handsome revenue from taxation. The Russian had as yet done no more than scratch the surface of the vast region stretching from the Urals to the Pacific, but at least he had taken possession of it. Though the population was very scattered it had quickly struck deep roots. From village to village, from post to post, settlement continued to the very borders of Manchuria; hence the attraction of a more organized way of life, which began to appeal, if not to the peasant, at least to the military or merchant adventurer. The essential features of the Russian colonization of Asia were beginning to emerge.

This progressive occupation of Siberian land by the Russians was not altogether unconnected with the consolidation and progress of the Russian positions in central Asia where Russia had also been expanding for more than half a century.

At Baku the watchtower had been converted into a lighthouse, but in 1880 the future oil capital was still lit at night only by Cossack torches. The town was wholly Eastern in appearance, that dusty East characteristic of central Asia in the nineteenth century. The ships in the ports took on Tartar crews. The railway from Batum to Tiflis had not yet been extended as far as this, but agriculture was progressive at the expense of hunting and fishing. Cotton was flourishing. French missions, in 1848, had arrived to observe the progress of silk manufacture and to attempt to direct its trade towards Lyons. These textile crops in Caucasia were very successful at the time of the American Civil War. The vine did extremely well there, and was soon producing the best wines in Russia. Tobacco soon followed. Meanwhile the primitive industry was being expanded. Almost modern equipment began to replace the old tools of wood and stone. With the exploitation of copper and naphtha, Georgia came to life under the protection of Russia. In Transcaucasia Russia's advance found its point of equilibrium in 1880 when it came into contact with Turks and Persians, but the same could not be said east of the Caspian. There everything was still in a state of flux, and in 1880 Merv was still independent, a relic perhaps of past splendour, yet at the end of the eighteenth century this famous city had been almost destroyed in the course of its struggles against the Emir of Bukhara. Its population had been deported almost in its entirety to the rival city. In the nineteenth century it numbered only a few thousand inhabitants, sheltered within the imposing-looking walls. It kept alive the tradition of the old caravan capitals of central Asia, for the nomad Turkmen still pitched their tents under the city walls during fairs. All around it stretched the oasis, the irrigated area where corn and sorghum gave yields of one hundred per cent, but not far beyond was sand and swamp, both equally treacherous: these men of Merv were chiefly robbers and still had a bad reputation in 1880. Never-the less, habits were changing: the area was pacified by the Russian conquerors and already the nomad encampments were turning into fixed villages and gradually growing into large townships.

Bukhara had lost its warlike impetuosity, though not because it had resumed its fine past as the intellectual capital of Asia. The ruins of this Rome of Islam were as strong and solid as its faith had once been, and the most sordid poverty went hand in hand with the skilled craftsmanship of some of the last of its leather workers and cotton or silk weavers. But Bukhara was a Russian protectorate. It was from Russia that it obtained the manufactured goods in common use, and it was through Bukhara that tea made its way towards Russia from Afghanistan. But whether Russian trade and a Russian protectorate had the power to save Bukhara from destruction was not yet clear. The century was marked by a series of disasters: each year the inhabitants emigrated by hundreds, sometimes by thousands, northward or in the direction of Samarkand. Bukhara seemed to be giving up the struggle against the encroaching sand dunes from the desert. Its canals were silting up, its suburbs were buried. Central Asia, the land of marvels, had become the land of ruins and it was precisely this threat from the desert, combined with the decay of its important trade, which gave a powerful impetus to the Russian advance.

The Tsar was the protector not only of Bukhara but also of Kiva. Here, however, up to 1863, the Khans were not only independent but actually prided themselves on the Russian Christians they had captured and enslaved. The Russian slaves had revolted; they were tortured, massacred, hacked in pieces. Russian troops came to save those who survived, though many more died on the long return journey. The Russian troops found admirable ruins, but few inhabitants. They had fled. Those who remained were besotted with opium and hashish.

Moving eastward again to Samarkand we find ourselves once more in Russia. Tamburlaine's city had become the capital of a province and around the ancient streets with their famous ruins, new suburbs had sprung up, inhabited by Russian merchants. Old and new blended harmoniously in the centre of a cultivated zone in which the ruins of the old walls of the head of Islam were still standing here and there. The tomb of Tamburlaine was overgrown with bushes. With the arrival of the Russians, the Zerafchan had returned to life, and soon all the surrounding regions with it. The Ferghana was the richest of these Asian valleys, once its irrigation canals were restored, the trees in the orchards renewed and the cotton and mulberry plantations which fed the silk worm recultivated. The produce was exported to Russia in loaded caravans which brought back consignments of tools, utensils and cloth from Nijni-Novgorod. Some of these goods also went to enrich the bazaars of Tashkent, the leading city in central Asia, which vied with Tiflis for recognition as the chief Russian city in Asia. More than one hundred thousand inhabitants of every race crowded its still ill-defined streets, surrounded by houses of dried mud. But the Russian quarter was already easily distinguished, with its solidly built houses surrounded by gardens. Remnants of disease still dominated the old Tashkent, and whole districts had had to be evacuated, since half the Russian soldiers were afflicted with goitre. There had even been an attempt to move the site of the bazaar. Nevertheless Tashkent was developing rapidly and producing enough money to endow the nearby leper asylum with alms and to order the newest literary works and the very latest products of fashion and good taste from Europe.

For centuries central Asia had controlled the East-West relations of Eurasia until the English conquest seemed to have robbed it of its last chances of survival. But now it gradually came back to life as Russia's economic influence was extended. The Russian economy was still very rudimentary by European standards, but this in itself meant that it could graft itself effectively on to these primitive countries. The railway was not to come for many years, but the long files of horses, heavy wagons, and flat-bottomed boats were a continual source of wonder.

Even the slowness of postal communications helped on the Russian conquest. In St Petersburg, in other words more than 1,250 miles from the area of operations, ministers and diplomatic officials would reassure the chancelleries of Europe as to the peaceful intentions of the Tsar, and assure them that the advance of Russian troops had finally reached its ultimate limit; and influential military circles would endorse these assurances, which they believed to be sincere. But on the actual spot the small armed groups in the most forward positions, the light infantrymen, continued to live the life of Cossacks, Tolstoy's stirring picture of whom has already been mentioned: the soldiers would perhaps have liked in their heart of hearts to settle down and stop moving forward, if only they could obtain a piece of land. But the endless skirmishes with the opposing Kirghiz cavalry continually drew them on. There was always the spur of a hill to be captured, a dune to be outflanked, an old fort to be occupied, a village or a town to be cleaned up, a group of Russian slaves to be set free. The decay of the central Asian trade routes had created this vacuum, which kept drawing the Russian peoples onwards. This forward movement awoke a lively response in the Russian trading population, and particularly among the Jews. In a city which had barely been completely conquered the first operations were not without danger, and the merchant risked his life, but for what handsome profits! Soon, newly rich, he returned to his little native town flushed with success, which proved a strong incentive to new departures. The peasant soon followed, for the rights of property were not yet rooted deep enough in the Russian soul to tie the peasant to the land.

One important result of the abolition of serfdom had been to encourage that love of travel which, from time to time, obsesses the Russian soul. Change, sometimes for the worse but change at all costs, is an old saying in the Ukraine. It was an atavistic cast of mind going back to the remote struggles of Russian Christianity against the pillaging Muslims, and it relieved a host of pent-up bitterness which had been accumulating ever since the days of Genghis Khan and Tamburlaine, and which no agricultural technique could efface as long as Russia remained so close to a nomad culture. It played a bigger role in the Russianization of the regions bordering on Muscovy than all the ukases issued from St Petersburg by the Tsars.

This irresistible movement, which carried the full weight of Russia's power so decisively into the frontier areas, was halted in central Asia only when it came up against Persia and Afghanistan. They had the support of the English, who were beginning to reach these areas at about that time after the long voyage around Africa or through Suez. With Russia checked in central Asia, this racing tide fell back like breaking surf along the Tianshan and reached the Amur River and the borders of China. The Russians hesitated to enter China but continued to send in their luxury-laden caravans and tried to win the goodwill of Peking, which was alarmed by the barbarians from the sea. The Russian drive reached Mongolia and Manchuria through the activities of businessmen. A *camarilla*, eager to carve out great estates in the frontier areas, went as far afield as the Pacific and even appeared in Korea. For the first time no buffer state separated the power of Russia from the maritime capitalist powers. The first check to Russian expansion came from Japan.

13
Changes in Europe and Africa

BOTH the success of European institutions in America and their failure in Asia had adverse effects on Europe itself. The one brought competition, the other, resistance. These were the underlying causes for the long-lasting crisis which set in at the end of the nineteenth century and forced Europe to push to the extreme its programmes of industrialization and social reform. The demands of capitalism had never been so exigent or its imperialism so blatant. One continent, Africa, still remained free. It had been ignored during the years when America and Asia were easy to conquer and had also been impenetrable until adequate methods and techniques were available; but now it was seen as the last world left for Europe to conquer. It represented Europe's last great victory in a series which stretched around the world, and carried European influence to every continent. Europe had reached the height of its power. Yet at the very heart of Europe, numerous regions had more or less escaped the influence of industrial civilization, particularly the regions contiguous to Russia.

In effect there seemed to be two Europes, one linked to Asia, the other washed by the Atlantic. This second Europe, however, was not wholly maritime, for the great continent of Africa was within easy reach. The interior of Africa was until then both feared and unknown, but now Europeans attempted to penetrate it.

THE BURGEONING OF INDUSTRY
FROM 1880 TO 1895

By 1873 the last echoes of the Parisian revolution had died away and the hopes it had aroused among small groups of advanced thinkers from Budapest to Warsaw had vanished. Bismarck had brought his war to a successful conclusion. Calm reigned in Europe for almost half a century.

Yet in the next twenty years, a succession of crises transformed the structure of societies and the destiny of nations. A major factor in these crises was the fantastic rise in world production which meant that the European markets were facing stiff competition for the first time. These crises were reflected in the periodic financial fluctuations which had occurred from the beginning of industrial capitalism.

Outward Appearances: Financial Crises

This new crisis was first apparent in Vienna, where it touched off a series of bankruptcies which wrecked the precarious financial institutions of Germany. Financiers in Switzerland had been cautious, and were therefore very little affected, but the new Italy was badly shaken. France survived the crisis fairly well. The war of 1871 and the great financial effort required during the years 1871–3 to pay the indemnities laid down at Frankfurt had clipped the wings of speculation. On the other hand, London was the scene of activity. From March to June 1873 the discount rate of the Bank of England rose steadily from three and a half per cent to seven per cent. Yet in spite of this rise, gold drained away from the City and crossed to the continent notwithstanding England's gold credits on France. On 7 November 1873 the English bank rate rose to nine per cent. One reason was that the wave of bankruptcies had no sooner begun to spread over the continent, in the summer of 1873, than the Atlantic economy was called on to face a wave of American bankruptcies. Liabilities amounting to over two hundred million dollars could not be met and more than half of them were placed in New York alone. Prices on the stock exchanges collapsed. At the Bank of England there was thought of suspending Peel's Act. Then English credit strengthened rapidly. The Governors of the Old Lady of Threadneedle Street returned a rather curt refusal to the presumptuous offer made her by that Berlin *parvenu*, the Bank of Prussia. It had now become the Bank of Germany and was rich with French gold. The general uneasiness showed itself in a permanent demand for gold, the price of which rose everywhere, gradually creating a climate of anxiety. In addition so much silver was being produced from the mines of Nevada and Mexico that its relationship with gold collapsed. In twenty years silver was devalued by half. Silver coins were still common currency, even in England, and they were now regarded almost as paper money. The Imperial Bank of Austria was in serious difficulty, since its important metal reserves were in silver. In the United States of America the owners of silver mines started an energetic campaign for the defence of the silver standard. In fact, though the minting of silver continued, from then on bank reserves were only in gold; many business firms lost their independence in this tightening up of financial discipline and closed down. In 1878 the City of Glasgow Bank had to suspend payments; the result was a chain of disasters which lasted through the next two years. Its effects were all the worse since the Bank of Glasgow was not a limited company, so that the shareholders had to bear losses much greater than the capital subscribed and had to liquidate their personal property.

The year 1883 saw a great French bankruptcy case, that of the *Union Générale*, which was deeply involved in the affairs of the railways and in industrial expansion as well as insurance, then in full swing. In 1890 there was another serious scare, but this time in England, where Baring's Bank, one of the oldest-established and safest in the country, went bankrupt through having been over-venturesome in Argentina, where the Government had recklessly abandoned all scruples about foreign currency. Although 8 November 1890 was a Saturday, the most influential financiers in the City went to their offices to decide the fate of one of the most powerful families in England which was liquidating its own bankruptcy. For months it took all the vigilance of the British Government and of a committee of famous bankers who had decided to cover the Bank of England, for the affair not to assume the proportions of a national disaster.

Finally, about 1896, not before a new wave of bankruptcies had again swept over America and Europe, the situation appeared to be in hand. At last the bank rate was stabilized. Credit became cheap; the movement of gold from one country to another was organized on the basis of the deficits or surpluses of each country's balance of payments. This was the beginning of the epoch of financial orthodoxy, which lasted until 1914.

This series of financial disasters had some important consequences. Gold was substituted for silver as the monetary standard, and a new demand for gold arose just as it had done in Europe in 1845, when it touched off the great revolutions of 1848. The clamour for gold, at all events, was soon satisfied by the systematic exploitation of the African and Australian reserves, an operation which could now be carried out more economically than ever before, thanks to the new dynamite which allowed the ground to be excavated cheaply. The economies certainly needed some such reinforcement of precious metal, since the new gold standard now applied not only to the millions of inhabitants in the Old World but also to the millions of America and Africa, and was also beginning to penetrate into Asia through Russia, India and Japan. China alone retained her old silver currency. Naturally the development of paper money and cheques made up for the deficiency of metal coinage. In Austria and Germany, where banking was still too recent to meet all the demands, the technique of the postal cheque was devised.

Competition took a new turn. The basis of Europe's economic activity in 1885 was still agricultural. In Great Britain the population of the towns was, it is true, already much greater than that of the country areas, but British agriculture employed more labour. Germany and France had more peasants than town-dwellers. Now this age-old foundation on which Europe's economy rested was shattered by a phenomenon quite new in history: massive quantities of agricultural produce began to arrive in Europe from overseas. The path for this invasion had been opened up by England, which had been choosing to buy foreign foodstuffs for a long time even if they were expensive, in order to be able to sell more industrial products and to be sure of making money on trade and transport. We noted the growing activity of the rural areas of America, Africa and Australia in the 1880s. Everywhere enormous harvests were choking up the farms, so that great sheds had to be built and the first silos were introduced. Prices fell in the great new markets of Chicago and Buenos Aires, and Europe could no longer control world prices. Ships crammed with corn sailed into French and German harbours to dump the surplus not required in London; the result was a general drop in world prices. The statistical graphs showed a halt in the continuous rise in prices which had buoyed up Europe's activity since 1850.

This drop affected different countries in different ways, but by and large in twenty-five years it represented a nominal loss of fifty per cent on commerical stocks and realizable assets. Agriculture was the first to be affected; but later industry was the victim of its own expansion. Europe was not only worried by American competition; competition within Europe itself and within each nation had become as keen as it had been in 1830, when the middle classes had suffered a severe shock. As in the 1840s, the clamour for gold brought a fall in prices.

This poses a problem: a drop in prices lasting only a few years had led to the revolutions of 1848, yet this new drop lasting twenty-five years had produced practically no visible change in European events. The solution is that the very structure of Europe was changing in depth. Its industry was stronger, it had a more flexible financial system, and a commercial system which could reabsorb stocks more easily. It had at its disposal an amazing accumulation of inventions which were waiting in the laboratories until they could be used. The fall in prices forced producers to do their utmost to make better use of the new methods and techniques.

We have already noted that in England, which was already highly developed, the events of 1848 had led to major demographic and social changes rather than to political revolution. Half a century later the same phenomenon was occurring on the continent of Europe, from the North Sea to the Vistula. Using its technological banking potential, western and central continental Europe transformed its methods and its whole organization.

Events in France: Industrialization

It is unnecessary to labour the point already made that French agriculture strongly resisted any innovation affecting its structure and its equipment. In 1882 it was France which had the highest proportion of smallholders and they were still predominant in 1892; there had in fact been a slight increase, from 2,150,000 to 2,200,000. Similarly, the number of farmers had risen slightly from 970,000 to 1,000,000 and the number of *métayers* (farmers paying rent in kind) from 342,000 to 344,000. Taken all together these figures revealed a marked number of new land proprietors, bringing the total to the record figure of 3,100,000. During the same period the number of agricultural workers dropped from 3,400,000 to 3,000,000. The French, then, remained unchangingly devoted to their small farms. and their smallholdings, and still resisted any industrialization of the countryside. Nevertheless, a careful analysis would show that this small farm was no longer quite the same in 1900 as it had been in 1880. First its area had increased a little. Several large farms had been so hard hit by the fall in agricultural prices that they were put up for sale. The number of farms of more than 250 acres fell appreciably, and thrifty peasants bought small plots for a reasonable figure. So the small farm was increasing in size at the expense of the large one; but it also increased at the expense of the very small one. Day-labourers who had a small plot of land of less than a hectare left the countryside, attracted by the rise of industry in the towns. In the country, wages were becoming more difficult to earn, and remained at the same low level. The small owner, therefore, seized the opportunity to buy up portions of field and additional garden plots. On an average the gain was fairly meagre, hardly more than a hectare, but for farmers working ten or so hectares (25 acres), it was a source of new confidence; it filled them with optimism, and gave them a new incentive to remain attached to the land and to farming.

Moreover, the peasants did even better; they also bought new equipment. They ventured to agricultural shows and to exhibitions of farm equipment in the neighbouring town, and acquired new plant. True, there was as yet no question of using the powerful American and English combined harvesters: they bought chiefly hay-making and mowing machines. To possess one's own threshing machine became the hallmark of success, and within fifteen years their number doubled. Weeders were the cheapest implement, and ten times as many of these were bought in the same period. Certain regions seemed particularly progressive, for instance Haute-Garonne, where the number of mowing machines and binders increased tenfold within ten years. Within the same period, the use of fertilizers became more systematic; after the popularity of guano, farmers cautiously began trying out the synthetic nitrogenized manures and especially basic slag, which could be obtained cheaply near the government foundries. Production was also reorganized to meet requirements, less corn was grown, more potatoes and much more beet. In 1900 sugar production reached ten times its level of 1870. Sheep were given up, since their wool could certainly not compete with that of Australia and the Argentine, and the byres were filled with two or three additional horned animals which the town butcher would buy at a fairly good price. Their pigs were protected against the cheap pork from Germany or America with the help of the Government, which fixed high import duties. These changes did not amount to an agrarian revolution, but they indicated a slightly more progressive approach to the old traditional farming methods.

In the French countryside of 1890, some men were lucky, others unlucky, and fate selected both impartially from amongst very small landowners and very large ones, from farmers with an average holding of a hundred acres and those with large farms of 125 acres. France continued to be the country of the small and medium farm. This fairly homogeneous peasant class began to organize itself into embryo societies; though the *Société des Agriculteurs de France* was more anxious to make complaints to the Government than to teach the countryside. In Loir-et-Cher a famous syndicate, founded in 1883, made arrangements to buy manure cheaply.

Certain agricultural syndicates took timely advantage of the law of 1884.

All these associations laid their grievances before the Government, and their complaints were all the stronger since the vines were threatened not only by foreign competition but by the dreaded phylloxera which cut down production by two-thirds in 1890, and made it necessary to import wine from Italy and Spain. The Government dealt with these complaints by protectionism. Méline, the protector of agriculture, was supported by the members of the rural syndicates who soon numbered half a million; he made France adopt a strongly protectionist customs policy and tried to convert all the states in Europe to the same policy of protection against the American agricultural invasion. It was also at this period that Parliament enacted a series of specialized laws connected with vines and wine which hindered France's entire agricultural policy in the twentieth century.

The way in which the marketing of new products, such as fruit and vegetables, was organized was also indicative of the slight but unmistakable advance in French agriculture.

The PLM Railway Company was interested in the construction of an irrigation canal and the producers formed themselves into local and regional unions to ensure the quality of their produce and the exploitation of markets. This tendency towards organization also affected dairy produce. A new feature was the granting of loans by the *Banque de France* to the groups of producers, though it was, of course, covered by the state against attendant risks. The peasants were still making complaints in 1900 against the farmers-general, intendants and *métayers* as they were still occasionally called; but the grievances of the proletariat were finding expression in strikes, in the Nièvre for instance, which were a prelude to the great vineyard strikes of 1907.

A major revival was taking place in France towards 1890, just as it was in the world as a whole, but it affected agriculture less than industry. French industry had previously been the most backward of all, but it became the quickest to develop. The year 1890 saw the greatest migration from the countryside to the towns. The great landed proprietors left their country homes and settled in Paris. Whatever capital they had been able to amass by selling lands, town houses and *châteaux* they invested in industry. The farm labourers went to form the urban proletariat. Thus from 1875 to 1900 coal production doubled while imports of coal trebled. The output of cast-iron doubled and that of steel was almost tenfold. Phosphorous ores were exploited by the Thomas-Gilchrist process and France became the second country in the world for ore; Bessemer and Thomas steel, thanks to coke, was either made in France or imported from Germany and England and supplied most of France's needs. It was a great time for builders of blast furnaces and coking ovens. Le Creusot acquired steam-hammers and rolling-mills, and the north began to develop into a great metal and chemical region. Steel plates and girders were made in the urban centres, now surrounded by entirely new factories ; Belleville made boilers and Saint-Denis built rolling-mills; the workshops of Eiffel were constructed at Levallois-Perret. The future automobile industry was already building the Darracq works. Paris ceased to be a city of craftsmanship and became industrial. This great industrial advance of the 1880s can best be measured by the increase in the use of the steam engine: their number rose rapidly between 1885 and 1892. This did not mean that France had suddenly become industrialized at one fell swoop. But there had never before been such an effort at modernization; in Normandy the textile industry was strongly concentrated at Elbeuf, where the number of mills dropped abruptly from two hundred and fifty to twenty-five. This effort was all the more astonishing and admirable since France had lost the industries in the east, the fine spinning-mills, the machine-tool works at Mulhouse, part of the ironworks and all the coalfields in Lorraine.

A new period was opening in French history: silkworms were no longer being raised in the Rhône Valley, but Lyons became the world silk market. The markets at Le Havre, Roubaix and Tourcoing put French industries in a favourable position to compete in world trade. Better still, France led the world in the hydro-electric industry, thanks to Bergès. The French launched the processes of electrolysis for the making of aluminium and the techniques of reinforced concrete.

There was marked progress in the fleet too, in spite of the curious attachment to tradition (France was one of the few countries where the number of sailing-ships went on increasing after 1870, and wooden ships were still being built). The French liners were the finest in the world on the Le Havre–New York run, and withstood the competition with English and German rivals. French ship-building techniques in iron and steel gained the same high reputation as the designs of the last sailing ships had had sixty years earlier.

Events in Germany: Phenomenal Development of Industry

France was the country in which the 1890s marked the most abrupt turning-point of industrialization, but Germany's industrial drive had not lost its impetus – quite the reverse. In the early stages, German agriculture had remained solidly organized around large farms, in spite of a trend, analogous to that in France, towards the development of the medium-sized farm at the expense of the very small one and of the large one. Half Bavaria was still no doubt predominantly a land of small farms where land tenure was on the French pattern, though the farms were noticeably larger than in France; but there were still only large farms in Mecklenburg. This persistance of the large estate was apparently connected with the division of common lands and the redistribution of fields, which finally came to an end in the 1890s. It was a difficult task. In Brunswick, the first country affected, the change was completed only in 1905. This agrarian reform was, however, a remarkable achievement. Some areas in the west resisted it at first, and Alsace never abandoned its opposition to the movement. But there was a marked development in sugar beet and even more extensive cultivation of

the potato than in France; as in France, too, there were changes in livestock; sheep were no longer kept and the number of pigs was greatly increased. But, in contrast to France, Germany sowed more wheat and increased her yields. She was still not producing enough corn for her needs,
but harvests were steadily increasing. Several sandy wastes and marsh-
lands in the north-east were reclaimed. This transformation of German
agriculture was supported throughout by the development of banking,
which had made great strides by 1860. All the establishments created on
the Prussian model, central co-operative banks and co-operative agricultural societies were merged into an Imperial Union, working in association with the *Raiffeisen* Union. At the beginning of the twentieth century,
the co-operatives had in all four million members, and one-third of these
co-operatives were affiliated to credit societies.

Thus the German peasantry remained economically more effective than
the French, worked in better conditions, and were better integrated into
the financial movement.

As in France, the development of the medium-sized German farm drove
the very small farmer to the towns. Between 1885 and 1900, the number of
working miners doubled, while during the same period the concentration
of mining concerns substantially increased the number of workers per pit.
With an average of more than a thousand workers per mine, German business was among the most concentrated in the world. German iron production
had almost equalled that of Great Britain in 1900; the same year the German
steel output already exceeded the British amount and was three times as
great as that of France. There was a marked move towards concentration in
industries which had previously been dispersed, such as cutlery at Solingen or
silk at Crefeld, although the introduction of electricity was bringing a new
lease of life to various country factories. The concentration of the German
silk industry at Crefeld between 1890 and 1905 was so successful that it became a threat to the Lyons market. A parallel process of industrialization
was affecting the spinning and weaving districts. Whereas in 1880 two-thirds
of the weavers were still small craftsmen working in their homes, twenty
years later all the workers were employed in huge mills. In spinning, the
hand-worker was nothing but a memory. There was now hardly any hand-
work except in the flax and hemp industries. The number of German cotton
spindles and looms had been increased by the contribution from Alsace,
so that there were slightly more than in France, and though the industry
was late in developing it became well-established in the European market.
By dint of technical improvements and a systematic study of cheap production, German yarn and cloths became famous for both their mediocrity
and their cheapness. They sold admirably in South America or in Turkey,
and even in England. On the whole it was the cheapness of its goods which
gained Germany a place in the international markets, in spite of her rivals'
attempts to denounce German 'shoddiness'. In fact, in self-protection the
English imposed on all goods a label of origin. At first the mark 'Made in Germany' was associated with goods of very poor quality, but about 1900 the

famous label became a piece of propaganda for German trade ; the middlemen in the City soon noticed that even some of their Dominions' customers were deserting them to deal direct with Germany.

Naturally, it was in the chemical and electrical industries that German progress was most spectacular. Within twenty years, the production of sulphuric acid increased tenfold, and superphosphates were already in general use. Ammonia made even more progress, and artificial dyes were being exported in large quantities. In 1882 German statistics did not include workers in electricity, but twenty years later they numbered more than one hundred thousand. They made the electrical dredgers which caused a sensation at the Frankfurt and Paris exhibitions, and even electric ploughs.

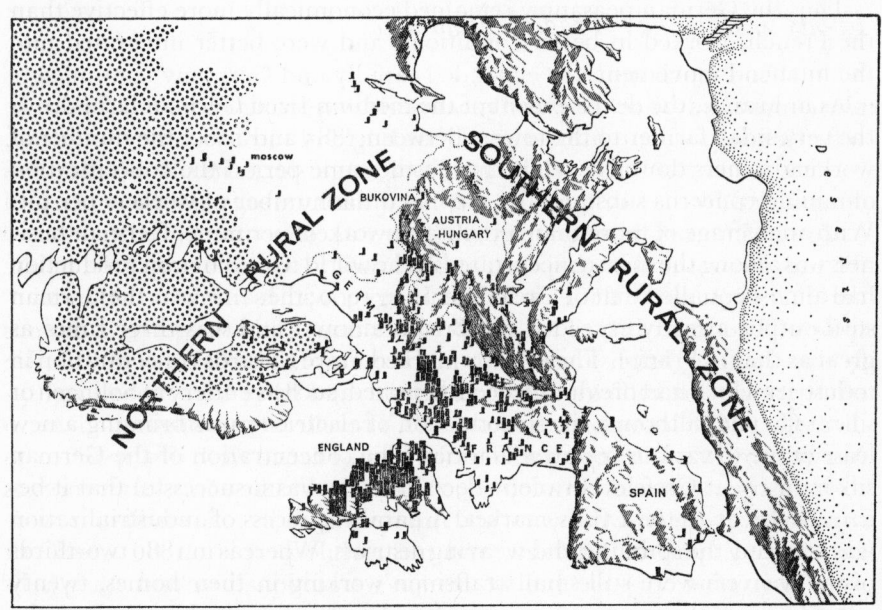

(the black blocks designate the industrial centres)

29 The Economy of Europe c. 1880

From 1887 the telephone became exceedingly popular. As early as 1890 Germany was a large exporter of electric cables, and in 1900 she cornered the market. All this production was dominated by two great firms, Siemens and the *Allgemeine Edison Gesellschaft* which was launched in 1883, and soon became transformed under the skilful management of Rathenau, one of the most powerful figures of European capitalism. All this industry greatly stimulated Germany's large-scale trade. The German fleet, after 1890, was built at record speed. Fine steel ships were launched on the North Atlantic routes, and although they were newcomers they were soon in the first rank of competition. Bismarck had abandoned the policy of free trade which had served him so well in the sixties, in favour of *Realpolitik*, a protectionist policy. He imposed moderate duties on corn and manufactured goods in 1890, and made them heavier after 1890 at the moment when American and French protectionism was becoming more clearly defined. In 1902, Germany had the best planned system of customs duties, devised by Caprivi's government, and income from it provided subsidies for the export industries. This business acumen irritated the old-established trading nations, and England denounced its treaty with Germany to protect Canada against an invasion of products 'made in Germany'. Almost everywhere Germany gained the reputation of dumping in order to conquer the markets.

Events in England : Trade Predominates

So in 1880 French industry expanded rapidly and Germany continued its phenomenal advance. England meanwhile was living on its great past. In 1884 Randolph Churchill declared that England's iron industry was dead, 'as dead as mutton', its coal industry was languishing, its silk industry was dead, killed by the foreigner, its woollen industry was *in articulo mortis*, and its cotton industry was seriously ill. This was, of course, a rather gloomy picture. He was making a speech at Blackpool to try to convince the public that it must support the Fair Trade League, which demanded the imposition of a customs duty of ten to fifteen per cent. Only the goods of nations freely admitting English goods would be exempt. The years of the Jubilee celebrations were difficult ones for England, and there were many Englishmen who put their complaints into words. Travellers returning from Sweden Norway, Switzerland or even Germany and France were disappointed to see their country so slow to adopt electricity. Hydraulic dams, new processes in metallurgy, electric furnaces, and improvements in coke distillation were all frowned upon in England, and meanwhile people on the continent were beginning to poke fun at Britain's traditionalism and smug self-satisfaction.

Many of these British anxieties were justified. Of course English blast-furnaces were being rebuilt, but they were no longer the kings of steel. American or German plant was producing more than that of England in 1900. Electro-metallurgy had made scarcely any headway in Great Britain and its metallurgists ridiculed the progress made on the continent and in America in special steels; yet these steels could be turned at immense speed and by 1900 they had transformed the market for machine tools to the great advantage of America. America also led the way in pneumatic machines, steam-hammers, and riveters, which were increasingly being used, and even in shipbuilding. English industrialists were very slow to adopt the new coke ovens for the recovery of the new ammonia gas. The English Aluminium Company was not formed until 1895 to exploit the processes which America and France had already introduced some years previously.

The electrification of English coal-mines had barely begun in the 1890s. Many worthy French and German mineowners were indignant at the antiquated gear of England's coal-mines; the equipment was installed with little apparent regard for the miner's life, and it was so cheap simply because it was so primitive. It was not only in the art of building that England had remained backward. The country had made amazing progress in the years 1830–70, but seemed now to have lost all its economic supremacy.

This may have been true of industry perhaps, but not of finance. The new developments lowered prices and changed the direction of the flow of goods, but at the same time the circulation of foodstuffs around the world increased appreciably; and this benefited freight, insurance, the activity of ports, of pools and banks. England adapted itself well to the new financial conditions between 1880 and 1900, and if it could afford to neglect its industry it was because its commercial power was at its height. If business was slack in Europe at any time, it was sure to be flourishing in China or Japan. If the price of agricultural produce dropped, all the better for the pockets of consumers in London or Glasgow. And the development of new industries benefited England indirectly. The new rubber industry was slow to catch on in England, but it was the English who shipped it and bonded half the world's rubber production, until in 1905 English financiers encouraged planters to settle in Malaya. With a rare flexibility England weathered the years of crisis and competition, not so much modernizing itself as skilfully manœuvring both its fleet and its capital, steering them always into the main stream of trade and keeping them away from reefs. When the fresh rise in prices led amongst other phemonena to an increase in gold production, it was soon apparent that the sources of these new treasures were all in the hands of England, exploited by English machines and English dynamite, and soon guarded by English soldiers.

England's strength lay in its genius for making good investments rather than pushing on with the modernization of the country, but there were risks inherent in this policy, and particularly the risk of unemployment. The trade union statistics show high levels of unemployment at various times between 1885 and 1895. It may have been good business to choose German steel it if cost less, rather than home-produced steel, but it threw many men out of a job. Actually the threat was not particularly heavy, and there was a great boom in building. Houses, offices and modern blocks typical of the later years of Queen Victoria's long reign were built at a great rate. As this century, which had been such a great one for England, drew to its close, peace and quiet, calm and comfort prevailed. The privileged regarded the earth, as Lord Asquith said in later years, as the playground of the rich. England was a country good to live in in those days, making progress in hygiene and with fairly good wages. Many English emigrants returned home about 1900.

Moreover, at this same period England was making a slow but determined effort at modernization. A law was passed allowing municipalities to build electric factories. The chemical industry, long regarded by the majority of English businessmen as a German monopoly, began to take advantage of the wealth of England's coal. The springs of industry were wound up once again.

RURAL LOYALTIES

The North and North-East: Modernization of Agriculture

To the north of Europe's vast industrial backbone lay a broad agricultural belt stretching from Ireland to Finland and covering Scandinavia.

This zone, so different in character, opened up at the very gates of the great cities of steel and steam, to which it offered so violent a contrast. Ireland in the nineteenth century presented a strange and tragic spectacle. Poverty there had been extreme in the eighteenth century, but it seemed at the opening of the industrial century as if things were about to change, because of the recent discovery of the potato. It was cultivated everywhere and the yields were good in spite of primitive methods because of the suitable soil and climate, so that it ensured an almost completely adequate food supply. A great wave of hope swept the country. Even the English were beginning to display comparative tolerance, and they allowed the tithe on their Catholic subjects for the benefit of the Church of England to be collected with the farm rent. The Irish Bill brought Catholics into the English Parliament. The position of the Irish peasants had improved. The population increased in a few years; between 1800 and 1845 it rose from six to eight millions. The towns expanded, life became more civilized.

The Irishman has always had in his speech a strain of poetry, a lively wit often envied by his English neighbour. Great orators popularized the English language, the old Erse was lost. Matthews, an earnest preacher, succeeded in converting the Irish to sobriety. A country-wide movement closed the drink shops and converted almost the whole country, village after village. The peasants began to save a little. Some grew accustomed to working in England's industrial cities where they were given the hardest jobs ('what on earth should we do without the Irish?') and, by depriving themselves, sent their savings to their families which had remained in Ireland.

Since they had been forcibly compelled to abandon the old system of collective ownership, the Irish had begun to realize the advantages of individual ownership, though these peasant holdings, often tiny, were redivided into even smaller plots each time they were handed down. The old pagan traditions preserved by poverty and loneliness began to disappear, and lingered on only in a few of the islands. Railway lines were built from Belfast and Dublin. A little trade brought life to the countryside. English landowners began to go and look after their vast estates on the spot.

All this surge of hope came to a tragic end with the famine of the black years of 1846–7. The potatoes developed a disease; the harvest was practically non-existent; famine threatened, the small herds of pigs were soon eaten, cattle could barely crawl about in the inadequate fields and died there. The peasants carried these starving animals to the stables but this made no difference, for exclusive concentration on potatoes had led to the neglect of hay and fodder. On the roads, in the hamlets, death struck mercilessly. It was a famine as disastrous as any in the darkest eras of the Middle Ages and people soon stopped burying the dead. Huts, cabins, whole villages were burned down to get rid of the corpses. In the towns, the healthy no longer even cast a glance at the weakling who dropped in the streets. It was difficult to count the number of victims, but there must have been between one and two millions. In a few years the population fell to a figure below that of the eighteenth century. Naturally, emigration had completed the work of the famine; all who could get to a port set sail for America and left their country which they sadly called 'the poor old lady'. The emigration itself was tragic enough. More than a third of the emigrants died on the voyage or on disembarking. By 1880, paradoxically, there were more Irish in America, particularly in the United States, than in Ireland itself.

But the disaster was followed by a period of new growth. The peasant farm was somewhat enlarged by so many departures. English landowners took advantage of the cheapness of land to round off their estates, but at the same time some large estates were divided to the profit of the small ones. The English Parliament had some pity at last and granted the Irish tenant the right to receive compensation if evicted by an English landlord. During the famine a few subsidies had been paid out. Above all the Irish exiles in America had found it easy enough to get work since they were not afraid of heavy labouring, and they saved enough to send millions back to the old abandoned country. Sometimes of course the Irishmen in the homeland gave way to fits of black depression and forgot the good resolutions made before 'the troubles', so that some of the money went on liquor; but agriculture did benefit from it as well. A current of trade began to flow from Ireland to England, bringing corn and especially dairy produce and meat. Flax-growing provided the raw material for the textile industries of Scotland and even of Ireland, where an industrial area developed around Dublin and particularly Belfast. Dublin never regained the prosperity it had known before Cromwell but it began to look like a capital once more. American Ireland had saved European Ireland. Soon the countryside regained the mellow prosperity it had lost for centuries. In 1880 Ireland was on the way to becoming one of the finest agricultural countries in Europe.

Holland had experienced no such tragedies or hardships. It was, in fact, because she was so wealthy that she had been able to remain placid and untroubled on the agricultural fringe of Europe. This amazing country, which in the seventeenth century had set the world an example of modern organization, seemed to have forgotten its urban vocation in the nineteenth century and devoted all its effort to the countryside. Railways were introduced late, for there was already a fine system of canals; and the construction of railways across the unpredictable flats and dikes involved enormous work on bridges and viaducts, which needed continually to be strengthened in the light of experience.

Industrial technique penetrated Holland only gradually, but it was a tremendous help in conquering these lands: the old windmills were still turning, but steam pumps were more efficient and made it possible to plan such ambitious projects as the draining of the bed of the Zuyder-Zee. The country already had splendid achievements to its credit: the sea of Haarlem had been drained and islands lost for a hundred years had been recovered. From the end of the imperial wars in Holland up to 1880, the country had reclaimed 150,000 acres. It was rich land which responded excellently to the new agricultural techniques, the use of manures, the selection of seed and of stock. There again, the proximity of the consumer markets of England and Germany ensured a profitable flow of trade. The growing volume of shipping made it essential to dig the fine canal from Amsterdam to the sea, and Rotterdam in turn had to improve its stretch of estuary. These investments of capital were soon made to pay, thanks to the amount of traffic which increased with each fresh advance of German metallurgy.

The Dutch also had their Indian colonies which brought in revenue. Holland was prosperous enough to concentrate her ambitions on maintaining the neat and well-tended countryside, which had been typical of the Dutch since the finest periods of their history. They did not abandon their industrial activities, but concentrated on those which were in keeping with their traditions; luxury fabrics and lace, which was not yet being replaced by cotton; glassware and particularly food industries.

Denmark was also mainly agricultural and reaped the benefit of English free trade. There, the farmers were still content with poor-quality cereals for themselves but they grew more and more wheat which sold at a good price in England. A flourishing stock-breeding was soon started too, and came to be considered the finest in Europe. Denmark offered England its bacon, lard, dairy produce and beef. The Danish population doubled in sixty years. Although there were still important aristocratic estates in Denmark and enormous inequalities in wealth remained yet the development of the agricultural revolution worked out to the advantage of the small farmer who acquired more land, cleared moorland, took possession of the common lands, drained marshes and by care and thrift succeeded in swelling his bank balance. The Danish countryside was more prosperous even than the towns; education developed more quickly, there was scope for ambition, and the countryman was more active in politics than the townsman. Naturally Copenhagen remained an important centre, favoured by its admirable site: nevertheless there were few industries and little fishing, and agricultural trade and shipping were its mainstay.

The Scandinavian countries were all agricultural. In the three Nordic countries there was certainly a marked trend towards urbanization, but except perhaps in Norway it never reached the same proportions as in industrial Europe. The population was not immobile; here as elsewhere a progressive countryside meant a deserted countryside. But from 1875 the towns which attracted the northern migrants were those of America. The progress of Scandinavian agriculture assisted England's towns by feeding them and the towns of the United States by populating them. This agricultural advance took two forms. First of all numerous clearings were made in the peat bogs, the moorland and the forest areas: within ten years (1865–75) two and a quarter million acres were brought into cultivation. In Sweden the government gave considerable help with the draining of lands flooded by lakes. Norway was reclaiming her fiords. The victors of this battle were small farmers, who soon became small landed proprietors and settled firmly on their new lands to bring up large families in a Lutheran and Republican atmosphere. Even the Laps took part in this expansion.

A more sensible method of farming was adopted. More care was taken over stock-breeding. Scandinavian breeds were formed by a continuous and increasing adaptation of genuine Nordic elements. Scandinavia exported foodstuffs, whilst the newsprint and cellulose industries gave the forests a new value, and the woodcutters moved ever farther north, covering the rivers with innumerable log rafts. The Norwegian or Swedish peasant owned his own land. If he were a farmer, he was protected against serfdom by the tradition of a country into which it had never been introduced, since it was restricted to the south of the Skagerrak. Then, too, collective ownership persisted stubbornly in the north. In the south the vagaries of the civil code on the French model were experienced only after 1850.

Railways had not been started until the second half of the nineteenth century and were slow to develop. Denmark was intersected by the sea, Sweden by lakes and Norway by mountains, so that each called for great feats of engineering. The railway network was not yet sufficiently developed for the great mineral deposits of the northern regions to be exploited, and Swedish industry in the central areas still retained its traditional character based on good craftsmanship and excellent ores. There was a sudden movement towards urban expansion especially in Norway, round about 1880, caused by the coastal shipping and the fishing. The cod and herring fishing kept to its medieval techniques until the end of the century, though it widened in scope and it was able to send copious supplies to the German and English markets.

The movement of change had not yet penetrated to Finland where a Swedish aristocracy (self-styled) passed under Russian rule as a 'Western' people. The peasants living in their smoky dug-outs, hollowed out of the ground, took their first steps forward only where they adopted the Russian *isba* built of round logs. Finland had been equally free from serfdom, but the rule of the seigneurs was restrictive and the government clashed violently with it in the attempt to give the peasants a little more land. The railway was still so recent an innovation that it was not yet possible to speak of modernization.

On the opposite side of the Gulf of Finland, the Finnish peoples fared little better in the matter of land, with this small difference, that the Germans disputed the ownership of the land with the Swedes and introduced serfdom. When Russia became the new master the peasants were offered freedom on condition that they were converted to the Orthodox Church, but they often had to go to faraway Siberia to enjoy it, for on the spot the Germans ruled and even succeeded in imposing Protestantism in the country districts near the cities whose trade they controlled. The landless peasant remained closely dependent on the seigneur. In 1880 a small movement began to take shape in favour of individual ownership but it benefited only a very restricted number of native inhabitants.

The peoples of northern Europe reveal certain common characteristics in their economic systems, above all an attachment to agriculture; but the Slav population which formed the eastern fringe, the intermediate zone between Europe proper and Russia, is more difficult to define briefly. We have seen that part of Bohemia became re-attached to the great industrial backbone just as southern Poland did, but beyond the Carpathians, Slovakia, northern Poland and Lithuania retained all their ancient characteristics. In fact the whole of the region between Warsaw and the North Sea up to 1878 was fairly similar in structure to that of the Baltic and Finnish countries. It formed an enormous group of servile peasants dominated by a few great lords, Polish or German in Posnania, Austrian in Galicia, Russian in the east. Trade was entirely in the hands of Germans, Rhenish Jews who were all-powerful in the cities.

Poland's revolutionary struggles were the product of an old-fashioned Polish patriotism and were rapidly suppressed by Russia. But they had the paradoxical effect, in the Russian zone at least, of hastening the liberation of the serfs and developing a small peasant farm on something approaching Western lines. The Russians were more skilful than the Austrians in Galicia; they wished to destroy the influence of the arrogant Polish landowners, and they steered the conflict between them and the peasant classes into economic spheres. The estates of the nobility were dismembered, villages and farms given back to the peasants, lands redistributed. At the same time the peasant was allowed to keep his old communal institutions analogous to those of the Russian *mir*. He used them as a kind of trade union to enable him to fight against the Jewish or German moneylender. When a straightforward system of landownership in German Poland had been established, it ended after a brief opposition in the peasant's subjection to the landowner. But the composite Russian régime gave this Polish peasant a chance to develop his vocation: agriculture improved in quality and quantity at the expense of the dismembered seigniorial estate, and the rural population increased noticeably. Within twenty years it rose from four to seven millions. The peasants moved out of the hamlets to the villages and from the villages to the towns, and provided the labour pool of an industrial Poland, which made marked progress. The same phenomena were occurring in Lithuania, at the expense of the German and Polish rulers. Here the reform of serfdom had the effect of westernizing Poland. The success of this policy of landownership not only enabled the Russians to wean the mass of the Polish people away from the heroic, but short-sighted patriotism of the seigneurs, but made Russianization bearable. It also made tolerable the attempts of the Orthodox Church to supplant Catholicism, and the compulsory use of the Russian language in schools. This obligation did not prevent a surprising growth in the number of Russian schools paid for by peasant contributions; they increased fourfold within ten years. It is true that in the privacy of their homes the Polish people remained faithful to their religion, their language and their country. But their attitude towards their Russian masters was different from that towards their old aristocratic rulers. Economically and socially the Russians were seen as liberators all the more readily since the oppressive power of the landowners had been strengthened in the German and Austrian zones, and since urban capitalism, urban trade and money-lending remained in the hands of foreigners. The Polish noble looked to the West, the people to the East.

The East and South-East: Prisoners of their History

Wretched though the *Wasser Polaken* might be, the Ruthenians were even more so. This hinterland of Europe was a curious crossroads of the East. Races, languages and religions cut across each other in an incredible confusion, and economic life was completely controlled by the Jews. The Ruthenian sometimes felt himself a Russian at heart though he had his own language and practised the Orthodox religion. The racial, linguistic and religious influence of the Poles extended to the Upper Dnieper, but Hungarians and Rumanians also penetrated as far as the Dnieper, whilst the Czechs crossed the Carpathians.

Bukovina was famous in 1880 for the scene of political confusion it presented. There were for example eight or ten religions currently being practised there. This mixture and confusion were increased at the end of the nineteenth century when a start was made on exploiting the resources of the subsoil and the hitherto neglected naphtha. This drew fresh waves of immigrants of every nationality from all the surrounding areas. The people benefited hardly at all. A primitive agriculture barely enabled them to keep alive in the good years, and to renew their debts with the obliging Jews when times were bad. Here the reform of serfdom or the rights of property had very little meaning – every town was a law unto itself. It was a relic of the old Europe of feudal days, before the social movements brought reforms and led eventually to capitalism.

Moving southward, we come to Transleithania, the Hungarian half of the double eagle. The traveller arriving from the north was immediately struck by one most unusual feature – there were very few trees, sometimes none at all. The Alföld stretched for almost twenty-five thousand square miles with no growth but plants and the few shrubs bordering the roads near the villages. As in China, the peasant's fuel in these parts was cowdung. The lands of the *puszta* were rich enough not to need manuring. As on the Asian steppes, flocks and herds roamed about in the care of shepherds; this way of life was a fashionable source of inspiration to the Romantics and was illustrated by Petöfi. The uniformity of the countryside created an illusion of racial unity in this pocket where the Eastern steppes came up against the mountains of Europe. There was certainly a unity of landscape, but far more important was the unity of language. Though the Magyar tongue prevailed, the Magyars themselves were not really in control of the country. They had long been aware of the delicacy of their position, surrounded as they were by such a variety of Slavs who were beginning to realize their common claims against the Hungarian overlord. Like Turkey, Hungary was beginning to look like an Asian enclave planted in the middle of Europe. Though the formidable courage of this race of horsemen had compelled the Habsburgs to concede their rule over the plains of the Empire, it seemed that the dual monarchy might become a triple one: there were in fact too many Slavs.

As for the German masters, they were firmly installed in the Alpine mountain regions, in control of the passes and the great valleys, of the fortress from which they had started the conquest of the lowlands. But today it was the very diversity of Austria which paralysed it. The Austrians had certainly made great efforts to finish the dense network of railways in the 1860s, but the difficulties were immense. Then came 1873: we have seen how the crisis which shook Europe broke first in Vienna. The disaster of 1883 followed, when the Austrian railways played a decisive part in the failure of the *Union Générale*. The die was cast. Austria had missed the opportunity for industrialization in Hungary and could no longer follow the rhythm of development in rival countries.

Nevertheless Vienna still retained its aristocratic air, chiefly because the Viennese plain was effectively industrialized on Western lines and the Alpine country region had almost caught up with the movement of modernization. The radius affected by this revitalization was limited, but it accounts in part for the extraordinary vitality of Vienna. The Austrian monarchy had been doing everything possible to consolidate its position for the past hundred years and had at least succeeded in making Vienna the gala capital of Europe. The land of Mozart and Haydn had become that of Strauss. His waltzes were still full of the imperial splendour which set all Europe dancing, delighting each generation afresh with their unusual rhythms, drawing wild applause alike from the Sunday crowds in the parks and from the aristocratic circles which were the last remnants of the feudalism of the *ancien régime*. The palaces of these nobles had now shed yesterday's gilt baroque only to adopt the ornate modern style based on the

latest botanical fashions, and which became all the rage in London, Milan
and Barcelona. It was the prestige enjoyed by this ancient aristocracy and
its old-world standards of honour which held the Empire together. Its
officials were intensely proud of their calling, its soldiers gloried in their
high vocation, and its priests were tolerant because they were troubled by
no doubts. Vienna lived on its past, it set Europe an example of wonderful

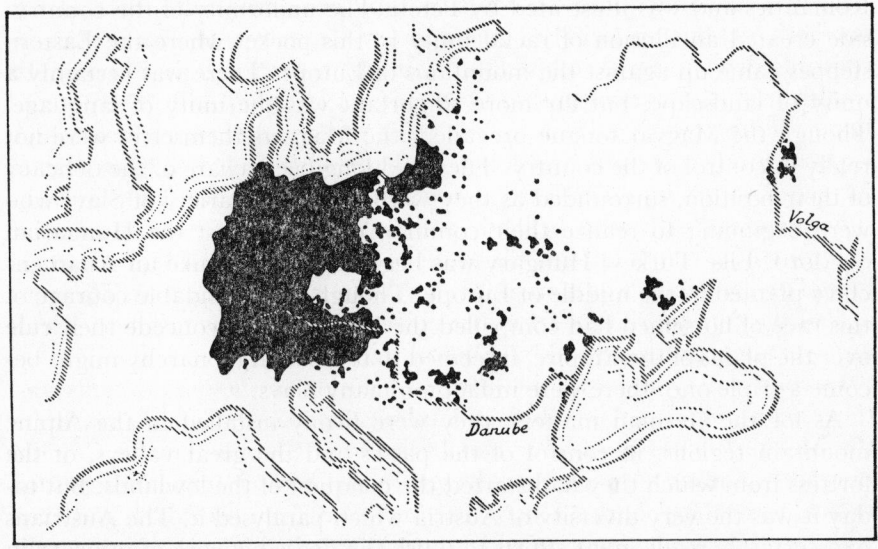

30 German-speaking Population of Central and Eastern Europe c. 1880

solidarity, and resisted the assaults of nationalism by diplomacy and a kind
of resigned wisdom which made the Austro-Hungarian yoke bearable. All
its subjects were eager to be educated in German-speaking schools while
waiting for the day when, like Italy, they would break free from the antiquated imperial city.

To the east the German people were pushing forward everywhere and
colonizing the Slav lands.

Italy: Capitalism Builds Unity

Italy had succeeded in winning independence and had forged a national
unity. What a railway had failed to do in Austria it had achieved in Italy.
As in Germany the construction of the peninsular railway had prepared
the ground for political unification. Brindisi could claim to be playing a
pivotal role in the new Mediterranean economy, although it had still to
be connected up with the great continental axes. In Italy every form of
transport was slowed down by the presence of the Papal States cutting

across the country like a scarf from one sea to the other; the administrative indifference of the Papacy enraged engineers and businessmen who were battling against the keenest international competition. Above all, the richest part of the country was in the hands of the Austrians, whose financial administration was cumbersome and inefficient. On the other hand Genoa which had lost its independence in 1815, when it joined up with Piedmont, was enjoying a genuine prosperity and was sufficiently vigorous to threaten the Austrians in Trieste.

Italy's economic progress could not be compared with that of the northern nations, especially contemporary Germany. It was not an irresistible drive towards industrialization which carried Italy to unity. Its wealth was still agricultural, and in spite of spinning mills, textiles and luxury industries of all kinds, it was trade in agricultural products which kept the lovely museum cities going. In that respect Italy was more akin to France than to any other European country. Like France, Italy was fortunate enough to have a brilliant political ideology, at once speculative and romantic, which imbued the unification movement with the idea that love of one's country was more important than material interests. The most ardent patriots had full belief in the power of French revolutionary ideals and were never discouraged by military setbacks.

Cavour is a typical example of the evolution of these sentiments and these needs. He was the godson of Pauline Bonaparte (Camillo's father – the Marquis Benso di Cavour had been Great Chamberlain to Camillo Borghese) and as a young man began by deliberately expounding such radical ideas that Charles Albert kept him away from his Court, and even withdrew him from Genoa to which he was attached. Cavour himself tells how he learned to moderate his passions and to appreciate the delicate situation in which his country was placed, between the threat of Papal excommunication and Austrian bayonets. He travelled, got to know England, and wrote a penetrating book on the English public assistance scheme. He realized the progress being made by Germany. Most important of all, he made many close friendships with Frenchmen, and this aristocrat, like so many Italian patriots, learned in Paris that it was the progress of the people which would forge the future. Debarred from holding any public office but a modest post on his country's statistical commission, he devoted himself to running and improving the family estates. He drained and ploughed and introduced new breeds, did an extensive trade in food produce, made money, studied economics, founded schools and hospitals and even tried his hand at industry. He founded an agrarian association and published a great many practical articles in his newspaper. He believed the rôle of the railways to be ethical rather than economic. In spite of this activity, Cavour was suspect to the monarchists in power and to the democrats in opposition, for he had to pursue a delicately-balanced policy which would enable agricultural Italy to profit from the industrial revolutions of northern Europe. He started a new newspaper, *Il Risorgimento*, in 1848. His political beginnings were marked by setbacks which gave him time to forge more solid links with London and Paris. He made the acquaintance of Louis Napoleon. Following England's example, on his return to Piedmont he freed the corn trade and was instrumental in promoting the railway from Genoa to Turin. The rest is history: his activities during the Crimean War and at the Congress of Paris, and the way in which he served Italy 'in the only way permissible in the existing state of Europe'. He succeeded at last in winning popularity through his friendship with France, and with good reason, since the Emperor's intervention drove the Austrians from Milan and enabled Piedmont to annex Tuscany, Parma, Modena and Romagna, and to transform itself into the Kingdom of Upper Italy. Cavour finally wrested from Napoleon III the authority to install himself in Naples in place of the Republicans and Garibaldi when the latter drove the Bourbons out of it.

After Cavour's death, his policy was carried on, but by then it was not France which was the leading industrial power on the continent, but Prussia. Each Prussian victory brought the young kingdom of Italy its share in the expansion; Venice after Sadowa, and Rome after Sedan.

The achievement of Italian unity was followed by an outburst of activity. Italian engineers won general admiration, and their bridges and canals were examples to the rest of Europe. In industry, Italy tried to develop away from the old crafts for which the country had been famous; but there was little coal, and the iron on Elba was not sufficient for the whole country. There were fortunately rather more resources for the chemical industry. In order to succeed in heavy industry, Italy had to rely more on ingenuity than on natural resources. Italy had been the first to introduce commerce into Europe and now the country's efforts were concentrated on it again. The elements of a transoceanic fleet were evolved from the extensive coastal shipping, and the first Italian vessels began to cross the Atlantic.

Nevertheless the excessive population presented a serious problem. Its density was too high, and was caused by a high birth rate rather than by longevity. Italy was therefore still at the stage which Europe had first reached on the eve of the industrial changes. There were few country districts in Italy except in the north which did not show the two infallible signs of poverty: famine and rickets. Italy, like England, exported as many able-bodied men as she could to America, but she also developed her own brand of emigration; large numbers of Italians slipped secretly across frontiers to France, Switzerland and North Africa. These emigrants remained loyal to the families they had left behind in Italy, and thus made susbtantial contributions to the state, whose finances showed a continual deficit.

But this emigration was not enough to compensate for deficiencies of industrialization. Ignorance and poverty kept alive certain picturesque features with which the Italians could well have dispensed, and maintained a body of peasants who were little more than relics left over from bygone centuries. One of the picturesque elements was banditry. In 1865, brigands were still the real rulers of the country districts of Palermo, for example, where they had their own law, the *omerta*, which they claimed went back to the days of the Normans. When the farmer harvested his corn, his oil or his wine, he had to pay tribute. At the end of the century according to official statistics the Mafia still numbered thousands of members who exploited the general fear of risks and the hatred felt for the gendarme who received his orders from Rome. The situation was serious not only in Sicily, but also in Calabria, and in many regions in southern and central Italy.

All this was the legacy of the wretched past. Venice had reached the lowest point of its decadence round about the 1840s when its palaces were in ruins, its squares were overgrown with grass, and its population dwindled to less than one hundred thousand inhabitants. At the close of the century the city was reviving and there were almost one hundred and fifty thousand inhabitants. New houses were built, the glass and textile industries were in full production, and maritime trade was making a fresh start. The same was true of Milan; of Naples, which was beginning to develop; and of Rome, the new secular capital, where the historical ruins were being classified and protected, and new and modern administrative buildings were being built.

Spain: Capitalism Encourages Disorder

Italy was being reorganized on modern lines, but Spain had not the same opportunity for doing so. The natural resources of Spain were exploited by foreign capital, and by English, French and Belgian engineers. For example, from 1861 the Carthagena zinc mines brought as many as twenty-five thousand people to live in the vicinity of Las Herrerias mines. The majority of Spain's railways too were built by foreign capital and engineers, and sometimes at a heavy loss, for the geography of the peninsula put so many obstacles in the way of the constructors. All these thousands of millions of pounds invested by foreigners shored up the economy of a country whose own inhabitants seemed to reject the demands of the modern world in order to cling to what remained of their past. The budget showed a continual deficit and the bulk of Spain's expenditure went on the upkeep of its army. This numbered two hundred thousand and was recruited with much difficulty by a system of conscription which gave exemption to cripples, invalids, defaulters, and those who were bought out; the latter class grew as the national finances became more and more shaky. A considerable part of this army was permanently immobilized in Cuba and the Philippines. Since the revolutions of 1855 the monasteries had emptied, but as Catholicism remained the state religion ecclesiastics formed a caste far more numerous than the businessmen. No one took the trouble to verify a nobleman's claim to his title: the number of hidalgos apparently amounted to something like a million. It was through this hard crust of age-old traditions that modernist ideas had to penetrate. In Spain as everywhere the reformers attempted to win adherents in the poverty-stricken country areas and towns, and among the discontented lower middle classes. Since there was no satisfactory outlet available in industrial life, the urge to change led to continual revolts; it was the root cause of an insecurity which never really succeeded in changing the country but unleashed an unending chain of disorders. There were movements against the clergy, against the monks, against the aristocracy, against the royal family. From 1835 to 1868 the crisis was latent. From 1868 to 1880, after driving out Isabella II, Spain tried every possible expedient: a military dictatorship, monarchy (with an Italian prince), a republic ... Though Isabella's son reigned from 1876, he was unable to win over the legitimists of the north; from the Basque provinces to Catalonia, these recognized none but Don Carlos. That explained why Spain's military expenditure was so excessively high.

This perpetual civil war had an economic motive. The railways had helped to keep Madrid the most important city in Spain. It had nearly half a million inhabitants who made their living by genuine industrial activity. But the plateaux around it had emptied. Spain's entire population, outside the capital, appeared to be ebbing away to the coasts, attracted by the new maritime ventures, and by vine-growing. The region of Cadiz, for instance, supported two hundred thousand hard-working citizens. Some went to Santander, Santiago, Bilbao, or Carthagena, and many to the incomparable Barcelona, which clung tenaciously to its activity and showed every sign of becoming one of the most prosperous Mediterranean cities in the French style. Between Madrid, which was isolated at the centre and needed to set up a strong union at all costs, and these provinces which clung to their regional independence there was a continual struggle. Foreign capital gave as much support to local capitalism as it did to the construction of the railway which favoured Madrid, and so gave ammunition to both sides: the very modernization of Spain kept alive the conflict it sought to bring to a close.

INDUSTRIAL EUROPE SPREADS INTO AFRICA

European settlement in Africa was one of the outstanding phenomena of the late nineteenth century. In order to get there, the Europeans had had to cross the barrier which Islam had erected across the world from India to the Atlantic. This had already been extensively breached by France, as we have seen, through the newly-emerging nationalisms. Once this gap had been widened, Africa was open to every influence of the Western world.

The Defeat of Islam

For a full understanding of the situation, we must go first to Teheran, a capital reft by Russian and English ambitions. From 1857 the Shah had

been travelling abroad and forming economic alliances. In 1864 the telegraph was working and astounding the crowds, whilst the learned men of
Islam looked inside the wire for the hole through which the messages were
transmitted. About 1870 a modern city was growing up around the huge
English bank, known as the Imperial Bank, and endowed with the magical
telegraphic address of 'Pehlevi' (a name which was to become that of a
ruling house). This city soon boasted gas and trams. Good roads were
constructed to link it up with the Caspian and the Persian Gulf. Here,
between the equally balanced power of Russia and England, a new
nation emerged which no longer owed anything to the 'unity' of Islam.
It adopted Western numerals (known as Arabic though the Arabs
count by letters) and the decimal coinages. French (and Western)
thought brought a new stimulus to education. In 1896 when the ruler did
not appear enough of a reformer, he fell victim to a plot. Progress swept
him away.

As for Turkey, it was cut off on the eastern flank by England's advance
to India, by Russia's advance across the steppes and by progress in Persia
itself. It is true that the Sultan Mejid had achieved a master-stroke and
was posing as victor in the Crimean War, which ended the quarrel over the
Holy Places between Russia and the West with the fall of Sebastopol.
Constantinople was growing. The sultans abandoned the old Seraglio and
built new palaces on the Bosphorus, to the north of the Golden Horn. The
suburbs of Galata with their many foreign inhabitants thus became the
centre of the city. The Sultan Abdul Hamid, who was detested by the
West, hoped to take advantage of this revival to re-establish the unity of
Islam. He intrigued with Bismarck, strengthened his army, surrounded
himself with Arabs and assumed the title of Caliph, which none of his predecessors had ventured to do. But his attempt to restore Islam did not succeed. Hated and lonely, he went in fear of his life, hiding first in one room
then in another, terrified by the Young Turk movement which had succeeded in assassinating his predecessor. These Young Turks, carried away
by the success of the Young Persians in Teheran (1896), abandoned the
turban for the fez and took an interest in the economic advance which enabled Trebizond to benefit from the Persian renaissance. The Sultan-
Caliph's great problem was to win them over with all speed by making
himself the champion of modernism.

It was not the old masters of the Mediterranean, Italy and Spain, which
reaped the benefit of its commercial revival; nor was it Turkey, although
on the map the Sultan's nominal possessions were still considerable. But
they were rarely put to any good use. If an attempt was made to bring
fertile lands which had been lying fallow into cultivation, it turned out that
they belonged to a mosque, or to the Sultan. The wretched farmer found
himself in prison and his goods confiscated by the Seraglio, and not without a substantial rake-off for the local authorities.

For the Sultan's one over-riding and incessant preoccupation was to get
money, a lot of money. One excellent reform was the reduction of the vast

army to a well-equipped, well-disciplined corps of one hundred thousand men. At far less cost to itself, the sovereign power was now more secure against the revolts of subject peoples, but it was also more exposed to the danger of praetorian revolts. As further economy the Turk wrote off two-thirds of his fighting fleet, so as to be spared the trouble of equipping and maintaining it. Turkey's strategic position had until recently made it the focal point of the ambitions of neighbouring nations. Now these nations were conferring together to ensure that, under the close supervision of them all, no single one should reap the benefit of an easy windfall. Thanks to their efforts, the last of the sultans were left free to enjoy the pomp and luxury of power without any of its accompanying responsibilities.

So in the gardens of the Seraglio and the new palaces costly summer-houses and follies were built and valuable furniture and precious objects were installed. Six thousand servants were barely enough for this fabulous household, which also included a host of parasitic retainers. The food contracts show that one thousand two hundred sheep a day were taken into the palace kitchens. Although he had reduced his administrative expenses as much as possible, and encouraged the extortion of money out of his subjects, the Sultan did not scruple to borrow money to keep up this luxurious way of life. He was encouraged in this since he always found one or other of the Western nations eager to seek his favour.

The land was still rich and the people were stubborn, so the rural economy with its strong tradition of craftsmanship kept alive, in spite of the pretentious way of life of the court. Constantinople remained the city of mirages: six hundred thousand inhabitants were still herded together in wretched wooden shacks and the watchmen on the Galata Tower discovered five or six major fires a week in the quarter. The city was a medley of races, religions, nationalities. Yet the Franks, tolerated by the easy-going Sultan since it was in his interests to do so, seized the bulk of the business and built in stone; the suburb of Pera replaced the Phanariotes. When the railway linking Constantinople with Vienna was completed it became an advance-post of the European economy.

For a hundred years the collapse of the Turkish Empire had been confidently awaited; it was expected that Constantinople would become a market for Western goods. But there was no evidence of this in 1895. The masterpieces of craftsmanship still displayed in the bazaar seemed rather to prove the permanence of the economic and human structure of the Muslim worlds of continental Asia. And although it went underground the slave market was nevertheless very busy. Although the Christians were more numerous they were less active in local politics: the Greeks looked to Athens, the Armenians to Russia. The various Muslim peoples, in turn, were more preoccupied with their own countries of origin than with the fate of the old capital, and with every year that passed they drew a little farther away from the Turks, leaving it to them to criticize the Seraglio and its antiquated politics. The Sultan, in spite of his ambitions, was no longer regarded as master of a world, the head of a religion covering the globe, but as a local potentate whose insensate extravagance could no longer be justified. The young generation of Turks in particular were ready to abandon dreams of world-wide domination in order to work for the effective creation of a limited country run on modern lines. Whether or not Constantinople was to predominate in Turkey, it could no longer claim to do so in Asia, Africa or the Mediterranean, which had been taken over by the economy of the West.

In Egypt the Albanian Pharaohs were carrying on with their programme: roads, canals, towns and palaces transformed the country. Ismail built Ismailia and improved Alexandria, the population of which rose from two thousand inhaibitants in 1800 to four hundred thousand in 1900, catching up with that of Cairo. The total population of Egypt reached almost ten millions at the end of the century. This was all accompanied by a great drive for education, and an expansion of the universities and even of popular education.

This progress was spectacular but short-lived. The Egyptian people, the fellaheen, suddenly realized that they belonged to a nation and called on Araby 'the Egyptian' against their Albanian masters who represented the hated Turkish rule. Turkey's influence had been incautiously revealed when Sultan Abdul Hamid deposed the Khedive Ismail in 1879. Ismail's successor, the young Tewfik, was in a most difficult position. His predecessors had spent wildly and borrowed at heavy interest. It had been necessary to do so in order to modernize the country, but the creditors were pressing; Tewfik, caught between Egyptian nationalism, the claims of the Turkish Sultan, and the demands of French and English bankers, was compelled to accept the 'protection' of England. The English acted singlehanded in 1881 when France delayed over her reply.

The whole of North Africa was therefore cut off from Arabia, from which its conquerors had set out ten centuries earlier.

Europe's Future in Africa

We have described how the failure of the old-established Mediterranean countries to exploit their sea had enabled France to gain a footing in Algeria; and it is easy to see now how the French were able to extend their field of action to the whole of North Africa. First there was a sudden increase in the French and European populations in Algeria. This had three causes: the Crémieux decree granting naturalization to the Jews, the immigrations of Spaniards, Italians and Maltese who were also eligible for naturalization, and the considerable French immigration since 1871. Some Arabs objected, some considered naturalization themselves, although they hesitated for fear of betraying the Law and the Prophet. In any case the major language was either French or Sabir, and work was done more and more on European lines. Unfortunately much of the work consisted of cutting down the woods spared by the gigantic fires of 1865, 1881 and many others caused by imprudent new colonists. But farms also were being built, with earthen floors, on the lands granted to settlers by the state. It was hard work. The draining of the Mitija was also a miracle of rural heroism. More than fifty villages were founded for the refugees from Alsace and Lorraine. Work was started on a land register which even allotted some ground to the natives. In addition, improvements were made in the organization of workers, the miners were being exploited, roads were opened up, and caravan traffic across the Sahara had been resumed. The volume of shipping increased at the ports and new districts were built in Algiers around the old Kasbah and along the busy port.

The railway followed the coast and had reached the very heart of Tunisia, taking French power as far as Tunis. It had been laid down by the French, whose task was made easier by the imprudence of the Bey. He was nominally a Turkish official, but in fact independent; he had borrowed money from all over Europe, especially from France, without thinking too much about how it was to be repaid. It was to put his finances on a sounder footing that the Treaty of Bardo in 1881 associated a French resident with the government of the country. The army of occupation numbered forty-three thousand men, and although it was quickly reduced to ten thousand, it brought in its train a crowd of Algerians, more Arab than French, who followed their new rulers hoping to improve their frugal way of life by accompanying the spearhead of the modernization drive. At all events, the French were now firmly entrenched in Algeria and the way was prepared for the supremacy of the French language and way of life, as well as for French institutions, in spite of the other Europeans, particularly the Italians, who up to that time were the most numerous and the most active.

The new French influence not only resulted in the efficient ordering of the budget, which doubled from 1883 to 1886, but also vastly improved the city of Tunis. New quarters were built in what had previously been the refuse dump, which the Jews had been obliged to empty from time to time. The drainage of land for building brought Tunis nearer the sea, where a great artificial harbour was planned in the creek with its picturesque fishermen. These were the first stages of a far-reaching programme. As the tribes fleeing from the Christians made their way towards southern Algeria, a growing number of immigrants was arriving from the Mediterranean countries, and these all helped to draw the country away from its Eastern traditions and to link it to the modern way of life, which was dominated by French speculation. At the other end of the Atlas range the supervision of the Algerian borders led to the exploration of Morocco. The most daring of these explorations was that of Charles de Foucauld who crossed the Atlas Mountains and travelled across areas of the south where hardly anyone had ventured before. The region of Rabat at Fez was, however, better known, and people from every nation could be found travelling there. The question then arose whether Morocco should be independent, under international supervision, or French. In any case Morocco was opening up to foreign influence. The Moroccans were no longer forbidden to offer hospitality to the Christians. European greed found effective ways of flattering the Sultan. His personal fortune was mixed up with that of the state, after the Turkish custom, but he had no need to borrow, for the income from his taxes and the gifts which accompanied them was substantial. French settlement in what was still called Barbary China was to be no easy task. The process was the result of a vast international movement which involved Europe in the seizure of the whole of Africa.

Europe's appropriation of Africa was the greatest outcome of its drive to expand, the last and strongest of the series which emanated from the old world. And no other power, even among those which competed with Europe for Asia, thought of disputing the European claim to Africa. Nevertheless, Africa only forms a single continent for the convenience of modern geographical classification; in reality this great and varied land mass is criss-crossed by innumerable trends and currents. Its Atlantic coast, as we have seen, had long been exploited by the slave-traders. Then the traders seeking gold, ivory, fruit, cocoa and wood established their trade settlements, but as yet did not venture into the interior. But the progress of steam navigation and the creation of ports of call stocked with the coal these ships required meant that the coastal ports were being developed. Then Faidherbe emerged from the island of Gorea, occupied Dakar and ventured a little way into the interior. All around these coastal bases patches of oil began to appear in the sea. The same phenomena occurred in the east as in the west. In the east, for instance, the Piedmontese Sabato explored a region which gradually began to take shape as Eritrea, around Massawa. England penetrated up the Zambesi and German merchants traded around Zanzibar. Along the whole of this coastal belt the traces of the great commercial empire of Zanzibar formed a powerful motive for penetration inland. The Arabs by the Red Sea, along the route from India, had as we have seen developed a kind of thalassocracy. The Sultan of Zanzibar claimed sovereign power over the territories in the interior of Africa into which Arab caravans penetrated in search of slaves, spices and ivory, which he re-sold to India. These warlike caravans relied for their defence on young Negroes, kidnapped and trained to serve as escorts. They no longer bothered greatly about concealing the routes they followed, and so opened up the way to adventurers from Europe. Something in the nature of a European condominium in fact controlled the Sultan of Zanzibar, who was soon consoled for the loss of his empire since the pressure of Christian competition quickly filled his coffers. Lastly, there was an extensive thrust into the interior from the Dutch territories in South Africa. The north seemed to fall into an easy division between the English in Egypt and the French in Tunisia and Algeria; the Italians tried to gain a foothold somewhere in between.

There remained central Africa itself. The problems it raised were complicated by a geographical error. From ancient times there had been argument about the course of the Nile, the miracle river of the desert. It was known from Negro folk-lore and from several explorations that there were enormous lakes in the centre of Africa; it was out of this lake Zaïre that the Nile was believed to flow, as well as the river which emptied itself into the kingdom of the Congo. At the end of the eighteenth century the Portuguese had made a last attempt to link up Angola with Mozambique. Little is known about what these Pombeïros achieved on their journey, which continued into the early years of the nineteenth century. Once again in 1843 Graça followed in their footsteps, apparently with no more success. The Portuguese were followed by the English. From 1887 they penetrated inland in their turn, in search of the central empire which might possibly have become the refuge of the mythical Prester John. In 1870 Livingstone set out, followed a few years later by Stanley.

The Partition of Africa

This time a new era was beginning. Western explorers were becoming increasingly confident in their methods, their tools, ships, weapons, and medicine chest. They drew up more accurate maps, and were quicker at understanding native dialects; among the Bantu tribes, for instance, forty, and ultimately fifty, variant dialects were recorded. Then Stanley undertook his fantastic expedition on the Livingstone (as he wished to re-name the old Zaïre which in the end retained the more politic name of Congo). The journey covered twelve thousand miles of jungle, forest, reeds, lakes, cataracts, waterfalls and mountains, including the Mountains of the Devil! It took three years and cost hundreds of lives, three or four of the casualties being white men. Stanley was, however, the first to give an informed description of the heart of Africa (1877). On landing at Marseilles he found waiting for him two emissaries from the King of the Belgians. For the past fifteen years Leopold had been looking for a colonial venture, not so much because he was an explorer at heart but because he was a far-sighted businessman and had shrewdly appraised the wealth which skilful exploitation of these new worlds had heaped up in England's coffers. Stanley would have preferred to work for England, but the latter rejected the explorer's offers. Consequently he agreed to become Leopold's man, or rather, officially the representative of an association which was called in succession the *Association de Géographes*, then the *Internationale Africaine*, then the *Études du Haut-Congo*, and finally emerged as the *Association Internationale du Haut-Congo*. Its aim was to root out the remnants of slavery from the Congo and to carry to the Negroes the Gospel and the benefits of civilization. It was to work through national committees in several countries. It would perhaps be more to the point to ask what was Leopold's aim: it was to gain a vast stretch of territory for himself, and the means which would enable him to do this were the credits which the Belgian banks were obliged to grant their king. Leopoldville was founded in 1882 by Stanley, who had gone back to the Congo in fulfilment of the Association's statute which sought to 'set up civilized establishments along the banks, to conquer the country by peaceful means, to cast it in a new mould more in keeping with modern ideas, to foster states in the bosom of which the European trader would fraternize with the Negro, the African trader, and from which murder and the slave trade would be banished for ever'. Meanwhile in order to resume the exploration of the country, this time from west to east and moving towards the Nile, Stanley made an agreement with the Arabs and used their squads of slave hunters. It is only fair to note that while Belgian money was enabling the European to replace the Arab, a movement was growing to transform numerous Negro states, previously warlike, into agricultural countries where manioc was grown, the forest cleared, and agricultural produce sold rather than prisoners of war. But during these early years the Congo was far from bringing Leopold the quick profits he had been expecting.

This did not, however, prevent the Belgian venture from arousing much keen jealousy. For more than ten years Savornan de Brazza, starting from the Gabon estuary, had been pushing into the interior on expeditions which took him too to the Congo. He recruited troops on the spot and exploited native rivalries to establish himself in an enormous tract of country. He laid claim to Stanley's river and established an impregnable post on the banks with a garrison consisting of four Negroes.

The Germans in Zanzibar, for their part, made many marches westward in order to annex as much as they could of the region of the Great Lakes. In such circumstances the *Association Internationale* did not appear a very formidable rival: there was open talk in Berlin of carving out a good empire at its expense. The Portuguese in Mozambique and Angola fought bitterly to assert their historic rights, and England suddenly gave them noble support after having considered sharing with Germany. In short, central Africa became a great centre of rivalry between the European powers. There was, however, no question of actual war: however eager the new nations were to paint the maps of the world in symbolical colours, the forests, swamps, and fevers of Africa did not inspire them with the requisite greed. Each power was concerned mainly with playing off its rivals. It used its traders and engaged in diplomatic disputes, the more readily since both Leopold and Portugal appeared an easy prey. Bismarck suggested that France should convene an international conference on Africa in Paris. France affected to prefer Berlin. The purpose was to ensure 'the most favourable conditions for the development of trade and civilization in Africa'. In practice the Act of 1885 established a kind of working rule: Stanley, Brazza and the Germans in south-west and east Africa, the English in the Sudan and the south, majestically presided over the distribution of flags. The 'conqueror' arriving in a village negotiated with the chief, offered him gifts, all with the greatest solemnity, and handed him the flag of his own nation: the conquest was completed. Brazza found flags a more valuable item of baggage than footwear. In future, treaties were to be notified to the European chanceries. Each power naturally had great bundles of treaties, except perhaps England, which more often than not merely marked her zones of influence on the map, often not even bothering to go here, accustomed as she was to being the only nation on the spot. Moreover, and this was the most important of all, the Act of Berlin granted to each owner of a stretch of coast first claim to its hinterland. This effectively barred England's route to the north. On the other hand, in return for heavy sacrifices on the banks of the Congo River, the Congo was recognized as an independent state, charged only with the obligation to leave trade free and equal for all. The Brussels Parliament resigned itself in turn, with reluctance, to allow its constitutional King to become an absolute monarch in the Congo. France was momentarily appeased by the promise of a right of pre-emption and allowed the measure to go through.

Leopold, though sovereign ruler, was short of money and deeply in debt and the Congo, far from bringing money in, swallowed up enormous amounts of capital. The Belgian Bank was no longer adequate, and the Belgian Government was forced to lend millions to its sovereign. He had to negotiate the right to establish customs duties in order to bring in the resources needed for the abolition of slavery. No sooner had he obtained this concession than the world witnessed the strange spectacle of Leopold behaving as a landowner more brutally than the harshest slave-master in pre-abolitionist America. It was the rule of the Chicote, a whip made of hippopotamus hide. It was all the easier for the régime to go unchallenged since the last Arab rivals were crushed in 1893. Negroes were recruited compulsorily, populations were transplanted, and forced labour was instituted particularly in the rubber plantations; 'red rubber' as the opposition called it. Leopold became the most colossal landowner in the world, living sumptuously in Europe, building palaces and collecting mistresses on an equally lavish scale.

There were sporadic insurrections, some indignation, and a good deal of jealousy. Nevertheless, the change which had come over the management of affairs in the Congo had noticeable repercussions in several other parts of Africa. France took possession of Madagascar, and England of Zanzibar: each allowed the other a more or less free rein. But Madagascar was shaken by revolts; costly expeditions had to be sent and many lives sacrificed. It was found necessary to depose Queen Ranavalona and introduce direct rule. In the Niger, France and England had joined forces to oppose the claims of Samory, the champion of Islam. The French, in pursuit of slave hunters, reached the Chad: thus at last achieving the internal link between west and north Africa. It was chiefly in order to extend this internal domination as far as the region of the Upper Nile and of Bahr El-Ghazal that the Marchand expedition set out in 1896 from the Congo in the direction of the Sudan. Two years later, after innumerable adventures, it reached the post of Fashoda only a few days before the English expedition commanded by Kitchener arrived at the same point, having come up the Nile. Although France was traditionally a militant nation she ceded Fashoda to the English. In colonial territories French policy was peaceful, more concerned with human contacts and economic progress than with spectacular *coups*.

A whole generation of young colonial leaders was now growing up, following in the great tradition of the Faidherbes and the Brazzas, and adding new lustre to it by their magnificent achievements. There was Galliéni on the Niger and in Madagascar, Laperrine in the Sahara and Charles de Foucauld exploring unknown Morocco. Lyautey has described how this new spirit came into being. In 1889 he was received at Saigon by Galliéni, who asked him for the books and papers he had brought in his kitbag (the tactical manual, army service book and other aide-memoires). Galliéni firmly tied them up into a parcel. 'Forget the lot,' he said, 'nothing they contain has anything to do with our job out here. We have to begin by observing, listening, reflecting and re-reading Joseph Chaillez: colonial policy is not so much a matter of continual expansion as of carefully planned progress. A European capital cannot possibly administer or govern by *its* methods, its laws and its European officials . . . In order to pacify a country one has to use peaceful means.'

The brilliance of France's industrial development during these years enabled it to rely confidently on this policy that was so essentially English in conception; at this time England, whose economic superiority was now threatened, was embarking on the most terrible war in the whole of her colonial history in South Africa, although its record there had been one of great tolerance up to that point.

Conclusion

Danger Ahead

ONE CAPITALISM OUSTS ANOTHER

IN 1890 the stock exchanges of London, Paris, Berlin and New York controlled the economic progress of the whole world. The liberal middle class had reached the height of its power and influence. There was, however, a tremendous difference between the businessman of 1890 and the bourgeois of 1830. An entirely new society was coming into being which called for a new type of person, was organized in new ways and used new methods. Above all it was preoccupied with a new and unusual source of anxiety. Hitherto the European bourgeois had made money at the expense of the other classes and the other continents; it had left it to providence to take care of poverty and relied on progress to eradicate it. In 1890, those in control of Europe's economic life were obliged to organize and integrate the European working classes who were now powerful enough to make themselves felt as an essential factor in this evolution; they were also forced to reassess Europe's place in a world which had itself awakened to new life.

We have noted that the economic history of the 1880s posed this problem in the form of a paradox. These years saw the introduction of a range of technical processes invented in the new scientific laboratories which had the effect of stimulating the economy even further. During these years, too, great factories were set up on the continent with modernized plant, and the mechanical civilization they created was far more powerful than the one which excited the progressives in 1850. But at the same time this period was marked by the biggest drop in prices yet experienced in Europe's history, and that without the accompaniment of revolution or of war; a profound transformation of society was taking place.

The year 1850 had been, as we have seen, that of the railway, and the vogue for railways persisted up to 1880, when Freycinet drew up his grandiose projects for it in France. The fact was that the business world was under the illusion that the mileage returns from lines built in 1880 would equal that of the lines built in 1850. Unfortunately, it is quite obvious that branch lines of small secondary centres, on which moreover traffic was slower, could never bring in as much as the great main lines. In 1882 thousands of miles of track built by the French Government could not find a bidder, and the exchequer had to bear the cost until almost the end of the century. Furthermore, the *Compagnie de l'Ouest*, for instance, managed its affairs so badly that it had to be nationalized in 1909. It was the same in Belgium; the state was obliged to buy back certain lines, and doubled its network in 1873; in 1880 it built three-quarters of the railways and almost completed the system in 1908. In Germany the completion of the railway system had largely been facilitated by the war indemnity paid by France. All the same the Prussian Government also had to buy back the networks of Hanover, Hesse and Nassau. The Imperial Government bought back the Alsace-Lorraine network and set up an organization that by and large turned the railways into a state concern though it was opposed by some countries, among them Bavaria. In Prussia the state lines increased from three thousand to nearly twenty-five thousand miles, while the private lines fell from something like eight thousand to less than two thousand. This concentration of railways in government hands is worth noting, since it could be considered the beginning of state capitalism. In the 1880s financiers were continually complaining of the small profits now to be made on the railways. The fact was that the concentration of lines, the simplified and reduced rates, no longer made profits possible except for very large concerns. By 1900, only the very big French companies had come near to repaying the credits borrowed from the government. Only the Prussian railways were bringing their owner, the government, substantial profits; moreover these remained outside parliamentary control and made possible a close connection between the railway and the military administrations. A similar situation was developing with the canals and roads; the age of individual enterprise on the English pattern of the 1830s was definitely over. Only vast organized systems could meet the costs and guarantee profits. These hard facts were obvious only to a very small group of thinkers who met with such a hostile reception when they forecast the end of small-scale middle-class enterprise that they did not dare express openly either their belief in 'state control' or their 'socialism'.

This trend towards concentration in transport was equally apparent in other spheres of economic life. Financiers were now familiar with the rhythm of crises. When the currency circulation of the bank of issue increased, the increased number of bills and acceptances indicated widespread activity by private enterprise. A large number of industrialists attempted to try their luck. The consumer's market, strongly influenced by advertisement and by a growing volume of publicity, made its choice from the mass of new products and those it rejected piled up in the factories which soon had to close down. Then the discount rate rose. Credit tightened. Reserves dwindled, the issue of paper currency slowed down and the crisis had arrived. The small manufacturer faced bankruptcy, total ruin, or at best the sale of his business at a low rate to a much larger concern whose floating capital was substantial enough to surmount the credit difficulties provoked by the rise in discount. Consequently there occurred vast ebbing and flowing movements of credit, which assumed an approximately five-yearly rhythm.

Each period of recession was characterized by concentration. This was so intense that private family capital, the bourgeois capital of the 1830s, could no longer cope with it. The joint stock company was essential, since that alone could make good in each phase of prosperity the retrenchments which had been imposed by the slump. In France, three hundred companies a year were being founded in 1880 and more than a thousand in 1900. In Germany there were more than two thousand new ones by 1885, and approximately four thousand by 1900; these latter figures included only the *Aktien Gesellschaft* or very large businesses, small limited liability companies being much more numerous.

A large number of these joint stock companies were banks, which were becoming more and more necessary to provide floating capital for businesses. The development of banks was widespread in England and in France, but in Germany it was phenomenal. In France the deposit banks already had two hundred and fifty branches in 1890 and the total passed the thousand mark at the beginning of the twentieth century. In Germany the banking organization was more complex. There were a great many regional and local banks, and it was by direct or indirect control of them that the great central organisms grew to vast proportions. At the opening of the twentieth century, the *Deutsche Bank* participated directly in the management of thirty banks and indirectly in that of fifty-seven. These growing organisms, sometimes monstrous in size, amassed a large quantity of deposits for the three great Western countries, France, England and Germany. These must have amounted to something like four hundred million pounds in 1880 and nearly two thousand million twenty years later. The bank completely dominated industrial credit. Any business concern however well equipped from which it withheld its support, especially in the rather risky economies such as that of Germany, would certainly go bankrupt or would be compelled to merge with a more important firm or one more favoured by the bank. Yet the bank was able to accumulate such vast deposits only by constant contact with a growing and increasingly trustful clientele. It was these who, in actual practice, controlled the placing of shares, thus playing in the distribution of long-term credit a rôle equivalent to the one they played in short-term credit. Hence the enormous power wielded by these enormous banking houses which erected their proud façades in the new capitals of 1900. In Germany, four great banks practically shared out between them the financial market of the whole Empire by a gentleman's agreement. The *Dresdner Bank*, for instance, controlled the steel and electrical industries, as well as business concerns in west Africa and Brazil; the *Deutsche Bank* was more concerned with communications, chemicals, and also the central European and Turkish markets.

Behind this concentration of banking and finance, an industrial concentration was also in progress. In France the owners of coalmines and foundries entered into joint agreements known as *comptoirs*. In 1876 in Germany the Westphalian coalmines had, as we have seen, agreed to fix prices, a move towards organization which was a reaction from the fever of the *Gründerjahre*. In 1890 came a further step: a cartel organized sales;

three years later it controlled half the country's production by a merger with the briquette union and the coke syndicate. Similarly, cartels were set up for steel, iron and metallurgical plant (the *Stahlwerksverband*). We have seen that from the beginning the electricity industry was concentrated. Under the direction of Rathenau, the AEG joined forces with Siemens to exercise almost absolute control over the whole of German production. The *Kalisyndikat* was created in the same way. Powerful new men came to the fore, amongst them Kirdorf, Thyssen and Krupp in the Rhineland.

In reality, economic power, though organized empirically, was nevertheless as closely knit as political power at the end of the nineteenth century, and it is important not to regard it merely as an outward expression of the personality of some captain of industry or influential financier. Industrial concentration proceeded at such a pace, because of technical progress and under the impact of the long slump, that in effect it created an economic administration. This was no longer on the classic lines of middle-class liberalism, but it employed an army of officials who were as active and influential in the nation as the officials in the public services.

The innumerable employees of the banking houses and the industrial managements really were officials. The hierarchy, though it may have been less obvious, nevertheless exerted great power; the head of the system was not parliament but the boards of directors. In principle these bodies were responsible to the general body of shareholders. In fact the majority of shareholders empowered their banks to negotiate on their behalf and the zeal and vigilance of a few bankers were all that was needed to ensure the stability of the board. Administrative officials dealt with one transaction after another whether or not there was any connection between them. Plurality of seats thus reinforced economic solidarity and added a new 'princely' hierarchy of directors, in which each man's rank was determined by the number of 'seats' at his disposal. It was a far cry from the middle-class employer paternally managing a small factory of some tens or even hundreds of workers. This was a polysynody of great aristocrats which exercised absolute control over hundreds of thousands or even millions of workers.

The new social régime needed new men to fill posts at every level of its hierarchies. Up to 1880 the problem of education had been chiefly a political one: the elector had to be educated, and the major subjects had been philosophy and the teaching of liberty, law and politics. After 1880 the problem was increasingly a technical one. The controversy on the problem of 'special' education in France towards 1870 provides an illustration. Whilst secondary education in the *lycées* continued to teach Latin rhetoric, Victor Duruy had selected for special education some young men who had not studied Latin but wished to be initiated into the modern disciplines of science. Classical instruction held its ground for nearly fifteen years against this despised competition; it made concessions; in order to save Latin it did away with the old-fashioned exercises in Latin verse, and split up the *bachot* so that the second part could be either scientific or philosophical, to the great despair of cultured minds for whom philosophy remained the true end of education. But the special education continued and began to attack the privileges of the *lycées* cautiously at first, then in strength; finally it organized a system of 'modern' education without Latin, and with its own literary and scientific divisions. In 1892 it triumphantly achieved parity with the old *bachot*. In 1894 the two teaching bodies were merged. This merger was all the more important since a marked increase in the numbers attending *lycées* took place at the same time. Every year this new economic way of life called for more officials, more engineers, more business managers: the old middle-class grounding in Latin and philosophy was no longer adequate.

England, as we have seen, remained sentimentally attached to its Victorian economy even after 1890. Its universities turned out clergymen and theologians: the sons of great families went there to acquire a veneer of culture.

Technical education was equally limited. An official report in 1884 deplored the total lack of elementary institutions, and the scarcity of higher education. It was customary in England for the businessman and the technician to be trained within the firm itself, which naturally made it much easier for sons to make a career in the family business in which they served an apprenticeship under covenant. Yet the incessant demand for labour which characterized this vigorously expanding economy did not deprive the poor man's sons of all hope: he too made his way in the world. Starting as one of many, he proudly attained a directorship forty years later. Nevertheless a systematic modern education was vitally necessary. Many English scientists (or scientists who had migrated to England) heard the call of science in the great public lectures of the Royal Society. When a well-known expert was lecturing, he easily attracted several hundred attentive listeners, most of whom had just come from the office, the laboratory or the shop, in search of a little knowledge. As in the age of enlightenment, it was through personal contacts, chance meetings, the friendship formed between an expert and his faithful disciple, that the experts of the future were recruited.

After 1850 the secularization of Oxford was decided upon, but it was not until 1870 that the monopoly of examinations was taken from the old medieval universities and that examining bodies were set up in London with power to grant degrees to the pupils of the independent schools. These were springing up here and there in cities such as Birmingham and Manchester. However, the well-known Industrial Museum at South Kensington was beginning to disseminate elementary and secondary technical education. Although the universities were slow to widen their scope, they began to acquire laboratories in modest premises presided over by some great scientist such as Faraday or Maxwell. Modern higher education began to take shape in 1880.

In France, too, higher education still preserved its middle-class character at about this same period. The lecture-halls of famous professors were crowded with fashionable people, men of learning and wealthy young men, rather than with students. It was not until 1875 and the advent of Liard that higher education began to be more concerned with turning out technicians than with philosophizing for the benefit of the cultured people. It was only at the end of the century that the faculties gradually overcame their administrative autonomy and were grouped into universities. We know how wretchedly equipped were the laboratories of Berthelot and especially of Pasteur. The great scientific movement was almost as slow to get under way in France as in England. Nevertheless France had her schools, *Polytechnique*, *Normale Supérieure* and *Centrale*, already long-established. To these new schools were being added, built in the same spirit; particularly the *École des Sciences Politiques* founded by Taine and Boutmy and intended to train suitable men for the new public and private administrative posts. Then too there was the *École des Hautes Études*, which through Duruy's foresight answered in advance the complaints set out by Renan in *La Réforme Intellectuelle et Morale* – a treatise in which the historian and the philologist deplore the lack of technical training in French culture. The great reformers of 1890 urged on the development of the university in the hope that it would succeed in absorbing all the special schools born of the imperial tradition.

Renan attributed part of Germany's victory to the excellence of its universities. These had, in fact, been regarded as a model throughout all the latter half of the nineteenth century. They had forged the idea of German unity and they celebrated the victory of the Empire as their victory. Most of the old universities had doubled their numbers. Faculties of political economy had been inspired by the teachings of List, while the faculties of philosophy split into two sections, history and sciences. The system of seminars brought masters and students into more direct contact for practical work also, and the system of the *Privat-dozent* enabled men of talent to use their popularity with the students in order to become candidates for official chairs, thus undermining the position of the old-fashioned lecturers by competition. Seminars and *Privat-dozents* competed with each other for students who made a point of going the rounds of three or four universities before settling down in one of them. This competition encouraged the public authorities of a university city to keep excellent libraries and laboratories, and led to a close liaison between research and teaching within the framework of the states of the Empire. The staff of German universities had such exceptional privileges that in contrast with the situation in France legislation sought rather to reduce than to extend them. In 1880, the imprisonment of members of university councils was actually limited to a fortnight! The life of the student guilds which Germans sometimes liked to trace back to the Middle Ages, with their curious customs (particularly the duel, the *Mensur*), dated in fact from the time when rapid progress took the universities from their medieval structure of the 1830s to the large-scale capitalist structure of the 1880s; so that in only two generations the whole of the middle-class era was spanned.

Economists, lawyers, engineers, technicians of every kind, armed with testimonials in England and diplomas in Germany, filled the new posts created by the capitalist economy. Renan made the suggestion that a country's educational system was a clear indication of its worth. Germany was methodical, erudite, ambitious, confident; England cautious, self-assured, haughty; and France divided between the technical achievements of her schools and the too-generalized culture of her university.

The 1880s also witnessed a general encouragement of primary education. The school set out to attract the most gifted young men of the nation in order to carry them towards posts in private businesses or with the government by a process known as 'social capillarity'. Schools were opened in the countryside. It need hardly be said that though the nation's hierarchies were being radically changed and Republican statesmen in France (Ferry and Berthelot in particular) did all they could to make the new capitalist structure democratic, it still remained easier for the rich than for the poor to attain the key positions. A curious instance of this was provided in France between 1789 and 1880. Higher education for girls created at the instigation of Camille Sée was at first free. It was a failure. The municipal schools could get no pupils. The idea was then conceived of making it appeal to its 'natural' clientèle, so the education consequently had to be paid for; and it was soon a great success. It is hardly necessary to recall here that the cost of the actual tuition represented only a fraction of the total cost incurred in a young man's education. The son of a peasant or a workman was hardly in a position to embark on the long course of secondary and advanced study. The lower middle classes sometimes went as far as the fourth grade, or to a public school in England, and there were various generous schemes afoot to carry education to wider sections of society; the University of Cambridge launched the University Extension movement, offering a course of popular lectures designed to cover the normal school syllabus in three years and enabling students who had passed a qualifying examination to take the final years of the university course. The popular universities in France, and even more in Belgium, also made provision for this movement, which continued throughout the expansive phase of the modern technocratic society.

The nineteenth century offered many striking instances of tradesmen's sons attaining the highest honours by way of either science or industry, but it was comparatively rare for such eminence to be achieved by the sons of peasants or of artisans, or by anyone from the ranks of those who in the 1830s were known as 'the people'. However, a middle-class parent still deplored the fact that he had to send his children to universities and schools in which they might have to rub shoulders with the sons of the people. A large new lower middle class was also emerging from which the army of officials was recruited; this class was dominated by powerful industrial and financial circles.

And what of the people? Michelet no longer regarded them as synonymous with the working class which had come into being in the great urban centres, and which might more fittingly be called the proletariat from 1880 onwards.

A SETBACK FOR THE MIDDLE CLASS

The closing years of the nineteenth century also brought about a growth in population. This time, however, the rise was due not to an increase in fertility, since this was in fact steadily declining, but to improved expectation of life. Although man's life-span now extended into the middle years of the fertility period, this increased longevity was from 1880 onwards no longer accompanied by a rise in the birth rate. The two-fold movement from the country to the town, and from the agricultural fringes of Europe towards the industrial areas of Europe or the New World, meant that populations were being shifted by rail or by boat on a hitherto unprecedented scale. The people were moving along the channels opened up by the techniques of capitalism. The rise in the birth rate was not very marked, and a few years later the rise was to slow down, then stop altogether.

The urban working population took on a new lease of life in this time of flux. Amongst these uprooted people the first stirrings of a new spirit were beginning, a feeling of brotherhood uniting all the workers of the world. Not that socialism had suddenly won the day: its growth in the early years was hesitant and impeded by the continual fluctuations of the economy. It was nevertheless favoured by a slight but continuous rise in wages. The great mechanized industries paid best and gradually absorbed the ragged proletariat, the victims of the sweating system, but not without terrible sufferings: the last days of the rural hand-loom weavers were agonizing whether it was in Cambresis, Silesia or Lancashire. Parliamentary investigations in every country revealed the poverty of these families, toiling away fourteen hours a day at their old looms to earn barely enough to buy bread. The fact was that mechanized industry now worked at such cheap rates that the craftsman was being driven out from many sections of the economy, and particularly from textile manufacture. In the factories, there was as yet no question of a systematic organization of work, and the multiplication of machines necessitated a new team work and created a new feeling of solidarity. In the towns the building of new housing estates for the newcomers brought working-class families into the closest contact with each other and created for them an urban setting which, though still rudimentary, was already establishing a uniform pattern of living amongst workers all over the world. Shrewd minds were shaping this new army for the coming class struggle; Marx believed he had seen the first signs of it in England twenty-five years ahead of the times.

A new working-class solidarity was beginning to emerge. In 1880 most of the workers were craftsmen in the direct tradition of the old guilds, and the rapid or gradual disappearance of the old rules had unleashed rivalries which set tradesman against tradesman. The people of 1900 still bore the mark of the harsh treatment meted out to them by the early liberalism, but pressure of circumstances forced the working classes to recognize that solidarity was far more essential than competition. The poor began to realize that it was foolish to try to succeed in isolation. Shared migrations and the common difficulties involved in settling on new lands or in the vast collective tenements and new suburbs gave them a better opportunity to bring about communal improvements in material conditions. Common funds, capable of financing common action, came into being side by side with the old savings banks advocated by the philanthropists of 1830. Mutual aid societies and unions were modelled on the pattern of those in Germany, which claimed to be the inventor of social insurance.

The great problem was the recruitment of labour. Labour exchanges were a French idea of about 1848, which had gradually gained ground under the Second Empire without any backing from the public authorities, who preferred their own system of employment bureaux run by each mayoralty. Other countries took up this idea and it almost succeeded in Austria and Belgium. The power of the unions in England succeeded in establishing it there. Each union tried to control the labour market by employing a special secretariat; they also made use of publicity which was timid by modern standards but nevertheless well-planned. In 1876 at Philadelphia, in 1880 at Le Havre, workers' conferences put the question of labour exchanges on their agenda. In 1888 the Paris Municipal Council granted the Paris Labour Exchange a huge office block in the Rue Jean-Jacques Rousseau. It included an assembly hall seating one thousand five hundred. The early days were difficult. The Caterers' Bureau succeeded in finding employment for two-thirds of its members, but the labourers were not nearly so well served. It was also not clear whether the Exchange should support other needs of the workers. Numerous though the exchanges were, they were soon quite inadequate and it was necessary to plan the building of a Central Exchange near the Place de la République.

In any move towards working-class solidarity, the problem of labour recruitment involved that of wages. The laws of 1871 in England and of 1884 in France opened up a wide field of action to the unions: each new crisis led to fresh unrest and agitation among the workers. Sometimes the new proletariat would erupt with an isolated act of anarchy; sometimes a group plotted together; there was the attempt to dynamite Wilhelm II at the unveiling of the statue of *Germania* in 1889, and the French *Chambre des Députés* in 1896. President Carnot was assassinated in 1898, King Umberto in 1900. The working-class organizations openly condemned these anarchist moves, and the International excluded anarchist theorists from its membership. Anarchism, a label rather than a programme, was abandoned almost everywhere except in Spain. For though the anarchist movement had its theorists like Kropotkin, it was chiefly the symbol of a discontent which working-class organization alone could cure. This derived its strength from the struggle for better living conditions, higher wages and more stable employment. Once strikes were legalized in 1880 they were widely used in times of crisis. Strikes affected the exploitation of raw material in the Borinage and in the Ruhr; and were used with even greater effect against the means of communication (as in the Italian telegraph service in 1893). A strike could rally enormous crowds around its committees; there were as many as thirty-five thousand in St Petersburg in 1896. As the proletariat organized itself, it grew increasingly conscious of its strength. Jules Guesde reproached the Germans with not putting enough revolutionary fire into their action. Pelloutier urged the use of the general strike. The ground was prepared for the great waves of general revolutionary strikes which marked the opening years of the twentieth century.

This movement had a considerable revolutionary element in it and originated largely in Paris. In 1880 Paris was undoubtedly the city in which large-scale industry was the least developed of any in the world. Average-sized businesses with craftsmen operating in suburban workshops were still the rule. In this respect, French working-class agitators used similar methods to those of 1789, and the quarrels of the Commune were revived after twenty years. But it was in France, too, that the struggle for working-class education was strongest, precisely because the frontier between the proletariat and the lower-middle class was less clearly defined. It was this democratic opinion which supported Ferry's educational programme and gave colour and strength to the work of Pelloutier, a bourgeois in the service of the people. Outside France, the demands of the workers were more closely linked to their conditions of work. Americans were the first to stipulate an eight-hour day, and the celebration of the First of May as Labour Day. Differences began to emerge in temperament and outlook between the various countries. Their delegates clashed in speeches and motions at international conferences. At Zurich in 1893, a great Dutch trade unionist reminded his audience that chauvinism existed among socialists just as among the middle classes. In 1889, the year of the birth of the Second International, the Congress of Paris was divided between socialists and trade unionists. As for the Germans, they had turned socialism into an enormous political party of more than a million members in 1890; but it grew too quickly, lost its fighting strength, and collaborated in parliament with the middle-class parties.

Amidst all this upheaval and conflict of ideas, one fact was indisputable: the proletariat existed and its strength was growing. Intellectuals of every order recognized it, from Lyautey to Léon Bourgeois. Sorel discussed the problem of violence, the English discussed Henri George's book on progress and poverty; the readiest answers to the proletarian problems of the day were found in Karl Marx.

In 1887, the young Lenin was seventeen when he learned that his brother had been hanged for complicity in a plot to kill Alexander III. In his subsequent embittered search for a more effectual way of reviving and emancipating the people, it was in the works of Karl Marx that he discovered the guidance he was seeking.

A SETBACK FOR EUROPE

The 1890s marked the zenith of European power; Europe's conquests were still continuing in Africa and Asia, but it was the peak of the graph. And though the decline may not yet have been perceptible, the forces of opposition were already lining up and taking up positions of strength. The United States in their westward advance and Russia in its thrust eastward were becoming imperialist powers that were soon to surpass Europe in strength.

We left the United States on the verge of imperialism, poised on the shores of two oceans and eager to exert their young strength over both. The attempt was made in 1895 and the first victories were astounding. At first Madrid feared nothing and suspected nothing; revolts in Cuba were only too frequent. The usual way of dealing with them was to send a few troops and a ruthless general. But this time there was a new feature. Cuba's complaints were noisily and prominently ventilated in the press, first of New York, then of all the states. Though American mobilization was clumsy and its navy mediocre, its forces demoralized the Spanish troops who were a long way from their base, and were beaten before ever they fought. As a result, Cuba became an American protectorate, Porto-Rico was annexed and bought for twenty million dollars. This sum almost equalled the indemnity received by the United States after the Boxer risings; they had used the indemnity to attract large numbers of Chinese students to the States. The Filipinos were skilfully won over by an agrarian reform, which secularized monastic property and greatly increased the number of small farms. The north Pacific became a zone of American influence.

It is in the context of this great westward expansion of the United States that the history of Japan assumes its full significance. The furthest spearhead of the American thrust touched Japan in 1854; the Americans had then been forced to withdraw at the time of the Civil War and Japan was left to work out its own transformation. By the time the Americans returned they had only to set themselves up as protectors of the new nation. The Japanese proved themselves the best of all America's pupils. Victory over China had won Japan the Liaotung peninsula, but its possession was disputed by Europe. The Japanese were finally obliged to return it against an indemnity of thirty million taels, which China could get together only by appealing to Russia. This gave Russian capitalism the chance to make a bold move, and it took over at China's expense a territory almost equivalent to the Japanese conquests; it extended as far as Port Arthur and included control of Manchuria. In December 1895 a Russo-Chinese bank was opened in St Petersburg, and three months later it opened a branch in Shanghai. The great Parisian houses, particularly the *Crédit Lyonnais*, the *Banque de Paris* and Hottinger took part in the transaction; for some years past French savings had been deeply involved in the Russian economy. Russian capitalism had crossed the whole of Siberia and reached the China seas by the land route.

Parallel to the changes in America in the 1840s, so developments of equal importance were taking place in Russia during the same period. After the vacillations and uncertainties which followed the great reforms of the 1860s there had been a marked advance, at first demographic: in the later years of the century, Russia's population increased by thirty millions. The great fair of Nijni-Novgorod in 1896 astonished the world; it was a real international exhibition comprising ten thousand exhibitors, amongst whom were Chinese, Japanese, Persians and Europeans. This last great survival of Europe's medieval trade had now become an ultra-modern showpiece. Exhibits of the most famous craftsmanship in the world created a sensation, but so did the modern plant and equipment manufactured by ancient Russia. Already statistics showed Russia to have eighteen thousand factories and more than a million workers, using three hundred thousand horse-power of steam. Output of coal and cast-iron remained poor, but an immense effort was getting under way everywhere: there were, it was claimed, two hundred and thirty-five thousand men at work in the Urals. The progress in naphtha production was very considerable; a first pipeline was functioning in Transcaucasia. In the science of petroleum, the Russians were so brilliant that American technicians were soon turning to them for the solution of their problems.

Changes in rural life were less clearly defined. There were great variations in livestock because of the chronic insecurity of stock-breeding, but a determined effort was being made to find out more about the different strains and their diseases, about the land and its requirements. Russian laboratories also made the most outstanding contributions of the twentieth century to the study of soils and their treatment, which led to a true agronomic revolution whose effects were apparent in the twentieth century in every country and particularly in the United States. Most of the agricultural produce, moreover, was exported, and thus stimulated the development of a growing merchant fleet. The Russian Trading and Shipping Company owned eighty ships of one hundred and forty thousand tons. In 1877 a new company was founded, which was sufficiently unusual to deserve mention; it was not a capitalist creation on English lines, but was started by national subscription just after the Russo-Turkish war of 1877, accompanied by a campaign explaining the urgent need to develop transport. This 'volunteers' fleet soon numbered fifteen vessels. Once the capital had been assembled, this national enterprise became a private one (1883).

In the field of transport, however, Russia's truly great achievement was in the development of transcontinental railways. With the help of French industry the railways had already been extended as far as Merv and soon Tashkent. The pace of progress quickened after De Witt came to power in 1892; his career had been in railways and he hastened the building of the Trans-Siberian, for which construction yards had been opened the previous year. Rivers, swamps and rocky spurs were crossed. In ten years the whole continent had been crossed, the last obstacles being the Baikalia tunnels. Already capitalists and engineers were busy in Manchuria, and plans were going ahead to reach Peking. There was also a tentative project to carry the southern line on towards Persia and even India. This meant in effect that overland lines would short-circuit the shipping routes which for three hundred years had been draining Asia's trade towards western Europe and the Atlantic. A self-important and unscrupulous group was busily intriguing on the fringes of the government – the Russian equivalent to American 'Grantism'. Companies were founded to exploit the distant territories which the railway had suddenly brought within reach of Europe. When there was talk of mineral wealth in Korea it was a question of forestalling Japanese claims: woodcutters, soldiers and workmen disguised as peasants infiltrated into the peninsula and paved the way for capitalist conquest. Statesmen like Bezzobradzov, service-chiefs like Admiral Alexeyev, and bankers like the Gunzburgs were already making a name for themselves with this sort of project. De Witt himself became uneasy and gave warning against the dangers to which this uncontrolled spirit of adventure was exposing the Empire. But he admonished and implored in vain. The capitalist group succeeded in opening a free-water port in the Liaotung peninsula which enabled it to control both China and Oceania.

These great movements of expansion were accompanied by a real advance in education and culture. Although police kept a strict watch on academic establishments and bookshops, schools and books multiplied. Villages subscribed to get schoolmasters, advertised for them, went to the cities to look for them. It was a point of honour with the Zemstvos to open as many schools as possible. To celebrate the marriage of Nicholas II, the Moscow Zemstvo prided itself on opening twenty new schools. Russian literature was popular all over the West, particularly in France.

A good deal of capital was needed to finance so much activity. We have stressed the difference between American and Russian institutions. The expansion of America may have been greater but Russia's was amazing in view of her poor banking facilities. However, St Petersburg had found considerable resources in France. It was the age when the great Jewish families in the old Russian cities, the traditional representatives of big business, set up large banking concerns. Once they were protected by court privilege and had become very wealthy, they were granted the Russian nationality previously refused them. They opened sumptous offices in Paris and set up small courts which fashionable artists and literary critics did not disdain to frequent. Close contacts were established with the French credit network. For twenty years the *Crédit Lyonnais* devoted much of its energies to placing Russian loans. Whilst finance was hard at work, the Grand Dukes were amusing themselves in Paris. In this way they gave the most spectacular publicity to Russian credit. At the 1900 exhibition the French people, who had risen up four times in rebellion against its own princes, gave an enthusiastic welcome to the Russian princes. As a result the Russian budget was the only one in the world which showed a substantial surplus every year. The gold debt rose by three thousand million francs in the last years of the century, yet the interest on this debt was not increased. Public infatuation, especially among the French public, was such that it permitted skilful reconversions, investments at par, and above par. Russia's finances were the soundest in the world thanks to the French treasury.

Thus, from London, New York and San Francisco, a wave of expanding capitalism reached the China Seas, while at the same time a bid for economic domination from London, Paris and St Petersburg was developing; though certainly smaller in scope, it was no less intense, and its influence extended as far afield as Mukden and Port Arthur.

A new world was indeed emerging at the close of the century, a world in which the two great new powers were attracting both intellectual curiosity and financial resources. It foreshadowed the world in which we are living today. Its general outlines were even more clearly discernible at the close of the nineteenth century than at the beginning of the twentieth, and two generations were to go by before the picture was complete. It is tempting to suggest that it was precisely the rapid progress of Japan which halted both America and Russia; but it was chiefly the instability of Russian capitalism and the national rivalries of the Western worlds which gave Japan the great chance of appearing to check the two new colossi during the next fifty years.

The essential features of Russian and American development had already been determined by the railway and the steamship. When Stephenson demonstrated his first engine the *Rocket* to a group of pioneers and incredulous transport contractors at the beginning of the century, he was setting in motion forces which changed the whole world. He was opening the way for economic exploitation of the great continents. Up till then the Westerners had only explored their coastlines; they were the sons of Mediterranean sailors and did not willingly venture over high mountains and across vast rivers. Grandiose though Saint-Simon's dream may have appeared, it was soon surpassed. In any case his Mediterranean system stopped at Baghdad, whereas the fate of the world was to be played out in the seas around Korea. The railway age brought with it a wealth of invention and a great eagerness for conquest; it gave the world a new youth, so that within four generations the pattern of the past thousand years was swept away.

In 1780 we described London as the capital of the seafaring world, and Berlin as the city most typical of the continental civilizations. A century later the capital of the seas had shifted westwards towards America, and the centre of the continents had been shifted far to the east by the expansion of Russian Asia. We described Paris of 1780 as being between two worlds. In 1900 it was the whole of Europe which was threatened by these new expansions, for Europe was the hinge and pivot on which they turned. There was no guarantee that a replanning of the European railway system would ensure unity; it seemed possible that Europe would break somewhere, perhaps on the Channel, the Rhine, or the Vistula under the weight of these two new gigantic wings. It was a question which the generations of the future had to answer in blood and fire. The end of the eighteenth century held no intimation of the profound crises which were to come in the 1880s, which compelled societies which had remained stable for centuries to make fundamental changes in their structure, their tools and their way of thinking. But these crises themselves stemmed directly from the development of new worlds.

The Europe of 1900 knew nothing of the world catastrophes which were to come. It was dazzled by its own success and proud of the triumph of its unique civilization; 'like the Berecynthian in her chariot', it exulted in having brought forth so many gods.

But the new science which had been the foundation of Europe's success was undergoing profound modification; and its centre of growth would perhaps no longer even be in Europe.

A SETBACK FOR NEWTON

There had always been some contradictions implicit in the accepted scientific principles of the nineteenth century. On the whole they were dismissed as insignificant until Einstein in 1905 gave an unforeseen direction to the controversy. He showed that the ideas of absolute time and space were fictions of the mind. Two vital concepts which had been the basis of all intellectual effort since Newton and Kant were therefore being challenged.

Einstein's conviction was, indeed, far from being unanimously shared. Here again a generation would have to go by before it was generally accepted. Nor did his discovery, which we regard as belonging to the twentieth century, spontaneously appear in 1905. It was prepared by half a century of critical and original thinking by men whose work must at this point be mentioned.

In England about the middle of the century the mathematicians had been lulled to sleep, as we have said, on the downy pillow of Newtonian fame. Pedagogues and philosophers spent their time criticizing the mental paralysis which mathematical disciplines inflicted on students, although it must be admitted that they themselves seemed quite incapable of doing anything to remedy the situation. But one of the most original minds of the age distinguished himself by his defence of mathematics. George Boole, the son of a small shopkeeper, had tried various ways of making a living – business, the Church and the University. He achieved fame by a work of unusual daring in which he suddenly brought new life to logic if not to metaphysics (which remained as entrenched in tradition as it had always been). His book was entitled *An Investigation of the Laws of Thought, on which are founded the Mathematical Theories of Logic and Probabilities*, a study of 'the operations of the mind by which reasoning is achieved', and which he expressed in terms of calculus. Boole's work did not revolutionize contemporary thinking, but it already marked the opening of a new era, that of the axiomatic.

At about the same time the German Clausius, making a special study of temperatures, and observing their tendency to equilibrium in a closed system, revealed a general tendency of the universe: work is changed into heat; the lower the temperatures, the more they tend to fall; energy is degraded. In order to measure this reduction, Clausius suggested the idea of entropy, which has assumed such importance in the twentieth century.

Proof of its importance is furnished by a study of the kinetic theory of gases. In 1848 Joule had succeeded in calculating an approximate figure for the speed of molecules by establishing the relationship between the speed, volume, pressure and temperature of gases. The total available energy of molecules in a closed system is measured by the total heat of the gas, and the energy of each molecule contributes to the temperature of the gas. These startling observations confirmed Mariotte's Law for approximate values but invalidated it for more accurate observations; the same applied to the theories of Boyle, Avogadro and the whole group of physicists of the 1800s. It was noted that molecules tended to achieve the arrangement which would most probably produce a levelling out of heat in a system; this introduced the notion of entropy into the theory of gases and thus into the composition of matter. It should be recalled that this notion of the most probable was related to the probability theory which had been the subject of study from the seventeenth to the nineteenth centuries, and had been clarified by the gifted Gauss. Thus thermodynamics and the constitution of matter introduced into science a revolutionary form of determinism: statistical determinism. The approximate number of molecules per cubic centimetre was established, and observation of this movement of molecules showed that it did not always proceed in a straight line: it took all the refinements of mathematics that we mentioned earlier to calculate the molecular energy of a few diatoms.

All this represented a transformation and expansion of the conclusions to be drawn from the surprising observations made by Brown. As early as 1827 he noted the small movement of particles in collision with the molecules of the liquid in which they were immersed. Soon Maxwell linked up all this body of reasoning and observation by showing that the sun's rays warmed the molecules and made them bounce off the surface of the ground, particularly if they were very absorbent, in short very dark. So a small mill with arms white on one side and black on the other could be made to revolve in sunlight.

This molecular study of gases had, one may well imagine, many repercussions in the sphere of chemistry. Newton had foreseen it and Berthelot almost formulated it in his work on the speed of chemical reaction. The whole question was, however, reopened in 1850 by Wilhelmy. From monomolecular to dimolecular phenomena, all this movement was related to the principles of thermodynamics, and resulted in the law of action of chemical mass in 1864. The speed of reaction could change under the action of a substance which was present in an active state but not yet itself transformed. This was the idea of catalysis, formulated by Berzélius and studied by Berthelot. It resulted in 1880 in the definition of enzymes, which have been the subject of a good deal of study since then.

In studying solutions it was noticed that the speed of diffusion varied according to the substance, and Graham distinguished colloids from crystalloids. Applied to solutions, electricity produced marvellous results. In 1840 Faraday had easily explained numerous phenomena by calculating the speed of displacement of ions to electrodes, and electricity adopted the ion as its atom. By 1860 the relative speed of ions was calculated with comparative accuracy. The discoveries of Clausius were of the greatest help, and the relationships between the composition of matter and electrical phenomena were clarified towards the end of the century. The relationships between the electrical properties of solutions and osmotic pressures were also worked out. Thus the ground was being prepared for the twentieth-century discovery that electricity lay at the very centre of the composition of matter – a body of knowledge which was still theoretical and was not to be applied until the twentieth century.

From 1850 to 1900 there was an astounding variety of discoveries in every sphere, the relationships of which were sensed by the most distinguished minds, though they could not always reduce them to the unity of a formula. From this extraordinarily widespread creative activity, the finest example that can be given is in the branch of science unrelated to all the preceding ones. About the middle of the century, Foucault and Bensen tried to apply the principles of thermodynamics to the composition of the universe, and in this way they gave a great impetus to the spectral study of the stars. Newton had indicated the importance of this without reaching any decisive conclusion on the subject. The movement of rays across the microscope revealed the speed of displacement of the source of light. This spectral analysis led on to the discovery of substances in the sun which were not found on the earth for another twenty years (as for instance helium, detected in the solar spectrum in 1878, and not on earth until the end of the century). Thus infra-red and ultra-violet rays too came to be studied. Most important of all, however, was the fact that all this research suggested a solution to the problem of the velocity of light.

In 1887, Michelson in Chicago reached an amazing truth: working on the effects of motion on the velocity of light, he obtained a series of results which had only one possible explanation: the velocity of light is invariable whatever the relative speeds of the sources of light and of the observer, a discovery which rendered classical mechanics and the principal hypotheses of Newton completely out of date.

Towards the end of the nineteenth century then, a whole age of scientific thought was drawing to its close. At the very time when the United States was supplanting the old Europe, when Asia was awakening, when the social structure of Europe was being transformed, Newton's star was waning in the scientific sky and the principles of general mechanics were superseded.

CONCLUSION

There could be no more fitting or thought-provoking theme with which to conclude. European expansion had originated with the conviction that the earth was round, and that man would therefore have to reconsider the position he had assigned himself in the universe. From the age of Tycho-Brahé and Kepler to that of Newton and Laplace, who finally completed the system, ships had steered by this new knowledge of the heavens and gained the mastery of the seas, conquered unclaimed territory all over the world and assumed control of the coastal areas which fringed the ancient civilizations.

The possession of great territories and the control of communications encircling the globe were new factors which rendered the old methods of political and economic government completely out of date. Businessmen and industrialists, using the new techniques which had also been developed by science, overthrew the old courtly society founded on privilege, initiated economic liberty, founded a system of credit and created belief in the future and in progress. The result was a victory for those who were proud to be called the middle classes. It was they who controlled the cities, industry and commerce, and the world.

Every advance in science contributed during those years to the wealth and authority of the middle classes and did much to renew and strengthen the power of Europe. Yet just as the privileged few of the *ancien régime* had been unable to gain control of scientific progress, so the middle classes of Victorian Europe were unable to retain the monopoly of its benefits for long. Society underwent a series of structural changes, as a result of which the middle classes were swamped by a rising tide of technicians drawn from the ranks of the people and educated in the new schools. From Monge to Gauss and Lobachevsky the new mathematics spread across the continent to Russia; from Fresnel to Michelson the most brilliant research crossed the Atlantic. Scientific thought found a solution to the problems propounded by Michelson in the geometries arising directly out of Lobachevsky's work. Just as the Vatican Library had been powerless to keep Galileo's thought enclosed within its walls, so the laboratories and libraries of Europe did not prevent science from re-entering the world; they had, in fact, thrust it out themselves.

The European middle classes were proud of their triumphs, but were they justified in claiming them as their own? They were surely the triumphs of science, and they themselves were merely its instruments, suitable enough because they believed in science implicitly. The laboratories and libraries of America and Asia undermined the foundations on which the power of the European middle classes had rested. It was not long before they began to feel uneasy at the growth of technocracies and socialisms and the rise of new continents. Soon they were being gradually deprived of their power and by exactly the same forces that they had themselves employed to despoil the privileged of a previous generation – by belief in progress and respect for its laws.

Even the deadliest of wars do not achieve their purpose, since their ultimate effect is to speed up evolution. Science and humanity are one, an the future of knowledge will decide the future of the world.

Bibliography

ANSTEY, V. *The Economic Development of India.* 1929.

ARIES, PH. *L'enfant et la vie familiale sous l'ancien régime.* 1960.

ASHTON, T.S. *An Economic History of England in the Eighteenth Century.* 1955.

BAKER, J.N.L. *A History of Geographical Exploration and Discovery.* 1937.

BEAU DE LOMENIE, E. *Les responsabilités des dynasties bourgeoises* (3 vols).

BELLET and DARVILLE, W. *Les plus grandes entreprises du monde.*

BERNAL, J.D. *Science and Industry in the Nineteenth Century.* 1953.

BIGO, R. *Les bases historiques de la finance moderne.*

BIRNIE, A. *Histoire économique de l'Europe, 1760–1932.*
An Economic History of the British Isles. 1935.

BLOCH, M. *Esquisse d'une histoire monétaire de l'Europe.* 1954.
Les caractères originaux de l'histoire rurale française (2 vols).

BLUM, J. *Lord and Peasant in Russia from the Ninth to the Nineteenth Century.* 1961.

BOUTHOUL, G. *La population dans le monde.* 1935.

BOWDEN, KARPOVITCH and USHER. *Economic History of Europe since 1750.*

BOWMAN, L. *Pioneer Settlement.* 1931.

BRIGGS, A. *Age of Improvement, 1780–1867.* 1959.
Victorian People, 1851–1867. 1965.
Victorian Cities. 1963.

BROGLIE, L. DE *Savants et découvertes.*

BRUFORD, W.H. *Germany in the Eighteenth Century.* 1965.

BRUUN, G. *Europe and the French Imperium.* 1954.

CAMERON, R.E. *France and the Economic Development of Europe 1800–1914.* 1961.

CAULLERY, M. *Le problème de l'évolution.*
La société française depuis le XVIIᵉ siècle.

CARR SAUNDERS, A.M. *World Population.* 1936.

CHASLES, M. *Rapport sur les progrès de la géometrie.* 1870.

CHAUNU, P. *L'Amérique et les Amériques.* 1964.

CHEVALIER, L. *Classes laborieuses, classes dangereuses à Paris dans la première moitié du dix-neuvième siècle.* 1958.
La formation de la population parisienne au dix-neuvième siècle. 1950.

CIPOLLA, C. *The Economic History of World Population.* 1962.

CLAPHAM, J.H. *An Economic History of Modern Britain. I: The Early Railway Age, 1820–50. II: Free Trade and Steel, 1850–86. III: Machines and National Rivalries, 1887–1914, with an epilogue, 1914–29.*
The Economic Development of France and Germany, 1815–1914.
The Bank of England.

CLARK, C. *The Conditions of Economic Progress.* 1940.

CLOUGH, S.B. and COLE, C.W. *Economic History of Europe.*

COLE, G.D.H. *Life of William Cobbett.*

COLLINS, I. *The Age of Progress: A Survey of European History from 1789–1870.* 1964.

COLQUHOUN, A. *China in Transformation.*
Congrès internationaux de la population.

COURT, W. M. B. *A Concise Economic History of Britain.*

CROCE, B. *A History of Europe in the Nineteenth Century.* 1965.

CROUZET, M. (ed.) *Le dix-neuvième siècle (Histoire Générale des civilisations).* 1955.

CURTIN, P. D. *The Image of Africa; British Ideas and Action, 1780–1850.* 1965.

DAUMARD, A. *La Bourgeoisie parisienne de 1815 a 1848.* 1963.

DAUMARD and FURET. *Structures et relations sociales à Paris au milieu du dix-huitième siècle.* 1961.

DECARY and CASTEL. *Migrations intérieures récentes des populations malgaches.* 1941.

DION, R. *Essai sur la formation du paysage rural français.* 1943.

DOUGLAS, R. K. *China.*

DUMONT, A. *Dépopulation et civilisation.* 1890.

DUNHAM, A. L. *La révolution industrielle en France, 1815–48.*

DURKHEIM, E. *De la division du travail social.* 1893.

DUVEAU, G. *La vie ouvrière en France sous le Second Empire.* 1946.

ENGELS, F. *The Origin of the Family, Private Property and the State.*

EPSTEIM *From Opium War to Liberation.*

FÈBVRE, L. *La terre et l'évolution humaine.* 1922.

FIRCKS *Bevölkerungslehre und Bevölkerungspolitik.* 1898.

FLORINSKY, M. *Russia, II.* 1953.

GALLAGHER and ROBINSON *Africa and the Victorians.* 1961.

GLASS, D. V. *Population Policies and Movements in Europe.* 1940.

GOODFELLOW, D. M. *Modern Economic History of South Africa.* 1930.

GUILLET, E. C. *Pioneer Days in Upper Canada.* 1965.

HACKER, L. and HENDRICK, B. *The United States since 1865.* 1946.

HALBWACHS, M., SAUVY, A. and ULMER. *Le point de vue du nombre. Encyclopédie française,* vol. VI. 1936.

HALEVY, E. *History of the English People in the Nineteenth Century.*

HARTWELL, M. *The Industrial Revolution.* (Historical Association Leaflet.) 1965.

HEATON, H. *Histoire économique de l'Europe* (2 vols.). 1950, 1952.

HENDERSON, W. O. *The Industrial Revolution on the Continent; Germany, France, Russia 1800–1914.*

HOBSBAWM, E. *The Age of Revolution.* 1962.

HOLBORN, H. *A History of Modern Germany.* 1959.

HUBER, M. *Cours de démographie.* 1938–41.

HUETZ DE LEMPS, A. *Australie et Nouvelle-Zélande.* 1954.

JANET, P. *La Famille.* 1919.

KEYSER, E. *Bevölkerungsgeschichte Deutschlands.* 1941.

LABROUSSE, C.-E. *La crise de l'économie française à la fin de l'Ancien Régime et au début de la Révolution.* 1943.

LANDRY, A. *La révolution démographique.* 1934.

LANG, O. *Chinese Family and Society.* 1946.

LATOURETTE *A History of Modern China.*

LATTIMORE, O. *The Making of Modern China.* 1954.

LEFÈBVRE, G. *La Grande Peur de 1789.*

LEMAITRE, J. *Les contemporains.*

LE PLAY *Les ouvriers des Deux Mondes.* 1878.

LEVASSEUR, E. *La population de la France.* 1889–92.

LINDER, R. *Die Schwedische Landerbevölkerungs unter dem Einfluss der Industrialisierung.* 1938.

LORIMER and OSBORN *Dynamics of Population.* 1934.

LYASCHENKO, P. *History of the Russian National Economy.* 1947.

MACKENZIE, K. *The Banking Systems of Great Britain, France, Germany and the USA.* 1945.

MANTOUX, P. *La révolution industrielle en Angleterre.* 1906.

MAVOR, J. *Economic History of Russia.* 1925.

MILIOUKOV, L., SEIGNOBOS, C. and EISENMANN, L. *Histoire de la Russie.* 1932.

MONDAINI *La colonisation anglaise.* 1925.

MORAZÉ, C. *La France bourgeoise.* 1946.
Introduction à l'histoire économique.
Les trois âges du Brésil.

MORRISON and COMMAGER *The Growth of the American Republic* (vols. 1 & 2). 1962.

ORSI, P. *Histoire de l'Italie moderne.* 1911.

PANNIKAR, K. *The Future of South East Asia, An Indian View. Asia and Western Dominance, A Survey of the Vasco da Gama Epoch of Asian History, 1498–1954.* 1954.

PARNABY, O. W. *Britain and the Labor Trade in the South-West Pacific.* 1964.

PEARL, R. *The Natural History of Population.* 1939.

PHILIP, P.-D. and WOOD, G. L. *The Peopling of Australia.* 1928.

PILON, E. *La vie de famille en France au XVIIIᵉ siecle.* 1928.

POINCARÉ, H. *Dernières pensées.*
La valeur de la science.
Les fondements de la géométrie.

POPPER, K. *The Open Society and its Enemies.*

PORTUS, G.-V. *Australia. An Economic Interpretation.*

REDFORD, A. *Labour Migration in England, 1800–1850.*

REEVES, W.-P. *New Zealand.*

REINHARD, M. *Histoire de la population mondiale 1700–1949.*

RENOUVIN, P. *Transformation de la Chine et du Japon de 1850 à 1952.*

RIST, CH. *Précis des mécanismes économiques élémentaires.* 1947.

ROESSLE, R. *Die pathologische Anatomie der Familie.* 1940.

ROUPNEL, G. *Histoire de la campagne française.*

SAGNAC, P. *La formation de la société française moderne.*

SCHNABEL, F. *Deutsche Geschichte in XIX Jahrhundert.*

SÉE, H. and SCHNERB, R. *Histoire économique de la France* (2 vols).
Les origines du capitalisme moderne.

SIMIAND, F. *Le salaire, l'évolution sociale et la monnaie.* 1932.

SOYESHIMA, Michimasa: *Oriental Interpretation of the Far-Eastern Problem.*

SUNDBARG, C. *Bevölkerengsstatiskik Schwedens, 1750–1900.*

TATON, R. *Histoire du calcul.*

TAWNEY *Land and Labour in China.* 1932.

THOMAS, D. S. *Social Aspects of the Business Cycles.* 1927.

THOMPSON and GARRATT *Rise and Fulfilment of British Rule in India.* 1934.

TOLEDANO, A. D. *La vie de famille en France sous la Restauration et la Monarchie de Juillet.* 1943.

TREVELYAN, G. M. *English Social History.* 1942.

USHER, A. P. *A History of Mechanical Inventions.*

VACCHINO, A. *La populazione italiana. Storia delle populazione e demografia italiana.* 1941.

VANDENBOSCH, A. *The Dutch East Indies.* 1941.

VAN SOMEREN BRAND *Les grandes cultures du monde.*

WEBER, M. *Gesammelte Aufsätze zur Social- und Wirtschaftsgeschichte.* 1924.

WILLCOX, W. F. *Studies in American Demography.* 1940.

SOME NINETEENTH-CENTURY TRAVELLERS

ALCOCK, SIR R. *Art and Art Industries in Japan.* 1871.

ARDENNE DE TIZAC, H. *d' La sculpture chinoise.* 1931.

AUBERT, L. *Les maîtres de l'estampe japonaise.* 2nd ed. 1922.

BALLOT, M. J. *La céramique chinoise* (Louvre Museum).

BRUCE, J. *Travels to Discover the Source of the Nile in the Years 1768–73.*

BURNES, M. A. *Voyages de l'embouchure de l'Indus à Lahore, Caboul, Balh et à Boukhara et retour par la Perse, pendant les années 1831, 1832, 1833.*

BUSHELL, S. W. *Chinese Art* (Victoria and Albert Museum, 1924).

CAILLÉ, R. *Le voyage de R. Caillé à Tombouctou et à travers l'Afrique, 1824–1828.*

CORNET, CAPT. *Au Tchad. Trois and chez les Sennoussites, les Ouaddaiens et les Kirdis.* 1910.

COSTE and FLANDIN *Voyage en Perse* (with an atlas).

DEMIDOFF, A. DE *Voyage dans la Russie méridionale et la Crimée par la Hongrie, la Valachie et la Moldavie.* 1840.

DJELAL ESSAD *Constantinople.* 1909.

DOOLITTLE *The Social Life of the Chinese.* 1866.

DU HALDE, FA J.-B. *Description de la Chine.* 1736–1737.

DUMONT D'URVILLE *Voyage pittoresque autour du monde.*

GANDAR (the elder) *Le canal impérial. Étude historique et descriptive.* 1894.

GUIMET, E. *Promenades japonaises* (2 vols). 1879–80.

HOMMAIRE DE HELL, X. *Voyages en Turquie et en Perse exécutés par ordre du gouvernement français, en 1846–48.*

HUC. FA. REGIS *Souvenirs d'un voyage dans la Tartarie, le Thibet et la Chine.* 1850. *L'Empire chinois.* 1855.

KOULOMZINE, A. M. DE *Le Transsibérien.* 1904.

LA PÉROUSE *Voyage autour du monde.* 1797.

LE BON, DR G. *Les civilisations de l'Inde.* 1887. *La civilisation des Arabes.* 1884.

LIVINGSTONE, D. *Exploration à l'intérieur de l'Afrique Australe.* 1881.

MAGE, E. *Voyage dans le Soudan occidental, 1863–1866*

NANSEN, F. *In Nacht und Eis. Die Norwegische Polar-Expedition, 1893–1896.*

NORDENSKIOLD, A. E. *Voyage de la 'Vega' autour de l'Asie et de l'Europe.* 1883. *Nouvelle bibliothèque des voyages.* Paris, Lecointe, 1823–30.

PALGRAVE, W. G. *Une année de voyage en Arabie centrale, 1862–63.*

PALLAS *Russie et Asie septentrionale, 1788–1793.*

PARODE, MISS *The Beauties of the Bosphorus.*

PLAYFAIR *Cities and Towns of China, a Dictionary.* 1880.

SOLTYKOFF, FA. *Voyage dans l'Lnde.* *Voyage de Perse.* Le Cou, 1854.

STANLEY, H. M. *Divers voyages.*

SVEN HEDIN *Durch Asiens Wüsten. Drei Jahre auf neuen Wegen, in Pamir, Lopnor, Tibet und China.* 1899.

SYKES *The Taiping Rebellion in China.* 1863.

VAMBERY, ARM. *Voyage d'un faux derviche dans l'Asie centrale.* 1865.

Index

d'Abbans, Jouffroy, 160
Abbas, Kajar, 183
Abdul Hamid, 11, 366, 368
Abel, Henri, 249 n
Abingdon, 105
Aboukir Bay, 161
Abyssinia, 45
Acapulco, 68
Acre, 38
Adam, Robert, 146
Adelaide, 172
Aden, 62
Afghanistan, 70, 173, 180, 183, 340, 342
Africa, xv, 4, 30, 38, 39, 42–5, 160, 183,
    184–6, 343, 345, 368–74
d'Agoult, Marie, 153
Agra, 57, 315
Agriculture:
    Australian, 293
    Central European, 19–20
    Chinese, 65, 321–2
    English, 12, 101–2, 105, 221, 253, 345
    French, 25, 232–3, 345, 346–8, 349–50
    German, 16, 130, 131, 133, 202, 225,
        226, 345, 349–50
    Indian, 175–6, 312
    Irish, 354–5
    Japanese, 308
    Javanese, 330–1
    North American, 53, 164–5, 167, 282–5
    Russian, 333–5, 339, 388
    Scandinavian, 356–7
    South African, 294–6
    South American, 297–9, 302
    Spanish, 28
    Turkish, 366
Albuquerque, 62
Alembert, 84, 85
Aleppo, 38
Alexander I, 105, 156, 178
Alexander II, 179, 248, 332
Alexander III, 386
Alexeyev, Admiral, 389
Algeria, 184, 240, 368–9
Algiers, 41, 185, 186, 369
Alsace, 129, 216, 241, 349, 369
Altay, 69, 338
Amazon, xiii

America, xiv, xv, 4, 5, 25, 27, 45–55,
    101, 160, 161, 177, 202, 205, 225,
    258, 345 (see also USA and South
    America)
Amiens, 199
Amiens, Treaty of, 161
Amoy, 178
Ampère, 87, 88, 251
Amsterdam, 6, 9, 24, 63, 194, 234, 356
Andrezieux, 198
Angola, 361, 372
Annam, 329, 330
Antwerp, 198, 234
Anzin, 26, 115, 126, 195, 237
Arabia, 368
Archangel, 70
Architecture:
    Austrian, 361
    English, 10, 265
    French, 264
    German, 7, 146, 265
    Indian, 315
Argentina, 96, 170, 172, 221, 299–301,
    345
Argout, 142
Aristocracy:
    British, 11, 142, 203
    French, 112, 115, 126, 143
    German, 18
    Polish, 20
    Russian, 73, 180, 183, 331
    South American, 168
    Spanish, 27
    Viennese, 361
Arizona, 277
Armenia, 71, 182
Armies:
    Chinese, 69, 326–7
    Egyptian, 184
    English, 296
    French, 116, 124, 185–6
    Japanese, 307
    Prussian, 16, 230
    Russian, 71, 341–2
    South American, 170
    Spanish, 27, 364
    Turkish, 38–9, 184, 367
Artois, 126

Ashley, Lord, 142
Aspdin, Joseph, 219
Asquith, Lord, 353
Athens, 36, 367
Atlanta, 279
Attiret, Father, 67
Auber, 151
Augsburg, 195
Aurengzeb, 57, 61
Australia, 172, 203, 208, 209, 221, 224,
    293, 328, 345
Austria, 21, 77, 79, 131, 135, 146, 152,
    154, 156, 158, 179, 192, 200, 207,
    208, 212, 228–30, 231, 234, 236 239,
    360
Auvergne, 124, 237
Avogadro, 87, 392

Babeuf, Gracchus, 145
Bach, J.S., 19, 152
Baden, 228
Bahia, 51
Bakewell, 101
Baku, 183, 339
Ballot, Charles, 121
Baltimore, 288
Balzac, 128
Banking, 100–1, 105–6, 108, 110, 127–8,
    140, 143, 162, 172, 194, 203, 209,
    210–4, 231, 241–2, 306, 344–5, 379
Barcelona, 29, 365
Baring, 172, 194
Barras, 117, 118
Basra, 62
Batavia, 62–3, 68, 321, 330–1
Bateson, 254
Batum, 183, 339
Baudelaire, 245, 266, 270
Bauwens, 122
Bavaria, 131, 132, 135, 200, 225, 228–31,
    269, 349, 378
Bayonne, 122
Bazard, 144
Beauharnais, Josephine de, 117, 119, 146,
    161
Beaumarchais, 5
Bebel, 231
Beethoven, 151, 152, 153, 268
Belfast, 355
Belgium, 178, 196, 198, 202, 217, 229,
    233, 371–2, 378, 383
Bell, Graham, 288
Bengal, 57, 174, 312

Bensen, 393
Bentham, Jeremy, 137, 138, 148, 255, 256
Beresford, 163
Bergès, 349
Berlin, xiii, xiv, 7, 15–16, 21, 27, 85, 129,
    130, 131, 151, 192, 194, 200, 201, 207,
    226, 229, 260, 265, 372, 390
Berlioz, 153, 154
Bernadotte of Sweden, 161
Bernard, Claude, 81
Berthelot, 250, 254, 262, 287, 382, 383,
    392
Berthollet, 105
Bertschneider, 323
Berzelius, 87, 250, 392
Bessemer, 4, 217, 224, 237, 290, 348
Bethune, 237
Bezzobradzov, 389
Bichat, 81, 90
Biedermeyer, 146
Bilbao, 29, 365
Birmingham, 6, 13, 14, 104, 381
Bismarck, xiv, 229–31, 243, 343, 352,
    366, 372
Blanc, Louis, 144
Bloch, Marc, 233
Bohemia, 261, 358
Bokhara, 71
Bolivar, 169
Bolivia, 297
Bologna, 32
Bombay, 60, 175, 313–6
Bonaparte, (See Napoleon)
Bonington, 149
Bonn, 200
Boole, George, 391
Bordeaux, 6, 24, 26, 109, 199
Borodin, 70
Borsig, 133, 226
Boston, 52, 53
Boston, Yorks, 105
Botany Bay, 293
Bouillaud, 81
Boulanvilliers, 155
Boulton, Matthew, 3, 14, 146
Boulogne, 199
Bourgeois, Leon, 386
Boutmy, 382
Boyle, 392
Bradford, 13
Braganza, 162
Brandenberg, 132
Branly, 247
Brazil, 30, 47, 51, 162, 170, 221, 299,
    301–4

Brazza, Savornan de, 372
Bremen, 228, 229, 234
Breslau, 16, 261
Bright, 81
Brindisi, 192, 229, 362
Brisgau, 19
Bristol, 6, 13, 43, 104
British Museum, 11
Broussais, 81
Brown, 392
Brucke, 229, 230
Brussels, 152
Budapest, 207
Buddhism, 59, 68, 305
Buenos Aires, 48–9, 163, 169, 170, 172, 299, 301, 345
Buffalo, 288
Buffalo Bill, 283
Buffon, 89, 253
Bugeaud, 186
Bukhara, 340
Bukovinia, 359
Burlington, 283
Burma, 320, 331

Cadiz, 28–9, 365
Cairo, 40, 185, 368
Calais, 125
Calcutta, 58, 185, 313–6
California, 208–9, 277, 284, 287
Callao, 48, 49, 172, 297, 321
Cambaceres, 95
Cambodia, 240
Cambresis, 125, 144
Cambridge, 85, 223, 247, 383
Canada, 5, 54, 203, 221, 224, 352
Canaletto, 31
Canova, 32
Canton, 65, 68, 177, 178, 317, 319, 326
Cape of Good Hope, 43, 44, 294
Cape Verde Islands, 43
Caracas, 50
Carlsbad, 4
Carlyle, 125, 137, 255
Carnegie, 290
Carnot, President, 385
Carnot, Sadi, 250
Caste system, 59, 60, 175–6
Castille, 28
Catherine the Great, 5, 20, 21, 70, 73, 93, 95, 178, 335
Catholicism, 30, 329, 364–5
Caucasus, 182, 339–40
Cauchy, 85, 249

Cavaignac, 206
Cavendish, 247
Cavour, 262–3
Cawnpore, 312
Ceara, 302
Celebes, 63
Ceramics, Chinese, 65, 324
Ceylon, 314
Chaillez, 374
Chaillot, 123
Chambers, 253
Champagne, 237
Champollian, 145
Chandernagor, 58
Chappe, 194
Charenton, 194
Charles II of England, 60
Charles III of Sicily, 95
Charles III of Spain, 27–9, 167
Charles X of France, 186
Charleston, 53, 279
Chartism:
    English, 205, 208
    French, 206
Chateaubriand, 139, 147, 155, 156
Châtelet, Madame de, 84
Chénier, Andre, 148
Cherkasky, Prince, 332
Chesme, 73, 184
Chevalier, Michel, 193
Chicago, 283, 286–7, 345, 393
Chile, 48, 168, 297, 298
China, xv, 5, 8, 56, 63–9, 106, 160, 176–8, 183, 209, 238, 275, 276, 286, 304, 305, 309, 311, 317–31, 345, 353, 387
Chippendale, 146
Cholar, 328
Chopin, 153
Chungaria, 64
Cincinnati, 217
Civier, 90
Clapham, 230
Clary, Désirée, 161
Clausius, 255, 392, 393
Clementini, 152
Clermont, 24
Cleveland, 287, 288
Cleveland, President, 292
Clive, 59, 61
Cobbett, 137
Cobden, 103, 138, 140, 198, 204, 220
Cochin China, 68, 240, 329
Cockerill, 122
Coeur, Jacques, 120

Colbert, 7, 95, 96, 110, 125, 128, 134, 233
Coleridge, 255
Cologne, 208, 226, 228
Colonisation, 73, 164, 166, 171, 186,
    221–2, 292, 311–7, 329–31, 337–42,
    356, 365, 368–74, 387
Colorado, 277
Columbus, Christopher, 27, 83, 273
Commentry, 237
Committee of Public Safety, 116–17
Comte, Auguste, 247, 303
Communications (Railways, Roads,
    Telegraph), xiv, 66, 70, 128, 129,
    132, 135, 139, 142, 154, 191–202,
    214–5, 288–9, 293, 297, 303, 309,
    314–5, 323, 336, 341, 351, 355, 360,
    361, 377–8, 386, 388, 390
Condorcet, 114
Congo, 44, 371–2, 373
Constable, 149
Constant, Benjamin, 117
Constantinople, 36, 41–2, 70, 71, 73, 80,
    177, 182, 184, 237, 238, 319, 366,
    367
Cook, James, 91
Cook, Jay, 281
Copenhagen, 7, 41, 88, 357
Corn Laws, 203, 204, 208, 219, 223
Corneille, 5, 150
Coromandel, 61
Corot, 267
Corsica, 25
Cossacks, 71, 181, 333, 341
Coulomb, 88
Courbet, 245, 266–7
Courrières, 237
Cracow, 200, 205
Crefeld, 134, 228, 350
Creil, 200
Crimean War, 179, 223, 229, 238, 312,
    336, 363, 366
Cromwell, 12, 110, 355
Cuba, 164, 364, 387
Cugnot, 160
Curacao, 54
Custine, 119, 131
Cuvier, 89
Cuyp, 149
Cuzco, 49, 296
Czartoryski, Grand Duke Constantin, 157
Czechoslovakia, 157

Dakar, 370
Dalhousie, Lord, 312, 314

Dalton, 85, 87, 88
Damascus, 38, 62
Danton, 116
Danzig, 7, 17, 20, 96, 106, 204, 225,
    261
Darmstadt, 262
Darwin, Charles, 90, 91, 253, 254, 255,
    270
Darwin, Erasmus, 253
Daumier, 136, 148, 245, 266
David, 32, 147, 148, 150
Decamps, 149
Decazes, 140
Deccan, 61
Dedekind, 248 n
Delacroix, 148, 149, 150, 153
Delaroche, 149
Delbruck, 231
Delescluzes, 148
Delessert, 118
Delhi, 57, 311, 315
Deliniers, 163
Denain, 237
Denmark, 19, 161, 220
Denver, 283, 286
Deprez, 120
Descamps, 266
Descartes, 84, 86
Detroit, 287
Devries, 254
De Witt, 337
Dickens, Charles, 142, 144
Diderot, 3, 8, 23, 253
Digoin, 123
Dijon, 199
Dilke, 275
Dirichlet, 247, 249 n
Disraeli, 224, 275
Don Carlos, 365
Donges, 263
Dortmund, 228
Douglas, 122
Dresden, 7, 17, 151, 152, 200, 261, 268
Drury, Admiral, 177
Dublin, 355
Dufaure, 243
Dumas, Alexandre, 136
Dumas, Jean-Baptiste, 262
Dundee, 104
Dupleix, 61
Dupont de Nemours, 114
Dupré, 149
Durham, 217
Duruy, Victor, 380, 382
Dusseldorf, 226

East India Company, 14, 57–9, 61, 101, 106, 174, 255, 311
Eastern question, 8
Edison, Thomas Alva, 288–9
Education, 12, 67, 92, 222, 224, 292, 310, 317, 325, 333, 359, 368, 380–3, 386, 389
Egypt, 40, 183, 184, 238, 241, 368, 370
Einstein, 391
Eisenstein, 247
Elberfeld, 134
Eldorado, 277
Elgin, Lord, 319
Enclosure Acts, 13, 101
Encyclopédie, 8, 114
Encyclopedists, 83, 136, 246, 251
Enfantin, 195, 275
Engels, 145, 158, 205
England, xiv, 4, 6, 9–15, 22, 30, 39, 43, 47, 73, 77, 79, 82, 85, 93, 97, 100–9, 119, 121, 124, 125, 128, 133, 135, 136–45, 146, 171–3, 168, 172, 177, 178, 184, 186, 193, 194, 196, 202–5, 210, 214, 216–24, 229, 233, 238, 247, 257, 265, 273, 274, 319, 330, 344, 352–4, 368, 379, 381, 384
Ensival, 122
Erivan, 182
Eritrea, 370
Essen, 133, 212, 261
Esterhazy, 152
Estremadura, 28
Euler, 8
Eugénie, Empress, 243, 256, 275

Faidherbe, 370, 374
Faraday, 85, 88, 250, 252, 381, 393
Fashoda, 373
Febvre, Lucien, 84
Fermat, 84, 89, 249
Ferrero, Guglielmo, 119
Ferry, Jules, 244, 383, 386
Feuerbach, 145
Fez, 369
Fichte, 19, 156
Finances (See also Banking):
  American, 165, 280–2, 291–2
  Austrian, 229
  Belgian, 213–4
  English, 12, 105, 107, 138, 202–4, 209, 216, 221, 353
  European, 343–6, 378–9
  French, 26, 109–11, 114–20, 127–8, 139, 206–7, 209, 213, 234–5, 242–3

German, 212–3, 214, 228
Indian, 175, 176
Italian, 362
Japanese, 306–7
Papal, 32
Russian, 333, 337, 389–90
South American, 301
Spanish, 364
Finland, 161, 354, 357–8
Flanders, 22, 125, 241
Flaubert, 233, 256, 264, 266
Florida, 165
Floridablanca, Count of, 29
Fontaine, 147, 252
Foochow, 178
Formosa, 69, 325, 326
Forster, 247
Foucauld, Charles de, 374
Foucault, 393
Fouquier-Tinville, 117
Fourchamboult, 237
Fourier, 87, 275
Fox, Charles James, 59
France, 4, 5, 19, 21–6, 51, 63, 77, 79, 82, 84, 94–6, 98, 100, 101, 104, 107, 109–29, 133, 135, 136–45, 146, 148–54, 155, 160, 165, 177, 180, 183, 184, 185, 192, 194, 198–200, 202, 204, 205–7, 211–12, 214, 216, 217, 223, 229, 232–44, 247, 254, 257, 262, 264–5, 319, 329, 344, 346–9, 368–70, 377–9, 380, 381–2
Frankfurt, 7, 9, 19, 96, 140, 207, 344
Franklin, 22, 53
Frederick II, 8, 16, 21, 26, 39, 95, 130, 131, 133
Frederick William IV, 200, 205, 207
French East India Company, 173
French Revolution, 3, 8, 77, 85, 100, 103, 113–9, 123, 128, 147, 178, 185, 227
Fresnel, 88, 394
Freycinet, 243, 378
Fulton, 160, 273

Gaboon, 251
Galicia, 157, 205, 358
Galileo, 84, 85, 87, 394
Gall, 89
Gallieni, 374
Galton, Francis, 254
Galvani, 88
Garibaldi, 363
Garnier, Francis, 330

Gauss, 85, 88, 89, 90, 202, 247–8, 254, 392, 394
Gay-Lussac, 87, 91, 262
Genoa, 34, 122, 229, 287, 362
George, Henri, 386
Georgia, 183, 340
Gerbillon, Father, 63
Géricault, 148, 149, 150
Germain, Henri, 211
Germany, 3, 7, 15–19, 21, 22, 31, 77, 82, 85, 92, 96, 98, 100, 105, 121, 122, 128, 129–35, 137, 140, 141, 145–6, 149–54, 156, 158–9, 193, 194, 195, 200–2, 204, 205, 207, 208, 212, 214–5, 220, 224–32, 239, 257, 262–3, 288, 349–52, 372, 378, 379, 382–3
Gibraltar, 41, 183
Giessen, 262, 263
Gilbert Incorporations, 141
Gilchrist, 218
Gironde, 116
Gladstone, 138, 139, 223–4, 293
Glasgow, 104, 105, 107, 196, 251, 344, 353
Gluck, 152, 268
Godunov, 180, 181
Goethe, 4, 8, 18, 32, 146, 150, 151, 152, 154, 156, 266, 268
Gold rush, 208–9, 277, 287, 293
Gondar, 45
Goodyear, 251
Gorea, 370
Goreie, 44
Gotland, 70
Gottingen, 202
Gouin, 199
Gould, Jay, 282
Goya, 29, 32
Graca, 371
Graham, 393
Gramme, 252, 261
Grant, President, 276, 279
Greece, 238
Greuze, 4
Greville, 142
Grillparzer, 18, 159
Gros, 148, 150
Guardi, 31
Guatemala, 169
Guesde, Jules, 386
Guilds, 14, 141, 208
Guinea, 42
Guizot, 127, 140, 144, 149, 206, 223
Gunzburg, 389
Gurkhas, 173
Guys, Constantin, 266

Habeas Corpus, 93
Hachette, 252
Hall, Marshall, 90
Hamburg, 7, 19, 108, 135, 140, 152, 164, 200, 212, 228, 229, 230, 234, 263
Hamilton, 87, 165
Hangchow, 323, 325
Hankow, 317, 324
Hanoi, 330
Hanover, 130, 132, 261, 378
Hansa, 10
Hartig, 24
Hashirobi, 307
Hastings, Warren, 58
Hauptmann, Gerhart, 141
Haussmann, 242–3, 256, 257
Hawai, 291, 292
Hayange, 237
Haydn, 8, 151, 152
Hegel, 92, 145, 156, 246
Heilmann, 129, 220, 241
Helmholtz, 87, 246
Henry, 252
Henry IV, 141
Herculanum, 4, 145
Herder, 158
Hermitte, 249
Hérold, 151
Hesse, 378
Hildesheim, 226
Hoche, 119, 131
Hofmann, 251, 263
Holland, 19, 31, 39, 63, 96, 129, 186, 201, 204, 205, 220, 233, 330, 356
Honan, 177
Hong Kong, XIII, 68, 178
Hottentots, 171
Hottinger, 118
Hugo, Victor, 151, 153, 236, 245, 268, 270, 329
Humboldt, 91
Hume, 255
Hungary, 21, 79, 157, 207, 228, 230, 360
Huskisson, 108, 220
Huxley, T.H., 91, 253
Hwang-Ho, xiii

Ile Bourbon, 45
India, xv, 5, 40, 56–62, 101, 106, 156, 158, 160, 173–6, 177, 179, 221, 229, 234, 238, 241, 273, 275, 287, 296, 311–17, 345
India Bill, 59
India Company, 55

Indo-China, 329
Indonesia, 69
Indret, 111
Industrialisation (See also communications), xiv, 6, 14, 15, 17, 21, 26, 77, 100, 104, 121-7, 128-9, 131, 133, 137, 141, 142, 143, 166, 180, 201-2, 204, 212, 216-44, 251, 256, 287-90, 303-4, 309, 335-6, 348-54, 363, 374, 384-6, 388
Ingres, 136, 147, 150
Innsbruck, 19
Inquisition, 27
Iowa, 284
Ireland, 79, 203, 220, 221, 223-4, 354-5
Isabella, II, 365
Isabey, 149
Ispahan, 72
Italy, 4, 14, 19, 30-5, 96, 119, 121, 154, 156, 158, 186, 192, 202, 204, 205, 238, 239, 263, 266, 344, 361-4
Iturbide, 169

Jackson, 165, 292
Jacobites, 117
Jacquard, 220
Jahn, Père, 18
Jansenists, 63
Japan, xiv, 68, 162, 177, 276, 304-10, 326-7, 342, 345, 353, 387, 390
Jaures, 112
Java, 63, 251, 330-1
Jefferson, 53, 165
Jena, 18, 89
Jefferson, 53, 165
Jenner, 80
Jerusalem, 38
Jesuits, 63, 64, 114, 177, 300
Jews, 19, 21, 34, 38, 41, 42, 70, 73, 127, 184, 195, 211, 335, 342, 358, 359, 368, 369, 389
Johannesburg, 296
John VI of Braganza, 170, 303
Joliet, 287
Joseph II, 8, 20, 21, 77, 132
Jouffroy, 148, 155
Joule, 88, 250, 392
Junkers, 132
Junot, 162

Kaffirs, 171-2
Kamchatka, 69
Kammer, 249 n

Kanake, 291
Kant, 92, 150, 156, 158, 246, 268, 391
Karamsin, 24
Kashgaria, 64, 177, 319, 320
Kashmir, 60, 175
Kelvin, Lord, 250
Kensington, 286
Kentucky, 54
Kepler, 84, 86, 394
Kiangsi, 65
Kia-King, 177
Kiel, 202
Kien-Lung, 176, 318
Kiev, 335
Kingte, 324
Kirdorf, 380
Kitchener, 373
Kiukiang, 317
Kiva, 340
Koenigsberg, 17
Kollar, 157, 158
Koran, 60
Korea, 309, 326, 342, 389, 390
Kossuth, 158
Koxinga, 68
Kreutzer, 151
Kronecker, 249
Kropotkin, 385
Kruger, 296
Krupp, 134, 212, 296, 380
Kublai Khan, 304
Kudlish, 207
Kuhlmann, 262
Kulja, 320
Kyoto, 304-6

La Bruyère, 4, 111
Laennec, 81
La Fayette, 5
Lafitte, 124, 140, 149, 192
Lagrange, 85, 89, 247
La Guavia, 50
Lamarck, 90, 253
Lamartine, 186, 232
La Mettrie, 90
Lanchow, 323
La Paz, 49
Laperrine, 374
Laplace, 85, 86, 247, 249, 275, 394
La Plata, 48-9
Laramie, 283
La Rochefoucauld-Liancourt, 25, 111
Lassalle, 231

Lavoisier, 26, 87, 90, 114
Law, 55, 110, 113, 114–5, 120
Lebeau, 145
Lebon, 250
La Chapelier, 141
Lecomte, Father, 66
La Couteux, 118
Le Creusot, 26, 111, 115, 123, 128, 194, 199, 237, 296, 348
Leeds, 13
Legal and Political Systems, 14, 24, 92–9, 113–4, 132, 141–3, 175, 179, 186, 208, 292, 307, 326, 331, 332, 333
Legendre, 97, 249
Leghorn, 34, 41, 121, 122
Le Havre, 129, 199, 234, 241, 349, 385
Leibnitz, 92
Leibniz, 275
Leipzig, 18, 152, 195, 200, 267
Lejeune, 251
Lenin, 337, 386
Lenoir, E., 250
Lenoir, Richard, 122–3
Lens, 237
Leopold of Belgium, 371, 372, 373
Leopoldville, 371
Lepère, 275
Leroux, 145
Lescarpelles, 237
Lesseps, Ferdinand de, 275
Lessing, 149, 153, 156
Levantine ports, 38
Leverrier, 89
Liard, 382
Liebig, Justus, 90, 250, 262, 321
Lille, 124, 205, 237, 263
Lima, 49, 297, 321
Lincoln, Abraham, 277–9
Linde, 157
Linnaeus, 89
Lisbon, 30, 122, 123, 162, 170, 303
List, Frederick, 195, 200, 201, 227, 382
Liszt, 153
Litterature, xiv, 18, 103, 107, 149–51, 154–59, 255, 266, 270, 326, 386
Liverpool, 6, 13, 24, 43, 104, 185, 220
Livingstone, 371
Lobachevsky, 248, 394
Locke, 91
Loire-et-Cher, 347
London, xiii, xiv, 7, 9–12, 21, 26, 27, 30, 43, 53, 59, 80, 104, 105, 107, 108, 125, 130, 144, 152, 162, 172, 174, 185, 194, 202, 209, 220, 259, 261, 274, 312, 344, 346, 353, 390

Loos, 237, 263
Lopez, Solano, 300
Lorraine, 95, 129, 216, 349, 369
Los Angeles, 50, 277
Loti, 326
Louis XII, 233
Louis XIV, 7, 275
Louis XV, 63, 109, 120, 192, 256
Louis XVI, 5, 22, 23, 77, 109, 110, 113, 123, 128, 140, 147
Louis XVIII, 81, 124
Louis, Guillaume, 121
Louis-Philippe, 122, 127, 186, 193, 210, 234, 235, 242, 244, 266
Louisiana, 96, 290
Lourenco-Marques, 296
Louviers, 122
Lucknow, 312
Luddites, 107
Ludwig II of Bavaria, 269
Luxemburg, 206
Lyautey, 374, 386
Lyell, 90
Lyons, 6, 24, 123, 124, 127, 142, 199, 234, 236, 349, 350

Mably, 53
Macadam, 191
Macao, 8, 177, 178
Mackintosh, 251
Macquart, 80
Madagascar, 45, 62, 373, 374
Madras, 61, 174–5, 313, 314
Madrid, 28, 168, 365, 387
Mafia, 364
Magdeburg, 195
Magyars, 158, 360
Mahmud II, 184
Mainz, 17, 200
Malabar, 61
Malacca, 330
Malaya, xiii, 353
Mallet, 118
Malta, 145
Malthus, 81, 90, 103, 142, 253
Manby, Aaron, 194
Manchester, 13, 104, 107, 124, 144, 220, 381
Manchuria, 326, 339, 342, 387, 388
Manchus, 64, 69, 317, 327
Manet, 267
Manila, 62, 68
Mannheim, 18, 151
Manteuffel, 225

Mantz, Paul, 265
Marchand, 373
Marco Polo, 325
Maria Luisa, 30
Maria Theresa, 16
Marie Antoinette, 26, 146
Marillac, 95
Mariotte, 392
Marrakesh, 41
Marseilles, 40, 109, 185, 212, 229, 234, 371
Marwitz, 132
Marx, Karl, 143, 145, 158, 205, 208, 231, 232
Maryland, 53, 164
Massachussetts, 284
Massawa, 360
Mateh-Sing, 319, 320
Matthews, 354
Maua, 276, 303
Maupertius, 8, 85
Maximilian, 240
Maxwell, 88, 247, 381, 392
Mazagan, 41
Mazzini, 156
Mecca, 38, 40, 62, 319
Mechlin, 198
Mecklenburg, 225, 349
Medicine, 80
Mehemet Ali, 184
Meissonier, 245, 264, 265
Meknes, 41
Melbourne, 172
Méline, 348
Memel, 17
Mendel, 89, 254
Mendeleef, 87, 287
Mendelssohn, 152
Mengs, 29
Menzel, 265
Merv, 340, 388
Messina, 33
Methodism, 167
Metternich, 157, 179, 205, 207
Metz, 243
Mexico, 50, 54, 63, 166, 168, 170, 209, 216, 239, 243, 258, 277, 344
Meyerbeer, 151
Michelangelo, 149, 265
Michelet, 112, 148, 155, 383
Michelson, 393, 394
Michigan, 290
Mickiewicz, 155
Middlesbrough, 217
Middleton, Sir Hugh, 12

Milan, 152
Mill, John Stuart, 219, 255
Millet, 245, 267
Milyutin, 331
Mimerel, 140
Minas-Geraes, 51
Mining, xiii, 26, 48, 50, 126, 128, 134, 195–6, 218, 226, 237, 287, 290, 291, 294–6, 302, 323, 336, 338, 344, 350, 353, 364, 379
Minnesota, 284
Mirès, 242, 243
Missouri, 166
Mitsubishi, 307, 309
Mitusi, 306, 309
Mogador, 41
Mogul Empire, 173
Mohammedanism, 60, 177, 183, 316, 319, 320, 365–6
Mokha, 62
Molière, 80
Mollien, 106, 120
Moltke, 231
Moluccas, 63
Monaco, 35
Monge, 116, 117, 252, 394
Mongolia, 64, 342
Mongols, 70, 319, 327
Monroe Doctrine, 172
Montague, Lord, 11
Montalivet, 243
Montesquieu, 31, 72, 93, 113, 137, 225
Montevideo, 49, 170, 299, 301
Moreau, 131
Morgan, J. Pierpoint, 282, 290
Mormons, 167
Morny, 233, 257
Morocco, 41, 184, 370, 374
Morvilliers, 53
Moscheles, 152
Moscow, 70, 71, 73, 107, 161, 180, 336–7
Mozambique, 371, 372
Mozart, 8, 32, 151, 152, 153
Mulhouse, 128–9, 220, 241, 349
Muller, 89
Munich, 7, 17, 152, 200, 207, 265
Murger, 264
Music, 70, 151–3, 267–9, 360–1

Nana Sahib, 312
Nancy, 95, 199
Nanking, 317, 324
Nantes, 6, 109
    Edict of, 44

Napier, Lord, 177
Naples, 33, 122, 152, 194, 363
Napoleon I, 86, 95, 106, 107, 117, 119–21, 123, 131, 132, 139, 148, 160, 161, 163, 173, 184, 192, 210, 233, 236, 244, 266
Napoleon III, xiv, 207, 211, 213, 215, 223, 231–3, 235, 237, 240, 256, 275, 363
Nassau, 378
Nationalism, 5, 155–9, 168, 170, 179, 183, 201, 205, 207, 208, 308–9, 363, 365, 366, 368
Navarino, 184
Navarre, 28
Necker, 111, 113
Nepal, 60
Nevada, 344
Newcastle, 196
New England, 284
New Granada, 50
New Orleans, 165, 166, 279
Newton, 48, 85, 86, 87, 88, 91, 246, 254, 391, 392, 393, 394
New York, 52, 53, 166, 172, 202, 275, 279, 285–7, 288, 344, 387, 390
New Zealand, 203
Ney, 124
Nice, 35
Nicholas I, 179
Nicholas II, 96, 157, 336, 389
Nijni-Novgorod, 7, 73, 341, 388
Ning-Po, 68, 178
Nobel, 263
Normandy, 124, 233, 349
North, Lord, 93
Nova Scotia, 55
Norway, 161, 178, 180, 276, 352, 357
Nuremburg, 17, 129, 200

Oberhausen, 133
O'Connor, 205
Odessa, 73, 335
Oerstedt, 88, 251
Offenbach, 151, 256
Omaha, 283, 286
Orange, 293
Orleans, Duke of, 26, 111, 115
Ormuz, 62
Ostend, 198
Owen, Robert, 142, 145
Oxford, 85, 142, 223, 247, 381

Pagannini, 152
Painting, fine arts, 29, 146–51, 245, 264–7
Palermo, 33, 364
Palestine, 38
Palmerston, 223, 224, 235, 238
Panama, 47
Panchaud, iii
Paraguay, 48, 170, 300, 302
Paris, xiii, xiv, 17, 21, 23, 26, 53, 54, 56, 64, 85, 101, 108, 113–9, 122, 124, 125, 127, 130, 136, 142, 144, 151, 152, 155, 178, 184, 192, 194, 199, 208, 212, 215, 229, 234, 237, 251, 256, 259–60, 264, 288, 348, 349, 362, 385, 386, 390
Pascal, 84, 147, 248
Pasteur, 89, 247, 254, 382
Pedro I of Brazil, 171
Pedro II of Brazil, 171, 302, 303
Peel, Sir Robert, 13, 108, 138, 204, 219, 223, 344
Peking, 64, 65–7, 69, 177, 310, 317–20, 326, 342, 389
Pelloutier, 386
Pennsylvania, 164, 166, 288, 290
Percier, 147, 149
Pereire, 198, 199, 211, 241, 242–3
Périer, Claude, 118, 123, 140
Perrache, 24
Perrégaux, 118
Peru, 49, 170, 221, 297, 328
Perry, Commodore, 305
Persia, 38, 62, 69, 70, 71, 72, 173, 179, 181, 183, 184, 342, 366, 389
Peter III of Russia, 71
Peter the Great, 311, 336
Pétin-Guadet, 237
Petofi, 360
Philadelphia, 53, 385
Philippines, 62, 68, 364
Pichegru, 117
Piedmont, 34, 362, 363
Pillau, 17
Pithole City, 286
Pitt, William, 14, 59, 106, 138
Pittsburgh, 288
Pizarro, 297
Poincaré, 249
Poitou, 237
Poland, 5, 8, 20, 21, 69, 71, 72, 73, 79, 96, 131, 156, 157, 161, 179, 181, 205, 358–9
Pombal, 30
Pomerania, 17

Pompeii 4, 145
Poor Laws, 102
Pontchartrain, 95
Polulation, 78, 79, 82, 164, 180, 185, 203, 257–61, 286, 293, 300, 308, 324, 363, 385
Portalis, 95
Port Arthur, 326, 387, 390
Port Elizabeth, 172, 294
Porto Alegre, 302
Porto Rico, 387
Portugal, 30, 51, 68, 162, 220, 303, 372
Pothier, 95
Potosi, 49
Potsdam, 146
Prague, 19, 158, 200
Pre-Raphaelites, 265
Pressburg, 158
Pretoria, 295–6
Priestley, 90
Proudhon, 144, 206, 208, 235, 256, 267, 268
Prussia, 21, 79, 109, 129, 131, 132, 135, 157, 192, 200, 204, 212, 224–32, 236, 240, 378
Puccini, 268
Puerto Cabello, 50
Pugachev, 71, 73
Punta Arenas, 298
Pupin, Michael, 288
Pushkin, 71, 178

Quebec, 54
Quesnay, 64
Quetelet, 90, 254
Quichua, Indians, 296–7
Quinet, 148, 155, 156
Quinsay, 325
Quito, 50

Rabat, 369
Racine, 150
Radcliffe, 138
Raiffaisen, Friedrich-Wilhelm, 213, 350
Rambouillet, 25, 111, 133
Ramleh, 38
Ranavalona, Queen, 373
Rathenau, 352
Récamier, Mme., 117, 118
Religion:
    Abyssinia, 45
    America, 167
    China, 67–8, 177
    India, 59, 173, 316

Indo-China, 329
Japan, 305
Portugal, 30
Turkey, 40
Renan, 254, 382, 383
Rheims, 122
Rhodes, Cecil, 296
Rhodesia, 296
Ricardo, 107
Riemann, 249 n
Riesener, 146
Riga, 332
Rio de Janeiro, xiii, 51, 106, 162, 171, 172, 302
Rio de la Plata, 169, 170
Rio Grande do Sul, 302
Robespierre, 116
Rockefeller, 287, 290
Romanticism, xiv, 145, 148–54, 208
Rome, 4, 32, 146, 152, 207, 363
Roon, 230
Rosas, 170, 299
Rossetti, 265
Rossini, 151
Rothschild, Nathan de, 19
Rothschilds, 124, 172, 194, 198, 199, 211, 229, 242
Rotterdam, 356
Roubaix, 124, 128, 220, 349
Rouen, 220, 234
Rouget de Lisle, 122
Rousseau, Jean-Jacques, 2, 23, 113
Rousseau, Theodore, 149
Rowlandson, 266
Royal Society, 12, 85, 89, 91, 252, 381
Ruhmkorff, 252
Ruhrort, 133
Rumania, 96, 238
Rumford, Count, 87
Russia, 20, 21, 31, 38, 56, 69–73, 79, 96, 122, 157, 160, 161, 177, 178–83, 207, 223, 229, 261, 288, 291, 311, 320, 326, 331–42, 345, 358–9, 366, 367, 387–90, 394

Saigon, 321, 374, 329
Sadowa, 230, 363
Saint-Etienne, 198
Saint-Germain, 199
St Helena, 44
Saint-Hilaire, Geoffroy, 253
Saint-Omer, 237
St Petersburg, 20, 73, 122, 123, 178, 337, 341, 386, 387, 389

Saint Quentin, 220
Saint-Simon, 144, 238, 256
Samarine, 332
Samarkand, 71, 340, 341
Samory, 373
Salonica, 38
Sand, George, 153
San Domingo, 54, 55
San Francisco, 209, 263, 275, 277, 321,
    390
San Martino, 169
San Paulo, 302
San Sebastian, 50
Santa Fé, 49, 50, 299
Santander, 365
Santiago, 48, 169, 298, 365
Saussure, 90
Savary, 128
Savigny, 95
Savoy, 211
Saxony, 8, 79, 96, 131, 132, 133, 135,
    202, 226, 233
Say, Jean Baptiste, 258
Schelling, 81
Schiller, 18, 150, 151, 154, 156, 269
Schneider, 199, 237
Schopenhauer, 268
Schubert, 153
Schumann, 152, 153
Schulze-Delitzsch, 213, 230
Science, xiii, 4, 8, 83–92, 245–55, 381,
    391–4
Scotland, 105, 196, 203, 209, 217, 355
Scribe, 151
Sebastopol, 239, 366
Sedan, 122, 240, 243, 363
Sée, Camille, 383
Seraglio, 366
Serbia, 238
Serfdom, 19–20, 23, 132–3, 207, 208, 225,
    227, 332, 342, 358–9
Seringapatam, 173
Shah Abbas, 62
Shanghai, 178, 319, 321, 325, 387
Shipping, 161–2, 163, 185, 194, 217–8,
    219, 238, 273–5, 291, 305, 309–10,
    349, 352, 363, 369, 388, 390
Siam, 330
Siberia, 181, 332, 337–9, 358, 387
Sicily, 33, 205, 364
Siemens, 201, 202, 261, 290, 352
Sieyès, 117, 119, 120, 155
Silesia, 131, 133, 201, 226
Singapore, 321, 330
Sining, 323

Sismondi, 144
Skagerrak, 357
Slavery, 42–4, 53–5, 63, 65, 93, 140, 164,
    166, 171, 182, 184, 221, 277, 302,
    328, 367, 371
Slavs, 157–8, 358, 360
Smith, Joseph, 167
Socialism, xiv, 143, 144–5, 206, 208,
    231, 234, 384, 386
Sorel, 386
South Africa, 171–2, 224, 261, 370
South America, 98, 163, 167–71, 261,
    296–304, 350
Spain, 27–30, 96, 107, 133, 162, 163, 165,
    169, 233, 263, 364–5, 385
Spencer, 255, 256
Speransky, 178, 179
Spy, 254
Stanley, 371–2
Stendhal, 125, 148
Stephenson, George, 196, 390
Sterne, Laurence, 4, 8
Stettin, 17, 200
Stockholm, 263
Stolypin, 337
Strasbourg, 199
Strauss, 360–1
Stuttgart, 151, 207
Suez Canal, 275, 316, 342
Suffren, 5, 56, 61, 162
Sun Yat Sen, 326
Sutter, Captain, 208
Swabia, 19, 132
Sweden, 19, 21, 69, 105, 161, 177, 178,
    352, 357
Switzerland, 19, 96, 220, 229, 268, 344,
    352
Sydney, 293
Syr Daria, 71
Syria, 37, 239
Szafarzik, 158

Taine, 382
Tali, 320
Talleyrand, 114, 120, 139
Tallien, Mme, 117
Tambulaine, 341, 342
Tartary, 69
Tashkent, 341, 388
Taylor, 292
Teheran, 72, 183, 366
Ternaux, 121–3
Tewfik, 368
Texas, 166, 290

Textiles, 218, 227, 236–7, 241, 290, 301, 316, 339–40, 349, 350, 355
Thackeray, 107
Thaes, Albrecht, 131
Thierry, Augustin, 155
Thiers, 126–7, 140, 144, 198, 223, 235, 240, 243
Thomas, 218
Thysson, 380
Tian-Shan, 69
Tibet, 64, 69, 320
Tientsin, 317, 319, 321
Tiepolo, 31
Tiflis, 71, 182, 339, 341
Tiradentes, 51
Tocqueville, de, 223, 238
Tokyo, 305–6, 310
Tolstoy, 71, 341
Tongking, 68, 330
Toulouse, 199
Tourane, 329
Tourcoing, 124, 128, 349
Townsend, 13
Trade, xiii, 6, 8, 13–14, 21, 27, 38, 43, 48, 60, 62, 69–70, 97, 101, 105, 108, 127, 133–5, 137, 161–2, 172, 178, 181, 183, 186, 194, 219–23, 227–9, 231, 234, 238, 276, 309, 313, 324, 327–8, 330, 342, 352, 370
Trade Unions, 142, 222, 309, 323, 353, 385, 386
Trafalgar, Battle of, 120
Transcaucasia, 340
Travel, 4, 22, 192–3, 197, 342, 352
Trieste, 185, 229, 231, 234
Tripoli, 38, 41
Troyes, 199
Tsu-hi, Empress, 321, 326, 327
Tsului-Cheng, 323
Tunis, 31, 41, 369
Turin, 85, 207
Turkestan, 70
Turkey, 36–42, 71, 72, 73, 179, 181, 182, 183, 184, 186, 231, 350, 360, 366
Tuscany, 34, 363
Tyrol, 19

Ukraine, 71, 332, 335, 342
Umberto, King, 385
United States of America, 52–3, 54, 102, 106, 108, 162, 163–7, 172, 176, 205, 209, 217, 220, 221, 225, 238, 263, 273, 276–92, 326, 328, 344, 387

Urban development, xiii, xiv, 6, 13, 26, 66, 81, 104, 130, 143, 201, 204, 232, 241–2, 258–61, 263, 285–7, 301
Ure, 137
Uruguay, 96, 299–301
Utrecht, Treaty of, 47, 162

Vaal, xiii
Valencia, 27
Valmy, 4
Valparaiso, 48, 298
Van Beer, 90
Van den Bosch, 330
Vanderbilt, 282
Venezuela, 50
Venice, 30–1, 34, 363
Ventavon, Father, 64
Verbiest, Father, 63
Verdi, 275
Vergennes, 5
Verlegers, 141
Versailles, 4, 7, 20, 22, 109, 125, 230
Verviers, 122
Victoria, Queen, 311, 353
Vienna, 7, 19, 24, 38, 151, 152, 158, 192, 194, 200, 207, 260, 344, 360
Vienna, Congress of, 135, 164, 184, 186
Vigny, 151, 198, 264
Ville d'Avray, 266
Villeneuve, 37
Villeroi, 24
Viollet-le-Duc, 264, 265
Viotti, 151
Virgil, 5
Virginia, 53, 163
Vladivostock, 276
Volta, 88
Voltaire, 3, 5, 29, 83, 84, 89, 93, 95, 113

Wagner, 150, 151, 153, 267–9
Wales, 203, 217
Wallace, Alfred Russell, 253
Walpole, 13
Warsaw, 73, 157, 358
Washington, 162, 278, 279
Waterloo, 124
Watt, James, 14, 123
Watteau, 149
Webb, Mary, 103
Weber, 153, 247, 268
Wedgewood, 14, 146
Weierstrass, 249
Weights and Measures, 97–8

Wellesley, 173
Wellington, 107
Wendel, 237
Werther, 18
West Indies, 47, 54
Westphalia, 96, 131, 133, 201, 226
Whitelock, 163
Whitworth, 218
Wieck, Clara (Schumann), 152
Wilberforce, 93, 140, 164
Wilhelmy, 392
Wilkinson, 14, 26
William I of Prussia, 230, 231
William II of Prussia, 385
William IV of England, 173
William IV of Prussia, 157
Winckelmann, 4, 146, 149
Witt, de, 388, 389
Wren, Sir Christopher, 9

Würtemburg, 79, 135, 186, 225, 228, 230
Würtemburg, Duke of, 18

Yakub, 320
Yedo, 304–6
Young, Arthur, 22, 25, 101, 102, 130, 233
Young, James, 88
Yuan Che-Kai, 327
Yucatan, 51
Yunnan, 320

Zanzibar, 229, 370, 372, 373
Zanzibar, Sultan of, 184, 370
Zollverein, 200–1, 228–31
Zulus, 172
Zurich, 386